**W9-AAF-368**

WITHIN REASON

WITHIN REASON

A Life of Spinoza

MARGARET GULLAN-WHUR

ST. MARTIN'S PRESS
NEW YORK

THOMAS DUNNE BOOKS.
An imprint of St. Martin's Press.

ISBN 0-312-25358-3

First published in Great Britain by Jonathan Cape

First U.S. Edition: March 2000

10 9 8 7 6 5 4 3 2 1

For the *Vereniging Het Spinozahuis*
and Tom Sorell

CONTENTS

LIST OF ILLUSTRATIONS
AND TRANSLATION ACKNOWLEDGEMENTS

1 Map of Amsterdam (1647)
2 The Beth Haim at Ouderkerk, the Jewish burial place outside Amsterdam, engraving by Romeyn de Hooghe (by permission of Rijksmuseum, Amsterdam)
3 The Nes, Amsterdam (Historisch-topografische Atlas of the Gemeentearchief of Amsterdam, by permission)
4 René Descartes, portrait by David Beck (by permission of the Royal Swedish Academy of Sciences, Stockholm)
5 Henry Oldenburg, portrait by Jan van Cleff (by permission of the President and Council of the Royal Society, London)
6 Christiaan Huygens, plaquette by Jean-Jacques Clérion (by permission of the Academisch Historisch Museum, University of Leiden)
7 Coenraad van Beuningen, engraving by Cornelis Meyssens (by permission of the Rijksmuseum, Amsterdam)
8 Spinoza's room at Rijnsburg (photograph by Jeremy Gullan-Whur)
9 Spinoza's home, 72–4 Paviljoensgracht, The Hague (photograph by Theo van der Werf)
10 Johan de Witt, portrait by Adriaen Hanneman (by permission of the Museum Boijmans Van Beuningen, Rotterdam)
11 William III, portrait by Adriaen Hanneman of the prince aged 14 (1664), painted for the English Court (The Royal Collection, Her Majesty the Queen, by permission)
12 Atrocities of the French invasion, 1673, engraving by Romeyn de Hooghe (by permission of the British Library, Shelf Mark 591 d.21)
13 The Battle of the Texel, 11–21 August 1673, painting by Willem van de Velde the Younger (National Maritime Museum London, by permission)
14 Letter to Joh. Georg Graevius, 14 December 1673 (Royal Library Copenhagen)
15 Spinoza's seal, from a letter to Gottfried Wilhelm Leibniz, 9 November 1671 (Niedersächsische Landesbibliothek, Hannover)
16 Spinoza, engraved frontispiece of the *Opera Posthuma*, 1677 (Vereniging Het Spinozahuis)

The author and publishers thank the following for permission to use translations:

Curley, Edwin, *The Collected Works of Spinoza*. Copyright © 1985 by Princeton University Press. Selections reprinted by permission of Princeton University Press.

Spinoza: The Letters, translated by Samuel Shirley, with an introduction and notes by Steven Barbone, Lee Rice and Jacob Adler. Copyright © 1995 by Hackett Publishing Company. All rights reserved. Selections reprinted by permission of Hackett Publishing Company.

The Philosophical Writings of Descartes, 2 vols., translated by J. Cottingham, R. Stoothoff and D. Murdoch, Cambridge University Press, 1985. *The Philosophical Writings of Descartes*, Volume III: *The Correspondence*, translated by J. Cottingham, R. Stoothof, D. Murdoch and A. Kenny, Cambridge University Press, 1991. Selections reprinted by permission of Cambridge University Press.

Spinoza: The Political Works. The Tractatus theologico – politicus in part and the Tractatus politicus in full. Edited and translated with an introduction and notes by A.G. Wernham, Oxford University Press, 1958. Selections reprinted by permission of Oxford University Press.

ACKNOWLEDGEMENTS, TECHNICALITIES AND A CONFESSION

Anyone embarking on a biography of Spinoza soon realises why so few have been attempted during the twentieth century. Facts lie buried in obscure documents written in half a dozen European languages, and some – to echo the frustration of the editor of the Dutch edition of the *Posthumous Works* – 'may still be in the possession of someone or other'.

It would have been impossible to complete this life of Spinoza by myself. It did not prove enough to learn Dutch in order to get into the records and scholarly literature often ignored due to that language's inaccessibility. The framework from which old documents derive their meaning requires expert interpretation. My greatest debt is to Theo van der Werf, secretary of the *Vereniging Het Spinozahuis* (Spinoza-House Society), who has been supportive for almost ten years, photocopying ancient or esoteric literature, allowing me to examine Spinoza's reconstructed library, pointing out areas already researched, researching with me, and recently communicating only in Dutch. Here is the address of the society he serves so well: *Vereniging Het Spinozahuis*, Paganinidreef 66, 2253 SK Voorschoten, The Netherlands.

There has also been indispensable help from other sources. Adri Offenberg and the staff of the Rosenthaliana Library, University of Amsterdam, have been available for discussion, and Elsa Strietman of the University of Cambridge has pored with me over baffling phrases in seventeenth-century Dutch. Marco Frangiotti of the University of Florianopolis, Brazil, translated the Portuguese text of António Borges Coelho, which provides the most recent information on Spinoza's forebears. Rivka La Fontaine and David Hart advised on Sephardi-Jewish matters, Rivka also helping with Hebrew and Dutch texts and with research. Odette Vlessing of the Amsterdam archives has given her time and spirited interest in Spinoza, as one of several outstanding personalities amongst the Portuguese-Jewish community of the Dutch 'Golden Age'. Ian Campbell took such thoroughgoing professional interest in Spinoza's illness that, after all possible chronicled symptoms had been collated and fed into Medline Computer Research, an appendix on this neglected topic resulted. Jeremy Gullan-Whur, Jan Beames and Colin Foale, who were responsible for exclusions and inclusions when at last a typescript of sorts was ready to read, may only now see how important their critical role has been. Jeremy has also contributed a mini-archive of photographs from our research and sailing trips in Holland. I want, too, on a vital count without which there would certainly have been no biography, to thank my university teachers and examiners in Spinoza's philosophy – Peter Bell, Susan James, Anthony Savile, Tom Sorell and Arnold Zuboff.

By way of transition into the technical section of this introductory note, a number of earlier researchers into Spinoza's personal and historical background on whose published works I have drawn are thanked and, in the case of those no longer alive, warmly remembered. If Spinoza's philosophy depended in a sense – as I believe it did, despite his refusal to pay his intellectual debts – on the thinking of earlier philosophers, my research depends to a greater extent on the meticulous work of (in particular, but in no particular order) Edwin Curley, K.O. Meinsma, J. Freudenthal, A.G. Wernham, A.M. Vaz Dias, W.G. van der Tak, J.I. Israel, Yosef Kaplan, I.S. Révah, Lewis Feuer, Yirmiyahu Yovel, Herbert H. Rowen, C. Louise Thijssen-Schoute and Léon Poliakov. Wim Klever, Piet Steenbakkers and António Borges Coelho are especially credited for recent research. The general histories of A.Th. van Deursen, Pieter Geyl and Simon Schama confirmed at an early stage that some apparently odd emphases in Spinoza's life and writing remain unintelligible unless interpreted in a seventeenth-century Dutch context.

I am also grateful to the editorial and production team at Jonathan Cape, and especially to Jörg Hensgen for his sustained commitment to the point of the book, and to creating an appropriate material form for conveying this. With the latter inspiration in mind, quotations from Spinoza's works and letters are distinguished throughout by being printed in italics, without speech marks. To prevent disruption of the text, reference numbers are avoided, but all quotations are given references in the source notes (as are, page by page, historical and archive details). Many of these have never been translated into English; several have never been published. Claims made in the text are identified by key phrases, for example, **Spinoza liked beer**: Letter 72, to Schuller, 18 Nov. 1675. Commentators credited in the source notes are not named in the text because they add confusingly to the many seventeenth-century characters. Except for one discussion in the final pages of the book, only J.M. Lucas, Johannes Colerus and the philosopher Pierre Bayle, seventeenth-century writers on Spinoza's life, are referred to by name. All translation is mine, unless otherwise stated.

On historical technicalities, the mismatch of Dutch and English dating in the seventeenth century is occasionally a minor obstruction. The Gregorian 'new-style' calendar used in Holland ran ten days ahead of the Julian calendar still current in England.

The bibliography is restricted for reasons of space to books used in writing this biography. Since it may not cover the needs of people new to Spinoza's philosophy, I recommend *Spinoza: An Introduction to his Philosophical Thought*, by Stuart Hampshire, Penguin Books, revised edition 1987, and *Spinoza*, by Roger Scruton, Past Masters Series, Oxford University Press, 1986. These books elucidate Spinoza's philosophy, but their biographical sections are inaccurate. People wanting to go straight to Spinoza's texts will find a choice of good paperback translations of *Ethics*.

I acknowledge no precedent in taking as basic a handful of Spinoza's principles. These agitate throughout the narrative, and allow individual judgement on whether Spinoza succeeded in living in accordance with them. Spinoza claimed that human beings were parts or aspects of a single, unified nature, that God was identical with nature, and that reason, not revelation or unanalysed experience, supplied the truth of any aspect of *God, or Nature*. Logical inference was his yardstick for drawing conclusions in all areas of human concern, including emotion. He believed – an ancient assumption – that the ordering of the universe was causally logical. Reasons and causes being thus identical, the paradigm of *adequate* knowledge was mathematics. In an informal sense, mathematical rationality consisted for him in measuring particular claims against *common notions*, ideas reflecting *the common properties of things*. He believed this reasoning process provided sufficient everyday practice in deductive inference to keep imagination, opinion, passion and prejudice under control. Fundamentally, too, he held that the mind was *the idea of the body*, and that any human thought must be considered in this perspective. These axiomatic beliefs are central planks in Spinoza's complex philosophy, and they serve the biographer well when exploring the interface between his mind and his life.

I also blame no one for my claim that Spinoza was a lonely and emotional man who lacked close friends. This belief is based on the best available evidence – Spinoza's own words – and it defies opinion that he had life-long devotees, although on hitherto unnoticed grounds I suggest that the young Dutch merchant Simon de Vries may have wanted, or even had, a homosexual friendship with the philosopher. The late nineteenth-century revival of interest in a philosopher who had for 200 years been generally vilified resulted, understandably, in excessively flattering accounts of his life and character. The need for a more balanced appraisal produces, paradoxically, a more lovable person. In my view Spinoza was an intellectually supercilious man, whose arrogance seldom tallied with his criterion for rational self-esteem, and whose testiness was ingrained. Having examined his temperament in relation to his illness, it is found to accord with his own principle that the causes of mental states are not to be understood as physical, but as lying deep in the network of earlier ideas.

So to the confession. Spinoza would detest this book. He would consider it *inadequate*, a mere calculus of probabilities and a distraction from his principles, which he believed to be, like Euclid's, deducible from self-evident axioms without recourse to context. *Euclid, who only wrote of matters very simple and easily understood, can easily be comprehended by anyone in any language . . . We need make no researches concerning the life, the pursuits, or the habits of the author; nor need we inquire in what language, nor when he wrote, nor the vicissitudes of his book, nor its various readings, nor how, nor by whose advice it has been received.* Only Euclid and Spinoza, it would seem, demonstrated truth to this standard. Not even the great mathematician and scientist René Descartes, still alive until Spinoza was sixteen, escaped censure. To help sort out the muddles he thought Descartes had left, Spinoza published an orderly reconstruction of his principles. Lesser thinkers were mercilessly toppled: a treatise by a professor of philosophy, for example, was glanced at in a bookshop. *From the little I then read of it, I judged it not worth reading through, and far less answering. So I left the book lying there, and its author to remain such as he was. I smiled as I reflected that the ignorant are usually the most venturesome and most ready to write.*

What chance has a biographer of meeting his standards of accuracy? Spinoza possessed only one biography among his 160 mainly scientific, lexicographical, classical and political books, namely a Dutch translation of the exile years of Charles II of England. It was probably a gift, and he never found it worthy of mention.

It is therefore under the sceptical stare of those brilliant brown eyes that I claim events in his life to have a bearing on his philosophy. Recent research has revealed with piecemeal slowness who his parents and grandparents were, and continues to throw flickering light on how the throng of elusive personages whose names pepper documents were related to him by blood or marriage. We may never know if the face on the book cover, which was almost certainly not painted from life, was based on a lost original or modelled on the engraving (Plate 16) that was commissioned after Spinoza died, and which is thought to be a reliable likeness. Personal details in letters were fastidiously removed by Spinoza or his editors.

But the date of his birth was etched into the posthumous engraving, on the orders of those who knew him well enough to be sure of it. This, with other archive data, takes us securely to the quarter between Amsterdam's South Kerk and St Anthonie's Gate where, on 24 November 1632, Spinoza was born to Hana Debora, second wife of the 44-year-old merchant Michael de Espinosa, and barely more than half her husband's age.

THE FAMILY OF SPINOZA

according to evidence supplied in the source notes

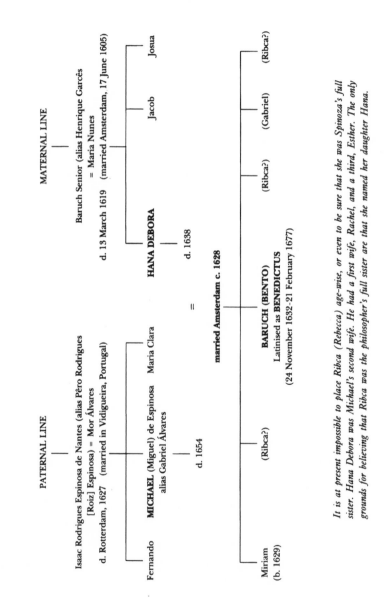

It is at present impossible to place Ribca (Rebecca) age-wise, or even to be sure that she was Spinoza's full sister. Hana Debora was Michael's second wife. He had a first wife, Rachel, and a third, Esther. The only grounds for believing that Ribca was the philosopher's full sister are that she named her daughter Hana.

STADHOLDERS OF THE UNITED PROVINCES OF THE NETHERLANDS

discussed in this book

Prince Willem I ('The Silent') of Orange
(b. 1533, d. 1584)
Stadholder 1544-84

Count Maurits of Nassau
(refused the title of the Prince of Orange)
(b. 1567, d. 1625)
Stadholder 1584-1625

Prince Frederik Hendrik of Orange
(b. 1584, d. 1647)
Stadholder 1625-47

Prince Willem II of Orange
(b. 1626, d. 1650)
Stadholder 1647-50
(married Mary,
daughter of Charles I of England)

Prince William III of Orange
(b. 1650, d. 1702)
Stadholder 1672-1702
King of England 1689-1702,
joint ruler with his wife Mary (d. 1694),
daughter of James II of England

Stadholder   I use a capital S when referring to the member of the House of Orange governing the province of Holland, living at The Hague, and regarded as a national leader by the Dutch people. When a lower-case s is used, I am talking of the role of stadholder in general or referring to the governor of one or more of the six outlying provinces of Utrecht, Gelderland, Overijssel, Drenthe, Groningen, Friesland and Zeeland.

William III is given the English version of the forename to distinguish him from his father and great-grandfather, and to highlight his role as the future joint ruler of England.

THE UNITED PROVINCES OF THE
NETHERLANDS, *1648*

ONE

Amsterdam: November 1632

I only know from report the date of my birth, who my parents were, and similar things, which I have never doubted . . . [But] men relate in chronicles and histories their own opinions rather than actual events, so that one and the same event is so differently related by two men of different opinions, that it seems like two separate occurrences; and, further, it is very easy to gather from historical chronicles the personal opinions of the historian.

Despite the dank North Sea fog that defied Aristotle's law of non-contradiction – for it did not rain, yet it rained – the baby was blessed to be born in Amsterdam. The Spanish might take the dozen or more towns that stood between the city's windmill-studded walls and the borders of the United Provinces, but Amsterdam itself was impregnable. The watch need only open the St Anthonie sluice gates, let in the sea, send it roaring down to engulf the low-lying ground of the polders, and drown the approaching enemy. In 1632 the Spanish army still crouched in the southern Netherlands. Its best battalions had been sent to the Rhineland, leaving only miserable and mutinous pikemen in the garrisons, but it remained a threat to the seven independent northern Provinces of the Dutch Republic. Spain did not intend to lose the Dutch-speaking principality of Liège to the 'rebels' in the north, so each time the Prince of Orange tried to re-take Spanish-held towns and territories, his troops were held off until reinforcements arrived. The Spanish were hated by the north Netherlanders: the very word *Spanjaard* was coined by the northern Dutch to turn the usual *Spanjool* into an insult by rhyming it with *veinzaard* and *snoodaard* – hypocrite and villain. The Portuguese, allies of Spain until 1640 and thereafter plunderers of Dutch shipping and usurpers of its trading posts, were likewise loathed. In this respect the infant was still further blessed: his family was Portuguese, but Jewish, persecuted and effectively expelled by the Inquisition, and protected by the Dutch.

Southernmost towns in the rich and populous Province of Holland (just one of the seven United Provinces) suffered from their proximity to the border with the Spanish Netherlands. The ancient trading port of

Dordrecht, for example, stood at the confluence of rivers blockaded to keep food from the enemy. It had stagnated commercially during eighty years of war with Spain while the upstart Amsterdam, taking over from Spanish-held Antwerp as the headquarters of Dutch commerce and trading, flourished and expanded until its Stock Exchange and *Wisselbank* became the financial hub of Europe. The city's prosperity was partly due to the skills and worldwide contacts of its Iberian refugee Jewish merchants, one of whom was Michael (Miguel) de Espinosa. Amsterdam's council delighted in the ability of its Jewish merchant venturers to evade or trick the Madrid maritime customs vigilantes, who singled out Dutch ships for capture. These refugees from Portugal succeeded in smuggling in silver bullion from Spain and precious shipments from Morocco via contacts in Fez and Tangier and the coastal cities of southern Spain. Records show the De Espinosas trading with the Middle East via Salé in Morocco. The little boy was therefore triply blessed because, until war with Spain finally ended in 1648, the burgomasters put a special value on his father's occupation.

Michael de Espinosa, born around 1587, was the son of a prosperous Lisbon merchant who had fled the city's Inquisition first for Vidigueira, in southern Portugal, and then, as the Inquisition of Évora took hold, for Nantes. Michael eventually moved to Amsterdam, where he joined his father's brother Abraham and married Abraham's daughter Rachel. His 84-year-old father Isaac, finally following on from France to the Netherlands, did not make it to Amsterdam alive. The old man never saw the warehouse on the Prinsengracht filled with sugar, brazil wood, candied ginger and dried fruit, to which Michael kept the key, nor his grandson (by Rachel) named Isaak after him, nor the synagogue on the Houtgracht, close to Uncle Abraham's large house. In 1627 his corpse was brought to the city by boat along the network of rivers and canals from the country village of Rotterdam where he died, to be laid in the Jewish cemetery alongside his sister Sara, Michael's first wife Rachel and two of their infants. All were carried away, perhaps, by the plague that rolled across Europe, hitting Amsterdam every year from 1622 to 1628, with a toll of 35,000 dead.

By the time this child was born, mourning was a chronic state of mind for Michael. Yet Amsterdam had brought him a satisfaction beyond sadness. He could at last practise his religion openly. He could stand if he wished at an open window, his prayer shawl draped over his tall black hat, singing sacred Hebrew phrases with Hispanic cantorial ecstasy. The days were gone when he must hide the Sabbath light in a pitcher, then glance all around before jabbing on a hat to mouth a hasty blessing before the meal. In Spain and Portugal Jews had risked their lives if they observed food rituals, kept Hebrew books or were circumcised, and France had proved no easy refuge either. Jews were officially expelled from Nantes in 1615, when Uncle Abraham left for Amsterdam. The child was blessed again, then, in being born in this tolerant metropolis, as his teacher Rabbi Menasseh ben Israel would make plain when petitioning Lord Protector Cromwell to readmit Jews to England: 'In the Low Countries the Jews are received with great charity and benevolency, and especially in this most renowned city of Amsterdam.'

In the eyes of the Jewish community, the baby with the typical dark looks and olive skin of the Portuguese Jew had all the blessedness and freedom he could ever want. He was safe from sudden death at the end of a pike (the invader would make Jews special targets); he could legitimately prosper; and he could exult in his ancestral faith to the point of rabbinical renown. Perhaps a sense of privilege moved the merchant to give his second son, by his second wife Hana Debora, the sacral name of Baruch, Hebrew for 'blessed one', although another reason for this is suggested shortly. Bento, the name that Spinoza used as a merchant, was the Portuguese version of the Spanish 'Benito', and also meant 'blessed'. In Latin, Benedictus covered the sense of it, but Michael would not willingly have used this alternative. Not that studying Latin was rare among Jews: publishing in that language of scholarship was necessary if trans-European academic notice was sought, and there were several Latin scholars in the Amsterdam community, among them Menasseh ben Israel. Even Rabbi Morteira (who seems to have been a fairly close friend of Uncle Abraham's, since he was a signatory to Abraham's conferring of power of attorney on Michael in 1625, and attended Rachel's funeral as a mourner), who abhorred all Christians, distinguished the roman language from the Roman Church when he quoted the Stoic Marcus Aurelius in synagogue sermons. No, it was the association of *benedictus* with Catholicism that repelled: Michael must have seen in the eye of distant memory the priest's hand poised, two fingers raised to make the sign of the cross, at the mass that all Jews were forced to attend. Few Jews would learn Latin in Holland. Perfecting Hebrew was task enough for those still struggling with the rudiments of Judaic ritual and Law. The first arrivals at the turn of the century had had to bring the learned Joseph Pardo from Venice to be their first rabbi, and in 1627 the 613 Commandments were printed, so that 'all of us who come from Portugal and Spain and for our sins do not understand Hebrew shall rightly know what they are'. The community's largely self-taught sages rejoiced that children born into practice of the Law – future Dutch Jews – would equal themselves in its understanding before they were of age, and Michael's enrolment of his sons in synagogue classes and societies, and his refusal to use other than their sacral names, shows that he wanted them to be maximally orthodox. He had

3

signed his Hebrew Grammar 'Miguel de Spinosa', but he buried his first wife as 'Rachel', not Raquel, and his name was chiselled 'Michael' on Hana Debora's gravestone.

To Latinise one's name was, for any scholar, to send a signal to the world, but for Hispanic Jews names had long been flashpoints of identity and emotion, and for them alias-using was a habit and an art. Non-Hebrew names had deflected attention from their Jewishness in Iberia. On emigrating they often changed their names again – making research into family backgrounds difficult. The Spanish consul in Amsterdam reported, 'It is a custom among the members of this nation to assume as many names as they please, either for purposes of deceit or in order not to jeopardise their relations who still bear their [true] name in Spain.' Spinoza, a first-generation Dutch Jew, usually added just the single initial 'B', which explains why biographers seldom coincide on his forename. But while Spinoza suppressed the connotations of his different forenames, and often failed to sign his letters at all, it is the biographer's task to interpret the signals they emit. As a merchant he was Bento, and for family reasons given below he is likely to have been called that by his mother. At school, and to his father, he was Baruch. As a Dutch Jew striving to make a mark as a scholar, he was Benedictus. As the creator of a unique philosophy, we call him Spinoza – a name he almost never used in that curt Northern form.

Being Baruch was a filial duty. Slowly the name became a deadweight which denied his philosophical project, and he abandoned it as surely as some Jewish hand eventually scratched it out in one of the synagogue's membership registers. That said, Michael's anguished past and yearning for a return to Israel dominated Bento's childhood, and we need to apprehend the burden of atavistic sorrow and frustration set to descend on the boy at birth if we are to appreciate both the extent of his rational detachment from it and the strand of Hispanic Jewishness inextricably woven into his mentality.

Bento may have known no family in the Amsterdam Hispanic Jewish community which had not endured a relative tortured, hanged or burned during the Inquisition purges that tore across the Iberian Peninsula. We now have grounds for believing that his own family had suffered typically. The 'Gabriel Álvares Dispinosa' who appears in Amsterdam records as the son-in-law of 'Manuel Rodrigues Dispinosa', and who came from Vidiguiera, appears in Portuguese Inquisition registers as Pêro Roiz's second son. 'Pêro Roiz' was the alias of old Isaac Espinosa, son of Fernão Espinhosa and brother of Abraham. Roiz is an abbreviation of Rodrigues, as is shown in a document referring to 'Abraham Espinosa de Nantes alias Manuel Roiz Espinosa'. The brothers' paternal grandmother can be traced to Vidigueira, in the south. As Jews living in Portugal in the early to mid sixteenth century they were well assimilated and respected, although denied political or economic power. Conversion to Christianity was not enforced there until the 1580s. Once organised, however, the Portuguese Inquisition rivalled the established Spanish process in ferocity. The punishment for practising Jewish ritual was baptism, often forcible. For proselytising Gentiles it was death. Most of Michael's paternal family, the Espinosas, had at once fled or hidden. His father Isaac had made for Vidiguiera, where he married Mor Álvares, Michael's mother. But when the terror reached Vidiguiera in 1596 almost all the Álvares family was taken to gaol, and a horrifying sequence of treachery and cruelty, documented by the Inquisition of Évora, ensued. Mor's father and aunt, compromised by links with Vidiguiera's system of justice, denounced her and her brothers as practising Jews. Mor had, in fact, already left for France with Isaac and their children. The Inquisition record states that 'All these people [Isaac de Espinosa, his wife Mor Álvares, and three children, Fernando, Gabriel or Miguel, and Maria Clara – "slim, fair-skinned and with charming eyes"] fled before pardon.' But other family members were arrested. Some narrowly escaped hanging. Mor's brother, tortured four times, finally denounced his aunt. If Michael remembered the dreaded *autos-da-fés*, the compulsory public declarations of faith he had seen as a boy, he would have told Bento with revulsion of the *sanbenitos*, yellow robes slashed with black crosses, which surviving 'penitents' had to wear thereafter at mass, and in the street on religious feast days.

Michael may have noticed the secularity, difficulty in accepting humble status, and skill in dissembling of the Spanish Jews who, throughout the sixteenth century, had trickled into Portugal. For centuries they had been given royal protection, and such privilege had been responsible for the outbursts of public envy and hatred which had in 1390 made half the Spanish-Jewish population convert to Christianity. The pious, including physicians and lawyers educated at the great universities of Salamanca and Toledo, and fabulously rich royal agents and financiers, had preferred to join the Jews of Portugal. It was they who had taught the Portuguese how to wear a Christian mask while secretly keeping the Law; how to let their children be brought up as Catholics until they were old enough to keep silent; how to attend mass without bowing to images. As a result many Jews wavered between the two creeds for a lifetime, some being circumcised on their deathbeds, others converting late to Catholicism. Some, more often Portuguese, wholly resisted Christianity, as no doubt Michael told his son with a mixture of bitterness and pride, for Spinoza would write that while Spanish Jews, being considered worthy of positions of honour, converted and identified themselves so closely with native-born Spaniards that *no*

5

traces and even no memory of them remained in Spain, *precisely the opposite happened to those who were forced by the king of Portugal to embrace the religion of his kingdom, for although they were converted, they continued to live apart from the rest of the community, simply because he declared them unworthy of any position of honour.* It was not, of course, true that all Portuguese Jews kept the faith, or that Spaniards of Jewish birth did not, but this general European opinion pervades travellers' reports and documents, which refer to all Iberian Jews as 'the Portuguese' or 'the Portuguese people of the nation'. In Amsterdam the community usually called itself the *nação* rather than the *nación*, and synagogue announcements were made in Portuguese.

Yet Spinoza's life and work testify not only to a powerful Spanish-Jewish influence in Amsterdam, but to a personal attraction to things Spanish. He owned numerous Spanish literary texts – poetry, rhetoric, comedy and criticism – and chose to use a Spanish translation of Calvin's *Institutes*. Traces of a cross-cultural intellectual concept of God much admired in Spain and written about extensively in that language are found in his first work, the *Short Treatise*, and in some of his last reflections, in *Ethics* Part 5. He is reported to have told some visiting Spaniards in 1659 that he would like to visit their country, a comment that might be dismissed as politeness, had he not acquired much later than that a book called *Voyage in Spain*. These interests, added to his common Spanish surname (associated with a town near Burgos) and a lack of any affectionate mention of Portugal, may explain the once-held belief that he was Spanish. This was refuted in the 1930s when the first documents relating his father to Vidigueira were found. However, several business documents and letters have a *tilde* in the signature (Spiñoza), and after Michael died the family firm was renamed 'Bento y Gabriel Despinoza', using a Spanish 'y' rather than a Portuguese 'e' for 'and'.

I believe that Spinoza may have had Spanish connections his father did not share. Justifying this claim involves in the first place clarifying his maternal line. On 17 June 1605, in Amsterdam, Maria Nunes married Henrique Garcês, alias Baruch Senior (Señor), a distinguished founder-member of the first Amsterdam synagogue. Another document reveals that 'Maria Nunes Garses' was the mother of two sons called Josua and Jacob Senior and 'of the wife of Micael Espinoza'. Elsewhere Josua Senior is recorded as 'son of Garcez'. In this way the parents of *a* 'wife of Micael Espinoza' are established. But which wife? Can we be sure that Garcês and Nunes were Hana Debora's parents and Bento's grandparents? Well, we can eliminate the other two wives. Michael's third wife Esther (surname Fernandes or De Solis) is stated in her marriage entry of 1641 to have come 'from Lisbon, about 40 years old, with no parents alive', and to have been

6

previously unmarried. To be a daughter of the Garcês/Nunes union she would have had to be born four years before their wedding and to have returned to Lisbon to live – an act of extraordinary bravado. Michael's first wife Rachel was the daughter of Abraham Espinosa. We know this from a notarial document of 1639, which states that Jacob Espinosa was the son and heir of the said Abraham Espinosa, and that Michael Despinosa had been married to his sister. Rachel died in 1627, and synagogue funeral or memorial dues were paid then by Michael, Abraham and Jacob Espinosa (and Rabbi Morteira). There is one small piece of evidence linking Hana Debora further with Maria Nunes. Henrique Garcês died in 1619, but Maria Nunes was still alive in 1638, when she was a witness at the wedding of 'David' Senior, aged twenty-seven, to the 17-year-old Ester Rodrigues Portalagre, whose 'aunt', named as Hana Debora Espinosa, was also a witness. If Hana Debora, who was then at the oldest thirty-two (and perhaps less than twenty-seven), is accepted as a Garcês-Nunes daughter and a sister of Josua and Jacob Senior (one of whom may have had the alias 'David Senior'), then she had illustrious Spanish connections on her mother's side.

At this point we turn to Portuguese Inquisition records. Maria Nunes came from Oporto or Ponte de Lima, where her uncle was burned by the Inquisition of Coimbra in 1588, and a second cousin, Luis da Cunha, was arrested in 1618. The name of this Padua-trained physician matches that of an author, previously untraceable, of one of Spinoza's books. This *Obra Devota* is in Spanish, and it may be that some of Maria's forebears came from Spain, for there is evidence that several of her cousins, including 'Padre Bento', were *conversos* who became Spanish Jesuits. One was the rector at Alcalá in 1556, and the mayor of Toledo in 1565–8. Another, Henrique Henriques, taught philosophy and theology at that time at Córdova and Salamanca, where he tutored the immensely influential (Jewish-born) Vatican advisor on philosophy and theology, Francisco Suárez, traces of whose views are found in Spinoza's texts. At least one 'Senior' gravestone in the Dutch Jewish cemetery is inscribed in Spanish, and a rare Jewish Edition bible, published in Amsterdam in 1602, in Spanish, was found in Spinoza's library alongside even older books in that language.

Little Bento would know his mother for less than six years, yet after her death her family's affairs would impinge on the De Espinosas, and personal contact with them may have added to the already strong Spanish cultural influence at the synagogue, where both ancient traditions and modern literary and philosophical trends in Spain were avidly debated. Michael treated his in-laws well – to his own cost, it will emerge – but the evidence points to his nursing a Portuguese cast of mind, in which Portuguese nationalism was fused with orthodox religious zeal of a specifically

7

Portuguese intensity. It is hard to believe Michael could ever have been thought Spanish, for neither his sojourn in France nor the thirty years he subsequently spent in The Netherlands persuaded him to speak anything but Portuguese. To the end of his life he had documents translated into that language before he would sign them. He married first his Portuguese cousin Rachel, then Bento's Portuguese-speaking mother Hana Debora, and three years after her death Esther, who arrived directly from Lisbon. His gravestone bears only a laconic Portuguese inscription. As to his religious commitment, in 1633 he became a synagogue *parnas*, a governor bound to strict interpretation of the Law, and eligible for election to the Jewish governing body, the *mahamad* (council of fifteen), empowered to discipline rabbis. In 1635 he would be elected *parnas* of the school, in 1637 *parnas* of the new enlarged congregation, and in 1649–50 he would serve on the *mahamad*. He was almost certainly a fervent Messianist: most of the *nação* believed that the Messiah would be one of themselves, and rabbi Menasseh ben Israel would in 1650 dedicate the Portuguese edition of his Messianic book *Hope of Israel* to Michael, as one of seven *parnasim*.

The thousand or so Iberian Jews living in Amsterdam when Bento was born were by no means, then, unified in racial or religious commitment, and Bento would witness much malice and dissension among the 'marranos'. (Both converted and unconverted Iberian Jews were known as 'marranos'. This was not a term of abuse, being originally a combination of the old Castilian word for pork and the Arabic *mahram* – 'forbidden for some'. In medieval Spain it had made fun of Jewish dietary rules, but it had none of the venom of the later *chueta*, the derisive distortion of 'Jew' into 'swine', and it is still used by Jews to distinguish those who fled the Peninsula from the later orthodox 'Sephardi' – this term was not introduced until 1851 – the Jews of *Sepharad*, the 'cities of the south'.) To Amsterdammers, degrees of Jewish commitment were immaterial. At the turn of the seventeenth century the Dutch could not tell Hispanic Jews from Spanish Catholics, and during one prayer meeting the magistrates had the rabbi arrested as a spy.

To be sure, the marranos looked nothing like the medieval Jews of caricature and myth, or the few Polish and German Jews (then called *Hooghduytsen*, not Ashkenazi) who lived in the city. The English traveller Peter Mundy wrote after visiting Amsterdam in the early 1630s, 'The Jewes [are] either all, or most, Portugalls, Ritch Merchants, nott evill esteem'd off, living in liberty, wealth and ease.' Their well-cut doublets and knee-breeches showed them to be men of affairs: the quality and colour of their silk and satin, lace and camel-hair made them typical *hidalgos* (a term used with pride by the marranos, but with resentment by the Dutch, for whom it meant less 'gentlemen' than 'arrogant invaders'). In Spain and Portugal the

8

taste had been for opulence and embellishment, and it had been expedient there for Jews to dress like their Christian peers. While some of the older men had neat pointed beards, they merely kept to the high fashion of their youth, their immaculate goatees jutting at the requisite angle above the pleated gauze ruffs they still wore. (Art experts do not think Rembrandt's paintings, although of this date, represent their clothes reliably; he often made his sitters dress up.) The full beard trimmed only with scissors had long been abandoned by most, and perhaps not unwillingly, for the marranos were Iberian in temperament, looks and, to no small extent, in blood. It is recorded that almost all the inhabitants of eleventh-century Spain had looked more Arab or African than the other Europeans of their day, and many historians believe that the obsession centuries later with 'cleanness' from Jewish or Moorish blood was futile. Few Spaniards, from King Ferdinand and the infamous enforcer of his Jewish solution, Torquemada, to Teresa of Avila (later to be made Spain's patron saint) were 'clean'. Luther, Erasmus and Willem the Silent, founder of the United Provinces, claimed that most Spaniards had Jewish blood. But while these enemies of Spain were obviously making political capital, the fact was that when, in 1562, the Portuguese bishops demanded that Jews wear badges, it was because the Jews looked exactly like everyone else.

In turn, the marranos, even when in the eighteenth century some adopted Dutch names and spoke Dutch at home, revered their Hispanic past. One, accused of setting fire to a Spanish ship, was censured by another: 'Much as he may feel rejected by his native country, no Spanish-born Hebrew should commit such an outrage against his fatherland.' Portuguese loyalty was equally strong: when Portugal rebelled against Spain, the Nunes da Costa family sent King John a warship and munitions. In sum, the marranos preserved their southern character even as they flaunted their newfound freedom of worship, and neither practice endeared them to the Dutch. Their sheer exoticness in the eyes of these neighbours has rarely been brought out in descriptions of Spinoza's background. The marranos were conspicuous in looks, manners and worship, in which, paradoxically – and understandably confusingly for the Dutch – Catholic elements were integrated. In 1598 it had been suggested that Portuguese immigrants might buy citizens' rights 'in the hope that they are Christians', although they would still be banned from public office. But when the Calvinists realised that these immigrants were Jews, they criticised other rituals – for example, the festooning of bridges with greenery on the Feast of Tabernacles – and were backed in this by the Reformed Church Council of Amsterdam. In 1612 the city authorities acted on complaints by threatening to demolish any 'temple' that the 'Portuguese Jews' built. So it was that, following recommendations for controlling the Jews, proposed by the jurist Hugo de Groot (Grotius), the rented house on the Houtgracht that held the Beth Jacob synagogue kept its anonymous façade even after it was bought, while its interior had been dramatically and beautifully altered. Michael's ornate signature adorns the 1630 bill of purchase.

There were complaints, too, about extravagance and gaudy attire, and the *parnasim* warned against displaying finery, except in the synagogue or at home. This irked most marranos, especially the wealthier merchants (arms dealers and diamond merchants, for example) and the 'court Jews' (envoys and agents), who had seen at close hand the French fashions of the Prince of Orange's entourage, his superb Spanish-Barbary carriage mares and his gilded ship of state; who had perhaps raised funds for his politicking or had walked alongside the previous Stadholder in the funeral procession of the marrano Samuel Palache, former ambassador and clever capturer of Spanish ships. At first the Jews had been told to live in the easterly quarter, called the Vloyenburg or 'Vloenburch', a raised area designed as a flood (*vloed*) barrier for the Amstel river, but Grotius had not endorsed the council's demand that they stay there, and some bought houses with double flights of stone steps in west Amsterdam, on the fashionable Herengracht or Keizersgracht. The style and status of these grandees are evident from their tombstones in the Jewish cemetery. Many of these monuments date from later centuries, but an English visitor wrote in 1641 about the 'Sepulchers . . . some of them very stately, and of cost' that he had seen. There are also numerous references to a typical *hidalgo* marrano manner, which consisted in varied measures of floridity, fastidious gentility, sycophancy, dignity and straight boasting. Of Spinoza, even when sick, living in humble lodgings and calling himself a 'good republican', it was said:

> He had a courteousness which was more like the Court than that of the commercial city in which he was born . . . There was something about his clothes which usually distinguishes a gentleman.

Such civility would not stop him displaying the less attractive features of *hidalguia*.

There was no ignoring the marrano presence. At the Stock Exchange all 'Portuguese' merchants with accounts automatically sat at the front, and by 1620 there were 114 Jewish accounts at the *Wisselbank* – 9.5 per cent of the total. Uncle Abraham had prospered in Antwerp, and had held accounts at the *Wisselbank* in 1625 and 1628. Michael, who would have Exchange accounts in the better times of 1642 and 1651–2, gave generously to synagogue funds, although his shipments suffered from piracy, storm

damage, raisin-rot, shipwreck and confiscation, and fluctuated with compli-
cations caused by the eighty years' war against Spain, the recession of
1649–50 and the Dutch-English war of 1652–4. He never owned his home –
it belonged to one Willem Kick, perhaps the Amsterdam silk merchant of
that name – but by 1651 he lived in a row of houses mainly inhabited by rich
marranos, and probably looked affluent to the Dutch merchants he met,
who on pain of censure by the ecclesiastical court of the Dutch Reformed
Church concealed their riches. The marranos, whose rabbis were usually
involved in business – Isaac Aboab de Fonseca was one of five members of
the *mahamad* who were chief shareholders in the Dutch West India
Company – were mystified by the drabness of many Dutch merchants, some
of whom sold their best cloth to France while buying coarse broadcloth to
wear. Portraits show, however, that the ubiquitous black was often satin,
and the white collar lace, and that inside merchant homes were costly
carpets and paintings, fine porcelain and exquisitely carved furniture – and,
in the closet of one soberly clad citizen, a pile of red satin underwear.

Of all the tensions that distanced the marranos from the Dutch, attitudes
to the female sex were among the most destructive. Amsterdammers
complained that the 'Portuguese' were 'insatiably given unto women'. It was
observed that in Portugal 'they allow brothel-houses, and will give their sons
money or leave to go to them sooner than the tavern'. In Spain and
Portugal, bedding the servants or any other available woman had also been
an acceptable peccadillo shared with Christian gentlemen, and the habit died
hard. In the United Provinces, Jews were not officially allowed Dutch
servants, yet they employed Christians and took on Dutch apprentices.
They were forbidden to have casual sexual relations with Dutch women, or
to marry them, yet a burgomaster objected in 1619 that 'many Jews fleeing
from Portugal had so conducted themselves and intermarried with the
daughters of this country that it tended to great obloquy'. There were
regular complaints of Jews 'abusing the daughters of the Christians serving
them'. In 1621 'a child from the house' of Michael's uncle Abraham de
Espinosa was buried in the Jewish cemetery and a maidservant dismissed.
His uncle, then in his sixties, if not older, and the maid were both arrested,
but released, and Abraham remained a *parnas* of the Beth Jacob community
until he died in 1637. In the eighteenth century a leading Amsterdam
marrano would reflect that *passion des femmes* had been one of the chief
failings of the *nação* as Dutch citizens.

It might, in the seventeenth century, have been hard to find a European
community more disposed to deny its women equality than one that was
both Portuguese and Jewish. The marranos confined their wives and
daughters to the house, unless accompanied, when they must be veiled. As

late as 1731 the Jewish authorities informed the burgomasters of Amsterdam that their unmarried daughters 'never go out and do not understand Dutch'. In Dutch and English eyes they were 'restrained and made prisoners'. This was as much a Portuguese as a Jewish custom. In 1651, in Lisbon, Dom Francisco Manuel de Mello cautioned that wives should not appear at table if a man from outside the family came to dinner, and an English sailor reported a little later:

> The men that are married are given much to jealousy, and will not permit any stranger to come where their wives are, much less to see them, but will keep them out of sight as much as they possibly can . . . all their women, both married and unmarried, go with a black veil over their heads and reaching down to their legs, all being covered except their eyes.

Spaniards living in Brazil made fun of this, and Spanish Catholic reformers began to see, ahead of the Portuguese, that women might bind children early to the faith if taught to read and to study the catechism. But female education was strictly curtailed. Sister Juana Inés de la Cruz, for example, entered a Mexican convent because she saw no other chance to study, but her theological critiques scandalised, and she died under Inquisition threat. Dom Francisco of Lisbon held that for women 'the best book is the cushion and the embroidering-frame', and Rabbi Eliezer warned that 'Who teaches his daughter the Torah teaches her nonsense', implying that she could make nothing of its wisdom. Yet an intelligent girl could progress through secret study, and as medieval non-Jewish women made names for themselves as scholars, the problem of female learning was addressed in the Jewish code *Shulchan Aruch*, of 1565. This ruled that a woman could be called to the Reading of the Law but that modesty must prevent her from complying. The marranos, more than other Jews, preferred their womenfolk unlettered. After 1623, when it became obligatory to sign Dutch civic marriage registers, many brides marked them with a cross, Bento's elder sister Miriam among them. His stepmother Esther, who brought him up after Hana Debora's death when he was barely six, wrote with difficulty; her sister not at all. Even sacred scripture was kept from marrano women, who were taught by their mothers to obey just three ritual rules: they must light the Sabbath candles (praying if young to be granted male children, bright in the study of the Torah); put aside a pinch of dough for an offering; and maintain menstrual seclusion. Women trained in these *mitzvoth* had often preserved the faith in Iberia in families where the men lapsed, yet they were given no place in the community's spiritual or intellectual life. A modern Jewish scholar admits that 'nothing in the Jewish Bible or rabbinical literature denies the relative superiority of the male child' and that the distinction is 'even more pronounced in their passage from childhood to adulthood'. It is conceded, too, that these frustrated women were often carping, domineering and weepy, hence the religious counsel, 'A man should always be careful lest he vex his wife: for as her tears come easily . . . though all other gates be shut, the gate of tears is never closed.'

In The Netherlands, on the other hand, a good many Dutch women had minds disciplined by education, as Bento would soon find out. The best-educated wrote and spoke Latin and transcribed in Greek. Some, such as the Visscher sisters and Anna Maria van Schurman, were profoundly erudite. The latter, who published a 'Logick Exercise' called *The Learned Maid, or Whether a Maid may also be a Scholar*, studied under Descartes, as did Princess Elizabeth of Bohemia, whose mental powers Descartes also eulogised, and whom the English philosopher Henry More thought 'infinitely wiser and more philosophical than all the savants and philosophers, not only women, but men, of Europe'. Van Schurman made no such claim. 'Though women cannot be equalled for their wit with those more excellent men who are "eagles in the clouds", yet . . . not a few are found of so good a wit, that they may be admitted to studies, not without fruit.' Women were excluded from public office even in the Dutch Republic, although many excelled in business (as did a very few marrano wives) and governed orphanages, hospitals, old-age homes and houses of correction, as many group portraits of such boards bear witness. But the Spanish priest Vivés, son of persecuted and converted Jews, had written in his *Office and Duties of a Husband* that the manners of Dutch men and women 'agree not with nature', since 'to the woman nature hath given a fearful, covetous and humble mind'. It was necessary, on the other hand, for the man's 'noble, high and diligent mind to be busy and to be occupied abroad', and 'natural' for him to rule.

The marranos – like other Europeans – found the women of the United Provinces unfeminine. All Iberians were horrified to see Dutch (and English) women alone in the streets, kissing and embracing publicly. Nor did Dutch women seem to have any reserve at home. The Englishman Owen Felltham reported that 'The woman there is the head of the house.' Dutch husbands themselves sometimes complained of their 'breeches-wearing' wives, and the civic authorities, aware of this, fixed fines for husband-beating at a higher rate than that for wife-beating. To many foreigners Dutch women seemed big, strong and bossy. Some were. A magistrate's wife in 's-Hertogenbosch pitted a female army against the Spanish: in Haarlem, housewives hauled cauldrons of boiling liquid to the ramparts to pour on enemy heads. 'Jan the Washerman', the hag-ridden husband of Dutch cartoon, was a grim spectre to the marranos, who did not want their wives to pick up the presumptions of Dutch women. This may be why many kept their families away from the Herengracht or Keizersgracht, although they could afford to live there.

How much marrano sentiment clung to Spinoza? It would be easy to view his misogyny as culturally induced and explore it no further. When, for instance, he refers to *the inconstancy and deceptiveness of women, and their other, often sung vices,* he gestures to centuries of scorn and subjugation of wives, daughters and sisters. A 'singing' of women's vices was a feature of the community into which he was born. But his philosophy consists, in an important dimension, in reasoning from universal or eternal principles – axioms or *common notions* that are the *foundations of our reasoning,* and throw light on particular circumstances. *Philosophy is based on common notions, and must be built on the study of nature alone.* It is generally thought that, in line with this doctrine, Spinoza's programmes for social, political and religious reform, for example, are free of emotional intensity regarding the suffering of his forebears. This was the result of reasoning, looking into the causes of violent feelings and relating them, as effects, to general causal principles in human nature, rather than unthinkingly imitating or despising them. He saw anti-Semitism as just one expression of human bigotry, it being born of *inadequate ideas* – for him, imagination, association, hearsay, passion, opinion and prejudice – and exacerbated by Jewish law and ritual which, he said, had been devised for the *political organisation and worldly prosperity* of the ancient Hebrews, and were now obsolete and provocative:

As for the fact that they have survived their dispersion and the loss of their state for so many years, there is nothing miraculous in that, since they have incurred universal hatred by cutting themselves off completely from all other peoples; and not only by practising a form of worship opposed to that of the rest, but also by preserving the mark of circumcision with such devoutness.

The latter he likened to the trademark pigtail of the Chinese.

Spinoza does not seem, however, to have submitted to testing by first principles the view of women that he inherited. Instead, we find, starting around 1661–2 and hardening over the course of his lifetime, negative pronouncements on their whimpering, partiality, foolish pity, superstition, inconstancy, deceptiveness, weakness and mental inferiority. Modern philosophers tend, with an eye to political correctness, to blur signs of his misogyny. For example, the Latin *muliebris* or Dutch *vrouwelijk* ('woman-ish') is translated as 'unmanly'. But 'womanish' is what Spinoza means. Indeed, it is hard to neutralise the gibe he makes in connection with Jewish ritual: *Did not the principles of their religion make them effeminate, I should be quite convinced that some day when the opportunity arises – so mutable are human affairs – they will establish their state once more.*

Spinoza's doctrine allows for differences in female mentality reflecting differences in their bodies. For him, the mind was the idea of the body. In so far as a woman's body differed from that of a man, the mind must differ accordingly. But it is also to be inferred from his principles that, when reasoning efficiently, the sexes must agree, since reason distinguishes the *common notions* that are by definition agreed by all minds. Spinoza should, therefore, have argued for a common male-female mentality, at least to the extent that he argued for the common human nature of ethnic groups wrongly judged diverse 'races'. But he did not. Instead, he left a chasm between his principles and his opinions, which will bother us considerably, as it bothered one of his contemporaries:

> The most part of philosophers walk by no other rule than that of the vulgar . . . Men may think . . . their principles are probably sufficient to discover which of the two sexes have naturally the advantage over the other; but none can think so but such who either know them not or are pre-possessed thereby. The knowledge of ourselves is absolutely necessary to enable us, for the handling of the question aright; and especially, the knowledge of our body, which is the organ of sciences; after the same manner as for to know how telescopes and Glasses of Approach magnifie the objects; we must know the fashion of them . . . The notions of natural things are necessary, and we form them always after the same manner. Adam had them as we have; children have them as old men, and women as men.

The writer of this 1676 treatise, François Boulain de la Barre, could have been chiding philosophers other than Spinoza. His compatriot Nicolas Malebranche, for instance, thought it was generally true that due to 'the delicacy of the brain fibres' in women 'everything abstract is incomprehensible to them'. But since optics was one of Spinoza's known preoccupations, he seems especially accused here by the reference to magnifying lenses. De la Barre also seems to echo concepts found in Spinoza's *Theologico-Political Treatise*, published in 1670:

> *All things are determined to exist and act in a fixed and definite way by the universal laws of nature . . . Reflection on human nature is all that is needed to understand it, this law can certainly be conceived in Adam as easily as in any other man, in a solitary as well as a social being . . . It is universal, i.e. common to all men, for I have deduced it from human nature in general.*

The Frenchman is unlikely to have read by 1676, when his own treatise was first printed in French, a work of Spinoza's that was published in 1677, and which stated that *All men have one and the same nature: it is power and culture which mislead us.* He may, however, have heard similar sentiments via the French political refugees who lived in The Hague and with whom Spinoza had a considerable amount of contact in the last years of his life. Moreover, whether directed specifically at Spinoza or not, Boulain de la Barre's pertinent rap on the knuckles accentuates the tension in Spinoza's view of women, and makes us seek either a logical or a psychological explanation for it. The author of the very early *La vie de Spinosa* says that Spinoza did not marry 'either because he feared the ill-temper of a woman, or because the love of philosophy took him up completely'. This author (whom I accept, although conclusive evidence is lacking, to be Jean Maximilien Lucas) is, like Spinoza's other early biographer, John Colerus, sometimes confused, and we cannot tell from this comment if he or Spinoza found women ill-tempered. But his comment prompts us to wonder whether it could have been on grounds of a particular paternal prejudice, rather than a general cultural one, that Spinoza apparently considered female minds *less fitted for abstract reasoning* than those of *uneducated peasants.* If Michael held this view we would expect Spinoza to denounce it as prejudice, but there is no reference to a father's grumbling in his writings. Did he witness his father treating women with contempt? Did his mother display extreme irrationality in the few years that her little boy knew her?

The meagre reports we have of Michael's wives leave them almost totally hidden behind their veils. Only one action, one remark, of Hana Debora's is recorded. Two months before she died, when Bento was nearly six, both his parents lay ill. A lawyer was sent with two witnesses to seek Michael's acceptance of a bill of exchange, but before 'Senhor Miguel despinoza' could speak, Hana Debora cried, 'Because of the illness that has befallen my husband, the bill of exchange will not be accepted.' Michael made no response, and the agent left, to report a 'default of acceptance'. Hana Debora was, then, a woman capable of making decisions when close to dying and Michael, who would live for another sixteen years, a man inclined to let her.

A final, bleak report on Bento's father's relations with his wives concerns the placing of his body in the Jewish cemetery. Michael was not buried anywhere near his first wife Rachel, nor alongside Bento's mother Hana Debora, nor in the grave dug only five months earlier for his third wife Esther, to whom he had been married the longest. Nor was he put in a chronologically ordered row, as were Rachel and his father Isaac. It has been suggested that, because he was a synagogue dignitary but could not afford a family plot, he was laid on the higher ground of the cemetery, out of danger of flooding. His gravestone, its simple lettering still clearly legible today, lies not far from Morteira's and Menasseh's. The same biographer concludes from the stone's curt epitaph that Michael was a sceptic about an afterlife, but the inscription expresses hope for a blessed future for him. Segregation from his wives could have resulted from wrangles between his children over which of their mothers he should lie with in death. Any quarrel – and we shall see what a quarrelsome family the De Espinosas were – would have lain between Bento, Gabriel and their sister or half-sister Ribca, since Isaak (who was probably Rachel's son) and Miriam (Bento's full sister) were by then dead.

Let us briefly ponder the parentage of these ill-documented siblings. Gabriel is assumed to be younger than Bento, because after Michael's death the family firm was called 'Bento y Gabriel Despinoza', and to be Hana Debora's son on grounds of Jewish Law in relation to Esther's will, for Esther left everything to Michael. However, I am told that this only means she had no other children by other husbands, and we know she was not previously married. More significantly, if Gabriel had been born to Esther, he would have been a partner in the family firm aged fourteen at the oldest: his name first appears in 1655. Finally, it seems to have passed unnoticed that, in the *Notta dos irmaos desta Santa Hebra* of 1637, 'Abraham Espinosa seu filho' is written beneath Michael's and Isaak's names, but above Baruch's. An 'Abraham Espiñosa' is also listed a few places below the scored-out name of Baruch in the Ets Haim register.

Ribca could have been Rachel's, Hana Debora's or Esther's daughter. Colerus says she was older than Miriam, and this has led one biographer to make her Rachel's daughter. Others state without evidence that she was Esther's daughter and, since she married Miriam's widower and could read and speak Dutch, it is tempting to think she was younger than her sister. But if she were Esther's daughter, then she was eleven years old or under when she translated Dutch legalese into Portuguese for Michael in 1652. I think, mainly because she is known to have named her only daughter Hana, that she was Bento's full sister.

All we know of the father's view of women, then, is that he obeyed Judaic Law by remarrying swiftly after the death of each wife; that he let Hana Debora's daughter Miriam remain illiterate, although her grandmother Maria Nunes had signed her marriage entry with a reasonably fluent and firm hand; and that he let Ribca read and speak Dutch.

We have gleaned what we can from family history, and must now look to the boy.

TWO

Amsterdam: 1632–42

Anyone who saw clearly that by committing knavery he would enjoy a more perfect and better life, or essence, than by pursuing virtue, would be a lunatic if he did not commit it. For knavery would be virtue with regard to so faulty a human nature.

His first memory may have been of the *ledikant*, the bed with red curtains that was said to be the only family inheritance he would accept, and which the inventory of his possessions shows he kept until death. He may have been born among its heavy feather bags. Michael perhaps lay hidden behind its curtains while the bill of exchange was presented. The *ledikant* (*lit de camp*, or *lit à la française*) was originally designed for the battle field: Rembrandt's '*Lit a la française*' shows a canopy draped like a wigwam. Although the notary was admitted to the 'bedroom', this was probably a ground-floor reception room, as was usual in those tall, narrow-staired houses where the hoist under the gables could raise a heavy object on ropes to roof height, yet still not get it through the casement. Bedrooms were rare in the seventeenth century: paintings often show bedsteads or wall-cupboard bunks in parlours.

Just before his sixth birthday Bento probably saw his dead mother's face on the *ledikant*'s pillows. Did he see Hana Debora put into her coffin, and the coffin loaded into a canal-boat at the landing stage in front of the synagogue? He may have sat in the barge with the men while it was towed by a horseman to the Beth Haim at Ouderkerk, the burial ground of the Jews. No Jew wanted to lie in Christian consecrated ground, or break the Judaic law that a cemetery be fifty ells from the nearest house, and the marranos had pleaded from the first to buy their own piece of earth. The Beth Haim lay on the Amstel river, just south-east of the city. Funeral processions might take the dyke path, but boat-travel was easy and, since Jewish cortèges had to pay tolls when passing churches, these barges became a familiar sight. A sign above the former landing-stage to the cemetery, inscribed in 1616, marks the river as the point of entry, not the road. There was much ritual wailing and flamboyant fluttering of vast silk handkerchiefs, and in the early days wilder displays of grief. These brought complaints from the Dutch, whose own obsequies were perfunctory. Twice the bailiffs had to deal with hostile picketing from Amsterdammers, and the Jews were ordered to act more modestly. Once landed, Hana Debora's corpse would have been carried into the cleansing-house for the rituals of *taharah* (washing) and *rondeamentos* (the seven times circling of the dead), before being buried in a shroud like all other dead persons, to show the equality in death, at least, that God accorded to all. But on many of the beautiful gravestones in the Beth Haim cemetery the space left for eulogy to a widow remains bare. Did anyone comfort Bento with the words of the Spanish priest Vivés, that the best mother is a dead one? Did anyone mention Vivés's report of two bereaved sons, one of whom was thankful his mother never showed him any affection, and the other sure that his academic success was due to her death? Small wonder if the little boy climbed thoughtfully on to the *ledikant* he would later take from lodging to lodging; whose pillows would bear the force of the yearnings, jealousies, fears and tears chronicled only in teasing snatches; whose feather bags would be the silent guardians of his sexual jealousy, loneliness and grief.

Close by the bedstead will have belched a peat fire, or a pile of wood flotsam. Wood was expensive in the water-covered Netherlands, and most was imported from Denmark or further north. It floated, tied to ships, to be stored on or around the Houtgracht ('wood canal'). The marranos felt the damp North Sea cold severely: Rabbi Morteira received as part of his stipend a hundred baskets of peat a year. But peat smoke clogged the lungs, especially when aggravated by the fumes of cheap oil, cheap candles and tobacco. The marranos dominated both the importing of tobacco and its processing in Amsterdam. In 1651 Michael de Espinosa would receive a consignment of pipes from Algeria. (It was believed until this century that tobacco had medicinal properties. Culpeper lists it as good for rheumatic pains and all cold diseases: 'Tobacco is a great expeller of phlegm when smoked in a pipe.' One prominent physician swore that smoking alone had saved him from death during the 1635 plague epidemic.) Spinoza survived outbreaks of the plague that swept Dutch cities in 1635, 1655 and 1663–4, but 'he did not enjoy good health at any time in the whole of his life' and his lungs, diseased by tuberculosis and glass dust, would finally give out when he was forty-four. The smoke that clung to the curtains of the *ledikant* in his childhood would be a permanent feature: his pipe was his pleasure, his landlord said, until the day he died.

There were books, too – Spanish, Portuguese, Hebrew and French – some of them gifts or polite purchases from Menasseh ben Israel, from his pen or his new printing press, the first in Amsterdam, set up in 1627 when

Menasseh was just twenty-three. Bento would die with very old volumes still in his book cupboard, some of them, such as the gift of Menasseh to Michael mentioned earlier, alien to his thinking and perhaps untouched for years.

There would have been candles, tallow or wax, in that childhood home. Lighting was a measure of wealth throughout Europe. Wax candles were the most costly, and burned cleanest. For Jews, lighting also symbolised a particular spiritual illumination: 'The commandment is a lamp, and the teaching (Torah) is light.' The quality of the Sabbath light therefore mattered above all. Tallow was permitted if wax could not be afforded: candles must simply be as good as possible, as a humble expression of the greater lights that burned in the synagogue, where candles of best beeswax were suspended in fine glass lamps or glowed in the eight-branched candlestick. Spinoza's interest in the symbolism of light as joining the mind of man to the mind of God amounted to a firm resolve to substitute the natural light of reason for the irrational light of faith, superstition and divine revelation.

Until his early twenties only Jewish lights shone on Bento. In his infancy they dominated the tiny, beautifully carved and decorated Beth Jacob, which in the early 1630s was one of three small synagogues on the Houtgracht. In 1638 the houses containing the Beth Jacob and Beth Israel synagogues were sold, and the most easterly Neveh Shalom was luxuriously enlarged to house a united and expanded Talmud Torah congregation. Bento may have accompanied Michael and Isaak on weekday evenings when the pious worshipped, but he would also have seen the theatricality of the Sabbath, when reading, liturgy, ritual and chanting could extend from nine until half-past twelve in the morning, and again from three o'clock until evening. This assembly of recently Judaised marranos and curious non-Jewish visitors seems to have been at least partly an occasion for displaying status. Visitors noted that some men talked incessantly, rarely joining in the singing. (Were they doing business, forbidden on the Sabbath, under their prayer shawls?) Perhaps they were feigning nonchalance at being excluded by their birth from the ceremonial. All marranos, Jews of the South, could boast of being of royal David's blood, but the superiority of those of supremely select lineage was driven home each Sabbath. The Portuguese, as we know, considered themselves spiritually élite. 'One of their Rabbies', it was reported by a visitor to Amsterdam in 1633, 'walks up and down and in Portuguese magnifies the messias [sic] to come . . .' for 'the Jews hold that the Messiah shall come out of that tribe that speak the Portuguese language.' This belief, fed largely by the predictions of the mystic Isaac Luria, gripped many in the community. There were further discriminations. The 'Sons of

Aaron', representing the priests, carried the *Torah*, the five books of Moses, covered in cloth of gold and decorated with pendant gold bells. The 'Sons of Levi' sang the psalms of David. Yet the humblest male present, perhaps a German-Jewish servant, standing well back with popping eyes (for, to the *Hooghduytsen*, the marranos seemed an odd group of Jews), took precedence over the proudest of wives. 'The women were secluded from the men,' wrote another visitor in 1641, 'being seated in certain galleries by themselves, and having their heads mabbl'd with linnen, after a fantasticall and somewhat extraordinary fashion.'

The marrano Sabbath service also included a Moorish or Middle Eastern mix of singing, ululation and swaying, which shocked some of the Dutch. Music was banned by the Dutch Reformed Church because it was said to lead to lasciviousness: Mundy writes that in Amsterdam 'organs are nott played till the people depart', and then only tunes unconnected with dancing or drinking were allowed. But uplifting arpeggios from the virtuoso Jan Sweelinck were, like the tinkling virginals permitted in Dutch parlours, cold in comparison with the marranos' haunting Hebrew and Spanish rhythms, which pulsated with passion through the soft strings of the vihuela, or renaissance guitar. The brilliant young rabbi Aboab de Fonseca played the harp. One hymn was a love-song, referring to the bridegroom Israel and his bride, the Sabbath. There were elements, too, of mysticism and frenzy – a Spanish rather than Jewish arcane spiritual intensity, mingled in the older marranos' memories with searing sun, cobalt-blue skies and riotous religious festivals. At Purim the singing subsided into a boisterous party in celebration of 'Saint' Esther; grotesque masks were worn, and mild drunkenness allowed. It is unlikely that the lyricism and theatricality of services, which an eye-witness says included a Catholic-inspired kissing of prayer-shawls and using of 'incense-pans', did other than enthral a little boy of Mediterranean blood. Spinoza would claim that since *those things are good which bring about the preservation of the proportion of motion and rest the human body's parts have to another* – here came a side-swipe at the puritanical strictures of Calvinism and other Protestant sects – *nothing forbids our pleasure except a savage and sad superstition.* He recommended enhancing the health of one's mind and body with good food, entertainment, recreation and delights for all the senses. But he himself failed to look after his body or nourish his spirits, and when, in his last writings, we find perceptible but complex revulsions blended with a yearning for incorruptible intellectual *joy*, we shall recall the aesthetic ecstasy of the Sabbath.

There were also melodramatic quarrels in the synagogue, such as those that flared before the setting up of the rival Beth Israel synagogue in 1618, or during Morteira's furious excommunication of Menasseh ben Israel in

1640 – for just one day – which preceded a scandalous Jewish suicide that same year, of which more later. An eye-witness reported that 'Their elders sometimes fall together by the ears in the very synagogue, and with the holy utensils, as Candlesticks, Incense-pans, and suchlike, break one another's pates' – a claim supported by Grotius's prohibition on weapons being taken into a Jewish gathering, and the *ad hoc* condition for excommunication imposed by the *parnasim* in 1639: 'For entering the synagogue with staff in hand'.

Violence at the synagogue intensified the insecurity of a home life rocked by death and disputes. What did the six-year-old make of the row with Cousin Jacob of Grancairo? Jacob's sister Rachel had died in 1627, and his father Abraham in 1637. Jacob, as Abraham's 'son and legal heir', came hotfoot from Palestine where he ran a branch of the family firm. In December 1637 Michael petitioned that his cousin be allowed to take his father's place on the board of a synagogue charity. A year later Jacob amicably accepted a small sum from Michael as 'good payment' for partnership trading profits, and promised that no further claim would be made, but soon afterwards he and Michael admitted that 'between them a matter of controversy had arisen because of a certain inheritance'. The 'matter' was to be settled by arbitration, and failure to comply with the decision of the three appointed Portuguese merchants would result in a fine of 400 guilders, 'half of which will be used for the poor of this city and the other half for the poor of the Jewish nation'. Only towards the end of March were the 'disputes and differences' resolved. Michael was now required to pay 640 guilders, and was left only with the 'remainders, debts, shares and credit, none excepted, as could be collected' in relation to 'the joint trading venture he had with the father of the said Jacob d'Espinosa'. Times were clearly not good. It must have cost Jacob more than he gained to abandon his business and come from Palestine, and it was humiliating for Michael to have to expose his accounts to others. Yet reason had prevailed over passion, and there are no further reports of discord.

Spinoza would later painstakingly demonstrate the origins of destructive passions, and their capacity to enslave and destroy society. This was a general thesis based on universal principles of human nature, but the microcosm of society presented in family life required special attention. In his last work, the *Political Treatise*, he would write, *It is true that the quarrels which arise between parents and children are generally more frequent and bitter than quarrels between masters and slaves, yet it is not conducive to good family management to make the father a master, and to treat children as slaves.* He need not have had his own father in mind, despite a report that 'In his boyhood he already roused his father's dislike against him because, although destined for commerce, he devoted himself entirely to letters.' Living in rented rooms in private homes for almost all his adult life would give Spinoza plenty of exposure to filial friction. The evidence is that he tried to please Michael, and to minimise the shame he brought him, by remaining a dutiful member of the synagogue congregation until his father had died. Subtle signs of warm recollection will emerge in later years, when Michael is a dim memory to us all.

Some synagogue poses were judicious. Bento would have understood that aliases, track-covering and passwords must remain a reality of life in Amsterdam if relatives in Iberia were not to be compromised. Homesick *conversos* loitered, for example, hoping to earn safe-conduct passes to Spain by gleaning economic information or surnames. Many older marranos still found it hard, anyway, to mouth their Hebrew names. None forgot the tragedy of a careless betrayal. All had heard of families such as the one wiped out by the Inquisition after one of its children was asked his name by a Christian and replied, 'At home it is Abraham, but outside, Francisquito.' Michael seems to have dropped his alias of 'Gabriel Álvares' (his maternal grandfather's name) as soon as possible, but his son Baruch would show awareness of the wisdom of Iberian camouflage. He would trade under the name of Bento. He would withhold publication of most of his texts, and hide, on the title page of his 1670 *Theologico-Political Treatise*, behind the initials B.d.S. and a falsely stated Hamburg publisher. His personal motto, engraved on his seal and cut into his memorial stone, was *Caute* ('with caution'). *The virtue of a free man is seen to be as great in avoiding dangers as in overcoming them.* But these were reminders to himself that self-preservation was wise and he needed such reminders, because his astonishing indiscretions show that he was not naturally cautious. He often trusted too much, and had to backtrack or prevaricate. He increasingly put himself in danger by speaking out sharply. He specially loathed false piety – one of several kinds of posing with which he would have nothing to do – and is said to have let his scorn for this show even as a child. Lucas recounts how 'the teachings of his father, who was a man of good sense' led him at an early age to distinguish religious hypocrisy – bowing and scraping, preaching and posing – from true piety. Lucas's claim, made credible by examples of similar behaviour in later years, is that Spinoza had 'a ready and penetrating wit', which 'embarrassed his teacher', but which prompted Michael to trust him and perhaps to test him at the age of ten:

[His father] instructed him to go and collect some money which a certain old woman in Amsterdam owed him. When he entered her house and found her reading the Bible she motioned to him to wait until she finished her prayer; when she had finished it, the child told her his errand, and this good old woman, after counting her money out to him, said, as she pointed to it on the table, 'Here is what I owe your father. May you some day be as upright a man as he; he has never departed from the Law of Moses, and heaven will only bless you in the measure in which you imitate him.' As she was concluding these remarks she picked up the money in order to put it into the child's bag, but, having observed that this woman had the marks of false piety against which his father had warned him, he wanted to count it after her in spite of all her resistance. He found that he had to ask for two ducats [gold or silver coins much sought-after by merchants] which the pious widow had dropped into a drawer through a slit specially made on the top of the table, and so he was confirmed in his thought. Elated by his success in this adventure, and by the praise of his father, he watched these sort of people with more care than before, and he made such fine fun of them that everybody was astonished.

It is the last sentence that makes the strongest connection with Spinoza. Such cockiness readily foreshadows his rousing of Rabbi Morteira's fury by (it is said) sending him a message that 'he knew the gravity of his threats, and that, in return for the trouble he had taken to teach him the Hebrew language, he was quite willing to show him how to excommunicate him'. There is ample evidence in Spinoza's later life not only of his distrust of *external acts of piety and worship*, which he distinguished from the *inward piety and inward worship of God*, but of his sarcasm and shortness with those he thought fools. Long after he had vowed not to mock human failings, when he was a sick man whose passions, we might think, must be all but stilled by pain, loss and disgust, a direct challenge to his wits still provoked petulant contempt. *Descartes's principles of natural things*, he wrote, when a correspondent seemed inclined to prefer the dead French philosopher's concept of physical matter to his own, *are useless, not to say absurd*.

As he grew older, he reserved his most biting replies for those he thought should know better than to exhibit irrationality. Time and again he would confront the people most dangerous to his ambitions, rather than the indifferent or the simple-minded. Those who made no claim to achieving clear and distinct ideas were humoured, or gently corrected. So why was the old woman of the ducat story hammered so hard? Was it because she was a woman that he knew he could guarantee an appreciative response to his 'fine fun'? Did he think the lattices on the synagogue galleries had been put up to conceal the foolish irreverence of females? Or did he think the *inconstancy and deceptiveness of women* lay at the core of false piety? Perhaps the little boy was elated at being, at last, one of the merchants and away from the clutching veils. We may wonder who looked after four disturbed children under ten in the years between his mother's death and Michael's remarriage in 1641.

Yet there is no need to suppose, despite the constraints of an inward-looking community and an entirely Jewish primary education, that the greater world of Amsterdam and Dutch affairs failed to make an impression on the boy. A ten-minute westward walk from his home would stamp on anyone a set of colourful and conflicting impressions. Turn through the alley into the Breestraat, past the dwellings of rich but devout marranos and the house bought in 1639 by the painter Rembrandt van Rijn. Pass, perhaps, that odd man himself, although Rembrandt was likely to ignore the black-clad merchant with his equally dapper sons, preferring to use as models the more biblically evocative *Hooghduytsen*, from whom he bought the old robes and hats that he made his sitters wear. Evidence defies the myth that the painter made friends with marranos, or that they liked him. One marrano turned down a commissioned portrait saying it was no likeness: Rembrandt demanded immediate payment. A neighbour complained about the noise he made. Even Menasseh ben Israel, with his correctly scissor-trimmed beard, who was eager to chat, prompt to supply details of Jewish mysticism for the painter's depictions of Belshazzar and Faust, and would later commission book illustrations from Rembrandt, seems not to have held his interest for longer than it took to sketch him. The apprentice Govaert Flinck would be left to paint Menasseh's portrait. Spinoza and Rembrandt would not have had much to say to one another. Both valued the individual *ziel*, but this Dutch word, which did duty for both 'soul' and 'mind', was for the painter some ineffable, indefinable 'soul', whereas for Spinoza it meant 'mind', the ideas of an individual. Despite efforts at finding connections in the lives of Spinoza and Rembrandt, there is no evidence that they ever acknowledged each other's existence.

Just beyond Rembrandt's house they must cross the St Anthonie *Sluis* where the North Sea was held in check, forced back from the canals and the Amstel river by the acclaimed methods of Dutch water control. Nearby, across a wide walled cemetery, bells rang out from the soaring South Kerk spire, its gold-painted cupola and brass carillon glinting, its railed gallery, scrolls and pediments belying its stark whitewashed interior. The exterior, being Catholic-built, would have resonance for the marranos, but if they saw inside it (and why should they, enjoying as they now did the luxury of never having to enter a church?) they would find it oddly bare, and the trading guilds' coats of arms in every window undignified. French travellers contrasted the 'very sad nudity' of the Reformed churches with the beauty of the older churches and the town halls of Utrecht, Delft and Gouda – and the Amsterdam synagogue. Michael would have skirted the cemetery, and could not have conceived that his son Baruch would – through no wish of his own – be buried in just such a Christian catacomb. Bento, for his part, with only the Amsterdam synagogue for comparison, might have had mixed feelings. He might have noted with relief the simplicity and apparent neutrality of the church's interior, but he would soon learn that its harsh brilliance served only to reflect the white light of Calvinist prescription. 'Scripture . . . dispels the darkness . . .' It would take time for him to distinguish between rational enlightenment and that which merely 'lit up'. For a while, as a young adult, he would be attracted to the yet more severely unadorned meeting-halls of radical Protestant groups who rejected clerical organisation – the Mennonites, Collegiants and Quakers, of whom some were so puritan that they saw Calvinists as prone to sinful frivolity. But here, too, enlightenment failed to match the light of reason. Most of Spinoza's so-called free-thinking friends would be at core Christian. They never grasped that sectarian devotion alienated. Even as Spinoza was mustering all possible argument to show that only universal concepts could unite diverse social groups, his Dutch friend Pieter Balling would be testifying in his *The Light upon the Candlestick* to the mystic inner light of 'Christ, the Spirit, the Word etc.', which must 'infallibly discover sin and evil, to reprove and convince thereof'. This view of enlightenment differed little from Calvin's dictum that knowledge of God came only when the mind was illuminated through 'the internal teacher, the Spirit', and not 'till we have begun to be displeased with ourselves'.

On through the old city wall at Kloveniersburgwal and up the Old High Street, stepping aloofly through the jostling crowds in the measured Iberian manner that other Europeans found so funny. Michael's family would seem, despite their soft camel-hair clothes and the buckles on their shoes, and perhaps also their deep lace cuffs and canions – the deep ruffles or ribbons at wrist and calf introduced by Frederik Hendrik from France as 'tabliers de galant' – sober compared with the flamboyant patrician marranos who clattered by on horseback, or the turbanned Turks, or the beggars who lived in slums beneath the outer walls. The city, seething with misfits and described by a seventeenth-century French philosopher as 'the great ark of the refugees', drew varying opinions from foreigners. The practical charity, discipline and training given to felons and 'that sort of unnecessary vermin which frequents fairs', and the spectacular lotteries that funded such enterprise, were approved, but most visitors were scandalised at the laxity of the Reformed Church in allowing open religious dissent. To some it seemed that in Amsterdam people could worship as they pleased. Lutherans, Anabaptists, Catholics, any sect could a establish a congregation; there were more dissenters' churches than Dutch Reformed. Descartes thought the whole country 'a refuge for Catholics', as well he might, since the council of Egmond, where he lived latterly, steadfastly ignored a declaration against 'the wickedness of popery' sent it by the States General in 1588. But the English poet Andrew Marvell shrewdly isolated self-interest in the city's welcome:

> Hence Amsterdam, Turk-Christian-Pagan-Jew,
> Staple of Sects and Mint of Schism grew;
> That Bank of Conscience, where not one so strange
> Opinion finds but Credit, and Exchange.

And his countryman Felltham noted the all-seeing eye and tight grip of the regents, the magistrates, burgomasters, aldermen and councillors who would strike Montesquieu as truly 'a kind of king'. Felltham grasped that in the United Provinces religious correctness was coextensively political correctness, and that blasphemy and heresy were punishable offences. 'You may be what devil you will so you push not the State with your horns.' There must, as Grotius had decreed, be no disturbance of the peace: 'Atheists and impious people should not be tolerated in any good republic.' Grotius had ordered all Jews over fourteen years old to state their faith in God, Moses, the prophets and the afterlife. It may not have been true, as one anonymous pamphlet advised, that before applying for a position in government 'you must go to church, and not neglect one sermon, then you will come to the notice of the lords'. But it is, in the view of one historian, fair to say that 'anyone who did not want to miss a single opportunity would do well to place himself among the Calvinists', and that lists of magistrates and deputies affirm that civic honour required conformity. Once appointed, magistrates assumed the divine rights that Calvin allowed them:

> The Lord has not only testified that the function of magistrates has his approbation and acceptance, but has eminently commended it to us by dignifying it with the most honourable titles ... Civil magistracy is a calling not only holy and legitimate, but far the most sacred and honourable in human life.

Just as Spinoza understood that Spanish Jews had been eligible for public office whereas Portuguese Jews had not, and would before long discover that German and Polish Jews had been allowed neither wealth nor honour in eastern Europe, so he would before long perceive the glass walls that surrounded the apparent freedom of foreigners and religious dissenters in Amsterdam. It remained easy to be a member of a hated minority.

Did Bento want to venture, as a young child, beyond his father's clear-cut parameters in the city of Amsterdam, which narrowly encompassed the eastern sector, the Exchange and the Prinsengracht? Despite the pride the marranos took in their distinctive appearance, he seems to have grasped early on that standing out from the crowd through dressing either too well or too shabbily (like the strict Mennonite sect from whom the isolated present-day Amish of Pennsylvania descend, who wore only shapeless, frayed-edged tunics and trousers) caused hostility and distrust. *If someone dresses expensively in order to be honoured for that, then he seeks an esteem that arises from self-love, not from any regard for his fellow men. But if someone sees that men disdain his wisdom, by which he could be helpful to his fellow-men, and trample it underfoot because he dresses badly, then he does well if he provides himself with clothing that will not shock them, thereby becoming like his fellow men in order to win them over and help them.* Some of the marranos had sensed this from the start, and had set aside their richest clothes for synagogue wear, buying plain silk or starched linen collars for the city. Some of those who had, or wanted, professional friendships with non-Jews, such as Menasseh ben Israel and Dr Ephraim Bueno, sat for their portraits dressed in unrelieved black. In one sense Spinoza approved this Jewish tradition of 'bettering the instruction' of the native-born, for it was the expedient reverse of setting oneself apart. Representations invariably show him in black with a plain white collar. The inventory of his clothes includes coat and breeches in camel-hair; two camel-hair cloaks; two black hats; gloves; a leather waistcoat; black and grey shoes and a pair of silver buckles; a cotton cravat with detachable collars; sets of 'bands and cuffs' (canions)?; and four cotton handkerchiefs, plus one 'chequered' one. 'Nose-cloths' were not unusual in Holland, although they were rarely the fashion accessories flourished by the French and Spanish.

One of the reasons Michael could hold his head high was that he was not a Catholic. The trump card of the marranos as they sought acceptance in Amsterdam had been that they had been brutally treated by papists, and they played on the fact that another religious sect was more loathed than themselves. Marauding Spanish forces in the Provinces had included Walloons, Germans, Italians, Burgundians and English, as well as Span- iards, but all had been at least nominally Catholic, and, for many republicans, hatred of the Spaniards was still inextricably mixed with detestation for papery. Older people had during the years of revolt seen the banners flaunted before the town walls – *'Per Fide Catholica et Mercede Nostra'* ('For the Catholic Faith and Our Lady') – and horrific barbarism on the part of invading troops had inculcated a view of brutality as a Catholic attribute. The Dutch did not know that the Spanish commanders were themselves so appalled at the behaviour of their pikemen that the question, 'Are we here or in Flanders?' became entrenched in Spanish discourse after 1572 as a rebuke for disgraceful behaviour. Catholics were thought to be treacherous, too, after the papist Count Rennenburg suddenly surrendered the territory of Groningen to Philip II in 1580. Papists, it was muttered, were not to be trusted, not even those who sacrificed '*goet ende bloet*' (goods and blood) to the Republic, or became *klopjes*, Catholic virgins who took no vows, but visited the sick and gave charity to anyone in need. The atrocities of 1572 were retold in a book for children printed in 1615, so a new generation learned the stereotypes and slogans. Then, in 1629, when Amersfoort was taken and Hilversum was burned, and villagers were ordered to arm every sixth man with an axe or spade, old memories flooded back.

In Spinoza's childhood the Roman Catholics of Amsterdam were well advised to lie low. Even Joost van den Vondel, popular patriotic poet of the city, seriously dismayed his neighbours when he converted in 1641. One unfortunate incident or pernicious rumour could result in a public outcry, shattering individual friendships. Bento heard these sudden outbursts of passion and hysterical accusation, for they happened right there on the streets of Amsterdam, and he observed their roots in prejudice. *If someone has been affected with joy or sadness by someone of a class, or nation, different from his own he will love or hate, not only that person, but everyone of the same class or nation.* He would eventually publish a polemical treatise of staggering bluntness, imploring those capable of using reason to see the destruction and cruelty wrought through religious prejudice. But he also insisted that minority groups could bring loathing on themselves. The Jews, for example:

> *believed that their kingdom was God's kingdom, and that they alone were God's children, the other nations being his enemies – and therefore the object of their implacable hatred (for such hatred they regarded as piety, see Psalm 139, verses 21 and 22) – nothing could be more abhorrent to them than to swear allegiance and promise obedience to some foreigner . . . And the common reason for the continual growth of hatred was also present; for the Gentiles must have regarded the Jews with the most bitter hatred.*

The exclusion of Portuguese Jews from office had, in Spinoza's view, exacerbated holier-than-thou religious bigotry in the 'Portuguese', and the effect this had in Iberia seemed to be perpetuated in Holland. The Dutch of the streets may have pulled their infants tighter to them as the De Espinosas passed. ('Espinoza' they must spell it now, if their servants and business associates were not to hiss the 's' with northern sharpness.) This family, if not Catholic or Spanish, must be 'Portuguese', and the expectation of the ignorant, who had no share in the wealth that these strange Israelites created, would be that beneath their ruffles and refinement they were as brutal as Spanish pikemen and as prone to child murder and blood-drinking as any shabby Jewish pedlar. The latter slanders, embedded in folklore, would be spread anew with the sudden influx of *Hooghduytsen* Jews in 1648. In the 1630s there was, according to Mundy, the English visitor quoted earlier, no ghetto, no alarming, alien presence and no victimisation.

But treatises imploring freedom of speech and religious toleration are not written in a climate in which toleration is thought to prevail. *I marked the fierce controversies of philosophers raging in Church and State, the source of bitter hatred and dissension, the ready instruments of sedition and other ills innumerable* . . . Yet Spinoza's political works (the 1670 *Theologico-Political Treatise* and the 1677 *Political Treatise*) are not, either, the ranting of a victimised underdog. When as a child Bento accompanied Michael, he could walk tall as the typical son of a typical proud marrano, going about his lawful business, unlikely to provoke civil disruption or much envy. The wealth and royal protection of the Castilian Jewish élite had by the late fourteenth century provoked general hatred, but in Amsterdam, on the whole, the marrano merchants set an approved commercial pace, as noted wryly by Descartes: 'In this large town where I live, everyone but myself is engaged in trade, and hence is so attentive to his own profit that I could live here all my life without ever being noticed by a soul.' As with the question of conspicuous spending there was, to be sure, a small problem over shady practice. The Dutch winked at the duplicity of Jewish merchant venturers at sea, but resented their lack of scruples in Amsterdam. No church-going Dutchman, not even the slave trader with stone Negro heads either side of his doorway to show the source of his fortune, wanted to be denounced as a trader in gold and silver, or a lombard (*lommerd* is the Dutch word for a pawnbroker), since private money-lending was thought sinful by the Reformed Church, an occupation contrary to the word of God. To stop Jews prospering unduly they were hemmed with legal restrictions and excluded from guilds. Yet marrano wealth was often a mirage, for like other European Jews they disguised poverty and debt, a form of pride that baffled the tax-collectors. Grotius complained in 1640:

> I had imagined that the members of the Amsterdam synagogue were both wealthy and liberal. Now I realise I was mistaken. However, I am not sure whether to believe that they tell the truth, or that they wish to appear poorer than they are in reality, in order to evade taxes.

The widowed German-Jewish businesswoman Glückel of Hameln (1646–1724) admitted:

My business was large, for I had extensive credit with Jews and non-Jews. I afflicted myself in the heat of summer and in the snow of winter I stood there in my shop all day; and though I possessed less than others thought, I wished always to be held in honour and not, God forbid, dependent on my children, sitting at another's table.

Yet by and large the Hispanic Jews of Amsterdam occupied throughout Spinoza's lifetime a uniquely admired position, which he could not have failed to note. He saw early, too, a need for good citizenship, because it was impossible to walk the streets of Amsterdam without witnessing sin and its wages. Michael might, in his confidence as a Jew 'nott ill-esteem'd', make a short detour from the High Street to show his children the *Spinhuis* gaol on the Oudezijds Achterburgwal where, for a stuiver or two – the price of a loaf of bread – convicted women could be watched serving their sentences, spinning in subdued rows under the warder's platform. The *Rasphuis*, in the Heiligenweg, was the degrading alternative for men. Did Bento ever see convicts shuffling, shackled, through its grand gateway to start their sentences? Inside, their sweating bodies would be covered in a fine glistening coat of red brazil-wood dust as they sawed interminably, condemned to reducing, each day, a set amount of brazil wood to brilliant red powder. If they failed, or otherwise offended, they were subjected to the terrifying system of intimidation of the 'drowning cell', which constantly refilled with water – made blood-red by the brazil-wood dust that coated the prisoners' bodies – and where death was avoided only by ceaseless pumping. This was the calculated realisation of the worst of Dutch nightmares. Michael, a conformist to the core of his being, could not have envisaged how close his second son would come to a *Rasphuis* sentence. Bento's constitution being weak (Lucas says he 'had learnt to suffer since his most tender youth'), he would, of course, have died there: a lawyer acquaintance, sentenced for heresy, perished after a year. The punishments of the *mahamad* kept most Jews away from the magistrates, but the reputation of the *Rasphuis* was for most Hollanders the ultimate deterrent, and while no one denied that the Dutch were pugnacious ('A hundred Netherlanders, a hundred knives,' quipped a popular writer), the republic was known less for its lawlessness than for its fiercesome penalties and ubiquitous gibbets. On this question Spinoza would have mixed views. An individual could not, he said, be called a just person *because he fears the gallows*. To be *just*, it was necessary to understand. *He who gives every man his own because he knows the real reason and necessity for law, acts with constancy of purpose and of his own volition, not another's, and hence is rightly called just.* He would, I think, half-believe for a while that most people could to some extent be brought to reason; to see

31

that their true advantage was the common advantage, and to agree to abide by the laws of the State. *We can best show how much our skill and understanding are worth by educating men so that at last they live according to the command of their own understanding.* But while he abhorred rule through fear, he knew from the first day Michael hid him beneath his cloak and flattened himself and his boys against a wall to let the *grauw* – the mindless mob, enraged by as little as cheating at cards or a mocking greeting – pursue its revenge, that *no society can exist without government and force, and hence without laws to control and restrain the unruly appetites and impulses of men.* His protest at the persecution of reasoning dissidents was distinct from his belief that the law must have teeth.

There were other sinks of humanity that a good Jew should avoid. Did Michael hurry his boys past the *musicos* and taverns which crowded the area between the Jodenbreestraat and the Old Kerk, where the prostitutes gathered to greet constant incursions of sailors? The girls were renowned for their boldness. An Englishman traveller of the time tells of 'the most impudent whores I have heard of who would if they saw a stranger pull him by the coat and invite him into their house'. What did little Bento think of the street-women, knowing, being Portuguese, what they were for; seeing some of them paying for their impudence in the *Spinhuis*; hearing, perhaps, oblique rebukes from the *parnasim* in the synagogue regarding fathers, brothers, uncles? We cannot fill with documented facts the gap between wide-eyed childhood curiosity and the voluminous comment Spinoza devotes to lust in his texts. But the life-long high-mindedness that most scholars and biographers assign him may be mistaken. Even if he did not seek out prostitutes, as he grew a little older would a 'good-looking' youth with 'clear skin', 'fine features' and 'black curl'd hair' reaching to his shoulders avoid those clutching arms? Spinoza knew all about sexual ecstasy. *As far as sensual pleasure [libido] is concerned, the mind is so caught up in it, as if at peace in a true good, that it is quite prevented from thinking of anything else.* Did he mean by libidinous excess only the procuring of sensual pleasure, or marital indulgence too? In the later cold light of rational analysis and an apparently celibate existence, he did not distinguish. *Lust is also a desire for and love of joining one body to another. Whether this desire for sexual union is moderate or not, it is usually called lust.* While Spinoza's remarks on prostitutes often came directly from Terence or Ovid, nothing, textual or anecdotal, rules out carnal experience for him (with either sex). What is ruled in, on the other hand, is a strong interest in the topic. One commentator believes that 'Physical, sexual love to Spinoza partook of a bestial, degrading nature', but I find no cause to judge his experiences or his views to be that crude. They are sufficiently subtle to require several examinations.

And so to the Dam (pictured on the book cover), the great square bustling with townsfolk and foreigners, where the New Kerk and the fish market, the old town hall and the *Wisselbank* fronted the harbour. The noisy and chaotic Stock Exchange – a *confusion de confusiones* despaired one later marrano, who thought histrionics had no place in business affairs – stood back a little from the harbour, but was also close to 'the hundreds of sail' – the great ships that crowded the quays to the envy of foreigners, and seemed hardly inconvenienced by the dangers and detours caused by the war with Spain. Michael, and perhaps Isaak, certainly Gabriel, who would become a successful international trader, may have turned without a glance into the kingdom of commerce, or crossed five more canal bridges to the Prinsengracht warehouse, keenly eyeing the Herengracht houses on the way. The De Espinosas may have known that those houses were filled with fine Smyrna rugs, splendid Turkish tulips costing up to a thousand guilders a bulb, and Ming or porcelain vases to hold their blooms, a delicate funnel displaying each. Porcelain arrived by the shipload from the East until Blue Delft, its Dutch imitation, became popular.

Bento saw with his own eyes the rewards of industry and risk. He could have built, with gratitude and complacency, on the wealth and honour Michael had begun to accrue. Gabriel did; Isaak would not live to manhood. But there is possibly more evidence for Spinoza's scorn of devoting one's life to material gain than for any other characteristic bar his arrogance. Truly, he did not share the view that *usually occupies the mind of the masses more than anything else. For they can imagine hardly any species of joy without the accompanying idea of money as its cause.* His glee at recovering the ducats from the crone lay more in debunking pretence than in acquiring riches. To please his father he took seriously the task of becoming a merchant, but his ease in turning his back on the work after 1656, and his penny-pinching habits, bear out his claim that *those who know the true use of money ... live contentedly with little.* Yet he saw no harm in spending if it did not inhibit clear thinking. Hispanic exuberance would whisper even in his last, sick days. *Things like feasting, gambling, personal adornment, and so forth must be judged as excessive or otherwise in relation to the wealth of each individual, so that no general law can determine what is excessive and what is not.*

At the point where the slim ellipse through the city centre had almost returned to its starting-point Bento might, when too old to hold his father's hand, have slipped away northwards from the South Kerk to the Weigh House in the centre of the New Market. For there, on the upper floor, reached by a little staircase through a doorway inscribed *Theatrum*

Anatomicum (it is still there), the corpses of criminals were publicly dissected by surgeons the day after a hanging. These 'anatomies' were entertainment for many, but for Bento they are likely to have been an important stimulus towards building on the natural philosophy (science) taught at school, and keeping up with current research in physiology. In 1632–3 Rembrandt produced his 'Anatomy Lesson' of Dr Tulp, the sinews of the dead man's arm exposed, seven surgeons watching intently. Rembrandt did not include the rabble of gawping onlookers and rapt students, for his commission obliged him to show only, and flatteringly, the eight surgeons, who were not necessarily present but who would pay him and then hang his painting in their college. Not even Descartes, craning perhaps over the corpse, was depicted. Descartes would probably be studying in the anatomy theatre of the university of Leiden by the time Bento was old enough to sneak up the Weigh House stairs, but he had researched his *Treatise on Man* in Amsterdam between 1629 and 1633, while living on the Prinsengracht.

Descartes's treatise was complete and ready for printing in 1633 when word came of Galileo's Vatican Inquisition. He at once hid the manuscript, deciding it must be published only posthumously. Fame would not bring honour if this work offended, and a theory which, it was said, 'boasts that all phenomena in the world can be explained only by motion and substance', and therefore seemed to assert autonomous functioning for the body and deny God's power, was wisely kept from official eyes. The heretical implications of Descartes's picture of man-as-machine would in no way be dispelled, as its author had hoped, by his claim in his *Meditations* of 1642 that 'I, that is, my soul, by which I am what I am, am not merely present in my body as a pilot in his ship, but am very closely joined and, as it were, intermingled with it.' Still less did Descartes reassure his readers by proposing that the body and soul, separate substances, interacted in the pineal gland of the brain of humans, although many animals also had this gland but were denied souls by Descartes. *Meditations* 'demonstrated' to no one either 'the immortality of the soul' or 'the distinction between the human soul and the body', as its first and second subtitles claimed. Sorbonne theologians asked, 'You say "I am a thinking thing"; but how do you know you are not corporeal motion? . . . What if its nature were limited by the duration of the body, and God had endowed it with just so much strength and existence as to ensure that it came to an end with the death of the body?' The alleged atheist Thomas Hobbes was happy to find holes in Descartes's argument: 'It does not seem to be a valid argument to say, "I am thinking, therefore I am thought", or "I am using my intellect, hence I am an intellect", ' he challenged. 'On the contrary it may well be the case that mind will be nothing but the motions in certain parts of an organic body.'

Descartes eventually withdrew his claim that he could *prove* the immortality of the soul, and fell back on the received view that belief in non-physical soul-stuff depended entirely on faith.

The seeds of Spinoza's dissatisfaction with the Cartesian account of the mind-body relation were sown sometime between 1641, when Cartesian medicine had been banned by most Netherlands universities (but *Meditations* was available in Latin), and 1656, when it was rumoured that Bento de Espinosa doubted the existence of an immortal soul. Spinoza's own mind-body theory, once in permanent shape, would leave Descartes's standing in terms of flouting religious dogma. His denial of free will, and belief that nature dictated and constituted the contents of minds, was taken to be atheism and also materialism, the view that everything was matter. The philosopher would deny both these characterisations, however. He claimed only to provide a logically and empirically superior scientific explanation of the relationship of God to matter and, as deduced from that thesis, of the human mind to the human body. Descartes had himself taught that science must match the exactness of mathematics, but he did not equate mathematics with divine thought, as would Spinoza. Descartes believed that mathematical truths must be 'something less than, and subject to, the incomprehensible power of God', who could act in ways uncapturable by mathematical laws. Spinoza disagreed: since God's mind just was the laws of the universe, he held, if we got our mathematics right, we would know God's mind. The *essence* or precise nature of things, he said, *is to be sought ... from the laws inscribed in these things, as in their true codes.* Willingness to live in a *sanctuary of ignorance* and superstition would, he later declared, *have caused the truth to be hidden from the human race to eternity if mathematics, which is concerned not with ends but only with the essences and properties of figures, had not shown men another standard of truth.* He would far exceed Descartes's methodological ideal by requiring the same standard of certainty in research into all areas of human interest. In correcting the Cartesian theory of mind he simply, he said, dispensed with the unscientific, unquantifiable force on which it depended:

> *I cannot wonder enough that a philosopher of his [Descartes's] calibre – one who had firmly decided to deduce nothing except from principles known through themselves, and to affirm nothing which he did not perceive clearly and distinctly, one who had so often censured the scholastics for wishing to explain obscure things by occult qualities – that such a philosopher should assume a hypothesis more occult than any occult quality.*

Was Spinoza in fact preoccupied with the problem of the union of body and *ziel* because death had early, and constantly, flashed their apparent disunion before his eyes? No: sudden and tragic death was familiar to all in his day. While Hana Debora's loss may figure obscurely in his psychological orientation to women, his theory of mind is deduced from first principles of Nature – that is, from the necessary relation of God's mind to God's body, the universe. When he writes that *A free man thinks of nothing less than of death, and his wisdom is a meditation on life, not on death*, we have no cause to say that in this respect he was not free. Being free was knowing adequately, and obeying the laws of nature. Logical difficulties in his mind-body thesis and his explanation of the *ziel*'s fate after death persist, but they have never been assigned to neurotic morbidity.

The public sights of the city were probably the sum of young Bento's Dutch education, the confinement of his Jewish upbringing being clear from his slowness in learning the language of Amsterdam. In 1665, at almost thirty-three, his Dutch still was not fluent. *I really wish that I could write to you in the language in which I was brought up*, he wrote frustratedly in a letter in Dutch. *I could possibly express my thoughts better. Kindly excuse it, and correct the errors yourself.* Since 1620 the synagogue teachers of the *Talmud Torah* school had given free education to male marranos, and in 1637 the Ets Haim society was formed to fund a higher college of education. Learning elsewhere was unthinkable for a *parnas*'s son, even had Grotius not ordered segregated instruction for Jews. Daily life was governed by rituals and timetables that deliberately minimised contact with non-Jews.

Home life, too, was increasingly governed by synagogue cycles and encyclics as Michael's prestige there developed. The year 1637 was one of honour for him: he became a *parnas* of the Beth Jacob, a member of the charitable 'Holy Society for the matrimony of orphans and young girls', which allocated dowries, and a founder-subscriber, with his two little sons, to the new Ets Haim society. The following year he was surely part of the official welcoming party for Stadholder Frederik Hendrik and his guest, Queen Mother Marie de Médicis, on their visit to the newly enlarged and refurbished synagogue on the Houtgracht. Rabbi Morteira had been at her Court until Jews were expelled from France in 1615. Did the five-year-old Bento stand proudly in the synagogue? Were the De Espinosa children taken to see the parade of the guilds and troops, the buildings draped with bunting, the water masques and tournaments in the harbour? Michael's piety would not have stopped him savouring such theatricality. And if in 1638 Bento had been too young, he must surely have been present at the visit of Queen Henrietta Maria in 1642, when his father was *parnas* of the big united congregation, and Menasseh delivered a splendid address 'in the name of his *naçao*', which he then published in Dutch, Portuguese and

Latin. Such grand events were not the norm, however. Usually Bento's days brought long hours of lessons: in Hebrew alphabet and spelling; in reading; in studying 'something of the five Books of Moses with their crucial accents and pauses'. Classes lasted from eight in the morning until eleven, then from two until five, or in winter until the time of the evening synagogue service. The boys were expected to practise Castilian Spanish at home, rather than the colloquial Judaeo-Spanish Ladino, and to learn from their parents to observe the many *mitzvoth* of proper religious conduct. (The need for new arrivals to know these rules suggests that Michael may have lived at first with Uncle Abraham, whose house was also on the Houtgracht.) In 1643 Menasseh produced an instruction-book for the community, with an appendix for 'the most noble and chaste ladies of the *naçao.*' So badly was it needed that it was reissued up to 1710.

As yet Bento was not taught by rabbis. He was too young for the displays of brilliant exegesis from Morteira and Aboab, which provoked questioning and mild dissension in clever older boys, but which never challenged the central tenets of Judaism. *I was imbued from my boyhood up with the ordinary opinions about the scriptures.* Yet he cannot have failed, at barely eight years old, to hear of, if not see, the retribution that fell on Uriel d'Acosta, a Spanish *converso* who came to Amsterdam as a law student in 1618, yearning to be reborn in his ancestral religion. Seriously disillusioned by the rabbinical Judaism he found, d'Acosta challenged – insulted – the authority of the synagogue leaders, who eventually formally banned him from the community. He fled to Hamburg, but after seven years and a German-Jewish expulsion he returned, to be readmitted to the Beth Jacob during one of Michael's terms as *parnas*, after abject recantation. But his cavilling began again, and this time, we are told, purportedly by d'Acosta himself, he was condemned to public confession and thirty-nine lashes. Michael may not have condoned this terrifying re-enactment of the street flagellation of *auto-da-fé* (or of the cruel ritual punishment of Deuteronomy) since he was not a *parnas* in 1640. But both he and his family may have witnessed it.

> The Amsterdam Jews set their children upon me in the streets, who insulted me in a body as I walked along, abusing and railing at me, crying out, There goes a heretick . . . They spit upon me as they passed by me in the streets, and encouraged their children to do the same . . . During the time of the whipping they sang a psalm . . . I prostrated myself [at the synagogue door] whilst all both old and young, passed over me, stepping with one foot on the lower part of my legs . . .

D'Acosta then shot himself.

37

We might wonder how any child could fail to be marked by such an event, especially one who later admitted to a dread of 'brawling'. But while it was an atrocity, we may have to accept that it did not traumatise Bento. Apart from constant drilling by adults into seeing d'Acosta as a sinister figure, the boy would have known that the Jewish community was as brutal as the Dutch: he is said later to have been twice physically attacked by marranos. A Dutch historian comments that the 'exceedingly nasty' Dutch punishments for criminals reflected a recognition that violence was always just beneath the surface, and Spinoza's writings also reflect this. D'Acosta's fate would receive no direct mention, but the phenomenon of suicide was analysed. People might kill themselves, Spinoza suggested, from such diverse pressures as compulsion by a tyrant, as happened to Seneca, or false ideas of their own true natures. *No one, unless he is defeated by causes external, and contrary, to his nature, neglects to seek his own advantage, or to preserve his own being.* And his powerful disgust, conceivably already in place, towards *Pharisees* who *instigate religious Inquisitions* by putting observation of the Law of Moses before true piety, would echo d'Acosta's phraseology. Nor do I think we can altogether distance Spinoza from d'Acosta's desperate need to escape social pressures.

> *I saw that I was in the greatest danger, and that I was forced to seek a remedy with all my strength, however uncertain it might be – like a man suffering from a fatal illness, who, foreseeing certain death unless he employs a remedy, is forced to seek it, however uncertain, with all his strength. For all his hope lies there.*

Spinoza's early childhood is, as I have said, sparsely documented. Yet it happens that we have touched on all the major themes of his philosophy, and seen the genesis of the conflicting forces in his character on which that philosophy would in some respects founder.

THREE

Amsterdam: 1643–56

Honour has this great disadvantage: to pursue it we must direct our lives according to other men's powers of understanding – fleeing what they commonly flee and seeking what they commonly seek.

Bento made excellent progress in the Jewish school. Colerus writes that 'Spinoza showed from his childhood, and in his younger years, that nature had not been unkind to him' and that 'His quick fancy, and his ready and penetrating wit were easily perceived'. Lucas says he had 'a brilliant mind' and that 'He was not yet fifteen years old when he raised difficulties which the most learned among the Jews found it hard to solve'. These eulogies aside, later events show that Bento must have been industrious in the elementary classes of the *Talmud Torah*. He did not go on to the higher *medras*, which would have prepared him for the rabbinate and where he would have studied the *Talmud*, the post-biblical Judaism on which he owned commentaries but to which he makes little reference; yet, despite abandoning his Jewish education relatively young, he would teach Hebrew and Scripture in a well-respected Amsterdam school by the time he was twenty-four. Jarig Jelles, a Dutch merchant who traded with Michael's family in the 1630s, recalled that Bento was 'trained in letters from childhood, and busy for many years of his youth with theology in particular'. Following Spanish tradition, he was also taught mathematics and science, and judging by his exceptional skill in applied mathematics when in his twenties, his awareness of its adequacy for measuring truth may have surfaced when he was quite young. He became fluent in the Castilian needed to read classical Spanish literature and the mystical religious works that preoccupied many marranos. He would have perfected Hebrew, too, with its rhetorical and poetic subtleties, and studied the Pentateuch (the five books of Moses) in the light of this. In short, he was swept towards *bar-mitzvah* by the educational and *halachic* systems of the Portuguese-Jewish community and, judging by his exceptional school progress and the episode of the ducats, used his 'ready and penetrating wit' to champion his father's ideals.

Conformity and transparent respect may have been his only means of getting attention and approval, for he occupied no psychologically special place in his family. He was not the eldest son; he was the third and middle child. His mother, who might have favoured him, was dead. Without assigning his stepmother Esther or his sisters Miriam and Ribca any particular vices, we may assume that as a typical Portuguese-Jewish boy he is likely to have preferred male company from the day he perceived the superiority of the male child in his culture and the significance of *bar-mitzvah*. He was already a member of the Ets Haim society, whereas his stepmother and sisters were merely tolerated in the synagogue gallery. Girls, to quote a Jewish manual, 'passed into adulthood with hardly a ripple of public acknowledgement'. Not only was their intelligence ignored; Vivès affirms that for Iberians and Jews a premium was put on female silence in the presence of men. Away from men, their conversation consisted of what a growing Bento must have seen as fan-fluttering emotion and uninformed opinion. There is no reason to suppose he doubted the received view that the serpent of Eden solicited Eve because women were by nature gullible and garrulous, any more than he would have disputed that the *caquetoire* armchairs common in his day were so named because women sat in them to cackle. As a young child, why would he doubt what his eyes seemed daily to affirm? That, he believed with Descartes, was how children learned.

The men, too, may have loudly lamented news of relatives caught by the Inquisition, and quarrelled over the perilous passage of ships during the last years of the eighty-year war with Spain. Nor would they have talked coolly about recent scandals involving marrano denials of the special destiny of the *naçao*, namely the distinction of being chosen by God to produce the long-awaited Messiah. Such denial was heresy: Menasseh had stated this in his *De Termino Vitae* of 1639, and would restate it in his *Hope of Israel* (1650). Messianic belief had alone sustained many faithful Jews in Iberia, and pious marranos invariably reacted to mockery of it with fury. As a seven-year-old, Bento would have absorbed community distress without questioning, but a Bento approaching *bar-mitzvah* age probably eyed each angry face with that quizzical expression captured in every representation of him, as he noted the lack of coherent argument against the well-made challenges thrown by sceptics. An incipient urge to measure all human claims against a mathematical yardstick, added to a perception of Jewish insularity and a greater awareness of Dutch objectives than his elders (he was, after all, Amsterdam-born, a Dutch Jew), may soon have blunted his sympathy.

There is a sense in which the marrano disputes of Bento's childhood, and his own subsequent expulsion from the Jewish community, are a Jewish affliction, and as such they are amply covered in Jewish literature. However, many of the articles of faith that marrano rebels found unacceptable were also tenets of Christianity to which adherence was demanded by Grotius. Others were anthropological or scientific, as much the concern of an atheist as a Christian or Jew, and as pertinent to twentieth-century thinkers as to seventeenth-century zealots. I therefore set the disputes of the late 1640s and early 1650s in a broad European context while respecting the particular pain and affront of the Amsterdam 'Portuguese'. The opinions of Isaac de la Peyrère, a marrano-turned-Calvinist, would not burst forth on Europe in published form until 1655, during his visit to Amsterdam, but they were circulated in manuscript from 1643, commented on by intellectuals of all creeds and rejected by the marranos with bitterness and wounded pride. De la Peyrère, who moved in a Sorbonne circle that included Pierre Gassendi, Thomas Hobbes, the priest Marin Mersenne (Descartes's mentor and critic) and, around 1640, Grotius, questioned the received Judaeo-Christian view that humankind's origins lay in Eden. In arguing for the pre-eminence of natural history over revealed religion he claimed, for example, that Israel's antiquity was far outdated by China's or Egypt's, and that races such as the Eskimos and American Indians could not have sprung from Adam. His thesis, the *Prae-Adamitae* (owned by Spinoza), appealed to non-Jewish natural philosophers, and swelled a rising tide of literature and scientific experiment which urged that knowledge was derived from the laws of nature rather than the Law of God. It offended Christians in having as its scriptural basis a passage in St Paul's Epistle to the Romans, and was refuted by Grotius in 1648. It was also banned by Cardinal Richelieu, to whom it was dedicated, and was burned in Paris in 1656.

It is not hard to see how Jews were especially vulnerable to de la Peyrère's denials of the authorship of the Books of Moses, of the accuracy of biblical texts, of the tenet that the world was only 6,000 years old, of the dogma that Adam (or any Jew) was the first man, and of the history of the Jews as the history of the world. To no one were these denials more abhorrent than Michael de Espinosa and the rabbis who were his friends. Michael attended up to his death the discussion group of Saul Levi Morteira, founded in 1643. This *yeshivah*, called the Keter Torah – 'Crown of the Law' – was ultra-orthodox and fervently Messianistic, supportive of Menasseh's claim that the redemption of Israel through a marrano Messiah was fast approaching. Morteira, believed by Lucas to be the teacher whom Spinoza's 'doubts embarrassed', was the moral watchdog of the united synagogue, morals meaning the ritual rules or *halachah*. Most marranos accepted his rebukes and hasty excommunications (Lucas says he was responsible for most of these in Spinoza's time) knowing that they were motivated by a need for Jewish solidarity. Morteira prided himself on his reasoning. He taught that Christianity stood contrary to reason and that it was intellectually impossible to sustain any other creed but Judaism. But his belief that 'a man who is a philosopher is wicked' was blatant contradiction of this claim, and his proofs were limited to the mystical-cosmological cabala, or Oral Law, based on the revelations of Ezekiel, whose denial Menasseh, following the revered Jewish sage Maimonides, claimed to be heresy. His outpourings were so arrogant, and his hatred of non-Jews so intense, that his tracts could not be circulated. The *parnasim* kept him from Christian theologians, free-thinkers and the curious who came to the synagogue.

It will prove important that passions (*paixoes*) were in principle deplored by the rabbis in relation to the Jewish religion. A Jewish scholar writes that the Portuguese word was:

> laden with clear ideological and cultural implications, condemned not only enthusiasm [taken in its original sense of possession or raving] but also everything that signified a challenge to the existing order. A person guided by *paixoes*, that is, by desires, urges, and the sum of irrational operations, negated the political and social order. *Paixoes* were considered a symptom of illness; anyone subject to them must be kept at a distance until cured.

Until a community institution was opened, anyone afflicted by *paixoes* was committed to the *dolhuis*, the Amsterdam asylum. Here lay the origins of Spinoza's concern with the destructive effects of passion: an analytically minded schoolboy must disentangle rational objections to De la Peyrère's views from marrano emotion at marrano betrayal.

Bento would have been encouraged, following *bar-mitzvah*, to join a men's discussion group, and it is likely on the grounds of Lucas's testament (whose details are discussed shortly), and marrano puns on the name 'Espinosa' in connection with 'thorns' (*espinos*) ensnaring Morteira's 'Crown of the Law', that while he did not enrol in Morteira's rabbinical class, he attended his leisure-time *yeshivah*. We must pause here to consider why it was that Bento dropped out of higher education but subsequently took part in the most testing of the community's bible-study groups. There are three possible explanations for his surprising omission from the higher *Medras* registers. We have ruled out the idea that he was too stupid. The remaining explanations are that he *did* enrol, despite the lack of documentation; that he was prevented from enrolling; or that he refused to enrol. On the first, there is no sign of a subsequent deletion of his name as there is in the membership roll of the Ets Haim society. Moreover, he would have been listed had he enrolled, since he would have received a grant from the Ets Haim foundation. On the second, however bad Michael's finances might be, a synagogue official and founder-member of the Ets Haim trust for higher education is unlikely to have stopped his son from undertaking rabbinical study. On the third, I suggest that he deployed tricks of marrano dissimulation and made excuses not to enrol, taking care that his too-eloquent eyes showed no aversion to the calling of a rabbi, only regret that he must turn it down. Lucas writes that Bento knew 'his doubts embarrassed his teacher. Being afraid to irritate him, he pretended to be very satisfied with his answers, contenting himself with writing them down in order to make use of them at the proper time and place.' Anyone who has endured the trial of having a parent closely involved in one's education will empathise here. Baruch's father was a friend and governor of his teachers: the boy may have been known only as 'Michael's son', a torment intensified after Isaak ('son of Michael Espinoza' in the burial register) died when Bento was not yet seventeen. Expectations now fell even more heavily on the intelligent second son. Yet in another respect Isaak's death was sadly timely: Baruch could say he was needed during the day to help run his father's business.

Somewhere between boyhood and banishment from the synagogue his conformity to Jewish law became strained. While it was aptly noted by a contemporary that 'As he had a geometrical mind, and as he wanted to find a reason for everything, he soon perceived that the teaching of the rabbis was not for him', I do not think it can be right to say that 'he was a great enemy of dissimulation, hence declared freely his doubts and his belief'. It is as unlikely that he declared his doubts as that he carped at his school teachers, although one suspects his expressive face revealed disagreement enough. I incline instead to the view that Bento would have mulled over complaints such as D'Acosta's, and would have had questions ready for De la Peyrère on his 1654 visit to Amsterdam.

It would, on several counts, have been foolish for him to raise his voice before then. The first is rational. There were so many challenges to marrano thinking at that time that only a D'Acosta would have shrieked out every misgiving. It was wiser to avoid betraying scorn at, for example, the obsession of rabbis Morteira, Ben Israel and Aboab de Fonseca with the cabala. As a child Bento would have heard Morteira's sermons, full of cabalistic allusions. These immensely capable minds pored over biblical texts, seeking from the shape, arrangement and pauses between the Hebrew letters secret mathematical laws of the universe, which for them confirmed Messianic destiny. Spinoza would write in due course, *I have read and known cabalistic triflers whose insanity provokes my unceasing astonishment.* Now, he merely scorned the gullibility of his teachers in assuming that they scrutinised unaltered biblical texts. He dared not point out that *the Word of*

God is faulty, mutilated, tampered with, and inconsistent, and the original of the covenant which God made with the Jews has been lost, or express his opinion *that such objectors are in danger of turning religion into superstition, and worshipping paper and ink instead of God's Word.* (How he would have snorted at the suggestion made centuries later that his own doctrine was true because the equal numerology of the letters making up the words *Elohim* and *Hatevah* meant that God 'must be' equivalent to Nature!) While his critical faculties were almost certainly furiously active during his teenage years, we have no cause to think that any concrete ideas emerged during this period of questioning and ground clearing. The road to original thought is littered with rejected notions, and in 1659 he would admit he was still 'searching'. When in 1656 he grievously offended the *mahamad*, he did not do so with a well-argued battery of confutations or a d'Acosta-style tirade, but by showing in various ways his disdain for Jewish authority.

The second motive for biting his tongue was benevolence. Bento probably had no wish to humiliate his father within his inestimably precious newfound Jewish circle.

The third motive was skin-saving expediency. Every Jewish boy had a lively sense of the punitive power of the *mahamad*. An edict of excommunication meant expulsion not only from synagogue, friends and community but from one's (inevitably linked) livelihood. The elders would not tolerate the merest whiff of religious defiance, and peccadilloes such as over-friendliness with non-Jews and minor infringements of ritual counted as such. Let us be precise. In 1639 the *mahamad* of the newly united synagogue added fresh grounds for banishment to the heresies listed by Grotius (which were, to recap, belief in an external creator-God, in the divine revelation of Moses and the prophets, in an immortal afterlife, and in angels), and the following officially coded Jewish offences: (i) contempt for a rabbi, even after his death; (ii) despising the words of the sages and the Torah; and (iii) causing a multitude to profane the divine name. The new grounds for excommunication or *cherem*, unsanctioned by Law and clearly local panic measures, were, broadly: (a) opposing the decisions of the *mahamad* in speech or writing; (b) entering the synagogue with staff in hand; and (c) discoursing with non-Jews on religious matters. Specifically, Article 33 stated that business disputes be put to arbitration by the *mahamad*, as in the case of Michael and Jacob de Espinosa. Bento would need to be sure of what he was saying to risk home, livelihood and his father's blessing. The evidence suggests he was not yet sure enough, and that disobeying Article 33 could have been at least partly responsible for his expulsion.

Against this background occurred events that put the *naçao* in a less favourable Dutch light than previously. To its growing intolerance of independent thought was added a surprising display of Jewish racial discrimination. In 1648, Cossak and Swedish persecution in eastern Europe brought an influx of impoverished but mainly educated and orthodox Jews to Amsterdam. The marranos, struggling to keep their own affairs in order, found each new shipload of these shabby Jews mortifying, and while certain 'important Jews' housed and fed them, at first in two warehouses, the marranos did not greet them as kin. Many frankly looked down on these 'children of Jacob', not only for their inferior lineage – they did not share their own distinguished destiny of producing the Messiah – but also for the menial occupations most were forced to take up. Like themselves, these Jews were excluded from retail trade, but unlike themselves most had no wealth to invest in importing and wholesaling, and no useful contacts abroad. Since 1635 German and east European Jews (among themselves by no means a unified community) had been urged to set up their own synagogue. Now, many marranos avoided them altogether. This discrimination did not please the Dutch authorities any more than did the apparently arbitrary criteria for excommunication currently in force in the *Talmud Torah* synagogue. The Dutch had only one thing against the new immigrants, and it was not their poverty. The work ethic of Jews was well known: neither 'Portuguese' nor 'German' had proved criminal or wanted Dutch charity. For this reason they were increasingly welcome in some European countries and in new-world colonies. In 1652–3 the Duke of Modena would issue three charters inviting them to settle in Italy. But their strictness over ritual upset social harmony by inflaming Gentile imaginations. The *Remonstrantie* had recommended freedom for the Jews to print anything but their *Talmud*, whose instructions for ritual might rekindle Dutch rumours of vile Jewish practices, and the marranos were aware that this aspect of their worship bothered all European civil authorities. As early as 1616 a rabbi had warned that 'each may freely follow his own belief but may not openly show that he is of a different faith from the inhabitants of the city'. *Hooghduytsen* ritual therefore drew attention to the marranos' persisting isolationism.

The past suffering of the new arrivals is not in its details relevant to Bento's story, but the boy would undoubtedly hear the chronicles of Cossak, German, Polish and Swedish pogroms. While his later writing poignantly addresses the question of racial oppression, it also sternly upholds, on grounds of logical necessity, the Dutch precept that racial and religious differences must not be paraded. Any religious or racial concept that applied only to one section of society could not, by definition, he said, be universally true. In the case of Judaism, its *sacred rites, or at any rate those in the Old Testament, were ordained for the Jews alone, and adapted to their political organisation . . . and consequently contribute nothing to blessedness and virtue, but*

45

relate only to the election of the Jews, i.e. to their temporal welfare and the peace of their state; and for this reason could only have been useful while that state survived. Consequently, no sectarian precept could legitimately constitute a basis for the *religious inquisitions* instigated by the Pharisees and imputed to the Amsterdam *mahamad* by d'Acosta and others. (The common use of the term 'inquisition' by one religious denomination of another shows a general awareness of the injustice of religious oppression: the Remonstrants of Antwerp had called the Calvinist rulers of the north 'little monsters of the new Holland Inquisition'. An anonymous Jewish writing of around 1617 warns repeatedly that 'Inquisition' would result from disobeying Dutch law.)

The political crisis that developed in the United Provinces during the late 1640s must have added to Bento's doubts about the attitude of practising Jews to the society that had taken them in. Not only was he a Dutch Jew, he was also a 'Hollander', a resident of the rich Province of Holland, whose delegates from the powerful voting towns of Amsterdam, The Hague, Leiden and Dordrecht dominated the decisions of the delegates and town representatives of the other six Provinces at the States General at The Hague, and thought nothing of defying Stadholder Frederik Hendrik. Amsterdam in particular harboured many die-hard republicans. Spinoza's experience of regent rule, and his ambition of influencing this ruling élite, make it necessary to outline the events precipitating the crisis of 1648–50.

We have only touched on the privation wrought by constant threats of invasion by Spain and its allies. In 1634 free bread had been given to 20,000 people following rioting when supplies of wheat, blocked by the Swedish army, failed to reach the Provinces. By 1641 all Provinces but Zeeland had voted to stop fighting Spain and sue for peace. Zeelanders, living at the estuaries of the southern waterways, had not only seen Breda and smaller towns retaken, but had had steady work converting merchant-ships to warships, and had seen them put to sea, to return intact and victorious. Glory had come in 1639, when Admiral Tromp dealt the Spanish their worst sea defeat since 1588. Yet while Dutch seamen had become the envy and terror of Europe ('worth a million of ours,' wrote Felltham grudgingly, 'for they in boisterous rudeness can work, and live, and toil, whereas ours will rather laze themselves to poverty'), and many Dutch people could more readily see the value of maintaining a war-fleet to protect their international trading than an army which seemed to achieve little, the admiralty's coffers were now empty. The Treaty of Münster of 1648, which ended eighty years of conflict with Spain and formally divided The Netherlands into northern Dutch and Spanish south, saw jubilation. For the marranos, peace brought special joy. Portugal's 1640 split from Spain had given them new trading

46

breaks in sugar, tobacco, arms and munitions, Baltic grain and timber. Now, links with Spain and Antwerp could also be reopened. Michael's *Wisselbank* record reflects these booms: in 1651 he traded with forty-eight firms or merchants, and his account stood at almost 62,000 guilders.

Yet rancour and dissension soon overshadowed the 1648 peace celebrations. Dordrecht's expectations of an upturn in trade were dashed by impositions of tolls on the waterways by both Dutch and Spanish authorities. The cold, wet summer of 1648 brought failed harvest, and famine. Leiden found its textile industry (already depressed by the weather which prevented bleaching by the sun) competing with the cheap labour and cheap cloth of the newly retaken town of Maastricht. As recession bit in Zeeland, Brabant and Holland, it was sourly acknowledged that Spain could no longer be blamed for all ills, and the formidable deputies of the States of Holland, many of whom – for example the De Witts of Dordrecht – were lawyers, told the other delegates that all internal problems originated with the House of Orange. Willem I ('the Silent') had in 1544 been appointed by the Habsburgs as governor, and by rebelling on behalf of the Dutch had honoured the original role of stadholder as 'servant'. He had been saviour-count, military liberator and religious reformer, and while both he and his son Count Maurits of Nassau had governed as military leaders, neither had shown any desire to rule as a monarch. Willem had often declined the crown offered him by grateful north-Netherlanders; Maurits refused his hereditary title of Prince of Orange. (The latter had, however, crushed the faction of regents which in 1619 challenged his command of the army, and had involved himself in politics and religion to retain his own power.)

Regent families such as the De Witts did not hold Maurits in affectionate memory, and had come to loathe his brother and successor Frederik Hendrik for his dynastic ambitions. In 1641 Frederik Hendrik had succeeded in marrying his son (later Willem II) to the 10-year-old daughter of Charles I of England, and now courted royal status by squandering sparse Dutch State funds on military aid for Charles against Cromwell, and on sycophantic indulgence of the Stuart child bride. Jacob Cats, who as Grand Pensionary held the highest government office in the land, dutifully addressed him as 'great sovereign'. When Frederik Hendrik died in 1647 many Holland regents united against the wilful Prince Willem II, who in their view should not have had succession to various Provinces settled on him at birth, and who now, as Stadholder of six provinces and stadholder-elect of the seventh, wanted alliance with France and an assault on the Spanish in Brussels and Antwerp. Willem was said to plot the replacement of Holland regents by 'servile officers' or 'Church owls' who would vote to finance his army. We have noted the loyalty, gratitude and empathy of the marranos towards the Princes of Orange, and, as Willem set about realising his father's monarchist ambitions, and the States General denied him funds for an army, he turned to Amsterdam money-lenders in order to retain control of the army. But within two years it became evident that he could not recruit 'servile' representatives by legal means, and he took to canvassing for support with a military escort. The beheading of Charles I in 1649 did not deter him, or abash his haughty wife, Mary Stuart. Yet, while almost all Dutch people were horrified at the execution of a king by his own people, some welcomed the new English government, and hoped that events in England might subdue Willem, and persuade him that economic self-interest had now superseded national military honour as a priority. However, the Prince's response to towns that refused his demands for army funding was to deliver veiled threats and secretly to accept his cousin's offer to take Amsterdam by force. The assault failed because the burgomasters of Amsterdam were informed by the night-post rider from Hamburg that armed troops had assembled at Ouderkerk. As cannons were primed, drawbridges shut and a rider was dispatched to the mystery commander at Ouderkerk warning him to bring his men no closer, lest the city council feel compelled to use 'all the means provided by God and nature to repel them' – that is, to open the sluices – 'Every merchant [was] as brave as a count.' Every merchant? Had the marranos known who approached the city they would have stayed at home. Banned from public office and from bearing arms or joining the watch, they did not love the regents, and wanted Willem granted the means to retake Antwerp.

Willem withdrew from the planned assault. As it happened, he withdrew for good, for he died a few months later of smallpox. For more than twenty years the newborn son he left (the future William III) would be subject to stadholderless republican rule, which the Jews of Amsterdam seem to have accepted in silence, as well they might given the powerful residual anti-Orangist feeling in the city. Before Willem's death an anonymous pamphleteer had predicted, 'He hath cast so foul an aspersion upon his stock and lineage, that all the water in the sea is not able to wash it off . . . he shall become such a loathing to all posterity, and by all true-hearted Hollanders he shall be hated to the very death for it.'

On this subject Bento probably stayed silent at home, and indeed his sister Miriam's wedding to the rabbinical student Samuel de Casseres on 2 June 1650 may have dominated family discussion. Michael stayed away from the now obligatory banns-reading and registration at the Christian New Church, although stepmother Esther assisted. Michael 'gave his consent to the marriage', surely joyfully: De Casseres was already a distinguished Amsterdam figure and would in 1660 deliver Morteira's funeral oration. But the 1651 trading upturn came too late to allay worries over dowry and expenses. Shortly afterwards Michael took over the administration of the synagogue loan fund, and a cryptic note next to the record of his appointment in the Book of Agreements reads, 'That it may be to his benefit!'

Bento may also have kept quiet because if his disapproval of Stadholder rule (made plain in later years) was already in place, it had undoubtedly been put there by non-Jewish friends. He began, in the early 1650s, to meet Dutch merchants who argued that the stadholders were subtly altering their legitimate role, and that he should support a republican replacement for the 73-year-old Grand Pensionary Cats, who had been Willem's dupe. Cause for preferring democracy was, they could have pointed out, implicit in Calvin's lame defence of princely tyranny:

> In almost all ages we see that some princes, careless about all their duties on which they ought to have been intent, live, without solicitude in luxurious sloth; others, bent on their own interest, venally prostitute all rights, privileges, judgements and enactments; others pillage poor people of their money, and afterwards squander it in insane largesse . . . But if we have respect to the word of God, it will . . . make us subject not only to the authority of those princes who honestly and faithfully perform their duty towards us, but all princes, by whatever means they have so become.

Calvin's view still had force, a hundred years on, with the old, the poor and the noble. But there were few nobles, and while large cities had more representatives and thus more votes, those votes rarely reflected the views of the Orangist masses.

Most voting representatives of the towns of Holland believed the Provinces' best interests would be served by a new political order, and Bento could not have failed to notice two incidents which symbolised the desire of the Amsterdam council to terminate Orange power and bolster their own republican interests. Firstly, the beautiful old town hall on the Dam, much admired by foreigners, had burned to the ground while its razing was already underway. When the walls of its replacement rose in the early 1650s the vast building was seen to lack a stately entrance, and its sculpture and commissioned paintings to reflect divine blessing on the mercantile fathers, who for the first time appointed their own nine-man council (councillors, unlike burgomasters and aldermen, held their seats for life) without an imposed Stadholder shortlist. Secondly, late in 1650 floods spectacularly collapsed the St Anthonie's dyke at the Houtewael, which held back the North Sea, giving rise to claims of divine fury, a washing clean of the Dutch slate of iniquity and a sign to a new Noah. The flood tore past the Vloyenburg to the south-easterly polders, ravaging the Beth Haim.

Planks for a new Noah's Ark were laid at The Hague's Great Assembly of 1651, which ratified the Dutch Reformed Church as the State religion of the United Provinces. In that Assembly sat the 25-year-old lawyer Johan de Witt, recently elected permanent Deputy of Dort to the States of Holland. By 1653 he would replace his fellow townsman Jacob Cats as Grand Pensionary of the United Provinces, and be regarded by most regents, merchants and free-thinkers as the new Noah.

Dutch politics would have shifted now into focus for Bento, now out, in the kaleidoscopic impact of events and impressions of 1650–1. Descartes had died suddenly in 1649, at the Swedish Court of his patron and pupil Queen Christina. His philosophy was banned in most Dutch universities, but his *Opera Philosophica*, minus the *Treatise on Man* and *Rules for the Direction of the Mind*, was available in bookshops. The copy that Bento owned was published in 1650. Did the young Jew have Latin enough to tackle Descartes? Colerus reports that 'Because he had a great mind to learn the Latin tongue, they gave him at first a German master.' If 'they' were the Jewish elders, the master may have been a German Jew in need of employment. But this may not have happened: Spanish nuances in Spinoza's Latin texts suggest that Morteira or some other rabbi may have helped him. (Menasseh would never have found the time. In 1648 the publisher-rabbi complained, 'Two hours are spent in the Temple every day; six in the school; one and a half in the public Academy and the private one of the Peyreras, in which I hold the office of president; two in proof-reading for my printing press, where everything passes through my hands; from eleven to twelve I have appointments with all those who need assistance in their affairs or pay me visits.' In the early 1650s he researched and wrote three books on Jewish themes and was immersed in plans for his visit to England, so was even busier.) No one would have stopped Bento learning Latin, had he wanted to add that burden of learning to his other studies. The one subject for which Jews were admitted to the universities was medicine (the first Dutch Jew took his doctorate there in March 1633) and for this proficiency in Latin was required. Bento may have let it be thought that he wanted to study medicine. This may, in fact, have been his intention. By 1650 he no longer attended the synagogue school, but his interest in anatomy could have been obvious: within five years he would count three physicians and two would-be medical students as friends, and by his late twenties he had started formulating his challenge to Descartes's account of the mind-body relation. Only high esteem for the study, and perhaps envy of a rich boy's chance of taking it up, can have led him to recommend a young Dutch merchant friend drawn to philosophy to 'go through the whole medical course' instead. It is possible, given the length of time between Bento's leaving school and the eye of the elders being alerted to his behaviour, that Michael was, before Isaak died, and again after business prospered and Gabriel showed a flair for it, receptive to his studious son's plans for a career in medicine. But no early or latter-day biographer has ever suggested this, and if the urge seized Bento, it passed.

The physicians of the *nação* could not help Miriam. She died in September 1651 while giving Michael a grandson, Daniel. Spinoza never mentioned either Miriam or Ribca, who must, although there is no record of this, have married Miriam's widower Rabbi Samuel de Casseres soon after Miriam's death. Historical data shows that she would have three children by him by the time he died in 1660: her son Michael, described as the son of Samuel de Casseres on his gravestone, died in 1695 at the age of roughly forty-two. Ribca's children would grow up knowing Uncle Bento as the family's black sheep, just as Uncle Bento Henriques of Hamburg and Reccife, Hana Debora's great-uncle and the bane of Michael's and Joshua Senior's trading, comes over as the bad lot of Spinoza's maternal line.

In the six years following his brother or half-brother Isaak's death, much of Bento's attention must have been devoted, willingly or unwillingly, to the anxieties of shipping and wholesaling. Spanish harassment at sea had given way to hostile interception by the English, whose Admiralty confiscated in July 1651 a cargo of pipes and Algerian oil en route from Portugal 'belonging to Michael de Espinosa'. In November that year the ship *Prince* was captured on its way from the Canary Islands, and had to be reclaimed from London at Michael's expense. These stresses were the lot of non-Jewish Amsterdam merchants too: some of the paintings inscribed with endearments to 'our cargo ship' that hung in their parlours still survive. The outpouring of emotion in a marrano household over each shipping disaster may be appreciated. Now, things suddenly got worse. The English (and French) resented the new Dutch domination of shipping from the Baltic to the Levant and, despite admitting that Low Country sailors were 'the whip of Spain, and the arm wherewith they pull away his Indies', the English were ready to declare war on the United Provinces. An excuse was found in the summer of 1652, when Tromp refused to dip his colours to Admiral Blake, and the first of the three Anglo-Dutch naval wars of Spinoza's lifetime began a few days later. It wore down Michael's resistance to calamity. In August 1652 he sold to his bereaved son-in-law Samuel de Casseres a ship's interest, with whatever profit or loss accrued to it. The same year two bills were served on Michael regarding the costs of a forcible delay of a Dutch ship in Rouen. These notices were translated by 'his daughter' in August and by 'a servant' in October. Miriam, in any case illiterate, had already died, so we assume this daughter was Ribca. Michael denied the charges, but paid up.

Perhaps Michael had at last run out of fighting spirit. On 23 October 1652, Portuguese notary licentiates arrived at the Houtgracht home to record the last will and testament of his third wife Esther. In the document she requested 'an honest burial for her body' and left 'all her movable and immovable possessions, nothing excepted' to Senhor Michael d'Espinoza. But while the document stated that she was too weak to sign, Esther would not die for almost a year (14 October 1653). Once again the house was shadowed by morbid emotion and who can say what other acrimony. Why did Esther make a will, when under Jewish law she could not have married without a *ketubah* contract? Did Michael coerce her into doing so while she was poorly, or did an unnecessary and hysterical dramatic outburst contribute to Bento's harsh view of *womanish tears*? One of Spinoza's landlords says he was unsympathetic to those who grumbled when they were ill: 'Ever since he began to be in a languishing condition, he always expressed, in all his sufferings, a truly Stoical constancy; even so as to reprove others, when they happened to complain, and to show in their sickness little courage or too great a sensibility.' Michael's own life was nearly over. His depleted household consisted of a wife who was either hysterically or terminally ill, and two outwardly dutiful grown sons, the feisty Ribca by now being married.

Did Michael realise how tedious his son found trading? An embarrassing disaffinity for commercial confrontation is shown in a documented incident I recount ahead of its time (1655) to offset the gleeful approach to debt-collecting suggested by Bento's early ducat-recovering. A marrano called Anthonij Alvares, who, given his surname, may have been a relation of Michael's (his brother Fernando and his sister Maria Clara may also have come to Amsterdam), owed Michael's firm 500 florins. Bento held a bill of exchange for the debt, but Alvares first postponed payment for weeks, then gave Bento an order for payment against his brother, who refused to honour it. Bento took Alvares to court and succeeded in having him held in custody. When called to the inn 'The Four Hollanders' on the Nes, to come to an agreement, witnesses testified that 'the said Anthonij Alvares hit the requisitionist [Bento] on the head with his fist without there having been spoken a word in return and without the requisitionist doing anything'. On leaving this futile encounter Bento was attacked again, this time by Alvares's brother, who 'was standing in front of the inn and hit the plaintiff on the head with his fist without any cause, so that his hat fell off and the said [brother] took the requisitionist's hat and threw it in the gutter and stepped on it'. Bento had to pay the expenses of the arrest to the chief sheriff, the witnesses and the inn-keeper, and while he was promised repayment for these and for 'damages and interests suffered by the requisitionist as a result of the default of payment' there is no record that he recovered this debt, or any other for which he requested legal assistance from the Court of Holland. (There is more to be said on his applying to this authority over the heads of the elders.)

Bento's use of the Dutch language had its first testing when he took on business responsibilities, and while Michael may have conceded the benefit of this, he may have worried about its fostering of 'over-friendliness with non-Jews'. He would have seen Bento talking, for example, to the merchant Jarig Jelles, who lived close to the Exchange on the present-day Damrak, at that time lapped by harbour water, and also traded in dried fruit. Let us envisage the start of Spinoza's friendship with Jarig, in the place it is likely to have occurred, the courtyard of the Exchange. The elegant Portuguese youth, perhaps with silk collar, confers with the gentle north Hollander twelve years his senior who, being a member of the Mennonites, an Anabaptist sect established in The Netherlands before Calvinism, is wearing modest, course-cloth black. Each sees his father standing not far away: Jelles Senior was an Exchange Broker from 1629 to 1654. Each signals by his dress – less exotic by several degrees than his father's – a desire to find common ground. Jarig's Flemish Mennonite sect is not as puritanical as his parents' Frisian Mennonite branch, which allowed only long, baggy, fringed and starch-free clothing. But Jarig, too, frowns on frivolity in dress and other worldly vanities, including – importantly for the future of the friendship – academic learning. The fathers stand stiffly back from the encounter, isolated in their religions yet bonded by the strength of their prejudices. Each endorses his own community's commitment to the harsh rituals of public condemnation and formal ostracism and expulsion which keep his community free of 'the infection of sin'. The hostility of the fathers is tangible and real: the growing sympathy of the sons (I maintain, against a popular view that Jelles was Spinoza's close friend and disciple) little more than an ideological urge towards brotherly harmony. Michael would have been agitated to know that his son's chats with this odd fellow were not about raisins, and that in 1653 Jelles would make 'his flourishing and profitable shop over to an honest man' so that he could study philosophy. But the Mennonite would never philosophise on Spinoza's intellectual level, or become a free-thinker in the sense to which Spinoza aspired. He had not been to Latin school, and his demand that everything the philosopher wrote be translated into Dutch sprang from Mennonite principle, not educational deprivation. A refusal to see that Latin unified across nationality and religion was one instance of Jarig's blindness. It is in fact remarkable, given Jelles's privileged exposure to Spinoza's doctrine, how many basic Spinozistic tenets he would manage to misread or resist. I have concluded from all I can learn that Jarig valued Bento's shunning of personal honour and knowledge of natural science above his philosophy. Spinoza, in turn, remained grateful for Jarig's sincere charity, and tolerated the 'feelings' (*gevoelens*) that constituted his Mennonite faith. But, their correspondence suggests, he had no great expectations of his intellect.

Another Amsterdam merchant, Simon de Vries, was about three years younger than Bento, so in 1653 was only eighteen. A great-nephew of the patriot-poet Vondel, he lived with his wealthy family on the Singel. It was he who would, on Spinoza's advice, agree to study medicine. Simon's family was respected, but it was neither patrician nor Calvinist. On his mother's side the poet Vondel (a German-born hosier who invested modestly in ships' cargoes) became, as we know, a Catholic, as did several De Vries children. Other family members, including Simon's father, were liberal Mennonites. Simon's fierce desire to stretch his understanding radiates from his letters, and Bento seems to have been fond of him since, untypically, he stayed at the De Vries country estate at Schiedam for weeks on end.

By 1653 Bento is also likely to have met Pieter Balling, the free-thinking merchant with Quaker sympathies whose beliefs were, like Jarig's, too radically Christian to let him endorse Spinoza's mature philosophy, and whose treatise on spiritual inner light I mentioned earlier in passing. Pieter was a registered Amsterdam citizen (*poorter*) and agent for Spanish merchants. He spoke Castilian fluently. Unlike Simon or Jarig he was married, with children. A decade later he would with immense dedication translate Spinoza's *Descartes's Principles of Philosophy* into Dutch from Latin, motivated no doubt by its inaccessibility to Jarig and other non-Latin-reading friends. But the Dutch publication would throw Spinoza's work into the open arena of common ignorance and prejudice, and would bring its author only aggravation, and Spinoza later begged that no more of his work be translated into Dutch. The chief bond between Bento and these early Dutch-merchant friends was their desire for religious harmony, and there can be no more impressive tribute to the unifying power of this impulse than the tenacity of their affections despite differences of view. It is unclear, despite religious and trading affinities, how well these friends knew each other in the early 1650s, but soon their interests would converge with devotion on the young Portuguese merchant who at present struggled through a thick Hispanic accent to converse with them.

Two topics may have dominated their talk in 1653, given the changes that came about in Bento's life soon after that time. The first was the question of national security and political change. It would have been difficult to avoid passing an opinion on this in 1653. In July Johan de Witt was promoted to Grand Pensionary, and by the end of July the naval war with England was in crisis following Admiral Tromp's death at sea in a three-day battle lost to the English. The fleet did not sail from Amsterdam, but from Texel in the north or Zeeland in the south, but its progress was the talk of all. De Witt, said the merchants of Amsterdam, would swiftly bring the war to a proper conclusion. Any man from Dordrecht would know the importance of peace for trading. His draft proposal for stadholderless government by elected representation (his *Deductie*) seemed on the right track, too, although to most European governments the proposal seemed foolhardy. French ambassador Pierre Chanut shared a widespread fear that under a 'democracy', which he took to mean an appeal to public opinion, 'the people are made the judges of their magistrates'. But this was not De Witt's intention. His statecraft shows he shared Cicero's (and Cats's) view that power should stay in the hands of a political aristocracy; that the masses judge, as Cicero said, 'not as a result of rational choice or balanced assessment but usually on impulse and a wave of emotion'. Yet numbers of the powerless, possessionless proletariat who traditionally hated the regents and supported the warrior-counts of Orange now seemed inclined to listen to him. The national identity of the Protestant Dutch Republic had been conceived in proletarian protest, but it had always lacked a political channel of expression. Leiden university, for example, had been given in 1587 to the town as a thank-you from Willem the Silent for its resistance to the Spanish, but few of its inhabitants could make use of it. The only books in most Dutch homes were the 1637 States bible and the didactic but humorous works of Jacob Cats, written patronisingly for an underclass to whom nobody listened. Admiral Tromp, who boasted that his 'mother washed the sailor's shirts and starched collars for money', had told the States that the ships were too dilapidated for battle and had been ignored. Was the new Grand Pensionary about to offer the common people a voice in government?

Johan de Witt, quietly walking the streets of Amsterdam and The Hague, knew he could build on the expectant mood expressed by the people's poet Vondel. Vondel, ever the extoller of Amsterdam's prosperity, and of the Dutch language which was now, at last, used in the Council of State at The Hague, was crowned poet laureate in 1653, and began at once to manipulate public opinion. While the ageing, Orangist Cats had written reassuringly that 'It is a work of skill and worthy to be praised/ To be allowed to be godly and at the same time rich', Vondel hinted at the reason for most people's lack of riches when in 1654 he gave Lucifer, in his eponymous religious drama, the post in heaven of 'stadholder'. Vondel thus set the tone for the quiet ideological revolution that would take the place of the bloodbath predicted in 1650. De Witt made no rash, inflammatory moves. He did not (yet) legislate against the House of Orange, only *for* government by citizens. This sounded promising, and when in 1654 the Republic, as it now truly was, had to concede defeat to England, hopes of De Witt remained high. Here was no Cromwell, set to turn a 'Commonwealth or Free-State' into a mock monarchy. (Spinoza would later accuse the English of choosing *after much bloodshed* a *king by a different name*.) No Hollander wanted De Witt to assume the role of Stadholder, for Stadholder partisans wanted a return to military rule by a member of the House of Orange, while radical republicans wanted 'true freedom'. De Witt played his hand cannily, creating an impression of toleration by refraining from controversy, while carefully binding himself by marriage to the most prominent regent family he could find. He was rejected by the daughter of Dr Tulp, one of the richest and most influential of Amsterdam's magistrates (who, despite his frivolous name 'tulip', was an implacable opponent of extravagance and frivolity) but was accepted by the 19-year-old heiress Wendela Bicker, daughter of one of the Amsterdam regents who had averted Willem's 1650 coup. He would marry her in February 1655, so presenting himself to the burghers of Amsterdam as a Grand Pensionary with whom they should try to keep 'good correspondence'. Some Amsterdam regents may even have hoped to see the seat of government move from The Hague's moated *Binnenhof*, once the palace of the Counts of Holland, but since 1572 owned by the States General, to their city.

Gossip at the Exchange would have helped draw Bento beyond the little world of the Vloyenburg. Dates cannot be precise, but it is clear that by the time the Jewish elders decided Michael's son must go, he was not short of Dutch friends or places to harbour him, and the scraps of evidence we have suggest that by the early 1650s he had already sought out liberal-minded Dutchmen who would, in the widest sense, broaden his education. In Lucas's opinion, Spinoza was forced to find a living among Christians and *then* started new studies:

> He had so little intercourse with the Jews for some time that he was obliged to associate with Christians, and he formed ties of friendship with intellectual people who told him that it was a pity that he knew neither Greek nor Latin . . . He himself fully realised of what importance it was to find the means of mastering Greek and Latin, as he was not born rich and no influential friends to help him on . . . He was thinking about it incessantly and spoke of it whenever he met people.

But this account does not convince. True, to earn a living as a Jewish scholar Bento would need Latin and Greek: he knew from Menasseh that since the most learned Jews avoided Gentiles, opportunities were plentiful for anyone who would translate and interpret Scripture for non-Jews. Latin would be helpful; Greek essential for working on the New Testament books. But it is now generally held by researchers that Spinoza's seeking and finding of sympathetic Gentiles such as Jelles, Balling and Simon de Vries (and other, more abrasive and capable intellects to be introduced shortly) began *before* he loosened his ties with the marrano community. His earliest scholarly interests show that he wanted Latin for his own reading, especially for works Menasseh did not see fit to have translated into Spanish and printed at his press, and that somehow he learned Latin before he left the Jewish community. What is not disputed by anyone is that some part of his loyalty drifted unobtrusively away from Judaism while he was still accepted in the synagogue.

Learning the truth involved doubting, and perhaps a Dutch friend told him the simple but stimulating analogy offered by Descartes to the Sorbonne Jesuit Pierre Bourdin:

> Suppose [someone] had a basket full of apples and, being worried that some of the apples were rotten, wanted to take out the rotten ones to prevent the rot spreading. How would he proceed? Would he not begin by tipping the whole lot out of the basket? And would not the next step be to cast his eye over each apple in turn, and pick up and put back in the basket only those he saw to be sound, leaving the others? In just the same way, those who have never philosophised correctly have various opinions in their minds which they have begun to store up since childhood, and which they therefore have reason to believe may be in many cases false. They then attempt to separate the false beliefs from the others, so as to prevent their contaminating the rest and making the whole lot uncertain.

Doubt had brought success with the old woman and the ducats, and Spinoza is said to have been 'charmed with that maxim of Descartes which says, That nothing ought to be admitted as True, but what has been proved by good and solid reasons'. But the works of Descartes would have horrified the rabbis; indeed it has been suggested that Spinoza's possession of the Frenchman's texts would have been grounds enough for excommunication. No Hollander youth studied them at Latin school, either, where religious studies were rigidly monitored. But, like Rembrandt, who had been to Latin school and so could cope with the classical history and mythology he needed for his paintings, Christian boys had an advantage over Bento. It would have nettled anyone with his interests to see Descartes's *Meditations*, Hobbes's *De*

Cive or Christiaan Huygens's mathematical *Theoremata* being carried out of bookshops by people he knew to be his intellectual inferiors. When at last he ventured into an Amsterdam *boekhandel* he must have fingered with longing the leather-bound stacks hot from printing presses in Amsterdam or Leiden, although he would have noticed that for every solidly bound quarto or octavo tome of philosophy, law, medicine, anatomy, physics, mathematics, microscopy, astronomy and chemistry there were two or more duodecimo (pocket-sized) treatises on theology, the outpourings of university clergy and bishops. Disputes on Christian doctrine had entered public awareness in the 1640s, and dissension between reactionaries and humanists about the true basis of religious authority and conditions for 'salvation' would dominate the Dutch press throughout Spinoza's lifetime. The Dutch left no market opportunity unexploited, and censorship abroad also created a clamour for illicit texts which the States General, pressed by the deputies of Holland, was keen to satisfy. Books and pamphlets forbidden elsewhere were sent to the Provinces for printing and distribution. Descartes's *Discourse and Essays*, objectionable to the Catholic Church, was first published anonymously at Leiden in 1637, and his *Principles* in Amsterdam in 1644.

Book stores selling such works generated a literal meeting of minds, for progressive thinkers congregated in the dim and poky rooms of those old Amsterdam shops. By the late 1640s or early 1650s, when Bento still struggled with Dutch conversation, he would have wanted to join in this volatile cosmopolitan debate. The realisation that without Latin he had no access to seminal texts may have made the prospect of rigid rabbinical instruction repellant, and driven him into teaching himself the international language of scholarship at quite an early age. The number of Latin dictionaries and grammars that Spinoza owned which were published between 1635 and 1654 suggests he was buying Latin texts while learning the grammar and simultaneously translating between Spanish, Hebrew, Portuguese, Italian, German and Dutch.

No bookshop in Amsterdam was more likely to attract free-thinkers than Franciscus (in Dutch, Frans) van den Enden's. This oldest and most intellectually able of Bento's first non-Jewish friends was born in Antwerp in 1602. He was a polymath, a classical scholar who, having graduated in law and medicine, might call himself 'Master' and 'Doctor'. He came to Amsterdam sometime between 1645 and 1650, and by 1650 had registered as a bookseller in the Nes, in which narrow, noisy street he lived with his family in a corner house called '*In de Konst-Winkel*' – 'in the art shop'. There he sold paintings and books. Van den Enden (or Ende – the pronunciation is the same) was Jesuit-trained but had left the Order, or been dismissed from it. In 1642 he had married a Polish Catholic woman, who bore him between 1643 and 1651 five daughters and a son. All were baptised as Catholics, but by the early 1650s Frans himself was no longer Catholic, or Christian, at heart. Although careful to preserve a God-fearing veneer (to the end of his days 'he was Catholic with Catholics and Protestant with Protestants'), he was generally judged an atheist. At that time atheists were thought not only to deny a creator God but also to live in godless profligacy and immorality. Frans would be execrated for sowing 'seeds of atheism in the minds of young boys', and the 'great penchant for women' of this 'little' man would be remarked on when he was seventy. He may have left the Jesuits, said this informant, because he knew he could not entirely have resisted females. At fifty, however, bankrupt (but his debts paid off by friends) and with a brood of children under seven years old – including an eldest daughter, Clara Maria, said to be 'somewhat lame and deformed' – it is hard to see how he could have cut a dissolute figure. Yet by 1657 he had published a play called *Philedonius, or Lusthart* (Lusty-Heart), the story of a Don Juan who in his old age was forced to return to virtue, and by the early 1660s he would openly be advocating free love and easy divorce.

If Bento encountered Frans before 1652 he may have known nothing more about him than that he sold and understood the Cartesian philosophy. That would have been attraction enough. Simon, Jarig or Pieter could have told him about the shop, whose owner (like Pieter) spoke fluent Spanish, or Menasseh could have heard of it from Rembrandt, whose pupil Leendert van Beyeren lodged at Frans's house in the Nes. After 1652, however, Frans made his erudition known in the city, moved out to a better address on the Singel and opened a school giving instruction in 'Latin and Greek', or classical languages and 'the new philosophy'. Just as he may have shown skill in engineering a painless bankruptcy, it is a measure of Frans's canny self-marketing that he succeeded in opening a school, for Catholics were debarred from teaching. In 1673 they were still 'not admitted to any publick charges'. The schoolmaster was at most an infrequent visitor to the disguised Catholic church 'de Posthoorn' in the Brouwersgracht, but was known there since little Clara Maria, at least, remained a Catholic. Her mass-going might have seemed to threaten the school, for at ten years old she 'understood the Latin tongue, as well as music, so perfectly that she was able to teach her father's scholars in his absence'. Here was a Catholic openly teaching. But censures against Catholics were rarely enforced for fear of bloodshed and martyrdom claims. De Witt, who had asked rhetorically in his *Deductie* whether the hearts and souls of the Dutch were not 'united and bound together by the spiritual and divine bond of one and the same religion?', infuriated Reformed Church leaders by renewing edicts against 'false believers' and then, like the church council of Egmond, doing nothing when they were flouted.

Clara Maria was probably between ten and twelve when Bento met her, and it is said *she* taught him Latin: 'The Latin language he learned with avidity under the guidance and auspices of a learned young woman' – Van den Enden's eldest daughter. But the celebrated Cats suggests that Clara Maria, like Anna van Schurman, was freakish even for a Dutch girl:

> Although a clever maiden may be found
> One swallow, as we say, does not a summer make.

So let us consider the enormity of this situation for a Portuguese Jew, who may never have seen a girl reading, let alone tutoring males. He knew 'The richest merchants of that city entrusted [Van den Enden] with the instruction of their children', and we might think that he accepted this humiliation as a painful but necessary adaptation to Dutch life, and hid his discomfort behind a mask of *hidalguia*. But apparently he did not cold-shoulder the little girl, a portrait of whom is sadly lost, but who, it was noted, had a 'beautiful face' and 'a great deal of wit, a great capacity and a jovial humour, which wrought upon the heart of Spinoza'. Any impact Clara Maria had in this way would have been intensified when, sometime between Michael's death in 1654 and the synagogue expulsion of 1656, Bento moved into the Van den Enden home. We shall return to her then.

Had the marranos known of this 'over-friendliness with non-Jews' and 'discoursing with non-Jews on religious matters', they would have been incensed. Did Michael know, or was he too sick, and Bento too subtle, for these visits to be noticed? Bento may have been a withdrawn and enigmatic presence in the Houtgracht house as his stepmother sank into the last stages of her illness, and his father shifted more and more duties on to him as he neared his own death. An old order would pass from Bento with Michael's passing in March 1654. The transition would be as natural and organic for Bento as for Michael, for (Spinozistically speaking) the 'push' from an internal determining nature was the same for both. One would return to his natural elements in death; the other would assemble his natural elements and move on in life. But from the marrano viewpoint, Michael's demise was a progression within *halachah*, and so a proper 'following' (the word *halachah* is derived from the Hebrew 'to follow'), whereas Baruch's deviation from *halachah* was judged an unnatural sundering. Baruch de Espinosa has been described by Amsterdam Jews as a 'lost son'.

In 1654 the few men of Michael's family who bore his corpse to the Beth Haim had a more immediate worry: his debts. The prosperity of the last few years had not wiped them out, and he left his family so badly off that Bento was not eligible for wealth tax during his remaining two years at the synagogue. Death had revealed the common Jewish tendency to live on credit. Michael's trusteeship since June 1638 (five months before Hana Debora's death) of the bankrupt Henriques estate, and acceptance of at least one bill of exchange on its behalf, may also have consumed his profits. Whatever Bento's private thoughts, and whether or not he observed the Jewish practice of secluding himself at home for a week, seated on a low stool wearing a torn upper garment, records show that he honoured Michael with public *kaddish* – prayers for the peace of his soul. Only respect for his father can explain his pledging of a subscription to the synagogue to replace Michael's, and to keep this up not only in accordance with the orthodox eleven-month period of mourning but for two years, until shortly before he was banned from the community.

We do not know why Bento believed he was heir to his mother's estate in a way that those who seem, by force of dating evidence, to have been his siblings were not, but during Michael's lifetime he 'took it upon himself to pay a few debts of the said estates so that afterwards he could more easily act as heir of his said father'. After Michael died he was challenged by 'Duarte Rodrigues . . . and the curators of the estate of Pedro Henriques'. Instead of asking for Jewish mediation as was required by Article 33 of the 1639 regulations – perhaps fearing that the outcome of it might be bankruptcy – he appealed to the civil authorities as a 'privileged creditor' and also, being under twenty-five, as a 'minor':

> Louis Crayer, appointed by the Orphan-Masters of the city of Amsterdam as guardian of Bento de Spinosa, minor son of the late Michael de Spinosa, in his life merchant in the aforementioned city, respectfully brings to your notice that to the same Bento de Spinosa a considerable sum is due from the estate left by his mother from the above mentioned Michael de Spinosa, without having received to his contentment anything from the fruit of this in his father's lifetime.

The results of the inquiry did not favour Spinoza's claim:

> And although the said Bento de Spinosa should have acted as a privileged creditor with preference to others . . . it now appears that the said inheritance is encumbered with many arrears to the extent that the said inheritance would be extremely detrimental to the said Bento de Spinosa [who] has come to the conclusion that it would be best to abstain from it in all respects.

But having ensured that his 'claim on his mother's goods will be given preference above all other creditors' (a puzzling judgement if he was not Hana Debora's only surviving child), he is said by Colerus to have demanded only the *ledikant*. Colerus makes no reference to the *Fiat Mandate of Indemnity of the Supreme Council in Holland*: he says merely that 'his father's succession was to be divided between him and his sisters, to which they were condemned in law, though they had left no stone unturned to exclude him from it'. Bento had only one sister now, as far as we know, namely Ribca. Did Colerus mean 'siblings', not 'sisters'? Neither Ribca nor Gabriel was specifically 'condemned in law' although four claimants to Michael's estate were named. However, if we note the date on the *Fiat* (March 1656) we recognise that by then Michael had been dead for two years, and Bento was very close to the excommunication which would come that July. He may already have quit the family home, which we recall that Michael did not, in any case, own. Fear among the De Espinosas that what little of Michael's remained might slip away from his sanctuary on the Houtgracht is understandable. It is also plausible, looking at Spinoza's library, that he made off with Michael's and Abraham's books, some of which may have been carried tenderly from Portugal to Nantes, and then to Amsterdam. He may have taken his maternal grandparents' books, too. Here I think of Da Cunha's *Obra Devota*, the old Spanish bible and other venerable tomes, all of which were probably heirlooms. Besides that red-curtained canopy-bed, he took the fine camel-hair clothes he had been able to invest in, and I think also the silver buckles and silver knife found among his possessions, for he would not have bought these later, and they would not have made suitable presents, given his humble lifestyle. I conclude that he surrendered any money to his kin, but bonded himself to his parents with visible, valuable, emotionally charged artifacts. Even as he consciously let Jewish wealth and Jewish honour slip through his fingers, he pulled to himself its southern, sensual consolations.

Events after Michael's death suggest that Bento no longer felt the same need to disguise his belief that Jewish rulings were dispensable, and some of its dogma preposterous. Lucas depicts Morteira as mutating from admiration at 'the conduct and genius of his disciple' and mystification that 'He could not understand how a young man of such penetration could be so modest' to asking some of his advanced pupils to find out 'his real views'. When this happened, according to Lucas, Bento was torn between fobbing off Morteira's intermediaries with platitudes, and instructing them:

> [He] did not answer them for some time; but seeing that he was pressed he told them smiling that they had Moses and the Prophets who were true

Israelites, and that these had decided about everything, and that they ought to follow them without hesitation if they were truly Israelites.

This response rings true because it is echoed in a similar riposte made by Spinoza years later to an inflexible Calvinist businessman. *If it is your conviction that God speaks more clearly and effectually through Holy Scripture than through the light of the natural understanding . . . you have good reason to adapt your understanding to the opinions which you ascribe to Holy Scripture. Indeed, I myself could do no other.* Unfortunately he did not then excuse himself to the students and vanish into the streets of Amsterdam but, Lucas says, let himself be provoked into answering such questions as 'Has God a body?' Lucas has him replying, 'Since nothing is to be found in the [Jewish] bible about the non-material or incorporeal, there is nothing objectionable in believing that God is a body. All the more so since, as the Prophet says, God is great, and it is impossible to comprehend greatness without a body.' This thought is expressed, without reference to prophets, in his earliest texts.

Did arrogance trap Bento into indiscretion when he was asked directly for his views on scripture? It was easy enough to keep mum about secret reading and new friends, even to listen to confessions of faith or superstition, if he lowered his eyes to hide their mocking glitter. But resisting the urge to instruct when he had 'a burning desire for knowledge', as Jarig recalled of him, may have been beyond him. Such unwise responses at crucial moments will become familiar for, I have suggested, *Caute* was Bento's maxim, not a description of him. It is hard to see him remaining silent if highly educated sceptical marranos such as de la Peyrère, or the Christian-born Daniel de Ribera, in 1655 on the point of fleeing the *mahamad*'s 'inquisition', or Juan de Prado (a Toledo-trained physician, the tenth Jewish medical practitioner on the Amsterdam register) who arrived in 1656, pressed him on the relation of God and the soul to nature. What does surprise is that, once suspicions were aroused, it took so long to convince 'the Rabbi that he was mistaken in having a good opinion of him'. One Jewish scholar suggests, 'There was no precise idea of Spinoza's doctrines, nor any attempt to answer them directly at the time.' Certainly, responses along the lines of I-don't-see-why-not were not positive heresy. Lucas says that, when charged directly by the elders, 'The accused retorted that . . . he would admit what they said . . . if it was not necessary to support it with incontestable reasons.' In 1656, then, there was probably no worked-out thesis, merely an urge towards basing belief on what must, logically, be true.

Another researcher claims that Spinoza was not expelled for heresy at all: that he did not present the same case as De Prado or Ribera, but had unforgivably 'threatened the whole system of mutual credit and trust, which was essential for the Portuguese trade' by going above the heads of the Jewish community authorities to the Dutch civil courts:

> ... the son of a former *parnas* who had been responsible for the community's pawnshop had accused his late father of withholding from him his share of his predeceased mother's estate, had himself declared a minor at the age of 23 although he had been conducting trade independently in the previous two years, had another Jew taken into custody by the sheriff's officers and had sought refuge with the civil authorities without letting the Jewish leadership settle his affairs internally.

This claim is in some ways similar to one made by an earlier researcher, in which Spinoza's chief offence was considered his objectionably close trading and social relations with non-Jews. It emphasises the dire import of Articles 12 and 33 in the 1639 regulations, the first of which stresses the authority of the *mahamad* in all community affairs. Article 33 required, as noted earlier, that business disputes be put to arbitration by the *mahamad* before any recourse to the civil authorities was made, on pain of excommunication. The researcher quoted above believes that the precedent for this ruling lay in the Synagogue Schism of 1618, when the civil authorities were called in to arbitrate, and that the text of the ban read against Spinoza closely resembles one used then. Another commentator points out that the *mahamad* which judged Spinoza was a 'commercial aristocracy' that included – to recap – five chief shareholders of the Dutch West India Company, among them Rabbi Aboab, and probably minor shareholders, too. Such a *mahamad* could conceivably have been as concerned with preserving Jewish solidarity in trading and control in community affairs as defending Judaic Law. Points of tension had certainly shifted since the writing of an anonymous Jewish text in 1617 (taken to be a response by *nação* elders to Grotius's *Remonstrantie*), which warned repeatedly about proselytising and sexual offences, but did not threaten boycott for financial misconduct.

It is possible, then, that Bento *could* have been excommunicated for offending the Jewish governors in matters of business, not religion. But *was* he? It has been argued that the wording of a writ of excommunication used against three men maintaining 'harmful and heretical beliefs' and 'entirely denying the Oral Law [the cabala] which is the foundation and underpinning of our Holy Law' also matched the formulation used in Bento's case. Moreover, with regard to exposing community affairs to the city council, we have seen that Uncle Abraham appeared before the magistrates in 1620, but was neither excommunicated nor deposed as *parnas*. We would be better able to judge this 'no-heresy' claim if we knew whether Spinoza was offered the same statement of retraction as was read out by De Prado a few days after his excommunication by the same board of elders. This mentioned only disobedience to 'God and his Holy Law'.

Let us reserve judgement while looking deeper. We have noted Bento's likely sympathy with de la Peyrère's claim that there were people before Adam – *most men refuse to admit that this story* [of Eden] *is a parable at all, and insist that it is a straightforward record of fact* – and that Jewish history was its own history alone, not that of the world. His mature views on this would be set down in his *Theologico-Political Treatise* fifteen years hence, as part of an argument designed to show that the Jews (like any other human sub-group) *could not*, by the laws of nature, differ from other human beings. *Human nature, Jew as well as Gentile, has always been the same.* If the Jews turned out to be a successful race it was due to their *social organisation . . . In short, their life was a continual practice of obedience . . . This, I think, is the most effective means of influencing men's minds that can be devised.* These views may have been drafted in the 1650s, but no text for a formal *Apology* to the synagogue (rumoured to have been written in Spanish and sent to the *mahamad*) has been found, and it is now thought that none was sent, at least before the *cherem* was enforced, since an official reply would have followed. Afterwards, communication between apostate and elders was disallowed. Whether or not anything was written down or sent, judging by the disjointed text of Spinoza's *Short Treatise*, completed in the early 1660s, a 1650s' version of Bento's views could not have sufficiently resembled the eloquent *Theologico-Political Treatise* of 1670 for long passages to be identical. It may or may not be significant that the devout Amsterdam marrano De Barrios, recalling in 1683 that Spinoza had been 'ejected from Amsterdam' for, as he vaguely put it, 'bad opinions', referred only to a claim the philosopher made in the *Theologico-Political Treatise*, namely that 'the Jews have no obligation to observe the Mosaic Law since they have no state'.

Accepting that Bento's doubts did not in 1656 have the makings of a coherent thesis makes it easier to understand Morteira's initial patience. Lucas tells us the rabbi was slow to do more than ask Bento sadly 'Whether he was mindful of the good example he had set him? Whether his rebellion was the fruit of the pains that he had taken with his education? And if he was not afraid of falling into the hands of the living God? The scandal was already great, but there was still time for him to repent.' Menasseh said nothing, since he had left Amsterdam the previous December on his two-year visit to London to seek the readmission of Jews. His own agenda always came first, and he was hurrying to meet Queen Christina at Antwerp before sailing to England, to tell her he had received no payment for books sent to Sweden. But there is no reason to think Menasseh would have tried to reverse the *mahamad*'s decision. He might have thought Baruch's offences less serious than those of Ribera, for until 5 December 1655 Spinoza still attended the synagogue, pledged to its funds (although paying neither tax nor trading dues) and made no open criticism, whereas Ribera defied the Amsterdam elders and does not seem to have applied officially to join the community. A 1644 regulation stated that Jews arriving from 'any land belonging to Spain or Portugal ... shall not be numbered [in the congregation] without asking beforehand before the whole congregation for forgiveness from the Blessed Lord and his Holy Torah'. Records were kept of supplicants from 1644 to 1724, and Ribera does not seem to have been listed, although the pious De Barrios is named. We know D'Acosta's direct challenge to the authority of the *mahamad* incurred its rage and retribution. Ribera's derision of Jewish history was also of greater concern to the marranos than any abstruse cosmological theory, of which the rabbis themselves propounded several. Speculations about the emanation of God within the world of matter were part of the marrano heritage, and also widely discussed by Christian Neoplatonists and Hermeticists: Calvin had preached and written in the 1530s against the subversive doctrines that attracted the educated of many creeds. But the God of such Hermetic or Neoplatonic theories remained super-natural or spiritual, *in*, not *of*, nature. In 1703 David Nieto, marrano rabbi in London, was rescued from excommunication by this distinction after he preached that 'God and Nature are one and the same'. Spinoza would equate God with Nature, leaving nothing spiritual beyond nature. But this absolute denial of the miracles, demons and angels that were articles of faith for marranos was not necessarily formulated in 1656.

Ribera, on the other hand, was blatantly sceptical about all aspects of the Law. He openly ridiculed the divine revelations and miracles of Moses. His insulting remarks on this – 'Moses our teacher was a great magician'; on the falsity of the Law – 'a law for children'; on the beginning of the world – it had none, at least as so described by the Jews; and on 'the *dicta* of our sages' were the more inflammatory because Ribera flagrantly abandoned many rules of *halachah*, which he dismissed as senseless rituals carried out 'not because of religious merit, but because everyone else is doing it'. He was said to have sent his servant out for Gentile food, including pork; to have publicly regretted his circumcision; and to have stayed away from the synagogue after being allocated a seat. An inquiry was set up, and those who had heard him belittle Judaism united intimidatingly to testify against him. Morteira threatened. Aboab de Fonseca, back in Amsterdam from Brazil, and shaken at its loss to Portugal following twelve years of war and Inquisitional horror, was in no mood to take insults from those whose easy existence in Amsterdam gave them leisure to concoct sophistries and attack the preservers of the faith. The *mahamad*'s punitive fury apart, Amsterdam held little attraction for a fugitive in 1655. Plague raged, and England's recent declaration of war on Spain ruined hopes that the republic's surrender would end cargo losses and lift the trading depression. Ribera lay low, then emigrated to England where he found it expedient, for a while, to become an Anglican. Ultimately, he reverted to Catholicism.

In comparison with Ribera, Baruch might have seemed tractable. No one accused him of infringing ritual laws: the inquiry set up to discuss Baruch d'Espinosa's case is said to have found 'nothing impious'. Yet real animosity to him surfaced around this time. It was in April 1655 that the assault at 'The Four Hollanders' took place. He was also attacked (Bayle reports) 'on leaving the theatre, by a Jew, who stabbed him with a knife. The wound was slight, but he believed that it was the assassin's intention to kill him.' Colerus says the attempted stabbing took place outside 'the old Portuguese synagogue', and adds that Spinoza 'avoided the blow, which reached no further than his clothes'. A concentration of resentment at either location is perfectly plausible. Van den Enden, for example, loved dramatics. He followed up his first school play (a tableau based on Virgil, performed by his pupils at a wedding reception in 1654, with Vondel, whose shop in the Warmoesstraat was close to the Konstwinkel, providing a Dutch commentary) with school plays performed in the Amsterdam theatre. Bento could have been leaving that theatre with the Van den Enden family when he was attacked. Knife-attacks were not, as we have heard, rare events at the time. An assault near the synagogue could equally have been the result of a grievance, or a trading dispute connected with the troubled firm of 'Bento y Gabriel de Espinosa'. But Spinoza was said in the 1670s to have 'kept still the coat that was run thro' with the dagger, as a memorial of that event'. If so, it was surely less as a sour memento of the Jews than a caution that a man of peace could attract brutality.

Whatever the cause of the attack, there was now a crisis in the marrano community in which Bento was implicated but, again, was not the central figure. Juan (now Daniel) De Prado's welcome was short-lived. He was given work, as were as many refugees as possible, but one of his Latin pupils soon objected that not only had Dr De Prado urged him to abandon Hebrew as 'one great mass of confusion', but had also asked him, 'What cause have we to believe in the Law of Moses rather than in the teachings of the various other sects?' De Prado has been accused of single-handedly leading Bento astray, and there are several central concepts in Spinoza's philosophy which De Prado, like Van den Enden, might say reflected his own views. In 1659 De Prado and 'one Espinosa' would be reported to the Spanish Inquisition for identical heresies. We shall consider this circumstance at the proper time, but at this crucial point in Bento's life, when De Prado began to raise his voice among the marranos, a mere seven months before Bento's ban, I confine comment to the ways in which De Prado, alone, offended. He was accused of openly denying the special providence and vocation of the Jewish nation, the superiority of the Jewish religion, the supernatural revelation that was the foundation of Mosaic Law, and the miracles that were seminal to Jewish history. The Latin pupil reports him as claiming that 'the world is uncreated, but exists in eternity', and that the soul's survival is 'impossible and irreconcilable with what the intellect dictates'. All these views are more or less consistent with Spinoza's mature philosophy, and Bento may have been giving De Prado's voluble opinions thought; but he is not recorded in the synagogue annals as asserting them in 1656. De Prado retracted them as fast as he had uttered them, reading out an apology formulated by the *mahamad*. He struggled vainly against a second threat of *cherem* in 1657, and within a few years of being excommunicated left the Provinces for Antwerp. There, he asked the Spanish authorities for permission to return to Spain and Catholicism and, being refused, embraced debauchery with such abandon that De Barrios condemned him in verse.

It is now clear, I think, that Baruch de Espinosa's case lay outside the marrano norm. His muted insolence was neither standard youthful questioning nor outright heresy. While De la Peyrère was clearly an obdurate *converso*, and Ribera and Prado, who blustered and retracted, would show by embracing Catholicism that they did, after all, accept revealed religion, something in Baruch's sinisterly calm demeanour suggested a rational ground-clearing of the mind. His friendliness with free-thinkers and discussion of religious matters with them; his alienation from rabbinical students and deference to Dutch jurisdiction implicitly expressed rejection of Jewish authority and showed his behaviour to be no temporary lapse. The elders knew he had deserted them in his heart, and they set about silencing him before he could produce 'incontestable reasons' or again humiliate them before the civil authorities. They offered him, according to rumour, a pension 'to engage him to remain among 'em, and to appear now and then in their synagogues', which Bento is said to have refused. If this desperate proposition was indeed made – and the text of the ban mentions that they tried 'various ways and means to dissuade him from his evil ways' – this was a back-handed gesture of respect, for there is no record of such a bribe being offered to D'Acosta, De la Peyrère, Ribera or De Prado.

Morteira is then alleged to have insisted on *cherem* 'not for ordinary reasons but for execrable blasphemies against Moses and against God'. Morteira has been accused of personal revenge, not only by non-Jews such as Lucas, but by many generations of Jews. Yet the *mahamad*'s decision to declare Spinoza a heretic was, using hindsight, justified on at least the counts of discoursing with non-Jews on religious matters, disobeying the elders, fraternising and litigating outside the Jewish community and – probably – possessing banned 'writings', such as Descartes's. A suspicion that he also disbelieved the credos considered crucial by Grotius would not only compound these statutory offences, but make him by Dutch law liable to 'death or corporeal punishment, according to the merits of the case'. The *mahamad* wanted any Jew brought into line before that scandalous denouement was reached (which is why d'Acosta was given so many chances to recant). But when finally told that his choice was 'repentance or punishment', Spinoza is said to have answered Morteira back, saying 'he knew the gravity of his threats, and that, in return for the trouble he had taken to teach him the Hebrew language, he was quite willing to show him how to excommunicate him'. Bento knew, of course, that rabbis had no power of excommunication; they merely consented to the decision of the *mahamad*. But it happened that Morteira was at that time a member of the *mahamad*. Is it likely that Bento made this silly remark? By 1656 he should have been so practised in guardedness that any such retort was at most muttered as he walked away, his back to Morteira. Yet I think he probably did say it, for we find such sarcastic compliments in his letters. *I hardly believe our correspondence can be for our mutual instruction . . . I owe you many and sincere thanks for having confided in me in time your method of philosophising.* Whether Morteira heard him or not, Bento's manner is likely to have been edged with an insolence that would be taken as contempt. This characteristic of Spinoza's, which would throughout his life infuriate those who thought religious dogma conferred right, truth and virtue on their views, may have swept away any hesitancy Morteira felt over desiring the excommunication of his dead friend's son.

Was Bento, then, as guilty of narcissism as d'Acosta, Ribera and De Prado? He never admitted to *pride*, the false sense of one's merit which made such self-love an irrational emotion. *When this imagination concerns the man who thinks more highly of himself than is just, it is called Pride, and it is a species of madness, because the man dreams, with open eyes, that he can do all those things which he achieves only in his imagination.* Spinoza would distinguish this from self-esteem early on. *Legitimate self-esteem . . . is only attributed to one who knows his perfections according to his true worth, without passion, and without regard to others' esteem of him.* He would argue later that because such a view resulted from a wholly rational appraisal of one's own nature, *self-esteem is really the highest thing we can hope for.* While vanity would creep in during Spinoza's later years, the outcome of the 1656 rupture suggests that any ideological assurance had a sure grounding in his nature. Ribera's and De Prado's self-love would turn to feed on fresh fantasies, but only unshakeable self-esteem, an absolute conviction that it was right to question, and if necessary to preserve himself by eschewing past instruction, can account for Spinoza's subsequent composure. On being told that the date for reading the ban had been set (it would be in late July), he was said to 'prepare himself for retirement'. This does not mean that to avoid the unpleasantness of *cherem* he hid himself at home. That would have been pointless since he had, anyway, to leave. A ban made living or trading with Gabriel impossible the very word *cherem* meant 'separation'. He is therefore now commonly believed to have dismantled the bedstead, packed his books and removed himself to the house of Frans van den Enden, who had 'offered to look after him'. He is said to have declared (Lucas does not say to whom):

> They do not force me to do anything that I would not have done of my own accord if I did not dread scandal; but, since they want it that way, I enter gladly on the path that is opened to me, with the consolation that my departure will be more innocent than was the exodus of the early Hebrews from Egypt. Although my subsistence is no better secured than was theirs, I take away nothing from anybody and, whatever injustice may be done to me, I can boast that people have nothing to reproach me with.

Was this Spinoza's final message to the Jews of Amsterdam? If so, did they grasp his insinuation that he, made to feel guilty all his life at escaping persecution, had himself been held a slave among the marranos? Michael, at least, would never hear those cutting words. And Baruch was spared a father's curse. Yet biblical parallels should not dominate our perception of his predicament. There is nothing essentially Jewish in the estrangement of a young person from the blood, goods and beliefs of childhood. The anguish of *cherem* reverberated that day through the streets of the city with an ageless, raceless sigh of bitter sorrow, which the Christians of Amsterdam, scouring their bibles for chapter and verse to support the rumour that behind the elegant façade of the synagogue a 'precentor blows a horn, and wax-candles are turned upside down so as to make them fall drop by drop into a vessel full of blood', failed to recognise.

There was no grotesque ritual but, without ceremony, a terse reading of the order of *cherem* from the Ark of the *Talmud Torah*:

> The Lords of the Mahamad announce that having long known of the evil opinions and acts of Baruch d'Espinosa, they have endeavoured by various means and promises to turn him from his evil ways. But having failed to

make him mend his wicked ways, and, on the contrary, daily receiving more information about the abominable heresies which he practised and taught, and about his monstrous deeds, and having for this numerous trustworthy witnesses who have deposed and born witness to this effect in the presence of the said Espinoza, they became convinced of the truth of this matter; and after all of this has been investigated in the presence of the honourable *Hachamim*, they have decided, with their consent, that the said Espinoza should be excommunicated and expelled from the people of Israel, as they now excommunicate him with the following ban:

By decree of the angels and by command of the holy men, we excommunicate, expel, curse and damn Baruch de Espinoza, with the consent of God, Blessed be he, and with the consent of the entire holy congregation, in front of these holy scrolls with the 613 precepts which are written therein; cursing him with the excommunication with which Joshua banned Jericho and with the curse which Elisha cursed the boys and with all the castigations which are written in the Book of the Law. Cursed be he by day, and cursed be he by night; cursed be he when he lies down, and cursed be he when he rises up. Cursed be he when he goes out, and cursed be he when he comes in. The Lord will not spare him, but then the anger of the Lord and his jealousy shall lie upon him, and the Lord shall blot out his name from under heaven. And the Lord shall separate him unto evil out of all the tribes of Israel, according to all the curses of the covenant that are written in this book of the Law. But you that cleave to the Lord your God are alive every one of you this day.

We order that nobody should communicate with him, neither in writing, nor accord him any favour, nor stay with him under the same roof nor within four cubits in his vicinity, nor shall he read any treatise composed or written by him.

The edict was unsigned, suggesting that hope still remained that within six weeks Bento would humble himself to their judgement, accept the inferior position that his involvement with Dutch civil law had brought on him, and retract anything that had offended. But he was not available for either humbling or shunning. He had removed himself to the ancient centre of Amsterdam, where the cacophonous hit-or-miss quarter-hourly chiming of church bells ceaselessly reminded him that *the same old song of the pharisees* would now be sung for him by Calvin.

FOUR

Amsterdam (and Ouderkerk?): 1656–60

I do not differentiate between God and nature in the way all those known to me have done . . . Man, as long as he is a part of Nature, must follow the laws of Nature. That is true religion [in Dutch, *Godsdienst*: God-service].

Abandoning Baruch and Bento to become Benedictus can only be conceived as blessedness if the chains of reasoning underlying Spinoza's actions during the next few years are grasped. Grasping them is not easy, for his actions were on the face of it odd. We would hardly have guessed, for example, that a man of twenty-four who had forfeited honour and potential wealth among his own people, because he doubted that any particular religious sect had a monopoly on truth, would apparently join another sect. We might also wonder why someone who had struggled to learn Latin would take up an apparently artisan trade, and why he would buy the very latest published Spanish literature when his income and Spanish contacts had been abruptly cut off. We might not, either, find a rational connection between *self-esteem* and going to live near the grave of a father whose beliefs had opposed that self-esteem.

In contrast, affection for a fascinating teenage girl (Clara Maria was thirteen during that bitter winter of 1656–7) is understandable. Her mother may by then have been dying. She was alive in 1652 when portraits of Frans 'and his house-wife' were listed in the bankruptcy inventory, but we know she died in Amsterdam, and a woman 'of the Cingel' bearing her name was buried on 7 May 1657. Benedictus may have felt the more for Clara Maria because she stayed cheerful, hiding her tears and putting laughter in place of hysteria or ritual lament. A boy who came for lessons later wrote a poem about this 'sweet and learned' girl, who not only had brains but could also draw, paint and sew. She probably pleased Bento by conversing willingly in Latin and exposing his ignorance, then confidently putting him right. She may also have found him attractive: as we know, several observers thought him handsome. Colerus reports that Spinoza grew very fond of her; in short, he reports, 'having often occasion to see and speak to her, [he] grew in love with her, and has often confessed that he designed to marry her'. While we have no grounds for believing that Spinoza ever had such a plan, we are unjustified in rejecting the idea out of hand. It is, for one thing, anachronistic to imply that Spinoza could not have desired the girl without having paedophile inclinations. It would have been perfectly natural for him to view her romantically or sexually. Jewish girls could marry at twelve and a half, and the records show that in Amsterdam they did. Dutch girls did not reach legal majority until they were twenty-five, but they could marry at sixteen, as De Witt's daughter would try to do, and were considered objects of desire, and marriageable, from the age of puberty. The East India Company asked for 'young daughters' to be shipped out for their Netherlands employees in the Far East. They could be fifteen, sixteen or seventeen, but well-developed 12-year-olds were accepted. No doubt Clara Maria was aware from her first days in Frans's schoolroom of older pupils' interest in her, and we shall see that the plays her father put on could not have left her ignorant about sexual power. It is also false to suppose that, being Jewish-born, Spinoza was not legally free to marry her. We know that, under the regulations of Grotius, Jews were forbidden to marry Dutch citizens, and the granting of Dutch citizenship to them in 1657 for the purposes of free passage while trading or travelling did not alter this ruling. But conversion was much encouraged by the predicants, and if a Jew was publicly baptised, or took a Christian oath in church, marriage was allowed. Spinoza's relationship to his host's daughter may always be obscure, but I suggest that what we know of her upbringing and character supports a view that he could have found her subtly, and not solely sexually, seductive.

Benedictus – the only manner in which we know he was addressed is Simon's 'Sr Benedictus Spinosa' – would have been the subject of talk from the day he moved into Frans's house on the Singel. It was unusual for Jews to spend time with Gentiles, but it was almost unheard of for them to fail to go home to eat unless forced to stay for diplomacy's sake, as in Menasseh's case when he was 'civilly entertained by Cromwell at his Table' while lodging in London's Strand. The distant and disdainful Portuguese merchants had always, when the Exchange closed for business, retired from Dutch life at a dignified pace, forming an orderly procession if in a company of more than two. But now that eastern European Jews earned their living where they could, as pedlars, tobacco workers, frippery dealers and fiddlers (the latter normally played in the taverns till eleven p.m.), the Sabbath eve rush to the Vloyenburg had become a feature of Amsterdam. Orthodox Jews avoided Dutch homes on principle. How could they dip in the *hutsepot* or take a slice off the *worst*, not knowing what mixture of milk and meat it contained? Cheese or butter appeared at every meal, and crabs and oysters, the butt of crude gags to the Dutch and forbidden to Jews, sometimes replaced the staple pickle-herring. The 'roots' (*groente* – vegetables, pronounced 'hroote') that the Dutch ate raw were derided by most foreigners. But if the young Van den Endens wanted to tease their elegant guest they would call him 'Mijnheer *Spinazie*' – Mister Spinach – a joke lingering in the Dutch jingle which claims that eating spinach makes you (clever) like Spinoza. Drinking beer with the family was no novelty for him: Dutch water was unsafe, especially Amsterdam's, and everyone drank small or simple (weak) beer. Although he liked beer – he would later accept half a barrel as a gift – Spinoza seems not to have been interested in food. Some years on he is said to have eaten nothing for days but raisins, butter and milk-gruel, and to have refused every invitation to dine. Raisins, the cornerstone of Michael's income, may have been a comfort since childhood, and no doubt Jarig kept him continually supplied. Benedictus's poor appetite may have been caused by his enfeebling lung condition rather than by Dutch food, which was claimed to fortify both physical and moral well-being. Colerus noted, as a physician acquaintance confirmed when Spinoza died, that he 'had been troubled with a pthyssick'. In the physician's opinion his illness was hereditary: Colerus mentioned only that Spinoza had had it 'above twenty years, which obliged him to keep a strict course of diet, and to be extremely sober in his meat and drink'.

Frans is said to have 'put him up in his own house without exacting any other return than that he should sometimes help him to instruct his pupils when able to do so', and Benedictus may regularly have sat down at the becarpeted table in Van den Enden's parlour to teach. We get a vivid impression of the contents of Frans's former home from the insolvency inventory of 1652, which shows that Benedictus is likely to have sat beneath paintings of Jesus, the saints and 'Prins Willem', with a clavichord and bed beside him. (The inventory shows beds in each room, including the kitchen.) It is unlikely that his Hebrew scholarship was enriched by the Dutch theologian and Hebraist Adam Boreel, as has been suggested, since Boreel was in England with Menasseh at this time, and in the later 1650s was learning from the Jewish rabbis who had been Bento's teachers. But Benedictus did have to get deeply into the New Testament, and for this he bought Greek lexicons, a grammar and a New Testament in Greek and Latin with a Hebrew commentary. He later admitted that he could not expound these Christian books well. *I do not possess a knowledge of Greek sufficiently exact for the task.* We might suppose that he learned Greek grudgingly and taught scripture under sufferance, as agreed for his keep. But events show this was not so. He was avidly concerned with the meddling of apostles and consistories – ecclesiastical councils or courts – with what seemed to him the very simple creed of Christ, and would rake the New Testament for the origins of Christian dogma and for evidence of St Paul's misunderstanding of the books of Moses.

Frans's classes were differently engrossing. It is worth mentioning that, as an ex-Jesuit, Frans's first manuals on natural philosophy would have been those of the Vatican-approved Suárez, who was taught, we recall, by Spinoza's grandmother's cousin, Henrique Henriques. Descartes is also said to have studied Suárez, carrying his *Disputationes* with him during his travels. Spinoza would sometimes refer to Suárez's teachings, but appears not to have owned his texts, and would be as aware as Descartes that science was moving ahead fast. Books on mathematics, astronomy, physics and anatomy were acquired at least as eagerly as his classical texts: Lucian, Virgil (three volumes), Tacitus (two), Livy, Aristotle, Aurelius, Hippocrates (two), Epictetus, Julius Caesar, Seneca (three), Homer, Pliny and Ovid (two), Curtius, Petronius, Plautus, Cicero, Justinian and Horace. How did he pay for them all? His library is usually rated as modest, but for a man who must daily face up to the smallness of his means it was vast. I have suggested that he bought books during the early 1650s when trading was good, and made off with Michael's, Abraham's and Nunes-Henriques-Senior books, too. Besides the Spanish texts mentioned, many of his books were published in the sixteenth century. Spinoza hoarded books, and took them as gifts. Van den Enden may have passed on his classical texts when he left for France in 1671, for his satire of Petronius was not published until 1669, and it is hard (but not impossible) to imagine Spinoza buying that tale of southern Italian *dolce vita* for himself at that bitter stage in his life. A Frenchman he met around that time who had a keen interest in Petronius may also have pressed it on him. If the classics were gifts, then Spinoza bought mainly mathematical, scientific and language texts in the 1650s, and this would make sense.

However kind the welcome, and congenial the chance to study, Benedictus must learn to live with his dependence on Van den Enden, and with the gossip of his pupils and neighbours. These would soon have identified the young teacher, whose typical *zwartheid* – thick, glossy dark hair, dusky olive skin, brilliant black eyes and 'long eyebrows' – immediately marked him off as 'Portuguese', with 'the renegade Jew' recently cursed and deprived of his Exchange seat. It is to be expected that for a while Benedictus kept a low profile in Amsterdam, toning down yet further the richness of his clothes (did he still use the silver buckles?), cultivating a not-too-fashionable pencil-line moustache and limiting his visits to trusted contacts such as Jarig, Simon and Pieter. These friends came anyway to Frans's house, not only to discuss the issue of religious freedom that preoccupied them all, but to learn as mature students. Being scientifically trained, Frans could show the superiority of Descartes's physics to the empirical experiments of Bacon by setting his treatises on natural philosophy in the same mathematical context as those of Galileo, Gassendi and the Danish astronomers Tycho Brahe and Christian Longomontanus – which their compatriot the Leiden student Niels Stensen (Steno), known to all these Amsterdammers, would augment. Benedictus may at first have assimilated all this in silence, but working with Van den Enden undoubtedly made him rapidly argumentative, perhaps in Latin alternating with Spanish (which would explain Spanish nuances in his Latin) rather than in his still shaky Dutch. Someone who had known Frans well would recall that he was an awesome talker, and we know that Benedictus did not care to be outwitted. He fast became familiar with the ancient Greek philosophers, most of whom would be rejected too soon for their texts to be bought. *The authority of Plato, Aristotle and Socrates carries little weight with me.* Descartes became Spinoza's 'greatest light', 'Master' and 'Guide', says Colerus; his works were 'greatly useful' to Spinoza, comments Jarig. The *distinguished man* would enjoy a decade – no more – of such esteem.

The young teacher of Hebrew made an impression in his own right. We know this because pupils later sought him out during their university years. One, Theodor Kerckring, although born in Hamburg, was the son of the Amsterdam merchant and company captain Dirck Kerckring. His mother Margaretha was the daughter of Dr Dirck Bas, a sometime Amsterdam Burgomaster and States-General Deputy. Theodor was seventeen in 1656: in 1659 he would register at Leiden University to study medicine. Thereafter he would achieve both fame and notoriety, and would dip in and out of Bento's life as a grating but compelling presence. In later years he would refer to 'Benedictus Spinosa' as a 'noble mathematician and philosopher', and it is likely that Benedictus taught mathematics at Frans's school, since such lessons would require a minimum of Dutch language. Another pupil, Joannes Casearius, as he called himself (although he claimed to be an Amsterdammer, and the name Casier appears in the city's baptismal records and Leiden's *Studentalbum* at appropriate dates), was a little older than Clara Maria. Spinoza would have profound influence on Jan Casier's life and, again, the destiny of this pupil reflects poignantly on Benedictus's. A third pupil, Albert Burgh, son of one of Amsterdam's wealthiest and most influential regents, later to be Treasurer-General of the United Provinces, would remain in touch with Spinoza, but in the far future would convert to Catholicism and rail at his former teacher's 'unspeakable blasphemy'. In return, Spinoza, nettled by all the features of ignorance and prejudice he could least abide, would plummet to a nadir of abuse.

Could Benedictus be said by this time to have any methodological principles over and above his conviction that belief must be based on what must, as guaranteed by a logic as watertight as mathematics, be true? His theory of knowledge preceded and underpinned his doctrine. It rested on certain deeply rooted guiding assumptions, one of which he had probably never questioned, and the other which he would within the next five years re-invent. The unquestioned assumption was that logical, mathematical and metaphysical necessity were identical. Consequently, reasons and causes were identical, and natural causes, being mathematically ordered in nature, could be known as eternal truths. This medieval assumption would not have worried his contemporaries. It was perfectly familiar to them. Descartes had also urged the use of rational deduction for establishing causes, claiming that mere sense perception – random observation of causes – distorts our view of things: 'If a cause allows all the phenomena to be clearly deduced from it, then it is virtually impossible that it should not be true.' For Spinoza, even more than for Descartes, whose earliest principles were also methodological, truth was established *a priori*, in the confined workshop of the head. For both philosophers, conclusions drawn *a posteriori*, after observation or experiment, supplied no truth for anyone unless intellectual analysis had preceded them. Rather than arguing from instances (*for how can he be sure that the experience of some particular cases can be a rule for him for all?*), Spinoza set himself to work out what must, by a logic equivalent to mathematics, be true. Any *adequate* or complete idea, conveying the truth about any really existing thing, was for Spinoza derived *from intellectual axioms alone, i.e. a deduction based on the pure power of the intellect, and following its order of apprehension.* Surpassing Descartes in logical rigour, he would cast aside the fruits of imagination, faith, passion and random experiment as bad apples. We need to take his intentions regarding the discovery of certain truth into account as we try to understand the confusing period in Spinoza's life between 1656 and 1660, although he neither provided, as promised in one of those early treatises, a systematic explanation of the function and flaws of empirical science, nor invariably stuck by his own methodological rules.

The second epistemological postulate would soon become a foundational plank in his philosophy. He believed the truth about singular phenomena or events could scarcely ever be known by human minds except in its most general features. (The modifying 'scarcely ever' contains a seriously worrying question about precisely how any singular phenomenon can be known *adequately*, and we shall confront it later.) The general truths we can know must be deduced from a *common notion*, whether that notion concerns a physical thing – a human body, for example – or a mental concept, such as religion. *Common notions* are described by Spinoza's editor (presumably with

Spinoza's approval) as axioms or postulates 'so clear and distinct that no one can deny his assent to them, provided only that he has rightly understood the terms themselves'. Although the properties of clarity, distinctness and self-evidence assigned to *common notions* were also Cartesian, Spinoza diverged from Descartes's traditional claim that 'common notions' were undeniably true just because they were innate ideas, planted in our minds at birth and accessible through intuition. When, after much thought, Spinoza propounded his quite different doctrine, he stressed that to be *common*, a thing or idea had to be exemplified either in all things or in all of a kind, such as humankind.

What is common to all things, and is equally in the part as in the whole, does not constitute the essence of any singular thing.

This was not a doctrine of universals, but a criterion of rational universality, a quasi-Socratic 'one over many' based on real instances in nature. For Spinoza, searching for truth involved – at least until his last years – looking beyond particular instances to what was universal because really instantiated in ideas or things – what was *common* to them. Although Spinoza did not argue for this principle until he wrote Part 2 of *Ethics*, around 1663–5, he asserted it in one of his two earliest treatises. *We must now establish something common from which these properties necessarily follow, or such that when it is given, they are necessarily given, and when it is taken away, they are taken away.* This doctrine dictated, for instance, that no person, group or sect could have a monopoly on truth: singular or factional ideas were simply not *common* to all minds. If, on the other hand, something a person or group believed *was* true, it was true for all people, times and places. It was known *sub specie aeternitatis* – under an aspect of eternity. Conversely, no singular or 'subjective' thought, conceived *sub specie durationis*, under an aspect of time and place, was adequate. *There are no inadequate or confused ideas except insofar as they are related to the singular mind of someone.* Spinoza would not recognise the word 'subjective' as we use it: he would take it merely to denote a thought held by a subject. Yet 'subjective' properly characterises his *singular thoughts or this or that thought*, the opinions, passions and sensations of any finite mind in so far as these remained unrelated, through rational examination, *to the common properties of things.*

Behind the bright eyes, primly closed lips and often enigmatic smile, a pitiless search for truth was underway. Morteira, who claimed to reason precisely himself, had probably sensed this meticulous internal calculation. It undoubtedly impressed the members of the philosophical study group, who would eventually – but not yet – cease to take Frans van den Enden's views as infallible, and instead build the circle round Benedictus. For the moment the new teacher was handicapped by his need to master languages, and by his inability to support himself without the protection and employment Frans offered. He was penniless, and the subject of gossip. He was also, I think, having lost his home and job and forfeited attachment to his brother (who, left to handle the firm's financial and social embarrassment, now used his sacral name 'Abraham' for business, so accentuating his Jewish identity and rejection of 'Benedictus'), handicapped emotionally. The elements of social solidarity and the ancient, emotionally charged belief-system that he had abandoned, left him in one dimension of human mentality – the one he thought he scorned – vulnerably naked. Even as principles governing all searches for indisputable truth were firming up, and should have acted as constraints or conditions of *necessary* and *universal* truth for fixing parameters of religious freedom, pain, a mixture of personal hurt, moral outrage and the rotten apple of clannishness disguised as brotherhood in religious practice, undermined his rational resolve. The following events strongly suggest that Spinoza was drawn, through that last misapprehension, which would only slowly be expunged from his psyche, into the heart of a Christian sect.

At some point he was introduced, possibly by Frans, but more probably by Jarig, Pieter or Simon, to a maverick elderly Englishman called Peter Serrarius, an ex-Calvinist pastor who now saw himself as a 'minister of the universal church'. How could Benedictus not want to meet a man with such a mission, a friend to Jews, displaced Jews and Christians alike? It is possible that, since Serrarius had worked with Menasseh, Benedictus had met him some time before. In the summer of 1656, with ecumenical ardour (and delight that peace now allowed English visitors to cross the North Sea), Serrarius opened his arms to a party of the relatively new and unknown religious sect of Quakers. Simon and Jarig may also have greeted them, for it was the Mennonites who organised meetings in a tanner's garret.

Benedictus could have met Quakers while still attending the synagogue, for William Caton and Samuel Fisher had visited it in 1655 and gone afterwards to Jewish homes (where they found the Jews 'a very hard, obstinate people in their way'). He may then have been attracted to their message of individual *inward* enlightenment, and avoidance of the *external acts of worship* that were not fundamental to true piety. He must have welcomed their denial of the literal truth of scripture, and their rejection of social divisions and church offices, and he would understandably have been drawn by the quiet, compelling personality of their Amsterdam leader, William Ames. Yet, mystifyingly, he seems to have been unaware that the Quaker movement, in its pre-institutionalised form, depended chiefly on religious ecstasy. While having no English (or so he would insinuate in 1665) Benedictus must have seen that the Friends were not enlightened by reason, but 'lit up', as this observer implies:

> The Enthusiasts, Quakers or Tremblers . . . remain seated a long time without speaking or stirring, often for one or two hours, and one hears nothing from them except moans, until one of them, feeling the agitation of the movement of the Spirit, gets up and says what the Spirit commands them to say . . . they challenge all those in the Assembly, begging and entreating them to speak, if someone has something to say to oppose them on what they have just said on the Spirit's behalf. It is that which causes the disputes and quarrels which come between them.

The bouts of passion that shattered Quaker silences did not always come from the many women present, although women also felt 'the movement of the spirit'. One adherent, born in 1654, would recall, 'I very well remember what odd sort of people about that time did flock to the Quakers in this country . . . they were also contradicted by Ames and others, and after many exorbitances they left'. These 'exorbitances', which recalled the tendencies of the English Ranters, included raving, 'singing, dancing, falling on the floor, coming in sackcloth and ashes . . . indulging in fearful denunciations and prophecies' and using 'blunt language'. Some witnesses 'spoke themselves dry'. Many Dutch thought the early Quakers shameless or mad. Ames, who offended in Amsterdam merely by keeping his hat on, was stoned by a mob at Gouda, and thrown into Rotterdam bedlam when he protested, the militia being alarmed by a 'passionate and giddy-headed man' accompanying him. Benedictus would fall victim to the early Quakers' typical mixture of piety and vitriol when some zealot added the following Foreword to his first, unpublished *Short Treatise*:

> Previously written in Latin by B.D.S. for the use of his pupils, who wished to devote themselves to the practice of ethics and true philosophy, and now translated into Dutch for the use of lovers of truth and virtue, so that those who boast so much on this subject, and press their dirt and filth on the simple as if it were ambergris, may one day have their mouths shut for them, and may stop blaming what they still do not understand – God, themselves, and how to help people have regard for one another's well-being: and to cure those who are sick of mind, through the spirit of gentleness and forbearance, following the example of the Lord Christ, our best teacher.

It has been suggested that Jarig Jelles wrote this Preface, but nothing like it appears in his letters, his *Confession* or his Preface to Spinoza's *Complete Works*. We would want to think that Jarig extracted himself from meetings that got out of hand, but the concept of obedience which dominated his faith may have made him sit through them in silence.

Spinoza does not mention the Quaker movement, but on the evidence we may have to concede that he not only became close to the Amsterdam Quakers, but was involved in their project of 'saving' the Jews. A move was afoot at the time to address Jewish communities in their own language, which was taken to be Hebrew. (Here is the first stumbling-block to believing Benedictus to be an accessory to this enterprise: in 1657 only schoolboys and scholars understood their ancestral tongue, as he well knew.) A translator was sought. Samuel Fisher was fluent in Hebrew, but by the time the work requiring translation had been composed in England, Fisher had left Amsterdam on a mission to convert the Pope, so was unavailable. Menasseh and Boreel being in London, Caton scoured Amsterdam for a substitute. Calvinist Hebraists wanted nothing to do with Quakerism and, not surprisingly given a spate of synagogue bans and the taboo on non-Judaic literature, Hebrew scholars also backed away. But late in 1657 Caton wrote to Margaret Fell, 'mother of the Quakers' and the author of *A Loving Salutation to the Seed of Abraham among the Jews, wherever they are scattered up and down upon the Face of the Earth*:

> I have been with a Jew and have showed him thy books. I have asked him what language would be the fittest for them he told me Portugees or Hebrew: for if it were in Hebrew they might understand it at Jerusalem or almost any other place of the world. And he hath undertaken to translate it for us, he being an expert in several languages.

The letter does not name or in any other way identify Benedictus as the translator, and indeed he could not have offered to transcribe from English into Hebrew. However:

> As touching thy book . . . I have gotten it translated into Dutch, because the Jew that is to translate it into Hebrew, could not translate it out of English; He hath it now, and is translating of it . . . the Jew remains very friendly in his way.

Given relevant synagogue excommunication records, it has been concluded by an eminent scholar that the person 'that by the Jews is cast out' or 'who hath been a Jew' was Spinoza.

If Benedictus was the translator, he surely did not foresee that *A Loving Salutation* would be repetitive, patronising and substanceless. He would have been told that the Englishwoman preached very well. Quaker women, following artisan tradition, strongly participated in all aspects of the movement's activities, and a Dutch Jew already forced to acknowledge the talents of Clara Maria may have expected something sparkling. Margaret Fell, wife of George Fox, the founder of the Society of Friends (Quakers), was said to have 'a beaming countenance' and 'a most sweet harmonious voice'. But her writing lacked charisma. The *Salutation* was not noticeably loving, nor was it intelligent enough to warrant translation into a scholars' language. Although 170 copies were 'greedily received' by the Amsterdam Jews, Ames himself seemed finally to realise that 'the common people of the Jews cannot speak Hebrew'. It is unlikely, however, that whatever language Fell had used, any Jew would have welcomed it, judging by this typical passage from its pages:

> Turn your minds to within, into the light, which convinceth of Sin and Evil. Here you will come to have your hearts circumcised, and the fore-skins of your hearts taken away ... Here you will come to have your hearts rent, and not your garments. If ever ye know peace and atonement with God, ye must come to the Light, to be proved by the Light, and tryed by the Light, and led by the Light, and guided by the Light ...

Fell's words were ignored, and the attempt to convert the Jews of Amsterdam was abandoned for, monotony, offensiveness and proselytising apart, the Quaker message was not universal. The Friends were not only essentially Christian – the Amsterdam mission was advised in 1657 to 'keep your meetings in the fear of the Lord and . . . stand in the cross' – but while observing such articles of faith, it was noted in 1673 that 'in their outpourings . . . they always add strong condemnations of *other Christians*' (my emphasis). Moreover, since Serrarius would sadly conclude that Quakerism was unlike primitive Christianity, and Van den Enden would later denounce 'stubborn Quakers' as a sect that threatened any truly Christ-like society, we must assume that the Dutch had expected to hear Christian precepts.

Is it possible that Benedictus was not the translator? Even if by 1657 he was able to translate from Dutch, we must surely doubt his willingness to 'missionise' any sect. And even if he approved the spirit of Fell's message, could he have thought it advisable, knowing that Hebrew was read only by educated Jews, to pass it to the likes of Morteira? It is possible that he delighted in the simple principle of the interiorisation of religion shared by all the free-thinkers he met in Amsterdam, and distinguished this from the *outward* trappings of Christian dogma as cleanly as he marked off the clashes that Quaker enthusiasts provoked in Dutch cities from the movement's message of social harmony. But many people thought he was, at that time, a Christian. In 1661 he was pointed out to a Dane as 'somebody who had become a Christian from a Jew, and was now nearly an atheist'. Robert Hooke, the English physicist, referred in his diary to 'Spinosa quakers'. It is remotely possible that, knowing a Jew could marry a Dutch woman if he converted to Christianity, Benedictus fleetingly went as far in that direction as his principles allowed him. But I find it harder to believe that he called himself a *christen* than that he translated Fell's book, because unless he misunderstood Christianity's tenets he could not, by his principle of rational universality, have affiliated himself to any Christian sect. Certainly he would for many years believe Jesus's central message to be non sect-specific. *Christ's mind had to be attuned to beliefs and concepts common to the human race, i.e. to notions which are universal and true. The spirit of Christ*, he thought, was demonstrated in all who *worship God by the exercise of justice and charity towards their neighbours*. Like many avowed Christians, he thought Christianity allowed that *The man who lives in a state where the Christian religion is forbidden is bound to abstain from those rites, and will still be able to live a blessed life.*

There is no doubting that for many years Spinoza took the *spirit of Christ* to be Christianity's criterion; that he learned this criterion from his first Christian friends and was told by them that the offensive aspects of the religion were attributable solely to its institutions and the power of Church consistories. Pieter's *Light upon the Candlestick*, Jarig's *Confession of the Universal Christian Faith* and Frans's *Liberal Political Propositions* all show the same refusal to equate ritual and rule with Christianity as would Spinoza:

> *As for Christian rites like Baptism, the Lord's Supper, [etc] . . . if any others were ever instituted by Christ or his Apostles (and so far I have no sufficient evidence for this) – they were instituted only as outward symbols of a universal church, and not as things which make any contribution to blessedness or have any intrinsic sanctity.*

However, despite Jesus's pronouncement in Matthew Chapter 22 that 'Thou shalt love the Lord thy God with all thy heart' and 'Thou shalt love thy neighbour as thyself' and that 'On these two commandments hang all the law and the prophets', one has only to read on in the Gospels to see that Christ's teaching was incompatible with what we already know of Spinoza's views. If we are to trust the Gospel chroniclers we must believe that Jesus taught, for example, that God was external to, and above, nature – a creator, judge and heavenly, caring Father – and that human souls were subject to final judgement. But these doctrinal differences aside, Spinoza cannot have believed any creed labelled 'Christian' would allay *the hate the Turks have against the Jews and the Christians, the Jews against the Turks and the Christians, and the Christians against the Jews and the Turks, etc.* Turks and Jews would not listen to Christ, whom they would see as an anti-prophet, any more than Christians and Turks would accept Jewish *halachah*, or Christians and Jews would revere Mohammed. No belief particular to one creed and incompatible with others could be described as a *common notion*.

Perhaps Benedictus was not misled, but chose from his first days as a religious sceptic and refugee to focus on the two indisputable principles of Christianity constantly preached in the Reformed Church with which he could hope profitably to work, namely internal godliness and the outward practice of justice and charity. The most bigoted of theologians or parish predicants must affirm these Christian virtues. At all events, he would cling to them during the storms of religious controversy that later flashed about his head when he made his loathing of *external* Christianity known. Yet I think his commitment to those who at that time gave him unjudgemental warmth, those whose soft pronunciation of *christen* contrasted appealingly with the teeth-baring hiss habitually resorted to by zealots, went deeper than rational approval of a simple maxim, for he did, as a matter of recorded fact, leave Amsterdam between 1660 and spring 1661 to live in an internationally known Protestant centre, where baptism by immersion in a tank fed by a brook was regularly practised.

There can be no doubting that the radical Protestants of Amsterdam opened their arms wide to Benedictus, and anyone who finds similarities in his writings to Jarig's and Pieter's over and above those just distinguished (I find few) also sets him squarely within that brotherhood which largely, in advocating irrational, sectarian beliefs, represented a contradiction of his principles. The marrano mysticism on which he was knowledgeable would have been as welcome to this fraternity as his Hebrew and knowledge of biblical history. Serrarius, for example, was, like Menasseh, a mystic. He probably abhorred Benedictus's 'geometric spirit' and must have rejoiced that it was in abeyance during the Amsterdam hunt for a *very simple universal faith*. But Serrarius and the Quakers symbolise an undertext in Benedictus's thinking between 1660 and, roughly, 1661–2. The face he would ultimately offer the world was gradually unveiled through the encouragement of a number of Leiden academics of diverse character and influence. It is perhaps least confusing to take an over-simplified view of the following events by looking on them as in a part a tussle for the intellectual soul of a talented young man, and in part an acknowledgement of the threat posed by his growing independence from the opinions impressed on him from all sides.

The 28-year-old Lodewijk Meyer, an occasional star of Van den Enden's study group, was destined to be Benedictus's first editor. He is easily seen to occupy a polarity opposing the evangelicals by the fact that Serrarius would publicly refute a treatise he wrote promoting a rational or philosophical understanding of scripture. We do not know exactly when Meyer met Spinoza, but in 1663 Benedictus referred to *the kindness and esteem you have always seen fit to show me*. After gaining a philosophy doctorate in 1658 Meyer would enrol in the medical school, a year before Kerckring. Meyer was a polymath: in 1650 he had so ably revised and amplified an existing 'Dutch Vocabulary' that it went into many editions over fifty years. He also wrote poetry, and would eventually pour all his exceptional abilities into his work with the Amsterdam theatre. His family were Lutherans, but he openly put criteria of clear thinking above passive religious obedience. He befriended, and knew socially, Simon de Vries – in 1658 composing a poem for his cousin's wedding – and probably knew Jarig, Pieter and Peter Serrarius. Benedictus did not own a copy of Meyer's 'Dutch Vocabulary', doubtless because he had no intention of composing anything in Dutch, yet Meyer stands out as a significant influence on him. Again and again we find evidence of his effective persuasion. It was Meyer who first identified *common notions* with axioms or postulates. He did not noticeably motivate Benedictus at this early stage, perhaps because the student-teacher had produced no words for him to savage, but by 1662 he would urge Spinoza to work with his 'geometrical spirit', instead of against it, and to cut out the Jewish mysticism that crept into his *Short Treatise*.

Spinoza and Meyer may first have met while Meyer was at home during the long Leiden university vacations, helping perhaps with Van den Enden's school productions at the Amsterdam municipal theatre. In 1657 and 1658 Frans put on three plays in Latin: his own *Philodonius*, and Terence's *Woman of Andros* and *Eunuchus*. The theatre, and Terence in particular, were disapproved of by the Reformed Church, and Frans's productions probably led some parents to withdraw pupils from the school. Terence had been made a slave in Carthage, but he may have been Iberian, and his indelicate subject matter was packaged in dialogue so delicate yet vibrant that it must improve anyone's Latin, if no one's morals. Did Benedictus act in these plays? They were long, and the prancing about they demanded may have been too much for him, but while he owned no text of Terence, Spinoza's *Ethics* contains so many paraphrases from *Eunuchus* and *Woman of Andros* that one scholar thinks we can guess which roles he took. Terence's subtle assigning of intelligence and sexual responsibility to women may have worked on the received view of women that Clara Maria and the Quaker women had already slightly unsettled, but it did not obliterate the plays' central theme of women as sex objects to be excited, exploited or seduced, and will have confirmed Benedictus's view of women as being, in their way, more manipulative than men. The question arises whether Frans, who thought marriage unnecessary, genuinely pardoned prostitution among Terence's privileged free-born ladies or, being a radical democrat, merely relished a slave's satirical view of patrician behaviour, but nothing suggests he was responsible for Spinoza's later sourness about women.

At some point the house on the Singel ceased to be a haven. There may have been little peace in a household where every belief and decision was questioned, yet where constraints like, yet unlike, those of his own family home subtly operated. The Houtgracht house might have been latterly tensely silent, but it may also have been a more satisfactory place for private study than Frans's educational hothouse, where school classes, study groups, rehearsals and possibly political activist meetings filled the house with visitors, and the brood of Van den Enden children demanded what may have seemed to Benedictus excessive attention. Dutch fathers took an unusually active part in bringing up their offspring, not only guiding them mentally into the outside world, but listening, comforting and physically tending them. Spinoza would never much like children: *childish* is as well-used a pejorative for him as *womanish*. He saw only sense-bound, impressionable young minds, to be taught to respect, then to reason, then to use that reason to reassess the respect they'd had. Clara Maria was differently demanding, inspiring in class, but probably exasperating outside it, being of exceptional intelligence yet tolerating the fanciful beliefs of what for Spinoza would remain the most superstition-ridden of sects – Catholicism. The girl could cut through others' mental mists easily enough: if he had shown her Fell's *Salutation* she'd surely have screeched with laughter at the Englishwoman's ramblings. She may have joined Frans's study groups and watched Benedictus's right eyebrow rise as she said her piece with perfect composure, or quipped mercilessly, perhaps at the expense of poor Jarig, on whom Latin was lost. The bedrock of blind faith on which any close friendship that developed between the high-spirited Dutch girl and the geometric-spirited philosopher would eventually founder had not yet been struck, and the two may have formed a rapport that transcended other misgivings. Benedictus may even have fixated on her allegiance to her Catholic faith, seen it as a challenge, his belief that women were mentally weak making Clara Maria's mind malleable in his eyes, her childhood conditioning easier to alter than a man's. To the end of his life he held that women could not be free, rational agents. *I added 'independent' to exclude women and servants, who are subject to their husbands and masters.* Given his background, he is unlikely to have believed, in the 1650s, that a young girl could hold out against her father: her faith was *stubbornness of superstition* indeed in the face of Frans's antipathy to institutionalised religion, and his powerful verbal gifts. Van den Enden would soon write that preachers of any kind were a 'ruinous pestilence of all peace and concord'. Spinoza agreed, reserving – we see – a special disapproval for Reformed Church theologians and the Catholic Church. Dutch historians who ignore all other aspects of his thinking find it necessary to mention his belief that the State must legislate on matters of religion. Did Clara Maria, laughing at them both, pull Benedictus along to 'de Posthoorn'? He may have gone readily, to listen to the Latin, to judge how papery failed Christ, to calculate how best to argue away such ridiculous superstition.

It may have been assumed that he would in due course move on. Family and pupils must surely have asked Benedictus what he wanted to study at Leiden, that centre of European research where so many students were foreigners that general conversation was in Latin. It must have seemed obvious that the brilliant Portuguese teacher would enrol there. Grotius had entered university at the age of eleven, Hobbes at fourteen and Jan de Witt at sixteen. Kerckring, who began learning Latin later than this, would be remembered as an *opsimath*, a late starter. Meyer, too, first registered at Leiden aged twenty-five.

Spinoza's name is not found in the registers of Leiden university, but his knowledge of Professor Heereboord's unpublished philosophy, for example, and the testimony of an Inquisition spy that he had studied there, suggest that he may have attended lectures as a free listener, perhaps in the company of Meyer, Kerckring or Steno, or friends yet to be introduced such as Johannes Hudde, who was studying medicine there and knew Van den Enden. (Hudde came from a Calvinist regent family, but he was a Cartesian and an excellent mathematician, and by 1666 a meeting of minds had grown between himself and Spinoza – on the topic of Cartesian mathematics, at least.) The reasons for Benedictus's non-enrolment seem, on the sparse evidence we have, to echo his ostracism of the higher *medras*. Poverty may, partly, have kept him away. He had no means at present of supporting himself without working during the day – and university students were forbidden to study at night – without accepting charity. As with the system of rabbinical instruction, he did not want to be told what to think. He would not have thought Leiden a fusty enclave: it was a lively research institute occupying a former convent building at the centre of a fortified industrial town of 50,000 people, where the destitute lived under the ramparts and the families of underpaid textile workers subsisted in slums. Apart from

Zaandam, Leiden was the biggest Dutch industrial conurbation, and De Witt may have learned something about economic conditions while he studied there. (He would certainly be amply advised – and Spinoza would be influenced – by the politically active Van den Hove brothers, sons of an immigrant Leiden cloth worker and still living there.) Yet whichever of the university's disciplines Spinoza chose, he would, as in the higher *medras*, have to submit to years of passive absorption of knowledge. *To pursue [honour] we must direct our lives according to other men's powers of understanding.* Since it is not clear who at Leiden could have helped Benedictus progress in philosophy – although similarities in Spinoza's ideas to those of certain contemporary professors are discussed later – Lucas may be closest to the real reasons behind Benedictus's lack of a Leiden degree when he says, 'As there were no authors to his liking, he had recourse to his own meditations, being resolved to ascertain how far they could reach.'

Perhaps Benedictus's pupils merely asked him what branch of natural philosophy drew him, assuming it would have some connection with mathematics. Frans's own specialty in the earth sciences was chemistry. He is said to have worked on nitre with a colleague, and Kerckring and other ex-pupils of Frans's would study under the iatrochemist Sylvius, an Amsterdam physician since 1641, made Leiden professor of medicine in 1658. But Benedictus, led perhaps by Leiden talk of the 'perspective glasse' or 'mathematicians' perspectil', also called the 'optic magnifying glasse', which had been developed into an 'optic tube' for magnifying heavenly bodies, became increasingly engrossed in his old textbook, the priest Scheiner's *Astronomy and Refraction*. Borelius's *De Vero Telescopii Inventore*, published in 1655, explained how Galileo's 'imperfect instrument', which supplied only an inverted image, had been improved by Father Scheiner, who first substituted a convex lens for Galileo's concave one, then added a second convex lens which inverted the image again, giving the observer a natural view of the object. *What* was seen interested Benedictus less than *how* it was accurately viewed through glass. The success of this depended on the accuracy of the Law of Refraction, first formulated at Leiden by Willibrord Snell, affirmed by Descartes in his *Optics* and currently being revised at Leiden by Christiaan Huygens. At three years older than Benedictus, Huygens was by then a celebrated scientist. In 1651 he had published an important book on mathematics, and by 1657 he had both discovered the nature of Saturn's rings and invented the pendulum clock.

Of all the opportunities Leiden offered, Benedictus might most have wanted to work with Huygens. He would around this time have begun his own investigations, starting, as we would expect, with mathematical theory – calculating the angle at which a ground lens would best bend parallel rays of light and bring them to a focus. Testing theories involved practical experiment, but theory dictated whether tools for making plane-convex rather than concave-convex lenses should be bought for the purpose. When, some years later, Spinoza asked Johannes Hudde for his *opinion and advice* before getting some new polishing tools made for himself, the information he wanted was not practical, but algebraic. Only when calculation was complete came lens preparation. Robert Hooke, who did not invent, but launched on the world, the compound 'microscope' – in 1656 a new word – stressed that expensive tools were not necessary for making simple 'glasses', and indeed spectacle-makers had experimented effectively with magnification since the twelfth century simply by curving one surface of flat glass. (The principle of the microscope or telescope – the placing of two or more lenses together in a tube – is credited to Zacharias Jansen, a spectacle-maker of Middelburg.) Now, numbers of amateur natural philosophers, stimulated by Descartes's *Optics*, were taking an interest in the construction of prisms and lenses. There were four main operations. First, a blank must be sawn from raw slab glass. For this a hacksaw blade wiped with ash and oil mixed with diamond grit (worked in by sawing on hard glass or quartz) was needed. Then black pitch was used to hold the lens in place while a centring spindle and lathe (or trepanning mill) rough-ground the curve to size and angle or radius. Next came fine grinding while maintaining the angles or radii. Finally, carborundum and polishing powders were used to complete the lenses. Such tools and materials were easily available in Amsterdam, and what other master would Benedictus need than Jan Glazemaker, friend of Van den Enden? Glazemaker, a Flemish Mennonite from a glass-making family living on the Prinsengracht, was now a Latin scholar. In recent years he had translated all Descartes's available philosophy into Dutch. But when he married in 1651 he gave his profession as 'glassmaker', and only in 1687 was he registered in the *poortersboek* as a translator. While the textbooks on glass-cutting and optics that Spinoza owned were not published until 1663 and 1668, he must have made lenses before then, for in 1661 he was observed to 'occupy himself with the construction of telescopes and microscopes', and the skills needed for that cannot have come easily. A three-year apprenticeship is still required for perfecting lens-grinding and polishing. In the mid-seventeenth century the arts of polishing and 'peeping' were gentlemanly hobbies, to the chagrin of committed researchers. The acclaimed microscopist Van Leeuwenhoek, born in the same year as Spinoza, refused to set up a school to teach gentlemen to 'polish glass', or to look through it, since 'I am convinced hardly one in a thousand is properly fitted to take up this study.'

So began Benedictus's science of optics, and with it the misleading legend that the philosopher took up menial labour in order to earn a crust.

Details of what Spinoza was doing in those Amsterdam years of 1657–60 are uncertain, but we have evidence that his Jewish attachments were not dead, and thereby some support for my belief that he missed his former life. Juan de Prado had not accepted the ban pronounced on him early in 1657, and in 1658 was still fighting the *mahamad*'s ruling. He saw himself as a much-needed reformer of Judaism, and only redoubled his bid for reinstatement when the elders offered him and his family assisted passages to a marrano community abroad. We might think Benedictus would have avoided this trouble-maker, but research into Inquisition records shows that the two were seen together in Amsterdam in 1659, shortly before De Prado finally took himself off to Antwerp.

In 1654, following a peace that amounted to surrender by the Dutch, England had declared war on Spain, and a certain priest, Fray Tomás Solano y Robles, had been taken prisoner. On his release in 1659, and en route for Spain, Fray Tomás stopped over in Amsterdam to find and question on behalf of the Madrid Inquisition a certain Lorenzo Escudero, now calling himself 'Abraham Israel'. In the company of this quarry he found one 'Dr Prado', who had with him 'one Espinosa', born in Holland and 'a good philosopher who has studied at Leiden' but was of 'no profession'. It is fascinating that Benedictus did not call himself a teacher or microscopist, but let it be thought he was a university-trained philosopher, and it is also significant that De Prado was *not* described as a philosopher, since this seems to reinforce the seventeenth-century rumour that he was 'a small philosopher and even less of a physician, mad in his reasoning, dauntless in his talk'. Fray Tomás gives us a valuable pictorial description of the two men. He states that 'Dr Prado' was tall and thin, very dark in his eyes, hair and complexion, and with a big nose. Curiously, the monk puts De Prado at thirty years old, whereas he was approaching fifty. Espinosa, on the other hand, is described as a short man of twenty-four, of handsome face (*de buena cara*) with light, clear skin and with black hair and eyes. An echoing description was given to the Inquisition by Captain Miguel Pérez de Maltranilla, a day after Fray Tomás's. The Captain, visiting a Canary Islands physician convalescing from leprosy in Amsterdam, stumbled on a discussion group at the sick physician's home, where he distinguished two men 'who had abandoned the Jewish religion' from two other, allegedly practising, Jews (who should not, of course, have been 'under the same roof or come within four cubits') of Benedictus or De Prado. De Maltranilla declared that De Prado was tall, with a thin face and black hair and beard, and was fifty years old, while Espinosa was a thin young man – 'his age is thirty-three' (he was not yet twenty-seven) with long black hair and a small black moustache. The Captain also remarked on Espinosa's 'beautiful face' and on his comment, which we noted earlier, that 'he had never seen Spain, but would like to'.

We do not know whose words Fray Tomás used when he summarised the confessions of Spinoza and De Prado, but apparently both spoke Castilian, both said they regretted being expelled from the synagogue, and both admitted that they were

> content to maintain the heresy of atheism, since they felt that there was no God except philosophically speaking (as they had declared) and that souls died with bodies, and that faith was unnecessary.

Does this summary approximate features of Benedictus's gradually crystallising doctrine? On the first avowal, while Spinoza did not acknowledge a theistic God (that is, supernatural, and enjoying a personal relation with His creatures), the question of whether he was an atheist in the commonly accepted sense is still open to debate, for *God, or Nature* really existed for Spinoza. Thus the second avowal is also wide of the mark. God did not just exist philosophically, but was all there is *existentially* speaking. On the third avowal, Spinozistic minds did not wholly die with bodies. They did not survive in any traditional sense, but some of the ideas that constituted minds could, as ideas, survive. Faith was, certainly, unnecessary for knowledge. Thus, although Solano's report is a major contribution to our knowledge of Spinoza's thought at this time, it is too crude to be said to express it. The report does however make sense of Peyrera's cryptic comment of 1659 that 'This world is but a barren ground, a field full of thistles and thorns [*abrojos y espinos*], a green meadow [*prado*] full of poisonous serpents.' These two men were still a menace to the marrano community.

Their renegade views should only have been whispered between themselves, or among sympathisers, in the same way that Benedictus discussed the thesis of *God, or Nature* with Van den Enden in a circumscribed study group. While he may no longer have been Frans's house guest, he was probably still teaching in the school, and he would be attending Van den Enden's classes and debating groups for some years to come. There is evidence that ideas began to flow between Frans and himself on the most basic level of philosophising, those grass-roots from which, Descartes had insisted, all natural science must grow:

> The whole of philosophy is like a tree. The roots are metaphysics, the trunk is physics, and the branches emerging from the trunk are all the

other sciences, which may be reduced to three principal ones, namely medicine, mechanics and morals.

Master and pupil discussed metaphysics, theories of what lay behind the physical; of what the physical might be; whether or not it was one independent substance, or many, or not distinct from other phenomena previously considered distinct substances, such as thought, or God. Until recently it was thought that their shared 'pantheistic' concepts, noted at the time by one of Frans's pupils, sprang from a mutual interest in Greek philosophy, but a stronger affinity between Frans's ideas and Spinoza's philosophy has now been found. In recently discovered pamphlets, published anonymously in 1662 and 1665, Van den Enden equates God with nature, says that human beings follow fixed laws of nature through cause and effect, and denies any difference of substance between mind and body. These are central tenets of Spinoza's, and they represent a dramatic divergence from other known views of the time. They do not, as I have mentioned, match well-disseminated Neoplatonic or Hermetic doctrines in which God was in some weaker sense extended by being 'in' Body; by 'informing' it. De Prado's *Dios de la naturaleza*, for example, created the universe and set it in motion, and Henry More wrote of 'Extension arising by gradual Emanation from the First and Primest Essence, which we call the Centre of the Spirit':

> An emanative effect is coexistent with the very substance of that which is said to be the cause thereof . . . Suppose God created the matter with an immediate power of moving itself, God indeed is the Prime Cause as well of the Motion as the matter, and yet nevertheless the Matter is rightly said to move itself. Finally this Secondary or Emanative Substance may rightly be called Substance, because it is a subject endued with certain powers and activities, and does not inhere as an Accident in any other Substance or Matter.

More had corresponded with Descartes on this, and Descartes had dismissed the notion that God could be material, even as a 'secondary' or inferior substance. Yet More held Descartes's mechanistic theories to be a greater danger to Christian theology than his own system, in which spirit pervaded the universe, and he was put in a state of consternation partway through reading one of Spinoza's texts when he grasped that a naturalistic God having no 'First and Primest Essence' other than the substance of the universe was postulated. Neither Van den Enden nor Spinoza held that there was a God before, or outside, nature. For Spinoza the two terms are interchangeable: wherever *God* is mentioned in his works and letters the word *Nature* may be substituted. One researcher believes Van den Enden formulated and passed on to Spinoza this and other central metaphysical tenets; indeed, he takes the schoolmaster to be 'a proto-Spinoza, the genius behind Spinoza'. Yet, while this researcher's discovery of Van den Enden's manuscripts leaves no room for doubt that the schoolmaster exchanged ideas with his famous pupil, if this claim is to be accepted its proponent must show that Frans had conceived the God or Nature doctrine *before he could have met Spinoza*. This has not yet been shown. The same researcher quotes a 1661 report that Franciscus had already 'communicated in manuscript to his friends some of his secret doctrines', and cites a 1670 claim that Johannes Bouwmeester (a physician friend of Meyer's and a future somewhat sceptical correspondent of Spinoza's) owned 'all the secret writings of Doctor Van den Enden'. In this case Bouwmeester, and anyone else who had read Frans's thoughts, would surely have protested if they thought Spinoza had hijacked the thesis. Bouwmeester gave no such hint, and indeed most of the Amsterdam group seem to have found Spinoza's thesis of *God, or Nature* unfamiliar. Benedictus expected this: when he at last let some of his views be circulated in his unpublished *Short Treatise on God, Man and His Well-Being*, he wrote near the end, *It only remains for me to say to the friends to whom I write this: do not be surprised at these novelties, for you know very well that it is no obstacle to the truth of a thing that it is not accepted by many*. This advice does not suggest that he knew he was repeating their teacher's views.

The flow of instruction may in fact have gone the other way, for certain elements in Van den Enden's and Spinoza's work, for example the notion of *the intellectual love of God*, were grounded in Hispano-Judaic teaching and had been written on by, among others, Menasseh ben Israel. Moreover in 1668 another of Frans's pupils or acquaintances, the Amsterdam physician and lawyer Adriaan Koerbagh, would be charged by Amsterdam's Reformed Church Council and its magistrates with promulgating specifically 'Hebrew' heresies which he was assumed to have been taught by Spinoza. (At present Koerbagh was still writing, under Sylvius at Leiden, a doctoral thesis on the causes of phthisis.) He would deny discussing the topic with Spinoza, or with Van den Enden, but would admit that he knew Buxtorf's Hebrew dictionary to be a source of information on occult cosmological matters. Spinoza owned Buxtorf's two-volume dictionary and thesaurus, as well as other books containing cabalic terms, and he did grant a partial anticipation of his doctrine of *God, or Nature* to *Some of the Hebrews* [who] *seem to have seen, as if through a cloud, that God, God's intellect, and the things understood by him are one and the same*. In fact, a Jewish scholar assures us, no esoteric Jewish metaphysical scheme quite says this, and Spinoza gave out that his view was unique to himself. In the spring of 1662, just as Van den Enden took his treatise containing the God-or-Nature concept to the printer's, and well before Koerbagh began to write, Benedictus would claim, *I do not differentiate between God and Nature in the way all those known to me have done.* We find nothing on Van den Enden, De Prado or Koerbagh in Spinoza's letters. This does not mean that he did not mention them: we know his letters were edited and identities deleted. He was also notoriously lax in acknowledging his intellectual debts. It is therefore more significant to note that none of these writers ever claimed him to have appropriated their ideas, and that the widely-read philosopher Leibniz said that he could recall no earlier one-substance claim than Spinoza's.

The confessions to Fray Tomás were not wise, and whether or not De Prado and Espinosa were aware that their names were lodged in Madrid's Inquisition records – De Prado would be questioned in Antwerp – it seems that around 1660 something frightened Benedictus in a way the *cherem* had not. His suspicion that he was an undesirable figure in Amsterdam was at least partly rational, grounded in a reasoned appraisal of his situation. No longer being a merchant, he contributed nothing to Amsterdam's mercantile economy. He was known to associate with free-thinkers, some of them notorious disturbers of the peace, one of them a schoolmaster who taught godless ideas. He was a wandering Jew who sought out other outcasts from the synagogue. But over and above these undesirable characteristics, something specific seems to have jolted him into realising that he must not be heard to deny basic Judaeo-Christian concepts. Perhaps information from the two orthodox Jews who overheard the confessions stung the *mahamad* into public protest, for Lucas says the elders petitioned the magistrates for a civil order driving him from the city, and that the burgomasters 'condemned the accused to exile for several months'. Lucas adds that the council gave in to Morteira to get 'rid of the importunate clamours of the most vexatious of all men'. But no evidence for a petition to the civic authorities exists, and by 1660 Morteira was dead. (Menasseh never returned to Amsterdam. He died at Middelburg in Zeeland in November 1657.) There may have been a warning from the Amsterdam council, or denouncements from pulpits, for while the magistrates found Jewish disputes irritating, the dignified rabbi Aboab de Fonseca would have sympathy from the Dutch authorities over blatant violations of Grotius's atheism condition. The city was rapidly expanding – soon the leafy canals would be fully ringed with brick buildings – but it was still small enough for verbal threats to reach individuals.

Whatever alarmed him, Benedictus's subsequent efforts to bind his friends to silence seem to spring from a chronic anxiety, which began about 1660. Fearing the evil reputation he was gaining, and searching for a

94

philosophical identity he did not yet have (he had committed nothing to paper, as far as we know), he seems temporarily to have gone into hiding. In May 1660 Jarig bought a large house on the Herengracht, and no doubt, and not for the first time, offered Benedictus protection and a home. But Colerus holds that:

> He was able to maintain himself with the work of his hands, and to mind his study, as he design'd to do. So that having no occasion to stay longer in Amsterdam, he left it, and took lodgings in the house of one of his acquaintance, who lived upon the road from Amsterdam to Auwerkerke. He spent his time there in studying, and working his glasses. When they were polished, his friends took care to send for them, to sell 'em, and to remit his money to him.

So let us place Benedictus for a short while, for want of other evidence, near Ouderkerk, close by the Ets Haim cemetery on the bend of the Amstel. He may still have been there when his sister Ribca was widowed in September 1660. This period – months, perhaps years – is thought to have seen some initial drafting of his first two treatises, one just over a hundred pages long, the other much longer. He must also have perfected his glass-working skills, and this involved time-consuming calculation and experiment. Yet there was time also for reflection as he walked, as he liked to do, along the lanes or the high dyke flanking the Amstel; perhaps stood beside his father's and Morteira's graves in the Beth Haim cemetery. He may not have chosen to live near that last shrine to *halachah*, but any musings there, softened perhaps by the curious forgiveness we bestow on dead presences, which do not answer back, cannot have undermined his self-esteem as much as disputing with two elderly, abrasive and possibly jealous physicians. He began to write prolifically, certain now that *Godsdienst* involved acknowledging that whatever was God should be given respect and love; that nature was not merely matter, but also all the thinking there could logically possibly be. Human beings must be respected as partial expressions of that one natural substance, that single, determining, natural force. *Man is a part of Nature, which must be coherent with the other parts . . . We do not ask, when we speak of the soul, what God can do, but only what follows from the laws of Nature.* There was more to this concept than Van den Enden or De Prado dreamed. Benedictus tried to convey it in the pages of his metaphysical *Short Treatise*. Realising while doing so that the mathematical cast of mind needed for deducing from nature's laws was lacking in most of his readers, he also composed a tract on the method of making clear deductions and distinctions. He called it *The Treatise on the Emendation of the Intellect.*

One report says that he shared his Ouderkerk home with 'someone' about whom nothing definite has been discovered, but who has been taken to be one of Amsterdam's *Collegianten*. The word simply meant 'gatherers', free-thinkers who convened to worship. They acknowledged no religious organisation or leaders, and so committed were they to respecting differences of view that although their movement was very well known, they were not listed as a sect or further described in a book published in 1673 called *The Religion of the Dutch*. Benedictus, still searching for a *very simple universal* form of *Godsdienst*, and apparently still failing to see alliances of the religiously like-minded as sects, was, it is supposed, drawn to their meetings in a house in the Rokin. There, he may have had pointed out to him persons of distinction, liberal regents like Coenraad van Beuningen, Pensioner for Amsterdam from 1650 to 1660, and an experienced diplomat, by 1660 second in influence in Holland only to De Witt. In my view, only knowledge of Van Beuningen's association with the Collegiant movement, and belief that this choice of religion was acceptable to State authority, makes Benedictus's next move rational, for around 1660–1, his discourses unfinished, 'in order to be less disturbed in his contemplations by friends in general [*gemene vrienden*], he left his birthplace, Amsterdam, and took up his abode in Rijnsburg'. This village, lying between Leiden and the North Sea, was the birthplace of the Collegiant movement and the venue several times a year of its main Assembly. Van Beuningen would later write of being fortified by 'religious conversations and exercises' while living there in his twenties, and Benedictus, whose *Short Treatise* betrays an unmistakable hunger for what may loosely be called spiritual uplift – how powerful must that childhood cultural influence have been – is said to have gone to live there with the unidentified 'someone' whose home he had latterly been sharing.

He cannot have known how fervently Van Beuningen shared the mystic visions of Serrarius. Nor may he have realised that the periwigged ambassador was not considered a model of rational behaviour even in those early days, decades before his sanity finally failed, when he would daub with blood on the walls of his Amsterdam house cabalistic signs, and words of Old Testament damnation.

FIVE

Rijnsburg: 1660–2

The way of understanding the nature of anything, of whatever kind, must always be the same, viz. through the universal laws and rules of nature . . . I have therefore regarded passions like love, hate, anger, envy, pride, pity, and other feelings which agitate the mind . . . as properties which belong to it in the same way as heat, cold, storm, thunder and the like belong to the nature of the atmosphere.

The travelling trunks probably reached Rijnsburg by water; if not by canal boat, then by horse and cart carried by sailing boat across the inland sea of Haarlem. Benedictus himself would have taken the L-shaped canal route that ran west from Amsterdam to Haarlem and, now, south to Leiden. The newly cut stretch had been opened in 1657, and although the horse-drawn canal boat or *trekschuit* which edged along it took seven hours by day and nine by night to reach Leiden from Amsterdam, the trip was comfortable and safe. It skirted the shallow inland Haarlemmer Meer, where dense mists could becalm a vessel, or violent side winds cause sharp, choppy waves, which threatened to overturn it. English voyagers seem to have dreaded the sea of Haarlem more than the North Sea: Sir William Brereton noted nervously that 'the boat rowled so much on one side that it went within less than a quarter of a yard of the water, the sail almost leaning into the water', and recalled the King of Bohemia's barge capsizing there in a sudden squall and the Prince drowning. Many lakes were drained between 1612 and 1640, but the vast Haarlemmer Meer defeated the engineers.

Spinoza would take the *trekschuit* many times to Amsterdam, Leiden and The Hague, and to the De Vries estate at Schiedam. Canal-barge travel was cheap, just a few stuivers, and no tow-boy dared overcharge since the rates set by law were 'vulgarly known'. On each journey the *trekschuit* passed through tracts of almost empty polder, where every village and farmhouse seemed served by a canal, a wide ditch or a river. This watery network created a strange vista in which sails appeared to glide through grass. When the canals and ditches froze in winter, the farmers put on skates to pull sledges, so getting about their work at double speed. Polder people were toughened by the constant loss of their livelihoods through strategic wartime flooding, and by laws confining their trading to local markets. They would not have dreamed of taking the *trekschuit*, but plied their own rafts and dugouts and, unless driven from the polders by poverty, never saw the larger towns. If Benedictus had climbed out of the cosy cabin of the *trekschuit* his dark looks, slight build and aloof air would have drawn curious looks from the blond and big-boned duck-hunters and reed-cutters of those backwaters. Few would be old enough to see him as a dreaded *Spanjaard*, for it was now over thirty years since that enemy's troops loomed out of the mists that so often blanketed the pasturelands, but blue eyes would nevertheless have stared at his *zwartheid* and his fine cloak. They would, indeed, have fixed on his shoes, since in such places only rich farmers wore them, and then only on Sundays. The village of Lange Dijk owned three pairs, for use by officials summoned to The Hague. Long pointed clogs daubed with cheap paint were the norm in the wetlands. (For economy's sake everything, including the canal boats, was painted with a compound of linseed oil and either of the common mineral dyes of yellow earth-ochre and carbon, or the two together, which made up shades of dull green.)

The difference between the cities and the frequently waterlogged farmlands of the Provinces drew comments from travellers, who blamed an unhealthy imbalance of the elements for the dull moist air which, some said, put even the dogs pulling rafts along the ditches into a state of lethargy. Without the flying arms of the windmills and the splashing of the ducks there would, some said, be no animation at all outside the cities. Most French visitors found everywhere but The Hague impossibly humid: Descartes had to put up a strong case in his letters for his love of Holland, where he had lived contentedly with his Dutch maid-mistress and their little girl. But foreigners liked the *trekschuit*'s restful way of getting from town to town, and praised the plump Dutch cows that sometimes blocked the tow-horse's way. Spinoza, too, never complained about those journeys as he did about walking in high winds. Hispanic Jews were traditionally town dwellers, yet he found the foliage beautiful and soothing, and his attempt to work in peace in the countryside did not fail because he disliked the bucolic. But he may have had views on slowness of mind, since he only mentions rustics in order to drive home limitations in human intelligence. For example:

They tell of a peasant who deluded himself into thinking that, outside his fields, there were no others. But one day he missed one of his cows, and had to go far away in search of her. He was astonished that outside his own small farm there were so very many others. Many philosophers must also be like that. They have deluded themselves into thinking that beyond this plot of ground, or little globe, on which they are, there is nothing more (because they have seen nothing more).

His consistent thesis was that the uneducated mind perceives everything *from the common order of Nature,* and that it takes abstract reasoning not only to submit those perceptions to reason, but to stick with the findings of reason. *When we look at the sun, we imagine it as about 200 feet away from us . . . even when we later come to know that it is more than 600 diameters of the earth away from us, we nevertheless imagine it is near.*

Spinoza would live for a decade with *boeren* for neighbours, but he never suggests that they hindered his philosophising in the way his educated acquaintances did. 'Although he took precautions to avoid all intercourse with his friends, his most intimate friends went to see him from time to time, and only left him again with reluctance.' It was admirers from Amsterdam, not local people, who paid the visits he found unprofitable. And generations of students have found his allusions to the confusions and passive perceptions of the country folk among whom he lived helpful in clarifying his philosophy. For example, we might not immediately see what he means when he claims that words can misrepresent ideas, if he did not show what he meant by demonstrating it through the agitation of a neighbour *whom I recently heard cry out that his courtyard had flown into his neighbour's hen.* The man's words failed to express his thought. Similarly, the ten-mile trudge through the dunes to The Hague from Rijnsburg elucidates his theory of the association of ideas. *For example a soldier, having seen traces of a horse in the sand, will immediately pass from the thought of a horse to the thought of a horseman, and from that to the thought of war, etc. But a farmer will pass from the thought of a horse to the thought of a plough.*

The canal boat from Amsterdam must take a left turn just north of Leiden to reach Rijnsburg. It could get there directly along a narrow brook or *vliet* with banks dappled to this day in summer by pink and purple ox-tongue, sheep sorrel, foxglove and wild rose, the water edged with yellow flags. From Leiden, one had to take the slow sailing-boat which meandered along the Rijn to the south of Rijnsburg, or the road, better than average because Rijnsburg had been the strategic base of the Earls of Holland. Rijnsburg's abbey had seen thirty abbesses of royal descent, and was the burial place of kings. But it was destroyed by fire during the 1573 siege of Leiden, and only its ruined south tower would have been visible to Benedictus on his arrival. More immediately obvious was the Collegiant meeting-hall on the right-hand bank, in the Moleneind near the windmill. Activist Remonstrants had built it in Count Maurits's day, but since 1625 it had been a more or less peaceable venue for the 'assembly of the free-minded'. The *trekschuit* carried on past it since the *Vliet* cut through Rijnsburg towards Katwijk and the coast. Benedictus stayed in it, for he was to lodge in a cottage built in 1660 by the surgeon Herman Hooman, at the western end of the village, on the Katwijkerlaan. Hooman's cottage bore physical witness to the anger and despair of the first *Rijnsburger Collegianten* in the verse by Dirck Camphuysen, vociferous champion of conscience as 'infallible judgement . . . the predicant in our hearts', painted on its outer wall:

ALAS! IF ALL MEN WERE BUT WISE
AND OF GOOD WILL AS WELL –
THE EARTH WOULD BE A PARADISE,
NOW IS IT MORE A HELL.

A stone engraved with the same words (not the one set into the wall of the cottage-cum-Spinoza Museum on the present-day Spinozalaan) was found inside the house in 1690.

As in Amsterdam all sects and both sexes were welcome at the Rijnsburg Collegiant meeting-hall. Was Benedictus really attracted to this gathering of dissenters, which three times a year took over the pretty, normally tranquil village? Drab Mennonite fringery nudged satin and lace and professional black tabard, and mingled with the motley of curious foreigners, cranks and convenors with an eye to the 'free table' provided for persons of no means. Living in Rijnsburg Benedictus presumably at times must have straightened his back from bending over the microscopes he now made for sale, put on his hat, and, probably with the Hooman family, made the 10-minute walk along the suddenly bustling Rapenburg and *Vliet*-side to the Windmill-End. Yet consider the proceedings in that crowded hall, where the silence that enveloped those waiting for enlightenment was intensified by the relentless grinding of mill sails just outside. A sudden outpouring of spiritual insight, a gleam of opinion charged with remorse or passion, could inflame the Collegiants as fast as the Quakers: in the 1620s a mutual outburst of testifying had resulted in a claim that the Holy Ghost had descended into the meeting-hall and selected 'Apostles'. Like the Quakers, Collegiants often used blunt language: Camphuysen had called any constraint on the human conscience 'filth'.

Nothing in Spinoza's writings endorses this sort of free speech, and he does not refer to the assembly or its devotees in any letter or text. Can we envisage him raising his voice in such a throng to test one of the arguments he was now struggling to clarify, or to warn against trusting in revelations and visions? The Collegiants were actually known as 'the sect of the prophets'. Moreover, the idea that they were in any strict sense free-thinkers was illusory. They were Christians. Baptism by full immersion was regularly practised in the *Vliet* before the hall, and by 1743 their remonstrant origins had faded in folk memory. The gatherers at the 'Great House' in the Moleneind were by then known locally as 'Quakers'. Spinoza could not, even when assailed by the unmathematical yearning that still overtook him at times (we soon see its fruits in the *Short Treatise*) have supported practices and precepts that encouraged superstition, and if he believed Van Beuningen's patronage set the Collegiant movement above reproach by Church or State he was misled. The diplomat was very rarely in the country, so was hardly a familiar figure at assemblies, and in any case his religious views were already regarded in political circles with disapproval or mirth.

Neither Lucas nor Colerus links Spinoza to the Collegiants, and his lack of reference to them in connection with the *very simple universal religion* he sought, together with the content of the manuscripts he completed while at Rijnsburg, suggests they played little part in his present pressing preoccupation. When failing light brought his optical work to a halt, and the door of his room ceased to burst open with customers and unexpected friends, he at last retrieved his treatises from their secret place and began what he called his *late-night studies*. 'He devoted himself to his studies far into the night,' it is said, 'and for the most part toiled . . . by lamplight from the tenth evening hour until the third.' Reason then – most of the time – drove him coldly. While the *Short Treatise* shows elements of Hispanic-Jewish mysticism, neither text displays the rambling revelation or *gevoelens* that glowed in Jarig. Spinoza could, and sometimes did, suffer turbulent emotion, but his deprecation of unexamined feeling as a guide to behaviour set him in opposition to Camphuysen's criteria for infallible religious knowledge, which were heart and *gemoed* – a gut sense of rightness. When, within a few years, he supplied what we would now call the psychology of the individual ('psychology' was not a seventeenth-century term) he did so as a logical exercise: *I shall consider human actions and appetites just as if it were a question of lines, planes and bodies.* Such, in fact, was his air of *gravitas* that one alleged portrait of him could be, save for that quizzical expression, Johan de Witt. The affinity is significant, for in more closely resembling that man of the world than the members of the spiritual brotherhood in whose midst he was living, Spinoza signalled an internal detachment from them. By September 1661 the Danish anatomist Oluf Borch, passing through Rijnsburg, was informed that there lived there:

somebody who had become a Christian from a Jew and was now nearly an atheist. He does not care about [*non curat*] the Old Testament. The New Testament, the Koran and the fables of Aesop would have the same weight according to him. But for the rest this man behaves quite sincerely without doing harm to other people; and he occupies himself with the construction of telescopes and microscopes.

Spinoza's alleged comment about religious authorities and Aesop's fables is so similar to his dismissal of biblical and philosophical icons that he may well have muttered it.

Did he come to Rijnsburg with hopes that the Collegiants failed to meet? We sense from Jarig's comments that any desire for personal or social brotherhood was short-lived. I find deep ambivalence in Spinoza's emotional needs, a swinging between claustrophobia and loneliness that would eventually create a recognisable rhythm in the philosopher's life. Philosophically speaking, his silence on the topic of the Collegiants, and his dissatisfaction with some aspects of what he was now writing, are the sole evidence that he neither formulated his metaphysical doctrine as he wished, nor saw his rational indignation over the suffering of religious dissidents result in a model for *a simple universal religion* or *a society of the kind that is desirable*. Taking the latter failure first, the kind of desirable society Benedictus wanted to see did not, despite the impressions received by foreigners, exist in the Dutch Republic. It was true that the State did not make the intense demands it did in Catholic countries, or in England, where, for example, the free-thinker John Bunyan was imprisoned in 1660 as an 'unauthorised person' who 'refused to leave off his preaching' under a new Act of Uniformity of 'Passive Obedience' to the dogma of the Church of England. Bunyan would be held in Bedford County gaol for twelve years, with a further short sentence in 1676, during which he began to write his *Pilgrim's Progress*. Gatherings of Quakers were called 'risings' and were broken up: in August 1663, diarist Samuel Pepys records, a hundred Quakers who had met in Southwark were clapped into Kingston gaol. Yet the law enshrining religious uniformity, which had been brought in to strengthen the restored monarchy was undermined by Charles II himself. He had married a Portuguese princess and now modelled his court on the flamboyant style of a Catholic monarchy. Pepys describes a confrontation between the new King and a quietly defiant Quaker woman:

This morning I stood by the King arguing with a pretty Quaker woman, that delivered to him a desire of hers in writing. The King showed her Sir J. Minnes, as a man the fittest for her quaking religion; she modestly saying nothing till he began seriously to discourse with her, arguing the truth of his spirit against hers; she replying still with these words, 'O King!', and thou'd all along.

It is not irrelevant to note how Pepys, on being elevated to the Navy Board, reflected the new anti-puritan order. On 22 January 1660 he decided to dispense with cloth shoe ties: 'This day I began to put buckles to my shoes.' (It was, coincidentally, Bunyan's prison task to make end-tags for shoe 'laces'.) In May he bought 'wide canons' (canions) in The Hague.

There were elements of Quaker egalitarianism and Collegiant anti-consistorialism that Spinoza may have thought would profit De Witt's attempt to impress democracy on a nation in which agitation erupted from time to time over suppression of the interests of the House of Orange. The Grand Pensionary's Act of Exclusion had caused fury when it became known, for while Cromwell had insisted as a peace condition in 1654 that Prince William (then aged four) be excluded in perpetuity from traditional stadholder offices, De Witt had gone along with this, even engineered the Act, some said, for his own personal ends. Still it was not fully obvious to all that De Witt wanted no court of his own. He was careless of his academic and artistic gifts, indifferent to his wife's fortune (though not to her influential family and friends) and content with a plain religion that preserved the peace, but his motives were not well understood and he had not set a safe tone in the land. Benedictus's rejection of Hispanic flamboyance, Mennonite dowdiness or patrician bewigged elegance – extremes of dress that he thought stopped people from listening to one another – was made plain in the *Short Treatise*. He would gradually adopt Quaker classlessness in his manner of speech, too. His 'awkward' Dutch, which he must now speak every day, remained plain. He did not, reported Lucas, 'affect polished and elegant diction'. Yet as we reach the point when at last we have evidence in his own words of what he believed, a tension must be acknowledged between his insistence that the general truths were *common* knowledge and his intellectual élitism. He did not choose to write in his mother tongue, Portuguese, or Castilian, the vehicle of marrano culture, and evidently thought that if he wrote in Dutch the chances of words coming apart from meanings were highest of all. It seems certain that all his texts were composed in Latin and translated by others into Dutch. Letters, too, were written in Latin for choice. (Spinoza's Latin is considered good: his editors had far less to do when preparing his scripts for publication than when correcting the 'Latinity' of, for example, one of his most brilliant and best-educated later correspondents.) That he composed only in Latin is not of itself a guarantee of intellectual élitism, but it happens that this was only the first of many indications that he wrote exclusively for an educated minority.

Already, we may be sure, Benedictus had seen a place for himself within De Witt's political vision, and believed that De Witt could make use of his outstanding abilities. Before long he would confide that he would like to influence *some men holding high positions in my country*. He may have believed that De Witt, a fellow mathematician, who had already separated by statute the studies of philosophy and theology in the universities, and, despite protests led by Gisbertus Voetius, professor of theology at Utrecht, allowed Cartesianism to be taught, was on his mental plane. Alas, Benedictus failed to appreciate the low value placed on abstract reasoning by apparently rational people in positions of influence. Pieter van den Hove, the Leiden political reformer, for example, would soon write that philosophy was 'ridiculous . . . adapted to extinguish all human wisdom'. De Witt was a pragmatist, thought by one historian to show no philosophical depth in his reflections, and by his biographer to be an 'unphilosophical Cartesian' devoid of 'theoretical freshness' even in politics.

Before making any approach to persons in authority, Benedictus knew that he must hone his disquieting doctrines into a *tour de force* of reason. We are not short of documentary evidence for what he thought and wanted to achieve while he lived in Herman Hooman's cottage, since his letters (the first is preserved from late summer 1661) and his growing early treatises tell us much, stilted as their language is by multiple translation. His motive for shunning company had been to put his central philosophical concepts into coherent written form. But these must have been months of desperate frustration for the ambitious young philosopher, for the metaphysical *Short Treatise* on which he laboured in Amsterdam and Rijnsburg would remain, despite all attempts at clarification, so obscure, so exotic in style and terminology that, far from making his views persuasive, it confused. It lacked the homogeneity of the *Treatise on the Emendation of the Intellect*, the stiff elegance of the geometrical demonstration of *Ethics*, or the thundering polemic of parts of the *Theologico-Political Treatise*. It was a ragbag of styles, and some of its most important statements (on, for example, the impossibility of there being more than one substance; on the consequent equivalence of God and nature; and on the equally entailed nature of the soul) are found in footnotes and Appendices. On the one hand the treatise followed Leiden professor Heereboord's traditional model for metaphysical exposition. The standard opener for medieval metaphysical treatises had been 'All Being is divided . . .', and Heereboord, too, headed his *De Materia*, *De Forma* and so on. Many of Benedictus's chapters were named, Heereboord-style, *Of God's necessary actions; Of Opinion, Belief, and Science,* etc. But on the other hand, elements of a broader education intruded disconcertingly. Classical aphorism alternated with analyses of the *affects* (emotions) apparently modelled on Descartes's *Passions of the Soul*. Concepts from marrano-cabalic mysticism were also given space, notably the notion of God as the *All-in-All*, and the belief that loving God *intellectually* could effect union with God's mind. These are found in the Lisbon-born Jew Judah Abravanel's *Dialoghi de Amore*, an old copy of which Spinoza owned in Spanish translation, and whose themes – striking oddly on twentieth-century ears and unfamiliar to his non-Jewish acquaintances in Amsterdam – would remain a subtle influence on Spinoza for the rest of his life.

Abravanel named his mouthpiece of wisdom Philo, evidently in reverential regard for the Alexandrian-Jewish writer of that name who propounded the view that man is wisdom and woman his sensual helpmate, the mere helper and ally of man. Abravanel's Philo, who represents manly wisdom, advises his lover Sophia that God must be the focus of love: that 'All that exists, exists through participation in Him'; that 'union in knowledge' or 'perfect cognitive union' with God's mind 'is the end of desire', and that 'human blessedness' consists neither in material goods nor pleasure but:

> in the activities and dispositions of the intellect, which are the most worthy, and to which all other human practices are but means. . . . The Active Intellect, which gives light to our power of understanding, is God most high . . . happiness lies in cognition of the divine intellect.

Spinoza's enthusiastic echoing of this view in the *Short Treatise* suggests to me a transferring of the yearning for a loving brotherhood united in its religious aspirations to a private, perfectly secure independent intellectual understanding of God, or Nature. *What a Union! What a Love!* he declared, endorsing Abravanel's choice of an eternal object of love above a human one. In one of two snatches of dialogue (in a chapter called 'What God is') he assigned the voice of human 'love and wanting possession' to a character called *Lust*. In the second he made his own *Theophilus* the instructor not only of Sophia (who until near the end only asks Philo questions) but of *Erasmus*, the revered Dutch humanist. While Spinoza would eventually prune Abravanel's concept of the intellectual love of God by discarding the marrano's sexually charged notion of union, the distinctive Hispanic-Jewish cast of Spinoza's *intellectual love of God* would be reintroduced with intense emphasis near the end of his life – at which point, having followed further developments in the philosopher's mind, I think we may draw close to understanding the philosopher's mingled misogyny and arrogance.

Meyer could have helped Benedictus reorganise his disjointed *Short Treatise* by instructing him in Dutch philosophical terminology, for in one expert opinion the lexicographer raised the Dutch philosophical language to such an apex of precision that translations of Descartes's texts made in the mid-seventeenth century have not since been bettered. Meyer, who may have assisted Descartes's Dutch translator Glazemaker both through his *Dutch Vocabulary* and in person, was perennially distressed by lack of clarity in discourse. In his 1658 philosophical doctoral thesis he had insisted that 'physics and ethics can and should be taught by means of demonstrations'. In 1663 he would write darkly about the mental chaos engendered by unstructured philosophical essays:

> The mind, which has longed for an unshakeable truth, and thought to find a quiet harbour where, after a safe and happy journey, it could at last reach the desired haven of knowledge, finds itself tossed about on a violent sea . . . hurled up and down endlessly by waves of uncertainty, without any hope of ever emerging from them.

Meyer would gradually persuade Benedictus to expound his novel and difficult concepts in the geometrical method as used by Euclid, in which propositions and proofs followed given Definitions, Postulates and Axioms. He may have encouraged him to add the brief geometrical demonstration which forms Appendix I of the *Short Treatise*, and the fragments sent with a letter in 1661. Meyer may himself have been stimulated by Professor Geulincx of Leiden, who in 1663 published a treatise set forth 'in the geometrical order and style'.

Spinoza's other early treatise, which he called the *Treatise on the Emendation of the Intellect, and on the way by which it is best directed toward the true knowledge of things*, experimented with yet another model of exposition. It opened with a longish declaration renouncing wealth, honour, and libidinous indulgence in favour of some *permanent good*. We know that these words voiced a genuine intention: Benedictus had already turned down rabbinical distinction, mercantile opportunities and a university career. But this opening was in fact as much a borrowing of form from earlier philosophers and literary diarists as anything in the *Short Treatise*. *I wondered whether perhaps it would be possible to reach my new goal – or at least the certainty of attaining it – without changing the conduct and plan of life which I shared with other men. Often I tried this, but in vain . . .* Resonance from Abravanel is obvious, but these lines also follow advice given by Professor

Heereboord in his 1657 *Modes of Inquiry and Expression*, namely that private reflection, autobiography and a specification of 'the foundation, object, and scope of the author's written treatise' should be added to disputation. (Since the professor died in 1661 without publishing that work, this suggests that Benedictus had attended his lectures, perhaps before moving to Rijnsburg.) Heereboord doubtless had in mind Descartes's *Discourse*, which starts by inviting readers to share the thoughts he had – while confined in a 'stove-heated room' during a cessation of fighting in Germany – about his education and 'the various occupations which men have in this life.' In the *Meditations* Descartes used a different personal-journey-of-enlightenment technique by making each of his six meditations a step in a philosophical argument. The roots of this attention-arresting tactic and subtly persuasive ploy were not, however, philosophical, but lay in the ancient narrative device of cajoling an audience into assent by forcing it to listen to a story of experience and discovery. Bunyan would do the same thing in his *Pilgrim's Progress*. In comparison to other writers, Spinoza's version of the autobiographical opening was curtailed, and perhaps he was already dubious about using it, for he never did so again. Taking Euclid as one's model meant abandoning biographical reflection for well-ordered demonstration.

The *Treatise on the Emendation of the Intellect* ran, after its modish opening, as a seamless lecture on *healing the intellect, and purifying it*. It was, in contrast to the metaphysical *Short Treatise*, a work of epistemology. The correct method of seeking the truth, Benedictus declared, requires us to reason from first principles, and to do this we must hone our reasoning faculties. He used the simple analogy of the development of increasingly efficient tools, which as time went on made evermore difficult tasks easy to achieve, to show the power of the active mind in furthering its own ability. *In the same way the intellect, by its inborn power, makes intellectual tools for itself, by which it acquires other powers for other intellectual works.* We have to scrutinise critically the kinds of knowledge we have, since sense perception, report, chance encounter, and so on do not furnish truth. We need to aspire to mathematical standards which involve, as a minimal condition, awareness of proportionality and meticulous attention to inference. While Spinoza's theory of *modes of perceiving* was as embryonic in the *Treatise on the Emendation of the Intellect* as in the *Short Treatise* he was as clear there on the need to *make accurate distinctions* and to *define problems precisely before striving for knowledge of them* as he would ever be. Much space was given to the causes of confused thinking, and complacency over trusting the evidence of the senses was ruthlessly exposed. It was not enough, he said, to admit that the senses were often deceptive; that the earth, for example, did not actually resemble *half an orange on a plate*, and that the sun – incredible thought –

was not in fact smaller than our world, but many times larger. To understand the causes of our deception we have to think about *how* the senses deceive.

I have suggested that Benedictus would not have written the *Treatise on the Emendation of the Intellect* had he been satisfied that the members of the Amsterdam study group knew how to reason. Even those studying at Leiden, being continually exposed to the traditional learning method of assimilation from ancient authority, were liable to forget to work from undeniable first principles. Descartes's concept of 'natural light' or intuition, which he claimed infallibly revealed clear and distinct ideas, did not always help in this respect, since it was grounded in St Augustine's notion of 'divine light', so could be confused with flashes of religious revelation. Spinoza did not deny that intuition could reveal self-evident truths in a single intellectual act, but his concept of intuition was not the same as Descartes's. It was more like doing instantaneous mental arithmetic, getting straight to the particular essence of a thing without going through stages of reasoning. He would warn his readers, *The things I have so far been able to know by this kind of knowledge have been very few*, and he advised them instead to reason, to make inferences from definitions or axioms.

It was not that he thought his friends and pupils especially dull-witted. Throughout Spinoza's life his opinion of the capacity of anyone but himself to reason properly on any matter was low. He rarely deferred to anyone. During the Rijnsburg years his intellectual narcissism, masked to us in Amsterdam because we were not lashed by his own words except via hearsay, began to be evident, as each consecutive correspondent disappointed him. The disapproval of this supremely uncompromising rationalist fell heavily on most of his contemporaries' efforts at philosophising, including, as we shall see shortly, their projects in natural philosophy – their science. Judging by his correspondence, Benedictus must have devoted a good deal more time to science in his first months in Rijnsburg than has so far been suggested, and we soon turn to extraordinary developments in that context. But it needs to be said first that there was in fact for Spinoza no place for any other kind of understanding but *scientia*, knowledge. For him, all *scientia* was science, and the only valid science was mathematical science. Geometry expressed the mathematical ordering of the material world, and logical implication and inference expressed the mathematical ordering of thought. That was, he said, how humans knew *God, or Nature* in any of its manifestations, including their own natures. He saw no distinction between discoveries in natural science and a search for knowledge and Jarig's Preface to the *Complete Works* played him false by making one:

Besides his preoccupation with knowledge (*wetenschappen*) he had taken up a particular training in optics, and in the grinding and polishing of magnifying glasses and [lenses for] telescopes.

No search for knowledge could, for Spinoza, come apart from some scientific methodology. That was a consistent principle. His later *Ethics* assertion – quoted as a heading to this chapter, that the nature of anything whatsoever could only be known through the laws of nature, is equally firmly stated in his earliest works:

> *An idea is called true when it shows us the thing as it is in itself, and false when it shows us the thing otherwise than it is. For ideas are nothing but narratives, or mental histories of nature . . . We require no tools except the truth itself and good reasoning.*

This ruthlessly minimal standard of truth and knowledge accounts for the desire, which became more earnest and intense during each year of his life, to get into the very mind of *God, or Nature* through the paradigm of mathematics. Spinoza is often called the supreme rationalist philosopher, since for him nothing whatsoever escaped the searchlight of logical reasoning. Other philosophers of his age, including Descartes, allowed for ignorance, for faith in religion; for mystery and miracle in nature; for demonic possession of mind. But, for Spinoza, everything was in principle knowable through reason, because nature was rationally (that is, logically or mathematically) ordered. While human minds, being fragments of all the intelligence that exists, could not know all truths, they could know certain general truths (laws of nature) and could grasp that the truth about particulars must be deducible in principle from those general laws. This, alone, was the basis for knowledge *sub specie aeternitatis*.

He could not see how any intelligent person could fail to agree with him on this, and he began to expose his annoyance at confusion or dissension. *A philosopher is supposed to know what is the difference between fiction and a clear and distinct conception*, he told his first recorded correspondent crossly. From 1662 onwards his increased use of the geometrical method would allow for a curt *Q.E.D.* in his texts, and he tried to match that finality in his correspondence. But he often snapped out his conclusions without using formal proofs, so coming across as tetchy, evasive or, as the philosopher Bayle among others observed, missing the point. So often did his exasperation rise that one commentator believes 'the rebellious marrano philosopher' used the geometrical method as a form of self-discipline, to help him control his 'violent attacks' and 'viciously grotesque descriptions' of the religiously orthodox, and that intolerance and emotional agitation intrude in the non-geometrical portions of *Ethics*. While later events make this a thought to ponder, we can, I think, be sensitive to the frustration and intellectual loneliness underlying at least some of his sharpness.

As he sat at his candle or lamp-lit table at Hoomans's cottage, his window open against the summer heat, his collar probably tossed aside and the tassel ties of his shirt hanging loose, the bestial night-time sounds of the countryside competing with the scratching of his quill as he rapidly added and scored out passages, Benedictus seems to have felt himself a lone spokesman for reason. Even in dialogue with trained intellects he felt himself as thwarted by prejudice, triviality and superstition as he had among his father's people. During the year in which he turned thirty and began to consolidate his philosophical position, some bonds of affection tightened, yet mental isolation is evident in his letters, and I think the 'circles' he is said to have moved in may, after he left Amsterdam, have amounted to no more than temporary and fragile associations of convenience. It is difficult to find any fundamental metaphysical agreement between Spinoza and those who are supposed to have been his disciples or friends of like mind. Attachments of ideological sympathy such as antagonism to the mental tyranny of bigots described by Van den Enden as 'holy hypocrites' did not add up to unified religious-scientific endeavour. In the case of Jarig and other radical protestants Benedictus's expectation was low: his frustration was chiefly directed at those most privileged in terms of education and opportunity, the university men. I have taken the Spanish priest's deposition and Benedictus's knowledge of Professor Heereboord's philosophy as evidence that he attended lectures at Leiden as an outsider sometime between 1657 and 1660, and I have suggested that he chose not to enrol there because he thought his education would be, like rabbinical training, passive. He still, we shall see, admired some aspects of Leiden medicine, but had no opinion of Leiden philosophy. Although Professor Heereboord stood out among Dutch university philosophers for his intrepid promotion of Cartesianism, many scholars thought he got its doctrines wrong, partly because he insisted on synthesising it with older systems. Descartes had protested to him about this in 1647.

It is absolutely clear from his correspondence that by 1661 Benedictus also considered himself an authority in matters of natural philosophy, and his clarity on this aspect of knowledge does not seem to have been affected by the confusion or immaturity we have talked about in relation to some parts of his *Short Treatise*. Acquaintances from Van den Enden's tuition groups (Steno, Meyer and Hudde, for example) and ex-pupils, including Theodor Kerckring and Jan Casier, were at Leiden university. Adriaan

Koerbagh had just qualified as a doctor of law and was practising in Amsterdam. All probably visited him. All seemed, like Koerbagh, set to find themselves places of prestige in the world. All but Casier studied some branch of natural philosophy. (Jan had enrolled at Leiden to study philosophy but in 1661, at nineteen, re-registered as a student of theology. Heereboord died that year, and this may have had something to do with Jan's change of direction, to which we shall return.) Kerckring took a straightforward medical path. He had already produced from his studies in chemistry a treatise on alchemy, a copy of which he may have given Benedictus, since it was found in his library. The student physician is likely to have visited Rijnsburg since he would soon own a 'most excellent microscope, made by that noble mathematician and philosopher Benedictus Spinosa, which enables me to see the lymphatic vascular bundles'. Kerckring knew that the excellence of his mechanical device depended on mathematical calculations, but he does not seem to have relied much on mathematical principles in his own investigations. Instead, with empirical zest, he researched both chemistry and anatomy by travelling round towns and villages looking for exceptional cases. His later anatomical observations, specialising in the foetus, are still praised, but there was nothing exceptional in his treatise on antimony: that dissertation was just one more claim from a natural scientist that he had discovered a secret formula for extracting gold from mercury and antimony. Benedictus passed no opinion on this project, and did not prejudge the alchemical claim. For, if anything in physical nature was simply a rearrangement of basic elements, it was no more inconceivable that mercury should combine with the bluish-white flaky crystals of antimony to make gold than that water and an onion-like vegetable should combine to produce a superbly striped, waxy tulip flower. One needed to know the laws governing chemical reactions before judging whether the project was futile. Years later, on Jarig's behalf, Spinoza would question a silversmith, and the physician to William, Prince of Orange, on the supposed scientific basis of alchemy. Afterwards he remained mildly sceptical, but still withheld judgement. But eventually he did lose interest in alchemy. In 1675 he told a young Amsterdam physician that he had not tried to make gold, and did not intend to, either. *For the more I think about it, the more I am convinced that you have not made gold, but have insufficiently separated out what was hidden in the antimony.*

The painstaking investigation of mineral properties was not the objective of most alchemists, however, who up to and including Newton preserved the Renaissance belief that alchemy involved harnessing the 'Natural Magick' that pervaded the universe. Kerckring's alchemical treatise includes the information that:

Unicorn's horn drives away all poison from itself. For example, a spider placed within a circle made of unicorn's horn cannot get out of the circle ... On purpose have I brought such rude and vulgar examples, because the force and true virtue of antimony lies deeply hid and it is to be deeply inquired after.

Many 'mechanical philosophers' who prided themselves on studying only real things felt able to hold with equal conviction *both* that everything in nature was reducible to moving particles, *and* that supernatural powers could disrupt that natural pattern. The miracles, spirits, witches and demons that Benedictus ridiculed would remain the stock-in-trade of scientific discourse for centuries to come, and scientists may still endorse the 1635 view of Thomas Browne, who qualified in medicine at Leiden, that 'They that doubt of [witches] do not only deny them, but spirits: and are obliquely, and upon consequence, a sort of atheist.' Robert Boyle, of the Royal Society, held that there could be no more convincing proof of the falsity of atheism than the confirmation of a supernatural event. Such testimony from this celebrated prober of nature's secrets had the effect of exciting new interest in witchcraft and sorcery, and confirming the superstitions of ordinary folk, who had always put as much faith in magic as in medicine, and often preferred occult cures to herbal ones. The tooth-drawer's relieving of pain, for example, was thought to lie more in his incantation and sheep's skull than in his surgery. Learned physicians also prescribed quack cures, including the Royal Touch for 'King's-Evil Swellings'. Charles II touched thousands of sufferers a year. Isaac Beeckmann, physician, mathematician and advisor to Descartes and De Witt, recommended eating a 'hair of the hare' for stones. Pepys, now a member of the Royal Society, jotted down 'charms', sacred verses for staunching blood, expelling thorns and curing cramps and burns. Late twentieth-century scientists will obviously sympathise with Spinoza's impatience with such superstition, but in its day his denunciation was as astonishing and absurd to most people as is the modern philosophical theory of eliminative materialism, which maintains that what we call 'the mental' is mythical, since everything is, we know, mere matter.

Yet, while approving Spinoza's rejection of the supernatural, many natural scientists might want to exchange the term 'supreme rationalist' for 'manic rationalist' regarding Spinoza's view of good science. There can be few periods in human history in which greater solid and practical advances were made in humankind's knowledge of its world than in the mid-seventeenth century, yet Spinoza thought failure to research from a starting-point of mathematical reasoning invalidated most of the scientific conclusions of his contemporaries. He strongly opposed the inductive method of generalising from observed instances to so-called 'laws of nature', that is, *the Method of proceeding of the Empiricists and the new Philosophers, who want to do everything through experience... In this way no one will ever perceive anything in natural things except accidents.* For Spinoza, certainties about the universe did not lie in empirical generalisations, but were deductions, *based on the pure power of the intellect and following its order of apprehension.* But despite their admiration for the mathematical science of Galileo and Descartes, most natural philosophers of the time who prided themselves on studying real things were producing countless examples, or cases, to prove their discoveries true. Kerckring, for instance, was studying chemistry and anatomy at the most progressive school of medicine in Europe, where methodology was strictly experimental. His professor, Sylvius (Franciscus de le Boe), so entirely rejected all past 'dogmatic' systems that he refused to consider any *a priori* theory. For him, all medical knowledge had to be *a posteriori*, the result of practical experiment. Indeed, Sylvius denied having any 'basic doctrine' at all. The ten *Disputationes* containing his working principles were based on student notes taken down between 1659 and 1663. He was the first clinician at Leiden to introduce sickbed consultations, and he is immortalised by his discovery of the *Fissure of Sylvius* in the brain. Sylvius did not accept alchemical speculation, and denied the existence of magic, so he would not have thought much of Kerckring's treatise. But the professor's scepticism was directed at the hypothesising involved, not the tests. He personally vested all truth in observation and experiment. It is thought today that he drew hasty medical conclusions from too low a number of observed cases, so displaying a credulity as damaging to good science as a belief in occult magical forces, and in this respect his principle of experiment failed to advance knowledge of real things any further than Francis Bacon's. Bacon died in 1627 of a chill caught while stuffing a fowl with snow to see how long its flesh could be preserved, and Spinoza might consider his death due reward for the folly of doing science *from the common order of Nature* (although in fact Bacon died because he was subsequently put in an unused, damp bed). Benedictus would rebuke members of the English Royal Society for trying to learn from such haphazard means, yet he acknowledged that experiment displayed instances of the ways in which the laws of Nature worked, and he made practical tests of his own. Ironically, he accelerated his own death by inhaling glass-dust.

Benedictus was not interested in celebrity in an international scientific arena, and was not ready to publish the metaphysical thesis on which he believed all knowledge rested. This priority should not be doubted. His apparent efforts to penetrate through mystical concentration to the rationale underpinning the universe were integral to this belief. He knew his thesis was both unclear and unsafe to publicise. Yet news had begun to spread of an iconoclastic world-view now being formulated in a quiet sand-swept lane in Holland, and Benedictus's first overseas correspondent visited him in the summer of 1661. Henry Oldenburg was forty-seven years old, a German cousin of Leiden professor Johannes Koch (Coccejus) and like him an untidy-looking man of theologically tidy mind. Coccejus, although interested in Descartes's philosophy, was a stalwart of the Reformed Church. Henry had also gained a Master of Theology degree at Bremen before moving to England, and Benedictus must have realised that caution was advisable when discussing religion with him, since his piety was considered obtrusive, even for that God-obsessed period. However, Oldenburg's faith was mental bedrock buried beneath congenial intellectual curiosity. It would be exposed only after years of excoriating criticism of his beliefs by Spinoza. Oldenburg had earned his living in England, apart from a brief commission as a German diplomat during the 1650s Anglo-Dutch war, by tutoring. His duties had included the customary European educational tour, and he had accompanied one pupil to Oxford, where he met Robert Boyle, to whom he would later be connected by marriage. Boyle (the 'very tall' – six foot – son of an adventurer from Kent, who was made Earl of Cork after serving the English crown in Ireland) fired his interest in natural philosophy, and Henry joined the Philosophical Group of Gresham College, founded around 1645. Boyle proposed him as its Secretary, probably because he was well travelled, spoke five languages and kept up an immense correspondence, before Gresham College was granted a royal charter in 1662 and became the Royal Society. Charles II, who presented the Society's mace, had a laboratory at Whitehall and a 35-foot-long telescope in his garden. But he seldom visited the college, and Pepys records mainly the King's jokes about the Society's work, such as 'spending time only in weighing of ayre'.

Oldenburg's compulsion for striking up relations with experimental thinkers was the basis on which his friendship with Spinoza developed. That summer of 1661 he had made his way from Leiden to Rijnsburg, perhaps alone, to meet the man who had made a name for himself in the university without being a member of it. We can visualise the oddly-matched pair sitting in what must have seemed to Oldenburg quaint surroundings, the sounds of farm labouring and the lowing of cows punctuating the flow of Latin or German which, possibly because Benedictus kept changing the subject as Henry drove frantically to the heart of his developing metaphysic, did not much enlighten either. Yet the correspondence which began immediately afterwards would reveal not only

Spinoza's philosophy but in turn his aspiration, arrogance and fear. It would persist through the first year of the brutal Anglo-Dutch war of 1665–7, resume in 1675, and turn sour only shortly before the deaths of both men, at the point when the Secretary finally grasped what the philosopher was saying. It began with a letter from Henry:

> With such reluctance did I recently tear myself away from your side when visiting you at your retreat at Rijnsburg, that no sooner am I back in England than I am endeavouring to join you again, as far as possible, at least by exchange of letters. Substantial learning, combined with humility and courtesy – all of which nature and diligence have so amply bestowed on you – hold such an allurement as to gain the affection of any men of quality and of liberal education. Come then, most excellent Sir, let us join hands in unfeigned friendship, and let us assiduously cultivate that friendship with devotion and service of every kind . . .
>
> In Rijnsburg we conversed about God, about infinite Extension and Thought, about the difference and agreement of these attributes, and about the nature of the union of the human soul with the body, and also about the principles of the Cartesian and Baconian philosophy. But since we then spoke about such important topics as through a lattice-window and only in a cursory way, and in the meantime all these things continue to torment me . . .

Henry wanted to hear more of Spinoza's views. Benedictus promised *diligently to foster* relations with '*Hendry*' – as in an effort at English he addressed him on the outside of one letter – and, because he could not resist a chance to instruct, opened the lattice a little. He warned, however, that *I shall attempt to explain my views on the subjects we spoke of, although I do not think this will be the means of binding you more closely to me unless I have your kind indulgence.* As it happens, Henry did not understand what he was told, and it is fortunate for us that for well over a decade he did not, or this kinsman of Coccejus might have brought a long and interesting correspondence to an immediate halt.

On Henry's questioning regarding *the errors of others* Benedictus not only succeeded in deflecting attention from his own views of the human soul, on which he remained silent, but wasted no time in informing him that all the great Verulam's (Bacon's) principles and procedures fell short of proper standards of rationality. Bacon had based all his conclusions on randomly collected and categorised data: he had further contended that the aim of observation and experiment was to discover the 'forms' of natural phenomena, most of which turned out to be occult or unknown, so had no explanatory value.

But Bacon's vision of new knowledge through the immediate observation of natural phenomena had stimulated the new scientific methodology. Bacon, it was, who had dismissed Aristotle's science as 'laying down the law to nature'. Bacon's recommendation of an experimental college of natural philosophy had been the stimulus for Gresham College and the Royal Society. In attacking Bacon, therefore, Benedictus came close to hacking at the foundation stone of the Royal Society. Had he merely criticised Bacon's version of inductive procedure, luminaries such as Hooke, Boyle and Huygens, who were proud to be known as 'Mechanical' philosophers, might have agreed with him. In the past decade Hooke had devised the air-pump and the first efficient compound microscope. He would soon astonish Europe with the detailed drawings of fleas, feathers etc. in his 1665 *Micrographia*, a 'treatise on sixty microscopic observations, where,' Oldenburg summarised for Benedictus, 'there are many bold but philosophic assertions, that is, in accordance with mechanical principles'. Hooke would, among other seminal scientific achievements, isolate the 'cell' of modern biology. Boyle, with Hooke's help, crowned his experiments on air with a statement in the Appendix to the second edition of *New Experiments Physico-Mechanical, touching the Spring of the Air and its Effects, made for the most part in a new Pneumatical Engine* on the relation of pressure to volume in gases, a statement now enshrined as Boyle's Law. Features of Boyle's 'new chemistry' also remain undisputed to this day. The Royal Society was thus a temple erected to empirical science, dedicated to replacing substantial 'forms' with insights into the real, observed properties of things.

However, in Benedictus's view its work, not being grounded in rational principles, was permanently liable to error, and he disparaged either wholescale or in some measure the findings of almost all the projects proudly explained to him by Oldenburg. The latter's equability in the face of Spinoza's carping criticism and occasionally faulty science is impressive. In 1663 Henry would reiterate that 'Our Royal Society is earnestly and actively pursuing its purpose, confining itself within the limits of experiment and observation, avoiding all debatable digressions.' Only a genuine commitment to exchanging scientific research data can have prompted the Secretary to go on explaining the work of the Royal Society after sending Benedictus the gift of a Latin version of Boyle's *Certain Physiological Essays*, on Nitre, Fluidity and Solidity, and receiving in return a generally scathing denouncement covering dozens of pages. To run slightly ahead – Spinoza's reply was not made until April 1662 – he curtly informed Boyle via Henry that no one could confirm the source of the motion of particles *by chemical or any other experiments, but only by demonstration and by calculating. For it is by reason and calculation that we divide bodies to infinity, and consequently also the forces required to move them.* He further denigrated Boyle's achievement by claiming that he repeated old work and added nothing to *other experiments readily available . . . I do not know why the esteemed author strives so earnestly to draw this conclusion* [i.e. that tangible, or secondary qualities depend only on motion, shape, etc.] *from this experiment of his, since it has already been abundantly proved by Verulam, and later by Descartes.* And as a final put-down, he pitted his own experimental findings against those of the lugubrious researcher on almost every count. Forced to test hypotheses with cheap, ready-to-hand materials, in checking the influence of particle-shape on fluidity he replaced Boyle's olive oil with milk and butter.

After two years of such deprecation Oldenburg finally passed on from Boyle some brief but courteous responses to Benedictus's attempt at demolishing his achievements. The sage of Rijnsburg took umbrage. *The learned Mr Boyle, too, I thank very much for being so good as to reply to my observations, in however cursory and preoccupied a way.* And Spinoza discharged a last, devastatingly sarcastic shot. *For my part I did not imagine – indeed I could never have been convinced – that the learned gentleman had no other object in his Treatise on Nitre than merely to demonstrate that the puerile and frivolous doctrine of Substantial Forms and Qualities rests on a weak foundation.* Benedictus was now accusing Boyle of working within an outdated paradigm of science. It is true that Oldenburg had in September 1661 stressed as a basic assumption of the college 'that the forms and qualities of things can best be explained by the principles of mechanics, and all Nature's effects are produced by motion, figure, texture and their various combinations, and that there is no need to have recourse to inexplicable forms and occult qualities, the refuge of ignorance'. Benedictus, disappointed that Boyle had no radically new theory of chemistry to offer, was nonetheless aware by the time he reached the conclusion of his letter that he had insulted him. *If it seems more advisable to you to consign these thoughts to the fire than to pass them on to the learned Mr Boyle, they are in your hands. Do as you please, so long as you believe me to be a most devoted and loving friend to you and to the noble Mr Boyle. I am sorry that my slender resources prevent me from showing this otherwise than in words.*

Boyle's and Spinoza's dispute constituted a legitimate scientific debate since – using centuries of hindsight – both had right on their side. Boyle's discoveries are to this day the pride of the Royal Society because so many seem to have hit on laws of nature, whereas few of Spinoza's specific scientific conclusions, either deductively or experimentally derived, are thought to be of scientific interest. It is thought that ultimately Spinoza added nothing original to optical theory, despite studying refraction so intently that his lenses 'sold pretty dear', possibly to Huygens himself, whose own ocular lens is still the type most widely used. Nor can we protest that his research was stolen by the formidably ambitious and wealthy Huygens who, we shall see, was happy to take note of the penniless philosopher's theories and methods of lens preparation, while taking care not to pass on his own. No: Huygens was not the Dutch master of microscopy. The laurels for seventeenth-century research went to Anthonie van Leeuwenhoek, who built in all 247 single-lens microscopes, using a secret technique for grinding some of the lenses, which magnified objects beyond anything his competitors could achieve. Van Leeuwenhoek painstakingly drew and described the 'little animals' he saw, and over the years posted 165 packages of these observations (written in Dutch) to the Royal Society in London. In 1718, at the age of eighty-six, the draper was at last made a Fellow of the Royal Society. Spinoza, on the other hand, seems to have taken no serious interest in optics after 1671, when the great German polymath and philosopher Leibniz consulted him on the extent to which rays could be collected after refraction. Leibniz considered him an outstanding microscopist, but thought 'Monsieurs Swammerdam, Malpigi and Leeuwenhoek the best observers of our day'. Spinoza kept a small lens-polishing mill, and for a time a microscope: his last landlord said he 'observed also, with a microscope, the different parts of the smallest insects, from whence he drew such consequences as seemed to agree best with his discoveries'. But no microscope was found when he died. Nor need we believe he ever owned a cumbersome wooden workbench of the type now displayed in the Rijnsberg museum-cottage. His rooms were always small, and no reference is made to one. At his death his toolbox held some 'glasses in poor condition, among them one good one, and a small quantity of glass and tin tubing'. The tubing was used in construction of microscopes. It is possible that Spinoza's optical studies were, from the start, a cover, a distraction that gave his visitors and correspondents an excuse to contact him without fear of being censured for keeping disreputable company. But Spinoza would not have disputed on optical matters at length in his letters, or written a *Treatise on the Rainbow* (which Jarig and Colerus suggest he later burned, thinking it unsatisfactory), had his interest in optics not been genuine. He was, like many others in his day, an able amateur.

Few dispute, however, the extraordinary vision of Spinoza's inner eye. While he was not a distinguished natural scientist, he interestingly anticipated much later ways of looking at nature. First, he debunked the supernatural in a manner uniquely open and forceful for his day, leaving no doubt, despite calling Nature *God*, that the God of the Bible and the Koran had gone the way of spirits and demons, and that everything that happened was natural, and naturally caused. Miracles, for example, were logically and practically impossible:

> *Nature herself is God under another name, and our ignorance of the power of God is co-extensive with our ignorance of nature ... Nothing happens in nature which does not follow from her laws.*

Next, he made *God or Nature* one indivisible whole. Nature's 'parts' were not discrete, but differently arranged particles, differentiations within one substance. To summarise:

> *It is nonsense, bordering on madness, to hold that extended Substance is composed of parts or bodies really distinct from one another ... If there were different substances which were not related to a single being, then their union would be impossible. Bodies are distinguished from one another by reason of motion and rest, speed and slowness, and not by reason of substance ... If we proceed in this way we shall easily conceive the whole of Nature as one Individual, whose parts, i.e. all bodies, vary in infinite ways, without any change in the whole Individual.*

Nature was indivisible. Its laws were therefore at some general level interconnected. Local laws were deducible, though not always by human minds, from general laws:

> *In the examination of natural phenomena we try first to investigate what is common to all nature – such, for instance, as motion and rest and their laws and rules, which nature always observes, and through which she continually works – and then we proceed to what is less universal.*

He insisted that we remember this principle when doing science or we might – like the parasitic worms that he watched through his microscope aimlessly colliding with each other in the blood – conclude that local natural phenomena were cut off from nature's comprehensive scheme, and actually happened haphazardly, or through a miracle. He told Henry:

> *[The worm] could have no idea as to how all the parts are controlled by the overall nature of blood and compelled to mutual adaptation as the overall nature of the blood requires, so as to agree with one another in a definite way ... Now all the bodies in Nature can and should be conceived in the same way as we have here conceived the blood: for all bodies are surrounded by others and are reciprocally determined to exist and to act in a fixed and determinate way, the same the same ratio of motion and rest being preserved in them taken all together, that is, in the universe as a whole. Hence it follows*

that every body, in so far as it exists as modified in a definite way, must be considered as a part of the whole universe, and as agreeing with the whole and cohering with the other parts.

Finally, the principle on which this entire thesis depended was the internal disposition of matter to create its own motion. Whereas in Cartesian physics and in all ensuing mechanical theory motion came apart from rest – matter was considered inanimate until it moved – *God or Nature*'s force was not external, but internal. This Spinozistic doctrine would not have an echo in formal science for 300 years, since in every mechanical theory from Descartes, Boyle, Leibniz and Newton onwards there has been a gap between assertions about the mechanical behaviour of bodies and explanation of the underlying force that moves them. For Spinoza, nothing but the intrinsically dynamic nature of all partial expressions of a unified, active and causally productive nature can explain force, and grasping this is a matter of mathematics. It is tempting to see his doctrine as a prototypical field theory, anticipating modern physics, and while in the view of most philosophers of science certain features bind it to the mechanical theory of the seventeenth century, making the claim an exaggeration, Spinoza's conception was remarkable for his time, and obviously difficult to explain in terms of mechanical theory. When pressed on his theory of motion he not surprisingly disappointed questioners. He could not explain exactly what *motion-and-rest* was, and never formulated a conservation law that could be universally applied.

But his physics was seamless in its explanatory scope. Nothing escaped the single unified system that was both God and Nature, and every discovery he made confirmed the integration of *Homo sapiens* with the whole of nature. His science was an *intellectual love of God, or Nature*. Science, philosophy and religion merged when he looked through a microscope, saw his own hands appear ugly as they revealed their interconnections with other animal matter. We can surely liken this rapture to the recognised euphoria of a scientist fitting an anomaly into a system like a piece into a jigsaw, or finding a 'beautiful theory'.

No aspect of existence eluded his system. There could be only a natural explanation of the most sublime of our mental states, because none lay outside nature. Whereas Descartes (in the way of most subsequent philosophers) directed the analytical power of philosophy to just some objects, Spinoza thought that the mathematical ordering underlying every process of thought, including emotions, must be grasped at all times. Feeling was a species of thinking, and thinking without reasoning, he said, was the cause of all human problems. Passions (for Spinoza never induced or influenced by physical causes, as Descartes had supposed) were caused by inadequate perceptions, such as opinion or imagination. *We maintain that knowledge is the proximate cause of all the 'Passions' of the soul.* Even love and joy would, if so caused, *tend to our destruction.* Only if caused by true perceptions, or understood through reason, could they benefit us. This thesis was rudimentary in the *Short Treatise*, but it was clear enough. Once sadness, for example, was understood it could not engulf the mind. *He who uses his intellect properly must know God* (Nature) *first ... It follows incontrovertibly that someone who uses his intellect properly cannot fall into sadness ... It is necessary to be freed of it, because it hinders us.* It was because Benedictus believed this so firmly that he looked at the scientific causes of the 'omens' afflicting Pieter Balling when Pieter's little boy was close to death. The philosopher's sympathy went out to his friend when the child died, but was reined in by rational judgment. *This, dear friend, is my opinion about the problem you raise.*

Spinoza's stern view of the *affects* was established in Rijnsburg. By the time he had rejigged the material of the *Short Treatise* for the mature thesis of *Ethics*, he had conceived a formally structured thesis which would today be called a theory of cognitive therapy, a programme dedicated to uncovering the confused thoughts of the past causing present misapprehensions. This was strictly a science of the mind, in contrast to Descartes's thesis that made sadness a partly physical 'unpleasant listlessness', which could not, and perhaps should not, be reasoned away. When Descartes's father and five-year-old daughter Francine suddenly died, he resented the attempts of others to 'free' him from his grief:

> I am not one of those who think that tears and sadness are appropriate only to women, and that to appear a stout-hearted man one must force oneself to put on a calm expression at all times. Not long ago, I suffered the loss of two people who were very close to me and I found that those who wanted to shield me from sadness only increased it, whereas I was consoled by the kindness of those whom I saw to be touched by my grief.

Spinoza did, however, deprecate *womanish tears* and *womanish compassion*. Whenever we come across the term *womanish*, with its connotations of weakness and stupidity, I suggest we check whether his attitude is justified by his doctrine. *Could* Spinoza have found eternal human truth in the grief prized by Descartes, or *must* he firmly maintain that *someone who uses his intellect properly cannot fall into sadness?* He would always hold that the passions of a group were not merely a hindrance, but dangerous, since an aggregate of inadequate *gevoelens* could only generate further unreliable emotions. But he would, later, modify his view that in all cases of emotion we are passive, by marking off rational emotions from irrational passion. Possibly because he needed to be able to include as active thinking a powerful love that at times took over his own mind during his last years, he would allow that *An affect that arises from reason is necessarily related to the common properties of things.* In the early 1660s, however, he seems to have deplored Descartes's approach on metaphysical grounds. This does not mean, of course, that the affects had no hold over him personally. Those who feel nothing do not propose, in an extravagantly protracted thesis, a way out of the mental anguish caused by hatred, envy and anger. But Benedictus seems to have been precociously stoical during the early years of his banishment, and to have shown during his twenties the *good sense and strength of character* he believed had helped Pieter Balling to *scorn the adversities of fortune, or what are thought of as such.* This description refers of course to Spinoza's controlled behaviour, not his disposition. The tears and lamentation which would at least once wildly defy the guidance of reason; the burrowing into the agony of sexual jealousy of *Ethics* Part 3; the obsessional preoccupation with the *intellectual love of God* in *Ethics* Part 5; and the outbursts of petulance or fury in his letters reveal (I think) enduring Hispanic sensitivity and the suffering of strong emotions. His last landlord testified that 'He had the command of his anger, and if at any time he was uneasy in his mind, it did not appear outwardly; or if he happened to express his grief by some gestures, or by some words, he never failed to retire immediately, for fear of doing an unbecoming thing.' His last landlord knew only too well, as events will show, the powerful feelings that his lodger sometimes had to control.

By 1662, as he approached thirty, Spinoza believed that he had inferred the real nature of the passions. He certainly, he thought, had Love and Desire better sorted than had Descartes in his late middle age. He abhorred Descartes's fusing of 'concupiscent' and 'benevolent' love, and his resulting belief that 'purely intellectual joy . . . can scarcely fail to be accompanied by the joy that is a passion'. In the *Short Treatise* Benedictus distinguished two kinds of joy according to the Jewish mystical notion, stressed by Abravanel, of the directing of Love on a corruptible, or on an eternal, object:

> *As far as the corruptible are concerned . . . loving them, and uniting ourselves with them, does not strengthen our nature at all. For they are weak, and the one cripple cannot support the other. And not only do they not help us, but they are even harmful to us.*
>
> *. . . Love is a union with an object that our intellect judges to be good and magnificent; and by that we understand a union such that the lover and the*

*loved come to be one and the same thing, or form a whole together. So he who
unites with corruptible things is always miserable.*

This judgement, which does not fade out in later writings on the subject of
sex, stands in conflict with Spinoza's metaphysical and epistemological
doctrines. He taught that all is natural, and that whatever is common to all
human nature is in some sense eternal. He deduced from this thesis, as is
discussed later in more depth, that there could be nothing absolutely good
or evil: good or evil was whatever advantaged or disadvantaged us. We use
the terms 'good' and 'evil' as we perceive this to be so. It is odd, then, that
Spinoza should express more disgust at coitus than Descartes, who put God
outside natural processes and the self outside the mortal body, yet saw
sexual love as a feature of God's perfect plan. Descartes wrote that

> . . . attraction comes from the perfections we imagine in a person who we
> think capable of becoming a second self. For nature has established a
> difference in sex between human beings, as in animals lacking reason, and
> with this she has also implanted certain impressions in the brain which
> bring it about that at a certain age and time we regard ourselves as
> deficient – as forming one half of a whole.

In the *Short Treatise* and the *Treatise on the Emendation of the Intellect*
Spinoza took a tougher line on sensual gratification than he ever would
again. In the former, as we have just seen, he dismissed a link between
happiness and sexual desire. In the latter, his version of the classical notion
of post-coital misery – *after the enjoyment of sensual pleasure [libidinem] the
greatest sadness follows* – seems as impregnated with genuine feeling as the
autobiographical disclaimers of honour and wealth which immediately
follow it. His treatment of the topic in *Ethics* Part 3 shows a stronger sense
of personal involvement with it, but if, as has often been suggested, Spinoza
suffered psychological scarring from a sexual relationship, it had almost
certainly happened by the time the *Short Treatise* and the *Treatise on the
Emendation of the Intellect* were put into the form in which we now read
them.

Again, we can try to isolate personal pain from what can be deduced from
basic metaphysical precepts. Passionate love, sexual desire (later to be linked
with jealousy and hatred) must, necessarily, by his logical scheme, interfere
with rational thinking. *[Solomon] did wrong, and acted in a manner unworthy
of a philosopher, by indulging in sensual pleasure.* This was not because
Solomon committed adultery: we recall that Benedictus believed that all lust
dulled the mind. Sexual passion was, he believed, a state of mind to be
eschewed if a higher (i.e. rational) satisfaction of mind was to be achieved.

But what law of nature dictates that it has no place in *the desire for physical union? As for marriage, it certainly agrees with reason if the desire for physical union is not generated only by external appearance but also by a love of begetting children and educating them wisely.* We are left wondering what pricked at the back of his mind among its all-but unconsciously held emotions and passive associations of ideas, where reason must battle to get a foothold. (We should not doubt that for Spinoza ideas could be unconscious. His doctrine depended on the causal power of unconsciously retained ideas which perpetuated prejudices and affected future attitudes and behaviour. Memory, for him imagination – a reflecting of image-making going on in the body – could so function that people remained unaware of thoughts which held their minds in bondage. Suicide, he said, sometimes resulted from such hidden mental causes.)

Why is almost everyone who has written about Spinoza so sure that he did not want what most young men want? It is hardly far-fetched to suppose that he had slept, or wanted to sleep, with a woman or a man. Nor is it impossible to suspect that he might have left Amsterdam to escape a Quaker or Collegiant who had confused human warmth with sexual desire, or with whom, given his temperament and loneliness, he had become entangled. Benedictus probably had closer contact with liberated women there than was possible in Rijnsburg, among more watchful country neighbours, although pictures show that women formed a substantial proportion of the congregation at gatherings of the free-minded at the Moleneind meeting hall. Nor are we justified in sidestepping Colerus's anecdotes concerning Clara Maria. Why, for example, did Spinoza choose to correlate the harsh term *cripple* with human sexual love? By 1662 Clara Maria, nineteen years old and deformed in some way that did not detract from her appeal, would have been in Descartes's estimation a proper object of love. The philosopher was poverty-stricken, but while this, added to an apparent refusal of baptism (so Borch implies when he refers to the man who 'was now nearly an atheist') made thoughts of marriage unlikely, there is no reason to suppose attraction had withered. The passages on sexual jealousy in *Ethics* Part 3 were probably written in the mid-1660s. Scarring sexual experience seems tied to the years preceding 1662, but sexual emotion may still have been building up.

I have suggested that Clara Maria's appeal to Spinoza could have been complex, and only subliminally invested with sexual desire. She was clever and witty, a good teacher. He was having problems making his doctrine clear. Wit is a much-valued didactic agent in philosophy: analogies that draw laughter often impress concepts on the memory. For Spinoza, *laughter and joking* would be classified as *pure joy* – emotions that did not block out adequate ideas. He thought the use of cheerful wit legitimate. Mockery, on the other hand, was inadequate: it diffused a perspectival, jaundiced light. *I recognise a great difference between mockery . . . and laughter*, he said, and vowed more than once not to use it. But cheerful laughter (*risus*) did little work for him in his texts. He said he distinguished it from mockery, but he only ever used *risus* to mean ridicule, laughing *at*. One translator questions whether Spinoza confused mockery with laughter, or whether there was an early editorial error: had Spinoza perhaps meant *inrisione* (derision), not *risu?* Another translator assumes this at times. Spinoza's everyday sense of humour also seems to have been a little warped. His last landlord, who insisted that 'He was never seen very melancholy or very merry', nevertheless describes how he set some spiders to fight, and was apparently 'so pleased with that battle that he would sometimes break into laughter'. I am inclined to conclude after careful checking that humour was, for Spinoza – like caution – an aspiration, not a disposition. *Cheerfulness, which I have said is good, is more easily conceived than observed.*

I offer the suggestion that he was aware that derision sprang from inadequate thinking, and also that he was not getting the central precepts of his philosophy across. Henry Oldenburg had not only just shown intense interest in his metaphysical beliefs, but had in spirit invited Benedictus through the prestigious portals of Gresham College. What could have distracted him enough from these excitements to send Henry a hurtfully brief reply to his penetrating questions? *While preparing to go to Amsterdam to spend a week or two there*, Benedictus had scribbled, *I received your very welcome letter and read your objections to the three propositions which I sent you. On these alone I shall try to satisfy you, omitting the other matters for want of time.* Henry had responded, aggrieved: 'I very much regret that your journey to Amsterdam prevented you from answering all my doubts. I beg you to send me, as soon as your leisure permits, what was then omitted.' Benedictus's brusque reply can be interpreted in two ways. He might have seen Henry's questions as an unwelcome irritation, even a threat. If he spelled out his doctrines clearly, how soon would they get back to Cousin Coccejus? On the other hand, sections of his *Short Treatise* could be taken to Amsterdam and discussed with the group. He would receive advice there on how his theories on *God or Nature* could best be put to Henry – or withheld from him with equal grace. Yet the laconic explanations he had hurriedly sent off did not, on the whole, seem intended to puzzle:

Thirdly, things which have different attributes have nothing in common with one another, for as I have explained an attribute as that whose conception does not involve another thing. Fourth and last, of things which have nothing in common with one another, one cannot be the cause of another.

These sentences merely repeated the proofs Benedictus had previously sent. They would later form some of the first propositions of *Ethics*. He had then gone on to protest:

As for your contention that God has nothing formally in common with created things etc., I have maintained the exact opposite in my definition . . . I beg you, my friend, to consider that men are not created, but only begotten, and that their bodies already existed, but in a different form.

It is strange that he introduced these last contentious points at all, since while they were entailed by the existence of one absolutely infinite and indivisible substance, they had no place in the geometrical demonstration of this prime and prior assertion.

Caution, then, does not explain Benedictus's brusqueness. Was he perhaps bored by Henry's bragging about the college? He did not respond with compliments, and we have seen how little time he had for the Royal Society's scientific method. But if he was irritated by its enterprise, why did he subsequently send Henry reams on his own experimental findings? Lack of time, lack of trust and lack of interest in empirical science would never noticeably obstruct the rambling correspondence that passed between the two men for more than a decade. I am convinced that the snub was caused by Benedictus's frustration at his own lack of progress in communicating his central metaphysical concepts. Henry's difficulties over what Benedictus thought were obvious inferences had exacerbated the need to make them easier to understand. Benedictus's Amsterdam readers would prove to be, in the main, as baffled by the One Substance doctrine as Henry, being equally conditioned to Henry's Aristotelian notion of many separate substances. An Aristotelian substance was subject to change but could not go out of existence and remain a substance. Thus, for Henry, two men were two substances. For Descartes, a substance was defined by its principal attribute of thought or extension, yet he also believed that, in a secondary sense, there were more than two. Spinoza found this equivocation absurd. *By substance I understand what is in itself and is conceived through itself, i.e. that whose concept does not require the concept of another thing, from which it must be formed.* Only God met that criterion, and nothing could lie outside God. God was both extension (body) and thought (mind). Van den Enden may never have analysed the God-nature monism he asserted: Adriaan Koerbagh would cleverly clarify it (we shall find) in his own way.

The influence of Borellius, Tacquet, Clavius and Heereboord on the Leiden-educated Cartesians had also to be overcome. Meyer had suggested the geometrical method as a didactic aid, and Benedictus had tried it out with Henry. It had not worked. 'I warmly approve your geometrical style of proof,' Henry had lamented, 'but at the same time I blame my own obtuseness for not so readily grasping what you with such exactitude teach.' Benedictus needed the sounding-board of the group, and perhaps the effortless grip on conceptualisation that Clara Maria could provide if he could argue her out of her *stubbornness of superstition*. There is no reason to think he had given up in that area: he would wrestle with Henry's blind faith on and off for fourteen years.

Speculations about Clara Maria apart, the fact that Spinoza did not respond to Henry on Boyle's theories on nitre – that special interest of his former teacher – until he had visited Amsterdam at least once and probably twice, added to more testimony from Borch, suggests that when Benedictus took the *trekschuit* that October day he was bound for the Van den Enden home.

SIX

Rijnsburg and Voorburg: 1662–4

In the mind there is no free will, but the mind is determined to will this or that by a cause which is also determined by another . . . Nor can any man will or do anything but what God has decreed from eternity that he would will and do.

It was obvious now to most Hollanders that De Witt was, beneath a conciliatory veneer, an autocrat, yet it seemed that the Republic was in a safe pair of hands. The United Provinces had not been defeated since the loss of the 1652–4 English naval war, and towards the end of a prolonged conflict in the Baltic, during which De Witt had taken decisions with a specific view to serving Dutch commercial interests, his mediation had achieved first an alliance between England, France and the United Provinces, then negotiations between Denmark and Sweden, and finally, with the 1660 Treaty of Copenhagen, general peace. But the deputies noticed that he retained personal power by keeping his impressive knowledge of foreign affairs to himself, and it was later found that the alliance he forged with France in 1662 had included a secret pact. The Grand Pensionary's reason for wanting to reinforce Dutch-French friendship was well understood: he feared Charles II would join Louis XIV in fostering the cause of their mutual kinsman, young William, who, proud of his ancestry, already signed himself 'G', for Guillaume, Prince d'Orange. Charles's self-interest had not escaped De Witt when, exiled in Paris in 1653, the Stuart heir had asked for a wartime commission in the Dutch navy. De Witt had refused, knowing the instability that this undermining of loyalty to Cromwell would generate, and he had not been surprised when, after the Restoration, Princess Mary of Orange threatened to make Charles her son's guardian. Mary died in 1661, but William remained a potential pawn. For that reason De Witt was, by 1662, exceedingly wary of the Dutch army. He would not name a new field marshal, let alone contemplate restoring the office of captain general, that established privilege of the stadholders. He personally supervised the education of the Prince, who at thirteen impressed the French with his 'clear mind' and 'promising talents', but was so sickly that he appeared unlikely ever to ask for a military post.

De Witt had an ally in the Leiden lawyer and economist Pieter van den Hove, who in 1661 showed the Grand Pensionary a book he had written called *The True Interest and Political Maxims of the Republic of Holland*. De Witt approved it, and almost certainly added material to it, but he did not, as some thought, write the book, on whose title page Pieter's initials 'V.H.' appeared, and whose central, passionately republican, claim was that:

> the weakness of Holland was caused by their own stadholder and captain general, and on the other side, Holland by the present free government is enabled to make use of all its abundant strength for its own preservation.

This assertion was supported by detailed reports on industry, trading, colonising and defence, but also by vehement attacks on Willem II – one, concerning his abuse of the navy, added in the handwriting of De Witt himself. The book drew angry rebuttals from Orangists and Calvinists, but sold in vast numbers, and soon afterwards De Witt was re-elected for a third term of office. Van den Hove's book would be enlarged, outrageously emboldened and reissued under a new title (*Indication of the Salutary Political Foundations and Maxims of the Republic of Holland and West Friesland*), without De Witt's consent, in 1669, when the Republic was close to crisis. Its propaganda would then do the Grand Pensionary more harm than good. Spinoza seems to have bought neither version, but he owned and referred with approval to two rather more theoretical discourses published in 1661 and 1662. Both were inscribed 'V.H.', but the former had been written by Pieter's brother Jan, who had died in 1660. Pieter was not a theorist but a practical strategist or political 'economist', this epithet having been previously used only for the activities of housekeepers.

We now know, thanks to recent research, that in 1662 Frans van den Enden also produced a polemical pamphlet, written in Dutch, on the well-being of a free society. He later claimed he had not previously thought of writing a single line on politics, but we may doubt this, since in 1650 he had reproduced under his own name the demand for democratic rights made by the Dutch against Philip of Spain in 1587. His new project was, moreover, the result of a request by some Amsterdammers about to colonise the New Netherlands (America), who probably knew of Frans's interest in political reform. They had asked him to petition the city council on their behalf for an official permit, for protection, and for freedom from the taxes which, as Pieter van den Hove pointed out, brought hardship and 'great distaste among the people'. Frans rose amply to the challenge. In the ninety-odd pages of the *Kort Verhael van Nieuw Nederlandts* he not only petitioned the burgomasters as requested, but also supplied the emigrants with a

Constitution of 117 articles, at the same time voicing bitter disapproval of the current Dutch government.

Frans's *Kort Verhael* was not a systematic political thesis. It grew organically as new conditions occurred to him during the winter of 1661–2, and as he turned them separately into *Requesten*, *Vertogen* (remonstrances) and *Deducties* addressed to the city fathers. These arguments would be expanded into a second, equally unsystematic treatise published in 1665, which we consider now since its subject matter built on the *Kort Verhael*, and both preceded any worked-out political theory of Spinoza's. The second pamphlet, *Vrye Politijke Stellingen en consideratien van staat* (*Liberal Political Propositions and Considerations of a State*), outlined, Frans later admitted, a fourth kind of republic, dissimilar to those of Plato, Grotius or Thomas More. The sole foundation of his republic was the common best (*gemeene-beste*), as this was agreed upon by 'the whole people, together':

> Government by the people [*volksregering*] alone is free government; [it is] the only one which from its nature admits and includes continuous improvement.

Few in the seventeenth century who advocated government by the people had in mind the 'equal liberty' that Frans made his slogan. As we know, the proletarian power deplored by Cicero was feared and legislated against throughout Europe. For Jan van den Hove, for example, rule by 'the people' meant decision-making by a stratum of independent citizens, which excluded not only the dishonourable and the insane but servants, women and most wage-earners. De Witt, having no intention of introducing the institutionalised chaos that a democracy was perceived to entail, approved these strictures. Van den Enden's model republic, however, utterly excluded a paternalistic élite claiming a superior rational understanding of the 'common-best', and expressed furious resentment of the Holland regents. A note pasted inside the British Library first-edition *Vrye Politijke Stellingen* reads, 'It is especially curious for the exact principles of Chartism given in it; the author was an Owenist before R. Owen', and indeed Frans's polemic was a people's charter:

> I therefore understand, on the foregoing basis of equal liberty, the common best of a community of people to include a correspondingly equal measure of orders, laws and mutual help between more or less reasonable, more or less well-to-do people, male and female, parents and children, servants and served or ruler and ruled, as discovered through reason and experience. From this one can conclude . . . that each member, in his position [in life], is not only not weakened and injured but, on the

contrary, is strengthened for the common benefit, his desire and appetite more and more fostered, and his soul and body ever more advanced to greater well-being.

Viewed in a broad seventeenth-century context this document was, as political theory, crude and undeveloped. It did not, for instance, engage with the views of Hobbes in *De Cive* (1642), which was attacked, it has been said, in almost every scholarly dissertation in politics, law or theology of the second half of the seventeenth century. (Hobbes's 1651 *Leviathan* was, until 1667, available only in English.) Hobbes claimed that a state of nature, in which people were unrestrained by civil laws, consisted in 'a warre of all against all'. The two most certain maxims of human nature, were, he said, contention and fear. People only voluntarily contracted to live in civil agreement through fear. Van den Enden, in contrast, made his respect for the natural dignity of human beings dramatically clear when he not only forbade slavery ('an abominable thing') but urged the settlers to adopt the social and religious mores of the settlers' American Indian neighbours, whose lack of false piety and superstition resulted in a zest for living in the present, rather than fearing death or trying to earn an immortal soul, and a natural preference for free love and easy divorce. In *Vrye Politijke Stellingen* Frans wrote with admiration, as had Grotius, of 'our time-honoured forebears', who had shown wisdom in, among other 'important things', their even-handed training of young people. In another sense, then, Van den Enden's thesis was not politically empty, but anticipated Rousseau's eighteenth-century discourse 'On the Origin of Inequality', in which lessons to be learned from societies untouched by modern man's problems would be examined at great length. Frans's views also anticipated Rousseau's *Émile* by grounding social reform in education. As a devoted parent and teacher, Frans placed great weight on the capacity of a lovingly and carefully educated child – of however humble a background – to grow into a responsible adult concerned with the general good of society.

Before considering whether Frans passed on to Spinoza the fundamentals of his later political theory, we must distinguish the schoolmaster's success as an educator from his polemic. We have seen that Van den Enden taught, either in his school or through contact in study groups, individuals who would later show remarkable degrees of independent thinking and rational self-esteem, many of them leaving traces of their achievements in Dutch records. The school he opened later in Paris was famed for its excellence and visited by Leibniz, who made a special note of the young female assistant who spoke Latin and gave lessons in Euclidean geometry. This was Frans's youngest daughter Marianna. It seems, then, that Frans put his principle of drawing out the full potential of all individuals, including females, into practice. He almost certainly guided Spinoza in, for example, natural philosophy, by encouraging a realist approach to the study of natural phenomena. Van den Enden signed his pamphlets 'M.V.Z.H.', which he later explained stood for *Meest van zaken houdt*; 'he who most loves things'. He was not a visionary, but an empiricist who worked with the real materials he found. Spinoza was by inclination a rationalist system-builder, mathematician and metaphysician, yet he seems to have been made aware early on of the need to acquire knowledge of the properties of actually existing things. *Above all it is necessary for us always to deduce all our ideas from physical things, or from the real beings, proceeding, as far as possible, according to the series of causes, from one real being to another real being, in such a way that we do not pass over to universals and abstractions.*

But how much responsibility should we assign Van den Enden for Spinoza's eventual involvement in politics, or for specific details of his political theory? We have seen that the schoolmaster asserted belief in a naturalistic God and determinism in all things, including the human mind. In his *Vrye Politijke Stellingen* of 1665 he also expressed, in identical terminology, the three kinds of knowledge – *wanen* (opinion), *gelooven* (belief) and *klare kennissen* (clear knowledge) – that Spinoza specified in the *Short Treatise*. We cannot say conclusively that either man dreamed up this formulation. All we can say for certain is that Spinoza did not merely assert any of the above philosophical precepts, as did Frans, but argued for them and developed them over many years. By 1665 he would, in fact, have abandoned both the *Short Treatise* classification of *opinion, belief and clear modes of perception* and the four *modes of perceiving* of the *Treatise of the Emendation of the Intellect* for the three different kinds of *knowledge* of *Ethics* Part 2. As with metaphysics and epistemology, there would have been discussion between Van den Enden and his ex-pupil on the themes of the *Kort Verhael* and the *Vrye Politijke Stellingen*, for while Spinoza made no direct comment on them, his own political theory would so obviously coincide with some of the views expressed in them that in the nineteenth century, long before any factual connection between Spinoza and these anonymous Dutch-language pamphlets was found, the note pasted inside the British Library copy of the latter treatise states, 'Has much in connection with Spinoza's liberal ideas'.

Passages in the *Short Treatise* express a view similar to Frans's regarding the respect due to the determined nature and needs of all individuals when assessing the *common good* of a community. *Man is a part of the whole of nature, depends upon it, and is governed by it . . . this knowledge also serves to further the common good.* But mutually stimulating sources, such as the writings of the Van den Hoves and the Quakers' ringing theme of 'equal liberty', no more resulted in political theses of similar emphasis or depth than their shared metaphysical and epistemological commitments carried the same weight or produced the same inferences. One sceptical commentator considers Van den Enden's democracy to be a 'pedagogical project', and his thinking 'too unsystematic, too inconsistent and too temperamental' to have a place among the political philosophies of his day. Spinoza's disagreements with his teacher would not emerge clearly for years, but since some of Frans's views conflicted with principles that Benedictus had by 1662 firmly stated, they may already have negatively affected the relationship between the two men, and we look at them now.

There can, for example, have been no agreement on the starting-point for forming *a society of the kind that is desirable*. Frans would announce on the title page of *Vrye Politijke Stellingen*, 'The People's prosperity is the highest law, and their Voice is God's Voice.' For Spinoza this was putting the cart before the horse: for him, to attend to God's voice (statements of the most general laws of nature) was to be in a position to deduce the lesser laws governing humankind's highest good. In *Ethics* and the later political works recognition of this priority was made the first condition for founding a democracy. Attending to the dictates of universality was not equivalent to listening to cries for equality. Merely canvassing the will of 'the whole people, together' was *inadequate* knowledge. The schoolmaster should know that: it was implicit in the taxonomy of knowledge they had agreed that *gevoelen* did not reveal what was truly for the 'common best'. While Spinoza would argue for the right of human beings to live according to the powers of their own natures, he denied that a harmonious democracy could grow from natural appetites, *for by the laws of appetite individuals are drawn in different ways*. Frans, on the other hand, believed that intense passions did not derive from original, simple human nature, but that people were driven into them following various experiences. They could trust their most natural inclinations. Spinoza's much stricter criterion for fixing the *common good* was grounded in the belief that only deduction from axiomatic principles delivered moral, political, religious and social truths, and that a *desirable society* was possible only if designed and enforced by reasoning individuals. *The basis and aim of democracy . . . is precisely to avoid the follies of appetite, and to restrain men as far as possible within the bounds set by reason . . . Destroy this basis and the whole fabric will collapse at a touch*. This view developed in reaction to Hobbes's in *De Cive*, which Spinoza owned, but he may also have noted weaknesses in Frans's thesis.

Two further rifts, in attitude rather than theory, are likely to have proved divisive at this time. Van den Enden is said by 1662 to have been forbidden to give public lectures. By publishing in the Dutch language he had aligned himself with the pamphleteers of his day who deliberately exposed their polemic to the common people, whose volatile response was much feared. Spinoza, in contrast, would address his treatises, in Latin and with loftiness, to the educated alone. On the one hand, he did not *want* to write for those whose thinking was largely limited to opinion and feeling. He would make this plain in the Preface to his *Theologico-Political Treatise*: *The multitude, and those of like passions with the multitude, I ask not to read my book. I would rather that they should utterly neglect it, than that they should misinterpret it after their wont.* A slowly germinating intellectual élitism was fed by doubt that *common notions* – the basis of reasoning – were readily graspable. *To deduce points from intellectual notions alone usually requires a long string of propositions, as well as the greatest caution, insight, and restraint – all of which are rarely met with in human beings.* He was also aware that writing dissident views in the vernacular caused special offence to Church and State authorities. Reformed Church minute-books are filled with interrogations, demands for retractions, condemnations, impositions of fines and, occasionally, horrible physical punishments. (The Leiden *Kerkeraad*'s threat to excommunicate Pieter van den Hove for his 1662 book was mild.) By the time Spinoza published his first political treatise in 1670 that truth had been cruelly driven home by the annihilation of Adriaan Koerbagh. Frans, however, openly outlawed 'sect-inclined' predicants from his model New Netherlands republic, and in his later pamphlet especially attacked Church institutions, giving the 'deceitful' Catholic Church a particular flailing. He was 'bitter and incensed', says the editor of his pamphlets, as he wrote a 'blackbook' denunciation of all institutionalised religion. We might expect retribution from the Reformed Church, but Van den Enden's name does not feature in the *Kerkeraad*'s records for 1665. We might also expect his school to have been closed immediately, and in this respect Burgh's influential father Coenraad may have protected him. In 1664 the school would stage Meyer's version of *Medea*, this time with parts for two of Frans's younger daughters.

Parallels have been drawn by another commentator between Frans's blueprint for a republic and the contemporary proposal for a New Amsterdam 'commonwealth' of the pioneer settler Pieter Plockhoy. But while Plockhoy's plan was similarly designed to 'eschew the yoke of the Temporall and Spiritual Pharoahs', his emphasis on Christian teaching, artisan virtues and the sharing of resources without flouting existing laws seems correctly described as a co-operative enterprise, and expresses a very different spirit from Frans's largely paragraph-less tirade and militant demand for radical constitutional reform. Benedictus may in 1662 have been seriously alarmed by Frans's confrontational stance. He told Henry Oldenburg that he had no definite plan for the publication of his *short work*. *I am naturally afraid that the theologians of our time may take offence, and with their customary spleen, may attack me.* He may have disliked Frans's exposure of their shared metaphysical views, too, for in his *Short Treatise* he implored his few selected readers not to speak openly about its content. *As you are also aware of the character of the age in which we live, I would ask you urgently to be very careful about communicating these things to others.* By the following year he was evidently aware of a specific enemy, since he made guarded references to *that petty man* (*illum homunculum*). The man's identity is unknown, but Benedictus, familiar with the outcome of insulting the *mahamad*, needed no warning about antagonising authority. When he later agreed to have a supposedly innocuous work printed he told his editor:

I should like everyone to be able readily to accept that . . . you are chiefly concerned to make this little work welcome to all . . . This everyone will readily believe when he sees that no one is attacked, and that nothing is advanced which might be offensive to some person.

Self-preservation apart, Benedictus's sympathy with the current Dutch government contrasts sharply with Frans's animosity. We have no cause to think that in 1662 Spinoza thought the system of elected patrician representatives favoured by De Witt needed the drastic reform Van den Enden advocated. Spinoza may still have seen a liberal regent like Van Beuningen, a good republican who withstood the tyranny of the Reformed Church, as a role-model. At all events, his most mature political theory would confer the power to decide *the advantage of all* on a council composed of those who were judged to reason best – a political *aristocracy*. He would also accept most of Van den Hove's limitations on the bestowal of voting and other political rights, and confine them to an economically independent and male stratum of society.

In sum, while Frans may have been instrumental in turning Benedictus's deep grievances over sectarian differences into political awareness, differences in their approaches to realising a *desirable society* operated on so many levels that I think the younger man probably wanted nothing to do with his ex-mentor's project. The years 1662–5 cover a period in which Benedictus was intent on being taken as seriously as a philosopher as Descartes (who, it may be noted, did not involve himself in politics) and we should envisage him in 1662, when Frans sent off his string of petitions, turning his energies in other directions. He may have had difficulty in diverting Frans's attention to Boyle's work on nitre, but he seems to have achieved it, since his reply to Henry was sent off by May.

The ubiquitous Borch attended a discussion group in Amsterdam in April, and found that unorthodox religious views were held and taught by its members:

> There are here atheists and they are principally Cartesians, like Van den Enden, Glasemaker, etc.; and they also teach other people. They don't preach openly atheism, because they often speak about God, but by God they do understand nothing else than this whole universe, as appears more clearly from a certain Dutch writing, which was recently artificially written while the name of the author was suppressed.

I do not think Borch could have had Spinoza's work in mind when he referred to 'a certain Dutch writing'. Although, as we know, Benedictus was writing on these topics, he told Henry in the letter he wrote very soon afterwards, *I have written a complete short work on this subject, and also on the emendation of the intellect, and I am engaged in transcribing and correcting it. But sometimes I put the work aside . . .* The *Short Treatise* was therefore still in draft form in April 1662, and while Benedictus may have exaggerated its unpolished state as an excuse for not sending Henry a copy, it had not, and would not, be printed (that is, 'artificially written'). There is no evidence that it was much circulated even in manuscript, and it is thought it was abandoned soon after this date. It was, moreover, 'previously written in Latin' and only later translated by others into Dutch, so it was not at this date a 'Dutch writing'. Further, we know that Spinoza had resolved not to expose his thesis of *God, or Nature* until he had published a treatise so masterful in logical persuasion, yet so mild in content, that *Perhaps as a result there will be some men holding high positions in my country who will want to see other of my writing which I acknowledge as my own, and so will arrange that I can make them available to the public without risk of trouble.* Whose, then, was the printed tract Borch saw? Borch was aware, as we saw earlier, that Van den Enden 'had communicated in manuscript to his friends some of his secret doctrines'. These 'secret' writings were presumably in notebooks, not printed. But the anatomist may well have seen the just-completed *Kort Verhael*, which was in Dutch and made reference to God, or Nature.

Spinoza knew that to avoid notoriety he must be seen to eschew the company of political agitators. He may have left Frans's home in the first place for this reason. He need not, now, sleep under Frans's roof on his brief visits to the city. He could stay with Jarig on the Herengracht, or Simon on the Singel, or with Pieter Balling, Lodewijk Meyer or Jan Glazemaker, all at present of good reputation. Although the schoolmaster ran a liberal and loving home, his prodigious memory, immense breadth of intellectual capacity and overpowering self-assurance, coupled with dazzling rhetorical force, may have been more oppressive than Morteira's narrowness and invective. Meyer burned as spiritedly as Frans to reform republican society, but held quite different views on how a philosopher should act.

It may have been Meyer who suggested that if Benedictus would not or could not enrol at Leiden, but wanted to establish himself as a philosopher of merit, he should prove himself within the traditional domain of philosophy. He should demonstrate his expertise independently, but according to the criteria of his intellectual peers. The policy of separating philosophy from theology in the universities now made Cartesianism a permitted academic study, and the Amsterdam study circle craved understanding of it: Borch, to recall, described its members as 'principally Cartesians'. Lucas puts a more sinister gloss on this view by suggesting that Spinoza's criticisms of Descartes were becoming well enough known to irritate certain relatively liberal theologians who were 'prepossessed with the doctrines of this great genius, and jealous of the right, which they believe they have, of being infallible in their choice', and that when these clergymen were accused of atheism they turned their anger on Spinoza. Either way, the course of action that Benedictus took next constituted a movement away from Frans's influence and towards creating a reputation for himself. Frans may have begun to lose interest in Descartes (his *Kort Verhael* showed no Cartesian input) and, if so, a niche had opened up for Benedictus as tutor on this subject.

The Cartesian philosophy perplexed many scholars. By 1661 Glazemakers's Dutch translation of *Alle de werken van René Descartes*, and two volumes of Descartes's Correspondence, had been published by Rieuwerts in Amsterdam. But while Jarig and Simon (whose Latin is described as 'naïve and primitive') would welcome them, reading Descartes in the vernacular did not necessarily aid comprehension, since Descartes's concepts were not always clear in themselves. Claims that should have been presented in the *Principles*, for example, were better stated in the *Optics* and *Meditations*. Meyer had long thought that a geometric demonstration of Descartes's *Principles of Philosophy* was needed, since, he said, people tended to 'chatter and babble' about Cartesian doctrines without thoroughly understanding them. He had made a start on such a project himself but had, he said, been distracted by other occupations. Perhaps he bowed to Spinoza's greater skill as a Cartesian: Borch had singled out Hudde and Spinoza as perceiving and building more astutely on the ideas of Descartes than the others. Spinoza especially, the Dane wrote, 'excelled in the Cartesian philosophy', indeed 'superseded Descartes with his distinct and probable ideas'. But the Euclidean method of exposition is likely to have been Meyer's idea.

There had been, until now, no written queries from the study group (or none is preserved), but letters from De Vries and Meyer the following spring affirm that by then Benedictus was being appealed to for explication. Around then, I conclude, he took over as the Amsterdam study group's principal philosophy instructor. It was a role he much wanted, judging by the eagerness and authority with which he responded to questions. Yet, in the September of 1662, as he lugged his ancient overnight bag – listed among his possessions – across the canal bridges and up the Brouwersgracht to the Haarlemmer Poort, where the *trekschuit* left the city, he knew that he must, during the long months of the coming winter, largely *direct his life according to other men's powers of understanding*. He is unlikely to have wanted the labour of demonstrating someone else's principles. Philosophers of far less originality balk at this chore, despite granting it to be an indispensable part of their training. While he accepted the assignment as a rational move, he took steps to ensure that his winter of servitude, during which he would be isolated when the *trekschuit* could make no use of half-frozen canals, would not show him the unwelcome face of solitude, and that his own principles need not be neglected. (They would not be; it is thought he resumed work at once on the 'propositions' and 'demonstrations' over which Henry had long puzzled, for that winter the Amsterdam study group was studying them.)

It is also possible that he was concerned about finding the means to live, despite Lucas's report that he 'had no fear whatever of the consequences of poverty' and that 'he was liberal, lending of what little he had'. He would not have much time for preparing lenses or constructing microscopes, and is said to have refused all offers of financial help:

> It is scarcely credible how sober and frugal he was all the time. Not that he was reduced to so great a poverty, as not to be able to spend more, if he had been willing: he had friends enough, who offered him their purses and all manner of assistance. But he was naturally very sober, and could be satisfied with little; and he did not care that people should think he had lived, even but once, at the expense of other men.

Why such pride? His father may have lived for nearly two decades under Uncle Abraham's roof. His sister Ribca did all she could to siphon off funds for herself, finally lowering her dignity to claim on 'Baruch Espinosa's' pitifully tiny estate. His brother Gabriel would soon appoint a proxy to run the family firm and leave for Barbados, possibly on an assisted passage. Yet Colerus says that Spinoza was genuinely dismayed when, a few years later, after he had moved to Voorburg, Simon suddenly gave him a large sum of money:

> Simon de Vries of Amsterdam, who expresses a great love for him [cf. his letters] presented him one day with a sum of two thousand florins, to enable him to live a more easy life; but Spinoza, in the presence of his landlord, desired to be excused from accepting that money, on the pretence that he wanted nothing, and that if he received so much money it would infallibly divert him from his studies and occupations.

Let us look more deeply into this response, since Colerus's 'on the pretence' hints at dissimulation. It is possibly significant that Spinoza protested 'in the presence of his landlord'. In Rijnsburg his landlord Herman Hooman was a friend who might have kept a confidence, but telling a country landlord was often tantamount to telling the village. I think this was what Spinoza wanted. He had vowed to renounce wealth, and being sensitive to a perceived connection between extravagance and atheism, it mattered to him that he was seen to live in conspicuous frugality. But the rationale behind the construction of this image may have been complex, as much the result of shrewd forethought as his restraint in dress. He would have learned from Jarig and others the profoundly persuasive effect of Christ's self-imposed poverty, and may have decided to emulate that lifestyle. It may not have come altogether easily to him. Vibrancy of colour and sound, visual and tactile enjoyment had accompanied him from birth, and he did not despise all possessions. We know he could not stop himself from buying newly published Spanish literature, unrelated though it was to his work. Who knows if he could have held back, if funds were to hand, from replacing the camel-hair cloaks and leather shoes? (Most Dutch shoes were wooden-soled.) Privately, he may have believed money *could* divert him a little. More privately still, he is said to have decided 'to lay up no more money than would be necessary for him to have a decent burying, and that, as his parents had left him nothing, so his heirs and relations should not expect to get much by his death'. Spinoza was no simple hermit.

In autumn 1662 he also knew he must keep himself, materially, through the winter, while he produced the explanation of Cartesian principles that the study group needed. He must also find a way of forcing himself to explicate Descartes's philosophy, without deviation, albeit in the face of 'that Maxim of Descartes which says, That nothing ought to be admitted as

True, but what has been proved by good and solid Reasons'. To expound, without exposing his disapproval at what he believed was in large measure false, would be no small test of his self-esteem. A solution to both these pressures was at hand in the person of Jan Casearius (or Casier). Jan, now a Reformed Church ordinand, either asked, or was invited, to come from Leiden as a pupil and to write out, at Benedictus's dictation, a geometrical demonstration of the Second Part of Descartes's *Principles*. This arrangement must meet, at a stroke, the philosopher's needs. Jan would presumably pay for his lessons, and would at the same time act as a safeguard against unwise emendation. The Author was constrained, Meyer would explain in his Preface, to dictate only Descartes's propositions and opinions, and to draw inferences that could be validly deduced from Cartesian foundations.

It is not hard, when you have seen that chilly little parlour (as cold as a cellar even in high summer) on the Katwijkerweg, to visualise Jan and Benedictus seated before the peat stove, wearing house gowns over their shirtsleeves in the Dutch way, the *ledikant* crowding them in that small cottage room (separate bedrooms being, as we know, only for the rich and fashionable), thick leaded-glass panes obscuring the dank February landscape. Jan, whose swiftness and accuracy of intelligence are evident from his signature alone, and whose ability as a scribe, a meticulous describer of things external to himself, would ensure the immortality of his name in more than one respect, took down Spinoza's exposition of the physics of *Principles* Part 2 without a hitch. It is difficult to tell whether he contributed much conceptually. The Euclidian-style passages on Cartesian physics seem to run on briskly, apart from a protracted and flawed discussion of Zeno's paradox, which could have resulted from discussion of Leiden views on the topic. No doubt Jan grew used, as they worked, to the spasms of coughing that his teacher could not suppress. In 1665 Benedictus would ask for *conserve of red roses*, a remedy for phthisis approved by the contemporary herbalist physician Culpeper: 'The conserve of the red buds, before the flower quite opens, which are the more restringent, is of excellent use in consumptive cases, especially in spitting of blood.'

Winter 1662–3 was one of discontent for Benedictus. Jan was twenty, and if he provoked no waspishness in the maturing – too rapidly maturing – metaphysician of thirty-one, he was, nonetheless, worrying company. We would not know this, were it not for Simon de Vries's jealous outburst, and the biographer is grateful to Simon for encouraging the following (I hope sensitive) scrutiny of the man to whom the chronicles assign no consummated love, yet who evidently painfully experienced it. The deep but unequal affection that grew between Simon and Benedictus has, I think, been underestimated. That Simon adored Benedictus is clear from his open sentiments, his unquestioning acceptance of the philosopher's advice, his persistent generosity and, I believe on grounds given below, an erotic interest in him. Benedictus had returned to his Rijnsburg lodging to months of Cartesian instruction, which for reasons of expediency brought Jan Casier to share his lodgings. Simon told Benedictus that he had, as recommended, enrolled at Leiden. 'I have begun a course of anatomy,' he wrote, 'and am about half way through. When it is completed, I shall begin chemistry, and thus following your advice I shall go through the whole medical course.' Resentment of Jan's chance to study with Benedictus is understandable, for Simon's letters show how much he would have liked to work, one-to-one, on the foundations of the Cartesian philosophy, and to learn how his friend's doctrine differed from it. He wrote to Benedictus from Amsterdam in February 1663:

> As for our group, our procedure is as follows. One member (each has his turn) does the reading, explains how he understands it, and goes on to a complete demonstration, following the sequence and order of your propositions. Then if it should happen that we cannot satisfy one another, we have deemed it worthwhile to make a note of it and to write to you so that, if possible, it may be made clearer to us.

Why, Simon must have wondered, should he be sent to study medicine, while a blinkered theological student enjoyed private philosophical tuition? Just how great a torture Casier's visit caused Simon has not been much remarked on, yet during a quick reading of Terence's *The Eunuch* certain lines jump out. In that play a young Roman, Chaera, desperately desiring a slave-girl, envies the eunuch who serves her: '*O fortunatum istum eunuchum,*' he moans, 'talking with her, living under the same roof with her, sometimes taking his meals with her, at times sleeping near her.' Simon, familiar with the plays, wrote to Benedictus:

> Fortunate, yes most fortunate, is your companion Casuarius who dwells beneath the same roof, and can converse with you on the highest matters at breakfast, at dinner, and on your walks. But although we are physically so far apart, you have frequently been present in my thoughts, especially when I am immersed in your writings and hold them in my hand.

The translator points out that Casuarius, a misspelling of Casearius, has the meaning in Latin of 'miserable fellow'. Perhaps the pun was intended, just as the Terentian suggestions were meant to be picked up.

Benedictus, apparently more interested in the reception of his own philosophical ideas than in an intense relationship, responded by sending fond thoughts to the whole group:

My worthy friend,
 I have received your letter, long looked for, for which, and for your cordial feelings towards me, accept my warmest thanks. Your long absence has been no less regretted by me than by you, but at any rate I am glad that my late-night studies are of use to you and our friends, for in this way I talk with you [all] while we are apart.

What are we to make of Simon's perceptibly physical yearning, and Benedictus's deflection of it? There is no signed ending to either this or his next letter to Simon. Both end abruptly. Or have passages been erased? Human sexuality is subtle, and while any male visitors are likely to have shared, as was the custom, the ample depths of the *ledikant*, its curtains close over the relations they witnessed. The philosopher was, I have stressed, of sensuously warm Mediterranean blood, and physical embraces were the currency of his own people, as they were for the Dutch. Only once was he accused of promiscuity: a physician in The Hague declared, twenty years after Spinoza died, that he had excited youths to 'show no respect for women, and to give themselves over to debauchery'. No evidence has been found for this, nor, despite a recent suggestion in a Dutch novel, for an attraction to men. Nonetheless, it seems right to mention on the last count that same-sex bonds were neither uncommon nor much noticed in the Dutch Republic of the seventeenth century. A long period of toleration separated the violent persecution of homosexuals in the sixteenth century from the organised witch-hunt of the eighteenth, when punishment by fire and water was revived for some instances of 'the abominable sin of sodomy'. In the eighteenth century, public humiliations and banishments would be the norm (as they were in the seventeenth century for prostitutes who stole), but 10 per cent of those convicted would be put to death. A certain pastor found guilty committed suicide, yet his body was still punished: it was burned and dumped, weighted, in the river – as he would have been two centuries earlier. In the seventeenth century, however, prosecutions were rare, and homosexual soliciting was habitually ignored. In Amsterdam men met under the arches of certain bridges, or in the fish market near the Dam. In The Hague the popular haunt was the Vijverburg, the street crossed daily by De Witt en route for the Council Chambers at the Binnenhof, and by 1730 regarded as the site of the original corruption of Dutchmen by effeminate French diplomats. Yet those who were publicly disgraced, who were pilloried on raised platforms in the city of Amsterdam with placards

142

pinned or hung on them proclaiming their sins, were not said in Spinoza's day to practise anything 'unnatural'. Sins of the flesh were equally natural in Calvinist theology, and equally unholy. Debate raged as to whether sexual intercourse within marriage was 'moral', and Spinoza (as we have seen, and shall see again) had his say on this. But most people in that self-assured society did, anyway, what came naturally. Pregnancy outside marriage was overlooked unless breach of promise was involved, and ménages such as Rembrandt's and Descartes's, where master and servant lovingly cohabited, were commonplace. Sex had a cheerful, high profile: Johan de Witt and his fiancée Wendela Bicker had sent out wedding-invitation letters that explicitly mentioned their longed-for joining of bodies.

Benedictus, now a miserable exception to this common animal appetite, knew that to the Dutch Reformed Church no carnal lapse equalled in depravity a denial of the supernatural power of God and the authority of His ministers. His concern during Jan's visit was the latter. He therefore replied to Simon:

> There is no reason for you to envy Casearius. Indeed, there is no one who is more of a trouble [odiosus] to me, and no one with whom I have had to be more on my guard. So I should like you and all our acquaintances not to communicate my opinions to him until he will have reached a more mature age. As yet he is too boyish, unstable, and eager for novelty rather than for truth. Still, I am hopeful that he will correct these youthful faults in a few years' time. Indeed, as far as I can judge from his character, I am reasonably sure of this; and so his nature wins my affection.

Did Benedictus really think Jan would notice nothing for himself? Did he think he had not put across his own views? A youth who had given up philosophy for theology must have been acutely sensitive to Descartes's weak points, and could not fail, having been a schoolboy pupil of Benedictus's, to recognise his manner of expressing and suppressing scorn. Jan might never read the early drafts of parts of *Ethics*, which Benedictus wrote in the frozen silences of night, then hid and smuggled out as and when possible to the Amsterdam study group. But however scrupulously the philosopher muted his conclusions or averted his face to conceal that uncontrollable right eyebrow, the student must have deduced or sensed his constant irritation. I do not think Jan wrote out the most flagrant niggles and alternative doctrines which, despite Meyer's admonitions, found their way into Spinoza's pages, for Benedictus told Henry that he had given friends a manuscript *which I had previously dictated to a young man to whom I did not wish to teach my opinions openly.* It seems past belief, given his awareness of a need for caution, that he showed his pupil the *Appendix* or *Cogita*

Metaphysica (*Metaphysical Thoughts*), which he added to the exposition of *Descartes's Principles*, and perhaps wrote before Parts I and II. Nor would Jan have had a hand in the Preface to Part III, where Benedictus teetered on the brink of granting Descartes a thesis of natural evolution, rather than creation. The student left Rijnsburg abruptly. We shall consider the reasons for this shortly, but we may speculate that Benedictus was finding it more and more difficult to conceal the true implications of Cartesianism. The following paraphrase, for example, turned a tentative reflection of Descartes's into a claim:

> *Having thus set out the most universal principles of natural things . . . we may demonstrate how the stars, the earth and finally all those things we find in this visible world, could have arisen, as if from certain seeds – even though we may know very well that they never did arise that way.*

Spinoza's words are almost Descartes's own, but Descartes had shown diffidence. 'I shall even make some assumptions which are agreed to be false,' he had prefaced them nervously. In the French edition he had vehemently disclaimed them: 'So far from wishing my readers to believe everything I write, I propose to put forward certain propositions which I believe are absolutely false.' Descartes had seen that looking deeply into natural causes jeopardised the biblical tenet that 'Adam and Eve were born not as babies but were created as fully grown people.' Forewarned by Galileo's recantation, he was careful to disavow this logical conclusion. Benedictus conveyed this care with an irony that would not have been lost on any reader. *We only ascribe seeds fictitiously . . . in the manner of the Mathematicians.*

We do not know exactly why Jan left Rijnsburg ('our Author ended the instruction of his pupil at that point,' wrote Meyer), but he fits the profile of those students of Van den Enden's whose fathers 'took care in due time to remove them from the school of so pernicious and impious a Master'. Such a father may have had him first removed from the philosophy department and then, when he found out where he was living, removed from Leiden altogether. At all events Jan went, or was immediately sent, to Utrecht, to knuckle under the supervision of the inflexible Reformed Church theologian Voetius, he who had thundered for twenty-five years that Descartes was an atheist whose philosophy 'was pernicious to the Protestant religion and to the peace of the United Provinces'.

In July 1663 Spinoza told Henry Oldenburg:

> *[In Amsterdam] some of my friends requested me to provide them with a*

transcript of a certain treatise containing a short account of the Second part of Descartes's PRINCIPLES *demonstrated in the geometric style, and the main topics treated in Metaphysics . . . Then they asked me to prepare the First Part too by the same method, as soon as I could. Not to disappoint my friends, I immediately set about this work, completed it in two weeks and delivered it to my friends, who finally asked my permission to publish the whole thing.*

He was satisfied, then, that he had written nothing offensive. (The astonishingly brief *two weeks* further suggests he was getting sick of aggrandising Descartes's philosophy, and wanted to work on his own.) Meyer, his appointed editor – or perhaps self-appointed, since he had more or less commissioned the work and may have been going to bear the costs of printing – found sections of the work injudicious. He had implored Benedictus to consider himself 'obliged not to depart a hair's breadth from Descartes's opinion'. In so far as a commitment to a *God, or Nature* was logically entailed by Descartes's confusions and errors, lively intelligences would pick that up for themselves. Spinoza's ideas must not be made explicit.

Johannes Hudde may also have tried to keep the creative philosopher in line. Benedictus's letters to him exhibit a rare clarity and elegance, which suggests a true meeting of minds in the *ésprit géomètre.* Hudde's obsessional interest was mathematics, and he published a treatise on Descartes's *Geometry.* Although Hudde was more interested in philosophy than De Witt, his application of mathematical principles to the 'more useful' questions of daily life in Amsterdam was, like De Witt's, pragmatic. De Witt consulted him when using probability theory and mortality experience to produce a life insurance system (a scheme that has been praised as the foundation of modern actuarial science), and it has been noted that the Grand Pensionary's mathematics were also more precise and complex than usual in his letters to Hudde. Hudde eventually resisted the thesis of *God, or Nature,* as Benedictus acknowledged, around the time of the discussion on optics in the mid-1660s, with exceptional composure. *I understand that for the most part you suspend judgement about the proof which I sent you.* While he then sent Hudde an exceptionally clear informal argument for his conception of God, there is no evidence of further letters, and Hudde's later actions show that he would not have tolerated a general dissemination of Spinoza's doctrine. Hudde's uncle Cornelis Witsen was a prominent member of Amsterdam's city council and a ferocious hounder of religious dissidents, and it is quite possible that Hudde explicitly warned all members of the study group about him. Given the vicious treatment that Witsen would inflict on the young lawyer Koerbagh, Hudde's uncle would be my candidate for Spinoza's *homunculum*, were it not for the philosopher's frequent acid references to theologians.

Descartes's Principles seems finally agreed to have had its potential for shocking readers and Reformed Church leaders curtailed, and Meyer's efforts are evident in Benedictus's grudging acknowledgement. *Since this is a matter of no importance to me, if you think that it may give offence to some theologians, do as seems best to you.* Yet Meyer's sympathy and support for Spinoza's position are implicit throughout the Preface. Hudde, too, must in some sense have concurred on reading Meyer's recommendation that 'the best and surest method of seeking and teaching the truth in the sciences is that of the Mathematicians, who demonstrate their Conclusions from Definitions, Postulates and Axioms'. And Meyer had not borne the whole responsibility for circumspection. The badgering about caution had been two-way: it was Meyer whom Benedictus had begged *most earnestly to leave out what you wrote at the end against that petty man*, and to see that *nothing is advanced which might be offensive to some person.* All the same, there remained plenty to offend.

Jan Casier's participation in the preparation of *Descartes's Principles* helps us view it from the Protestant perspective which would scan it for atheism and heresy. Cartesian physics offended many Catholics, and a number of Protestant theologians. It may be recalled that Borch mentioned Descartes and atheism in one and the same breath – 'atheists and they are principally Cartesians'. This conflation would have amused Spinoza, who saw the pains Descartes took to preserve his non-natural creator God, even when such a God seemed to slip out of the great man's inferential net. Descartes himself had been mystified at suggestions of atheism in connection with his science: – 'I do not see why he' – an obscure French priest who had criticised him – 'associates atheism with explanation in terms of shape and motion, as if the two were somehow akin.' The connection was often made, however, and not only by the Catholics who saw with consternation the implications of Descartes's account of the movement of particles for the sacrament of the Eucharist. Transubstantiation – the changing of bread and wine into the body and blood of Christ – was rendered physically impossible. The Catholic convert Burgh would refer in the traditional sense to the invasive hand of God, via miracle, when he reminded Spinoza of 'the things done in witchcraft, and in spells simply by the utterance of certain words'. Descartes, who disallowed magic, was hard put to update that explanation, and his compatriot Pascal is said to have thought the great man 'would have liked, in all his philosophy, to have been able to do without God'.

It was irrational, therefore, for a disgraced Jew to suppose that he could gain himself a good reputation by expounding the principles of Descartes.

Still less could he hope to get away with a subtly sneering accentuation of each of Descartes's potentially heretical points, and a provocative Appendix. Rashness was compounded by Meyer's editorial signposting of Cartesian doctrines which, he wrote, the Author 'rejects as false, and concerning which he holds a different opinion', since it was in precisely those areas that Spinoza's apostasy lay. But Meyer must also have included disarming contemporary signals over and above the frequent use of hypotheticals and conditionals, and the occasional statement of religious orthodoxies, regardless of the logical hiccups these constituted in the flow of the argument.

The divergences from Cartesian principles to which Meyer admitted were these. First, the Author did not grant the human mind to be an independent thinking substance. A substance, according to scholastic definition, was the cause of itself, and while Descartes re-defined it as 'every thing in which whatever we perceive immediately resides, as in a subject, or to every thing by means of which whatever we perceive exists', it was clear that human minds could not meet his criterion for independence. Minds had to depend on something for God to be omnipotent. Even Descartes admitted they were 'created' substances. Benedictus forced himself to go along with Descartes until the very last chapters of the *Metaphysical Thoughts*, when he cunningly helped himself to a concept of Aquinas – one of the few authorities whom Descartes thought worthy of respect. *A created thing is that which presupposes nothing except God in order to exist.* How, Benedictus then asked, should God look for something outside himself with which to create minds? If God resorted to another substance to make his created substances, then minds would depend immediately on that other substance, not God. *The builder is forced to seek suitable material outside himself, but God sought no matter outside himself.* All minds were therefore parts of God.

What about bodies? *Whenever people say that God is everywhere they introduce him as a spectator at a play.* The hint he dropped in *Descartes's Principles* was that a *Being* that lacked physical expression could not be complete, and to suppose so was not only illogical, but irreverent. Descartes conceived God as 'perfect' Being, using the word in its evaluative sense, but Spinoza would always rely on the strict meaning of *perfectus* as 'perfected' or complete. That was what he would put so clearly to Hudde in 1666:

> *Since God's nature does not consist in one definite kind of being, but in being which is absolutely indeterminate being, his nature also demands all which perfectly expresses being; otherwise his nature would be determinate and deficient. This being so, it follows that there can be only one Being* [or substance], *God, which exists by its own force.*

147

That being so, human bodies could only be parts of God's body. Spinoza would argue formally in *Ethics* for his recasting of the concept of God. But we should not try to get ahead in understanding from those first readers of *Descartes's Principles of Philosophy*, few of whom grasped – not even those privy to his frank assertion in the *Short Treatise* – that human minds were parts or aspects of God's mind (all thought) and their bodies differentiations of God's body (the universe). Not even Meyer drew attention to the shocking tenet that there was only one substance, having a thinking and material nature, which was God. Yet he clarified the disturbing corollary of this monism, namely, that:

> Just as the human body is not extension absolutely, but only an extension determined in a certain way according to the laws of extended nature by motion and rest, so also the human Mind, or Soul, is not thought absolutely, but only a thought determined in a certain way according to the laws of thinking nature by ideas, a thought which, one infers, must exist when the human body begins to exist. From this definition, he [the Author] thinks, it is not difficult to demonstrate that the will is not distinct from the intellect, much less endowed with that liberty that Descartes ascribes to it.

No 'will', Spinoza argued, could alter the thoughts and beliefs we naturally have. Where would such a will come from? One thought might replace another swiftly in our minds, but not because some non-natural phenomenon had acted on it. *Hence, we also do not ask, when we speak of the soul, what God can do, but only what follows from the laws of nature.*

Meyer thirdly advised that the Author departed from Descartes on what humans could know: 'We must not fail to note that what is found in some places [viz. *that this or that surpasses the human understanding*] must be taken as said only on behalf of Descartes.' If this meant that no phenomenon surpassed human understanding (at least in its most general features), then this was a dangerous admission indeed for, in the critical eye of an orthodox theologian, such presumption was as iniquitous as denial of God. Descartes had, one theologian objected, 'thrown us into total *pyrrhonisme* [extreme scepticism] and confusion', and left the very foundation stones of religious dogma open to disbelief. The very existence of God seemed deniable after Descartes's shaky proof of it in *Meditations*. In that notoriously circular argument Descartes made all knowledge of truth depend on the certainty of the existence of God. But he had not made knowledge of God either prior or certain. He had only made existence of one's own mind, and then not its composition, certain, and, as we have seen, he had received criticism on this from all quarters. Huygens, an orthodox believer, had rejected most of

Descartes's principles at the age of fifteen or sixteen, and found his criterion for truth and arguments for the existence of God unpersuasive. Spinoza, finding Descartes's theory of knowledge unnecessarily limiting, made clear his opinion that Descartes underestimated the power of human reason, and consequently the foundations for knowledge in the sciences. He let slip his belief that we can have indisputably true ideas – for example, that the three angles of a triangle are equal to two right-angles – *even though we know nothing of God, or whether the author of our nature deceives us.*

The Spanish spies had thus heard correctly: De Espinosa did believe that 'faith was unnecessary'. Did the philosopher also, in arguing for one substance, of which people's minds and bodies were parts, indicate a belief that there was no God 'unless philosophically speaking'? Certainly his deistic God (a God known through reason, natural, and without 'personality') was a calculated alternative to the God people thought of as a superman.

I believe that a triangle, if it could speak, would likewise say that God is eminently triangular, and a circle that God's nature is eminently circular. In this way each would ascribe to God its own attributes, assuming itself to be like God and regarding all else as deformed.

Later remarks, such as *By the guidance of God, I mean the fixed and immutable order of Nature or the coherent system of natural things*, also made Spinoza appear to have subsumed God into Nature, so making the name of God redundant. It was rumoured in the eighteenth century that an early version of *Ethics* contained only the word 'nature'. What would have been lost were this so? That question is answerable only when the full quotient of aesthetic spirituality that Spinoza would later load into his concept of nature has been taken into account.

In April 1663, just after Jan left, and when Part I of *Descartes's Principles* remained undemonstrated, Benedictus decided to move away from Rijnsburg. He had written to Meyer on 20 April that *the time of my moving is rapidly approaching*. The *ledikant* was again dismantled, the small store of chattels and optical instruments boxed up, and a 15-kilometre *trekschuit* journey made to Voorburg, which lay within walking distance of The Hague. We are not told in so many words why Spinoza moved, but his edginess around the time Jan left makes us suspect a link between his abrupt departure and the references to a *petty man*. Spinoza had told Henry Oldenburg he had resolved to *keep silent rather than thrust my opinions on men against my Country's wishes and incur their hostility*, and we may be sure from other caveats quoted that he thought he had left nothing in his book on which he could be criticised. He had shrugged at Meyer's suggested revisions, and declined to alter his reflections in the *Cogita Metaphysica*. Had he taken these to Rieuwertz after the editing was finished? Somewhere in the slippage between Benedictus's certainty that his observations were either safe, because self-evidently true, or were Cartesian principles implicitly sanctioned by De Witt, and his incapacity to join Henry in declaring 'away with all fear of stirring up the pygmies *[homunculi]* of our time', reason was pushed to provide a clear dictate on what he should do. Disquiet was rational given the real phenomenon of *odium theologicum*, denunciation by the Church, which might result in the condemnation of a book without a page being read. The Sorbonne priest and logician Antoine Arnauld would, for instance, write in 1691, 'I have not read Spinoza's books at all. But I know they are very nasty books.'

Did Benedictus think that dissociating himself from Rijnsburg's centre for free-thinkers, and repositioning himself nearer the seat of government at The Hague, would safeguard his reputation? Lucas took the view that 'He attributed most of the vices of men to errors of the understanding, and fearing lest he himself should fall into such error, he buried himself still deeper in solitude, leaving the place where he was staying in order to go to Voorburg, where he believed it would be more peaceful.' This report suggests he had reached the limit of his willingness to compromise his opinions. We can certainly envisage his Christian acquaintances, including Jan, suggesting how regulation orthodoxies might blot out his sceptical voice. As the book went to the printer's he told Henry querulously that he had agreed to publication only *on condition that one of them, in my presence, should give it a more elegant style and add a short preface warning readers that I do not acknowledge everything in the treatise as my own views, 'since I have written in it quite a few things which are completely opposed to my own opinions'.* He had had enough manipulation.

But there would be no let-up. That cold, wet summer Benedictus was besieged by visitors. *Right from the time of my return to this village where I now live, I have scarcely been my own master because of friends who have been kind enough to call on me.* Simon may have lingered when expected to leave (although he could have been going on to the family house at Schiedam), since Benedictus told Meyer, *Our friend De Vries had promised to take this* [Meyer's Preface] *with him, but since he does not know when he is going back to you, I am sending it by someone else.* There is a degree of proof that Spinoza had lost interest in *Descartes's Principles*. The exposition of Part I had been hasty, even careless. He had asked Meyer to point out that *I composed it within two weeks. Thus forewarned, no one will imagine that what I present is so clear that it could not have been expounded more clearly* . . . Part III was unfinished, left as 'a fragment'. In July, when he had grumpily given Meyer leave to make whatever changes he thought for the best, Benedictus possibly gave the impression of washing his hands of the project. But there was deep ambivalence in his attitude to it. Frustrated as he may have been since April by defending Descartes on points he thought indefensible, Spinoza did not despise all Cartesian principles. True, he believed Descartes was, like Bacon, deluded at a basic metaphysical level. *The first and most important error is this, that they have gone far astray from knowledge of the first cause and origin of all things. Secondly, they have failed to understand the true nature of the human mind. Thirdly, they have never grasped the true cause of error. Only those who are completely destitute of all learning and scholarship can fail to see the critical importance of true knowledge of these three points.* But he used Cartesian mathematics as a springboard for discovery, and defended not only Descartes's methodology but many of his specific findings. Nor was he indifferent to his own Cartesian commentary's publication. The three letters sent to Meyer between April and August 1663 show intense involvement with it, and no one reading the title-page of the book, bound in octavo, could doubt the pride of one who less than a decade earlier had dreamed of learning Latin in order to read Descartes's opinions.

PARTS I AND II OF DESCARTES'S PRINCIPLES OF PHILOSOPHY
Demonstrated in the geometric manner,
By Benedictus de Spinoza, of Amsterdam

In which are briefly explained the more difficult problems
which arise both in the general and in
the special part of Metaphysics.

Amsterdam,
Johannes Rieuwertz
1663

Moreover, in 1664 Benedictus would add new passages to Pieter Balling's Dutch translation of the work. He permitted and abetted a Dutch translation? Either he considered his book no more contentious than Descartes's own writings, or he was pressurised by his non-Latin-reading friends into providing instruction for them and the general Dutch public. It is not clear that this brought him any advantage (and Jarig would have no time at all for Descartes) but Benedictus would also, within the year, send Pieter geometrical demonstrations of his own first metaphysical principles for translation into Dutch.

With the despatching of the first Latin edition to bookshops, Spinoza knew that he at last had a stake in Holland's genius. He must have hoped that the extraordinary ability Borch had pronounced him to have would be noted, and praised. But Amsterdam remained silent that autumn of 1663, for an old enemy had invaded it. The streets were full of nervous, preoccupied figures, kerchiefs and cloaks pulled close across their faces to keep out, not fog, but plague. The dank summer, following a harsh winter, had left them with little resistance to the disease, brought, it was thought, by ship from Smyrna. The air was already pungent with the fumes of burning brimstone, saltpetre and amber, the only known disinfectants other than tobacco. Dogs, believed to be carriers, were destroyed, but no one thought to blame the small black rat, although the ancient Hebrews had made gold images of mice and buboes (plague-swellings) to entreat God to lift pestilence from the land. By spring the tolling of bells at each death was relentless, and the dignity of church funerals was abandoned. Corpses were removed at night, hooked on poles to avoid contagion, hurled into carts and tossed into pits. By summer 1664 the 'tokens' of the disease, round red or blue spots which turned black (when death followed swiftly, for these buboes of congealed blood betokened decomposition), were discovered with terror in Edam, Alkmaar, Enkhuizen, Haarlem, Utrecht, The Hague, Delft, Schiedam, Rotterdam and Antwerp. God was offended indeed, said the Netherlanders, for a comet to appear; for the lindens to die by the canals. In 1625 an educated correspondent had written to Secretary Huygens, 'The plague has passed . . . if only we could say that the sin which brought it about has also passed.'

The aweful visitation, still believed to be caused by sin, obliterated the central message of the *Cogita Metaphysica* even for its Dutch translator. In the sad letter quoted earlier Benedictus tried to persuade Pieter that *As for the omens which you mention, namely, that when your child was still strong and well you heard groans such as those which he uttered when he was ill and just before he died, I am inclined to think that these were not real groans but only your imagination* . . . But the majority of minds were sealed against the scientific truth that *none of the effects of the imagination which are due to corporeal causes can ever be omens of things to come, because their causes do not involve any future things;* that nothing operated on nature but nature; that a book could not cause plague.

Pieter's *omens* could have concerned things other than his little boy's death (which may not have been recent: the only record of the burial of a 'child of Pieter Balling' is for 16 October 1661), since one 'Pieter Ballingh', living on the Burghwal opposite the Swan Brewery, was buried on 23 December 1664, in an emergency graveyard in the grounds of an old monastery, fourteen guilders being paid for the bier and boat-cover used for his brief obsequies.

SEVEN

Voorburg: 1664–5

The nature and efficacy of natural reason consists in deducing and proving the unknown from the known, or in carrying premises to their legitimate conclusions . . . The light of nature has no power to interpret scripture. A supernatural faculty is required for the task. What is meant by this supernatural faculty I will leave to its propounders to explain . . .

The idea that constitutes the formal being of the human mind is the idea of a body.

The canal linking Leiden and Amsterdam to The Hague ran within yards of Daniel Tydeman's tiny house, which stood between the tall-spired church and the long straight *Vliet* dug out by the Romans. Voorburg was a rural village, but Benedictus had not chosen to live in a peaceful part of it, for the Kerkstraat houses, huddled in a terrace and generally having only a gable loft above their ground floors, were flanked by the market place and a boat-servicing harbour beside the Vliet. Yet, while this lodging was feverishly cacophonous compared with the sleepy Katwijkerlaan, he never complained. The constructor of telescopes and microscopes fell in with the local artisan routine for some hours each day and, aware of the advantages of that odd little place, lived in *Mr Daniel Tydeman, painter*'s cottage for five years.

Just two things about the village annoyed him: delays in the mail and time-wasting visits. Frustration over the dispatch and delivery of mail was natural, since the Republic had a famously fast and on the whole efficient internal postal service, and a sea-mail link with England via Brielle, south of The Hague. Yet despite being so close to The Hague's busy post-office, Benedictus felt he did not benefit from it. He grumbled to Henry:

I wrote this letter last week, but I could not send it because the wind prevented my going to The Hague. That is the disadvantage of living in the country. Rarely do I receive a letter at the proper time, for unless an opportunity should arise for sending it in good time, one or two weeks go by before I receive it.

Vexation over visitors is less understandable, given Voorburg's focal position on the waterway system. Meyer had undoubtedly bowed to an impression Benedictus wanted to give when he wrote in his Preface to *Descartes's Principles* that the Author 'lives in the country, far from the city', because nothing was easier than getting to any Dutch city from Voorburg. The philosopher could leave home almost at the ringing of the horse-boy's bell to catch the *trekschuit*. Voorburg being on the way to everywhere (the canal system joined the River Schie at Delft, and continued south to Rotterdam and Dordrecht), he should have foreseen a continuous flow of callers. Friends on business must think they offended if they failed to stop off at his door: Simon must pass each time he travelled to Schiedam. Spinoza, who was, I believe, a profoundly emotional man who needed social contact more than he admitted, was nevertheless unwilling to give much time to anyone who neither helped disseminate his philosophical ideas nor added dignity to his reputation. This emerges increasingly.

He still feared for his good name. Benedictus had praised Pieter for the way in which he had stood up to *the adversities of fortune*, and had added, *Still, my anxiety increases day by day, and I therefore beg and beseech you not to regard it as burdensome to write to me without stint.* He had concluded his letter, *I have been very brief, I confess, but deliberately so, in order to give you material for writing to me at the first opportunity, etc.* This urgency hardly seems appropriate if Pieter had merely written in a state of superstitious terror, or was truly grieving, and we are led to wonder if Benedictus was worrying about Pieter on counts other than his tormenting imagination. There may have been unpleasantness for Pieter as Benedictus's Dutch translator: drafts of the first two Parts of *Ethics* (later called, if not then, *Of God*, and *Of the Nature and Origin of the Mind*) may have been discovered in his house. Since then Pieter had died and no new translator had come forward. It was beginning to look as though the publication of *Descartes's Principles* under his own name had been, in terms of acquiring a desirable reputation, a mistake.

The plague year of 1664 was a bitter year of backfiring for Spinoza, as he found that in the eyes of a very large number of people he had cast himself as a Cartesian, whose sinister interpretation of Descartes's principles served only to put back the day of acceptance of the Cartesian philosophy. So lastingly, indeed, was Spinoza's scholarship associated with the 'new philosophy' of Descartes that few of his contemporaries seem to have realised how fundamentally incompatible his principles were with it. No other text by Spinoza but *Descartes's Principles* was available to its wide market of Latin readers, and since Spinoza's oblique comments did not amount to an exposition of his own philosophy, this was not seen as an entirely distinct doctrine. Even after Spinoza's death, when *Ethics* was published and thoroughly examined, his principles were seen as perversions of Cartesian principles, and Descartes was condemned for having inspired them. In 1696 the French philosopher Pierre Bayle may have misled by stating in his *Dictionnaire Historique et Critique*, 'It is not wrong to think that the ill use he [Spinoza] made of some of this philosopher's maxims led him to the precipice [of atheism]', as did the Utrecht theologian du Vaucel, referring to the 'very wicked author' who, 'completely imbued with the philosophy of Descartes', evaded or dissolved the principal miracles of the Old Testament. Descartes, however, who had asserted God's externality to nature and His divine intervention in its workings, is not to be blamed. Only a Spinozist reading of Cartesianism – in effect a demolition of it – makes miracles dispensable, just as only Spinozism dissolves little daily miracles of 'free will'. Even Leibniz, who was perfectly clear on the differences between all Descartes's and Spinoza's ideas, referred in 1710 to 'Spinozism, which is an exaggerated Cartesianism'. The astronomer Nicholas Steno included Spinoza among 'certain friends in Holland who are altogether lost to Cartesian philosophy'. As a Catholic convert, Steno demanded in a letter addressed to 'The Reformer of the New Philosophy' that he demonstrate 'how the thinking thing [mind] and the extended thing [body] are united'. This essentially Cartesian frame of reference suggests that Steno had not grasped that for Spinoza neither minds nor bodies were 'things', but part-expressions of one 'thing'. The Leiden professor of philosophy Johannes de Raey, who had more reason than most to understand exactly in what Spinoza's originality lay, since he himself published in the 1650s a set of critical reflections on Descartes's theory of mind–body interaction, recalled years after Spinoza's death that in the 1660s he 'began to become famous' for his commentaries on Descartes. Schopenhauer, with two hundred years of others' philosophical reflections behind him, neatly summed up Spinoza's prime and gross divergence from Descartes which, as Spinoza endlessly stressed, made him a *non*-Cartesian:

> Spinoza's philosophy consists mainly in the negation of the double dualism between God and the World and between soul and body which his teacher Descartes had set up.

So few people were clear on this that some commentators are reluctant to admit that there were any 'Spinozists' at all in the seventeenth century but Spinoza himself. Benedictus may soon have realised that this was the price he must pay for publicly expounding Cartesian principles, since in January 1665 he would write huffily, *I have not thought about the work on Descartes nor have I given it any further consideration since it was published in Dutch.*
Irritation at this may partly explain the following querulous reproof sent

eventually, at a low point in June 1665, to the Amsterdam physician Johannes Bouwmeester. Bouwmeester had contributed a poem as a flattering foreword to *Descartes's Principles*, but in the (nearly two) years since its publication seemed uninterested in its writer's own beliefs. Benedictus wrote:

> *I don't know whether you have completely forgotten me, but there are many circumstances which make me think so. First, when I was about to set out on my journey and wanted to bid you good-bye, and felt sure, being invited by you yourself, that I would find you at home, I was told that you had gone to The Hague. I returned to Voorburg, confident that you would at least call on me in passing. But you ... have returned home without greeting your friend. Finally, I have waited three weeks, and in all that time I have seen no letter from you. So if you want to banish this opinion of mine, you will easily do so by a letter, in which you can also indicate some way of arranging our correspondence, of which we once talked in your house.*

Several rarely noted personality traits emerge from this piece of self-exposure. Loneliness, archness, naïvety, egotism and sycophancy succeed one another, and the request that Bouwmeester should interest himself in *arranging our correspondence* smacks superficially of parsimony, since postage was usually (as Descartes had felt the need to point out to Mersenne) paid by the recipient. More significantly, it betrays an underlying fear that the physician was backing away from his influence and doctrine, for the letter went on:

> *If you fear that I may communicate your letters to others to whom you would then become a laughing-stock, on this matter I give you my word that I shall henceforth regard them as sacred and shall not communicate them to any mortal without your leave.*

Bouwmeester may at some point in the past have excused himself from discussing Spinoza's doctrine openly on the grounds that he could not understand it, since the philosopher adds, *I have previously suspected and am practically certain that you have rather less confidence in your abilities than is right.* Yet Bouwmeester had been to the Amsterdam study meetings. He must have been thoroughly familiar with the outlines of Spinoza's work. This, after all, was the man entrusted with Van den Enden's secret writings.

Therein, perhaps, lay some of Benedictus's anxiety. He could, in this desperate letter, have been trying to stop Bouwmeester from taking Frans as the oracle. Bouwmeester *was* gifted, and he *was* philosophically inclined: he would translate from the Arabic of Ibn Tophails' *Improvement of Human*

Reason. But the questions that reached Benedictus a year later suggest Bouwmeester sympathised with Frans's opinion that freedom of reasoning included passion and random experience. Bouwmeester's response is not included with Spinoza's published correspondence, as promised, but its thrust was revealed in quotations within Spinoza's reply to it, and it exposed his doubt that a Method existed whereby *we can make sure and unwearied progress in the study of things of the highest importance.* The physician took the view that our 'thoughts are governed more by fortune than by skill', that is, that no method of reasoning ensuring certainty, and no *clear and distinct perceptions* – the technical term which for Descartes and Spinoza meant self-evidently true propositions, not subject to doubt – existed. Responding to this, Benedictus admitted that all but ideas of pure understanding *depend in the highest degree on chance* (he meant by 'chance' random experience: for a determinist there could be no true accidents), but he urged that if metaphysical problems are given *constant meditation and a most steadfast mind and purpose*, we can *distinguish between intellect and imagination, that is, between true ideas and the others*, and form *clear and distinct perceptions.* Bouwmeester seems not to have been convinced, for he appears to have written no more letters. Nor does it seem that he reacted to Benedictus's plea for him to translate the completed parts of *Ethics* into Dutch:

> *With regard to the third part of our philosophy [Ethics Part 3] I shall soon be sending some of it either to you, if you wish to be its translator, or to our friend De Vries. Although I had decided to send none of it until I had finished it, yet since it is turning out longer than expected, I don't want to keep you waiting too long.*

I conclude that Bouwmeester's interest was lost at least to some extent through epistemological and methodological disagreement, although he may also have felt uncomfortable about corresponding with Spinoza on such unsafe topics.

What was Simon de Vries doing at this time? No register shows the rich young man qualifying in medicine at Leiden. While it is hard to believe that this poor Latin scholar, persuaded as he was by Spinoza's philosophy in so far as he understood it, was a good choice of translator for *Ethics*, offering him the task may have been a kindness. Simon's mother, brother and sister-in-law were snatched by the Amsterdam plague within a fortnight in May–June 1664, leaving him bereaved in the grand empty home on the Keizersgracht. He may often have come to Voorburg, sharing his friend's cramped room or staying, as he could well afford, at the hospitable Herberg

De Swaen opposite St Maarten's church. How did his visits, and those of other Amsterdammers, reflect on the stubbornly impecunious philosopher?

Spinoza's consciousness of his public image, and his calculated manipulation of it, might seem to fly in the face of his belief that all our actions are the result of natural determination. His actions did not, however, in the sense of curbing nature with 'will', flout nature's laws. He was driven by an irresistible inner compulsion to preserve his mental project from external destruction and to present it, perfected, to his fellow human beings. His actions were therefore of a piece with his doctrine of an active internal endeavour. *Each thing, as far as it can by its own power, strives to persevere in its being.* Only a yielding to external pressure from another natural modification could deflect him from this striving. *I say that we act when something happens, in us or outside us, of which we are the adequate cause, i.e. when something inside or outside us follows from our nature, which can be clearly and distinctly understood through it alone. On the other hand, I say that we are acted on when something happens in us, or something follows from our nature, of which we are only a partial cause.* To expect him to accept Baconian epistemology, for example (as Bouwmeester might have preferred) was to expect him to deny his natural intellectual domain of mathematical truth.

As the plague subsided, response to the Dutch edition of *Descartes's Principles* began at last to trickle into Voorburg. Such letters were welcome even when, paid for and their seals broken, they revealed a distressing lack of comprehension. So few reactions of any merit are preserved between August 1663 and the latter part of 1665 that we must assume some letters were lost, or destroyed because their writers dared not let their interest in such matters be known. This attitude would be ludicrously exemplified thirty years later in the pussy-footing of Hudde and the English philosopher John Locke around the question of God's uniqueness. Neither would commit himself, throughout the debate that they conducted via Philips van Limborch, a liberal pastor and theologian of wide intellectual curiosity, to an honest conclusion, and their discourse eventually petered out unedifyingly. No letter to Spinoza from Van Beuningen, Van den Enden or anyone in the Amsterdam study group exists for those years, either. The silence can be partly explained. Bouwmeester, we know, was concerned about being *an object of mockery*, as others may also have been. Simon visited. Meyer and Koerbagh were, although Benedictus may not have known it at the time, writing their own philosophical treatises.

It is in my view a measure of the sparseness of Spinoza's following in the mid-1660s that he devoted many hours to answering the questions of Willem van Blijenbergh, grain-broker of Dort. This businessman, familiar to us from his tortured doubts over the morality of sleeping with his wife, had read *Descartes's Principles* in Balling's Dutch translation and now wanted further enlightenment:

> Above all, I long for what was promised in your book, a fuller expression of your opinions. I would rather have come to greet you verbally with what I finally trusted to my pen, but not knowing your dwelling place, then the contagious illness, and finally my profession, have put this off time after time.

Van Blijenbergh's many confusions over Spinoza's views have long been the butt of jokes, and it is in some ways surprising that Benedictus did not give up on him sooner than he did. But it is easy to forget that Van Blijenbergh had read only *Descartes's Principles* and its cryptic Appendix. He had seen neither of Spinoza's early treatises, nor any fragment of *Ethics*, and had not had the advantage of personal tuition. How should he have understood Spinozism? To appreciate his starting-point we have to imagine someone trying to figure out Orwell's brand of socialism from his satire on communism in *Animal Farm*. The broker had no Latin (he later learned it) so his letter was written, and had to be replied to, in Dutch, which Benedictus did not relish. It was to Van Blijenbergh that he wrote, *I really wish I could write to you in the language in which I was brought up*. It is impossible for a foreigner to judge if or why Benedictus was still not at home in the local language after eight years of living outside the Jewish community, debating with Jarig for many years on the topics he now addressed, using it on a daily basis since moving to Rijnsburg, and being in any case a skilled linguist. His Dutch seems richer, less repetitive and more apt to express philosophical concepts than Van Blijenbergh's. Should we suspect him of looking for an excuse not to enter into this correspondence? This is unlikely since it held attractions to which we need to be sensitive. To start with, a request for instruction from a Calvinist burgher who explicitly asked for enlightenment, as one 'who is driven by nothing but desire for pure truth', was well-nigh irresistible. Moreover, in asking for the judgements of 'The Esteemed B.D.S', rather than those of Descartes, about whose philosophy the book purported to be written, Van Blijenbergh seemed excitingly alert to the need to distinguish Spinozism from Cartesianism. Further, this wealthy burgher might have authority in regent circles. In short, he seemed just the sort of person whose interest Benedictus courted: it was among such thoughtful, independent individuals that he believed social and religious reform could begin. (Benedictus was not in a position to know that Van Blijenbergh was considered an upstart in Dordrecht, having changed his name from 'Van Blijberg' to that of a prominent regent family and come by his business partnership through marriage.)

Van Blijenbergh's promising introduction of himself was followed by a legitimate and important question:

> It follows then [you say] that God is not only the cause of the substance of the soul, but also of every movement or endeavour of the soul, which we call will, as you propose throughout, out of which proposition it necessarily seems to follow either that there is no evil in the soul's movement or will, or that God himself does that evil immediately.

If everything was in God, evil must either be in God or could not exist. This was a fair point. Pleased with the letter, Benedictus agreed that the difficulty that his *very learned and very wise* correspondent had isolated (which had been addressed in the *Short Treatise*) did indeed seem to follow, and that to solve it our concept of evil must be re-examined.

> *I cannot concede that sins and evil are something positive, and far less that something would exist or happen against God's will. But on the contrary, I say not only that sin is not something positive, but also that when we say that we sin against God, we are speaking figuratively, or in a human manner, as we do when we say that men sin against God ... We know that whatever there is, considered in itself, without respect to any other thing, involves perfection.*

The Calvinist knew no such thing! Everything did *not* involve perfection as far as he was concerned! Spinoza was asking him to suspend the accepted belief of his day that real demons (minions of a real devil) caused real evil in the world. Descartes had taken seriously, for the sake of his readers' beliefs, at least, the notion of a 'malicious demon' that could intrude false beliefs into our minds (although he did not explain what kind of substance might constitute the demon's mind). Van Blijenbergh was understandably perturbed and also, having read nothing of Spinoza's but *Descartes's Principles*, confused. His dismay need not (though in fact it did) spring from narrow sectarianism. Even for an atheist the notion that there is nothing positively evil perplexes. We may grant that some 'evils' exist only in our minds. Weeds, for example, are only evil as perceived: in the seventeenth century formal flower-beds included hedge garlic, now considered a garden menace. Cruelty, on the other hand, although described by Spinoza as a species of hate, in turn a manifestation of sadness (*all knowledge of evil is sadness*) and occasionally credible as the idea of a body striving to survive, often seems plainly and positively bad. Leibniz would criticise Spinoza's God containing all that is logically possible on this very issue:

Not all possibles can exist along with others; otherwise many absurdities would follow. Nothing, however unreasonable, could be conceived which would not be the world, not merely monsters but evil and wretched minds, and injustices, and there would be no reason for calling God good rather than evil, rather than unjust.

For Leibniz, God's free choice must consist in the best of compatible possibles. Spinoza's claim was that evil was logically deniable and therefore, necessarily, did not exist.

Deeply worried, Van Blijenbergh at once took advantage of Benedictus's assurance that if he was not satisfied he might ask more questions. Unfortunately for his chances with Spinoza, his verbose reply began with a piece of blatant prejudgement:

> I have two general rules under which I try to direct my philosophising: one is the clear and distinct understanding of my intellect; the other is the revealed word or will of God. According to the one I try to be a lover of truth, while by both I try to be a Christian philosopher. Whenever it happens, after a long inquiry, that my natural knowledge either seems to conflict with this word, or is not easily brought into agreement with it, this word has so much sway with me that I suspect the apprehensions I imagine to be clear, rather than put them above and against the truth which I find obligatory in that book.

Benedictus, repelled by this confession of closed-mindedness and by the confusion of the consequent twenty-eight pages, spent more time in his reply attacking the grain-broker's way of thinking than trying to answer his questions clearly. Yet posterity is indebted to Van Blijenbergh – famous for being the first not to see how evil could be merely *imagined* – for raising the topic and demanding further explanation, since while he did not receive a very satisfactory explanation from Spinoza, he may have prompted the inclusion of the Definitions of good and evil which appear rather late in *Ethics*, and the long Preface to Part 4.

D1. By good I understand what we certainly know to be useful to us.
D2. By evil, however, I shall understand what we certainly know prevents us being masters of some good.

Spinoza's doctrine of *common notions* can throw some light on his rejection of the traditional notion of evil as a fiction. It is for him an *abstraction*, a comparative notion, formed only *because we compare things with one another.* It does not represent any really existing property in any particular thing:

there is no real property of evil or of good in nature and therefore our use of these terms is unscientific. But while Spinoza's thesis may explain away in terms of relativistic evaluation or self-interest some of the actions we want to say are positively evil, it does not effectively dispel them all. The question of carnal relations being 'good' here but 'evil' there, for example, which later preoccupied Van Blijenbergh, is hard to construe in naturalistic terms except through Spinoza's chilly view that sexuality is *useful* only for procreation.

Van Blijenbergh had raised one of the genuine problems that Spinozism presents, and, especially in view of Spinoza's own free use of the terms good and evil in his texts in what often appears a totally conventional sense, did not deserve the snub he received:

> *When I read your first letter, I had the impression that our views nearly agreed. From your second letter, however . . . I realise that this is far from being so, and I see that we disagree not only in the conclusions to be drawn by a chain of reasoning from first principles, but in those very same first principles, so that I hardly believe that our correspondence can be for our mutual instruction. For I see that no proof, however firmly established according to the rules of logic, has any validity with you unless it agrees with the explanation which you, or other theologians of your acquaintance, assign to Holy Scripture . . . I plainly and unambiguously avow that I do not understand Holy Scripture, although I have devoted quite a number of years to its study. [But] . . . when an indisputable proof is presented to me, I find it impossible to entertain thoughts that cast doubt on it . . .*
>
> *To return to your letter, I owe you many and sincere thanks for having confided in me in time your method of philosophising, but I do not thank you for attributing to me the sort of opinions you want to read into my letter. What grounds did my letter give you for attributing to me these opinions . . . ?*

One sharp rebuke followed another as Benedictus insisted that the man was not using his reason. *If you had read my letter with more care . . . If you had apprehended by pure intellect the meaning . . . Again, if you had given a little thought . . .*

Benedictus was staying at Schiedam with Simon when he wrote this reply, in the bleakness of another harsh winter, in a house of shadows of the dead. A cold sense that his doctrine, too, could die if people like Van Blijenbergh could not be guided by reason may, on an unconscious level, have gripped him: at any rate the correspondence highlights a deep-rooted tension in Spinoza's early political philosophy. On the one hand he believed anyone who sought the truth could be educated into reasoning away their irrational opinions. Simply by understanding the difference between merely believing and knowing *in a mathematical way* they made a start in self-enlightenment. He had thought Van Blijenbergh wanted to be so educated because the man had said in his first letter not only that he wanted to find peace of mind through knowing the truth, but that metaphysical study was the most likely science to help him achieve this. Benedictus would later reproach him, *I considered you as a pure philosopher who (as many who judge themselves Christians allow) has no other touchstone of truth than natural intellect, not theology.* Reasoning involved clear thinking and a willingness to reject preconceptions. For religious, social and political harmony to come about, *Each one must have firmly resolved and contracted to direct everything by the dictate of reason alone (which no one dares to oppose openly lest he appear mindless).* This resolve he expected of Van Blijenbergh. But, while acknowledging that *common notions* are *clear and distinct only to those who have no prejudices,* Spinoza had not yet accepted, in full consciousness, that prejudice could block out reason even in those committed to reasoning: that people, not wanting to appear mindless, could contract to be guided by reason without subsequently being able to perceive its logical implications. De Witt had given up arguing with Reformed Church predicants and the theologians who indoctrinated them because he knew they were bigoted and would remain so. Not for another decade would Spinoza admit that such a supremely rational individual as Johan de Witt might also succumb to that brand of mental bondage. He would never admit that his own mind might be so shackled.

Van Blijenbergh, wounded by the philosopher's harshness but not deterred, could scarcely have opened his reply more rationally:

Since your letter was peppered here and there with touchy reprimands, I hardly knew what I should judge from it . . . You offered me your friendship from your heart, with a protestation that not only was the letter you had then received very agreeable to you, but that any following letters would be agreeable, too . . . After your request and promise, I thought a friendly and instructive reply would be coming. But I received a letter that did not have an odour of great friendship. You say that no demonstrations, no matter how clear they are, count with me; that I do not understand Descartes's opinions, that I mix up corporeal and spiritual [or mental – *geestelijk*] things too much, etc., so that we can no longer instruct one another by letter. To this I answer in a very friendly way that I certainly believe that you understand the things mentioned above better than I do, and that you more often distinguish corporeal things from spiritual things, for I am a beginner in metaphysics, whereas you have climbed to a higher level. That is why I sought to insinuate myself into your favour, to be instructed . . .

Excuse me if I formulate some more objections, as I am bound to do as long as I cannot understand the thing clearly. This happens only because I want to find out the truth, not because I want to distort your opinions. So I ask for a friendly answer to this trifle.

The rest of his letter – which was no trifle – was a compound of real insight, dogmatism and confusion. He first launched into a lengthy argument on the difference between the pious and the impious as theologically (not rationally) conceived. From there he moved on to ask, entirely philosophically, how it was possible to 'stray' from God if our essence follows immediately from God, or to show virtue in obeying God if we are all compelled to do so, anyway, by nature: 'Certainly those who stay away from evil things only because their nature finds them repellant have little virtue to boast about,' he wrote. Following this extension of their earlier discussion he veered off, however, into a cluster of questions on themes considered obsolete by Spinoza concerning, for example, the natures of those discrete substances so central to Aristotelian metaphysics, and only partly forsworn in Cartesianism. Benedictus had asserted in the Appendix to *Descartes's Principles* that *God is not composed of a coalition and union of substances*, but we have seen that the best of his pupils found his One Substance thesis difficult. Van Blijenbergh concluded his letter with a cheery promise, 'I must be in Leiden in a few weeks, and will give myself the pleasure of greeting you in passing', and a P.S., 'In my all-too great haste I have forgotten to include this question: whether with our caution we cannot forestall what would otherwise happen to us.'

Benedictus's reply was frigid. *I only repeated, briefly, your own words, and therefore I do not believe that I gave the slightest reason for offence . . . I thought, as I still think, that my writing could serve no useful purpose, and that therefore it was more advisable for me not to neglect my studies – which I would otherwise have to leave for so long – for things that can be of no use.* Nonetheless, in case he left room for criticism by not dealing with the last batch of questions, he added, *I shall now turn to the objections, to answer them again.* He then hammered home to Van Blijenbergh how he should proceed to think if he wished to call himself a philosopher. *Furthermore I should like it noted here that while we are speaking philosophically we must not use theological ways of speaking . . . Therefore, philosophically speaking . . .* But eventually, on the issue of those obsolete and self-contradictory concepts of discreet substances and free will, his tolerance gave out:

And here I think I have answered your objections (if I have understood them properly, for I sometimes doubt whether the conclusion you draw does not differ from the proposition which you undertake to prove) . . .

Regarding the other questions which you have added at the end of your letter, since one could as well ask a hundred in an hour, without ever coming to a conclusion about anything, and since you yourself do not much urge an answer, I shall leave them unanswered.

Surprisingly, however, the despised student was permitted to call. *For now I say only that I shall expect you at the arranged time, and that you will be very welcome to me.*

The philosopher had by that time returned from Schiedam after a stay of at least six weeks, chafing, no doubt, to work on *my Ethics, which I have not yet published*, this undoubtedly being the study he had been forced to put temporarily aside. Why, then, was Van Blijenbergh encouraged to come to Voorburg in person? I suggested Benedictus might have thought he was a regent; even, perhaps, as a native of Dordrecht, a friend of the De Witts. If so, Spinoza would have thought a visit from this Calvinist broker timely, for it seems a dispute had arisen during the previous winter over the appointment of a new pastor in Voorburg, in which the painter Daniel Tydeman had taken part and had involved him.

> The said Daniel Tydeman has living in his rented room an A [msterdammer?] Spinosa, born of Jewish parents, who is now (so it was said) an atheist or one who derides all religions, and therefore a harmful instrument in this republic, [as] so many learned men and preachers, among others the Reverend Lantman, who knew him well, can testify: he has written the petition presented (so the members of the Church Council imply) to the Burgomasters.

Archive research shows that 'Dominee Lantman' was Thaddeus de Lantman, or Landman, a fiery Calvinist, who took office in The Hague in 1663. Such scandal was the last sort of attention Benedictus wanted. It is difficult to believe he would willingly have become involved in parochial passions regarding a preacher, yet we know his clever asides incensed, and if Tydeman passed on a carelessly uttered sneer about preachers in general, whose *excessive authority and egotism* he would decry in a letter that autumn, this could have acted as a catalyst for village resentment. We do not know that any petition was passed to the burgomasters, but Spinoza's name was blackened locally, and it could only benefit him for Van Blijenbergh, clad in regent black, to be spotted alighting self-importantly from the *trekschuit*, a pocket-sized New Testament in his hand. Word would soon spread that a God-fearing Hollander of substance had entered Tydeman's door.

While this aspect of Van Blijenbergh's visit may have been a triumph, it was in all other respects unprofitable. A year or two back Simon had written to Benedictus that the study group could 'under your guidance, uphold truth against those who are religious and Christian in a superstitious way', but the philosopher must now finally recognise the awesome bondage effected by Calvinist indoctrination. He had tried to explain to Van Blijenbergh how distinct was true *Godsdienst* from the unthinking acceptance of scripture, but he had not budged his belief that reason must yield to the 'rules' of theology. Probably, in the recesses of the grain-broker's mind, had lodged all along Calvin's warning against philosophising:

> Philosophers indeed, with general consent, pretend that in the mind presides Reason, which like a lamp illuminates with its counsels, and like a queen, governs the will . . . But Augustine properly observes that pride was the first of all evils . . .

Later events suggest that three months of acquaintance with Van Blijenbergh contributed to a catharsis in Benedictus's life, for in the stinging *Theologico–Political Treatise* he started soon after this frustrating correspondence ceased, the philosopher would, with a tilt at all theologians – including Suárez, whose expression he borrowed here – address *those whose philosophy is hampered by the belief that Reason is a mere handmaid to Theology*.

The broker, unaware of what he was stirring up, climbed into the canal boat after their March meeting in a daze, and later wrote to Benedictus:

> When I had the honour of being with you time did not let me stay longer with you, and still less could my memory hold everything we discussed, notwithstanding that on leaving you I immediately collected all my thoughts in order to remember what I had heard. Therefore, in the next place I came to, I tried to jot down your opinions on paper for myself. But I found then that I had not remembered even a quarter of what was discussed. And therefore you must excuse me if I make myself difficult once again by asking about things where your opinions were not clear, or not well remembered.

The answer this time – politely – was No. Benedictus would have preferred, he wrote, to have communicated this decision verbally, and in the friendliest way. But the Calvinist's fresh volley of objections, sent in two quickfire letters, meant that the matter must be concluded at once. Van Blijenbergh had asked, said Benedictus, for proofs of *a great part of Ethics*. It was pointless to go on; senseless to seek solutions for new objections when the first stage in understanding, namely willingness to discuss how things must, necessarily, be, rather than how theologians of a particular persuasion interpreted them, had not been examined. The philosopher concluded, *I hope that when you have considered the matter you will willingly drop your request and nonetheless retain your affection towards me . . . Your affectionate Friend and Servant, B. de Spinoza.*

There was no response, and the Van Blijenbergh connection seemed amicably severed. Yet the intensely polarised views that their association had generated would burst forth on both sides some years later. Van Blijenbergh did, despite the confusion of his visit, catch some of the philosopher's words, for in 1674, when he abusively denounced Spinoza's 1670 *Theologico-Political Treatise* in a pamphlet, he recalled that Spinoza had told him personally that he intended 'to introduce a political religion'.

We may sense a growing inner rage in that defiant promise, for the desperate letter begging Bouwmeester to translate for him was sent that same month of June 1665. Disappointment at failing to convince Van Blijenbergh, and anxiety over village scandal, were now almost certainly compounded by knowing that Van den Enden's *Vrye Politijke Stellingen* was selling in the bookshops while *Ethics*, rising above those rantings in an immaculate sequence of propositions and proofs, remained hidden. Resentment at the protection of a schoolmaster who openly vilified regents and Reformed Church clerics but continued teaching, while he himself lived quietly and abused no one, yet was accused of perversion, is understandable. Benedictus may have felt mentally and physically sick when he wrote imploring Bouwmeester's interest in his doctrine, for at the same time he made a rare admission of ill health. While asking Bouwmeester to send him some promised conserve of red roses, he told him of his self-administered blood-letting for tertian fever, from which he had recently suffered two or three times.

He was thirty-three years old, and the work that had taken a decade to put on paper in a form which satisfied him had been brought to a halt. Letters of the next year or two show a surge of attention to optics, but this study provided only snatches of knowledge of a fragment of nature, whereas he knew that he was rapidly clarifying the ground rules for clear knowledge of all its aspects. He was undergoing spiritual death, if by that is meant a suspension of active internal endeavour. But was he failing to express his essence as a philosopher because external forces prevented it? If he looked hard at the chains of causes and effects that determined his present predicament, and at the obstacles he had to remove if his truth were to reach people's minds, then conflicting ideas, *vacillation of mind*, emerged. A drive to remain a traditional philosopher, a quiet mouthpiece of wisdom, alternated with a growing and equally determined urge to denounce the tyranny of religious institutions committed to preventing access to that wisdom. Henry Oldenburg, having no inkling of the startling nature of the mildest of Spinoza's views, had advised: 'I believe that nothing can be published more agreeable and more welcome to men who are truly learned and wise . . . That is what a man of your talent and character should look to, rather than what pleases the theologians of our age and fashion. They look not so much to truth as to what suits them.'

Benedictus knew such facile encouragement was worthless whichever approach he took, unless he could be sure of protection and endorsement from persons in positions of influence. But the callers he most wanted to see did not come near the Kerkstraat. Of this we can be moderately, although not entirely, sure. Had the Grand Pensionary, or Coenraad Burgh or the talented but eccentric Van Beuningen stepped off the canal barge at Voorburg, news of it would surely have reached Lucas or Colerus, even if the episodes were cut from Spinoza's papers. (A visit paid by Benedictus to Huygens, for example, appears in a letter from Spinoza preserved in Oldenburg's correspondence, but is deleted from Spinoza's.) It is of course more likely that Spinoza would have been received in The Hague, if patronised at all, by distinguished politicians. De Witt would have known of Spinoza's existence at least as early as 1663, when *Descartes's Principles of Philosophy* was published and discussed, and Lucas insists that he protected Spinoza, giving him a pension of 200 'francs', asking for lessons in mathematics and often consulting him on 'important matters'. However, reasons for doubting any of this to be true follow one another in relentless succession from now on. The least of these was the Grand Pensionary's workload. In one letter he complained that he must attend so many meetings, and so many people demanded to see him privately, that he had to work at his papers well into the night. In others he apologised to family and friends for failing to attend their gatherings.

The political events that preoccupied De Witt also kept Van Beuningen away from Holland for much of De Witt's administration. He was made ambassador to France in December 1664 despite the opinion of Count d'Estrades, French ambassador in The Hague, that he was better at spoiling a friendship than keeping it, and that he should be left at home to think philosophical thoughts. (If those thoughts were a foretaste of the visions and prophecies that would fill his pamphlets of 1672, then they were inspired by the mysticism of Menasseh ben Israel, De Labadie and Serrarius, not Spinoza. Van Beuningen's metaphysics, unimpeded by advances in science or the dictates of reason, remained those of Ezekiel.) While Van Beuningen was recalled in 1667 for urgent talks, he was at once sent back to Paris, where he remained until September 1668. After that he had spells in Münster, London and Brussels. De Witt ignored his pleas for a home posting, which included the lament that he was ridiculed for his poor horsemanship, 'and there is nothing more damaging here than to be ridiculous'. In fact, despite his 'outbursts and threats' as France began to look acquisitively at the eastern United Provinces in the late 1660s, the French government respected him for his culture and experience. Van Beuningen was a busy man at a time of constant political tension, and he may not have met Spinoza at all between 1660 and late 1668. Moreover, Spinoza showed no personal interest in the fact that the Dutch ambassador had been sent to France when he mentioned it to Oldenburg. Whether or not the two men met, the contempt that the diplomat's own religious beliefs later received in The Hague, and his somewhat frigid dealings with De Witt since their dispute over Dutch policy in the Baltic war, made him unlikely to mention the philosopher of Voorburg in or around the Binnenhof at this time. Later, as the diplomat's eminence increased in proportion to his spiritual instability, the likelihood diminished further.

Christiaan Huygens, however, may have strode the half-mile from the Hofwijk (his father's moated château, seemingly modelled on the hunting lodges of the Princes of Orange, but surrounded by formal gardens of mathematical precision) to discuss optics with the philosopher three years his junior. The attention was doubtless initially gratifying. Spinoza needed public recognition from Hollanders of good standing, and we may be sure that Huygens bowed and praised his optical instruments quite satisfyingly enough to impress the Kerkstraat neighbours. We can picture them together, the tall and the short; the rakishly bewigged patrician inventor, his fashionable French soft cravat a little askew; and the curly-haired *hidalgo* of exquisite manners, clad in fine but ageing street clothes, staring in rapt unison, now through a microscope, now at scribbled algebraic notation. Huygens's visits were not shopping trips for lenses. The polymath prided himself on his mechanical expertise, and did not want his lenses made by 'a Craftsman', as had Descartes. He had personally ground the lenses for the telescope through which he had discovered the rings of Saturn. If he bought any glasses from Spinoza he did so from curiosity, to compare their construction and power with his own. Conversation would have touched on lens-making, but would have been grounded in the mathematics on which both thought all accurate discovery depended, and where their meeting of minds was closest and most wary.

At first, judging by this report to Oldenburg, the philosopher was genuinely stimulated by Huygens's discoveries. *He has told me wonderful things about these microscopes [Hooke's], and also about certain telescopes made in Italy, with which they have been able to observe eclipses of Jupiter caused by the interposition of its satellites, and also a kind of shadow on Saturn as if made by a ring.* Also, *I have seen Kircher's Mundus Subterraneous at the house of Mr Huygens,* runs the passage cut out of Spinoza's correspondence but printed in Oldenburg's. But Spinoza did not have much time for Huygens's theorising, and soon put Henry wise regarding any supposed superiority of Huygens's science over that of Descartes:

> *As to what you say about my hinting that the Cartesian Rules of motion are nearly all wrong, if I remember correctly I said that Mr Huygens thinks so, and I did not assert that any of the Rules were wrong except for the sixth, regarding which I said I thought that Mr Huygens too was in error.*

It cannot have pleased Benedictus that Huygens, who had as a boy thought Descartes's principles 'conjectures and fictions', disagreed over the points on which he himself thought Descartes was right, while dismissing the errors exposed in *Descartes's Principles.* The philosopher went on to describe the new machine Huygens had made for turning plates in the polishing of dioptrical glasses, adding sniffily, *I don't yet know what success he has had with it, and, to tell the truth, I don't particularly want to know. For experience has taught me that in polishing spherical plates a free hand yields safer and better results than any tool.* He was unable to satisfy Henry's curiosity about the success of Huygens's pendulums in fixing longitudes at sea, and seemed altogether mildly irked at having to discuss another natural philosopher's work at all. Huygens was no more an icon for Benedictus than was Boyle and, as had happened over Boyle's experiments with nitre, Benedictus's impulse was to show himself the abler scientific theorist and practitioner. Polishing with hand instruments was obviously more convenient for someone living in a confined space than using a lathe, but Spinoza characteristically claimed it to be, anyway, superior. A handbook he later acquired, *The Art of Glass Cutting* by the chemist Antonio Neri, would further convince him of this. (There is, our modern expert says, still a place for hand-polishing lenses and prisms 'when work of high class has to be produced in small quantities'.)

Huygens, like Van Beuningen, was seldom in Holland. In the spring of 1666 he settled in Paris to help establish its Academy of Sciences, and did not finally move into the Hofwijk until 1687, when his father Constantijn died there aged ninety-one. His contacts with Spinoza were therefore spasmodic, and while superficially courteous they were fundamentally patronising: he referred in several letters to the 'Jew' or the 'Israelite'. His attentiveness to the little man round the corner was as motivated by self-interest as Benedictus's desire for it, and their relationship, always formal, seems quickly to have turned edgy. Neither claimed to be a friend of the other. Benedictus noticed that Huygens kept Boyle's *Treatise on Colours* and Hooke's *Micrographia* from him, but proudly rationalised this on the grounds that, since those books were in English, he could in any case have made nothing of them. Did he have any idea of the lengths Huygens went to in order to keep his optical discoveries a secret from his Dutch rivals? While in Paris Huygens made his brother at Hofwijk responsible for finding out details of Spinoza's and Hudde's progress, and warned him at the same time to plead ignorance if asked questions by either of them. (The brothers corresponded in French, and this, together with Huygens's lack of support for the Dutch during their wars with France, and his further snub to his homeland in failing to set up a research society there equivalent to the Royal Society or the Paris Académie Royale des Sciences, is still held against him in Holland.) However, Huygens appears to have retained a grudging esteem for Spinoza, for over and above his flattering competitiveness he allowed him one genuine scientific finding: 'It is true that experience confirms what is said by Spinoza, namely that the small objectives in the microscope represent the objects much more finely than the large ones.' In turn, acquaintance with an eminent scientist who was consulted on problems of practical urgency by Johan de Witt mattered to Benedictus, and his replies to Henry Oldenburg's questions show him accepting the reflected kudos of the contact, even as he shrugged off Huygens's claims to eminence as a natural philosopher.

Huygens's notorious secrecy partly accounts for Oldenburg's need to question Benedictus about the Francophile's work. In 1665 the Royal Society's secretary quizzed many of his correspondents about Huygens's marine chronometer (which the Royal Society thought insufficiently tested) and his new lens-polishing machine. Huygens was only too anxious to lodge claims with the Royal Society ahead of the likes of Hooke and Boyle, and had met Henry Oldenburg during his visit of 1661, yet his excuses for not answering Henry's many letters or thanking him for gifts of scientific treatises are manifold. He had lost his address, he said, although Oldenburg had told him in a recent letter that he lived 'about the middle of the Pall Mall, London'. He could not understand the Secretary's description of Hevelius's lens-polishing technique, Huygens said, and thought Oldenburg was confused. Henry had, in fact, as was his habit, copied verbatim what Hevelius had written. Huygens sent just one short note directly to Oldenburg. Apart from that, Huygens's English correspondents passed on rare, brusque messages from him, and the general sense when reading the Oldenburg correspondence is of a mild aversion towards Oldenburg on Huygens's part.

Huygens's decision to make the Académie Royale des Sciences his base may not have been wholly academic. For one thing, Paris stayed free of the plague in 1664, whereas Holland was ravaged. Concentrating in areas of over-population, it decimated the Vloyenburg's *Hooghduytsen* community. Those Jews who could afford to move away fled to Weycke, on the coast north-west of Amsterdam, or left the country. On 31 October 1664, the Amsterdam archives reveal, one 'Sr Bento Gabriel de Espinosa' (a confusion presumably resulting from the registered name of the firm) 'living in this city' gave full power of attorney to Moyses and David Juda Leon to look after his business affairs, to 'onload and receive all goods and merchandise and letters and bills of exchange', and to sell for him at a profit during his absence, for he was, he declared, about to leave for Barbados. His ship reached the West Indies, notwithstanding its violation of the renewed English Navigation Act (which limited imports in England and its colonies to English-owned ships or ships of the countries of origin) and its defiance of the English law requiring permission from Whitehall for all immigrants to His Majesty's Plantations. The ship may have been fitted out and financed by the marrano community, this being common practice. (Gabriel's widowed sister Ribca would also, sometime between 1679 and 1685 and with some of her children, take an assisted passage to the West Indies, to die in Curaçao of yellow fever in 1695.) Marrano emigrant-carrying merchantmen were welcome in the English colonies, Amsterdam Jews having created wealth in Barbados and Jamaica before English rule. But their safe passage from Amsterdam depended on a flagrantly exploited legal loophole, for whereas Dutch Jews were declared 'Dutch' in the 1648 Treaty terms, and the States General had proclaimed in 1657 that Dutch Jews were citizens of The Netherlands, and in travelling and trading must be treated as such, English hostility at sea now made it no advantage to be Dutch, so Emperor Caracala's bestowal of citizenship rights on all Jews of the Roman Empire was cited instead. Once more, Jews could safely sail where the Dutch could not. (We may, by the way, be sure that the 'Abraham Espinosa' was Michael's son because another Amsterdam Jew, Abraham Jessurun de Espinosa, is shown in a register of synagogue officials to have served three times as a *parnas* in Amsterdam between 1663 and 1676.)

No comment on Gabriel's departure is preserved in Spinoza's correspondence. Perhaps he knew nothing of it, although Jarig would have heard trading news through his manager.

Huygens's Francophilia could also have intensified as a second naval war finally erupted between the Dutch republic and England after almost five years of bitter trading rivalry. While looking for an excuse to declare war, the English had systematically strangled the Dutch carrying trade, using plague as grounds for stopping and imposing restrictions on those Dutch ships that did not transgress the Navigation Act. In September 1664 Pepys of the Admiralty recorded that a Dutch ship of 300 or 400 tonnes was cast ashore at Groningen, 'with all men aboard her dead of the plague'. Amsterdam, already demoralised by disease, looked to become, as it had in 1653, a city of empty wharves, where grass grew in the streets. In October 1664 the English snatched New Amsterdam without bloodshed, a loss that might have been avoided if the New Netherlands had listened to the many petitions (most of them more moderate than Van den Enden's) which had warned the States General since 1649 about the religious and commercial pressure imposed by the Dutch governors on both emigrants and indigenous Americans. Unless more attention was paid to their views, one delegation had predicted, 'The most terrible ruin will follow and this province will become the defenceless prey of its neighbours . . . The very name of New Netherlands will be lost and no Dutchman will any longer have any say in affairs here.' Despite petitions such as Frans's, and the granting of a few minor concessions to self-government, the colony had remained weak and disunited, an obvious target for the English. Before long, New Amsterdam was renamed New York.

England at last declared war six months later in March 1665, and the English fleet put to sea on 1 May, but no attack followed. In June Benedictus's letter to Bouwmeester expressed, among other agonies, a general Dutch mood of distrust and anxiety:

I hear much about English affairs, but nothing certain. The people do not cease suspecting all kinds of evil, and no one can find any reason why the fleet does not set sail. And indeed the situation does not yet seem secure.

The English were in fact unprepared, having underestimated both their financial resources and the ferocity of the plague, which had now reached their shores, the first for twenty years. This would reach a devastating peak in September, leaving Oldenburg, for one, in perpetual fear of it, and would drive the eminent out of London. Charles II left for Salisbury, and when the plague reached Salisbury he moved on to Oxford. He sent messengers to discover if Quakers were victims in London, or if all had been spared. So many were dead (Samuel Fisher among them) that the King was reassured that his rough treatment of them had not provoked divine retribution. He was, consequently, hopeful of a quick victory at sea.

The year 1665 did indeed bring misfortune for the Dutch. The English had deliberately declared war while Admiral De Ruyter, the only man who could unite the Dutch seamen, was still in the West Indies. De Witt, knowing he could no longer call on France for support, was forced to take command at Texel, where getting the ships out to sea through shallow channels was notoriously difficult. There were such numbers of workless poor in the Provinces that, despite plague mortality, De Witt found no shortage of the 'volunteers' he insisted on engaging for this most sickening form of warfare. At its first foray the Dutch fleet was shattered, losing sixteen ships sunk or captured, as well as three admirals, including supreme naval commander Obdam, off Lowestoft in June. De Witt reported this to the States General with 'bold face', and asked to be appointed Fleet Deputy, making Tromp's quick-tempered son Fleet Commander in name only. Later in August, when the pilots refused to take the ships out, claiming the wind was unfavourable for one strait and that there was too little water in the other, De Witt climbed into a small rowing boat to test the depth with lead for himself and found that nowhere was less than twenty feet deep. So astounded were the sailors at seeing their Grand Pensionary first dropping a lead line, then staying on board ship to see the whole fleet out through the channel (it took two days) that the strait became known as 'Witt's Diep'. At the welcoming ceremony for De Ruyter's return, De Witt remained aboard, sleeping in the anti-seasickness hammock Huygens had designed for him, which hung, pendulum-fashion, from a large ball. (That spring, Van den Enden had written imploring De Witt's interest in his own well-researched but costly proposals for improving the armament, manoeuvrability and impregnability of the Dutch warships. In 1667 he would, still vainly, send plans approved by shipwrights. Meanwhile, the brand-new, gilded-sterned *Zeven Provinciën*, which would serve for almost thirty years, became the navy's flagship in June 1666.) Having settled disputes among the officers, De Witt returned to The Hague, considering himself thereafter an expert in naval warfare and constantly travelling to Texel or Goeree near The Hook of Holland to question flagship decisions. In November the weather was so foul that despite insisting that only four wind directions, not twenty-two, could stop Dutch ships putting to sea, De Witt decided that God had signified 'as if with a finger' that the fleets should not meet. That same month Henry Oldenburg wrote to a friend:

> The Dutch Fleet have their Rendez-vous at Goree [*sic*] where De Witt is said to be, and to brag still of a resolution to come out once more before winter, and to find out the English. If he doth, I am apt to think, he comes out to seek what he hath no great mind to find.

Benedictus's correspondence with Oldenburg was not, as it happened, interrupted by the war. Peter Serrarius (who passed as English or Dutch) carried letters, which included bulletins on the war's progress, between them. Henry wrote to Spinoza:

> Kircher's *Subterranean World* has not yet appeared in our English world because of the plague, which hinders all communication. Then there is also this terrible war, which brings with it a veritable Iliad of woes, and very nearly eliminates all culture from the world . . . I believe that the whole of Europe will be involved in war next summer . . . Some of our philosophers who followed the King to Oxford hold frequent meetings there . . .

Benedictus replied that November, *There appears to be no hope of peace with the English . . . The Dutch at present have no thoughts of peace* . . . In his opinion, the clamouring from the Province of Overijsel to send the Prince of Orange to England as a mediator (the boy was then fourteen) was merely a ruse to undermine the authority of the States of Holland. Exchanges between the two were not always friendly, though they stopped well short of the coarser insults flying across the North Sea. Benedictus's praise of the Dutch navy, for example, expressed in a letter now lost or destroyed, affronted Henry, who pointed out:

> The courage which you hint is the subject of debate among you is of a bestial kind, not human. For if men acted under the guidance of reason, they would not so tear one another to pieces, as anyone can see.

Benedictus was as stung by this apt reproof as he had been by Van Blijenbergh's justified complaint about his impatience, and his reply (echoing Montaigne and Diogenes Laertius) that *these troubles move me neither to laughter nor again to tears, but rather to philosophising, and a closer observation of human nature*, was repeated in *Ethics* and the *Political Treatise*.

It was during this year of sickness, savagery and setback that Spinoza completed the bulk of the philosophical manifesto which, with an emphasis rarely remarked on, but pivotal to his retention of 'God' in the *God-Nature* equation, he called *Ethics*. Concentrated study at Voorburg during the winter of 1663–4 is indicated by a prolonged silence in the chronicles and correspondence, and the plague year of 1664 saw Parts 1 and 2 sufficiently polished to be translated into Dutch for private circulation. The macro-scheme of *Ethics* Part 1 (called *Of God*), which demonstrated the all-inclusiveness, self-containedness and unified system of determined causal effects of God, or Nature, had been drafted for some while. The postulates and axioms from which all further conclusions in *Ethics* were claimed to be deduced were, Spinoza believed, self-evident, but he supplied Proofs, and Scholia (explanations) to aid the establishing of his Propositions. Euclid had done no less. Deductions from this basic metaphysical picture were now also well established in the microscheme of *Ethics* Part 2 (entitled *Of the Nature and Origin of the Mind*).

It is not possible in a biography to give Spinoza's theory of mind, which remains problematic for scholars after many years of study, the prolonged discussion it requires, but to understand Spinoza and his expectations of others it is necessary to be familiar with its central concepts. *Ethics* Part 1 had argued that God's mind could not lie outside nature. It followed from this that human minds could not be non-natural. Since *God, or Nature* was all there was, or could logically (metaphysically) necessarily be, human beings were parts or *modes*, ways of being of that one substance. The mind being natural and a part of God under the attribute of thought, it could not exert free will. *Inadequate and confused ideas follow with the same necessity as adequate, or clear and distinct ideas.* Descartes had therefore to be wrong, argued Spinoza, in his claim that the essence of a person consisted in a non-natural soul having agency over intellect and body. Nor had Descartes been able to demonstrate that the soul was immortal – a matter of concern to seventeenth-century readers. Spinoza's interest in the immortality of the mind was real, but his understanding of what made mind eternal was as remote from standard views of the soul as a disembodied 'personality' as his *God, or Nature* was from standard views of God as a 'personality'. *What theologians understand by the word 'personalitas' is beyond me.* For Spinoza, *the eternal part of the mind is the intellect, through which we are said to act. But what we have shown to perish is the imagination, through which alone we are said to be acted upon.* As long as the 'soul' was viewed as those ideas that were eternal truths, Grotius's article of faith could be said, after a fashion, to be honoured. When this doctrine of a natural soul was finally made public it pleased almost no one. Leibniz (who at least understood it) protested:

For [Spinoza], the soul does not survive except through its ideal in God. But there is not the slightest reason for supposing that the soul is an idea: ideas are something purely abstract, as numbers or figures, and cannot act; they are abstract and universal. It is an illusion to say that souls are immortal because ideas are eternal.

Spinoza, unshackled by any obligation towards man-made standards of correctness, ruthlessly demonstrated what he believed must logically be the case. In the *Short Treatise* he had defined the soul as the idea of the body.

The *knowledge, Idea etc., of each particular thing which comes to exist is, we say, the soul of this particular thing.* He had supplied there a long and remarkably fully worked-out explanation of the relation of body to mind. In *Ethics*, the reader was expected to deduce this from first principles:

> *In God [or Nature] there is necessarily an idea, both of his essence and of everything that necessarily follows from his essence . . . The object of the idea constituting the human mind is the body.*

Any mind was the idea of a specific body. Any thought was a reflection of, or a precise parallel of, a state of that body. An angry thought, for example, had a specific physical counterpart in the brain, superficially discernible by humans in a glare, perhaps, or a red face.

This doctrine of 'parallelism' (our term, not Spinoza's) had evolved in physical proximity to Leiden, where Professors de Raey and Geulincx were attempting to make the Cartesian account both coherent and satisfactory to theologians. De Raey had written a treatise in 1654 which developed the medieval notion of a relation between the order of ideas and the order of physical objects. A key proposition in *Ethics* reads, *The order and connection of ideas is the same as the order and connection of things.* Geulincx, who had sought refuge at Leiden from Louvain in 1658 after daring to question Aristotelian metaphysics, had a Leiden doctorate in medicine, and he encouraged the medical students there to learn his doctrine of 'occasionalism', a version of parallelism. Like Spinoza, Geulincx denied Descartes's doctrine of mind-body interaction: he argued that mind could not move body, nor body mind, and that states of mind and states of body, such as those described above, must be a matter of constant conjunctions. Like Spinoza, Geulincx thought human bodies and minds were states of one substance, not individual substances. But, crucially, he believed that minds and bodies were modes of two diverse, physical and mental, substances. Neither Geulincx nor the French philosopher Malebranche, who also denied that mind could move body, and allowed 'occasional causes', would take the bold step of attempting to resolve the problem of the mind-body relation by making mind and body identical in substance. For both, the mental and physical remained distinct in order to preserve a non-natural soul, and both explained the coincidence of thoughts and correlative body states only by appealing, as had Descartes, to the external will of God.

No scholarship is needed to see that similarities between Spinoza's 'parallelism' and 'occasionalism' were real, but superficial. Yet while the latter was mysterious, Spinoza's doctrine of mind and body as two aspects of the same thing was, and still is, cryptic. In the *Short Treatise* Spinoza had appeared to make mind logically and causally dependent on body. *The essence of the soul consists only in the being of an idea . . . arising from the essence of an object which in fact exists in Nature.* Indeed, one might suspect from Spinoza's earliest writings on the soul that he was, like Hobbes, a materialist – one who believed all things were merely matter. Hobbes held that Mind just was Body: 'For the universe, being the aggregate of bodies, there is no real part thereof that is not also body.' This was a topic of enormous concern in the seventeenth century: Henry Oldenburg had in 1661 twice pressed Benedictus to tell him his criterion for distinguishing the attributes of Thought and Extension:

> It is still a matter of controversy as to what Thought is, whether it is a corporeal motion or a spiritual activity quite distinct from what is corporeal.

Having ignored Henry's first query, Benedictus seemed deliberately to fudge his reply to the second, plunging his correspondent into his argument for the infinity – but not absolute infinity – of the attributes, an argument Henry had admitted he did not understand, before concluding obscurely: *This one thing you will not deny, that extension, in so far as it is extension, is not thought.* In 1661 Spinoza, immersed in the *Short Treatise*, was perhaps still inclined to believe that ideas depended on the real objects they represented. By 1665, when *Ethics* Part 2 was drafted, he had declared mind to be neither supernatural substance nor body. It was *related to God's Nature as motion and rest are, and as are absolutely all natural things*, but not physical. Yet the equivocation noticeable in the *Short Treatise* and lingering in the letter to Oldenburg haunts *Ethics*. For are not the attributes of thought and extension identical if substance is unique and indivisible? Here and there in *Ethics* Spinoza seems to suggest that mind and body are just two ways of seeing one thing. *The thinking substance and the extended substance are one and the same substance, which is now comprehended under this attribute, now under that. So also a mode of extension and the idea of that mode are one and the same thing, but expressed in two ways.* But this explanation will not do, since Spinoza would also insist in *Ethics* that extension and thought express two diverse and incompatible causal powers. The causal force within modes of extension was motion and rest, he claimed, whereas modes of thought, *ideas*, were empowered only by implication and inference. *The power of the mind is intelligence itself.* Neither power, he stated, could operate on modes of the other attribute. *The body cannot determine the mind to thinking, and the mind cannot determine the body to motion.* How, then, could mind and body be identical?

The tension in Spinoza's doctrine of mind between identity and autonomy persists, but it does not affect our understanding of his doctrine of the intimate correlation of mental states with body states which, with a small piece of explanation I add in a moment, allows us to assess the rationality of his belief that women were deprived *by nature* of a *strength of mind and intellectual ability* equal to men's. Spinoza wrote *Ethics* Part 2 in Rijnsburg and Voorburg. In Voorburg, in the troubled times of 1664–5, he moved on from Part 2 to his study of emotion in *Ethics* Part 3, *On the Origin and Nature of the Affects*. He probably also wrote in Voorburg most of Part 4, *On Human Bondage, or the Powers of the Affects*. The separate Parts of *Ethics* may not have had those titles in the mid-1660s, for Benedictus told Bouwmeester, *I shall send it up to about the eightieth proposition* of Part 3, whereas Part 3 now contains only fifty-nine. But Part 4 probably contains material from the original Part 3, and this is the right place to examine the metaphysics of female mentality. The additional explanation that I suggested we need turns on the question of how a passion, by definition passive, can have positive power. In Spinoza's words, *we are driven about in many ways by external causes . . . like waves on the sea, driven by contrary winds, we toss about, not knowing our outcome and fate.* Our body is disturbed, spun out of control, by external impressions, and in parallel agitation our thinking processes are caught and whirled round by forces beyond its own power. That our mind is in *bondage* does not stop it from expressing the destructive power that drives it. Positive internal, intellectual power is needed to rationalise or stabilise one's emotions. Spinoza's withering comments show that he did not think women possessed that necessary intellectual power.

We saw early on that since, for Spinoza, the mind was the idea of the body, in so far as a woman's body differed from a man's, to this extent the natural power of a woman's mind also differed. But, as we also know, Spinoza's theory of truth depends on his stricture that those ideas which all minds have in common reflect common elements in the bodies of which they are the ideas. *There are certain ideas, or notions, common to all men. For all bodies agree in certain things.* For Spinoza, the mental tool used to apprehend these general truths and their corollaries is reason, and agreement between human beings is possible only if reason is used. If, therefore, he denies that agreement through reason is in principle possible for women, his psychotherapeutic and social theories in *Ethics* Parts 3 and 4 become radically limited, his doctrine of human salvation or blessedness in *Ethics* Part 5 is for men only, and the social contract theory and argument for a universal religion of the *Theologico-Political Treatise*, which depends on agreement in all human minds, collapses. Spinoza did not intend this. When he claimed that *common notions* were notions common to all *men*, he meant by *men* people, not males. He would reiterate this in his later *Theologico-Political Treatise*:

In the previous Chapter we showed that the Divine law which makes men truly blessed, and teaches them true living, is common to all men: indeed we deduced it from human nature in such a way that it must be regarded as innate in the human mind and, so to speak, engraved upon it.

He equated *Divine law* with reason, cause, power, virtue, good, advantage and freedom. He said it governed all true thought, and that blessedness depended on grasping it. Blessedness was in principle accessible to all. Spinoza must therefore somehow show, in defiance of his epistemological principle, that a specifically female mentality, reflecting a specifically female physiology, denies women the power of reasoning conferred by a more general law of human nature. François Boulain de la Barre, whose 1676 *Woman as Good as the Man, or, The Equality of Both Sexes*, was quoted near the start of this book, denied the general belief of his day that woman was physically either an incomplete man or – according to a view that developed in the sixteenth century and prevailed until at least the nineteenth – a totally different creature from man, uncontrollably dominated by a tyrannical and vaporous uterus. To recall, de la Barre chided philosophers who failed to make a proper investigation of the differences between women and men: 'Very far from examining the capacity, and real and natural difference betwixt them, which is one of the most curious, and probably also the most important questions of all natural or moral philosophy', their principles were insufficient 'to discover which of the two sexes have (naturally) the advantage of the other'. De la Barre stressed that 'The knowledge of ourselves is absolutely necessary to enable us, for the handling of the question aright; and especially, the knowledge of our body, which is the organ of sciences.' Yet, despite de la Barre's belief that women profited from book-learning, there was a sting in his counsel that they should study:

A woman cannot learn true knowledge without becoming thereby more humble and virtuous: And there is nothing more proper to depress the vapours, and to convince her of her weakness, than to consider all the movements of her Engine, the delicateness of her organs, the (almost) infinite number of alterations, and painful failings, to which she is subject.

De la Barre thus seemed to approximate Spinoza's claim that women were radically and inevitably disadvantaged. However, he went on to argue that except in situations requiring brute strength, women were capable of holding almost any public post, 'and there can be nothing else but custom shown, which remove women therefrom . . . For my part, I should be no more surprised to see a woman with a helmet on her head, than to see her with a crown; preside in a council of warre, as well as with a council of State.' Spinoza, on the other hand, would insist to the end of his life that *I am fully entitled to assert that women have not the same right as men by nature, but are necessarily inferior to them.* He did not mean by *right* 'rights', which are man-made and socially bestowed, but *right* in his sense of *the right and law of nature.* It seems from this that women were, for him, doomed to mental bondage, and indeed he did not consider them suited to rule or to have social control of any kind. Hobbes had argued that women were disempowered by the actions of males rather than by nature, using as an example successful rule by the all-female warrior Amazons. Spinoza countered this by pointing out that the Amazons simply displayed their lack of reason and disdain for social harmony by killing the males born to them. More is said on Spinoza's view of political power relations between the sexes at the point in his life when he addressed the topic.

Spinoza's thesis that the mind is the idea of the body was in a crude sense supported by the popular study of the physiology of women of his day, which was of such major interest that it took prime place in many anatomy books. The view of Aristotle and Galen that all the generative parts of men were to be found in atrophied form in women, and the allied Judaeo-Christian view that women, being formed from Adam's rib, were deficient males, had been superseded following this surge in anatomical study by the view that women were not stunted versions of, but utterly dissimilar to, men. This advance in understanding did not alter the creed regularly voiced by philosophers during following centuries that women were 'by nature' inferior. Their inferiority was now thought due to 'hysteria', that is, the effects of the womb (*husterikos*) on health, sexuality, intelligence, appearance and social and moral behaviour. This thesis was, roughly, chemical, since it depended on the ancient theory of humours. Women, it was agreed, had cold, damp temperaments. The womb, an internal flower that never opened for want of sunlight, was a cold, damp field that could rot male seed (a belief that ensured there was no question of male infertility). Few physicians challenged the Hippocratic view that the uterus caused most diseases in women, and was also responsible for their naturally gullible, sensuous, talkative, frivolous and vindictive dispositions. Ugly women, especially those with moist flesh, narrow faces, small eyes and straight noses, were, it was suggested, most ruled by cold, wet humours, and were therefore likely to be sterile, malignant, unintelligent and in all ways suited to the practice of witchcraft. This general view (give or take differences of opinion on witches, especially in the Dutch Republic, which stopped executing witches around 1600) persisted well into the eighteenth century, and even then few physicians or philosophers argued with it. Diderot, for example, believed that 'the senses govern, not the mind. [Woman] contains within herself an indomitable organ, susceptible to terrible spasms . . . Her head continues to speak the language of her senses even when they are dead.'

Spinoza owned works on female physiology, including the *Anatomical Works* of Jean Riolan, physician to the Queen Mother of France. The works of Riolan (Riolanus) were in the seventeenth century standard textbooks: all six volumes were translated into English by Nicholas Culpeper. Riolan's drawings were meticulous, but it is as well that Spinoza did not build his thesis (as his medical friends might have wanted him to) on this expert's rather less than accurate gynaecological and generative theory:

> The menstruous blood, which being more than a woman needs for her nourishment, is ordained to nourish the child in the womb, and when it is born drops out of the dugs in the form of milk . . . 'Tis very strange that a child should be formed out of the cavity of the womb; and it favours the opinion of Paracelsus and Amatus Lucitanus, that a child may be made in a glass of a man's seed and menstrual blood, placed in Horse's Dung, unless both of them, the one being the atheist, the other a Jew, were known to be imposters.

Riolan took the relatively modern and controversial line that the woman was not just a fertile or barren nurturing-ground, but also had seed in her 'Spermatick vessels'. When this 'two-seed' theory was rebutted in 1672 by the Dutch physician Régnier De Graaf, who claimed that all animals, including man, grew from female eggs, there was male outrage. How could woman, physiologically and psychologically flawed, have been given this vital procreational role? The timely discovery by Huygens and Van Leeuwenhoek of male spermatozoa relieved masculine indignity by reaffirming women's secondary, passive function.

Spinoza took care not to let his theory of mind be trapped in contemporary empirical theory. *No one has yet determined what the body can do, i.e. experience has not yet taught anyone what the body can do from the laws of nature alone, in so far as nature is considered to be only corporeal, and what the body can do only if it is determined by the mind.* He was interested only in working from those laws of nature that could be taken as unarguably true – *common notions* governing all instances of a kind. Such notions were true for all time, and could reveal a degree of the truth of any particular state or event. According to Spinozistic principle, then, any claim about the nature of women must be derived from an axiom or *common notion*, and any claim made about women which could not be inferred from such a notion was suspect.

He could claim as a deduction from first principles only this: specific mental predispositions in women reflected specifically female body states. He could not validly assert that nature *necessarily* had not conferred on women the same fundamental capacity for reasoning as men. Nor could he easily show (though nothing rules this out) that *common notions* were more likely to be obliterated by ideas of imagination, opinion and passion in women's minds than in men's. That tendency was, also, common to all people. Anyone, Spinoza eventually admitted – and he may have taken *Ethics* out of its hiding place to make amendments accommodating this – anyone, however habitually guided by reason, and regardless of sex or education, might find their reasoning swayed by emotion. *No one is so vigilant that he does not nod sometimes; even the most resolute and upright of men falter on occasions, and allow themselves to be overcome by their passions, especially when strength of mind is needed most.* Recognising a common human nature for all individuals was a crucial and fruitful – perhaps the single most useful – Spinozistic *common notion*, and his denial of equal natural reasoning power to women would undermine his doctrine if his foundational tenets did not let us modify it to a claim that a woman's natural reasoning power was necessarily threatened by the affects she endured to a greater extent than a man's. This weaker claim, which, as De la Barre implies, gives women something sobering to think about, is consistent with Spinoza's general thesis, although he never explains why or how specifically female body states should be reflected in the female mind as irrationality. But validity is not truth. We seem left with cases of men ruled by passion and opinion who are, according to Spinoza's weaker thesis, *necessarily* more rational than any woman, and women who habitually reason but whose conclusions must be doubted because they fall under some sub-law of necessary weakening by emotion.

Spinoza gives no demonstration of his view of women's mentality in *Ethics*. He merely asserts that certain mental weaknesses are *womanly*. For example, he claims that any law against killing animals is *based more on empty superstition and womanly compassion than sound reason*. He was probably referring to the Jewish law which decrees that animals must be killed only for food, and then with humane ritual and prayer. However, one Spinoza scholar assumes Spinoza to mean that women actually are squeamish, and extrapolates from this opinion to Spinoza's view of women as being unfit to rule. If their *muliebri misericordia* stops them killing animals, this scholar argues, how much more must it stop them killing men in battle? While this suggestion follows logically, it does not question whether it is actually true that women dislike killing living things. The female battalions of 's-Hertogenbosch and Haarlem, the special fines for husband-beaters, the housewives crowding beside the gibbets and the lusty quayside disembowellers of still-flapping fish suggest the reverse. Spinoza also implies or asserts without evidence that women are more superstitious than men, and that partiality is likewise a notably womanish trait. Yet in *Ethics* Part 3, and in later writings, the superstition and bias that strangled the rational faculties of women could also grip males in insane passion. Spinoza would reproach the Catholic zealot Burgh for being mad with superstition: *When you were in your senses . . . Who has bewitched you . . . ?* Further, males are shown to be weakened by a humiliating affect traditionally associated with their gender. *Nor are they thought to be less mad who burn with Love, and dream, both day and night, only of a lover . . . Men generally judge* [women's] *ability and wisdom by their beauty.* Spinoza made men victims of female seduction. He claimed that women induced irrationality and distorted political decisions. *A king that is prey to lust often manages everything to suit the whim of some concubine . . .* Yet he used this male weakness as evidence for his view that women, not men, were unfit to rule!

Ethics Part 3 was intended to provide a critical analysis of the passions, conducted in the same way as God and the Mind had been treated in Parts 1 and 2, namely geometrical demonstration based on undeniable first principles. Any emotion, Spinoza said, was a variant of one of three primary affects, namely joy, sadness or desire. These were three of six affects acknowledged by Descartes as 'primitive passions'. They were, for him, true type-ideas in human minds, and therefore *common notions. Ethics* Part 3 began soundly enough in this respect, for the discussion of Joy, Sadness and Desire remained appropriately general to all humans until well after the notions of Love and Hate (respectively species of Joy or Sadness, each *with the accompanying idea of an external cause*) had been introduced. Then the affect of jealousy, *a vacillation of mind born of Love and Hatred together, accompanied by the idea of another who is envied,* was touched on. The proposal that hatred and jealousy are relative to our interest or advantage seems indisputable. *So each one, from his own affect, judges, or evaluates, what is good and what is bad . . . The greedy man judges an abundance of money best, and poverty worst . . . To the envious nothing is more agreeable than the other's unhappiness.* But most of the discussion centred on – became obsessed with – the special case of jealousy in close sexual relationships:

> *If someone imagines the thing that he loves is united with another by as close, or by a closer, bond of friendship than that with which he alone possessed the thing, he will be affected with hate towards the thing he loves, and will envy*

185

the other. Moreover, *he is forced to join the image of the thing he loves to the image of him he hates.*

The focus became narrower as Benedictus turned exclusively to the passions and imaginings of males as directed on women, and detailed intensity began to take over the demonstration:

> *The latter reason is found, for the most part, in love towards a woman. For he who imagines that a woman he loves prostitutes herself to another will not only be saddened, because his own appetite is restrained, but also will be repelled by her, because he is forced to join the image of the thing he loves to the shameful parts and excretions of the other. To this, finally, is added the fact that she no longer receives the jealous man with the same countenance as she used to offer him.*

Propositions 31–9 of *Ethics* Part 3 need to be read in sequence if the muted howl of anguish which forms a subtext to the demonstration is to be clearly heard. It is not necessary to read them, however, to empathise with the final desolation of the man gripped by sexual jealousy and hatred. *If someone begins to hate a thing he loves, more of his appetites will be restrained than if he had not loved it.* Is this self-evident? Or only true in some cases? It certainly seems to have been the case that *for Benedictus* the appetite for women – so unsettlingly beautiful and desirable that they sent reason to the winds – entailed jealousy, hatred and finally disgust. *Love of a harlot [meretricius] moreover, i.e. a lust to procreate that arises from external appearance . . . easily passes into hate.* The prospect of sexual love in marriage elicited, as we saw earlier, all the pedantry of St Paul.

It is not possible to accept these views as conceived under an aspect of eternity. The inevitable alternative is, in Spinoza's own terms, that they were conceived under an aspect of duration, as *related to the singular mind of someone.* Was sexual jealousy, mingled with hatred, disgust and the implied presence of an *other,* a living issue for Spinoza around 1663–5? Only one woman has been romantically associated with Spinoza (although there may have been others in the Jewish community, or among the many Quakers and Collegiants of Amsterdam and Rijnsburg when he met when still in his twenties). Colerus reports that Kerckring also found Clara Maria attractive, but 'did soon perceive that he had a rival, and grew jealous of him. This moved him to redouble his care and his attendance, which he did with good success.' Kerckring did, in fact, marry Clara Maria van den Enden, in 1671. If we could prove that there was rivalry over Clara Maria in the mid-1660s, when the passages on sexual jealousy were evidently written – they are too diffused and too integral to the argument of *Ethics* Part 3 to have been added later – we could fix on a prime cause of the pain and misogyny that lodged terminally in Spinoza's mind about that time. Available scraps of information provide grounds for inclining both towards, and away, from that hypothesis.

Pointers towards early rivalry between Benedictus and Theodor over Clara Maria start with Colerus's description of Theodor as 'another scholar of Van den Ende . . . a native of Hamburg', inaccurate hearsay, but more descriptive of the schoolboy than the Amsterdam physician who eventually married Frans's daughter. We know, too, that Kerckring had wealthy parents living on the Keizersgracht, and had by 1661 made his professional mark at Leiden. Nothing would have prevented him from courting Clara Maria in grand style while in his twenties. Colerus reports that 'a necklace of pearls, of the value of two or three hundred pistoles, which he had *before* [my emphasis] presented to that young woman, did without doubt contribute to win her affection'. If Benedictus thought he had lost the girl he loved to another because her affections had been purchased, bitterness would be understandable. *He who imagines that a woman he loves prostitutes herself* . . . We have seen him reported as saying that 'if he received so much money it would infallibly divert him from his studies and occupations'. He might have feared competitive spending in relation to a woman, if not this woman. Sexual jealousy could have been aroused, too, by Kerckring's escalating interest in gynaecology. His praised *Observationes* would include microscope revelations about female genitalia amid its copious anecdotal information on aberrations in female anatomy. There is also the matter of the Lutheran Kerckring's sudden conversion to Catholicism. If Benedictus had thought he could persuade Van Blijenbergh out of his superstition, how much more must he have believed that reason would prevail with Kerckring and Clara Maria, two of the brightest intellects of Van den Enden's school? It is tempting, for want of documented opinion from Spinoza on Clara Maria, to see her through his eyes as Descartes saw his brilliant pupil Anna Maria van Schurman:

Voetius [Descartes's fierce opponent at Utrecht] has spoilt Mlle de Schurman: she had excellent gifts for poetry, painting and other gentle arts, but these last five or six years he has taken her over so completely that she cares for nothing but theological controversies, and this has made all decent people shun her.

That was in 1640. Since then Van Schurman had left behind her not only those 'gentle arts' but her expertise in Hebrew, Latin, Greek, Arabic and Syriac. All were dropped when, in her fifties, she joined the commune of the mystic preacher Jean de Labadie, who had introduced Van Beuningen to the Collegiants. Van Schurman had written that, 'It was excellently said . . . that Philosophy seeks Truth; Theology finds it; Religion possesseth it.' That view would persist. The most inspirational blue-stocking of her day would in 1673 expound in her philosophical *Eukleria* only the mystical version of Christian Neoplatonism in which she had for the past few years been instructed by De Labadie. Benedictus's jaundiced views on female rationality may have hardened on hearing how these two women, having sufficient analytical talent to use tools of reason when reflecting on God, should prefer to hover, like moths, in a light cast not by God through the laws of nature, but by human beings through imagination.

Did Clara Maria taint Kerckring with her mental confusion? There may have been no cause to envy or pity Theodor Kerckring in the mid-1660s. Although no date can be put on his conversion, it may have come about suddenly around the time of the marriage, long after the passages on sexual jealousy, which seem so painfully personal, were written. Only five months before the wedding Kerckring had signed a legally binding mutual deed of gift with a man named until now Pieter 'Hauthum' and considered totally mysterious. Records show, however, that Kerckring's father's sister Cornelia married a merchant named Pieter Hunthum in 1633. This Pieter Hunthum died in 1652. However, a second Pieter Hunthum is shown in Amsterdam marriage records to have been born in 1640, and his signature there matches that on the Kerckring-'Hauthum' affidavit. Since the name Hunthum, or Honthom, was rare in Amsterdam, it seems the pact was made between cousins. The 1670 deed states that the sum of 6,000 guilders would be paid to the survivor from the estate of whichever of them died, still a bachelor. Even if the agreement was made through self-interest on Kerckring's part (meaning that he intended to marry, and knew Pieter Hunthum did not, or suspected that Hunthum was seriously ill and would die before him), we have to conclude that Theodor spent the latter years of the 1660s in a relationship close enough for such a commitment to be made. Nothing suggests the friendship was homosexual: Hunthum also married in 1671, on 17 July, and fathered two children, who died in 1679 and 1681. But it may have been: Kerckring was described as an obsessionally committed research physician, whose commitment to the 27-year-old Clara Maria was made unexpectedly and, in the opinion of the poet who wrote the wedding oration, without passion.

Yet, if we are not deluded in seeing personal involvement in the excessive attention to the topic of sexual jealousy in *Ethics* Part 3, there was some significant *other*.

Spinoza believed he had dealt satisfactorily with the topic of male desire and jealousy, and had shown that a proper operation of the principles expounded in *Ethics* Parts 3 and 4 (that is, an examining of distressing mental states in relation to *common notions* governing the primary affects of joy, sadness or desire) should free any mind from the bondage of the emotions. *The more an affect is known to us, the more it is in our power . . . There is no affect of which we cannot form some clear and distinct concept.* In principle this foundational concept applied as well to women as to men. They, too, should be able to deal with their emotions through reason. But the tension between women as Spinoza experienced them – seductive, deceitful and maddening – and women viewed dispassionately as partakers in a common rational human mentality remained because, I think, he did not and could not examine *all* his thoughts. Way back in the chain of impressions and opinions which formed his judgements about women were thoughts he did not bring to the light of reason – unconscious thoughts he did not know he had. He saw clearly enough that a person might commit suicide because their mind was shackled by external pressures that crippled their power to reason. But he could not see the hidden mental causes of his misogyny.

No life is rational without understanding. The final Parts of *Ethics* consisted of necessary truths deduced from Propositions in earlier Parts concerning the way we should naturally – that is, in accordance with the most obviously true principles of human nature – live. Benedictus, perhaps not registering that to make proper use of these practical principles one must have passed satisfactorily through the self-analytical processes of *Ethics* Part 3, was convinced that his geometrical demonstration was fully concatenated, coherent and true. *For I do not presume that I have found the best philosophy, but I know that what I understand is the true one.* He may have wanted his ideas put to immediate use in the divided, hating, dying populace around him, and when *Ethics* Part 3 was finished he needed the three Parts translated into Dutch for that reason. At the end of *Ethics* Part 2 he had written, *This doctrine contributes to social life.* It would be no novelty to put geometrical deductions to the service of the community. Some of the most versatile mathematicians of the day, Hudde, Huygens and De Witt, were out there routinely demonstrating that mathematical solutions were true and in practice reliable. Benedictus, believing that humankind's blessedness lay solely in the applied conclusions of mathematical deduction in every possible arena of perception, including that sphere of mental activity we call the moral, longed to have such influence.

However, Hudde and De Witt did not try to marry the concepts of mathematics and ethics in the extraordinary manner that characterises Spinozism. Hudde, we know, backed away from Benedictus's arguments for

God, or Nature, although the question of a proof for God's uniqueness would bother him for life. De Witt had no interest in alternative naturalistic or humanist doctrines, or in logico-mathematical metaphysics. He was, as we have seen, a conventional Christian, and deviated from its orthodoxies only in his disgust at the failure of its pastors to implement Christ's principles of compassion and forbearance. That very year he wrote despairingly that the lack of mercy and sensitivity in his country would eventually lead to God withdrawing his grace from it. He did not condone dissident views which expressed hatred for Reformed Church leaders or preachers, since this constituted in itself disturbance of the peace. He would give the nod to a ban passed by Synod on Van den Hove's 1669 *Indication of the Salutary Political Foundations and Maxims of the Republic of Holland and West Friesland*, just because Pieter had reinserted the offensive passages he himself had deleted in 1661. In sum, while he may not have seen the fallacy in logic of *ad hominem* arguments, he recognised their counterproductivity.

This much Benedictus grasped about the Grand Pensionary's cast of mind. But his hope that De Witt would champion an iconoclastic philosophy whose underlying principles made institutionalised Christianity mere superstition was misplaced. De Witt disapproved of bigots, not of Christian fundamentalism. His focus of objection was the predicants, the parish preachers who (described by De Witt's prime biographer as under-educated, intransigent, pugnacious and generally socially slighted) saw Reformed religion as the only truth. 'Not the slightest change can be permitted in [this] religion, nor another tolerated alongside it,' wrote one of them in fury at Van den Hove's 1669 publication. 'It underpins civil society.' But De Witt also had personal reasons for disallowing abuse of individual predicants. They wielded precisely the power that could displace him. While preaching a kind of democracy based on the rightful inheritance of the earth by the poor, they detested the regents, defended the rights of kings and were to a man Orangist. They did not accept De Witt's authority and he, in turn, despairing of reasoning with them, sought to minimise their rabble-rousing effect on the masses by keeping a distance from them but seeming to acquiesce with their trivial complaints. It was all that De Witt, considered by some a devilish force, could do to silence them over his toleration of Cartesian teaching. He would not be advocating anything that might shatter his fragile concord with them, especially at this time, when he clearly doubted whether God was blessing his endeavours in the North Sea.

On 5 October 1665, while De Witt was at Goeree watching with increasing misgiving the winds turn against the Dutch, Jan Casearius took his preacher's examination before the ecclesiastical board of Amsterdam. This final commitment must have dismayed Benedictus, who had hoped that reason and maturity would dispel it. What could a brilliantly gifted scholar expect from such a post? Popular respect? *The ministries of the Church are regarded by the masses merely as dignities, her offices as posts of emolument . . . The spread of this misconception inflamed every worthless fellow with an intense desire to enter holy orders.* Jan's ordination was, in fact, a calamity from all viewpoints, not just Spinoza's. He had already been refused a degree in theology from Utrecht, so any hope of scholastic advancement was blocked. The Reformed Church received him grudgingly. The examining board reprimanded him for neglecting orthodox texts and debarred him, as a 'Spinozist', from taking up a living in the Republic. This may have come as a shock to Benedictus who, while deploring Jan's decision, wanted neither persecution for his pupil nor a blackening of the doctrine which, it now seemed, had after all provoked independent thought in the boy.

Something in the philosopher's resolve now shifted. In what appears, after examining all possible chronicles, to have been a watershed period in Spinoza's life, the fear and the crawling, the belief that he could win approval through outward conformity, were overthrown. The scandal of the Voorburg predicant, the gradual dropping away of former admirers, the shackled minds of Casier and Van Blijenbergh, the chilling portent from the Reformed Church Council of Amsterdam and, possibly, a perception that love was conditional on conversion to Catholicism, brought a crisis which caution could no longer counterbalance. He told Henry:

> *I am now writing a treatise on my views regarding Scripture. The reasons that move me to do so are these:*
> *1 The prejudices of theologians. For I know that these are the main obstacles that prevent men from giving their minds to philosophy. So I apply myself to exposing such prejudices and removing them from the minds of sensible people.*
> *2 The opinion of me held by the common people, who constantly accuse me of atheism. I am driven to avert this accusation, too, as far as I can.*
> *3 The freedom to philosophise and to say what we think. This I want to vindicate completely, for here it is in every way suppressed by the excessive authority and egotism of preachers.*

Was this plan rational? Or did the frustration observed in March by Van Blijenbergh make him see these reasons – all external events acting sorely upon him – as *Reason?*

Spinoza did not embark on his new philosophical enterprise from a position of strength. He had no steadfast patron but Jarig, no ready-made readership, no strongly supportive students of impressive social standing to guarantee it a benign reception. The power of Benedictus's intellect was as yet questioned by no one – that would not be the case towards the end of his life – but his doctrine was either generally disliked and rejected (this has already been made plain, and will be made plainer, in the writings of almost all those taken in the past to have been his disciples) or it was a thesis to be secretly approved, perhaps animatedly discussed, but never publicly acknowledged. Probably, the superficial compliments he received from acquaintances such as Kerckring told him very little. Other compliments were certainly empty. Henry Oldenburg, for example, who had urged him for the past four years to let nothing stop him disseminating his philosophy, privately seemed to find his present project a matter for laughter behind his hand. That same October of 1665 he wrote to Sir Robert Moray about the 'odd philosopher that lives in Holland, but no Hollander', and, despite realising the confidential nature of what Benedictus had told him, copied out the philosopher's plan, word for word, for the eyes of the Protestant fanatic Boyle, adding in a following letter:

Sgr Spinosa, who is very much your servant, entertains me with a discourse of his, concerning the agreement and coherence of the parts of the world with the whole; which is not unphilosophical, in my opinion, though it would perhaps be tedious to you, to have a letter filled with it; and this makes me forbeare to send it to you.

EIGHT

Voorburg: 1666–9

Faith has become a mere compound of credulity and prejudices – aye, prejudices, too, which degrade man from rational being to beast, which completely stifle the power of judgement between the true and the false, which seem, in fact, carefully fostered for the purpose of extinguishing the last spark of reason!

Spinoza had demonstrated in *Ethics* Part 4 the principles governing the content of the *Theologico-Political Treatise*. There he had argued without reference to any particular case (as was demanded by his doctrine of *common notions*) that reason was active and universal, but that particular instances of emotion and imagining were passive and *singular*, therefore only commonly held, reasoned ideas could unite. The triumph of the geometrical demonstration had been its concatenation of universal applicable principles, which constituted a framework for further philosophical inference. If you accepted those principles and reasoned from them, you could see for yourself what must follow. You could construct conditional *a priori* claims which governed conclusions further down that train of thought. If, for example, all human minds necessarily functioned within nature, then no human mind could furnish divinations or prophecies through some non-natural power. Self-evident principles could elicit agreement in cases of prejudiced or impassioned judgement. *Anyone who wishes to make men believe or dissent anything which is not self-evident must win their assent by deducing his doctrine from common ground.* In 1665 *Ethics* could have been amplified to include a fuller geometrical exposition of Spinozistic social and political principles than was eventually included. This could have formed a new Part, perhaps called 'Of Society'.

Arguably, then, Spinoza need not have meddled directly in the hornet's nest of what he called the *despotic statecraft* of the Dutch Reformed Church in order to expose its intolerance, any more than he need anticipate particular twentieth-century social and moral dilemmas for his *Ethics* doctrines to have relevance to them. Arguably, too, he chose a title fated to confuse, for his aim was to bring about the sundering of theology and

193

politics. My view is that Spinoza's strength as a philosopher lay in his skill as a rationalist metaphysician. It was to metaphysics that he always made first and final appeal. *The necessity of things touches metaphysics, the knowledge of which must always come first.* Each argument in the *Theologico-Politica(Treatise* was submitted to those first principles or laws of Nature. When, much later, he wrote his *Political Treatise* (not to be confused with the *Theologico-Political Treatise*) he restated those principles as *particularly relevant to the present treatise.*

Moreover, Spinoza considered history to be shaky ground on which to establish principles. *Belief in historical narratives, however well-grounded, cannot give us knowledge of God, and hence cannot give us love for him, either.* Perhaps, then, his decision to compare the ancient Israelite and modern Dutch states – two particular local phenomena – was neither entirely rational nor in accord with his own most effective natural power. It so thoroughly defied the scruples of De Witt that when in 1670 the Synod of North Holland made the first of many petitions from all provinces for a ban on the newly published *Theologico-Political Treatise*, the Grand Pensionary made no effort to protect it. While Spinoza's theories of social contract and the political obligation of the individual add footnotes to political theory on human rights, they may have been read more outside the Dutch Republic than within it.

Why did he sit up deep into each night, bibles in Hebrew, Greek, Latin and Spanish before him; his old Chaldean, Talmudic and Rabbinic commentaries piled alongside, and the writings of Jewish philosophers – perhaps hardly glanced at since his days at *Keter Torah* – to hand? His overt motivation is clear. He sought the right of the individual to express beliefs freely. This right, which he had earlier vainly sought from Jewish community leaders, could only be guaranteed, he argued, by giving secular government the charge of religious affairs. The points he made to Oldenburg (and to Van Blijenbergh in person) show his conviction that muted dissent on the part of individuals, and *laissez-faire* attitudes on the part of magistrates, did not add up to 'true freedom'. The Republic's famed religious toleration fell apart when confronted with open, articulate dissent. He wrote in the Preface:

> *Seeing that we have the rare happiness of living in a republic, where everyone's judgement is free and unshackled, and where each may worship God as his conscience dictates, and where freedom is esteemed before all things dear and precious, I have believed that I should be undertaking no ungrateful or unprofitable task, in demonstrating that not only can such freedom [freedom to philosophise] be granted without prejudice to [piety and] the public peace, but*

also, that without such freedom, piety cannot flourish nor the public peace be secure.

His commitment to *demonstrating* was a measure of his fear that his thesis would fail if insufficiently closely argued. Yet a fear that neither reason nor awesome biblical scholarship would succeed in cutting through his readers' religious conditioning is indicated by his calculated use of familiar Christian quotations. On the title-page, for example, he inscribed

John, Epistle I, Chapter IV, verse XIII
Hereby we learn that we abide in God, and he in us,
because he hath given us of his spirit.

In a further attempt to soften readers into acquiescence, he would advise that although religious precepts had no place in a discourse of reason, they were legitimate notions within their own sphere, since *theology is not bound to serve reason*. He also stressed the open-handedness with which he would approach scripture. *I determined to examine the Bible afresh in a careful, impartial and unfettered spirit, making no assumptions concerning it.*

However, few readers doubted that the treatise set out to undermine the foundations of faith; that its author had long accorded the Bible the status of folklore, and that he resorted to equivocation and irony when discussing sacred Jewish and Christian texts in order to manipulate orthodox beliefs. The title-page quotation was a case in point: when re-read to tally with Spinoza's doctrine that *Whatever is, is in God, and nothing can or be conceived without God*, St John's words were clearly seen by all to have been outrageously distorted. An English critic, while considering the author 'very well versed in the writings of Moses and the Prophets', rightly accused him of '*leger de main*'. Spinoza himself would point out in Chapter XIV that any sectarian could confirm his articles of faith from scripture: *This is why 'geen ketter zonder letter'* ['no heretic without a text'] *has long since become proverbial among the Dutch.* Shakespeare had gone further: 'The devil can cite Scripture to his purpose.' And that was the real fear of many, such as Pastor Colerus, Spinoza's biographer, who eventually vilified the book:

If what Spinosa affirms were true, one might indeed very well say that the Bible is a Wax-Nose, which may be turned and shaped at everyone's will; a glass through which everybody may exactly see what pleases his fancy; a Fool's Cap, which may be turned and fitted at one's pleasure a hundred several ways. The Lord confound thee, Satan, and stop thy mouth!

In the more measured view of one of Spinoza's liberal critics, Philips van

195

Limborch, by then professor at a Remonstrant college in Amsterdam, the *Theologico-Political Treatise*'s author 'teaches atheism cleverly and in disguised words. Certainly he frequently uses the names God, power, knowledge and divine will, but these are only words.' Another relatively free-minded physician from Utrecht wrote that despite his 'close examination of the controversies among Christians in Europe', its author 'thoroughly subverts all worship and religion, and prompts atheism by stealth'.

Was such a book likely either to further a good reception for *Ethics*, or to have been truly the result of rational, or *legitimate* self-esteem? On the first count, we shall see that although the *Theologico-Political Treatise* did not bear Spinoza's name, its reception prevented him from publishing anything more in his lifetime. On the second, we saw him complaining to Henry that he was *driven to* write this *Treatise* by the behaviour of others. External constraints do not engender, by Spinozistic definition, rational self-esteem, and on the basis of past behaviour and contemporary events I think we can discern a push to write the *Treatise* from an irrational form of pride. The work was riddled with snide attacks and occasionally showed fury: passion was implicit in the book and it excited passion in its readers. To compose a *Theologico-Political Treatise* at all was to enter the lists of political agitators, for it would challenge not only Church authorities and zealots, but the most peaceable-minded of church-goers. As the English diplomat Sir William Temple observed, and Johan de Witt was wearily aware, the Dutch were 'generally so bred up to the Bible that almost every cobbler is a Dutch doctor of divinity'. But Benedictus cannot have acknowledged either his own passion or the potential of his book to rouse it, for he would both open and conclude the *Theologico-Political Treatise* with words that, given what lay between them, seem curiously naïve:

> *[My treatise] contains nothing which I would not willingly submit to the examination and judgement of my country's rulers. If anything I have written is in their judgement contrary to my country's laws or detrimental to the general welfare I am ready to retract it. I know that, being human, I may have made errors; but I have taken great pains to avoid error, and, above all, to see that everything I wrote should be in complete accord with my country's laws, with piety, and with sound morals.*

Had Spinoza's thesis been in accord with the Republic's laws and its conception of piety it would have been redundant. Instead, at each cutting of his quill, he guaranteed offence.

What allowed him to deceive himself to the extent of completing and publishing this book without going through the editing process to which he had half-willingly submitted *Descartes's Principles*? He may have thought he had satisfied the condition Henry Oldenburg set him on hearing of the intended project. Henry had advised that if his treatise did not threaten the existence and providence of God all would be well, that true religion would remain unassailed and philosophical reflections could be excused. However, Benedictus could also have been motivated to ignore this advice and express his contentious doctrine as freely and as precisely as he could. Still sensitive to the achievements of others and to his standing in relation to them, he may around 1665–6 not only have felt pressurised by the tittle-tattle of the neighbours and the increasing enmity of preachers and university theologians, but also by the recent intrepid actions of some of his free-thinking friends in Amsterdam in writing treatises for publication on the very same issues that engrossed him. Van den Enden's Dutch-language *Vrye Politijke Stellingen*, with its cry for fresh political vision and a dispelling of sectarian and social prejudice, was now selling so well that a second print-run was needed in 1665. (The Mennonite Press of Pieter Arentzoon was not, however, re-used.) Meyer, too, was publishing a treatise, called *Philosophiae Sacrae Scripturae Interpres* (*Philosophy as the Expositor of Holy Scripture*). His account of how sacred scripture should be interpreted was given in the philologist's habitual cool classificatory fashion, and since it made no remotely blasphemous or *ad hominem* attacks, kept away from (almost) anything that could have connected its author with Spinoza, and appealed here and there to scholastic platitudes, it gave a superficial impression of political correctness. In its Dutch edition it would lull Dutch readers with examples taken from Vondel, Hooft and Constantijn Huygens. Yet its argument, once grasped, was devastating, for Meyer argued that philosophy – reason – alone was capable of interpreting scripture. This thesis not only undermined at a stroke all ancient and orthodox exegetical authority but, one commentator suggests, 'poses the question, if everything one reads in the bible is in philosophy, what purpose does the bible serve?' The theology faculty of Leiden university would soon send a formal complaint to the States of Holland about it, and many Cartesians would also feel compelled to dissociate themselves from the treatise. It was published anonymously, and this undoubtedly saved Meyer a summons from the *Kerkeraad*, but it was generally attributed to him at the time.

In the Epilogue of *Philosophiae S. Scripturae Interpres* Meyer referred, following a tribute to Descartes, to a forthcoming philosophical writing 'on God, on the rational soul, on the supreme happiness of man, and the means of achieving eternal life, pages which will be authorised by the interpretation of sacred scripture'. It would also contain plans for unifying 'the Church of Christ, which is divided by continuous schisms'. If this comment was meant to refer to Spinoza's work it does not obviously signify any one particular text but, as the scholar quoted above suggests, seems to hark back to the early *Short Treatise*.

What did Benedictus think of Meyer's book? The physician was an elegant wordsmith and an accomplished critic, and his editorial judgement had largely been deferred to over *Descartes's Principles*. But Meyer avoided (and was perhaps not capable of) creative metaphysics, innovative philosophy or skilled scriptural exegesis. Spinoza would, on the other hand, in his *Theologico-Political Treatise*, sweep aside all earlier inspiration, return to the grounding of all truth in the laws of nature, and flaunt his knowledge of biblical history and Hebrew philology. (Years later he would write what he claimed to be a uniquely explanatory *Hebrew Grammar*.) He probably thought himself the author *par excellence* of any *philosophiae sacrae scripturae interpres*, and may have been needled into bettering Meyer's instruction. One chapter of the *Theologico-Political Treatise* (Chapter VII, *De interpretatione Scripturae*) reflected Meyer's title, but in it Spinoza used his detailed knowledge of biblical history and the Hebrew language to show that we precisely cannot – in contrast to Meyer's claim – know whether what scripture teaches is true or not, because reason and revelation are incompatible. *Scripture very often treats of matters which cannot be deduced from principles known to reason: for it is chiefly made up of narratives and revelation.* Language changes, and the 'facts' of the bible do not add up. Readers were led to a radically different conclusion from Meyer's, namely that scripture cannot be rescued by reason, so that in reorganising Meyer's work Benedictus in a sense refuted it.

As we know, Spinoza was not in the habit of flattering anyone on their philosophising. Most correspondents were ruthlessly lectured on their misguided opinions and given instant alternative doctrines, which were outlined laconically, as if their thrust were evident to anyone but a fool. This tendency would intensify with age, notwithstanding the celebrity of some of his later correspondents. He had since 1661 made copies of his letters – an activity not associated with lacking a sense of one's own distinction. He never admitted he was wrong, or apologised; very rarely asked for advice; and did not consider he was intellectually indebted to earlier philosophers. (Meyer's scholarly commentator believes that the physician's *Interpres* is essential reading in connection with the *Theologico-Political Treatise* since it cites by name the authors in Spinoza's library who are never credited!) Descartes, who in truth had little input in this thesis, which denied faith, miracles, revelation and free will, but immersed itself in politics, would scarcely be acknowledged. Nor, considerably less justifiably, would Hobbes, apart from a Note to Chapter XVI, the chapter in which Spinoza most obviously drew on the Englishman's theory of the development of a commonwealth from a state of nature. The Van den Hove brothers would receive no plaudit until the later *Political Treatise*, where reference was made to *that shrewd Dutchman V.H.* Professors Geulincx and De Raey were never mentioned. Was Benedictus aware that Geulincx, well known to Meyer and said to have influenced him, had written the first part of a treatise called *Ethics*, which made love of reason and love of God (whose divine law was expressed in reason) central? This *Ethics* was posthumously published in 1675, two years before Spinoza's. Spinoza may not have deliberately hijacked the title '*Ethics*', any more than Geulincx would knowingly have used the name of a work that would undoubtedly be condemned. Yet, since Geulincx also wrote *De Deo, Anima rationali, summa hominis felicitate*, and had suffered religious persecution, we may wonder whether Meyer had Geulincx's work in mind in his Epilogue, rather than Spinoza's.

Van den Enden's model state, grounded in natural law, also seems to be debated in the *Theologico-Political Treatise* and rejected, again with no reference to its architect. Spinoza's thesis in Chapter XVI on the requirement for reason to prevail over natural right if there is to be agreement in society appears to contradict both Hobbes and Van den Enden on *how* agreement can be reached between individuals in a community. But Van den Enden's cry for the people's voice to be heard is expressed in Chapter XX – '*That in a free state everyone may think what he pleases, and say what he thinks.*' As a translator points out, this chapter is written in the same spirit as the declaration of the States General in 1587 that 'the late Prince of Orange and the States General had always . . . respected the difference in religious opinions'. This was the declaration printed under Van den Enden's name in 1650. Spinoza therefore endorsed Van den Enden's view that the State should respect, on the basis of a scientific understanding of the laws of nature, the rights of individuals with regard to freedom of thought and worship, and that in so doing the State conformed with God's guidance. *By the guidance of God, I mean the fixed and immutable order of Nature or the coherent system of natural things.* But he did not associate his plea to his country's rulers with the polemic of Frans van den Enden.

Adriaan Koerbagh, the Amsterdam physician now also qualified as a lawyer, published in 1664 a legal 'dictionary' using popular Dutch terminology. The book was blatantly geared to giving common people a greater understanding of, and thus a chance to stand up to, the legal system, but it drew no condemnation. However, in June 1666 Adriaan and his brother Johannes, predicant and doctor of theology, were summoned before the *Kerkeraad*, accused of 'very heretical and unwholesome ideas', and subsequently recalled to be excommunicated, the former predominantly for

199

his 'shameful and debauched lifestyle' – he was living with a mistress and child – the latter for preaching against Church doctrine. At this stage no connection was made with Spinoza, and the *Kerkeraad* seems to have been unaware that Koerbagh was composing a similar *woordenboek* to help ordinary people with their theology. Spinoza's opinion of Koerbagh's books is not preserved, and no copy of them or of Meyer's 1666 treatise is found in Spinoza's library. (The 'five little packets' listed at the end of the first inventory of Spinoza's books probably contained pamphlets, but could hardly have accommodated Meyer's bulky work.) Spinoza may have known that Koerbagh intended to write on the metaphysical questions they had all discussed, and we may assume he thought the lawyer's work must be less instructive than his *Ethics*. It is therefore possible that news of Koerbagh's enterprise also fed his desire to get this into a public arena.

Neither Benedictus's decision to write for publication, nor his reluctance to credit other thinkers, was based on envy as he defined it. *Envy is nothing but Hate, in so far as it is considered so to dispose a man that he is glad at another's ill fortune and saddened by his good fortune.* But he was a writer, and his friends were publishing, and on issues that had a decade earlier moved him deeply enough to make him sacrifice his family and livelihood. He wanted confirmation of his doctrine, but – following, perhaps, the unrewarding outcome of publishing *Descartes's Principles* in Dutch – he was more sure than ever that he was not going to target ordinary-language readers. Instead, he wanted to plug a lacuna in intellectual discourse:

> *Such, Philosophical Reader, are the questions I submit to your notice, counting on your approval . . . To the rest of mankind I care not to commend my treatise, for I cannot expect that it contains anything to please them: I know how deeply rooted are the prejudices embraced under the name of religion; I am aware that in the minds of the masses superstition is no less deeply rooted than fear . . . they are led to praise or blame by impulse rather than reason.*

Spinoza would so amply fill the gap in political theory that the aged Hobbes, asked to give the Duke of Devonshire his opinion on it, honoured the slightly-built little philosopher with an analogy from the sport of cabre-tossing. Spinoza had, he said, 'out throwne him a barres length, for he durst not write so boldly'.

Spinoza's 'political works' of 1670 and 1677 are most often compared, as a unit, with Hobbes's *De Cive*, Macchiavelli's *The Prince*, Jan van den Hove's *Politycke Weegschaal* and his brother Pieter's *Political Discourses*, and, in tandem with the work of these brothers, with Hobbes's *Leviathan*, on whose English text Jan van den Hove had drawn. This approach puts Spinoza's political thought in the context of the history of political theory. A biographer's central concern, however, is to consider each single work as a creative act arising from the development of a mind within a specific personal, social and political setting. On this view there is no place for including in a discussion of a book conceived in 1665-9 a political thesis composed almost a decade later, under very different circumstances. We stay, therefore, with the disturbing events of the late 1660s, which precipitated the mounting pile of notebooks, filled with that close-lined, rounded script, accumulating in Voorburg.

We are left in no doubt that during the years following the postponement of the publication of the first drafts of *Ethics*, Benedictus – we are drawing to the end of the stage when it is appropriate to use that name – was preparing openly to defy the tyranny of Jewish and Christian religious authorities. This tyranny, alone, was his target in the *Theologico-Political Treatise*, and his self-assurance on the issue was total. An admitted lack of expertise in Greek did not stop him from pointing out the mistakes of apostles and Popes; indeed, in Chapter IV he came close to correcting Jesus as he re-interpreted some of the more inconvenient utterances of that founder of the Christian faith. Spinoza's own view was that *the sole aim of philosophy is truth: the sole aim of faith obedience and piety, as I have abundantly shown. Moreover, philosophy is built on common notions, and must be built on the study of nature alone; whereas faith is based on history and language, and must be derived only from scripture and revelation.* Yet in Chapter IV he explained away Jesus's requirement of faith (*He obviously means no more than full assent of the mind*); his talking in parables (*Doubtless to those who were capable of understanding the mysteries of heaven he taught things as eternal truths*); and his appearing *to have written laws in God's name* on the basis of revelation (*For God made revelations to mankind through the mind of Christ as he had previously done through angels*) as no ordinary revelation, because *Christ perceived, truly and adequately what was revealed to him.* Christ's aberration in *ascribing such qualities as mercy, grace and anger to God* was put down to *adapting his words to the nature of the masses. The stupidity of the masses, and their failure to think, is the only reason why God is described as a legislator or king, and called just, merciful and so on.* These misrepresentations were used as premises for his conclusion to Chapter IV, namely that *Scripture entirely confirms the light of nature and the natural divine law.* The insincerity of these passages (as I read them, and as Spinoza's later statements on Christianity confirm them to be) was geared to weaning readers away from the *external* dogma disseminated from the pulpit and towards *true piety*. It does not nullify the genuine respect Spinoza always had for Jesus and what he took to be Jesus's foundational principles.

But as a tactical ploy it failed (as the display of scriptural quotation exegesis that Jarig Jelles included in his Preface to Spinoza's *Posthumous Works* would fail) to persuade the orthodoxly committed that this author did not, in fact, teach atheism. Criticism of the ancient Jewish State also badly backfired. The obsessional interest of Protestant Europe in biblical history and modern Jewish affairs meant that from the very first chapters (*Of Prophecy, Of Prophets, Of the Vocation of the Hebrews*) onward, Spinoza's writing had the potential for creating widespread disharmony in all quarters. For the history of the ancient Hebrews was inextricable from the Calvinist foundation of the Dutch Republic. The ultra-orthodox appealed as vociferously as did free-thinkers to the crusade of Willem the Silent, since, stimulated by Willem's stand against the Catholicism of Philip of Spain, the Dutch Reformed Church had developed alongside the nation's struggle for independence and had come to represent a struggle for national freedom. Its grounding in biblical history was reflected in popular paintings, in Christian names and in commonplace allusions. Willem himself had been known as 'our Moses'. In 1651 Cats had opened a session of the States General with the words, 'Ye Children of Israel'. To attempt to discredit the Republic's self-image as a people led out of the wilderness of Catholic repression by a divinely inspired leader – subtly mingled as this was with a Calvinist reading of predestination and election, prophecy, miracles and a specifically Orangist republic – by pointing out that the foundation of the Jewish State was a matter of practical necessity rather than intrinsic holiness, was to court hostility.

Modern Jewish affairs were also inextricably intertwined with Christian 'millenarianism' – the belief that since the great flood occurred 1,656 years after the Creation, a Second Coming or some other world crisis was to be expected at a point 1656 years after the birth of Jesus. Speculation on the form this great event would take varied from the astrology-based belief that the planetary system was running down and might shortly change form or disintegrate, to a conviction that the prophecies of Daniel and Revelation pointed to an imminent Day of Judgement. The urgency of the Quaker mission to convert the Jews had been tied to the Christian belief that there could be no Second Coming until this was accomplished. Conversely the Jews, especially the marranos, put enormous store on the redemption of their nation through the coming of the true Messiah. This expectation had never, as we know, been far from the thoughts of Menasseh ben Israel, who had preached and written extensively on its imminence and had, perhaps unwisely in view of the millenarian fever in London, boasted to Cromwell:

Although we cannot specify the exact moment of our redemption, we consider that it is now very close . . . Seeing our perseverance amid such great hardships, we judge that the Almighty has preserved us for rewards to come.

Yet it is not hard to envisage earlier, good-natured dispute between Menasseh, who called himself 'Portuguese, with a Dutch spirit', and Peter Serrarius, who yearned for spiritual reconciliation with the Jews, or later enthusiastic debate between Jean de Labadie, the ex-Jesuit and commune-leading mystic who swept Anna van Schurman into his wandering flock, and the convinced millenarist Coenraad van Beuningen. As 1656 came and passed the messianic scrabble for salvation did not lessen, and when in 1665 a rumour spread of the emergence in the Middle East of a self-proclaimed 'saviour of the Jews', who promised an immediate Jewish return to the Holy Land, and whose charismatic presence inspired reports of prophecies, visions and miracles, Jewish and Protestant communities throughout Europe became hugely excited, none more so than the Jews of Amsterdam. It is said the *Hooghduytsen* poured into the *Talmud Torah* synagogue to hear news of him. The 'Portuguese', long supporters of four holy communities living around Jerusalem, sent gifts of gold and silver to Sabbatai Zevi, the Greek-born 'Messiah' now in Gallipoli. Some set out for the Holy Land.

Spinoza would have heard about this for it was, apart from the dragging naval conflict, the talk of both the English and the Dutch. Isaac Newton, at twenty-three not yet elected to the Royal Society, but already formulating his law of gravitation, was a fervid millenarian, not only fascinated by its cosmological and astrological aspects, but inspired by its spiritual import to compose essays on the prophecies of Daniel, the Creation and the Apocalypse. Henry Oldenburg consulted, as usual, his best available source of information:

But I turn to politics. Here there is a widespread rumour that the Israelites, who have been dispersed for more than two thousand years, are to return to their homeland. Few hereabouts believe it, but many wish it . . . I am anxious to hear what the Jews in Amsterdam have heard about it, and how they are affected by so momentous an announcement, which, if true, is likely to bring about a world crisis.

The Jewish question was, as Oldenburg implied, an important political issue. But the Zevi hysteria, which no one had bothered to relate to rational principles, probably disgusted Spinoza, who made no reply on the point. Not that he would frown in the least at the notion of a return of the Jews to their land of origin. That *was* a rational possibility. *Did not the principles of their religion make them effeminate, I should be quite convinced that some day when the opportunity arises – so mutable are human affairs – they will establish their state once more, and that God will choose them afresh.* It was the sense in which 'chosen' was used that Spinoza rejected. The cherished notion of the Jews that they were 'chosen' (or in the Calvinist terminology that was the coinage of Dutch debate, 'elected') for special human qualities, and should thus expect special divine reward was, he argued, false. God's *choosing them afresh* meant the fulfilment of the Jews through the necessary laws of nature. Redemption of the Jews meant Jewish *advantage* or *usefulness* or *interest* (*utilitas*) as reason, alone, disclosed this. Passion and hatred would bring no real redemption. However, given the 613 superstitions that the Jews made central to their Law, a Zion of reason must have seemed to Spinoza a species of *chimaera*, a hybrid that could not exist.

The explosion of Jewish fervour over Sabbatai Zevi's triumphant progress through the Middle East to Jerusalem, and the accompanying alert watchfulness of the Christian community, would have guaranteed Spinoza an enormous readership had his book been completed at the time. So would the mortifying collapse of that Coming, and the lost hope of Jewish repatriation when in 1666 Zevi, having arrived in Jerusalem but having shocked the rabbis there by infringing *halachah*, left the city to cause disruption and scandal from Smyrna to Gallipoli. In Gallipoli he was arrested, taken to the Sultan's court at Adrianople and there, to escape execution, he denied his vocation and – shockingly to his Jewish followers – converted to Islam. This was not universally seen as apostasy: there had been too many enforced conversions of Jews in the past for that. De Labadie, a Protestant, declared that Zevi 'was not turned Turk, but a Jew as ever in the same hope and expectation as before'.

Spinoza made no political or philosophical capital out of the Zevi episode. The *Theologico-Political Treatise* was only part-written, but he said nothing. His view of the débâcle was nonetheless perfectly clear in his chapters on Jewish leadership. Prophets, who *only perceived God's revelation by the aid of imagination*, could not be relied on to transmit true knowledge. Theirs was not divine, but all-too human, inadequate guidance. Moses, for example, revealed God's commands through the medium of a faith which was through mental images adapted to his singular imagination, dependent on his own particular apprehension of God. Moses relied on these images to scare the Israelites into obedience ... *thus treating them as parents treat irrational children. ... Moses did not seek to convince the children of Israel by reason, but to bind them to covenant by oaths, and by gratitude for services; besides, he threatened the people with penalties for disobeying his laws, and held out rewards to encourage it to observe them. All these devices are means of inculcating obedience only, and not knowledge.* That was also the plan of the

Dutch Reformed Church. One historian claims that the best-known bible text in the land was 'Fear God and honour the King'.

Spinoza's exposition of the lessons to be learned from the origins of the Jewish religion (*rites* . . . *adapted to their political organisation*, valid only in relation *to their temporal welfare and the peace of their state*) constitutes a major strand of argument in the *Theologico-Political Treatise* and, before shifting our focus, as Spinoza would in the second half of his book, we should consider Jewish reaction to this. Although sparse, since Jews were forbidden to read anything written by him, and from the way that the *Treatise* was slanted towards interpretation and toleration by Christians probably did not take it to be addressed to them, Jewish opinion was, when it finally came in 1683, predictable:

> Benedito Espinosa, ejected from Amsterdam for his evil opinions, wrote a book which appears to be a pot of gold, but [is] a poisonous distillation [*licor*] in that the Jews have no obligation to observe the Mosaic Law since they have no state; and if they had not observed it in slavery they could not be distinguished from Moabites [etc.] and other nations, with the [consequent] loss of their king and their laws.

We may also want to reconsider at this point whether Spinoza could have included in the *Theologico-Political Treatise* the dissertation he was rumoured to have written in 1656 to justify himself to the elders of the synagogue. When describing his excommunication, I took the now generally accepted line that Spinoza did not in 1656 have sufficiently well formulated philosophical views to write a lucid *Apology*. However, we noted Lucas's report of some sharp comments on Jewish scripture, and those thoughts and others could – with or without an *Apology* having been written – have found their way into the *Theologico-Political Treatise*. Let us compare, for example, the reply on 'God's body' reportedly made to Morteira's student spies with what he now wrote. In the 1650s he had allegedly said:

> Since nothing is to be found in the [Jewish] Bible about the non-material or incorporeal, there is nothing objectionable in believing that God is a body. All the more so since, as the Prophet says, God is great, and it is impossible to comprehend greatness without a body.

Now Spinoza wrote:

> *The law of Moses . . . nowhere prescribed the belief that God is without a body, or even without form or figure . . . Nevertheless, the Bible clearly implies that*

God has a form, and that Moses when he heard God speaking was permitted to behold it, or at least its hinder parts.

As another example, on Spinoza's suspected early belief that Adam was not the first human being, we find him referring obliquely to *the story or parable of the first man*, and cryptically describing Adam as *the first man to whom God was revealed*. But these textual parallels are evidence for the reliability of Lucas's reports of his youthful beliefs rather than for the submission of an *Apology*, just as statements in the metaphysical works indicate the accuracy of the Inquisition spies De Maltranilla and Solano. The chapter of the *Theologico-Political Treatise* most often thought to incorporate the content of an earlier *Apology* is Chapter XIV. But while it provides a list of *necessary articles of faith* reflecting the *simple universal religion* which was much on his mind in Amsterdam, this chapter is written in such a completely different style from the early *Short Treatise* that it is difficult to imagine any part of it being lifted from an even earlier composition. Its argument also rests on New Testament details which Spinoza is unlikely, in the first half of the 1650s, to have met.

Although we have now seen how inextricable politics was from religion in the seventeenth century, and have suggested that Spinoza's title only served to emphasise this, there is a sense in which the theological and the political were quite sharply pulled apart in the *Theologico-Political Treatise*. At the end of Chapter XV, by which time Spinoza had impressed the distinction between philosophy and theology, he believed that he had prepared the ground for the argument promised in the *Treatise*'s subtitle, namely to *show that freedom to philosophise not only can be granted without detriment to piety and public peace; but cannot be destroyed without destroying them as well*. This was the political thesis towards which he had steered earlier discussion. He opened Chapter XVI:

> *So far I have been concerned to distinguish philosophy from theology, and to show that the latter allows everyone to philosophise in freedom. Now it is time to inquire how far this freedom of thought and expression extends in a good state.*

He would argue, first, for *the natural right of the individual*. The metaphysical underpinnings of this argument are more easily understood in a later context, but on the premise of the inalienable natural right of each individual, Spinoza proposed that:

> *a society can be formed without any opposition from natural law . . . and it was in particular democracy that I wished to discuss, because it seemed to be the*

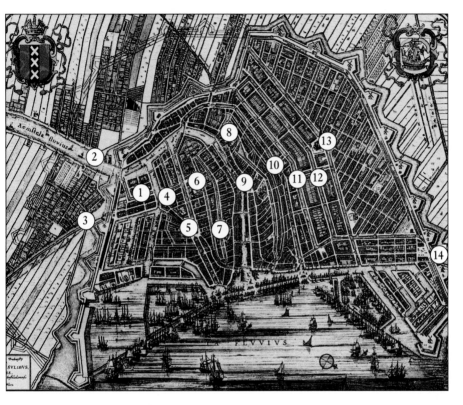

1. Map of Amsterdam 1647

1. Houtgracht: homes of Abraham de Espinosa de Nantes and Michael de Espinosa; the three
   earliest Portuguese-Jewish synagogues and the united Talmud Torah synagogue of 1638
2. River Amstel: the way to the Beth Haim at Ouderkerk
3. St Anthonie's dyke
4. South Kerk
5. Weigh House and *Theatrum Anatomicum*
6. Spinhuis
7. Oude Kerk
8. Rasphuis
9. Dam, Exchange and Town Hall
10. Singel
11. Herengracht
12. Keizersgracht
13. Westerkerk on the Prinsengracht
14. Haarlemmer Poort (*trekvaart* to Leiden and The Hague)

2. The Beth Haim at Ouderkerk, the Jewish burial place outside Amsterdam

3. The Nes, Amsterdam: the building on the right is 'In de Konst-Winkel'

4. René Descartes

5. Coenraad van Beuningen

6. Henry Oldenburg

7. Christiaan Huygens

8. Spinoza's room at Rijnsburg

9. Spinoza's last home,
72–4 Paviljoensgracht,
The Hague

10. Johan de Witt

11. William III,
aged 14

12. The French Invasion (1673)

13. The Battle of the Texel (11–21 August 1673)

14. Letter to Joh. Georg Graevius (14 December 1673)

15. *inset* Spinoza's seal

Natus Amstelod.
MDC. XXXII.
24 Novemb.

Denatus Hage Com
MDC. LXXVII.
21 Februa.

BENEDICTUS DE SPINOZA.

Cui natura, Deus, rerum cui cognitus ordo,
Hoc Spinofa ftatu, confpiciendus erat.
Expreffere viri faciem, fed pingere mentem
Zeuxidis artifices non valuere manus.
Illa viget fcriptis: illic fublimia tractat:
Huncquicunque cupis nofcere, fcripta lege.

16. Spinoza, engraved frontispiece of the *Opera Posthuma*

*most natural form of state, and to come nearest to preserving the freedom which
nature allows the individual.*

In this first, sketchy outline for a democracy individuals were encouraged, while retaining their natural right to live through appetite rather than reason if they were so determined by nature, to agree or *contract* rationally with other individuals to transfer their natural right to the *sovereign*, by whom Spinoza meant the figure of authority in whom a community collectively chose to invest the power of the State. Some conflict over this grounding of democracy in the voluntary agreement of individuals was evident, since those members of the community who did not give reasoned consent to a social contract were to be forced to comply. *No society can exist without government and force, and hence without laws to control and restrain the unruly appetites and impulses of men.* Spinoza thus replaced Hobbes's thesis that individuals would unite through fear, and Van den Enden's suggestion that the will of 'the whole people, aggregated' was sufficient to ensure a peaceful community, with a tentative general will theory. He admitted that the transfer of right was *in many respects purely theoretical* since the right to think freely, for example, could not be transferred. After reflecting on *Political Lessons Derived From The Jewish State* (Chapter XVIII), Spinoza affirmed that *When I said above that the sovereign had exclusive right over everything, and that all law depended entirely in his will, I was referring to religious law as well as to civil; for he must also be the interpreter and guardian of religious law.* He concluded the *Treatise* with a plea that the control of *external* religious practice should lie, not with Church leaders – *superstitious and ambitious men, who cannot tolerate liberal minds,* [and] *have gained such a reputation that their authority has more weight with the masses than that of the sovereign* – but with the *sovereign*, in the case of the Dutch Republic, *my country's rulers.* These should protect the natural right of individuals by setting only the broadest limits on religious practice, namely those that guarded against *danger to the peace of the state.*

In Descartes's view, Hobbes's main aim in *De Cive*, written in 1642, had been to show the necessity of supporting King Charles I, and indeed the Dutch translator of *Leviathan*, Abraham van Berckel, would be moved enough by Hobbes's arguments to become a vehement Orangist. Spinoza's proposal for a democracy, on the other hand, denied a place for a monarch in the Dutch Republic. He saw dangers not only in the transference of power to a hereditary monarch in a state unused to such rule, but in the office of Stadholder:

As for Holland, its Estates never had a king, as far as we know, but only counts; and the latter were never vested with the sovereignty. For as the High and Puissant Estates of Holland themselves make plain in the declaration they published in the time of Count Leicester, they always kept the authority to remind the aforesaid counts of their duty, and retained the power not only to defend this authority, and the freedom of the citizens, but also to get rid of their counts should these degenerate into tyrants, and to curb them so that they could do nothing without the permission and approval of the Estates. Thus sovereignty was always held by the Estates, and it was their sovereignty that the last count tried to usurp.

Here he recalled Willem II's 1650 bid for dictatorship. (He also, by referring only to the States of Holland, showed the prominence of this province and its assembly, and the relative domination of its counts of Orange-Nassau over other stadholders.) Despite almost certainly discussing the concept of sovereignty with Van den Enden and Adriaan Koerbagh (a 1664 pamphlet called *Souverainiteyt* is now thought to have been written by the latter), Spinoza did not clarify what he meant by the term 'sovereignty' until he wrote his *Political Treatise*:

The corporate right, which is defined by the power of a people, is generally called sovereignty, and is entirely vested in those who by common consent manage the affairs of state, i.e. who make, interpret and repeal laws, fortify cities, take decisions about war and peace, and so on. If such functions belong to a general assembly of the people, then the state is called a democracy; if to certain persons only, who have been chosen as members, it is called an aristocracy; and if, finally, the management of state affairs, and consequently the sovereignty, is vested in a single man, then it is called a monarchy.

Spinoza's loyalties were squarely with De Witt, and at this juncture he would not have appreciated the import of his final conditional for the Grand Pensionary's manner of governing (although he did by the time he came to write these words, around 1676). The present Dutch republic, he believed throughout De Witt's tenure of office, was, in its essentials – tyrannical consistories apart – a democracy in which true freedom could thrive. He wrote:

Take the city of Amsterdam, whose enjoyment of this freedom has made it great and admired by the whole world. In this flourishing state, this city without a peer, men of every race and sect live in the greatest harmony, and before they entrust their goods to anyone there are only two things that they want to know: whether he is rich or poor, and whether he is honest or dishonest. His religion or sect does not matter, for it has no influence on the decision of law-suits; and no sect whatsoever is so detested that its members (provided that they harm no one, give every man his own and live decent lives) are refused the protection of the civil authorities.

We may note here a comment made later by a presiding Dutch magistrate, that 'in our country, in the absence of public meetings or public writings, one did not look closely concerning the opinions which every individual harboured with regard to the Church'. This degree of free thought already being granted, all that was needed was a curbing of the power of the preachers and consistories, and Spinoza's *Treatise* was an appeal to the philosophically inclined to re-examine this major deterrent to political freedom. He did not argue for a supplanting of either De Witt or his élite band of regent deputies, whom he numbered, largely mistakenly, among the potentially philosophically inclined. His esteem for that aristocracy (a political ruling élite from which he was at present, although no longer a Jew, excluded) was partly responsible, I suggest, for the tension in his general will theory.

De Witt was not cast in the mould of philosopher-king, and while no one was more aware than he of the trampling of the hosts of Calvin over those who flaunted *freedom of judgement,* he found it expedient to accept the society-sobering judgements of the Church Councils, even when they showed more vindictiveness than Christian mercy. He was also, as we have seen, wary of the rabble-rousing power of the parish predicants, who generally assigned divine authority to Prince William (aged seventeen in 1667) and who challenged the judgements of De Witt, whom they thought had none, at every opportunity. The French ambassador d'Estrades, who had in 1663 thought the House of Orange 'entirely destroyed', and 'the States, that is, Monsieur de Witt' the sole Dutch political force, now reported to Louis XIV that the Grand Pensionary no longer had the power to push things through as before. The war with England also forced De Witt into making decisions he knew would be unpopular. The dismissal of William's tutor, for example, and the beheading of a French member of his entourage for treachery, led to talk of regent dictatorship and 'martyrdom' in the Orangist cause. De Witt was thus less willing than ever to overrule *Kerkeraad* decisions and, viewing his predicament from this perspective, it would that seem Spinoza was, during the four years it took to write the *Theologico-Political Treatise,* hacking diligently at the Grand Pensionary's slender support from the Reformed Church. For who must De Witt most humour, for the sake of quietening overtaxed and dissatisfied Dutch patriots, but that people's watchdog? Who must he most resemble, during those years of pressure to keep France as an ally, to bring the English naval war to a successful conclusion, to prevent Louis invading the Spanish

Netherlands and to keep the pugilistic Bishop of Münster's forces out of the eastern provinces, if not Moses? De Witt wanted least of all the support of an apostate *agent-provocateur* and most of all a miracle – a victory at sea.

Following a four-day battle off Flanders in June 1666, in which the Dutch navy triumphed, De Witt and his admirals hoped to inflict swift and total humiliation on the English. But in August the enemy fleet again put to sea, and although it was intercepted off Kent by Admiral de Ruyter, the ensuing overnight conflict ended in Dutch defeat. Pepys reported with glee 160 Dutch ships burned, ten or twelve fully laden with ship-building materials captured, and a false rumour that the Grand Pensionary's house had been besieged by the common people of Amsterdam (the city where De Witt had no house and where his standing was high) and that he had been 'forced to flee to the Prince of Orange'. De Witt had in fact used every gust of wind to get down the coastline to inspect the crippled ships in the Scheldt, and to deal there with a furious quarrel between De Ruyter and young Tromp. Aware that England was stricken by plague, he chafed to finish off its remaining ships, but the sickness of his own men prevented any instant retaliation. The devastation of much of London by the Great Fire that September may, however, have inspired his plan – confided only to his brother Cornelis, burgomaster of Dordrecht and now Fleet Delegate – to sail when least expected straight for the Medway, and to torch the English fleet within its Thames haven.

Much as De Witt wanted the English, and especially their King, intimidated by an alliance of Dutch and French sea power, for (wrote Van den Hove) 'England fears no potentate of Europe except the King of France', the ceasefire of winter of 1666–7 freed him to turn his back on the North Sea and face a threatened French invasion of the Spanish Netherlands. Temple believed that d'Estrades and De Witt were 'day and night together' and that De Witt was thought by all at The Hague 'to be too firmly linked with the French ever to be removed', but in fact De Witt held that to abandon Spain at this point was to make a present of the Spanish Netherlands to France, and thus make France neighbour to the Dutch. This no Dutchman wanted, for France was at best an unreliable ally. Van Beuningen, in Paris, found himself constantly compelled to remind Louis of his Treaty obligations, and in consequence brought a new complaint from Ambassador d'Estrades – that he was 'a prying, pressing man'. De Witt worked ceaselessly to preserve a French alliance and to convince Louis that young William of Orange was unworthy of attention, despite Charles II's wily championing of him, which included commissioning a portrait of the prince in armour (Plate 11).

This last move was one of several major errors that the Grand Pensionary made in the late 1660s. D'Estrades, reminded continually of William's lack of importance, had insulted him scandalously in 1664 by refusing to yield carriageway in The Hague. The 14-year-old prince had, eventually, climbed out of his carriage and walked off. In April 1666 William was made a 'Child of State'. His tutor, married to an English noblewoman, was dismissed, and his education taken over by the States of Holland in order to cut him off from contact with any other State enemies. At the same time, a resolution was passed forbidding the presentation of any foreign prince's recommendation on behalf of a Dutch subject's advancement. Sir William Temple, currently England's resident in Brussels, was told that De Witt had 'far greater power in the government than ever any Prince of Orange had', and that the boy now treated the Grand Pensionary coolly and should not be underrated. But Temple would also, during his long service in The Hague as English ambassador, see De Witt preparing William for an official role by giving him 'very just notions of everything relating to the State . . . to render him fit to govern'. Nonetheless, the cold youth who had come close to trusting his tutor, and had pleaded vainly with De Witt and D'Estrades to let him stay, assumed a new, icily courteous self-possession and a somewhat surprising robustness. When in the summer of 1667 the States of Holland warily offered him (under nominal command as Captain-General) a squadron of 8,000 men, provided he would sign away any further ambitions, William replied that he would willingly shed his blood for his country, but that since he was not less than his ancestors, he would wait for a greater future ambition. Meanwhile, sympathy and support spread from the Orangist Zeeland and Friesland deputies, who called for a life appointment and 'armour' for the prince, to voting towns throughout the Provinces. There had always been pockets of support for the House of Orange: the Leiden *Kerkeraad*'s anger with Pieter van den Hove was largely due to his insistence that the stadholders had brought the United Provinces close to ruin. Now, numerous town council proclamations demanding titles or responsibilities for young William were posted. However, the withdrawal of Münster's men after Charles's failure to send aid in the east temporarily silenced criticism of the Republic's weak and neglected army, and since the boy denied any attachment to his uncle and put off visiting his mother's homeland when invited, he remained a political puppet who was, for now, under control.

A victory at sea – that military arena in which no stadholder had achieved glory – was more badly needed than ever to stabilise both national feeling and De Witt's own position. It was this that the treacherous Buat, ex-commander of Willem II's guards, had worked to prevent. Charles II had pressed Buat to put it about that De Witt was prolonging the war, and during the first half of 1667 Pepys writes of the Dutch as being first 'in great straits, unable to get out their fleet', then 'high and insolent, look upon us as if come to beg a peace', then ready to make a treaty even while preparing their ships of war. By March, when Londoners were returning following the plague, and the burned houses were being rebuilt, rumours led the English to fortify the River Medway 'by a chain at the stakes, and [have] ships laid there with guns to keep the enemy from coming up to burn our ships'. Yet they were unprepared when eighty Dutch men-of-war first approached Harwich and then came right into the river estuary. 'Pressing orders for fire ships,' wrote Pepys, then, 'Lord! to see how backwardly things move at this pinch . . . the Dutch are fallen down from the Hope and the Shell-haven as low as Sheerness, and we do plainly at this time hear the guns play.' Finally, 'Home, where all our hearts do ake; for the news is true that the Dutch have broken the chain and burned our ships, and particularly "The Royal Charles" . . . And the truth is I do fear that the whole kingdom is undone.' Pepys was right: the English were forced to concede defeat, and signed the Treaty of Breda on 31 July 1667. The figurehead from the *Royal Charles*, which was towed back to Holland, still hangs in the Amsterdam Historical Museum. De Witt's leadership was credited, and both this and his brother's breathtakingly ruthless control of De Ruyter and the seamen were acknowledged in the ringing of church bells throughout the Provinces.

During an English post-defeat witch-hunt Henry Oldenburg was arrested as a suspected spy. 'Mr Oldenburg, our Secretary,' recorded Pepys, 'is put into the Tower for writing news to a virtuoso in France, with whom he constantly corresponds in philosophical matters; which makes it very unsafe at this time to write, or almost do any thing.' The 'virtuoso' may have been Huygens, who had been in loose contact with De Witt during the war years, and to whom Oldenburg wrote in French. Huygens had, as we know, largely ignored both the war and Henry. Spinoza, on the other hand, who had cheerfully passed on all he knew, had seemingly attracted no suspicion. After his correspondence with Oldenburg was curtailed, however, he ceased to mention current affairs in his letters. Perhaps he heard from Pieter Serrarius what had happened to Henry.

At the start of winter 1666–7 Benedictus had been, as his thirty-fourth birthday came and went, *living in solitude here in the country*. He was responding, with these words, to a query on the calculation of chances, a topic that had long intrigued Huygens, and which Hudde and De Witt had also studied. The identity of his correspondent, Johannes van der Meer, is conjectural, and since neither his querying letter nor the original of Spinoza's reply has been found, we may cynically wonder if Benedictus wrote out for himself this short statement of his theory literally as a cover –

an innocuous sheet or two in Dutch to place over the pages of the *Theologico-Political Treatise* if an inquisitive Hollander neighbour interrupted him. The *Treatise* was not scrambled into print but laboriously composed, the evidence suggests, behind a front of projects in natural philosophy, for the only letters preserved between June 1666 and January 1671 – a year after the book appeared in print – concern applied mathematics and physics. It was during this period that the normally phlegmatic Huygens, living in Paris (where he showed Van Beuningen the new moon through his telescope), became sufficiently flustered by Spinoza's progress in optics to fire off a series of letters on the topic – eight between September 1667 and May 1668. Had Van Beuningen, possibly keen to deflect Huygens's attention from Spinoza's philosophy, taunted the scientist by exaggerating the 'Israelite's' optical achievements? Compromised by his own free-thinking, and his nomination to an Amsterdam council that was becoming dominated by Reformed Church zealots, Van Beuningen may have wished Spinoza would confine himself to matters of physical vision. That Benedictus himself may have wanted to give that impression is suggested by the fact that, following the letter to Van der Meer, two missives were sent to Jarig Jelles in March 1667, on optics and alchemy. Then there is a gap for two and a half years, until a single letter to Jarig on water pressure is sent in September 1669. In it, Spinoza says he was *as busy as could be* with an experiment using wooden tubes and boards, which he had had made specially.

Was there no contact with other Dutch friends? There was not in all cases disagreement or rivalry. Simon, who had almost certainly kept up his visits, was dying. We do not know what disease took him, aged thirty-two, but it seems he knew beforehand that he would not survive:

> This same Simon de Vries being like to die, and having no wife or children, designed to make him his general heir; but Spinoza would never consent to it, and told him, that he should not think to leave his estate to anybody but to his brother [sic] who lived at Schiedam, feeling he was his nearest relation, and natural heir.

Simon had complied, while secretly arranging that the 'brother' (so Colerus calls him, but none seems to have been living; this must have been some other kinsman) should pay an annuity of 500 guilders to his now truly impoverished friend. On 17 September, soon after the Peace of Breda, Simon died 'a bachelor', and was buried in his mother's grave. There is only silence from Benedictus, a hugging of grief to himself, and a protesting of the pension payable out of Simon's considerable estate (part-shares in two

Amsterdam houses, the Schiedam house and pastureland). Reluctantly, he took 300 guilders. That he moved in 1668 to a room in a larger house is not significant unless he gave financial help to Tydeman, whose whole household uprooted with him and reinstalled itself in Voorburg's Herenstraat, a stone's throw from his present home, and even nearer the church.

The year 1668 opened with a lesser but still disquieting loss. Jan Casearius had failed to get the living he applied for in Smyrna in November 1666. As far as we can tell he did not try to win the favour of the overseas consistorial committee by decrying Spinoza. In the month of glory following the Chatham raid he married 22-year-old Isabella Brent. Both sets of parents were said to be dead, so Jan could (as Benedictus had) have felt set free from past scruples. But on 2 January 1668 he was again examined, and was this time appointed to Reformed Church service in Batavia. He probably left three months later on the *Sparendam*, which sailed to Colombo at that time, for he was well installed in his Indian station by September 1669. He may have seemed at that point to show dedication to the Dutch Reformed Church, but that would not prove so. Instead, 'The Spinozist clergyman of Cochin', as he would be remembered, gradually shed that unsteady loyalty as he found refuge in helping to collect and classify plant specimens for Cochin's Governor Van Reede. His Latin being much admired, he would edit and compose the text for the *Hortus Malabaricus*, proudly published in Amsterdam. Van Reede wrote that Casearius had 'feared that his style, to which the terminology of botanists and physicians was unknown, would not be up to the dignity of so great a work'. But the project, conducted in tents visited by curious local princes, was evidently a labour of love for Jan, who, burying his spiritual conflict in the task of producing 'clear and distinct knowledge' of the plants, was officially rebuked for his laxity as a predicant, ordered by letter to 'consult somewhat more the books of his profession than others outside it', and reminded of his obligation to learn Portuguese so that he could proselytise – strange irony – the Jews and Catholics of the region. There was, then, to be no forgetting of Benedictus Spinosa. In 1677, having become sick in body and mind and been given permission to leave that tropical, marshy and most unhealthy stretch of the Malabar coast, the 'most learned and reverend man, whom we loved so much, Casearius, was snatched away from us in the prime of life by bitter death'. He succumbed to dysentery (as did so many Europeans) in Batavia, en route for the Provinces with his family, after his ship had been struck by a thunderbolt and the main mast and topmast washed away. He died the same year as Spinoza, and his name is immortalised in an obscure Asian plant officially named *Casearia, Jacq.* of the family *Flacourtiaceae*.

The year 1668 darkened further. Since June 1666 both Adriaan and

Johannes Koerbagh had been watched, as was the rented house on the Rokin where Serrarius preached, and where the numbers of free-thinkers attending 'scandalous' assemblies had increased since Boreel's death in 1664 to hundreds. In the first days of 1668, the very week of Jan's acceptance for Reformed Church ministry, Predicant Johannes Koerbagh had a stormy meeting with the *Kerkeraad*, during which he claimed biblical support for all his views. He perplexed the Church Council sufficiently to be recalled several times without any charge being made, and indeed his impassioned appeal for the legitimacy of the Rokin services, based on St Paul's approval of the movement of the spirit in his first Letter to the Corinthians, makes confusion understandable. In February, following the discovery that his brother Adriaan was publishing a frankly heretical religious 'dictionary', the Church Council decided that this basically sound Christian had been corrupted at home. Adriaan's *Een Bloemhof van allerley lieflykhyd . . .* ('A Flower Garden of all sorts of loveliness . . .') inflamed at first glance, both in its title, which recalled the eponymous satirical and for some profane painting of the Dutchman Hieronymous Bosch, and its stark delivery, in which the central articles of Catholic and Calvinist worship and belief were defined, dictionary-style, in terms of secular and scientific understanding. 'Angels' and the 'Devil' were dismissed as fictions, 'Miracles' and 'Prophecy' as worthless superstition. 'Theologians want a miracle to be something other than or contrary to nature: this is false because nothing could be produced which was contrary or superior to nature . . . Since there is only one nature and nothing outside it, there can be no science except that of nature, and nothing outside it.' We should therefore, wrote Koerbagh, speak about God only in the context of physics. He coined a new word to stand for God or Nature, namely 'ipstantie', choosing this word because, like many other philosophers before and since Spinoza, he did not believe a 'substance' must necessarily be unique and independent, but nevertheless wanted to emphasise, as did Spinoza, that God, or Being, was the sole cause of itself (*ipse*), requiring no other thing for its existence. For Koerbagh, particulars were 'substances' or ways of subsisting within that unique *ipstantie* – a piece of terminology that could have constituted a welcome clarification to anyone trying to understand the One Substance doctrine. Under 'Concubine' he wrote that concubinage was not bad in itself but was, like polygamy, forbidden by law for good reasons. This judgement indicates a rejection (at least in principle) of Van den Enden's views in favour of Spinoza's. Moreover, Spinoza's love for *God, or Nature*, expressed in all his texts, was also echoed: 'In this consist our eternal happiness and salvation – in knowing in God's knowledge, and being in communion with God . . .'

While conceptual similarities such as these are undeniable, Koerbagh's philosophy was no straightforward affirmation of Spinoza's 'gospel', as has been suggested. Its independence and innovation are hinted at by Van Limborch's likening, in 1671, of Spinoza's view of God to that of 'someone' who had told him personally that there was only one unique *ipstantie* ('this barbarous word,' sniffed Van Limborch), which was God. Nor, conversely, did Spinoza expound 'Koerbaghism', since among other divergent and unacceptable doctrines in Adriaan's next book were aspects of the teaching of the Socinian sect which gathered at the Rokin meeting-house. The Socinians, despite denying the divinity of Jesus, the existence of the Holy Spirit and original sin, believed in sin, God's forgiveness and final judgement, and the dispatching of souls to paradise or purification before a final resurrection, with Jesus, of the same bodies that the faithful had in life. The inclusion of these precepts in Koerbagh's book is puzzling, since they reintroduce dualism, overturn his physics and make his thesis contradictory. Spinoza seems to have had little time for the sect. *Apart from the Socinians, I have never found any theologian so stupid as not to see that Holy Scripture very often speaks of God in merely human style.*

The Rokin meeting-house where Johannes still preached was now considered by the *Kerkeraad* a hotbed of apostasy, traceable – it appeared – to Adriaan's anti-bible. The council called for *Een Bloemhof*'s seizure and sent a deputation to the Town Hall to demand Adriaan's arrest. Adriaan fled to a safe haven on private property at Culemborg, south-east of Utrecht, which the States of Holland had no authority to enter. Meanwhile, the manuscript of his next book, in which the material of *Bloemhof* was expanded, was found at the printer's. This was sent, half-printed, to the chief officer of justice, or bailiff, Cornelis Witsen, the severe fundamentalist who was first cousin to Hudde's mother, Maria Witsen. Two copies were made for the magistrates to read. The book was called *Een ligt schijnende in duystere plaatsen* ('A Light Shining in Dark Places'), a title superficially similar to Balling's *The Light upon the Candlestick*. But Koerbagh's book shed, despite its Socinian inclusions, no hazy divine light. Here was the rasping of an exasperated academic, and when parts of the treatise were read aloud it created 'consternation of soul' in the assembly.

On 1 March 1668 preacher-brother Johannes was brought before the *Kerkeraad*. Once more, without denying his views, he managed to convince the board that he was a true believer who had chosen to shepherd souls into the fold of the Christian religion in unorthodox ways. He was released. But by late April Adriaan's whereabouts were known, and in early May the *Kerkeraad*'s frustration over this led to Johannes being re-arrested outside the Town Hall and taken down to the cells, where he was questioned. This time he was detained. He had not stopped preaching at the Rokin meeting-hall, and however much the doctor of theology thought his assembly resembled the early Christian Church, his preaching within it was subversive behaviour for a Reformed Church predicant. More immediately relevantly, he was said to have visited his brother, and to be receiving letters from him. By 18 May Bailiff Witsen was already demanding that Adriaan should be banned for life from Holland and West Friesland, and all his goods confiscated. A reward was put up by the municipal council for his capture, and eventually, in July, Adriaan was betrayed. He was in Leiden, the burgomasters were informed, at a particular address. The bailiff of Leiden was alerted and at dawn the room was raided. Adriaan was pulled from his bed and taken, shackled and under guard, to the dungeons of the Town Hall, Amsterdam.

The next day he was interrogated, the magistrates present including the newly elected alderman Johannes Hudde. The proceedings, recorded in the *Confessieboek*, show so great a persistence in getting at the sources of this 'fox in the vineyard' that this might have been the interrogation of a State enemy. We can only imagine Hudde's thoughts as he saw the free-thinker in chains, denying that anyone else had influenced his ideas; denying that (as far as he knew) anyone agreed with them; denying having spoken to his brother about them; denying that he had seen Van den Enden within the past six years; denying that he had read anything of Abraham van Berckel (although Van Berckel had been at Culemborg with him); admitting he had seen 'Spinosa', but denying that any part of his doctrine agreed with Spinoza's . . . Magistrate Bontemantel recorded in his journal that the prisoner appeared sad, but that although he said he wanted to be subjected to the Church and its rulings, he held adamantly to the views in his book on which he had been questioned. If Hudde had read *Een Ligt* he would have found a discussion of God's uniqueness with which he was more than familiar; a metaphysical scheme which almost matched that of the *Short Treatise*; attacks on superstition that owed as much to Van den Enden as Spinoza; and some patchy understanding of Hebrew teaching. Koerbagh had stated, for example, that many books of the bible were written by one Esdras (as had Meyer, in his *Philosophiae Interpres*). In the *Theologico-Political Treatise* Spinoza put forward the *hypothesis* that *Ezra set himself to give a complete account of the history of the Hebrew nation*. He may have expressed this personal view in a study-group session, or directly. But, on questioning, Adriaan's understanding of Hebrew did not extend to knowledge of what 'schabinot' (*sic*) might mean. He said he would have to look it up in Buxtorf's Hebrew dictionary (of which Spinoza owned two volumes). One biographer relates the word to *Hag Shavuoth*, the Jewish feast that Koerbagh mentioned under 'Pinxter' (Pentecost or Whitsun) in

Bloemhof. A Jewish scholar suggests, however, that the councillors were trying to get Koerbagh to tell them about *schechinat* or *schekinah*, the notion of God's immanence in nature. Koerbagh probably did not, in all sincerity, know the word, which is not mentioned by Spinoza. But Koerbagh also referred to the cabalic notion of the *All-in-All*, familiar to Spinoza from the rabbis' textbook and used by him in the *Short Treatise.* However, Koerbagh made his unique, all-inclusive Being or *ipstantie* consist solely in the two essential attributes of 'matter' and 'force' of the Neoplatonists, rather than the *extension and thought* of Spinoza. Hudde would have picked up differences between Koerbagh's view of *God, or Nature* and Spinoza's, and would also have observed that Koerbagh was not at home with Hebrew theology. It would not, however, have placated any Church Council member that Koerbagh's Socinian beliefs in bodily resurrection and redemption conflicted with his doctrine of the unity of all men with God in nature. Residual traces of Christian doctrine did not exonerate the lawyer from the wickedness of trying to alter the foundations of the common people's beliefs.

Preacher-brother Johannes was interrogated the following day, 20 July. He pleaded that he had now reflected in prison on his crimes for ten weeks, and that his brother, not he, had written the offending book, which he had not read. When asked if he thought *Een Ligt* was blasphemous, he would not answer. Four days later the board of magistrates called him again and he reluctantly admitted that, while the brothers had lived with their mother, his lawyer-brother had sometimes asked him, as a university-trained theologian, the origin of certain Hebrew words. The magistrates were not convinced that Johannes knew nothing about his brother's books, and interrogated him again, vainly, the next day.

On 27 July the magistrates met at 10 a.m., this time to watch Adriaan Koerbagh being tortured. His confession of the week before was then read to him. Bailiff Witsen, his appetite presumably whetted by this barbarism, immediately demanded that Koerbagh be taken up to the scaffold in front of the Town Hall, where his right thumb should be hacked off and his tongue pierced with a red-hot iron. The heretic should then, Witsen directed, be imprisoned for thirty years for his words, his writing and the printing of his blasphemous discourses. His fortune should be confiscated, and his books burned publicly or *in camera.* Koerbagh was asked if he had anything to say about this, and the broken man naturally replied that he was sorry. He was taken out by Witsen while the magistrates considered their judgement. It is not clear how a decision was reached, but nothing is recorded in the *Justitieboek,* and the scrawled judgement filling a margin of the *Confessieboek* suggests it was made with the same agitation that prompted an abandoning of the usual announcement from above the Town Hall, after its clock had struck. The sentence must be delivered *in camera*, it was agreed, in case the public showed curiosity about the books. Koerbagh was sentenced to ten years' imprisonment, then banishment from Holland, Zeeland and West Friesland. Further, added the margin note, 'The magistrates condemn the prisoner to a fine of 4000 gl., half for the *heer officier* and half for alms, besides another fine of 2000 gl. for the costs of his imprisonment, and expenses. And the books which shall be found must be suppressed.' Reference was made in the bottom left-hand corner of the margin to an '*Actum* 11 May', claimed to have been agreed by the bailiff and all the aldermen, and endorsed by Van Beuningen. Van Beuningen had been sent back to Paris after the Treaty of Breda, with the ambassadorial mission of establishing peace between France and Spain. He arrived there on 27 February 1668 after a journey of more than two weeks and was in the French capital, Huygens's correspondence testifies, on 29 June. He was not, therefore, in Amsterdam in either May or July 1668. In August – just after Koerbagh was condemned – he resigned from the council, although due to return to Holland that very September. Was Van Beuningen actually consulted at all on Koerbagh's sentence? Despite the firm views that the diplomat would express on religious dissidence when, in 1669, he was persuaded to rejoin the council as a burgomaster, we may doubt this.

Koerbagh had been given the worst possible punishment. When describing Spinoza's boyhood we imagined him seeing offenders being dragged, shackled, through the arched entrance of the *Rasphuis*. Spinoza must contemplate it now, for Adriaan was sent to this place of insufferable humiliation, set back in a lane between the Rokin and the Singel, on 29 July. In September – the month of Van Beuningen's repatriation, and of Jan Casier's safe arrival in Cochin – he was removed to a workhouse in a disused warehouse of the West-India Company where women and children, drunkards and debtors, were left to rot. He died a year later, in a state of mind which the pastor sent by the *Kerkeraad* to try to save his soul from 'the lakes of Satan' euphemistically described as 'decent' and 'repentant'.

It is unlikely that Cornelis Witsen of the Keizersgracht, buried seven months earlier, died in a similar mental state. He had attempted to settle a harsh punishment on Johannes, who had protested in his usual cryptic fashion that the charges against him were only 'ecclesiastical', 'justifiable by the Church'. The bailiff had demanded that Johannes be beaten *in camera*, fined according to the discretion of the judge and then imprisoned for twelve years, paying the costs thereof. After some argument Johannes was condemned to the costs of his earlier incarceration, bound to good behaviour and acquitted. But the next week he was recalled and told that his examinations must continue. In September 1669 he was still being warned to steer clear of assemblies that presented 'temptations', and it was decided to send a recommendation to all the Provinces that he should not be allowed into any pulpit. His involvement with 'heretical' meetings was questioned by the *Kerkeraad* until 1671, when references to him cease. He died at home in September 1672.

Why was Adriaan Koerbagh so exceptionally severely punished? It has been pointed out that between 1660 and 1710 only three writers on theological or political topics were sentenced to imprisonment in Amsterdam, and that these three alone had published in Dutch, the language of the common people. We know that Koerbagh was not put on the scaffold for fear that people would be stimulated to read his books. He had already put power in the hands of the masses with his *New Dictionary of Law*, and, fearing that people would not understand *Bloemhof*, he had clarified it for them in *Een Ligt*. Jan Casearius had presumably been accepted for the overseas ministry because, despite his obvious doubts and neglect of the bible, he had neither written nor preached offensively in the Dutch language. Against that line of argument, however, Van den Enden had published in Dutch against the Reformed Church. De Labadie, too, had written in Dutch about 'paradoxes' in scripture, and between 1666 and 1669, in which year he was living in Amsterdam and was brought before the *Kerkeraad*, he had some 60,000 followers. This was a cause for major alarm to the magistrates, and De Labadie's *Kerkeraad* inquisition ran through 1669–70. Yet the visionary received only the light penalty of expulsion from the Walloon Church. When he personally protested about this to Van Beuningen, the diplomat is said to have refused him protection, saying that as long as he stayed in the Walloon Church communion he must submit to its ordinances and discipline; but if he formed a new sect he would enjoy the protection that the State accorded all sorts of religions. This remarkable statement lifts the veil a little on the baffling Dutch 'blind eye'. One could, then, be a Collegiant or a Socinian outside the Church, but not a Collegiant, Socinian or otherwise a dissenter within it.

I think we must conclude that neither writing for the public in Dutch, nor attacking religious dogma, was alone, and of itself, responsible for Adriaan Koerbagh's savage sentence.

We may possibly glean more insight when we consider how little he recanted. Contrition, as Christ told the thieves crucified with him, was the Christian criterion for salvation (as it was for readmission to Jewish communities). Casearius displayed it, as did Johannes Koerbagh. Placatory and insincere noises may have been made by Van den Enden. Adriaan, on the other hand, failed to repent and took full responsibility for his notions. During his months on the run, *Bloemhof* and *Een Ligt* were read with escalating outrage, causing the consistory and magistrates to demand utter abjectness after his capture. What they got was a grudging apology made only after torture. Such defiance still excited depths of fear and horror in the seventeenth century, and the 'great consternation of soul' created by the discovery of *Een Ligt* may have sprung in part from a real dread of the work of the devil. We may recall that Johannes was told to eschew 'temptations', and that in September, when Adriaan was removed from the *Rasphuis*, probably already gravely ill, a pastor was sent to try to save his soul from 'the lakes of Satan'. The devil whom the lawyer had served seemed about to claim his soul, and lurked to ensnare his brother. The *Faustbuch*, which had gripped most of Europe before Marlowe dramatised the German scholar's pride and horrifying end, told of a scholar who rejected God's teachings and, having refused to repent, was carried off to hell by Mephistopheles, who had disguised himself as a monk. The devil could take any form while claiming the soul of an impenitent heretic. This was thought to have befallen Adriaan, an eye-witness wrote, for, as his bier was borne down the street for burial, a black hen alighted on the head-end and refused to move, despite a hail of stones and hats hurled by the *grauw*, the mob of 'hundreds' who believed 'the devil in the form of a black hen had taken away the wretch's soul'.

Koerbagh committed no offence, apart from writing in Dutch, that Spinoza did not duplicate in his *Theologico-Political Treatise*. And Spinoza would be regarded as an even more noisome instrument of the devil: 'One may very well doubt whether, amongst the many men whom the devil has hired to overthrow all Humane and Divine right', wrote a professor of divinity, 'any of 'em has been more busy about it than that Imposter, who was born to the great mischief of Church and State.' Moreover, Spinoza committed himself to the republican cause at a point when De Witt was not merely waning in popularity, but was becoming widely reviled. Soon after 1670 the Grand Pensionary would be engulfed in a national hatred, which would lead to all manner of baseless lies, such as a claim that a draft version of Spinoza's *Theologico-Political Treatise*, found on De Witt's bookcase, had been:

> produced in Hell by the renegade Jew in collaboration with the Devil, and published with the connivance of Mr Jan and his accomplices.

Spinoza would seem bound, then, not only to incur the same penalty from the *Kerkeraad* and magistrates as Adriaan Koerbagh but also, as a De Witt supporter, to stand in danger from the masses. Strictly he should not come under the jurisdiction of the Amsterdam Church and civil councils unless he used an Amsterdam printer, and the man he may have seen as the Torquemada of Amsterdam, Cornelis Witsen, was dead. But a series of *Kerkeraad* debates in March and April 1669 show the board resolving to intensify surveillance of the printers, in particular Rieuwertsz. Later that year Van Beuningen was made a burgomaster of Amsterdam, and chairman of the *Kerkeraad*, but the assiduous attention of that consistory to complaints from the pastors did not abate. A comedy performed in Latin in the Prinsengracht, for example, was said to have used wicked words, such as *vis* (force) for God.

The *Theologico-Political Treatise* was printed in 1670, anonymously and at huge risk to both author and printer. Its title-page gave as the publisher 'Henricus Künraht' of Hamburg, but it is thought to have been printed by Christoffel Koenraad, on account to Jan Rieuwertsz. Colerus wrote years later, bewildered:

> Conrad himself brought me some copies of that Treatise, and presented me with them, not knowing that it was a very pernicious book . . . It is certain that the magistrates and the Reverend Ministers of Hamburg had never permitted that so many impious things should have been printed and publicly sold in their city.

We are left to ponder the paradox of Spinoza's boldness, disparity of vision from the government he wished to serve, and curious confidence that he would not be punished. The fact is that he was never summoned before the magistrates. Why not? Van Limborch would suggest in 1702 that he had been tolerated because he admitted his atheism only to friends, and formed no sect. Jarig testified that Spinoza had never wanted his name attached to his 'knowledge'. Maybe his external aura of social and doctrinal modesty, set off by poverty and skill in a useful occupation, deflected personal animosity. Henry Oldenburg had been drawn to his 'humility' in Rijnsburg; Van Blijenbergh was by no means put off him in Voorburg. Yet no one doubted that by offering his *Treatise* even to a strictly Latin-reading public he gambled with a really existing malignant force. Leibniz, unnerved to hear in 1678 that one of his own letters to Spinoza had been printed in the volumes of Spinoza's posthumous works, had to be calmed. 'I have reprehended the publisher for giving your name in full . . . although I believe there is no danger in it, as your letter contains nothing but mathematics.'

Who paid for the printing of the *Theologico-Political Treatise*? Jarig? Some of the most perplexing Christian attestation in the work has a ring of Jarig's convictions as expressed in a *Confession* he later wrote. Neither Meyer nor Bouwmeester seems to have been interested in the project, and may, just as they had probably warned Koerbagh against publishing, have thought insane the behaviour of the philosopher they had tried to steer into a safe career. Spinoza would admit that *good friends* had advised against a Dutch translation of his *Treatise*. They may have begged him not publish the Latin version. On 26 November, a month after Koerbagh's death, these cronies met in a tavern in the Singel with the poet J.Antonides van der Goes, who had been at Van den Enden's school, to discuss forming a select arts society or academy called *Nil Volentibus Arduum* ('Nothing is hard for those who show will'). The eleven members would meet every Tuesday evening from five until eight, producing in rotation pieces on art, drama or poetry or letters, including Bouwmeester's translations of Ibn Tophail from Latin and Arabic. The club was exclusive indeed. Its detailed minutes did not mention Rieuwertz, Jelles or Spinoza and, at a meeting held eight years later, just two days after Spinoza died, there was no written recognition of that sad and unexpected event. It is possible, given the absence of letters from Meyer after 1663 and Bouwmeester after 1666, that they had kept their distance from Spinoza.

It has been suggested that between 1665 and 1669 Spinoza changed from being 'calm and benevolent' to uttering the 'ironical invective' found in the *Theologico-Political Treatise*, and that this was due to the Koerbagh heresy trial. The philosopher had always been sarcastic and anti-clerical, we know, yet it is possible that his exceptionally vituperative Preface, and forceful final pages, were added to an almost complete *Treatise*.

On Koerbagh's death he made no direct statement. He drew no comparison between Count Maurits's execution of the remonstrant leader Oldenbarnveldt, the Inquisition's persecution of marranos, the *mahamad*'s destruction of Uriel d'Acosta or the *Kerkeraad*'s annihilation of Koerbagh. Instead, he rose above these particular outrages to establish, in his final chapter, two general principles:

> *Men whose consciences are clear do not fear death or beg for mercy like criminals, since their minds are not tormented by remorse for deeds of shame; they think it is a merit, not a punishment, to die for a good cause, and an honour to die for freedom.*
>
> *I have thus shown that it is impossible to deprive men of freedom to say what they think ... For where attempts are made to deprive men of it, and where the opinions of the dissenters ... are called to account, the punishment inflicted on good men seems more like martyrdom than punishment, provokes instead of intimidating the rest, and moves them to pity if not to vengeance.*

NINE

The Hague: 1670–2

In a free man, a timely flight is considered to show as much tenacity as fighting . . . Human power is very limited and infinitely surpassed by the power of external causes. So we do not have an absolute power to adapt things outside us to our use.

Spinoza moved to The Hague sometime after 5 September 1669, when a last letter was sent from Voorburg. The *Theologico-Political Treatise* was probably complete when he took a second-floor back room in a substantial house on the corner of the southerly Stille Veerkade, sideways on to the broad residential canal of the Paviljoensgracht. Was his flight generated by *self-esteem*, a rational view of himself and his situation? He had said he was *driven* to write the *Treatise*. Was he now *driven* to this fifth removal? Lucas says that Spinoza positively chose The Hague, 'which he preferred to Amsterdam, because the air there was more healthy'. Yet it is hard to believe Spinoza saw Amsterdam as a choice, knowing that he could not hope for protection from Van Beuningen and Hudde. The two councillors had achieved nothing effective for Frans van den Enden, now nearly seventy and according to rumour 'not knowing which way to turn because he was known as being irreligious and leading an ill life'. Spinoza had probably heard that the old schoolmaster no longer attracted new pupils, and was planning to quit the city. He would leave for France early in 1671.

Hindsight confirms a cluster of needs prompting Spinoza's move to The Hague. The health issue was genuine. Physically, walking a mile may now have been impossible for him in the best of weather, for although the philosopher was only thirty-seven years old, it was 'a man of a very weak constitution, unhealthy and lean' whom Mevrouw Van der Werve took into her home. The chronicles suggest that he now showed clearly the symptoms of 'phithisis', noted in a 1655 doctoral dissertation as 'wasting away' and dense catarrh.

Colerus called his new landlady 'the widow'. In fact, her husband's name was still on the Rates List in 1670, and arrangements may have been made with Meester Van der Werve, a lawyer, with an eye to Spinoza's security.

But this is guesswork based on knowing the identity of the house owner from records. We do not know that Van der Werve was a free-thinker, although he may have been. The Hague was full of urbane individuals who outwardly preserved establishment values while, without attending noisy meetings or publishing anything contentious, conducted an underground discourse among themselves. Widow or not, a 50-year-old woman used to The Hague's constant coming and going of foreign emissaries, educated travellers and political refugees, would have felt safe with this frail and reserved gentleman, who kept much to his room but received visitors 'distinguished by their Quality, or by Civil and Military employments', and also, if the report is to be believed, 'young girls of good family who believed themselves superior, through their intelligence, to their sex'. If inclined to doubt that Spinoza had acquired this kind of following while living in Voorburg, as Colerus claims, we should remember that until 1670 he had published nothing flagrantly heretical. Moreover, many of the scholars and political refugees from abroad who had for decades converged on The Hague, especially those French who found Louis's absolute monarchy intolerable and were aware of Descartes's enjoyment of the relative freedom of the Dutch republic, suffered from *ennui*. While these émigrés, who had often been intensely politically active in France, chose The Hague for its climate and *conversation*, one, at least, deprecated the 'indolence' of life in that unusual, unfortified and in some respects un-Dutch administrative capital (which nursed at its heart, nonetheless, and not a stone's throw from the home of Johan de Witt, an ancient and vicious fortress-prison, the *Gevangenpoort*).

In 1669 Aglionby found The Hague's 'French quarter' especially elegant, and the English ambassador Sir William Temple thought that in those last years before war with France broke out all The Hague's inhabitants tried 'to imitate the French in their mien, their clothes, their way of talk, of eating, of gallantry or debauchery'. Fashions from the courts of Europe entered the Dutch republic via The Hague. The game of chess, for example, was almost exclusively the pastime of noblemen in The Netherlands of Spinoza's day: those who deplored the Dutch obsession with cards usually played draughts. Yet ivory and ebony chessmen are listed among Spinoza's effects. Hollanders would stroll through the wood past the stadholders' *Huis ten Bosch*, but while they admired it, they themselves did not necessarily dress up. The men often wore their dressing-gowns. And as Van Beuningen's amusing ploys to leave Paris, and William Wycherley's seventeenth-century fictional 'Monsieur Paris' (talking below) implied, the French found even those Dutch burghers who affected sophistication unstylish:

I did visit, you must know, one of de Principals of de State General . . . and did find his excellence weighing soap, ha, ha, ha, weighing soap, ma foi, for he was a wholesale chandeleer; and his Lady was taking de tale [tally?] of chandles wid her witer [white?] hands, ma foi, and de young lady, his excellence daughter, stringing Herring . . .

De Witt, who spoke perfect French and was said to dance with a grace outshining any Parisian, resisted courtly excess as he did fashionable French ideology. This was observed by Temple, who described him as walking 'on foot and alone' in the streets and employing one man to do 'all the menial service of his house'. The Grand Pensionary had preserved solid Dutch family conventions at home, bringing up his children with the strictness but open love that typified Netherlanders. In the late 1660s he had suffered bereavement and stress. His wife died, aged thirty-three, within months of their youngest daughter's death. In 1669 his eldest daughter Anna (sixteen years old and heiress to some of her mother's huge fortune) wanted to marry a youth whom Johan considered one of The Hague's many undesirable self-seekers. In fury he forbade her. 'I would rather take my children to the church to see them put into their graves,' he wrote. It would have been a rare Dutchman who disagreed with him.

It is a feature of De Witt's tragedy that while he stood strikingly apart from the French of The Hague, and distrusted the French King to the point of forging friendship with the enemy, Spain, he would be remembered by large numbers of Dutch people as a Francophile spy and traitor. Worries about France's designs had become, by 1671, serious. On the surface the Grand Pensionary remained composed, as he must, for despite his extraordinary achievement in developing the Peace of Breda into a Triple Alliance between England, Sweden and the United Provinces against France (which had brought him re-election in 1668, a doubling of his salary dating back to 1653, and an embarrassment of other pecuniary gifts from grateful Dutch councils), in 1669 a tangibly critical element coloured the burgomaster elections in Amsterdam, that former stronghold of support. Its deputies, who now included Van Beuningen, voted in favour of formally offering William of Orange the seat on the Council of State provided in principle by the Eternal Edict of 1666. Since the Council of State, which was distinct from the States of Holland and from the States General, had charge of the army, it was a matter of grave concern for De Witt when, in June 1669, the 19-year-old Prince firmly took his seat on it. By 1671 memories of his father Willem II's despotism had dimmed, so this news, added to a fresh spate of sermons reminding ordinary folk of Calvin's dictum that kings and princes were often by 'the wise arrangement of Divine Providence' the legitimate rulers, created a *Prinsgezind* clamour, which increasingly drowned out the few *Staatsgezind* (literally 'States-inclined' or 'following the States', but in effect, 'pro De Witt') voices still heard. The regents of Amsterdam, knowing Van Beuningen to be outstandingly well informed on foreign affairs, tended to take his advice, which nowadays often opposed De Witt's. De Witt could not, therefore, confront Orangist lobbying from the deputies of Zeeland with any hope of loyalty from Holland's deputies, and when Van den Hove, with excruciating timing, added to his revised *True Interest* passages attacking monarchs, princes, stadholders, captain-generals and religious authorities, the Grand Pensionary may have welcomed the civil ban put on the book by the States of Holland.

In the early spring of 1670 Amsterdam opposition to De Witt eased slightly when Van Beuningen was sent to England as Ambassador Extraordinary. But the reluctant diplomat sent gloomy news. A coincidence of anti-republican and Catholic interests had brought Louis and Charles together, and the English King had reneged on the anti-France clause of the Triple Alliance agreement, signing the Treaty of Dover just a week before Van Beuningen arrived. The latter naturally knew nothing of clauses committing France and England to deal a final blow to De Witt's presumptions and do 'what was possible' for the Prince of Orange by declaring war on the United Provinces in 1671 when joint forces were mustered. De Witt, although dismayed at the renewal of Anglo-French closeness, set about cultivating the friendship of both monarchs. He had been uneasy at Temple's abrupt recall in September 1669, but had not realised this was part of a plot to leave him without English friends. None of these formidable European leaders saw William of Orange as a force equal to any of them. Yet in November 1670, when the Prince finally visited his uncle, he showed displeasure at Charles's open contempt of Protestantism, closeness with Louis and his assumption that William, a member of the Dutch Council of State, would do as Charles told him. The King, taken aback, did not tell his nephew of war plans, but the Prince let slip that he sought De Witt's downfall.

Van Beuningen returned to Holland from England in December 1670, so he had not been in Holland when the 'pernicious book named *Tractatus Theologico-politicus*' was denounced by the Amsterdam *Kerkeraad* on 30 June, by the Synod of The Hague on 7 July, by the Synod of South Holland between 15 and 25 July, by the Amsterdam Synod on 28 July for being blasphemous and dangerous, by the Synod of North-Holland on 5 August, and by a host of other ecclesiastical boards. That Spinoza was alarmed at this is shown in his letter to Jarig of February 1671, in which he begged his frustrated non-Latin-reading devotee to stop a Dutch translation from being printed. *This is not only my request, but that of many of my good friends who would not like to see the book banned, as will undoubtedly happen if it is published in Dutch.* Consistory disapproval had brought the book into instant notoriety. Yet the Church councillors who condemned the *Tractatus Theologico-politicus* seem initially not to have known who wrote it. They may not have found links between this treatise and the named exponent of *Descartes's Principles of Philosophy*, since set side by side the two books made different impressions in their style, terminology and metaphysical commitment. The *Theologico-Political Treatise* moved towards explicating Spinoza's divergence from Descartes, although, we shall soon see, it did not do so clearly enough for all its readers. True, there were references to Cartesian physics and to things *I have already shown in another place*; but anyone who had read neither the *Short Treatise* nor the completed Parts of *Ethics* would have been unlikely to make a connection. The advertising of a publisher in Hamburg may also have deflected suspicion for a while.

That Spinoza was not at once publicly identified is a gift to anyone wanting to argue that his political and social philosophy was not original, but consisted in already well-circulated views. We know that, unique as his work was in providing sustained logical argument for the equation of God with nature, for the place of human beings within that unified system of *God, or Nature*, and for psychological social and political principles deduced from that same strictly defined matrix, it did not spring from a vacuum. We have seen that it expanded, adapted or refuted other naturalistic views, including the ancient, often cabalic or Neoplatonic cosmologies that Calvin had denounced as still tempting educated minds in Europe. Many readers who had explored this literature, as well as those who had read Hobbes and Van den Hove, would have felt on vaguely familiar ground with the material of Chapter XVI of the *Theologico-Political Treatise*, as Spinoza suspected they would when he addressed his treatise to the *Philosophical Reader*. It seems clear to me that the reception Spinoza expected had less to do with his old Amsterdam study group, now depleted and splintered, or with the nucleus of Cartesians who now began to see how radically he diverged from Descartes, than with the new acquaintance he is alleged to have made while living in Voorburg, who promised him a widespread following. This liberal readership of educated religious or political dissidents was not homogeneous, but in one significant dimension it consisted in the French *libertins* of The Hague and those whom they influenced both in the United Provinces and abroad, especially in Paris.

The *libertinisme* of this educated sector of French gentlefolk more or less adhered to a set of beliefs that had developed over a century. A battery of 'maxims' listed in 1623 esotericism; élitism (belief that only highly educated minds could grasp their truths); refusal to believe completely in scripture; a preference for nature as the sovereign power, and an 'imperative' of the demands of the senses; denial of angels and devils, and of the immortality of the soul; a refusal of standard morals, scruples and culpability; and the pursuit of happiness. By 1670 the long reign of their absolute monarch Louis XIV (who had come to the throne as a five-year-old in 1643) had put republican ideals at the top of this list. Those who reached Holland as political refugees were not always philosophically inclined. A distinction had long been made between *libertin érudit* and *libertin politique*, and it follows from the refugee status of many of these émigrés that political reformers and agitators abounded. To them, Spinoza was a useful polemicist who in his *Theologico-Political Treatise* pushed forward the historical, even anthropological, ideas initiated by Hobbes, and gave a fresh gloss to the republican theory of Jan van den Hove. Hovists were generally Dutch since the brothers published only in that language, but we know that many of the Hobbesians, 'Macchiavels' and religious speculators who admired Spinoza's political arguments as much as his Cartesianism were French. Hobbes, while living in Paris from 1640 to 1652, had built on theories that were already popular there, and Spinoza had, recognisably to this readership, built on Hobbes.

The French probably gave the *Theologico-Political Treatise* its most sympathetic response either in or beyond Spinoza's lifetime. In 1678 a French translation of the *Treatise*, called *The Key of the Sanctuary, by a wise man of our century*, would be printed in Leiden. This translation is usually considered the work of Gabriel de Saint-Glen, a gazette-writer and editor of an Amsterdam newspaper. A few scholars believe that he, not Lucas, who arrived in Amsterdam from Rouen aged twenty-seven in 1671, was the adulatory author of the oldest biography, *The Life of the late Mr de Spinosa*, although another admirer, De Boulainvilliers, has also been suggested. There was, in fact, no shortage of Frenchmen capable of listening to Spinoza's reminiscences and gleaning a smattering of his philosophy, and were I to guess who had paid 'Künraht' to print the 1670 Latin edition of the *Theologico-Political Treatise* in Amsterdam, I would suggest we need look no further than these émigrés, who wrote warmly of Spinoza and – Lucas being a typical example – promoted his ideas in so far as they understood them. *Libertins érudits* often had no strong political leanings, and would have provided fine cover for the publishing project. Being adept at hiding when necessary behind a façade of devout Catholicism they may not have struck the Amsterdam authorities as a likely source of support for Spinoza.

Libertinisme had long had widespread influence. Van den Enden may, like Juan de Prado, have come into contact with the movement before settling in

Amsterdam. Isaac de la Peyrère had been librarian to the Prince of Condé, a leading soldier and *libertin* who would soon impinge on Spinoza's life. Many sympathisers, unlike these writers, confined their doubts to discussions in private houses, were demographically obscure and often hid their antipathy to ecclesiastical discipline, but the distinct theologico-political views they held were demarcated clearly enough for many in the United Provinces to be labelled 'libertine'. The term had, during the course of Spinoza's adult years, broadened out in the Netherlands from its original French sense to include Erasmian humanists, political activists and radical Protestants who, like many of the French, did not necessarily endorse the *libertin* sexual laxity of the French Court, denounced by Calvin in 1545. Here was a widely diffused intellectual brotherhood, which regarded the author of the *Theologico-Political Treatise* as one of themselves.

But was he? A stock libertine creed was isolated by a Frenchman in a collection of letters he published as *The Religion of the Dutch* in 1673. He outlined it as a naturalistic view of God and the human mind:

> As for the *libertins*, it seems that as many of them as there are, they each have their private opinion. Most believe there is a single spirit of God, which is in all living things, which is dispersed throughout everything, which is and which lives in all creatures; that the substance and immortality of our soul is nothing other than this spirit of God; that God himself is nothing other than this spirit; that souls die with bodies; that sin is nothing, that it is only a simple opinion which disappears at once when we hold it of no account; that paradise is nothing but an illusion, an agreeable chimera which the theologians have invented in order to urge men to embrace what is called virtue.

This was not Spinozism, as the author of *La Religion des Hollandois* saw, not only by his inclusion of *libertinisme* as a Christian sect, but by going on to mention separately a celebrated *savant* called Spinosa, who was visited by all the inquiring minds of The Hague. It was the case that Spinoza's philosophy reflected certain *libertin* maxims, and some aspects of the new, broader libertinism, but it did not endorse the concept of God outlined above. Spinoza identified God with the universe, not with a spirit-God that lived *in* matter. This last pantheistic deity was the God of the Christian Neoplatonists, who did not go as far as the boldest of the *libertins* in rejecting the notion of an immortal soul but, like many of those same *libertins*, still attended church and did not want to be thought other than Christian.

Spinoza would, nonetheless, have relished a readership already disposed to think in a critical and metaphysical way, and may even have felt assured that he *could* publish on a currently popular theme without danger of personal recognition. Koerbagh may have hoped the same. I do not offer this thought with much confidence, however, since both Koerbagh and Spinoza exaggerated their trademark notions. Koerbagh forged a clear continuity between his dictionary format and his heretical definitions, and coined the word *ipstantie* as if to assert superior understanding of his topic. His *ipstantie* consisted in matter and force. Spinoza, in contrast, assigned essentially disparate force to each of God's attributes, and crucially accentuated *God, or Nature*'s expression of an attribute of thought, a natural, existential manifestation of all possible intelligence in the universe, including all the ideas that humankind enjoys at a sometimes disconcertingly superior level of reflection and wishes to call the spiritual.

However, in a letter written in 1671 Spinoza subtly played down his important difference of view. *I do not here inquire why it is the same, or not very different, to assert that all things emanate necessarily from God's nature and that the universe is God.* Deliberate prevarication is also suggested in the memoirs of an eminent *libertin* who lived in The Hague between 1665 and 1670. Spinoza probably met the Sieur de Saint-Évremond while living at Voorburg, since the Frenchman returned to London (and a generous pension from Charles II) at the point when the philosopher moved into the Stille Veerkade. Charles de Saint-Évremond was a gifted scholar, an ex-army officer who had been a favoured lieutenant of the Prince of Condé until he was overheard satirising him. He was also forced to flee the French royal Court, after witty letters criticising the royal family's links with Spain, and France's recent Treaty of the Pyrenees, were discovered, and he had left for England. Saint-Évremond would recall that Spinoza was 'esteem'd and courted by all the ingenious persons then at The Hague', but that the philosopher refusing to be drawn on the metaphysical views from which, said Saint-Évremond with considerable disapproval, Spinoza only 'cast off the mask' in *Ethics*, published posthumously. *Libertin* ideology did not, any more than did most Dutch anti-clericism and natural religion, deny God to be a non-natural creator, and Saint-Évremond, who despite when dying at the age of ninety refusing to receive a priest, nevertheless forbade anyone to describe him as other than a Roman Catholic. When *Ethics* was finally distributed in Paris, its 'atheism' caused the average *libertin* consternation. I have not previously hinted at *libertin* influence on Spinoza because I think there was not much, unless we accept some early indoctrination by Van den Enden and De Prado. Influence in The Hague years went chiefly the other way, and mainly through Spinoza's political theory.

Most French cosmopolites would have had no great desire to brave the mud of Voorburg's Kerkstraat, and Spinoza is likely to have visited Saint-Évremond rather than the other way round. Dutch dissidents, too, would have been glad to walk unobtrusively through the streets of The Hague to the Stille Veerkade. Ostensibly they may have called on Spinoza to buy lenses for their microscopes, or to discuss other aspects of natural philosophy, knowing better than to broadcast the identity of the lodger in the upstairs back room. Indeed, some were natural philosophers. Leibniz would come – but not for six years – on the strength of Spinoza's reputation in Paris. Others would come as 'Coccejans', professed proponents of the prudently laundered version of Cartesianism taught by Leiden Professor Coccejus. A widely read coded exposé of 1697, *The Life of Philopater*, claimed that the Calvinist theology professor Wittich (Wittichius), who had started teaching at Leiden in 1671, had been 'a great friend of Mr Spinosa'. The writer of *Philopater* claimed that Wittichius had let his students read the philosopher's most basic propositions on Being, and only eventually 'writ against the Ethicks of Spinoza for fear of being reputed a Spinozist ... an impious man and a libertine'. Colerus, among others, fiercely denied that Wittich was a Spinozist. (The publisher of *Philopater* – not the writer – was one of the three individuals exceptionally heavily penalised for blasphemy mentioned earlier. He was fined 4,000 guilders, given eight years' imprisonment and banned from Holland and West-Friesland for twenty-five years.)

The readership of the *Theologico-Political Treatise* was camouflaged by sophistry and precaution, and myriad justifications for reading the book (for example, to refute it) could be contrived. So, while it seems unlikely that a university theologian would visit Spinoza, we have to recognise the unique ethos spreading outwards from The Hague, for which Spinoza had almost undoubtedly gone there. He was, in the underground circles which, at times, and not always amicably, overlapped, known to be the author of the *Theologico-Political Treatise*. As was inevitable, this information leaked out to less sympathetic sources. As far afield as Bonn a certain pastor, sure that the author was one 'Zinospa' or 'Xinospa', who had previously written a work on Descartes's philosophy, denounced the book in a pamphlet published in Utrecht in 1671. Yet between the *Treatise*'s publication in 1670 and its banning by order of the States General in 1674 a pact of silence seems to have held among the Dutch. Philips van Limborch, for example, referred privately to 'the book of Spinoza' in his critical letter of September 1671, but did not openly condemn it until after Spinoza died. His letter was addressed to the liberal Utrecht physician Lambert van Velthuysen, who, besides having studied theology under Voetius, had also qualified in medicine at Utrecht under Descartes's friend and disciple Henricus Regius, who was forced around 1645 to stop including Descartes's views in his teaching. Dr Van Velthuysen's damning opinion of the *Theologico-Political*

Treatise was committed to paper and secretly circulated by Van Limborch by 1671, yet Van Velthuysen denied knowing the identity of the 'political theologian':

> I do not know of what nationality he is or what manner of life he pursues, and this is not of any importance. The methodical reasoning of the book itself is evidence enough that he is not unintelligent...

However, when Van Limborch's letter reached Van Velthuysen the following September it had no air of enlightening him on the author's identity, which Van Velthuysen knew, just as he knew that the 'paradoxical theologian' he had mentioned was Meyer (whose treatise was called, in full, *Philosophiae Sacrae Scripturae Interpres: Exercitatio Paradoxa in qua unam philosophiam etc.*). Despite his censorious review, Van Velthuysen did not publicly denounce Spinoza, and merely wrote in the Preface to his own works that he had talked with him often.

This avoidance of public denunciation marks the genesis of the clandestine intellectual underworld known to unite scientists, religious liberals and republicans in the early eighteenth century, which would became centred in The Hague and would later be known as 'the radical enlightenment'. Its 1670s' forerunners, a self-styled élite of scholarly *savants*, passed round and discussed unorthodox literature, and knew they could trust their own writings to be criticised out of earshot of those who would try to suppress them. This pact, with which Spinoza was now familiar, probably accounts for his certainty that his work would reach the minds for whom it had been written, and that, as the rose-design and motto of *Caute* on his signet seal demonstrated, his identity would be kept *sub rosa*. The rose, an emblem of confidentiality which had for centuries decorated the ceilings of banqueting halls and was in the sixteenth century set over confessionals, was adopted by an order of Rosicrucianism founded in Cassel, Germany in 1614 and, as one of the underground currents of the radical enlightenment, attracted intellectuals, including Leibniz. The Hague became a centre for the Brethren of the Rosy Cross, of whom Lucas is also said to have been one, and for the 'freemasons' associated with them, at that time forming Lodges throughout Europe. These adherents exchanged the secrets of cabala, alchemy and magic that Spinoza found ridiculous. It is, however, interesting to note that the philosopher's seal is first clearly observable on the letter he wrote to Leibniz in 1671, and this invites us to reflect briefly on his closeness to his new coterie of followers.

The French *libertins* were a comfort of sorts to Spinoza. While they were almost certainly the people with whom he declined to dine, they may have held an unconsciously irresistible attraction for him, not only in their proffered *fraternité*, to which we saw him succumb with the Quakers and Collegiants, but in their marrano-like political caution and dissimulation. (Did one of them give him his seal?) Moreover, although Lucas did not list French as one of Spinoza's spoken languages – and Lucas, being French, should know – the philosopher owned French books and dictionaries. Documents in French relating to Michael's business affairs in Nantes survive, and Spinoza may have used the language with faint nostalgia. Overall, he vacillated between working with the French and remaining aloof from them. Dissenters of countless eccentric persuasions, many of them French, would later and usually erroneously be called 'Spinozists', but by the time Spinoza moved to The Hague he knew that a leap in clear-headedness was required from any *libertin*, libertine or liberal Cartesian before he could acknowledge them as like-minded. He was, however, a willing subscriber to their practical policy of debate *sub rosa*. When he was sent a copy of Van Velthuysen's review by a third party (Jacob Ostens, leader of the Rotterdam collegiants and a surgeon), he referred when commenting on it to *this man . . . whoever he may be.*

Spinoza had, in fact, probably counted on a good review from Van Velthuysen, who had published an admiring exposition of Hobbes's *De Cive* in 1651, and a *Tract on idolatry and superstition*, and was known to oppose consistories, binding confessions of faith and oppression of Catholics. Instead, the physician summarised the arguments of the *Theologico-Political Treatise* coldly and for the most part accurately, although the theological gloss he put on some of Spinoza's arguments threatened at points to distort them. For example:

> . . . he locates man's highest pleasure in the cultivation of virtue, which he says is its own reward and the stage for the display of all that is finest. And so he holds that the man who understands things aright ought to devote himself to virtue not because of God's precepts and law, nor through any hope of reward or fear of punishment, but because he is enticed by the beauty of virtue and the joy which a man feels in the practise of virtue.

Virtue for Spinoza was obeying the precepts and law of *God, or nature* as known through reason.

No abuse sullied Van Velthuysen's measured paragraphs. There was no accusation of blasphemy, no abjuring of Satan, just a conviction that Spinoza 'envisaged such a God as can not move men to reverence for his divinity'. Spinoza was disgusted and disappointed, and his reply was bad-tempered and unwillingly sent. *You are doubtless surprised that I have kept you waiting so long; but I can hardly bring myself to answer that man's letter.* Yet a scholar tells us that 'In the original of this letter, the most contemptuous expressions are struck out and replaced by milder terms'. Spinoza had been a little offended at being judged 'not unintelligent', but he was deeply affronted at the charge of atheism . . . *It is in no equable spirit that he has passed judgement on me . . . But I think I see in what mire this man is stuck.* He was stuck, Spinoza angrily wrote, in the common assumption that those with no fear of death or damnation must *lead unbridled lives, and renounce all religion . . . Does that man, pray, renounce all religion who declares that God must be acknowledged as the highest good, and that he must be loved as such in a free spirit?* Spinoza had, after all, reiterated in the *Theologico-Political Treatise* the claim of the *Short Treatise* and the *Emendation of the Intellect* – also to be found in *Descartes's Principles* – that the *love of God*, or *the supreme happiness and blessedness of man, and the highest object and aim of all human actions* was his prime motivation. Van Velthuysen's charge of deism was also denied, which is puzzling, since deism is usually defined as knowing God through reason rather than faith. Spinoza must have had some other definition of the term in mind when he denounced deism as an *evil cause.* In 1675 he would write sarcastically to the Utrecht physician, denying that he was about to refute his critique. *I know that I never had in mind to rebut any of my adversaries, so undeserving of reply did they all seem to me . . . I would be much more obliged to you if you would put in writing the arguments which you believe you can bring against my treatise and append them to your manuscript.* Van Velthuysen presumably thought he had done so.

This correspondence marks a new cycle in Spinoza's life. Gone, almost, was the earlier paucity of intellectual response. Yet Spinoza would not take kindly to the well-made criticisms he began to receive. He could be as impatient and withering over profoundly perceptive objections as he had been over Van Blijenbergh's confusions, and accusations of atheism or blasphemy would continue to draw broadsides of fury or contempt that distracted from his reasoning. This tendency would peak in 1675.

Spinoza did not stay long with the widow Van der Werve because, Colerus says, 'he spent a little too much for his boarding'. This was something on which Colerus may well have been right, since when he himself was appointed pastor of the Lutheran church in The Hague in 1693, he moved with his wife and children into the house previously owned by the Van der Werves, and used Spinoza's upstairs back room as his study. While there is no reason to suppose this room was grand, Spinoza still claimed, despite the De Vries annuity, to be hard up. Quarterly accounts found among his papers after his death show how little he spent on food and drink. We know he refused financial help and hospitality because he 'did not care that people should think he had lived, even but once, at the expense of other men', and we might think his accounts were also an affectation, perhaps even a shrewd communication of his temperance to posterity. On one occasion he accepted half a barrel of beer, but insisted when thanking the donor that he would *repay him in whatever way I may*. Yet his illness may truly have given him stomach only for the 'milk-soop done with butter' or 'gruel done with raisins or butter' that he often chose, and financially he may truly have been, as Colerus reports him saying, 'like the serpent, who forms a circle with his tail in his mouth; to denote that he had nothing left at the year's end'. The De Vries pension amounted to 300 guilders. When, in 1671, Spinoza moved round the corner to the Paviljoensgracht, to the home of Hendrik van der Spyck or Spijk, variously documented as a master painter specializing in murals or portraits, and a military paymaster, his upstairs rooms cost him eighty guilders a year. This rent, added to moderate beer-drinking, pipe-smoking, book-buying, book-giving, mail-receiving and other expenses (we know, for instance, that he paid a barber) can have left him little. Geulincx was said to be 'terribly poor' on an annual salary of 300 guilders. If the Stille Veerkade rent was higher it is not surprising Spinoza moved.

Hendrik van der Spyck's house lay on the Paviljoensgracht, diagonally opposite, across the *gracht*, from the gracious walled gardens of the *Heilige-Geesthofje* (almshouses). It had been built in 1648 for the artist Van Goyen, and was bought by Hendrik's father from a son of the artist Jan Steen. It stood close to the southerly moat that marked the town boundary, not far from the Spui, where the *trekschuiten* left for Amsterdam, Leiden and Dordrecht. Here, Spinoza lodged once more with a young family. Hendrik was barely thirty in 1670, and by 1680 he and his young wife Ida Margareta would have four children under eight years old. Although Spinoza would experience in The Hague – that seemingly effete residential town, where carriages bearing the powerful and privileged bowled daily past his window – horror and grief such as he may never before have encountered, human warmth radiates from Colerus's account of the five or so years he spent with the Van der Spycks. Changes in Spinoza's character during those last years of struggle – the unexpected softening and hardening of attitudes we have glimpsed in the past, the redirection of his interests and the acquiring of something approaching congenial acquaintance – must be set against this affectionate and down-to-earth background. The philosopher did not particularly want carriages at his door. According to Colerus and Lucas, he was not to be seduced, any more than was De Witt, by the manners of the silk-clad social attention he now received. As a 'good republican', he did not 'affect polished and elegant diction' or buy a wig. He may have conversed with Saint-Évremond in French, but it is unlikely that he referred to 'Louis le Roi' in the flowery fashion of The Hague: plain Lodewijk probably did well enough. We know he would not dine out: according to Colerus he had no wish to dress up, either:

> An eminent councillor went to see him, and found him in a very slovenly morning-gown, whereupon the councillor chided him for it, and offered him a new one, to which he answered, 'Would I then be another man?

How we would like to know the identity of this 'councillor' (*raadsheer*), who could have been a magistrate, a States of Holland representative or a States General delegate.

The Van der Spycks, too busy to spy on what Spinoza did 'quietly in his own chamber', where he often stayed for three whole days or longer, cared for him not because he was ill and, despite his contrived ordinariness, a gentleman, but because they found him pleasant:

> If he was very frugal in his way of living his conversation was also very sweet and easy . . . He was besides very courteous and obliging, he would very often discourse with his landlady, especially when she lay in, and with the people of the house, when they happened to be sick or afflicted . . . When he staid at home, he was troublesome to nobody . . . When he happened to be tired by having applied himself too much to his philosophical meditations, he went downstairs to refresh himself, and discoursed with the people of the house any thing that might afford matter for an ordinary conversation, and even about trifles. He also took pleasure in smoking a pipe of tobacco . . .

While we cannot be sure that sustained political protection – as opposed to occasional wary patronage or curiosity – came from individuals in high places, Spinoza was protected at home. Not only did the Van der Spycks like him enough to defend his reputation; Hendrik would later be, as a *solliciteur militair*, a military paymaster responsible for advancing funds to fighting companies, and so in a position of trust and liaison with the magistrates. These companies were either long-established and socially select *schuttersgilden*, or raw platoons hastily recruited in response to the French invasion threat. In 1618 a portrait of the officers of The Hague's ancient Sint Sebastian guard had included the sitting magistrates of the day, but Frederik Hendrik had tried to divert the loyalty of these frighteningly powerful *schutters* by giving them a clubhouse and target range beside the Binnenhof. Although, now, all The Hague's companies were paid by, or answerable to, the States of Holland, the prestigious Blue Flag had remained stubbornly Orangist. Had Hendrik acted for this company, Spinoza might not, as a De Witt supporter, have survived Holland's *rampjaar* – disaster year – of 1672. However, neither military nor notarial records suggest that Hendrik had any strong connection with the political power base in The Hague during the philosopher's lifetime.

What was their lodger writing up there, day after day? The *Theologico-Political Treatise* was in print, and *Ethics*, or at least three Parts of it, lay locked in his desk – the desk eventually sent to Rieuwertsz with its contents. We must assume that since he laid it aside to write the *Treatise*, he was revising that enormously long Part 3, and creating Part 4. His letter of June 1665 (*I shall send it up to about the eightieth proposition*) being followed by one in September (*I am now writing a treatise on my views regarding Scripture*) suggest that additional material for Part 4 could not have been written until after the *Treatise* was complete. This additional material almost certainly consisted in the geometrical demonstration of Spinoza's political thesis, especially the *principle of our advantage*. He is likely to have discussed this, rather than his conception of God, with the *libertins politiques* of The Hague, since in the 1640s the theme of *advantage* or 'interest' was believed to have influenced Hobbes in Paris and, through Hobbes, Pieter van den Hove, who used the concept of interest and the *libertin* term 'maxim' in his title, *True Interest and Political Maxims*.

Ethics Part 4 contains, in my view, Spinoza's finest statements on the power of reason to unite individuals. It demonstrates without lessons from Jewish or Dutch history or comparisons with other political theories, but by inference from metaphysical principles established in earlier Parts of *Ethics*, the requirement for individuals to relate their own advantage to the common advantage, through reason. Indeed, so inseparable are the social and political theories of *Ethics* Part 4 from the earlier principles of *the striving of each thing to persevere in its being*, and the doctrine that only reason reveals *common notions*, that its final demonstration rests wholly on them. *A man who is guided by reason is not led to obey by fear, but in so far as he strives to preserve his being from the dictate of reason, i.e in so far as he strives to live freely, desires to maintain the principle of common life and common advantage.* Spinoza did not, however, demonstrate that all people could reason, or co-operate in a well-ordered society. Nor, judging by the title he chose for *Ethics* Part 4, *Of Human Bondage, or the Power of the Affects*, did he think such a Proof would be possible. Yet, in order to extrapolate as far as possible from his positive thesis; to squeeze out the last grains of truth on the extent to which human power could succeed in bringing about these personal and social advantages, he added an Appendix on *the right way of living*.

The political thesis of *Ethics* Part 4 expounded one set of logical inferences to be made from principles demonstrated earlier, but it ignored the consequences of another equally valid set of inferences, namely those derived from the natural incapacity of most people to reason. He would find himself forced to deduce from this principle in his later *Political Treatise*.

Spinoza may also have found it necessary to re-examine the inferences he had made from the primary passions in Parts 3 and 4, since in 1670 Meyer added a chapter called 'On The Passions' to an anthology compiled by the arts society *Nil Volentibus Arduum*. Bouwmeester contributed, too, continuing the same discussion. Meyer borrowed without acknowledgement from Descartes and Hobbes, and used so many Spinozistic definitions and concepts that we might think he had plundered the draft of *Ethics* Part 3 taken to Amsterdam by Spinoza in 1665. Perhaps he did, but his theory of the passions as *hartstochten* (urges or strivings of the heart) shows independent thought, and Meyer could just as well have enlightened Spinoza. For example, he poured scorn on Descartes's theory of the role of the pineal gland in mind-body interaction, which Spinoza would not do before *Ethics* Part 5 – not yet written if, as we suppose, he had been preoccupied with his *Theologico-Political Treatise* since 1665. The pineal gland, near the middle of the brain, had been proposed by Descartes in his last work *The Passions of the Soul* (and in his *Treatise on Man*, posthumously published only in 1664) as the 'the part of the body where [the soul] exercises its functions more particularly'. He conceived this explanation in response to critics unable to understand his thesis of mind-body interaction. But the pineal gland, however sensitive, remained material, and Steno had lectured in Paris in 1665 on the absurdity of this theory. It is natural that Spinoza, who is said to have sought Kerckring's advice on anatomy in 1673 while still working on *Ethics*, should consult medical friends on technical questions, and fierce debate on the topic plainly underlies the exceptionally long, argumentative Scholium *Ethics* Part 3 Proposition 2.

But this same Scholium is also evidence of Spinoza's isolation on the question of the causes and effects of the passions. His doctrine had been fully expounded by 1665 as a deduction from the basic metaphysic of *Ethics* Parts 1 and 2. By 1661 he had stated that Descartes did not know the true nature of the human mind or its specific states, and by 1662 he had given in 'Of the Human Soul' (Appendix II to the *Short Treatise*) an account of his mind-body theory. In his view Descartes had, despite making thought an essential attribute, not given it the independence it merited as a substance. For Descartes the passions, as we have seen, causally depended on, and sometimes were, physical. Spinoza, although making thought an attribute of one substance rather than a distinct substance, made it causally autonomous. He denied that 'animal spirits' or more sophisticated mechanisms carried messages from the body to the mind. Thus, no matter how similarly Meyer and others *described* specific emotions, if they held at the same time that passions were not wholly thought ('The passions are extraordinary motions of the heart,' wrote Meyer, 'caused by notions of good or evil, and perceived by the soul') and could control the body ('it is not the actuality but the conception of the thing which causes the extraordinary motion'), they diverged radically from Spinoza's view. In this view, passions sprang from thought-processes alone, and were explained through the laws of thought (inference and implication, called by Spinoza *logic*), although reflected in an underlying sequence of physical events, which was deduced from the laws of motion and rest and explained solely through its terminology:

> *In just the same way as thoughts and ideas are connected in the mind, so the affections of the body, or images of things are ordered and connected in the body.*

Reason, not body, interacted with the passions, making psychoanalysis possible. And, unacceptably to those who clung to the notion of a supernatural soul, 'will' had no causal role in either mind-decisions or body-actions. All were determined.

Meyer's account of the sub-category of the passions arising from aversion and enjoyment was from definition to example an elaboration of Cartesian theory, owing nothing to Spinoza. And whether or not Meyer's equable repetition of the classical view that sexual desire contains an element of tragedy resulted from experience (he is said to have been celibate), it serves to accentuate Spinoza's preoccupation with sexual jealousy.

This emotion may in 1671 have had its final test. Van den Enden's school closed down in 1670 after it was put about that he was the writer of an immoral political manifesto and a perverter of young minds. His daughters, aged from twenty to twenty-six, were, as Roman Catholics, hardly more acceptable as educators. Coenraad Burgh, now Treasurer-General of the United Provinces, may have remembered the girls with bitterness after his son Albert became a papist, and Steno's family may also have made the connection. Van den Enden's biographers, writing before his polemical tracts were discovered, believe that the Amsterdam *Kerkeraad*'s condemnation of Spinoza's *Theologico-Political Treatise* effectively killed the schoolmaster's chances of earning his living in the city. They quote a 1706 report which blamed Frans 'ill life' for influencing the 'notorious Jew', and suggest that Koerbagh had also been educated by him. (We might also call Meyer and Casearius 'victims' of that system had not, as was suggested earlier, Frans's principle of educating each pupil according to his or her personal capacity and appetite so obviously produced confident individuals who expressed themselves as they wished.) As his reputation worsened, Van den Enden lost his income. He had always been a poor businessman, and his home remained mortgaged, but this frustrated patriot and passionate republican was at sixty-eight, although disgraced, still full of fire and energy. Since at least 1650, when he had reproduced and distributed the 1587 Declaration, Frans had feared the United Provinces would degenerate into a vassal state through bad government. His 1662 petition had concluded with the words 'God preserve our land from starvation, etc.' His 1665 pamphlet had ended with a four-page polemic on Dutch mishandling of English bellicosity. Before and during the second naval war Frans had offered De Witt practical help. Now, aware that a French offensive was expected, and hearing on all sides criticism of De Witt, he laid plans to move to Paris. Why? One ex-pupil claimed he was invited by the King of France to be Councillor and Court Physician. This may have been a fantasy put about by the aggrieved ex-lawyer and physician, whose talents in these areas, like his expertise in chemistry, Latin, Greek, languages and drama, seemed no longer required in Holland. Certainly no Court appointment ever materialised, and given what did, the later report of a young Parisian – that Van den Enden was at this time weighing the suggestion of a French officer visiting Amsterdam that he should take an active part in a plot against Louis XIV – seems reliable. Yet the old man and one or more daughters travelled by ship to Toulon and Marseilles, lingering in the south with no apparent sense of urgency. On arriving in Paris they sought out only scholars for company and help, and soon, it is recorded, a school was set up in a beautiful big house on the Faubourg Picpus, beside open fields.

Frans had known he would need funds, and, having failed to recover a long-standing debt of 1,266 guilders from an artist, in September 1670 obtained cash for this IOU from none other than Theodor Kerckring, now an Amsterdam physician of immense wealth and some style. Kerckring, said to be an orthodox Lutheran and not noted as liberal or politically inclined, would seem on the face of it the least likely of Frans's former pupils to take on this obvious financial risk – artists were not often 'solid financially' – although the sum was small in relative terms. The physician had carefully built up his reputation and riches. He was famous not only for his anatomy and obstetrics, his alchemical claims and his findings on the 'little creatures' in Amsterdam's drinking water, which he asserted to cause such diseases as smallpox, but for his rare and valuable 'anatomical cabinet'. We know he collected human freaks, especially foetuses, and his skills in chemistry and dissection had obviously been combined to prolific purpose. Kerckring was perhaps, beneath his obsessional veneer, a poser. Grandiloquence distinguishes his *Spicilegium Anatomicum*, published at Leiden in 1670, in which he lavishly praises everyone with whom he has come into contact. Some would remember him for 'unreliability' and 'plagiarism'.

Kerckring's assistance for Frans is mysterious, but not as mysterious as the physician's pledging of 6,000 guilders to his cousin Pieter Hunthum just six months before he married Van den Enden's eldest daughter. Could Theodor possibly have seen Frans as a father-in-law when he relieved him of the artist's debt in September 1670? Had he loved Clara Maria for years, or had his close relationship with Hunthum not impressed the Amsterdam establishment on whose good will he depended? He may have decided he must present himself as a family man. Howsoever, the banns were called on 4 February 1671, and he and Clara Maria were married in the French Carmelite Chapel on the 27th, with Clara Maria's sister Margaretha Aldegondis as witness. A wintry chill permeates the affair. The poet who celebrated the nuptials in verse dwelt on the heroic efforts of Cupid, sent by Venus to awaken the passions of the pair and lure them from the squalor of the dissecting-room and the pure abstractions of the study, to make them view one another erotically. The poet presented both bride and groom as rare prizes, but as being thrust together by conspiracy. Indeed, if she whose mind had the capacity to 'pass through the clouds and the starry vault', yet would not enter a convent (her youngest sister Marianna would be 'put' in one in Paris), Frans would have had to make some arrangement for her. The most reliable source on Van den Enden's last years says that two daughters were left in Amsterdam with relatives, and a document of 1680 suggests that the couple, together with Margaretha Aldegondis, were still in Amsterdam then. Kerckring and Clara Maria travelled after that, via the Spanish Netherlands, France and Italy, to Kerckring's birthplace, Hamburg. A son, who would also become a physician, was born. Theodor would die in 1693, the son in 1709 and Clara Maria in 1710, in Italy, in the company of her father-confessor. Nothing suggests that Cupid ever achieved romantic love, for it was rumoured that the Hamburg physician 'of suspect morals' tried to murder his wife in order to marry her 'sister, or a servant'. (There is also scope for delving into the affairs of Pieter Hunthum, whose 'widow' died in 1703. Pieter seems to have been interred in Amstelveen in 1706, as the husband of another.)

We would have no interest in any of these details were it not for Colerus's insistence that Spinoza had been in love with Clara Maria. Colerus may have got this story from 'Elders of the Lutheran Church at Amsterdam' who complained of Van den Enden's sowing of the 'seeds of atheism', but these 'elders' may have been none other than Van der Spyck, who was by June 1699 one of their number. Of course we want to know Spinoza's reaction to the marriage, but unfortunately it is unavailable. Possibly he did not know of it, yet Van den Enden left for France immediately afterwards, and Spinoza would have heard of that. I suggested earlier that Van den Enden may have given Spinoza books before he left. There may also have been references to the affairs of the Van den Endens in letters to and from Jarig Jelles. The note of 19 April 1673, in which Spinoza is said to have referred to Kerckring in connection with 'some anatomical questions', was one of several letters destroyed by Spinoza's editors. We know this for sure because in 1710 a Dr Hallmann reported that the son of Jan Rieuwertz had admitted that:

> more letters had been found than had been printed; but they were of no consequence, so had been burned. But he had kept one letter, which was lying upstairs among his things. At last I persuaded him to fetch the letter and show it to me. It was a short letter written in Dutch on half a sheet of paper.

It could have contained personal news.

We certainly do not have to suppose that the strange, cool union in Amsterdam passed Spinoza by, and we may tentatively make a connection between that incident and a sensitivity about money. On 4 February 1671 the wedding banns were called. That same February, Spinoza made himself reply to Van Velthuysen's 'compendious summary', and was, we might think, unduly quick to relate accusations of atheism to money-making. *Atheists are usually inordinately fond of honours and riches, which I have always despised, as is known to all who are acquainted with me.* On 17 February he replied, equally touchily, and on a similar theme, to Jelles. He began, in justifiable agitation, by begging that the *Theologico-Political Treatise* should not be translated into Dutch, as *Professor* [name deleted – could it have been Wittich?] who *recently paid me a visit*, told him it had. Glazemaker had indeed already translated it, but Jelles would successfully stop it from being printed. Spinoza then turned to the subject of a booklet he had been sent, called *Homo Politicus*, which argued that all men, not just princes, acted chiefly from motives of greed and self-advancement, and that it was rational to do so. Spinoza ignored its fundamental question (of self-interest versus communal interest) to focus on *the restless and pitiable condition of those who are greedy for money and covet honours*, and resorted to a fable (that of Thales of Miletus) to drive home the point that *it is not out of necessity but from choice that the wise possess no riches*; that the wise could instantly be rich if they so desired. One commentator suggests Spinoza was pointing out that he had wilfully rejected the potentially lucrative life of a merchant. If anyone knew this it was Jarig Jelles, who had not only witnessed Spinoza's 'renunciation', but had regularly divested himself of his own worldly goods, and would in 1675 and 1681 make substantial charitable endowments.

So why was Jarig on the receiving end of this harangue? Well, my theory is that it was more or less at this point that Spinoza realised he could no longer afford to live in *Mevrouw* Van der Werve's house. Further, his brother Gabriel may already have been known in Amsterdam as a successful colonialist, having in January that year taken an oath of allegiance to the English Crown, after which Whitehall would 'prepare a bill to pass a Great Seal for making Abraham Espinosa of Jamaica, merchant, an alien born, a free denizen of England'. A document I have never seen quoted also lists 'Abraham Spinosa' as being granted, jointly with Moses Yessurun Cardosa, one hundred acres of land in St Andrew parish:

> in consideration that the individuals transfer themselves, their servants and slaves into the island in pursuance of a proclamation during the reign of King Charles II, and for the better encouragement to become planters, and diverse other good causes and considerations, on the annual payment of $\frac{1}{2}$d per acre.

Since, as noted earlier, an 'Abraham Jessurun de Espinosa' was periodically, between 1663 and 1676, an Amsterdam *parnas*, nothing prevents this Abraham, who had probably lived in Barbados for the previous six years and was among a very small number of Jews given land in Jamaica, from being the Gabriel of 'Bento y Gabriel despinoza', who later called himself 'Abraham Spinoza, son of Michael espinoza his heir'. Burial records cannot confirm his parentage, however, since an earthquake in June 1692, which killed several thousand people, sent the first Jewish synagogue and cemetery, sited in Port Royal, into the sea.

Jelles, still in Amsterdam, may have told Spinoza of Gabriel's good fortune. I suggest that any calculation of personal worth in terms of money and honour could have touched a nerve at this time, making Spinoza reassess the grounds of his own self-esteem and, possibly, channel into the safe outlet of invective over money strong feelings about the foolish marriage (foolish, of course, unless she wanted children) of Clara Maria. Whether or not this sour succession of thoughts occurred, the letter to Jarig shows that Spinoza stayed on good terms with Kerckring, whereas acid comments on the failure of women to rise above the petty and the sentimental, and to participate in society without manipulating through sexual attraction, would intrude in the latter Parts of *Ethics* and the *Political Treatise*, the latter not to be written for several years. No young lady of learning in The Hague seems to have disabused Spinoza of his view that, like the mass of the common people, women did not reason.

It must now be clear that Spinoza's lofty political ideology in *Ethics* Part 4, and his deliberate back-turning on the commercial interests which were the fount of Holland's prosperity, were ill-attuned to the problems of De Witt, who currently found himself casting around for any practical means of preserving Dutch sovereignty against invasion by the French. Never before had an army of 35,000 men threatened to assail one nation in Europe: never, perhaps, had the United Provinces been so surrounded by ill will. Louis XIV's megalomania had been used by the Bishop of Münster as an excuse to re-arm, and neighbouring German principalities promised Louis a clear path to invade the United Provinces. Huygens and Hudde were called on by the States of Holland to advise on the Nederrijn and Ijssel rivers, it being crucial to national defence that they remained unsilted. De Witt turned to Sweden, Denmark, Brandenburg and Austria for help, but met only prevarication or indifference. Only Spain agreed to send forces if Louis invaded, in exchange for Dutch help if he marched into the northern Spanish Netherlands. De Witt began urgently to build up the army – by April he thought he had 70,000 men – while trying to strengthen relations with England and keep open negotiations with France. But his last-minute mustering of infantry and calvary regiments under inexperienced field commanders caused head-shaking among Deputies and the Dutch public, most of whom would have been unsurprised to hear that French soldiers found the Dutch army a joke. De Witt had neglected the land forces for his sea warfare, everyone said, and now he either truly expected these hobbling regiments to serve him as a fighting force or, as they suspected (for no one thought him that foolish), he was secretly doing a deal with the French. In December 1671 the States of Holland ignored De Witt's protests after a burgomaster of the traditionally anti-Orange city of Amsterdam, angry at the burden on its commerce caused by recruiting, declared the person of William of Orange to be worth 20,000 men against the French, and elected the 21-year-old prince to the position of Captain General. De Witt had support, albeit mainly grudging, for his motion that William be made Captain General for one campaign only, and barred from election as stadholder in any province, but the Prince – so precipitating a turning-point in Dutch history – refused to agree to a temporary command. Eighteen months of meeting William in connection with sessions of the Council of State had convinced all that William 'was a man who could make himself obeyed by his impenetrable reserve, his immovable composure, his unconquerable obstinacy, and even by the curt and concise way in which he gave his orders', and on 24 February 1672 the young prince was voted, amid

245

public euphoria, Captain and Admiral General. By 27 June 'all military matters, directly or indirectly' had by States Resolution passed into his hands. By 1673 the hitherto amateurish role of company paymaster would be tightened up by law.

There was potential here for dissent between Spinoza and Hendrik van der Spyck, who, if already connected with the military, must now take his orders from officers acting only on Orangist authority, which Spinoza did not accept. (This would also hold for any other acquaintances with 'military employments'.) The philosopher had stated in the *Theologico-Political Treatise* that Dutch *sovereignty was always held by the Estates, and it was their sovereignty that the last count tried to usurp.* When Temple wrote of the sovereignty of the United Provinces he had this in mind. William was not a prince of The Netherlands but of a small principality in France, and while Calvin had taught that kings must sometimes take up arms for the infliction of public vengeance, this prince had no such right. On *Prinsgezind* fever, Spinoza's stance was also clear: no advantage (*utilitas*) could result from the passions of a people, aggregated. There is a hiatus in Spinoza's correspondence between November 1671 and February 1673, but the editors need not have removed anti-Orangist or pro-republic comments from his letters: his views were plain for all to see in the *Theologico-Political Treatise*.

The English precipitated a third Anglo-Dutch naval war in March 1672 by attacking Dutch merchant trading ships. De Witt, at once involving himself in naval policy, was warned that he could afford no mistakes, and his brother Cornelis, loathed for his arrogance, was monitored by a new deputy Fleet Commander. In April France declared war, and the Dutch and English fleets, warily watching each other in the North Sea, had not met when news came that Dutch fortresses had been seized. Cornelis at once ordered an attack, and the English were driven back at Sole Bay. But while the tattered fleets recovered Cornelis returned, sick, to The Hague, amid rumours that he had struck Admiral De Ruyter. Meanwhile the Prince, who had never seen battle, held operational army control with such aplomb on the eastern border that he quickly won the loyalty of field commanders sent by De Witt to undermine him. Soon pamphlets denouncing Johan and Cornelis as atheists, self-seekers, traitors and usurpers of princely power littered the Dutch streets. Only when it was added that Johan had embezzled States funds did he demand a States retraction. A (true) report spread that he had offered Louis Maastricht and other territory in return for peace, while French troops, in that exceptionally hot, dry summer, forded minor rivers and advanced on Utrecht. Dutch panic spread. A French aide recorded that 'The terror was so great that the Jews of Amsterdam sent me word that they would give two millions to the Prince of Condé [Commander of the French army, who planned to send 6,000 cavalry to Amsterdam] if he would save their quarter.' Late in June De Witt was attacked by Orangist fanatics in The Hague, and was slow to recover from his wounds. Louis's troops took Utrecht, and in mid-July the French Commandant was formally welcomed in the name of the municipal council by, among others, Lambert van Velthuysen. But the French did not advance because, despite the protests of landowners and dyke-cutters, the land south of Amsterdam, as far as the Waal, was flooded, leaving towns, farms and country estates under water at least waist high, into which no army commander could ride, let alone march his troops. Pieter van den Hove had in his 1669 *Indications* outlined plans for just such a 'trench'. The French described the inundation as an invasion of the Zuyder Zee, but it was not. Salting the land was avoided. However, word that this had happened was sent to the French to make them think that Holland, its agriculture ruined for generations to come, was not worth capturing.

While De Witt convalesced, the Eternal Edict was reversed by the States General, and the Prince of Orange, at once voted Stadholder of Holland and Zeeland, took his oath on 9 July. Late that month Cornelis was seized in Dordrecht, falsely charged with ordering William's assassination and flung into The Hague's odious Gevangenpoort to be interrogated under torture. De Witt called on the Prince, who was briefly in The Hague, and after an interview in which William referred all legal decisions to the States, and advised of dangers in the people's mood, Johan resigned, laying down his office in the Knights' Hall of the Binnenhof, the former palace of the counts of Holland, facing the Gevangenpoort. The hatred surrounding him was palpable. On 20 August, against advice, he entered the Gevangenpoort to pay Cornelis's 'trial' expenses, and to help him out to start the sentence of life banishment just passed on him. But, as the brothers tried to leave, a vengeful crowd armed with pikes and muskets forced them back in. All day the fortress was watched menacingly from surrounding rooftops (and fearfully by Johan's family, in his home a few doors away) as some of the town's militia gathered in blatant support of the *grauw*. In the afternoon the Spui's sluice-gates were shut, the drawbridges lowered and the canal-boats tied up to seal The Hague against mobs rumoured to be approaching from neighbouring villages. The *grauw*, hearing of this, howled for the traitors to be brought out and shot so that the town could be defended. At about five o'clock they shot at the door and broke it down, hauled out the brothers and dragged them to the high 'Green Sod' where the gallows stood, before the Binnenhof. The De Witts did not reach it alive: they were murdered on the way with blows, slashes and shot, chiefly by officers of the company of the Blue Flag. Then, in a vile delirium, their corpses were hung upside-down, stabbed, clubbed and shot again, and placards hung on them proclaiming 'Land Prince' and 'Water Prince' to mock their ambition. With unprecedented butchery, pieces of flesh were hacked off and sold as souvenirs, or roasted and eaten, not only 'by the canaille, but by chief burghers, silversmiths, shoemakers and others of like respectability, whereby can be judged how great a hatred possessed them'. By eight o'clock there was 'great joy amongst the people, as if a fair were going on'.

No one in Europe was left in any doubt about what had happened in The Hague. The English sailor Edward Barlow would later be told by Dutch seamen that their army:

> had taken some of their towns again from the French, and that which they had lost before was lost only through the treachery of John de Witt and his brother, two of their chief ministers of state, which had sold their provinces to the French; and for that treachery they had taken them two and hanged them upon the gallows and cut them in two-penny pieces.

Prince William, at Alphen, not far from his camp at Bodegraven between Leiden and Utrecht, was said by someone who was with him at the time to have been told of the deaths that evening at 7 p.m. and to have 'turned pale'. His grandmother Amalia said she was sorry 'such a noble mind' had died so shamefully. Huygens, in Paris, was appalled. De Witt had been unwise to show himself to the people, he wrote to his brother, but had committed no crime meriting death.

As the din and stench cut through the summer stink of the canals, Spinoza, not knowing the cause, may have closed his shutters in revulsion. *The mob is terrifying if unafraid.* Yet someone told him what had happened, never suspecting that the information would trigger a consummation of sorrow at the death of a good man; at the death of the world's first true republic. It is possible that the philosopher already knew; that he had been out, and, standing with those others in the thousand-strong crowd who were too horrified to speak, had witnessed the atrocity, for Lucas says, 'He shed tears when he saw his fellow-citizens rend to pieces one who was father to them all, and although he knew better than anybody what men are capable of, he could not but shudder at that cruel sight.' Perhaps he saw those mocking placards. At all events, Leibniz confirmed years later that Spinoza told him that he 'had been prompted, on the day of the massacre of the De Witts, to go out in the night and put up somewhere near the place a paper saying ULTIMI BARBARORUM [lowest of barbarians!]. Abuse in Latin would not have been understood by the rabble, but, chillingly, the crowd had not consisted entirely of 'canaille'. Spinoza's *Staatsgezind* presence would have been recognised, and his weak frame would not have got him home alive. 'But his host had shut the house to prevent his going out,' wrote Leibniz, 'for he would have been exposed to the risk of being torn to pieces.'

Lucas says that Spinoza 'soon got over this terrible incident', asking an inquirer calmly, 'Of what use would wisdom be to us if after falling into the passions of the people we had not the strength to raise ourselves by our own efforts?' Yet on this one occasion we would surely be right to envisage him dropping his placard in despair, climbing the stairs to the attic and, pulling across the red curtains of his *ledikant*, weeping into its suffocating mattresses.

TEN

The Hague and Utrecht: 1673

One man has another in his power . . . when he has inspired him with fear; or when he has bound him so closely by a service that he would rather please his benefactor than himself.

Most English people had not wanted a third naval war. Charles II had cajoled the House of Commons into granting funding for warships only by warning that, under the terms of the Triple Alliance, the fleet must be ready for a French attack. There was annoyance in 1672 over its pathetic performance at Sole Bay, and pity for the Dutch over their French invasion, but the Commons' wish to refuse funds for a further campaign was undone by emotive appeals to fears of Holland as a perennial sea-trading menace. However, in 1673 three lost sea battles, unsupported by the French, and thousands of pamphlets dumped by the Dutch warning the English of the 'Private cabal at Whitehall', ended backing for Charles. (Were the flyers William's first political thrust at his uncle?) Charles was forced to withdraw from the war, and in February 1674 signed away any prospect of gaining the river-mouth lands of Zeeland – the plunder Louis had secretly promised him at Dover, if victorious.

There was no noticeable glee in England over De Witt's murder. Temple, although he would return to The Hague as ambassador in 1674, to negotiate precariously between Charles and the intractable William, who daily found 'his authority rise with his credit among the people here', wrote, 'Thus ended one of the greatest lives of any subject in our age.' Felltham's sneer that 'The people are generally boorish . . . as churlish as their breeder Neptune, and without doubt very antient, for they were bred before manners were in fashion' had during the first Anglo-Dutch war appealed to folk memories of the ancient Batavians, savage boglanders who had defied the Romans from their watery lairs. Now, after twenty years of conflict, in which insults such as 'Dutch courage' were added to Marvell's view of the Dutch as 'pickled *heeren*' taking over from their 'pickled herring', the English were ready to believe that a typical outburst of drunken brutality had killed De Witt.

Some of the French saw the assassination as just another instance of the Dutch cussedness exploited by Willem the Silent and now expressed, in inimitable fashion, by his great-grandson William. (When Louis called for surrender the young Stadholder refused, telling States deputies that even if the land were taken, Dutch liberty and pure religion could survive, since ships could take 200,000 Dutch emigrants to India, where Amsterdam's Exchange and Leiden's university could be rebuilt in even greater glory.) One French diplomat, seeing the floodline as an act of near-demented violence, wrote:

> If they had not made use of an element as unstable as themselves there is every likelihood that by this time they would be under the yoke; but the obstinate fury of this rabble may be recognised chiefly in the fact that, although they perceive that God is punishing them, instead of humbling themselves they become more exasperated, and prefer to ruin and destroy their country and their subjects.

On the whole, although De Witt's murder was compared by some with the English regicide of 1649, the scandal suited France. 'This affair, which had produced much consternation among all honest men, could not fail to have a good effect upon the king's service,' wrote Utrecht's commandant, the Duke of Luxembourg. Army commander Condé, veteran warrior and notorious stock-market gambler (who had been offered a bribe by the Amsterdam Jews to spare them), was merely advised by his agent that the murder would keep down share prices, and so would unfortunately damage his speculations in the Indies.

The 52-year-old Prince of Bourbon-Condé, so bold in battle that his cousin Louis XIV had pardoned his six-year defection to Spain in order to regain his support, had never considered the invasion of the Netherlands wise, nor, despite the inexperience of its young Captain General, had he expected an easy conquest. He was therefore unsurprised on reaching Utrecht in April 1673 to find that no further advance had been made towards the Province of Holland. Instead, Colonel Jean Baptiste Stouppe, or Stoppa, Swiss aide to the commandant and, like councillor-physician Van Velthuysen, trained in theology, had become well enough acquainted with Van Velthuysen and Johannes Graevius, Dutch professor of rhetoric, to amass material for his book *The Religion of the Dutch*. The Utrecht authorities were curiously tolerant of Catholics, their States issuing only fourteen anti-Catholic placeats between 1636 and 1672, during which time the States of Holland put out 223. (They cannot, all the same, have much enjoyed the Corpus Christi procession that the French re-instituted, which bore the sacrament aloft through the streets of the city for the first time in a hundred years.) Stouppe, as we heard earlier, described in his book a celebrated *savant*, 'a very bad Jew and hardly a better Christian', whose opinions had attracted a number of followers, despite being set down in a book that 'had the essential purpose of destroying all religions, above all the Jewish and Christian, and opening the doors to atheism, libertinism, and freedom for all'. No Dutch theologian, Stouppe complained, had shown courage enough publicly to refute the *Tractatus Theologico-Politicus*. In this the Lieutenant was more or less right: only the critic of 'Zinospa' or 'Xinospa' had protested in print, although Utrecht's professor of philosophy Van Mansveldt had, when he died in 1671, left a hand-written attack.

Stouppe was considered a relatively liberal and humanitarian soldier, but there is no evidence that he would feel other than tainted by contact with Spinoza, and he was probably acting on orders, as Lucas suggests, when he invited the *Juif renegat* to visit the military quarters in Utrecht. Colerus reports that Stouppe 'writ several letters to Spinosa, from whom he received several answers; and at last he desired him to repair to Utrecht at a certain time'. No letter survives, and we may wonder if Spinoza found anything worthy of reply in the comments of a man who merely elaborated opinions presumably passed by Van Velthuysen. Spinoza would dismiss Van Mansveldt's book, after scanning it in a bookshop when it was eventually published in 1674, as *not worth reading through, and far less answering*, and its author as *ignorant*, although a copy of it was found in his personal library. The Van der Spycks' testimony suggests that at this time the shaken savant was more concerned with the desolate state of the Dutch than with answering screeds of theological prejudgement, and Stouppe may have guessed that some more appealing incentive than his criticism was needed to attract Spinoza to Utrecht, for the officer was, Colerus writes:

> so much the more desirous that [Spinoza] should come hither, because the Prince of Condé, who then took possession of the government of Utrecht, had a great mind to discourse with Spinoza: And it was confidently reported that his Highness was so well disposed to recommend him to the King, that he hoped to obtain easily a pension for him, provided he would be willing to dedicate one of his books to him. He received that letter with a passport.

What was going on? *The Religion of the Dutch* had gone to press within a month of Condé's arrival in Utrecht, so it would not be amended. Moreover, Stouppe knew full well that Spinoza's work, with its republican call for the freedom of each individual, must displease the French King.

Louis was an absolute monarch for whom the notion of human equality was laughable, and the right to free speech a monstrous threat. That very month he sent 12,000 cavalry, 20,000 foot soldiers and fifty-two cannons to besiege Maastricht, certain that the first drought or frost would allow army movement across the waterline and see Amsterdam taken, after which, the King said, 'nothing is to be looked for but total submission and abject slavery'. True, the *Theologico-Political Treatise* would have gratified Louis in its censure of papal authority and its assigning of control of religious affairs to the *sovereign* (read, of course, as 'monarch': as we know, Spinoza's *sovereign* was rarely a monarch: he very often used the word *summa potestas* – highest power – not *rex*).

> *Everyone knows what a tremendous weight the right and authority in matters of religion has with the people, and how all men hang on the lips of the person who has it; in fact he who has it may be said to have most control over their minds. Hence if anyone seeks to take it from the sovereign he is seeking to divide the sovereignty; and this will inevitably cause disputes and quarrels which can never be settled, just as it did of old between the kings and priests of the Jews.*

Louis quarrelled constantly with His Holiness and would have relished such backing. Hobbes's *Leviathan* had also condemned Roman Catholicism as the enemy of true religion since, among other iniquities, it falsely claimed the Church to be the Kingdom of God, and caused 'Darknesse' in subjects' minds by asserting a power superseding that of civil sovereigns. The *Theologico-Political Treatise* had further advised that *modern sovereigns, who have no prophets, and are not bound by law to recognize any* [need not] *allow religious dogmas to be confused with philosophy*. They should instead exercise reason and formulate conditions for free worship. Louis's insight into human nature was, Spinoza would have conceded, an element in his personal power. The King would, for example, write in his memoirs on the present Dutch war, 'The determination to flood the whole country was certainly rather violent, but what would not one do to save oneself from foreign domination?' This reflection, in its relating of a single instance to a universal truth of human nature, affirmed Spinoza's principles. But there was no other intellectual or political point of contact between them, and if Louis was told that Spinoza's doctrine matched Hobbes's sovereign-subject contract, which held through fear of compulsion and, being grounded in unconditional obedience, magnified the megalomania of any king, then he had been misled.

Leviathan had been printed in Latin in Amsterdam in 1668, and although no copy was found among Spinoza's books, it is assumed by commentators that he read it. He deplored Hobbes's social contract theory, and rejected his model commonwealth on many counts. Believing that *obedience is less a matter of the outward act than of the mind's inner activity*, and that the *hope of some greater good*, not fear, engendered it, he found the absolute monarchy of *Leviathan* abhorrent. As Bishop Bramhall had sarcastically put it in 1658, 'Who would not desire to live in [Hobbes's] commonwealth, where the sovereign may lawfully kill a thousand innocents every morning to his breakfast?' At this time Spinoza thought any kind of monarchy unsuited to the traditional *form* of the Dutch State, and while he would, years later, point out that the Dutch benefited from the financial burden of the House of Orange, since having to pay taxes had made them work hard and grow rich, he knew that rule by Louis would be pure oppression to the Dutch. The *Theologico-Political Treatise* had warned that *inward piety and inward worship of God are part of the inalienable right of the individual,* and that *the attempt to make men speak only as the sovereign prescribes, no matter how different and opposed their ideas may be, must always meet with very little success in a state; for even men of experience cannot hold their tongues, far less the mass of the people.* There could, in short, be no effective control over people's beliefs, and Spinoza's views were, it could be argued, a blueprint for anarchy. Graevius, who had already written to Leibniz about the 'Jew's' *liber pestilentissimus*, may have put Stouppe on to Spinoza with malicious intent and envisaged the heretical philosopher travelling calmly to his annihilation, for Condé must surely, in loyalty to Louis, take this troublemaker prisoner.

Condé, professional soldier, aristocrat and *libertin*, a relapsed Jesuit with no time for religion, was presently laid up with gout, and perhaps also trouble from his hand wound, sustained while crossing the Rhine. He was therefore unable to pursue his objective of inspecting conquered towns and trying to reduce the cruelties perpetrated by the French occupiers, which were among the most sadistic ever inflicted on Dutch villages. His respect for the humane Stouppe, added to his own vast and genuine intellectual curiosity, had led him into conversation with the Lieutenant, and at this time he was probably distracting himself by reading the *Theologico-Political Treatise*, while imploring his aides to find him company other than the Calvinist burghers who condemned theatre, dancing, fairs, playing cards, flirting and strong drink. The anti-clericist views that circulated in the smoking-rooms and libraries of France and England, where the educated and urbane had found Hobbes's making of religion an affair of State a relief, were evident in the *Treatise*'s Preface alone. A spirited dialogue between Spinoza and Condé might certainly have been anticipated: the French philosopher Nicolas Malebranche would be 'ravished' by the Prince's understanding of his work and the 'thousand honours' heaped upon him when he visited Condé's home at Chantilly for three days in 1683. (Malebranche, devout Catholic, may also have impressed the prince in a religious dimension since Condé, who had not received communion for twenty years, converted early in 1685.)

For his part, Spinoza knew that if Condé was familiar with Hobbes's political philosophy, his own mission was far from straightforward. Even if he kept the conversation clear of the metaphysical basis of his social and political theory, as he had with Saint-Évremond, their debate would be riddled with misunderstanding. Yet no Jewish-born political scientist, deprived by the terms of Grotius of public position and no longer believing, on grounds shortly made clear, that there existed *men holding high positions in my country who will want to see other of my writing*, could have refused such a summons. He set forth.

There was jeopardy at each step for the wheezy philosopher. First, it was necessary to take a roundabout, hazardous southerly route, skirting the floodlands and slipping between confrontations of Dutch gun-ships with French artillery at each patrolled river border. Once in Utrecht, he faced the *odium theologicum* of the city's Reformed Church dogmatists, whipped to a fine art by Voetius and already quietly mounting against himself. Entering the French army's quarters was an equally obvious danger, and Spinoza may at first have thought himself tricked when he discovered that earlier in July the Prince of Condé, his gout fully eased, had left the city for 's-Hertogenbosch. It is the case, as Lucas reported, that 'An order from the King had summoned the Prince elsewhere', for after two months of siege Maastricht had at last surrendered at the beginning of July. However:

M. de Luxembourg received Spinosa in the Prince's absence, showed him a thousand devotions, and assured him of the good will of His Highness. The crowd of courtiers did not awe our philosopher ... Although this kind of life was utterly opposed to his principles and his taste, he submitted to it with as much complacency as the courtiers themselves. The Prince, who wanted to see him, frequently sent word that he should wait for him. The inquisitive, who liked him and always found something new to like about him, were delighted that His Highness obliged him to wait for him.

Spinoza was in no danger: paradoxically, he was protected by the French from Dutch zealots. But to what end? The story of his sojourn in Utrecht is painful to anyone aware of his anguish over the collapse of the democracy whose advantage to all he had, at risk to himself, tried to foster. For several weeks this son of marranos (clad in old, well-cut clothes, perhaps flashing silver buckles and signet ring, probably speaking French, and bowing with Hispanic dignity) endured and enjoyed – the tension is implicit in Lucas's comment that 'he submitted to it with as much complacency as the courtiers themselves' – French food and wine in sympathetic surroundings, where music, miming and chess – perhaps he learned the game there – replaced solemn parochial carping. He daily submitted to questioning from French and Dutch alike, the latter politely disguising their outrage in deference to the *libertins*, who found him delightful. Van Velthuysen, as mentioned, recalled merely that they 'talked often'. We may assume it was more congenial for Spinoza to be with the French than the Dutch, since theological opposition to him afterwards hardened in the United Provinces, whereas good things were reported of him in Paris. In late 1675 he was told that 'the *Tractatus Theologico-Politicus* . . . is esteemed by many there, and there are eager inquiries as to where any more writings of the same author are published'. Relations with Van Velthuysen and Graevius, however, seem to have soured. A year later Spinoza admitted to Van Velthuysen that he had discussed with Joachim Nieuwstad, the Secretary of Utrecht, the possibility that he, Spinoza, might elucidate points in his *Treatise* with notes, adding in Van Velthuysen's criticism of it, and a reply to this, but had thought better of the idea. More immediately, a six-line note was sent that December from Spinoza to Graevius, insisting on the return of a letter Spinoza had lent him about the death of Descartes. The note professed friendship in its wording and in the inclusion of a forename, but it was sent by The Hague's night mail to Utrecht, landing the professor, it would seem, with a fine, for the French, intent on cutting Holland's communications, ordered mail to be sent to or from the province only by themselves, on pain of a hefty delivery charge.

Was sending the note by Dutch mail an act of vengeance on Spinoza's part? The only other letters he is known to have sent during the French occupation – save one to Heidelberg, soon to be discussed – were to Jelles in Amsterdam, and to a man at Gorinchem, a town in south Holland still held by the Dutch. It is possible: I think Spinoza especially loathed the theologians of Utrecht. When discussing Van Mansveldt's refutation of the *Treatise* just a month before the *Theologico-Political Treatise* was officially banned, a word had to be excised from Spinoza's letter: *It seemed to me that the* [word deleted] *set out their wares for sale in the same way as do shopkeepers, who always display the worse first. They say the devil is a crafty fellow, but in my opinion these people's resourcefulness far surpasses his in cunning.* The missing word could have been *theologen*, long loathed by Spinoza, and said by him in 1675 to be *intriguing against me everywhere*. But it may equally have been *sçavanten*, for the *college der sçavanten van Utrecht*, inspired by

Van Mansfeldt and now dominated by Van Velthuysen and Graevius, was well known by 1674 for its Cocceijan Cartesianism. It had attracted Leiden professors Heydanus and Wittich and others from farther afield, some of whom were thought to be secret Spinozists. The deleted word could also have been *Cartesianen*, Spinoza's view being that *the stupid Cartesians, in order to remove ... suspicion from themselves because they are thought to be on my side, cease not to denounce everywhere my opinions and writings.*

While Spinoza wanted the French to remove their armies from the Provinces, and had no wish to follow Van den Enden and Huygens to Paris, the tendency towards élitism that French intellectuals put in place of dogma in some measure left its mark on his writing, from the Preface of the *Theologico-Political Treatise* through *Ethics* Part 5 and the *Political Treatise*, in each of which Spinoza states that his project is not for the dull mind or the masses. But neither dulcet *conversation* nor dread of the discomfort of a return journey through the war zone could make him stay in Utrecht once he learned that the high-level talks for which he had taken the trouble to come must be cancelled, since Condé had gone back to France:

> After some weeks the Prince [of Condé] sent word that he could not return to Utrecht. All the inquisitive among the French were vexed, for our philosopher at once took his departure from them, in spite of the gratifying offers which M. de Luxembourg made.
>
> Monsieur Stouppe ... had assured him that he would willingly use his interest for him, and that he should not doubt to obtain a pension from the King's Liberality, at his recommendation ... Because he did not design to dedicate any book to the King of France, he refused the offer that was made him, with all the civility he was capable of.

Suddenly, accepting favours from the French was futile, and wrong. Futile because, as he is said to have remarked afterwards, 'all [the Prince's] power would not have supported him against the bigotry of the [French] court'; wrong because he now saw that he had taken French hospitality to no purpose, while his countrymen in the villages were being massacred and the people of Holland starved. The Dutch, lacking the butter, meat, bread and cheese that their lush pastures usually yielded, were thrown back on a diet of herrings. When, in the past, the Spanish had tried to starve the north Netherlanders into surrender, Count Maurits had called herrings the slingshot of David. The Goliath now casting a shadow over the Republic was France, and Spinoza, although sure (Colerus reports) that the people of The Hague knew he 'always aimed at the glory and welfare of the State', left Utrecht at once.

The Hague was in a wretchedly indefensible state. Barrels of treasury gold had long been sent to Amsterdam for safe keeping, and the idea of transferring government there, too, was frequently and urgently raised. Lack of ramparts and flood-devices kept the townsfolk edgy and alert, aware that if Maastricht had fallen, their town stood little chance – especially if treachery led the enemy to its heart:

> After [Spinoza's] return, the mob at The Hague were extremely incensed against him. They looked upon him as a spy, and whispered in one another's ears that they ought to kill so dangerous a man, who treated, without doubt, of State affairs, keeping so public a correspondence with the enemies.

Hendrik van der Spyck observed this local mood, 'and was afraid, not without reason, that the mob would break into the house, and perhaps plunder it, and then drag Spinosa out'. As the philosopher climbed from the *trekschuit* and rounded the Bierkade into the Paviljoensgracht, he may not have realised his life was in peril, and it is to be hoped that his cloak billowed, as it had once billowed in Amsterdam, against knife attack, for William's connivance at mob justice meant that Spinoza's death would have gone unpunished. Yet he was genuinely unafraid, indeed curiously buoyant, given the failure of his mission:

> Spinosa put [Hendrik] in heart again, and removed his fears as well as he could. Fear nothing, he said, upon my account. I can easily justify myself: There are people enough, and even some of the most considerable persons of the State, who know very well what put me upon that journey. But however, as soon as the mob make the least noise at your door, I'll go and meet 'em, tho' they were to treat me as they treated the good Heeren de Witt.

There is no report of an assault, yet I think we can infer, knowing that Spinoza 'spent the greatest part of his time quietly in his own chamber', and that 'once he did not go outside his lodgings during three whole months', that the philosopher reminded himself of his principle of *timely flight* and, unwilling or unable to leave The Hague, hid.

Who were the 'considerable persons of the State' said to have sanctioned his visit? Lucas says that Spinoza's 'friends persuaded him to set out on the journey', but this latter claim is hard to reconcile with the former. No person of influence, save the now immensely eminent Van Beuningen or his cousin Treasurer-General Coenraad Burgh, could have met both conditions, for William had contrived the downfall of all De Witt supporters. A cousin of the De Witts had been slaughtered by his own men while serving with the army. Pieter van den Hove, who had protested in print in 1669 that 'some lavish, ambitious and debauched people, whether rulers or subjects, might . . . under pretence of being of the prince's or captain-general's faction, turn this republic into a monarchy', had now fled the land. The Dutch ambassador told by De Witt to offer Louis Maastricht and other Dutch territory had also fled. As *Staatsgezinden* deputies dropped from the political scene William had not relaxed, but became increasingly autocratic and impetuous. Before long an eminent lawyer would observe that 'The Majesty of Orange was offended at the mere idea of the State having any impulse but what he was pleased to give it.' Indeed, William's stadholderate of all seven provinces made him monarch in all but name. Temple noted the changed atmosphere of The Hague, which was now either hectic, as officials and townsfolk fell over their feet to please William, or 'as dead as I have seen any great town . . . the Prince being gone into the field'.

Can we envisage Van Beuningen, William's confidant and escort at peace talks with the French, recommending as an emissary an apostate Jew rumoured to have 'published with the connivance of Mr Jan'? The diplomat had been in Brussels in August 1672, and in his absence had been short-listed for the position of Grand Pensionary when De Witt resigned. Of the three names put forward for election, Fagel, now 'a great creature of the Prince', received most votes. William expressly wanted Van Beuningen as an Amsterdam burgomaster because for twenty years he had challenged De Witt's judgement and had supported the Prince's foreign policy from the moment he became Captain General. Now, the rapport between the two was the best it would ever be. (They would quarrel irrevocably in 1683.) However, William's tendency to impetuous and harsh punishment is unlikely to have encouraged Van Beuningen to raise Spinoza's name with him. The Prince had shown no sign of forswearing the commitment to Calvinism he had let slip when Charles revealed his secret Catholicism, and may scarcely have tolerated Van Beuningen's own 1672 pamphlets, whose mystic prognostications of a French-wrought apocalypse, based like most cabalic extravagances on the book of Ezekiel, cast him as a volatile, Blake-like seer. Described in 1697 as a 'ridiculous prophet' and 'sottish thousand-yearist', Van Beuningen would in 1682 pay for the dissemination of the cabalic works of Jacob Boehme before descending into psychosis. (Visionary ravings aside, Van Beuningen's last papers affirm belief in the resurrection of the body, in miracles, in the reality of the devil, and in the truth of Holy Scripture.) William, with a realist discernment of power relations seasoned in boyhood, bound himself steadfastly to the Dutch Reformed Church, knowing that he could use its power to manipulate the masses. Spinoza, aware of this exploitation, added caustically when writing on how

Christians turn what could be true religion into superstition, *I doubt very much whether Kings will ever allow the application of a remedy for this evil.* Since it was noted by the French that two of the most 'violent' Calvinist preachers (one of them Dr Thaddeus de Lantman, or Landman) were attached to the House of Orange at The Hague, I conclude that Spinoza went to Utrecht through *libertin* liaison, and without William's blessing.

Mild anti-monarchist cynicism would not stop Spinoza concluding after rational analysis that, given The Netherlands' traditional system of government, some element of sovereignty was inextricable from the institution of hereditary stadholder rule:

> *The people of Holland thought that to gain their freedom they had only to secede from their count and cut of the head of the body politic; they never thought of reorganising their state, but left all its other parts in their original form; and so Holland has been left – comitatus sine comite – a body without a head, and the real government has been left without a name. Small wonder then that most of the subjects did not know in whose hands the sovereignty lay.*

The *Theologico-Political Treatise* allowed, and the *Political Treatise* would assert, that Dutch sovereignty must, from metaphysical necessity, be vested in the powerful person of William:

> *By the right and law of nature I simply mean the rules of each individual thing's nature, the rules whereby we conceive it as naturally determined to exist and to act in a definite way. Fish, for example, are determined by nature to swim, and the large to eat the smaller; so fish occupy the water, and the large eat the smaller, with perfect natural right. For there is no doubt that nature in the absolute sense has a perfect right to do anything in its power; i.e. that the right of nature extends as far as its power; the power of nature being nothing but the power of God, who has a perfect right to do anything. But the universal power of nature as a whole is simply the power of all individual things combined; hence each individual thing has a perfect right to do everything it can, in other words, its right extends to the limit of its power.*

Power acting on an individual through appetite, which was for Spinoza the very essence of human beings, and the natural force whereby they strive to preserve their own being, let in passion, opinion and prejudice. This sooner or later weakened that individual, since human appetite was not a uniting force. Maximum human power lay in the man guided by reason. *The power of the mind is defined by knowledge alone, whereas lack of power, or passion, is judged solely by the privation of knowledge . . . It is clear how much the wise man is capable of, and how much more powerful he is than one who is ignorant and is only driven by lust.*

The Prince was unlikely to be any more interested in this thesis than he was in disempowering the Reformed Church. In July 1674 his name, titles and arms would head a States ban on the *Theologico-Political Treatise*, together with Meyer's *Philosophia Scripturae Interpres* and 'the book called the Leviathan'. He would thereafter include Spinoza in his hawk-eyed dominion. He would not see the *Political Treatise* until after the philosopher was dead, but it would have been with his consent that all selling, reprinting and translating of '*B.D.S. Opera Posthuma*' was prohibited by law after it came out in Dutch. Spinoza's concession to Stadholder sovereignty would hardly have placated the Prince's anger, anyway, given his assessment of William's rise to power. *When the state is in desperate straits, and everyone, as often happens, is seized with panic, the citizens will take no account of the future or the laws, but will follow only the prompting of their immediate fear; they will all turn to the man who is renowned for his victories, release him from the laws* [a veiled reference to the overturning of the Eternal Edict], *create a disastrous precedent by prolonging his command, and entrust the entire commonwealth to his good faith.* The passage purported to paraphrase Machiavelli and to discuss the overthrow of the Roman State, but it was obviously directed at the Provinces' new Stadholder, as no doubt was the question: *If men are puffed up by appointment for a year, what can we expect of nobles who hold office without end?*

The Amsterdam *Kerkeraad* and magistrates were more intolerant of heterodoxy under Stadholder control than ever, and this may have made Spinoza humour Jarig Jelles when he came, as would seem inevitable, under the shadow of Reformed Church disapproval. Jelles sent Spinoza a draft of the *Confession of the Universal Christian Faith* he had written to 'stop the mouth of scandalmongers' slandering him in Amsterdam. In it, Jarig testified with immense conviction to the strange feeling or opinion (*gevoelens*) that sustained him spiritually. The 'conditions' for this feeling derived, he said, from the sixteenth-century Italian Protestant reformer Jacopo Aconzio (who had urged replacing dogma with meekness). Spinoza's influence might seem apparent in Jelles's emphasis on the 'necessity' of things, but Jelles's fatalism does not seem to me to express the active endeavour with which Spinoza believed individuals lived through their own essences. His certainty that we can know eternal truths may also appear to echo Spinoza's, but his guarantee was 'inner light' rather than mathematical proof. So strongly did Jelles cleave to Aconzio's 'judgement' that we may suspect he had instructed Spinoza in, rather than learning from him, the minimal definition of Christianity to which Spinoza clung for so long and which, added to the view of Jesus as God's eternal wisdom, strikes so oddly in the *Theologico-Political Treatise*. Jelles's 'feeling', in which he took refuge if 'going into details' was required (for example, on Cartesianism, with which he was now thoroughly disenchanted), swept out the rational along with the dogmatic. The mood of his treatise reflects the warmth he must have offered Spinoza, but its content shows the limited impact that Spinoza's doctrine had on the man who clung to Meyer's line that the role of philosophy was to display scripture's intrinsic truth. In sum, since Jarig put *gevoelen* before reason and obedience before knowledge, his passive *Godsdienst* constituted a negation of Spinoza's active *intellectual love of God*.

Three accounts of Spinoza's response to Jarig's *Confession* have survived. The actual text of his brief letter to Jelles, shown to Dr Hallmann by Rieuwertz, was, as we know, lost. In Rieuwertz's view, very few people were more advanced in the knowledge and love of God than Jelles, and Rieuwertz held that the 'certain friend outside the town' to whom Jelles had sent his *Confession* had responded, *I have read through your writings with pleasure, and found them such that I can change nothing in them.* Bayle paraphrases this same conciliatory reply. Hallmann, however, says that the brief letter shown him by Rieuwertz paid Jelles no compliments, but objected that 'on page 5 of the manuscript you assert that man is inclined by nature to evil, but through the Grace of God and the Spirit of Christ he becomes indifferent to Good and Evil'. Spinoza's response to this seems as strange as approbation for, rather than irritably suggesting that Jelles should bring his convoluted doctrine of good and evil into line with his own view that human beings are born with no sense of good or evil, and that the laws of nature dictate what is truly useful to them, he allegedly proposed the alternative statement, 'He who has the Spirit of Christ is necessarily impelled only to good'. Spinoza knew Jelles resisted his clever friend's doctrine in his heart, and would never be swayed by reason. He knew too that the dangers of heterodoxy were real, and he may have decided to support Jelles by eradicating any influence – however misunderstood – of his own.

Lucas seems to bind Spinoza's three-month period of seclusion to the year 1673 by referring in the same sentence to an important proposition made to Spinoza that spring – a proposition that contrasts significantly with Stouppe's summons to Utrecht, and leads us aptly into Spinoza's final and most imposing internal battle between reason and passion. An invitation came from J. Ludwig Fabritius, professor of Heidelberg university and Councillor to the Elector Palatine (on whose orders Fabritius was writing). The Elector was assembling celebrated intellectuals and Spinoza was asked, allegedly solely on the basis of a few chapters of *Descartes's Principles*, although it is also thought that the ideas of the *Theologico-Political Treatise* would have appealed to the Prince-Elector, 'to accept a regular Professor-ship of Philosophy'. 'You will,' wrote Fabritius, 'have the most extensive freedom in philosophising, which [His Serene Highness] believes you will not misuse to disturb the publicly established religion.'

Spinoza declined at once, partly on the grounds that *if I am to find time to instruct young students, I must give up my further progress in philosophy*, but mainly because he knew his freedom of thought and speech was at risk:

> *I do not know within what limits the freedom to philosophise must be confined if I am to avoid appearing to disturb the publicly established religion. For divisions arise not so much from an ardent devotion to religion as from the different dispositions of men, or through their love of contradiction which leads them to distort or to condemn all things, even those that are stated aright. Now since I have already experienced this while leading a private and solitary life, it would be much more to be feared after I have risen to this position of eminence.*

With hindsight, Spinoza must have seen that the two flattering invitations of spring 1673 bore identical price-tags: acceptance of either made him another man's creature. The offer of a professorship, on the face of it a chance for *timely flight* (although the French would burn down Heidelberg university the following year and its teachers would scatter), was instantly rejected because its trap was obvious, whereas for some reason Spinoza had not immediately foreseen that the French would exact the same conditions. (Did Louis, in fact, know anything about the offer of a pension, any more than he knew that Van den Enden had been invited to France as 'Councillor and Court Physician'?) These enticements had shown Spinoza wherein political liberty lay, and now, exultant at escaping mental subservience, he was only secondarily relieved that his body had survived. *Men whose consciences are clear do not fear death* . . . For Spinoza, loss of freedom consisted in bondage by passive ideas. Freedom lay in escape to a perpetually cold attic, where in the silence of night he occasionally found the *satisfaction of mind* that freed him. No wonder Hendrik found him eerily complacent.

ELEVEN

The Hague: 1674–5

Most esteemed Sir, I find that I have gone further than I intended, and I will trouble you no longer with matters which I know you will not concede, your first principles being far different my own, etc.

During his final years (for he had, on his return from Utrecht, only three and half to live) Spinoza's mind was dominated by the question of the power and right of the *free man*. He must at this time have been working on the fifth and last Part of *Ethics, On the Power of the Intellect, or on Human Freedom*, for in July 1675 he would confide to Henry Oldenburg that his *Five-Part Treatise* was ready for the printer. Introducing that final Part, he pledged himself to addressing the power of reason, to showing how reason could remove the destructive power of the affects and, through this thesis, to demonstrating the nature of *freedom of mind, or blessedness*. Yet he would seldom, as it happened, find freedom of mind when he sat down to write. Only the reflections of Part 5 brought a little blessedness and, given the assaults on his consciousness during the period we now share with him, it is hard to imagine how he came by such moments at all. *Ethics* was not printed in 1675 – he was strongly warned against it – and it is possible that the version of Part 5 found in the *Opera Posthuma* does not date from this period, but from later. Be that as it may, Spinoza does not emerge from this phase of his life as *free*, but as constantly grappling with minds held in bondage or with minds that bound his own in confusion. I believe the correspondence of these years, if read in isolation from the lofty assertions of *Ethics* Part 5, utterly debunks the myth of the philosopher's serenity and high-mindedness. With the exception of Spinoza's letters to his old friend Henry Oldenburg, it reveals snappiness, sloppiness and unremitting anxiety.

These characteristics are similar to those noted by the physician Abarbanel as symptoms of advanced phthisis. Once the corruption of the lungs had spread to the whole body, the physician observed, syrup of farfara stalks or distillation of oak could effect nothing, and the sufferer's 'tendency to violent passions and disturbances of the *anima*, especially gloom' took over in the terminal stages of the illness. Yet Spinoza had, as far back as his letters are preserved – that is, since Henry Oldenburg sent him Boyle's work on nitre – been irascible when forced to accept the theories of others. What the philosopher had always wanted most was a stimulating response to his ideas, and his tendency to welcome new acquaintance, to jump into any argument that promised to throw light or shadow on his ceaseless inner dialectic, and to jump out again fast when it failed to do so, was now exacerbated by frustration and worry over whether, following the posting of the civil ban on the *Theologico-Political Treatise*, any Dutchman would dare contact him. He therefore welcomed, despite its content, a letter from the disgraced *Staatsgezind* pensionary of Gorinchem, one Hugo Boxel, whom he may have met briefly in that town while travelling to Utrecht via the south:

> *Your letter, which I received yesterday, was most welcome, both because I wanted to have news of you, and because it assures me that you have not entirely forgotten me. And although some might think it a bad omen that ghosts or spectres should have been the occasion of your writing to me, I on the contrary, discern in this something of greater significance; for I reflect that not only real things but trifles and fancies can turn to my advantage.*

Spinoza's was a polite enough letter, but it did not treat the topic with the gentleness he had shown Balling, and it ended drily, *I beg you to tell me what kind of things are these ghosts or spirits, Are they children, fools or madmen? . . . Here I shall stop, until I hear from you what are the stories that have so convinced you that you think it absurd even to doubt them.*
Spinoza's scepticism about angels, apparitions and devils was rare for the period in which he lived, and there was no more to be gained from arguing with Boxel about spirits than with Van Blijenbergh about the devil. He must have known this. However, Boxel sent a fresh battery of argument and Spinoza, despite misgivings, could not stop himself sending off a six-page reply. Acidly he rejected Boxel's opinions and sources, including Pliny and Suetonius:

> *I am surprised that men of ability and judgement should squander their gift of eloquence and misuse it to persuade us of such rubbish . . . Let us see whether I, who deny that there are ghosts or Spirits, am thereby failing to understand those writers who have written on this subject, or whether you, who hold that such things exist, are not giving the writers more credibility than they deserve.*

Before systematically attacking Boxel's stories he indulged in a little flippancy:

> *On the one hand, you do not doubt the existence of spirits of the male sex, while*

on the other hand you doubt the existence of any of the female sex ... If this were really your opinion, it would be more in keeping with the popular imagination which makes God masculine rather than feminine. I am surprised that those who have seen naked spirits have not cast their eyes on the genital parts; perhaps they were too afraid, or ignorant of the difference.

Boxel was aggrieved. 'I say that spirits are like God because he is also a spirit ... As to their shape and constitution I say nothing, because this does not concern me.' The brief exchange of letters followed precisely the Van Blijenbergh pattern, Spinoza's arguments alternating with sardonic humour before degenerating into anger and dismissal. *That your conjecture regarding spectres and ghosts seems false and has not even a show of truth, I have demonstrated so clearly that I find nothing in your reply worthy of consideration.*

This final letter was sent in September or October 1674, around the time when troubling news came from France, and Spinoza may have been even less gripped by Boxel's problem than he made evident. Spinoza was a Dutch patriot, and his grief in 1672 at the catastrophic mishandling of the Provinces' affairs at every level of society had hardened into preoccupation with questions of peace and political autonomy. Worry over the loss of Dutch sovereignty to France had recently been a little alleviated, for in February 1674 Lorraine, Austria and Spain had acted to halt Louis's rampant ambition by forming a Grand Alliance with The Netherlands and Brandenburg. Most of the French camps squatting along the length of Holland's borders were now disbanded, their troops and artillery being needed outside the Dutch republic. But peace did not follow, and by the time the French were finally driven out and forced to return all land acquisitions in 1678, Spinoza was no longer alive. His last political work therefore conveys his apprehension that France would usurp the sovereignty and crush the character of the United Provinces:

Patricians [elected rulers in a political aristocracy] *will never take a fancy to foreign fashions, and disdain their native garb, if there is a law prescribing that patricians and candidates for promotion should be distinguished from the rest by a particular dress. And further measures can be devised in each state to suit the nature of its territory and the character of its people.*

Saint-Évremond had expressed the view that the loathing of the Dutch for 'violence' (oppression) exceeded their love of liberty, and Spinoza's view of an incident of autumn 1674 must include this perspective. Liberty was not, for him, a requirement for freedom: the *free man* knew that he could safeguard the rights of all only by abdicating some of his own. *A man who is guided by reason is more free in a State, where he lives according to a common decision, than in solitude, where he obeys only himself.* Yet Spinoza had seen good men destroyed by their attempts to lead others to true freedom, and the destruction of Frans van den Enden by the French that autumn must have been for him a matter of personal pain. It might possibly account for some of his own ill-nature during the following year, although I think other factors will make us treat that suggestion with scepticism.

Van den Enden had been running an exceptionally successful school in Paris. His family life, too, had blossomed. He lived with, and may have married, a mature, capable and attractive woman, and at least one of Clara Maria's sisters found a husband. But in late September 1674 the idyll fell apart. Frans's Amsterdam acquaintance Giles du Hamel de Latréaumont was, as had been rumoured, involved with other gentlefolk in a plot against Louis XIV led by De Latréaumont's mentor and ex-army commander, the Chevalier de Rohan.

Louis de Rohan was, through the blood of both his parents, a member of a great French family descending from the former kings of Brittany. All the Ducs De Rohan considered themselves of first royal rank, and their activities showed that they were, although loyal soldiers, bred to resentment of the Bourbon monarchs. It is not therefore surprising that all scions of this family were constantly watched by Louis XIV's agents. The plot devised under Van den Enden's roof was to stir up revolt in the already discontented *département* of Normandy, and to deliver the strategic port of Quillebeuf, near Rouen, to the Dutch fleet. Van den Enden's involvement could hardly be doubted, even if reports that he had planned to help set up a Franco-Dutch republic are discounted, for the main conspirators were overheard at the school by his paying guest Du Cause de Nazelle, first biographer of Van den Enden, who betrayed them. De Latréaumont died after being arrested, and de Rohan was captured in the royal chapel at Versailles. Van den Enden, having put Marianna in a Paris convent, was in Brussels making last arrangements for the rendezvous with the Dutch fleet. Returning to be told that De Rohan was in the Bastille, he at once fled for Brussels with his partner, but was caught at Le Bourget and also flung into the Bastille. Spinoza would have known of this by the time he wrote his second letter on ghosts to Boxel, for on 2 October bulletins in the Dutch newspapers on 'the trial of De Rohan' mentioned the arrest of a 'certain Hollander' said to have been associated with De Latréaumont. Spinoza's admirers Gabriel de Saint-Glen and Jean Lucas (now a gazette-writer for the Dutch newspapers, which incensed Louis XIV) may have been more immediate sources of news. On 13 November came the report that the Latin teacher 'born in Antwerp, and before that a Jesuit' had been found guilty of treason, and hanged, not being noble enough for decapitation by sword.

Spinoza gave his earliest Dutch mentor no obvious epitaph. The headmaster, famous for his fiery drama, polemic and rhetoric, had at the age of seventy-two converted these arts into revolutionary action. He was, recalled his betrayer, 'a spirit from a higher order' with 'the reputation of being one of the most learned men in Europe'. But Sophia, Duchess of Hanover, informed of the intrigue by her brother, was not sure he had been wise. She was:

> sorry that the mild humour of Van den Enden allowed himself to be persuaded by M. de Rohan into un-Christian treason against the king. It is better for these noble spirits to reason always, and to act, never.

Was Sophia, a cultured and well-read woman, voicing in this aphorism her own view, or that of her philosopher-sister Princess Elizabeth, the pupil of Descartes? Or of Leibniz, who in 1676 would enter the service of her husband's family? The letter from her brother had warned her that she would not find Van den Enden in Amsterdam on her forthcoming visit. As a princess of Bohemia brought up in Holland, Sophia may already have met Van den Enden there. Spinoza, who would not be driven into action by this latest State-sanctioned murder of a former friend, may at last have brought to some level of consciousness the assumption that had guided his reticence at the synagogue, his avoidance of religious rabble-rousers and his prudence over publishing. This assumption – that wise men reason rather than act – had been blocked when he made known his outrage at the murder of the De Witts, and when he went to Utrecht. Nor would he ever thoroughly explore the destructive function of passion in misinterpreting rational action, or the capacity of reason – even the frigid demonstrations of *Ethics* – to rouse passionate action. On a personal level there must have been anxiety over Van den Enden's predicament – Spinoza wrote in October that he was *completely distracted* – and dismay at his death. On a philosophical level, reaction to it is found in the analysis in his later *Political Treatise* of the rational role of an individual living under an intolerably oppressive or corrupt régime.

But I question whether Spinoza ever truly satisfied Sophia's maxim. No critic among those most bigoted, or most capable, correspondents yet to question the principles of his doctrine came as close to undermining his doctrine as did his own lapses in reasoning.

Reason often seemed, during the next year or more, to desert him when he wrote letters. He was, that October, weak, sleep-deprived and unwell. During the day Hendrik's tribe of young children filled the house with wailing and laughing, and callers brought him down his attic staircase to the parlour. When night fell, rather than collapsing in his *ledikant*, he lit his lamp and took on his severest intellectual challenges. From this, according to Lucas, a vicious circle of sickness and exhaustion resulted:

> Though there is nothing that drains one's strength so much as night-vigils, his vigils had become almost constant through the effects of a slight, slow fever which he contracted during his arduous meditations.

Spinoza admitted the pressure he tended to put on himself. Isolated from stimulating discourse by the reluctance of many learned individuals to seem to share his views, yet knowing that knowledge and advantage accrued from the interchange of ideas, he was both starved of tranquillity and internally driven to push his philosophy forward by exposing it to criticism. He could not resist, therefore, the penetrating questioning of a clever Leiden university graduate brought into his life by Georg Schuller, a young Amsterdam physician. Schuller, himself a competent metaphysician, passed on comments and questions from his friend, Ehrenfried Walther von Tschirnhaus, a very young German count of outstanding intellectual ability, who had enrolled at Leiden with Schuller to study medicine. Von Tschirnhaus had contracted but survived the Leiden plague of 1669, which had killed many professors, including Geulincx and Coccejus, and had inevitably fallen behind Schuller, who was now in practice. The Count was currently in Germany before starting his educational *grand tour*, but would be in Amsterdam that autumn. Spinoza wrote to Schuller that October, *Although I am at present fully occupied with other matters and my health is also causing me some concern, I feel impelled both by your exceptional courtesy and by your devotion to truth, which I particularly value, to satisfy your wish as far as my slender abilities allow.* And he replied to the first letter from Von Tschirnhaus, sent via Schuller, with assiduous care.

Von Tschirnhaus's association with Spinoza was the most testing, and should have been the most rewarding, of his philosophical career so far. Yet while scholars usually agree that Von Tschirnhaus got to grips with more of the perennial problems of Spinoza's doctrine than had anyone else, Spinoza did not during the following year make good use of this interest. The philosopher was persuaded into lending him a draft copy of *Ethics*, but resisted his well-made objections to a puzzling extent. The correspondence preserved after October 1674 shows little intellectual exhilaration on Spinoza's part, and a great deal of impatience that Von Tschirnhaus seemed either locked in Cartesian assumptions or wanted to get into aspects of natural philosophy that Spinoza was not prepared to discuss. To his suggestion that Spinoza should produce a 'General Physics' in order to clarify his theories of *Motion and Method*, Spinoza objected that *Since my views on these are not yet written out in due order, I reserve them for another occasion.* He had prevaricated in the *Treatise on the Emendation of the Intellect* on experiment and methodology, and in the *Short Treatise* on motion. *It belongs more properly to a treatise on natural science than here.* Quite simply, he could not explain his bold, futuristic theory of motion, in which the workings of an internal force (having no external origin) made *every particular corporeal thing nothing other than a proportion of motion-and-rest*, to be understood through calculation. The two definitions he gave Schuller in July did not find their way into *Ethics*, which Spinoza had suddenly decided, that very same month, to have printed.

To ask a reader for comments on a manuscript, then submit it for printing without waiting for a response, is an odd thing to do. It was also risky to consider travelling on the *trekschuit* with that incriminating bulk on his person. But perhaps he did not get that far:

> *While I was engaged on this business, a rumour became widespread that a certain book of mine about God was in the press, and in it I endeavour to show there is no God. This rumour found credence with many. So certain theologians, who may have started this rumour, seized the opportunity to complain of me before the Prince and the magistrates . . . I decided to postpone the publication I had in hand . . .*

Why had he chosen that moment to publish *Ethics*? He may have been led to think it was safe to do so. Von Tschirnhaus had in 1672, at the age of twenty-one (scarcely a year younger than Prince William), headed a volunteer regiment at the siege of Wesel. Spinoza, having by now spent two years in seclusion, may have falsely assumed that he had a protector in Von Tschirnhaus. If so, disillusionment was rapid and final. He now knew the theologians had William's ear, and he would not again attempt to publish his metaphysic. Was there a connection between this defeat and the increasingly offhand or irritable manner in which Spinoza would answer the Count's questions?

By 1675 Von Tschirnhaus had left Holland and was being deferred to in such élite centres of learning as London's Royal Society, but he was still forced to pussy-foot when making critical suggestions to Spinoza:

> Will you please let me have a proof of your assertion that the soul cannot perceive any more attributes of God than extension and thought. Although I can understand this quite clearly, yet I think that the contrary can be deduced from the Scholium to Prop. VII, Part II of *Ethics*, perhaps only because I do not sufficiently perceive the meaning of this Scholium. I have therefore resolved to explain how I come to this conclusion, earnestly

begging you, esteemed Sir, to come to my aid with your customary courtesy wherever I do not rightly follow your meaning . . . Perhaps these difficulties will all be removed by further reflection.

Spinoza's 'courtesy' amounted this time to a note which had so little bearing on Von Tschirnhaus's question that we might suspect editorial error in labelling it 'Reply to the Preceding', had it not been dated only sixteen days after Von Tschirnhaus's. The Count had misread Spinoza on a crucial point, but was left uncorrected. He had made the assumption that because *God, or Nature* expressed all possible attributes, man as a part of nature, did so too, and so must be able to apprehend attributes other than thought and extension. But the *Scholium* to which Von Tschirnhaus referred did not entail that, and Spinoza had earlier stressed that man was not a microcosm of substance but merely *a part* of it, expressing only thought and extension, and so unable to apprehend other attributes. In *Ethics* he had stated that:

> We neither feel nor perceive any singular things except bodies and modes of thinking . . . If the object of the mind were something else also, in addition to the body, then since nothing exists from which there does not follow some effect, then there would necessarily be an idea in our mind of some effect of it. But there is no effect of it.

On 29 July, just three weeks earlier, Spinoza had made precisely this point to Schuller, answering very fully the same question as had been asked by Von Tschirnhaus. So why did he fail to pick up a misapprehension he had only recently addressed? Perhaps he assumed that the contents of his reply to Schuller had been passed on to Von Tschirnhaus, for he had concluded, *Thus, most excellent Sir, I think I have answered your objections and those of your friend.* He might then have taken it for granted, without reading carefully, that Von Tschirnhaus was making a different objection.

Spinoza was not dangerously ill if he felt up to a boat journey and the buffeting pace of Amsterdam. Nor can he have suffered from mid-August heat, since summer 1675 was cold and wet: the perpetual rain caused a serious grain shortage. Perhaps a wave of depression, possibly connected with his illness, but linked to the realisation that he would never see *Ethics* in print, temporarily made discussion of his doctrine seem pointless. The curt, misdirected note to the Count was the only letter included in the *Opera Posthuma* for that August. I think something deeper was going on, and that Spinoza positively wanted to muddy the waters with Von Tschirnhaus. He was avoiding any aspect of his doctrine that might remind this cosmopolite of his very shocking view that man had no soul – if 'soul' was taken to be non-natural. Von Tschirnhaus had, in the first place, been wary of being known to consort with Spinoza, his first letter having been sent to Schuller, who had copied out a section of it. Spinoza knew that Von Tschirnhaus did not much like him; the Count's letters were formal and without warmth, and would remain so. The philosopher may have regretted handing over the draft of *Ethics* to him. Why would Von Tschirnhaus, who had either failed to put in a good word for him with William or been rebuffed by the Prince, hesitate now to report his new book? The point Spinoza was at pains to make in his hasty 'Reply to the Preceding' was that each and every individual mind, although a part of a single substance, had *no connection with the others*. He was making sure Von Tschirnhaus did not doubt that his doctrine allowed discrete selves, and perhaps hoping that he would think this guaranteed 'souls' of a politically acceptable sort.

A second shot had been fired at the philosopher that July. Before leaving London for Paris, Von Tschirnhaus had been introduced to a compatriot, the German-born Henry Oldenburg. Henry had long been released from the Tower, but had felt no impulse to react to the copy of the *Theologico-Political Treatise* that Spinoza is said to have sent him. He seems to have felt sincerely ambivalent about the quirky little philosopher. Schuller, who was amply Henry's match as a pursuer of eminent people, now informed Spinoza that:

> Mr Boyle and Oldenburg had formed a very strange idea of your character. [Von Tschirnhaus] has not only dispelled this, but has furthermore given them reasons that have induced them to return to a most worthy and favourable opinion of you, and also to hold in high esteem the *Tractatus Theologico-politicus.*

Alas, Henry was actually very distressed by Spinoza's book, and after making polite noises about it in June, and asking to hear more about Spinoza's 'very profound insight into the nature and powers of the human mind, and its union with the body', was alarmed to discover that he was considering publishing *Ethics.* 'Since . . . it is your intention to publish the Five-Part Treatise of yours,' he wrote in July, 'please allow me, out of your genuine affection for me, to advise you not to include in it anything which may seem in any way to undermine the practice of religious virtue.' A great deal of mental turmoil would elapse before Spinoza either answered Henry's letter or admitted Von Tschirnhaus to be a genuine seeker of the truth, but the next letter the philosopher wrote shows him realising, at last, that merely promulgating reason could provoke profound passion, and that the Count was a contact to be valued, not deflected. In view of the missives that now came at him like pistol shots from two Leiden graduates, now Catholic converts, he would have been obtuse to think otherwise.

Albert Burgh and Nils Stensen (Steno) had read the *Theologico-Political Treatise*, and both now saw their former friend as a purveyor of pernicious error, drawing on himself eternal damnation and leading others towards it. Burgh had studied philosophy at Leiden in the late 1660s, when Schuller and Von Tschirnhaus were there, and had promised, before leaving for Italy with friends in 1673, to let Spinoza know 'should anything worthy of note occur during my journey'. Spinoza seems to have been sure just before Burgh left that he shared his views: the graduate had appeared to have no patience with sectarianism, and was afterwards said to have mocked Catholic practices all the way to Rome. But when he reached the papal city he had been deeply impressed by a Dutch friar called Martin Harney. He converted to Catholicism, and probably made contact with Steno, since both wrote from Florence, and Spinoza later accused Burgh of following in Steno's *footsteps*. The young convert then fired off his letter to Spinoza and left Italy with the Dutch Dominican to walk barefoot back to Amsterdam. On the first of his twenty-seven pages of reproof to Spinoza he had written:

> The more I have admired you in the past for the penetration and acuity of your mind, the more do I now moan and lament for you. For although you are a man of outstanding talent, with a mind on which God has bestowed splendid gifts, a lover of truth and indeed a most eager one, yet you allow yourself to be entrapped and deceived [by] that most wretched and arrogant Prince of evil spirits. For what does all your philosophy amount to, except sheer illusion and chimera? Yet you entrust to it not only your peace of mind in this life, but the eternal salvation of your soul.

Solicitude evaporated as Burgh worked himself into a rage at Spinoza's 'deadly arrogance':

> Do you then dare think yourself greater than all those who have ever arisen in the State or the Church of God, the patriarchs, prophets, apostles, martyrs, doctors, confessors and virgins, the countless saints, and even, blasphemously, our Lord Jesus Christ himself? Do you alone surpass them in doctrine, in manner of life, and in all else? Will you, a sorry little creature, a vile little worm of the earth, nay mere ashes and food for worms, in your unspeakable blasphemy dare claim pre-eminence over the Incarnate, Infinite Wisdom of the Eternal Father?

... and so on until, as his anger burned out, the young zealot recalled his real message:

I have written you this letter with a truly Christian purpose, firstly, that you may know the love I bear you, Gentile though you be; and secondly, to ask you not to persist in ruining others as well as yourself.

This was a letter written in holy terror – a holding up of a crucifix to flash such white light that Spinoza must cower in Damascus-like submission. The Dominicans were a preaching order, and Brother Harney had trained Burgh fast. The impulse to evangelism would not last, but the monastic vocation did. Albert would repulse his parents' pleading and join a mendicant order of Franciscans in Brussels before returning to Rome.

The philosopher did not reply to Burgh's ranting for several months. *What I could scarcely believe when it was told me by others, I now at last learn from your letter; not only have you become a member of the Roman Church, as you say, but you are also its very keen champion . . . I had intended to make no reply to your letter . . . But some of my friends, who with me had formed great hopes for you from your excellent natural abilities, have strenuously urged me not to fail in the duties of a friend . . .* We come to Spinoza's response at the point when he wrote it, at the end of his watershed forty-third year.

Steno may have sent Spinoza his 1669 Leiden treatise on solids (it was found in the philosopher's library) and his reproach was ostensibly the cool appeal to reason of a friend. It was headed, 'To the Reformer of the New Philosophy, concerning the true philosophy':

> While public peace is what you seek, you are creating complete confusion, and while aiming to free yourself from all danger, you are exposing yourself quite unnecessarily to the gravest danger . . . I see shrouded in such darkness a man who was once my good friend, and even now, I hope, not unfriendly to me . . . And although your writings show you to be far removed from the truth, yet the love of peace and truth which I once perceived in you and is not yet extinguished in your darkness affords me some hope that you will give a ready hearing to our Church . . .

The astronomer had studied Spinoza's book closely, and made his points judiciously. Turning reluctantly from the credos of salvation and miracle, which had personally given him comfort, he assured Spinoza, 'I shall not speak of other matters subject to [the Church's] authority'. Instead, knowing that the accusation would sting, he charged him with materialism:

> Scrutinise your soul, for a thorough investigation will show you that it is dead . . . For it is a religion of bodies, not of souls, that you are advocating, and in the love of one's neighbour you discern actions necessary for the preservation of the individual and the propagation of the

species, whereas you pay very little or no regard to those actions whereby we acquire knowledge and love of our Author . . .

Gradually religious polemic took over once more:

> I am indeed fully convinced that to invent new principles explaining the nature of God, the soul, and the body, is just the same as to invent fictitious principles. Even reason tells us that it is inconsistent with divine providence that, while the holiest of men have failed to discover the true principles of these things for so many thousands of years, in our age they are to be disclosed for the first time by men who have not even attained to the perfection of moral virtues . . . As first-fruits of your repentance, offer to God a refutation of your errors which you yourself recognise through the illumination of the divine light, so that if your first writings have turned aside a thousand minds from the true knowledge of God, their recantation, corroborated by your own example, may bring back to him, accompanied by you like a second Augustine, a thousand thousand. This grace I pray for you with all my heart.

No reply to Steno has been found. Spinoza had been aware since his synagogue days of the futility of reasoning with religious fundamentalists, who had positively chosen to remain in bondage to superstition. But he still had no eye for the depths of entrenchment that could underlie what superficially appeared to be a genuine search for truth. The autumn brought more tests in this respect. Genuinely puzzled, still, at what it was in his doctrine that elicited passion in even those scholars supposed exceptionally mentally able, Spinoza at last replied to Henry Oldenburg's lukewarm praise of his *Tractatus Theologico-politicus*, asking him to *point out to me the passages in the Tractatus Theologico-politicus which have proved a stumbling-block to learned men.* (At the same time he asked Van Velthuysen to *put in writing the arguments which you believe you can bring against my treatise.*) While he waited for replies there came further anxiety, and a decision to make.

Schuller wrote asking if Von Tschirnhaus, now in Paris, might show 'your writings' (that is, the draft copy of *Ethics)* to Leibniz, whom he had met there. Leibniz, a brilliant young mathematician, had turned down an academic career (his father, and his mother's father, were professors at Leipzig) and was in 1672 secretary and emissary to Baron Boineberg. Sent on business to Paris, he had met Huygens and had succeeded, despite presenting disappointing research in London (his calculating machine failed to perform, and his claims concerning infinite series revealed ignorance of current work or, worse, plagiarism), in being elected a Fellow of the Royal Society in 1673, aged just twenty-seven. In Paris Leibniz had, as mentioned, visited Van den Enden's school, and in his *Theodicy*, written in close involvement with the Duchess Sophia and her daughter, Leibniz recalled Frans's boast that 'he would wager that his audiences would always pay attention to his words'. Leibniz added sourly that Van den Enden had certainly 'insinuated himself into M. Arnauld's good graces' – Arnauld being the revered priest and philosopher with whom Descartes had argued. According to Du Cause de Nazelle, the priest had found Van den Enden helpful with Hebrew and Syrian biblical texts. It would be some time before Arnauld took seriously Leibniz's metaphysical speculations: in 1686 the priest thought the summary he had been sent so shocking that he could not see what use the work could be. Van den Enden and Huygens, Leibniz's most stimulating rival, may have shown him Spinoza's *Descartes's Principles* and *Theologico-Political Treatise*. Leibniz, at that time engrossed in mathematics, repelled by the notion of a naturalistic God and not yet drawn to metaphysics, had sent Spinoza a copy of an essay on optics. 'Among your other achievements which fame has spread abroad,' he had written, 'I understand is your great skill in optics.'

Spinoza had in 1671 welcomed this approach. He had courteously sent on to Hudde the paper enclosed for him, and offered Leibniz a copy of the *Theologico-Political Treatise*. But in November 1675, when informed by Schuller that 'in metaphysical studies of God and the soul [Leibniz] is most skilled', Spinoza resorted to *sub rosa* dissemblance:

> *I believe I know Leibniz, of whom he writes, through correspondence, but I do not understand why he, a Councillor of Frankfurt, has gone to France. As far as I can judge from his letter, he seemed to me a person of liberal mind and well versed in every science. Still I think it imprudent to entrust my writings to him so hastily. I should like first to know what he is doing in France, and to hear our friend Tschirnhaus's opinion of him after a longer acquaintance and a closer knowledge of his character.*

Letters said to have passed between Leibniz and Spinoza on the subject of the *Theologico-Political Treatise* have not been found. But apart from Spinoza's patriotic suspicions about Leibniz's visits to Paris, and the likelihood that he had heard of the German's public moralising, the philosopher may have known that beneath any facile compliments lay some forceful condemnations of the *Treatise*. These would eventually be exposed in Leibniz's papers. To Von Tschirnhaus Spinoza sent gracious regards. *Greet that friend of ours in my name with all my duty, and if I can serve him in any way, let him command what he will.* Despite Spinoza's diffidence, Leibniz may have been shown *Ethics*, but in discussions with the philosopher the next year Leibniz would seem surprised at his 'strange metaphysic, full of paradoxes' and suggest a proof to reinforce the claim made in its first propositions.

Just as Spinoza sent his letter to Schuller that November, came Henry's selection of passages in the *Theologico-Political Treatise* 'which have proved a stumbling-block':

I refer in particular to those which appear to treat in an ambiguous way of God and Nature, which many people consider you have confused with each other. In addition, many are of the opinion that you take away the authority and validity of miracles, which almost all Christians are convinced form the sole basis on which the certainty of divine revelation can rest. Furthermore, they say that you are concealing your opinion with regard to Jesus Christ, Redeemer of the world, sole Mediator for mankind, and of his Incarnation and Atonement.

We might think this list of objections, with its oblique (or incredibly naive) rejection of Spinoza's central principles, would stun the philosopher into silence as a *coup de grâce*. Instead, for want of a reply from Van Velthuysen, Spinoza used these suggestions as a basis for his planned elucidation of contentious points in the *Theologico-Political Treatise*, and provided reasoned, and interesting, footnotes on that work. (These appeared only in the French edition, a fact that strengthens claims that his closest allies during those last years were the French émigrés, and also suggests they had put similar objections to him.) On the God/Nature equation he told Henry: *I entertain an opinion on God and Nature far different from that which modern Christians are wont to uphold. For I maintain that God is the immanent cause of all things, as the phrase is, and not the transient cause ... However, as to the view of certain people that the Tractatus Theologico-politicus rests on the identification of God with Nature (by the latter of which they understand a kind of mass or corporeal matter) they are quite mistaken.* In responding to the issue of miracles which Burgh, Steno and Oldenburg had all made pivotal to religious belief, he wrote imperturbably, *This I believe is the reason why Christians are distinguished from other people not by faith, nor charity, nor the other fruits of the Holy Spirit, but solely by an opinion they hold, namely because, as they all do, they rest their case simply on miracles, that is, on ignorance, which is the source of all wickedness.* On the question of his opinion of Christ, Spinoza rejected claims to Jesus's supernaturalism. *As to the additional teaching of certain doctrines, that God took upon himself human nature* [in Christ], *I have expressly indicated that I do not understand what they say. Indeed, to tell the truth, they seem to me to speak no less absurdly than one who might tell me that a circle has taken on the nature of a square.* Despite

277

Henry's protests in his next letter, Spinoza opened his riposte with intellectual exhilaration – *At last I see what it was that you urged me not to publish* – and expounded in even stronger terms his views on the sensitive topic of the resurrection. *Christ did not appear to the Senate, nor to Pilate, nor to any of the unbelievers . . . but only to the faithful according to their understanding . . .* A month later he would persist, *The passion, death and burial of Christ I accept literally, but his resurrection I understand in an allegorical sense.* The philosopher Pierre Bayle interestingly records in his *Dictionary* of 1697 that he had 'been assured that [Spinoza] said to his friends that if he had been able to convince himself of the resurrection of Lazarus, he would have broken his system into pieces and would have embraced without difficulty the ordinary faith of Christians'. This may have been Spinoza's precise response to the *libertins* of The Hague or the occupying French of Utrecht on this question. On determinism – the denial of free will, which made his doctrine entirely unacceptable to any Christian – he assured Henry, *This inevitability of things does not do away with either divine or human laws . . . the evils that follow from wicked deeds and passions are not less to be feared because they necessarily follow from them.*

Spinoza thus denied the central creeds of Christianity, making it impossible to call him a Christian. We know that since 1656, perhaps earlier, he had tried to pull Jesus's precept of the exercise of justice and charity towards one's neighbour apart from Christian dogma. He must have known, now, that he could not do this. He would cling to his belief that living in the *spirit of Christ* constituted true piety, but he would make his sour view of Christ's sacraments and supernaturalism evident.

At the end of December 1675, his reply to Henry dispatched, Spinoza began penning, as requested, his petition to Burgh. It made a mean ending to a less than noble year. Did Burgh bother to read on after its sarcastic opening? *I will concede that in the Roman Church there are to be found more instances of men of great learning and upright life than in any other Christian Church; for since this Church has more members, there will also be found in it more men of every character. Still, unless perchance you have lost your memory together with your reason, you will not be able to deny that in every Church there are very many honourable men who worship God with justice and charity.* Thereafter he answered Burgh sentence for sentence in abusive kind, berating him a dozen ways for his gullibility in giving *the title of mysteries for your absurd errors.*

Striking first at belief in a *prince of evil spirits*, then at miracles, Spinoza mocked the sacrament of Holy Communion. *Now these absurdities might so far be tolerated if you worshipped a God infinite and eternal, and not one whom Chastillon, in a town which the Dutch call Tiernan, gave the horses to eat, and was not punished.* He meant the Franco-Dutch Protestants who had seized the town from the Spanish in May 1635, and whose Huguenot general had ordered the consecrated communion host to be thrown to the horses. *O mindless youth [mente destitute], who has bewitched you into believing that you eat, and hold in your intestines, that which is supreme and eternal? You can give no grounds for your faith . . . You have become a slave of this Church not so much through love of God as fear of Hell, which is the single cause of superstition.* Burgh had attacked the monstrous vanity that let Spinoza believe himself superior in understanding to all previous religions and philosophies, telling him harshly: 'There is an easy remedy; turn away from your sins, try to realise the deadly arrogance of your wretched, insane way of reasoning.' Spinoza now hurled back the insult. *When you were in your senses, if I am not mistaken, you used to worship an infinite God . . . Do you take it for arrogance and pride that I resort to reason?* With sweeping disgust he turned to the self-interest of sectarian institutions. *The organisation of the Roman Church, which you so warmly praise, I admit is politic and a source of gain to many, nor would I believe there is any better arranged for deceiving the people and controlling men's minds if it were not for the organisation of the Mahomedan Church, which far surpasses it.* And in a final thrust, using the weapon of biblical knowledge of which he was vain and had used against Oldenburg and Meyer, perhaps even Koerbagh, he attacked Burgh's unfamiliarity with the foundation of his sect . . . *Examine the histories of the Church (of which I see you are quite ignorant) so as to realise how false are many Papal traditions, and through what . . . craft the Pope of Rome finally gained supremacy over the Church six hundred years after the birth of Christ.* This letter provides as mature a Spinozistic verdict on Catholicism as we shall get, for the philosopher died just over a year later, without mentioning the topic again.

There would be no more direct engagements with the shackled minds of zealots, but the philosopher's undignified lapses into invective had not ceased. Von Tschirnhaus would be reminded that *Cartesian principles of natural things are useless, not to say absurd.* There may have been other outbursts, too, for the published paragraphs of Spinoza's letters to the Count are extracts. The conflict was not over. He was not a *free man.*

TWELVE

The Hague: 1676–7

Love towards God must engage the mind most.
To have shown what ought to be done is not enough; the main problem is to show how it can be done.

While *Ethics* Part 5 may have been finished by July 1675, when Spinoza thought of having it printed, we need to look deeply into its subject matter now. For we have scarcely scratched the surface of Spinoza's personal search for freedom, witnessed only, perhaps, by his feeble night-time lamp. Consciously, his objective in *Ethics* Part 5 was to show the power and advantage of the wise man over the ignorant, and how that wise man, committed to living through the guidance of reason, might move on from the achievement of living harmoniously in society to the private satisfaction of mind Spinoza called *Salvation, or Blessedness, or Freedom, or Love or Joy.* This final thesis followed the logical trajectory set by *Ethics* Part 4, *On Human Bondage, or the Power of the Affects,* and he gave it the title, *On the Power of the Intellect, or on Human Freedom.* Unconsciously, however, Spinoza may have been longing to find refuge from his own destructive emotions. There is no doubting the disturbing intensity with which he eulogised that *intellectual love of God . . . which cannot be tainted by any of the vices that are in ordinary Love, but can always be greater and greater, and occupy the greatest part of the mind.* It is the nature of the intensity that demands clarification, and I suggest any interpretation must include Spinoza's vacillation between denying and embracing passion.

The lofty start to *Ethics* Part 5 degenerated into three contemptuous pages on Descartes's *occult hypothesis,* the theory of the body's interaction with a non-natural soul that Spinoza had refuted some three Parts of *Ethics* previously. And after that diatribe he still did not move the geometrical demonstration forward, as logic suggested he should, from the last passages of *Ethics* Part 4, by extrapolating from the state of mind of the individual who has learned to bear all calmly. Instead he offered two *remedies for the affects.* The first of these recalled the epistemic programme started in Part 3, which advised that if the mind actively reasoned in relation to its emotions, then these could not be passions (passive) but must instead further agency and advantage. The second was a desperate measure involving little reasoning. *The best thing, then, that we can do, so long as we do not have perfect knowledge of our affects, is to conceive a correct principle of living, or sure maxims of life, to commit them to memory, and to apply them constantly to the particular cases frequently encountered in life. In this way our imagination will be extensively affected by them, and we shall always have them ready.* It should not pass unnoticed that three of the five Parts of *Ethics* dealt with the problem of the affects, and I am sure that they represented an area of difficulty for this profoundly emotional man, who was evidently aware of the distorting shadows of inadequate ideas even as he wrote. I think we shall conclude, however, that while writing *Ethics* Part 5, Spinoza did not recognise the intensity or the origins of his own driving desire. The powerful urge to reach the *intellectual love of God*, a state of mind that soared beyond reason to the intersection of total rational mindfulness with ecstasy, created two tensions in *Ethics* Part 5, one in his theory of knowledge, the other in his own rational perspective. The first, philosophical, tension may remain insoluble but, like the threat to reason of the second, it is revealing of Spinoza the man.

On the first, epistemological issue, Spinoza made it clear that to achieve *joy* or the *greatest satisfaction of mind*, the *intellectual love of God*, the intellect must be maximally refined. This belief had, in fact, been implicit in his work from the start. In all previous texts he had insisted that loving *God, or Nature* arises from knowledge of *God, or Nature* of a superior kind. In the *Short Treatise* he had written about *a last kind of knowledge* that *produces love*. The same theme appeared early in the *Treatise on the Emendation of the Intellect*: only the *Perception we have when a thing is perceived through its essence alone* ensured truth, and satisfaction. *Love toward the eternal and infinite thing feeds the mind with a joy entirely exempt from sadness.* He had tried to put this notion into Descartes's mouth in *Descartes's Principles*. Descartes's proposition was: 'God's existence is known from the consideration of his nature alone.' Spinoza had added, *Almost all the knowledge of God's attributes, through which we are led to the love of him, or the highest blessedness . . .* In the *Theologico-Political Treatise* he had written that *the man whose main love and chief delight is the intellectual knowledge of the most perfect being, God, is necessarily most perfect, and shares most fully in supreme blessedness.* These earlier assertions had harmonised with Spinoza's tenet that to know general truths of *God, or Nature* was to be blessed. They had therefore, perhaps, been assimilated in passing. But in *Ethics* Part 5 the claim positively jarred; indeed, it undermined Spinoza's thesis, for while in the Preface he had promised that he would show only the immense power of reason over the affects, he went on to show that he did not think reason was the highest power of the mind. That greatest mental power he emphatically assigned to the third kind of knowledge, intuition, a kind of knowledge scarcely mentioned in the preceding Parts of *Ethics*, and given no important epistemic function there.

Suddenly, in *Ethics* Part 5, reason was relegated. *How much more powerful* [intuition] *is than the universal knowledge I have called knowledge of the second kind.* Intuition was not a tool for grappling, as reason must, with the inadequate ideas of imagination and opinion, but instant knowledge of the particular essences of singular things. *The more we understand singular things, the more we understand God.* Spinoza had always claimed this. He had written in his first treatises, *The essences of singular, changeable things are not to be drawn from their series, or order of existing . . . We call that clear knowledge which comes not from being convinced by reasons, but from being aware of and enjoying the thing itself.* Yet Spinoza had also admitted that intuition was a kind of knowledge rarely enjoyed by humans. *There seems to be a considerable difficulty in our being able to arrive at knowledge of these singular things . . . The things I have so far been able to know by this kind of knowledge are very few.* Now, however, he seemed to imply that intuition was requisite for contentment of mind: that reasoning one's way through systems of causes and effects in extension or thought could not, after all, furnish a view *sub specie aeternitatis* or make an individual *a free man*, and that in emphasising Descartes's term 'clear and distinct' to describe the ideas that only intuition affirmed, he was reverting to the Cartesian concept of intuition as 'divine light'.

One commentator suggests that for Spinoza reasoning always preceded intuition: 'As I gather scientific knowledge of my body and of my mind, as I close in, so to speak, on myself from all relevant causal angles, the ground is set for the third kind of knowledge.' This view, supported by Spinoza's examples of mathematical intuition, allows intuition a rational function, and puts *the intellectual Love of God* back into the arena of the scientist, where a 'beautiful' theory, however instantly known, is backed by previous inference and experiment. But this is not the same case as knowing individual essences. Moreover, the commentator who believes that reasoning must precede Spinozistic intuition goes on to exemplify intuitive knowledge only in connection with knowing the self and achieving 'salvation'. Indeed, only in the context of the joy of one *who understands himself and his affects clearly and distinctly*, and not in any other scientific context, did Spinoza claim, *Love towards God must engage the mind most.* For readers expecting to remain within a paradigm of reasoning, this thesis is confusing and disquieting.

It seems that we need to look again at the concept of *the intellectual Love of God*, whose Hispanic-Jewish roots we found clearly expressed, with those of the notion of the union of the mind with God, in Abravanel's *Dialogues of Love*. Like the medieval Jewish sage Maimonides, Abravanel had held that God was pure intellectual activity, and that union with this Active Intellect represented the highest human goal. This goal could be reached, Maimonides thought, by great philosophers, among whom he had included Moses. The former of these stimulating sources, both of whom wrote in the Sephardic-Cabalic-Neoplatonic tradition, inspired Menasseh ben Israel and other mystically inclined rabbis and Spanish writers with his cabalist vision. The second remained closer to the rational view propounded by Aristotle and later adapted, following a revival of interest in his work, by Aquinas and Suárez and, gingerly, Descartes. The core-concept of both traditions was that the human mind could partake in divine knowledge. We know this notion had attracted Spinoza as a young man on the two counts of acquiring mathematical-logical certainty, and achieving lasting and worthwhile happiness, and I have suggested that he passed on the notion of *the intellectual Love of God* to Van den Enden. Frans could already have been vaguely familiar with the concept of the human mind's union with God's mind, since the Spanish-Jewish cult emerged in Spain in tandem with the founding of the Jesuits (Society of Jesus) in 1534 by Ignatius Loyola, and was exploited by this Catholic order as a form of spiritual expression which the Reformation had inadvertently destroyed. Salamanca university, where Spinoza's kinsman Henriques taught philosophy and theology, had spawned during Henriques's time many proponents of intellectual, and ecstatic, mysticism both within and independently of Jesuit or Catholic commitment. All variants introduced themes from the biblical books of Hosea and the Psalms. Abravanel is described as a 'great precursor of the Spanish mystics', most of whose reflections are later thought to have resonance in the writings of Teresa of Avila, the Jewish-born Carmelite nun chosen as the country's patron saint. The immediacy of the mystic communion they promised also eventually attracted radical Protestants, such as the Quakers. But while respectful references to Suárez by these mystics show they believed their love of God to be intellectual, almost all expressed an emotionally or erotically charged style of worship in which the cognitive element was reduced or dissolved. During the four mental stages leading to union with the mind of God described by Teresa of Avila, for example, the intellect is seen as increasingly worthless, and the highest state of all 'a glorious folly, a heavenly madness, in which true wisdom is acquired'.

Spinoza approved neither this carefully structured leave-taking of rational thought nor the irrational yearning for inner light and sanctioning of hysteria of the sects who emulated it. Yet he had always aspired to

Abravanel's 'Active Intellect, which gives light to our power of understanding', and believed, with Abravanel, that 'Knowing and loving . . . are two activities . . . both are necessary to happiness'. It has been suggested that a yearning for such inner enlightenment, never quite satisfied by scientific methodology, had led Spinoza into his friendships with Balling, Jarig and others, and finally 'broke through the confines of his scientific system' in *Ethics* Part 5. Certainly the least semitically sensitised researcher who has read the *Short Treatise* recognises in *Ethics* Part 5 a similar wistfulness for communing with divine intellect, and can believe that this desire may have lodged at the back of Spinoza's mind since childhood, doing battle there with his belief that God was best replaced as a paradigm of truth by mathematics. I believe Spinoza's flight towards a higher plane of understanding in the last Part of *Ethics* may have been less the cogitation of an 'eagle in the clouds' (as Anna van Schurman granted the intelligence of 'more excellent men') than the escape into love seductively expressed by Abravanel, described to a small Bento by his father, Menasseh or Morteira, and developed to cult proportions since 1665 by Aboab in his Hispanic literary *yeshiva*. Abravanel's Philo ultimately advised his lover Sophia that it was 'time indeed for your sweet person to seek rest, while my mind keeps its usual anguished watch'. Philo's watch would be rewarded by a cognitive happiness, in which love 'born of reason' but 'not restricted or directed by reason' dissolved anguish. I suggest that Spinoza's longing for this state of blessedness was so intense that it tinged his view of Christ with envy, for while he sometimes snapped that Jesus was a prophet who spoke only from imagination, the philosopher also admitted that Christ *communed with God mind to mind*. Occasional doubts that Christ's intuition was any more rational than Abravanel's eroticism did not lessen his desire to share the *satisfaction* of mind it brought.

Poignant reminders of his own Jewish background may have been triggered for Spinoza in the 1670s, when the *parnasim* of the *Talmud Torah* synagogue bought the site of the St Anthonie's Gate at the eastern end of the Vloyenburg and, permission having been given by the city authorities, ordered the building of a new synagogue. This vast and lavishly equipped temple was opened in 1675, Aboab de Fonseca being unanimously chosen as its *hacham*. Soon afterwards Spinoza warned in his *Political Treatise* that the dimension of churches should be limited, to preserve public peace. However, while Spinoza may have deprecated the marranos' defiant ostentation, which had burgeoned in reaction to increased numbers of eastern European Jews in Amsterdam, loss of families to the West Indies and the reinstatement of Stadholder rule (William made use of marrano funding, and would do so even when living in England and fighting in

Ireland), there is evidence that in the 1670s his Judaic past began to reassert itself. In Spinoza's letter to Burgh he had shown unusually fervent sympathy for an Inquisition victim, news of whose death had reached Amsterdam during the 1640s, but whom he had not previously mentioned. *I myself know among others of a certain Judah called 'the faithful' who, in the midst of flames when he was already believed dead, began to sing the hymn which begins 'To thee, O God, I commit my soul', and so singing, died.* Now, too, he composed a *Hebrew Grammar*. Meyer would testify in the Preface to the Latin *Opera Posthuma* that Spinoza 'had always had it in mind to set forth a Hebrew Grammar demonstrated in the geometrical order', which would help those for whom 'up to this point the spirit of that sacred tongue had been obscure' and also 'show that the true pronunciation of the language had long perished'. Spinoza emphasised that his was the definitive handbook. *There are many who wrote of the Scriptures, but none who wrote a grammar of the Hebrew language*, he commented sniffily in its pages. *They wrote a grammar of the Scriptures, but not of the language.* We know that he had since his schooldays ridiculed his teachers' gullibility over the explanatory power of Hebrew phraseology as divined through numerology, and there is a slight sense of an old score being settled in this fiercely scientific exposition. The *Grammar* was not completed: there was reference to a second part on the rules of Hebrew syntax, yet no second part materialised. But an unfeigned love of the language, an early love possibly exploited by others in those vulnerable Amsterdam years when the Quakers needed a translator, shines through the pedantry. Spinoza seems to have dispensed with none of his Hebrew books, some of which, such as Maimonides's *Moreh Nebuchim* of 1515, were undoubtedly heirlooms. He had even – astonishingly – kept Del Medigo's cabalic texts (one on numerology) and Abravanel's *Hagadah Pesach*, a guide to ritual, which would surely have been treasured by the next generation of his family. (In 1674 Ribca's daughter Hana married one of the Portuguese-Jewish community's most devout scholars, Samuel Idanha, with whom she and Ribca would, sometime after 1679, emigrate to Curaçao.)

Perhaps, as he approached his mid-forties, his father's age when he was born, he took on Michael's *saudade*, the gloomy nostalgia for which Portuguese Jews were infamous, said to be rooted in grieving for King Sebastião, lost in Morocco in 1578, mingled with a longing for the Messiah to be born of the *naçao*. But whereas in the *Hebrew Grammar* any such incoherent, unexamined empathy was checked by the need for objective analysis, and in the letter to Burgh a trace of it had quickly been replaced with abuse of Catholicism, there is in *Ethics* Part 5 a disconcerting sense of private emotional absorption. During the frightening period of seclusion in the Paviljoensgracht in which Spinoza probably started writing this last 'demonstration', he may have anticipated violent death or rapid physical deterioration (*Perhaps, if I live long enough, I shall sometime discuss this with you more clearly*) and, like his forebears, sought to block his mind to all ideas but the eternal:

> *The intellectual Love of God, which arises from the third kind of knowledge, is eternal . . . Death is less harmful to us, the greater the mind's clear and distinct knowledge, and hence, the more the mind loves God . . . For the eternal part of the mind is the intellect.*

But if the nature of Spinoza's present love was rooted in past experience, its object, his iconoclastic *God, or Nature,* was not. Even Abravanel had thought God loved man in return, whereas for Spinoza, *God's love of men and the mind's intellectual love of God are one and the same.* The commentator who holds that *Ethics* Part 5 displays the breaking out of an old desire views with deep disquiet Spinoza's love for 'an entity of geometrical perfection and indifference', and wonders how the love towards God, which is untainted by envy or jealousy, and so on, can be said to constitute either affirmation of Spinoza's own essence or freedom of mind. He believes the only 'self' bothering Spinoza is Spinoza; that the *power of the intellect, or human freedom* is directed on Spinoza's own dominion over his affects, and that a 'streak of masochism' runs throughout Spinoza's doctrine of love which makes the intellectual love of God 'a form of self-hatred, a neurotic manifestation'. Further, he says, Spinoza's definition of love reflects his 'hatred of the body; he is indeed driving the harlot out of his images of love'. Love is, for Spinoza, this commentator believes, dissociated from the idea of union with the beloved object; 'love is rarefied, spiritualised, sublimated'. With respect to love, it is concluded, Spinoza's mind was neither free nor aware of itself: 'There was a component of enslavement here, of whose causes he was ignorant.' This very strong view may go further than is justified, but it compels careful scrutiny of *Ethics* Part 5, where we find, for example, that there is no mention of 'union' with *God, or Nature,* and that the term 'enslavement' seems the correct way to describe Spinoza's state of mind. I am going to propose an alternative understanding of this, which I think accounts for his conflict of aspiration in *Ethics* Part 5, and also explains what the Dutch call the 'black page' of the *Political Treatise,* where Spinoza states that women are incapable of reasoning as well as men and debars them from participating in government, from voting and, if possible, from influencing men by their presence or ideas. We return to this in the context of Spinoza's last, unfinished work, the *Political Treatise.*

The period of enforced seclusion after the visit to Utrecht saw the completion of *Ethics*, but not the termination of philosophical inquiry. Spinoza was now chronically sick and biologically aged: the grizzled grey halo and racked face of the 1677 engraving was said by those who knew him to be an excellent likeness. The night-vigils 'had become almost constant through the ill-effects of a slight, slow fever', this last being an indication that tuberculosis had taken irrevocable hold. But Spinoza seems, anyway, to have had an aversion to going to bed. The Van der Spycks said he 'came down' even when so poorly that he had to rest on a cupboard-bed in the front parlour. It was here, they said, and not in the *ledikant*, that he eventually died. Did the compulsion to get dressed daily spring, perhaps, from buried memories? His parents had taken to bed (that same bed he avoided?) and had never got out again. He may, unconsciously, have believed that in the *ledikant* lay death.

But once he had decided that a new treatise must be written he defied the inconvenience of his own demise. A letter sent in 1676 shows that, unwell and dispirited as he often was, he did not want to be distracted from this project. The letter, to 'A Friend', read, *I thank you most sincerely for the considerable trouble you take on my behalf. I should not let this opportunity* [words deleted] *if I were not engaged in a certain matter which I believe to be more important, and which I think will be more to your liking, namely, in composing a Political Treatise, which I began some time ago at your suggestion.* We can only guess at the identity of the 'Friend'. In 1674 Spinoza had briefly answered a query from Jelles on Hobbesian politics. Since the letter 'to a Friend' was used as a Preface to the *Political Treatise* in the *Posthumous Works*, to which Jelles wrote the Preface, I agree with the scholar who thinks it was probably sent to Jarig. On the opportunity offered there are no obvious leads: we must just note the greater priority of Spinoza's political interest at this point.

The project had no immediate link with the topics on which Von Tschirnhaus still pressed him, and Spinoza's answers to some of the most probing questioning with which he was ever honoured were curt and disappointing. On 'how, from Extension as conceived in your philosophy, the variety of things can be demonstrated a priori', for example, he would still prevaricate. *I think I have already made it quite clear that this is impossible ... I have not had the opportunity to arrange in due order anything on this subject.* The topic of knowledge of particular existences and essences would remain problematic, and the requested 'General Physics' would not be written. Nor was the political preoccupation connected with any of the issues on which Leibniz would tackle him when he visited The Hague in October 1676, on a circuitous route from Paris to Hanover, via London and

Amsterdam. Leibniz, like Von Tschirnhaus, wanted to know exactly how Spinoza's theory of motion differed from Descartes's. While forced to wait on board ship for six days at Sheerness for a wind favouring the crossing to Holland, he had composed a treatise on motion, in the form of a dialogue, and intended to discuss the question with the philosopher of whom he had heard so much. But he would get the impression that Spinoza 'did not see very well the faults of Descartes's laws of motion. He was surprised,' Leibniz would recall, 'when I began to show him they were inconsistent with the equality of cause and effect.' Surprised, perhaps, but not much interested. Spinoza could not explain his own novel doctrine of motion through mechanical theory, we know, but his scorn for Descartes's first principles of extension probably ensured that he had not bothered to examine the great man's laws of motion since he had defended all but one of them to Huygens in 1665.

Nor would Spinoza be impressed by the sophisticated metaphysical theory on the labyrinth of the 'composition of the continuum', which Leibniz was beginning to develop, or by his theory of monads, myriad minute substances (inspired, perhaps, by the teeming world of interconnected organisms revealed by microscopy), if the German's thesis depended on the Cartesian premise, which also underlay Huygens's empirical theory, that material things were inert unless pushed by an external, wilful divine hand. Leibniz, on the other hand, was curious about Spinoza's 'strange metaphysic' in which 'God was the substance of everything', and despite finding this principle as repugnant as Spinoza found any of Descartes's, he honoured it with meticulous analysis before rejecting it. Failing to make Spinoza's bold leap away from Descartes's belief in God as the *external* cause of bodies and motion, Leibniz told Arnauld in 1687 that 'everything happens in each substance in consequence of the first state which God gave it in creating it', and that mechanics could be studied without recourse to *a priori* metaphysical principles. Leibniz was not simply mollifying an influential priest here. Like most natural philosophers of his day, he remained a committed creationist, and all his writings affirm that God's will is the cause of the universal harmony of things, which governs the laws of motion, and that the cause of motion is mind, there being no motion, strictly speaking, as a real property of bodies.

After that autumn visit Leibniz reported that he 'spoke with [Spinoza] several times and for very long'. He recalled tackling him on *Ethics*'s first demonstrations of metaphysical necessity, arguing that the possibility that an absolutely perfect or complete (*perfectus*) Being must exist must be established before discussion of whether God could express all possible attributes was introduced. Spinoza, he recollected, would not at first accept his proof. Leibniz then produced another proof, which he believed Spinoza accepted. This is not the place to judge whether Spinoza's arguments and assumptions in *Ethics* Part 1 amount to a proof that nothing could count as a reason against the existence of *God*, but they do not obviously accommodate Leibniz's strictures, which Spinoza may have ignored. Like so many of the philosophical problems Spinoza's doctrine raised, this wrangle over 'sufficient reason' lingers on, as does the specific anomaly that Leibniz claims to have dissolved in his second proof, namely that God need not contain contradictions such as good and evil if God has not been demonstrated to express all that is possible. 'Such a God as the pious hold to would not be possible if the opinion of those is true who believe all possibles exist.' Spinoza believed that God expressed only that which was *logically* possible, and that logic could not bend to accommodate that to which the pious, in their prejudice and superstition, held.

Spinoza and his principles would remain thorns in Leibniz's consciousness and scattered writings, and he made constant references to both the man and his work. Spinoza, on the other hand, was withering or silent on the subject of this brilliant rationalist, not from menopausal resentment or fear of having his first principles unsettled, but from a conviction that those areas of his philosophy were indisputable. Leibniz was a neophyte of no philosophical consequence in 1676, but, were he *that most distinguished man* himself, what response would we expect from Spinoza to a defence of 'such a God as the pious hold to' but a raised eyebrow, a resigned nod and a handing back of the paper? If something in our belief had to be adjusted, it was our faulty view of good and evil, not God's capacity for expressing, existentially, compossibility. Nothing written by Leibniz, not even the 1671 *Note on Advanced Optics* sent with that first congratulatory letter, is preserved in Spinoza's library.

Disagreement and mental alienation were now habitual and not discomforting states of mind for Spinoza. The intellectual loneliness that had set him apart from every group or individual he had encountered since he was old enough to contemplate the fabric of others' minds amply satisfied the requirement of the twentieth-century philosopher Ludwig Wittgenstein (whom we would not want to envisage in dialogue with Spinoza) that 'the philosopher is not a citizen of *any* community of ideas. That is what makes him into a philosopher.'

However, he felt no such sense of natural rightness regarding his political theory. The *Political Treatise*, on which he was said to have embarked 'a short time before his death', offered an alternative set of inferences to those presented towards the end of Part 4. Although it would show in allusions and quotations that were instantly recognisable to politically aware readers that he engaged in a discourse extending from Terence and Livy through Machiavelli and Hobbes to Van den Hove, Spinoza's main aim in the *Political Treatise* was to construct an additional theorem – made necessary because the majority in any community would never be guided by reason – which was deducible from his own metaphysical and epistemological systems. In the model of democracy he had proposed in the *Theologico-Political Treatise*, harmony had resulted from universal rational agreement. A share in the State's *sovereignty* had been available to all who reasoned. But he had shown by his suggestion that consent might have to be compelled that he knew this contract was not ultimately workable. Now, following the national crisis of 1672, and perhaps also further reading of Hobbes and discussion with *libertins*, he declared that *the causes and natural foundations of the state are not to be sought in the precepts of reason*:

> *I have shown that reason can do a great deal to check and moderate the passions, but at the same time we saw that the way prescribed by reason is very difficult; so that those who believe that a crowd, or people divided over public affairs, can be induced to live by reason's dictate alone, are dreaming of the poets' golden age or of a fairy-tale.*

It was not in Spinoza's nature to admit he had been wrong. (*Repentance is not a virtue, nor does it arise from reason; instead, he who repents what he has done is twice wretched, or lacking in power.*) He did not, then, deny his earlier thesis, but augmented it. *To have shown what ought to be done is not enough; the main problem is to show how it can be done, i.e. how men, even when led by passion, may still have fixed and stable laws.* A new axiom was in place: *Men are necessarily subject to passions.*

The *Political Treatise* opened with a résumé of Spinoza's views on the problem for politics of the passions, then set out to reconcile the metaphysical *principle of our advantage* with a form of government that could contain the violence, greed and weakness which might unexpectedly shackle reason. The question of the *utilitas* (*advantage*, *usefulness* or 'interest') of the individual versus the common interest, or versus the interest of the State where this differed from the common interest) had, as mentioned, been debated before Hobbes first visited Paris in the 1630s. At that time Béthune, for example, wrote that 'the Reason of State is in effect nothing other than the reason of interest', and the Duc de Rohan (Prince of Léon and premier duke of the same proud Breton line as Van den Enden's accomplice Louis de Rohan) had exhorted heeding 'our own interest, guided by reason alone, which ought to be the rule of all our actions'. Hobbes had argued in *De Cive*, 'Forasmuch as the laws of nature are nought else but the dictates of reason

... unlesse a man endeavour to preserve the faculty of right reasoning, he cannot observe the Lawes of Nature'. But by the time he wrote *Leviathan*, Hobbes no longer believed that scientific reasoning, any more than prescription (that is, the 'oughts' and 'shoulds' pivotal to the success of De Rohan's theory) had the power to persuade men from their perceived interests. Among the human powers Hobbes now considered 'means to obtain some apparent good' were 'Strength, Forme, Prudence, Arts, Eloquence, Liberality ... Riches, Reputation and Friends'. If 'interest requires it' people set 'themselves against reason, as oft as reason is against them'.

Spinoza had conceded that *To have shown what* ought *to be done is not enough* (my emphasis), but as we know he did not accept that the laws of human nature generated a State where greed and fear must necessarily dominate, and he refused to contemplate a new social contract based on that premise. Instead, with what he admitted was no great originality, he undertook to examine the models of government discussed by almost all earlier political writers (including Van den Enden) of monarchy, political aristocracy and democracy. He subsequently made no mention of a contract, but proposed what must be for him a second-best democracy, a system which, as his subtitle showed, must operate under a monarchy or aristocracy, but which he chiefly cast within an aristocracy. This form of government took into account the failure to be guided by reason not only of the masses but of those most obviously endowed with reason. While a shortage of individuals habitually guided by reason meant that the sovereignty of a state must be vested *in certain persons only* – namely older men *whose private interests and advantage are bound up with the general welfare and the maintenance of peace* (in a monarchy they must be fifty years old or over; in an aristocracy, thirty) – these political patricians must also be monitored if tyranny was to be prevented. Spinoza therefore offered a *Political Treatise*:

> *Wherein it is shown how a Monarchy*
> *and an Aristocracy must be organised if*
> *they are not to degenerate into a Tyranny,*
> *and if the Peace and Freedom of the*
> *citizens is to remain intact.*

The *Treatise* was grounded in the view that no man whatsoever was consistently wise. *Those who confine to the common people the vices which exist in all human beings will perhaps greet my contentions with ridicule ... But all men have one and the same nature: it is power and culture which mislead us.*

Spinoza may have previously overestimated Johan de Witt's natural power, but he at last seemed to recognise where the man had gone wrong:

> *Pride is characteristic of rulers. Because long experience . . . gives such men a very thorough knowledge of affairs, it often happens that undue weight is attached to their advice, and that the condition of the entire state largely depends on their guidance; a situation which was the ruin of Holland. For this is bound to arouse a great deal of jealousy in the nobles . . . The sudden overthrow of this republic was not due to time wasted on deliberations, but to its defective condition and the fewness of its rulers.*

His conclusion seemed to be that no constitutional safeguard had existed to control De Witt's autonomy and pride in his own judgement, and in a disenchanted reproduction of the politics of Aristotle he promoted a *constitution established on correct principles*, a constitution *supported by reason and the common passions of men*:

> *It is really the goodness or badness of a state's constitution which determines the degree to which it will be subject to this malady. For when public liberty is based on insecure foundations it is never defended without risk; and to avoid running this risk the patricians choose as officials ambitious commoners, who, when revolution comes, are slaughtered like sacrificial animals to appease the anger of the enemies of freedom.*

Did Spinoza recognise, as he choked here on his own passion, how hard it would be for any constitution to provide a reliable safeguard? His long and carefully argued section on the probability that any passion could be overcome *by a stronger and contrary passion*, which he brought round to the *panic* that arises *when the state is in desperate straits*, shows that he did. Spinoza had in mind here the *panic* that had arisen in Holland in 1672:

> *First, in a well-organized state a panic like this does not arise without good reason; and so it, and the disturbance to which it leads, can be attributed to no cause which could not have been avoided by human foresight. Secondly, it must be noted that in a commonwealth such as I have described above it is impossible for any single man to have such an outstanding reputation for ability that he turns everyone's eyes upon himself: he must inevitably have numerous rivals, each with a considerable following. Thus even though panic does cause some disturbance in the commonwealth, no one will be able to get round the laws and appoint someone illegally to a military command without arousing the immediate opposition of the other candidates; and to settle the dispute it will be necessary in the end to revert to the laws once established and approved by all, and to arrange such matters in accordance with the existing constitution.*

De Witt might have failed the Dutch, but Spinoza evidently foresaw problems if 'the Majesty of Orange' was not promptly fenced about with constitutional restrictions.

Three further elements of the *Political Treatise* throw light on Spinoza's character in his last years. The first two stand out – in contrast to the element of 'enslavement' that mars the ending – as particular philosophical achievements. Indeed, Spinoza's treatment of the problem of the dissenting individual who chooses to remain in a State, and the extent to which a democratic constitution can stretch to allow this, may comprise his most lasting contribution to political theory. One political philosopher (writing, significantly, during the First World War) thought Spinoza's thesis of political obligation, which remained, ultimately, with the reasoning self, verged on 'inveterate irreverence towards the State'. But while Spinoza recognised that *devotion to some religious faith may lead one or two men to regard the laws of the state as the worst of all evils*, and insisted both that *true knowledge and love of God cannot be subject to anyone's command* and that *nobody can give up his power of judgement*, he still held that personal *right* must be sacrificed to the *law of the commonwealth*, since:

> it is quite inconceivable that every citizen should be allowed by a law of the commonwealth to live as his own judgement dictates . . . Men hold rights as a body . . . Peace cannot be achieved unless the general laws of the State are kept inviolate . . . Hence if the rational man has sometimes, by order of the commonwealth, to do what he knows to be opposed to reason, this inconvenience is far outweighed by the advantage which he derives from the actual existence of the political order.

That no constitution could build into itself scope for its own laws to be broken must be taken into consideration regarding the heroics of Frans van den Enden.

On the issue of religious freedom, for which Uriel d'Acosta and Koerbagh had paid with their lives, Spinoza made careful provision. *Godsdienst* was to be regularised under secular authority, and no member of the ruling élite might flagrantly dissent from this:

> All patricians . . . guardians and interpreters of the state religion . . . should be of the same faith, the very simple universal faith set out in the treatise referred to [the *Theologico-Political Treatise*]. For it is vitally important to prevent the patricians in particular not only from splitting up into sects and favouring different religious groups, but also from becoming prey to a superstition and seeking to deprive their subjects of the freedom to voice their beliefs.
>
> Although everyone should be given freedom to voice his beliefs, large

congregations should be forbidden; and so, while dissenters should be allowed to build as many churches as they wish, these churches must be small, of fixed dimensions, and situated some distance apart.

Faith was defended, but was not given a name. It *must not* have a name if the *Turks and the Jews and the Christians*, et cetera, were to worship in harmony. Christ was not mentioned in the mature political theorising of the *Political Treatise*, and only one reference to Christianity was made. It came in what I take to be Spinoza's ultimate statement on institutionalised religion:

Love finds its supreme expression when directed to the preservation of peace and the promotion of concord . . . a man truly does his duty if he gives everyone as much help as is consistent with the laws of the commonwealth, i.e. with peace and concord. As for outward rites, we may take it as certain that they cannot help or hinder a man at all in reaching true knowledge of God, and the love of him which is its necessary consequence; hence they are not to be esteemed of such importance as to justify a breach of the public peace and quiet. But of course I am not, by right of nature, i.e. (by Section 3 of the previous Chapter) by divine decree, a champion of religion. For I have no power, such as once belonged to Christ's disciples, to cast out unclean spirits and work miracles; and this power is obviously indispensable for the propagation of a religion in places where it is proscribed . . .

Each man, then, wherever he may be, can worship God with true piety, and take care of himself, and that is the duty of a private individual . . . But I must return to my subject.

Spinoza was not, *by right of nature, by divine decree, a champion of religion.* Here, at last, was his admission that he was not a religious man in the conventional sense. Here, too, was stifled lamentation for D'Acosta and Koerbagh. But here also was charity to Jarig and others whose faith was grounded in undiscriminating concern for the well-being of all. Colerus tells us that when Ida Margarita van der Spyck asked her lodger if he thought she could be saved through her Dutch Reformed Church religion, he assured her, 'Your religion's all right. You needn't look for another one in order to be saved, if you give yourself to a quiet and pious life.' Where worship remained untainted by superstition or theology, *true piety* did duty for *Godsdienst*. But this was a second-best endeavour, a lesser aspiration than the *intellectual love of God* in which lay humankind's highest blessedness.

We now return, via Spinoza's denial of political rights to women on the grounds of their inferior mentality, to the bondage of his own mind. We noted earlier that Spinoza doubted if the Jews would re-establish their State, since there was something fundamentally inadequate in their constitution.

Did not the principles of their religion make them effeminate, I should be quite convinced that some day when the opportunity arises . . . they will establish their state once more. In so far as the Jewish religion was ritual-bound and grounded in prophecy, it expressed, in Spinoza's view, something specifically female. His use of the word *effeminate* was not arbitrary, but the product of a sincere belief that female thinking was radically flawed. Whereas the seventeenth-century Frenchman François Boulain de la Barre held that women were well suited to controlling human affairs, and Frans van den Enden thought they should not only learn history, mathematics and medical science, but help choose 'community ministers', Spinoza expressly excluded all women, regardless of education or economic status, from political rights:

> *Absolutely everyone who is bound only by the laws of his country, and is otherwise independent, and who leads a decent life, has the right to vote in the supreme council and to undertake offices of state. I say expressly 'who is bound only by the laws of his country' to exclude aliens, who are regarded as subjects of another government. I added 'and is otherwise independent', to exclude women and servants, who are subject to their husbands and masters, and also children and wards, as long as they are under the control of their parents and guardians.*

Spinoza's exclusions verged on liberality in comparison with those of other seventeenth-century political writers, including Jan van den Hove. The stricture on women was, however, standard and is endorsed in Saint-Évremond's memoirs. Yet Spinoza can no more be pardoned for ordering exclusions on women on conventional grounds than he can for assuming marrano attitudes, and the weak empirical argument he offered did not strengthen his case: *If nature had made women equal to men, and had given them equal strength of mind and intellectual ability, in which human power and therefore human right mainly consists, surely among so many different nations some would be found where both sexes ruled on equal terms, and others where the men were ruled by the women.* Spinoza had committed himself to propounding only what was logically-metaphysically necessary, and he was therefore compelled to *demonstrate* that *women have not the same right as men by nature, but are necessarily inferior to them*; that women *could not*, from some cause equivalent to that dictating the radical mental inadequacy of infants and idiots, do so. He did not provide a proof, and no philosopher has managed to get him out of the hole he dug for himself.

One twentieth-century commentator, Alexandre Matheron, toys with allowing Spinoza the hypothesis that *if* women were economically independent, they *would* be suitable participants in political life, but admits that

Spinoza blasts away this possibility by implying that the laws of human nature expressed in the real power relations between men and women decree that if women were given political rights they would abuse them. Certainly, Spinoza's final lines in the *Political Treatise* form a crescendo of disapproval of female nature:

> *If we also consider human passions, and reflect that men generally love women out of mere lust, judge their ability and wisdom by their beauty, are highly indignant if the women they love show the slightest favour to others, and so on, we shall easily see that it is impossible for men and women to govern on equal terms without great damage to the peace. But I have said enough on this topic.*

> *Reliqua desiderantur.*
> The rest is wanting.

At this point Spinoza laid down his quill, for good. Matheron semi-flippantly concludes his own examination of the place of women in Spinoza's model democracy by proposing that, at this juncture, Spinoza realised the cruelty of the consequences of his principles, and found this realisation enough to make him stop, and die. Although Matheron thinks Spinoza exaggerates the role of women in political intrigue, he otherwise accepts his thesis, and doubts whether women inspired repugnance in him 'as is often said'. It was not the women themselves that repelled, Matheron claims, but 'something' in their natures. He then refers us to a passage in the *Treatise on the Emendation of the Intellect* which states that when *we understand nothing about the cause except what we consider in the effect*, we conclude that *there is something . . . some power* in the cause. Spinoza had in mind, of course, a real force in nature, not some 'occult power'. Matheron accepts the idea that for Spinoza there really was 'something' in female nature which disadvantaged women in the game of power relations, keeping all members of the human race under the rule of passion. This view narrows the focus of Spinoza's abhorrence to some essentially female power, which makes men *prey to lust*, prone to superstition, susceptible to passion or sentimentality and stunted in *strength of mind and intellectual ability*. Should such a mental power necessarily reflect a specifically female body state, Spinoza's claim would be non-pejorative and scientific. But we concluded earlier that the existence of women who reason consistently makes it only possible for Spinoza to claim that there is at most sometimes, in some women, a chemical imbalance or some such physical state with which destructive sexual power may be correlated.

I propose that the difficulties of *Ethics* Part 5, and the harsh views of the final 'black page' of the *Political Treatise*, are rooted less in Spinoza's doctrine of parallelism than in an assumption that permeated many ancient religions and, embedded in the theory of the humours, still dominated European conventional medicine in the seventeenth century. This was the notion that some elements in nature were male, active and intellectual, whereas other, female, elements were passive and sensual. Air and fire were considered the active elements; water and earth, the passive. In medicine, until well into the eighteenth century, they were thought to be contained in the human body as the humours of, respectively, blood, yellow bile, phlegm and black bile, and respectively in the temperament as sanguine, choleric, phlegmatic and melancholy. Spinoza did not overtly subscribe to this doctrine – that is, he did not mention it – and we know he took care not to trap his theory of mind in past or present observations. Yet, for him, the ideas of reason and intuition were *active* and *adequate*, while those of the first kind – imagination, opinion, hearsay, etc. – were *passive* and *inadequate*, and were solely responsible for the passions and for superstition. The former effected intellectual freedom; the latter shackled the mind. Abravanel may (although this plausible grounding for Spinoza's misogyny has not, to my knowledge, been explored) have been instrumental in fixing these metaphysical and epistemological polarities as male and female, for in his *Dialogues of Love* a sustained tension holds between Philo's instruction and Sophia's passive absorption of his wisdom. Philo tells the woman:

> Every man and woman has a masculine part which is perfect and active, to wit the intellect, and a feminine part which is imperfect and passive, to wit the body and matter . . . In the beginning, therefore, these two parts, masculine and feminine, were joined in absolute union in the perfect man whom God had made, so that the sentient and feminine body was the obedient servant of the masculine intellect and reason. There was then no division in man, and his whole life was intellectual.

But, says Philo, while man's intellect brought happiness, 'He began to find himself defective, because he had not a similar reason for affection for his feminine part. So God separated the masculine and feminine parts . . . they were separated for a good and necessary end.' Thus, when Sophia, persuaded of the superiority of Philo's intellectual love of God over their ordinary human love, pleads at last, 'I would not deny that I love you and desire union with your intellect – not that your intellect should be joined to mine, but mine to yours, as the lesser to the more perfect,' Philo recoils, appalled. 'Think on fulfilling your obligations to me,' he chides her, 'to which payment you are restrained by love, reason and virtue.'

Philo's fierce thrusting of Sophia back into her role of servant and purveyor of a meaner, human form of love sprang from horror at the prospect of contaminating his intellect with a woman's. Spinoza, judging by the harshness with which he excluded Abravanel's notions of a lovable and loving God, and his erotic fantasies, may have thought Philo had brought this nemesis on himself by likening the concept of love of, and union with, God, to coitus. Any notion of spiritual 'marriage' hinted at a conjunction of male and female, active and passive, adequate and inadequate – a hint on which Sophia had understandably seized. In *Ethics* Part 5 Spinoza rejected the notion that sexual union was a necessary, let alone sufficient, condition of love. *The definition of those authors who define Love as 'a will of the lover to join himself to the thing loved' expresses a property of Love, not its essence.* He had come to deplore the analogy made in Hispanic-Jewish tradition between coitus and union with God's mind. The medieval monk Bernard of Clairvaux had warned, 'Take heed that you bring chaste ears to this discourse of love; and when you think of two lovers, remember always that not a man and a woman are to be thought of, but the Word of God and a soul.' But the abbot's disclaimer came only after Bernard had characterised the threefold Mystical Way to God in three sensuous stages – Kisses of the Feet of Christ, Kisses of the Mouth of Christ, and Kisses of the Hand of Christ – and it came too late to blot out the explicit carnality of Hebrew poetry, or the sublimated sexuality of generations of nuns who called themselves the Brides of Christ. The echoes of sexual congress implicit in Menasseh's *Nishmat Hayyim* and Abravanel's *Dialogues* may long have mingled in Spinoza's memory with images of the aphrodisiac frenzy with which the Jewish hymn about the bridegroom Israel's greeting of his bride, the Sabbath, had been sung, and the *mahamad*'s conflicting warning that *paixoes*, desires and urges, were symptoms of illness.

For Spinoza, mystics who hijacked the notion of *the intellectual love of God* by deliberately replacing its element of active, rational understanding with passive faith or imagination effected a distortion that he invariably saw as *effeminate*.

In *Ethics* Part 5 he had set out to reinstate the *active* intellect as the means to loving and knowing *God, or Nature*. He wanted to counter theses such as that of Teresa of Avila, who compared the sudden and violent shock of rapture with being borne up on the wings of a 'powerful eagle . . . you realise, and indeed see, that you are being carried away, you know not whither'. The eagle, master of the air, traditionally symbolised the highest, keenest and most active knowledge, but Teresa, as had the Church when it built the eagle's image into the Bible lectern, wrested that faculty away from human intelligence, leaving the latter passive – *effeminate*. That is undoubtedly how Spinoza would have seen Kerckring's conversion to Catholicism – the weakening of the mind by a woman. In his extreme disgust at Burgh's surrender to faith and dogma he went further: we might almost accuse him of invoking another ancient prejudice against women as he demanded, *Who has bewitched you?* The philosopher's contempt was always proportionate to the potential ability of the enslaved mind. Those with ample intellectual capacity, especially those with mathematical minds, were derided for capitulating to *superstition*, since if a serious attempt at finding eternal truths and making deductions from them was to be made, imagination, superstition, sentiment and prophecy must be rigorously excluded. However, those not to be expected to enjoy the free life of the intellect, such as Jarig and Ida Margarita van der Spyck, were spared his invective:

> *Uneducated countrymen, nay even women, such as Hagar, Abraham's handmaid, were so gifted* [i.e. in imagination and prophecy]. *Nor is this contrary to ordinary experience and reason. Men of great imaginative power are less fitted for abstract reasoning, whereas those who excel in intellect and its use keep their imagination restrained and controlled, holding it in subjection, so to speak, lest it should usurp the place of reason.*

What must be *restrained and controlled*, held in *subjection lest it should usurp the place of reason*, was the female, passive component in nature, wherever it manifested itself. In being *womanish* and *effeminate*, it shackled reason in any mind, not only a woman's.

Yet Spinoza also yearned, with that very part of his mind he wanted to deny, for the escape from mental anguish described by Teresa, Abravanel and the host of his compatriots whose aesthetic and lyrical sensitivity he shared. So, while the *Political Treatise* democracy failed, in the end, to cohere with Spinoza's most basic principles, because the projection on women of an irrational force in nature was total, *Ethics* Part 5 confused because that *something* that must be *restrained and controlled*, held in *subjection* lest it usurp the place of reason, remained integrated in Spinoza's psyche. The philosopher sought *satisfaction of mind*, or *Love, or Blessedness*, or *Joy* in a state of vacillation, his own dreams and cravings battling with an assumption he had unconsciously assigned the status of metaphysical truth.

Spinoza did not experience the last, truly irrational action of a woman, for it was after he had died that Ribca visited The Hague to declare herself his heiress. There was nothing for her to inherit. The short list of his chattels and financial assets was reported by Colerus when listing its details as 'the inventory of a true philosopher'. Those goods, including the family books, must be sold to pay his debts, and on hearing this Ribca withdrew her claim.

Spinoza's character was not, ever, entirely harmonious or consistent. This did not make for easy or regular relationships, and I think we should not look for blessedness in that respect in his last year. 'Strong temper', 'scornful anger' and 'vehement outbursts' may be exaggerations, and his 'enslavement' no crippling sexual neurosis, but the inner tension that made him yearn for what he most deprecated – divine light beyond reason – and disdain what he most esteemed – forceful logical argument, such as that offered by Von Tschirnhaus and Leibniz – prevents us from summarising the outcomes of past attachments as the logically necessary conclusions to chains of implication constructed over the years. There are no tidy endings to the friendships he had made, just scrappy contacts, desultory estrangements and disrupted plans. For, quite apart from the complexity of his mental state, no one but Schuller suspected Spinoza's malady to be fatal. Leibniz, visiting the philosopher two months earlier, commented that he was 'sallow', but made no suggestion that he was ill. Colerus says, 'His landlord, and the people of the house did not believe that he was so near his end, even a little while before he died, and they had not the least thought of it.'

Which friends did he still have? The editing of his letters cannot disguise the extent to which any contact outside the four safe walls of the Paviljoensgracht house agitated him latterly. While it might often have been true, as Colerus reports, that 'if he happened to express his grief by some gestures, or some words, he never failed to retire immediately, for fear of doing an unbecoming thing', the biting sarcasm and invective regularly found in his last letters makes it easy to see why he recommended the use of maxims. Like the seal engraved *Caute*, they were the emergency kit of reason. The Van der Spycks, who missed little, mention no calls from long-standing friends, and I think Spinoza had few following Simon's death. His acquaintance had always been tangential and fluctuating, and we should not forget that more than once in earlier years he was said to have moved home to avoid social contact. Now, happy in his lodging and too weak to travel, he saw those who came.

He may have shed old friends, or been abandoned by them. No letter to or from Meyer, for example, appears after 1663. One textual expert suggests that the policy of editing out subject matter that was trivial, irrelevant or embarrassing (in a personal, political or religious sense) renders gaps in Spinoza's correspondence insignificant. But these criteria for exclusion do not explain why a thrashing-out of philosophical differences between, say, Meyer and Spinoza should be cut. There simply seems to have been none. It is held on early authority, and on the basis of certain characteristically elegant alterations in the Latin version of *Ethics*, reminiscent of Meyer's stylistic corrections in *Descartes's Principles*, that Meyer edited, or helped edit, Spinoza's work for the *Opera Posthuma*. But it has also been suggested, on the grounds that Spinoza humiliated Meyer by publicly belittling his *Philosophiae Scripturae Interpres* in the *Theologico-Political Treatise*, that the friendship had cooled, and that Meyer paid no last editorial tribute. The truth may be complex, for the worlds of academe and literature produce mingled respect, rancour and rivalry and, when an important writer dies, an undignified elbowing to get at his or her papers. We know there was some jostling to seize Spinoza's. Getting involved with editing or translating made this easy. Simon's kinsman, 'that friend of Schiedam', would from fond memory pay off some small material debts, but in the philosopher's prolific mental legacy lay real treasure. Even Leibniz considered coming to Amsterdam to sort through Spinoza's manuscripts when he heard that the 'famous Jew' had died, but dropped the notion on learning from Schuller that an *Opera Posthuma* was forthcoming. It has long been believed that Spinoza's original fair copy of *Ethics*, or a copy of that manuscript, was stolen by Schuller and offered for sale, via Leibniz, to the Duke of Hanover, and that the vendor withdrew his offer on finding that the *Opera Posthuma* was about to be printed. By 1678 Leibniz had received a copy of this in Hanover, sent perhaps by Schuller, who had richly expanded Spinoza's correspondence, and showed concern for him, arranging the dispatch, for example, of the half-barrel of beer that the philosopher was pleased to accept. But Schuller was not ultimately a friend. It is believed by recent researchers that he, not Meyer (whose initials 'L.M.' were used by Colerus, perhaps in frustrated speculation after Hendrik refused to supply a name), was the physician sent for by Spinoza and with him when he died, who:

> that very evening returned to Amsterdam by the night boat, without taking any care of the deceased. He was the more willing to dispense himself from that duty because immediately after the death of Spinoza he had taken a ducatoon [*dukaton* – a half-ducat] and some small change, which the deceased had left upon the table, and a knife with a silver handle; and so retired with his booty.

The inclusion and subsequent crossing out of Schuller's forenames on the inventory made that very day suggest he was present but wished to conceal the fact. His letters reveal that he gave conflicting accounts of the event, raked through Spinoza's possessions and books on Leibniz's behalf, and let it be thought that he had inherited rare books of Spinoza's.

This research also concludes that Meyer, Bouwmeester, Schuller and Pieter van Gent (another ex-Leiden university student with whom no personal contact is recorded) probably worked on the Latin version of the *Complete Works*. But Van Gent was merely making copies; Schuller's Latin was so poor that he cannot have contributed greatly; and Bouwmeester may have done little more than supply his own letters from Spinoza. Rieuwertz, Glazemaker and Jelles, meanwhile, completed and amended the Dutch version started by Pieter Balling. None of those mentioned (most of whom would be dead within six years of Spinoza) need have been a 'close friend' to have thought it worth involving themselves in the labour and printing costs of a book clamoured for abroad, after it was banned by the States of Holland as 'profane, blasphemous and atheistic' when the Dutch version was published in 1678. The editors did not co-operate much with one another, and they show in their textual alterations, even in the titles they gave the Parts of *Ethics* (only Part 1's title was expressed in equivalent form, as *De Deo*, or *Van God*), that each thought he knew best what Spinoza had intended. Jelles's Dutch Preface to the *Opera Posthuma*, translated into Latin by Meyer, reveals devotion to Spinoza, but estrangement from him. While turning it into Latin, Meyer weakened two of Jarig's avowals that Spinoza's philosophy accorded with Christian doctrine, purged his 'pulpit' style and altered some of Jarig's judgements on Spinoza's works. The Preface is riddled with around a hundred New Testament quotations, which – perhaps in an attempt to deflect Reformed Church hostility – cast a false light on Spinoza's doctrine. Jelles also wrote that Spinoza would have achieved great things in optics 'had not death snatched him away', but the philosopher's depleted store of glass-working tools, his near-silence on the topic since 1671 and his dissatisfaction with his *Treatise on the Rainbow*, which his editors knew was composed several years earlier, then abandoned (and, although conceivably hidden away by someone, was more probably burned), make this doubtful. Jarig admitted relying on 'the testimony of those with whom [Spinoza] lived', and on letters, for information on Spinoza's friends, scholarly contacts and recent activities. There is a faint plaintiveness, too, in his comments that Spinoza 'had withdrawn himself from all the world', and that his editors were publishing 'all that could be collected, that was of any worth, from among his posthumous papers and any copies kept by friends and acquaintances . . . It is believable that some work of our writer may still be in the possession of someone or other.'

Did Jarig keep nothing? His own exchange of letters was used for editing, then lost, destroyed perhaps by Rieuwertz with other correspondence he had thought 'of no consequence', or hidden in Amsterdam's *Oranjeappel* orphanage, where several letters were later discovered and where the editors may have worked. Perhaps Rieuwertz had burned or lost the Latin *Short Treatise*, too. Spinoza had translated into Latin some of the letters that passed between Jarig and himself on optics, alchemy and Hobbesian political theory. But in his Preface Jelles made no claim to close friendship, and I think this reflected no more than the truth, for only that one brief letter on Hobbesian politics, and possibly the even briefer note 'to a Friend', appeared after April 1673, when Spinoza received the draft of Jarig's Christian *Confession*. In that *Confession* the Mennonite had denied, with what looks like an oblique assault on the notion that fixed first principles are necessary to a search for truth, that he was proposing 'essential, fundamental and necessary articles of belief' or a 'universal symbol'. He was, he said, outlining a confession of faith universally acceptable to all Christians, as sanctioned by sure but unanalysable *gevoelens*. The philosopher may well have hidden from Jarig, whom he had personally, painstakingly instructed, but who rejected his doctrine to the end.

The twenty-first day of February 1677 fell on the Sunday before the pre-Lent carnival:

> On Sunday morning before church-time he went downstairs and chatted with his landlord and his wife. He had sent for a certain doctor L.M. from Amsterdam, who told the family to buy an old hen, and to cook it that morning, so that Spinoza could have the broth at mid-day. They did this, and he was already enjoying it when they came back from church. In the afternoon the family went back to church, leaving the doctor alone with him, but on coming out of church they heard that Spinoza had died at three o'clock, in the presence of that doctor.

Spinoza had always been, the Van der Spycks insisted, 'stoical or unfeeling' about his illness, and he made nothing of dying. He had come down to the parlour that morning as usual, to talk to Schuller. And while he had vowed not to *curse or laugh at the affects and actions of men*, we cannot but envisage the faint sardonic smile of the dead on his lips as a grand funeral and wine reception was arranged, and his body was borne, followed by six carriages and 'many illustrious persons', to the Dutch Reformed New Church in the Spui, where all that was left of Johan de Witt lay beneath the flagstones, and where Spinoza's own bones would decompose to the sound of ranting and dogma, and the tramping of the feet of the faithful.

POST MORTEM

There was no lack of pronouncement on the man and his work in the following months and years. We need not repeat the vilifications of those who found him unclean, or felt impelled to protest so publicly, just because he rejected biblical and church teaching. Nor need we reconsider the resentment of those for whom he remained a presumptuous, undeservedly renowned Neo-Cartesian. We need not, either, systematically explore the impact of Spinoza's thought on subsequent philosophy, since, while biography in the English language is sparse, good recent historical exegesis abounds. However, the maladroit or wilfully obtuse way in which Spinoza has been publicly judged demands reflection. It is as if the mental tensions I have uncovered, and tried to show are inseparable from the formal philosophy, disrupt critical obituary, just as they undermined the rational imperative of Spinoza himself. For any additions I have made to this proliferation of inadequacy I apologise, but, before handing over to future arbiters, I shall disturb the crust of past comment enough to release the principles that, in my view, Spinoza most sought to impress. Foremost among these was the requirement that individuals use their reason. This prime condition for mental enlightenment, the first philosophical plank young Baruch laid across the frail foundations of his formal education, asks twenty-first century readers to scour the following opinions – my own included – for partiality, and to allow the point of Spinoza's living philosophical experiment to emerge.

Leibniz, who met Spinoza and enjoyed a privileged acquaintance with *Ethics*, and, despite horror at what he found there, studied Spinoza's arguments carefully, had no doubt that this man aimed at the wholesale destruction of faith-based belief. We have already seen some of his reactions to specific Spinozistic claims. By 1704 this outstanding philosopher and well-travelled cosmopolite, sensitive to developing currents of opinion, feared precisely the influence of Spinoza's ideas on those in high places that the philosopher had sought in his lifetime. Far from withering for lack of dissemination following numerous publication bans, Leibniz believed that Spinoza's notions, having been seized on by 'disciples and imitators', were 'stealing gradually into the minds of men of high station who rule the rest and on whom affairs depend, and slithering into fashionable books, are inclining everything towards the universal revolution with which Europe is threatened'. The *Opera Posthuma* was not neglected during the last decades of the seventeenth century, as has sometimes been suggested. Instead, influential detractors began to manipulate opinion to ensure that Spinoza's philosophy was disgraced on logical grounds. This did not happen at once. John Locke, for example, a free-thinker in ill favour with the English Court and in the 1680s living in exile in Holland, ventured dangerously close to Spinozist influence. But as a committed Christian who made friends with Van Limborch in Amsterdam and Graevius in Leiden, and witnessed the long arm of English religious persecution in arresting anti-Catholics and other dissidents all round him, Locke avoided direct mention of Spinoza. Yet brief allusions in his 1690 *Essay Concerning Human Understanding* to a doctrine in which 'God, spirits, and body' were 'modifications' of the 'same common nature of substance', and to a material God, brought accusations of Spinozistic atheism against him. Spinoza did not, in fact, posit a God which was either modified or material, and Locke's sources may have been verbal and vague.

By 1697 an explicit, scholarly refutation had been published, and Leibniz expressed his relief that its author – 'the author of the finest of dictionaries' – Pierre Bayle, had ensured that Spinoza's 'pitiful or unintelligible' arguments were not only 'well held up to ridicule', but thrown into serious philosophical disrepute. Yet in his *Dictionnaire* Bayle effectively conceded the persuasive power of Spinoza's principles by calculatedly playing down their potential for religious and political agitation. Commenting archly that 'It is not true that his followers have been very numerous', Bayle set out to massage the beliefs of the orthodox and to assure the impressionable, or already impressed, that the greatest danger to them from Spinoza was of making themselves look foolish by defending him. Bayle had also to address the awkward fact of Spinoza's blameless life-style which, despite efforts at besmirching it – a pamphlet of 1695 testified that the philosopher had had 'an ill look' and 'bore a character of reprobation in his face', and a rumour would be put about that he had mocked the saying of grace when dining out – was widely known to have resembled the Christian ideal of frugality and abstention from sensory pleasure.

> Those who were acquainted with him, and the peasants of the village where he had lived in retirement for some time, all agree in saying that he was sociable, affable, honest, obliging and of a well-ordered morality. This is strange; but, after all, we should not be more surprised by this than to see people who live very bad lives even though they are completely

convinced of the Gospel. . . . All who have refuted the *Tractatus theologico–politicus* have found in it the seeds of atheism . . .

To the same end, Bayle chose to ignore Spinoza's ethical and humanitarian intentions, and interspersed, among a number of acutely reasoned arguments, a few which sacrificed scholarly attention to the philosopher's principles for popular prejudice:

> It is not as easy to deal with the difficulties contained in that work [the *Theologico–Political Treatise*] as to demolish completely the system that appeared in his *Opera Posthuma*; for this is the most monstrous hypothesis that could be imagined, the most absurd, and the most diametrically opposed to the most evident notions of our mind . . . It must not be forgotten that this impious man did not know the inevitable consequences of his theory, for he made fun of the apparition of spirits, and there is no philosopher who has less right to deny it. He ought to have recognised that everything in nature thinks, and that man is not the most enlightened and intelligent modification of the universe. He ought then to have admitted demons . . . If he had reasoned logically, he would not have treated the fear of hell as chimerical.

For Spinoza, no mode of extension was unaccompanied by, or in his unique sense identical with, an idea. Conversely, if an idea was logically impossible then it was a fiction, reflecting no really existing thing. Bayle had not followed this argument through. But his attacks were much admired, and were echoed in the comments of later philosophers and literary figures, who often appear not to have studied his work at first hand. The Irish bishop George Berkeley, for example, would in 1713, while deriding Spinoza's 'wild imaginations', seriously misjudge his theory of mind by imputing to him, by name, a materialism which put him on a par with Hobbes in believing that 'anything at all' could exist independently of a mind. David Hume, better informed, equally hastily dismissed in 1739, among his dismissals of other claims to knowledge of the substance of God and the world, Spinoza's 'hideous hypothesis' of 'two different systems of beings presented'. By speedily referring readers to 'Bayle's dictionary, article of Spinoza' for further enlightenment, Hume affirmed both his own lack of interest and Bayle's still-potent and damaging authority.

By the late eighteenth century Spinoza had, thanks largely to Bayle, little following among European literati, and his doctrine was treated mainly to flippant, sketchy and inaccurate second-hand interpretation. Voltaire wrote around 1772 in his *Satires*:

> Then a little Jew, with a long nose and wan complexion,
> Poor, but satisfied, thoughtful and solitary,

Spirit subtle and hollow, less read than celebrated,
Hidden beneath the mantle of Descartes, his master,
Walking with measured tread, approached the great Being.
Excuse me, he said, speaking very low,
But I think, between ourselves, that you don't exist.

Voltaire does not seem to have given Spinoza's *Opera Posthuma* much study, but borrowed from the vitriolic refutation of the Count de Boulainvilliers when discussing the metaphysical scheme and, like Hume, referred readers to Bayle's *Dictionary* for further analysis of it.

> Spinoza, in his famous book, so little read, speaks only of God . . . It is the first atheism which has proceeded by means of lemmas and theorems . . . Bayle, taking Spinoza's philosophy by the letter, reasoning from his own words, finds this doctrine contradictory and ridiculous. Indeed, what is it but a God of which all beings would be modifications, who would be gardener and plant, doctor and invalid, murderer and victim, destroyer and destroyed?

Spinoza was thus denied the thoughtful readership he sought. But the stigmas of atheism and incoherence which had flung his work into ignominy were beginning to fade in relation to the incompatibility of his philosophy with late eighteenth-century scepticism. Spinoza's battery of quasi-scholastic arguments for the necessary existence of God, and for the necessary self-containedness and all-inclusiveness of that one substance, *God, or Nature*, were now considered worthless speculation. Hume's early ridicule on this count had also targeted Spinoza's claim to human certainty about what were asserted to be the most common features and workings of really-existing attributes of thought and extension. This doctrine was now made dead wood in philosophical debate by the powerful arguments of Immanuel Kant (1724–1804), who in his vast investigations ignored Spinoza. Kant concurred with the Spinozistic principle that certain features of our experience may necessarily hold true for any instance of that experience, and that we can know this *a priori*, but any claim to knowledge of the 'thing-in-itself' was for him a gross 'rationalist extravagance'.

The process of whitewashing Spinoza's memory and reintroducing aspects of his thought other than his despised metaphysic is believed to have been initiated by the German Enlightenment thinker Gotthold Ephraim Lessing, who in 1780 astonished his contemporaries by not only giving Spinoza's work concentrated attention but by admitting that 'If I am to call myself after any master, I know no better'. Thereafter, Lessing conducted well-publicised but philosophically inexplicit defences of Spinoza against other German notables, and in 1785 the poet Johann Wolfgang von Goethe also declared himself a dedicated Spinozist.

> He does not prove the existence of God; existence *is* God. And though others miscall him atheist, I name and praise him as Theissimum even Christianissimum . . . I cannot say that I have ever read right through the great man's works, or even surveyed in my mind the whole structure of his thought. My way of thinking and living does not allow me to do so. But when I read him, I feel I understand him, I mean he never to my mind is inconsistent, and so he helps me greatly in my own way of thinking and acting.

Goethe's focus of interest lay in the broad theme of the interrelationship of all things in God, and in the thesis of *Ethics* Part 5, where Spinoza seemed to him to make morality consist in depersonalisation through a merging of self into God. The former emphasis precipitated Spinoza into popular consciousness as a pantheist: the latter pushed him back into the mould of contemplative or mystic ascetic. A greater distortion of Spinoza's intentions was affected by Goethe's and Lessing's more rigorously analytical compatriot Georg Wilhelm Friedrich Hegel, who, tremendously in sympathy with the 'profound thinker' of melancholy but 'mild and benevolent countenance', projected onto Spinoza something of his own absolute idealism. Hegel did not share Kant's scepticism about knowledge of the 'thing-in-itself', but took a clear line on what did really exist, which for him was solely mind, or spirit – a rational, unified whole. He believed Spinoza's one substance was also fundamentally immaterial, an 'ether'. 'Substance with Spinoza is only the Idea taken altogether abstractly, not in its vitality,' he claimed. 'Neither are extension and thought anything to him in themselves, but only externally; for their difference is a mere matter of the understanding.' But, observing that Spinoza, like himself, judged human thinking necessarily divine, Hegel overlooked Spinoza's stricture that thought was inseparable from body, and that all parts and aspects of body, being parts and aspects of God, were equally divine. Given Hegels's reading of Spinoza, it is not surprising that he denied Spinozism to have dealt 'the death blow to morality'.

> The allegations of those who accuse Spinoza of atheism are the direct opposite of the truth; with him there is too much God . . . Those who defame him in such a way as this are therefore not aiming at maintaining God but at maintaining the finite and the worldly; they do not fancy their own extinction and that of the world.

Hegel's non-Spinozistic Spinoza may, like Goethe's, have mistakenly affirmed for those enthralled by the defiantly irrational notions of the late eighteenth-century Romantic movement that Spinoza was in some sense their intellectual champion. In England, the idea that God was diffused in nature had been seized on by Samuel Taylor Coleridge and William Wordsworth, who had studied philosophy together in Germany for some months in 1799. Coleridge noted wryly that 'it is too true, and true frequent, that Bacon, Harrington, Machiavel, and Spinoza, are not read, because Hume, Condillac, and Voltaire *are*'. But while Coleridge counted *Ethics* as one of the three great works since the introduction of Christianity, and believed that at 'the common fountain-head' of 'the streams of knowing and being' in man, was the 'mysterious source whose being is knowledge, whose knowledge is being', he, like Wordsworth, saw divine spirit as invading nature, not as a constituent of it, and may inadvertently have given the impression that this Neoplatonic pantheism was Spinozistic. Thus, having suffered misconstrual as a materialist and an idealist, and having been more justly branded a rationalist of an extreme and anachronistic intensity, Spinoza became, and for some present-day deep ecologists remains, a panpsychist.

In 1850 Friedrich Nietzsche saw Spinoza in a quite differently fashionable light.

> That our modern natural sciences have entangled themselves so much with Spinoza's dogma (finally and most grossly in Darwinism) is probably owing to the origin of most of the enquirers into nature: they belong in this respect to the people, their forefathers have been poor and humble persons, who knew too well by immediate experience the difficulty of making a living . . . But as an investigator of nature, a person ought to emerge from his paltry human nook: and in nature the state of distress does not *prevail*, but superfluity, even prodigality to the extent of folly. The struggle for existence is only an *exception* . . .
>
> Do you not imagine some long-concealed blood-sucker in the background, which makes its beginning with the senses, and in the end retains or leaves behind nothing but bones and their rattling? – I mean categories and formulas and *words* (for you will pardon me in saying that what remains of Spinoza, *amor intellectualis dei*, is rattling and nothing more! What is *amor*, what is *deus* when they have lost every drop of blood?)

But George Eliot, who in 1854 began work on the first known English translation of *Ethics*, aligned herself with Goethe in admiration of Spinoza's noble view of a determined and common humanity. She wrote to a friend:

> Never to beat and bruise one's wings against the inevitable, but to know the whole force of one's soul towards the achievement of some possible

better, is the brief heading that need never be changed, however often the chapter of more special rules may have to be re-written.

Eliot did not, however, want her real name (Marian Evans) linked to her *Ethics* translation.

> By the way, when Spinoza comes out, be so good as not to mention *my* name in connection with it. I particularly wish not to be known as the translator of the *Ethics*, for reasons which it would be 'too tedious to mention'.

It is a measure of the extraordinary pliability of Spinoza's supposedly inflexible philosophy that we cannot tell from this comment whether she thought an association with Spinoza would damage her reputation, or believed her unmarried cohabitation with George Lewes (probably the first English biographer of Spinoza) would sit ill alongside the saintly notions she set out to publicise. Her translation was, in fact, rejected by her publisher, and was not printed until 1981. Spinoza's work was nevertheless increasingly discussed in Europe, and given a further variety of curious and incompatible glosses.

In 1880, more than two hundred years after Spinoza's death, the first serious movement towards a respectful public reconsideration of his life and work was made by the Dutch when a bronze statue, dedicated by an international roll of literary and philosophical figures, was erected outside what had recently been established as the philosopher's Paviljoensgracht home. Ordinary language translations and commentaries still useful today, such as J. Martineau's *Study of Spinoza* (1882) and H. Joachim's *Study of the Ethics of Spinoza* appeared, many readers being led to these texts by K. O. Meinsma's highly researched biography, *Spinoza en zijn Kring* (1896), translated into German in 1909; J. Freudenthal's invaluable collation of primary sources, *Die Lebensgeschichte Spinozas* (1899); E. Dunin Borkowski's *Der Junge Spinoza* (1910) and Frederick Pollock's *Spinoza, His Life and Philosophy* (1889 and 1912). Bertrand Russell confided in a letter of 1911 that 'Ever since I first read Pollock's book Spinoza has been one of the most important people in my world', and would eventually describe him in his *History of Western Philosophy* as

> the noblest and most lovable of the great philosophers. Intellectually some others have surpassed him, but ethically he is supreme. As a natural consequence he was considered, during his lifetime and for a century after his death, a man of appalling wickedness.

Yet Russell, while finding Spinoza worthy of praise, and invariably referring with accuracy to the specifics of his doctrine, added little to twentieth-century understanding of it. As a scientist of his time, Russell naturally sided with Hume and Kant in holding that its 'logical monism was incompatible with modern logic and scientific method'; that facts 'have to be discovered by observation, not by reasoning'.

> In forming a critical estimate of Spinoza's importance as a philosopher, it is necessary to distinguish his ethics from his metaphysics, and to consider how much of the former can survive the rejection of the latter . . .
>
> The value of such work [i.e. the ethical work] . . . belongs with practice and not with theory. Such theoretic importance as it may possess is only in relation to human nature, not in relation to the world in large.

Russell, having thus dismissed Spinoza as a scientist, focused his admiration on Spinoza's way of life and having, like Pollock, declared that 'I do not know of any occasion, in spite of great provocation, in which he was betrayed into the kind of heat or anger that his ethic condemned', joined Goethe and George Eliot in holding that 'Spinoza is concerned to show how it is possible to live nobly even when we recognise the limits of human power'.

Spinoza's good character had been reinstated, but in the English-speaking world there would be, apart from papers in narrowly circulated academic journals, little help available to explain the key concepts of his philosophy during the middle decades of the twentieth century. The philosopher George Santayana, delivering a paper to the *Societas Spinozana* (established in 1920) at its commemoration of the tercentenary of Spinoza's birth, located Spinoza's 'secret of peace' in his 'conception of eternal truth,' and found *Ethics* Part 5 to endorse 'animality qualified by reason' as the essence of man.

> Here we touch the crown of Spinoza's philosophy, that intellectual love of God in which the spirit was ultimately reconciled with universal power and universal truth . . . Insofar as we are able to understand the truth, we necessarily love the themes of an intense and unclouded vision, in which our imaginative faculty reaches its perfect function . . . From [man's] animality the highest flights of reason are by no means separable. The very life of spirit springs from animal predicaments; it moves by imposing on events a perspective and a moral urgency proper to some particular creature or some particular interest.

This interpretation precisely opposes earlier convictions that Spinoza sought and found peace through a depersonalisation of the self and its interests, especially its passions, and, in my view, neither this, nor Santayana's thesis, is Spinoza's. Spinoza did not ask human beings either to expunge their emotions to the extent that they lost touch with their individuality and best interest, or to use ideas of the imagination – always, for him, inadequate – to grasp their place in a universal 'moral' scheme. Thanks to such misleading interpretations, his statement near the end of *Ethics* Part 2 that the view *sub specie aeternitatis* was a rational and analytic understanding of particular events in relation to the whole, most readily apprehended by humans through universal principles governing events of the kind in question, was becoming fudged and lost to the greater reading public.

Harry Wolfson, in his impressively researched two-volume commentary of 1934, took yet another polarised approach. For Wolfson, Spinoza was not a revolutionary, but a thinker who 'chose to follow in the footsteps of rationalisers through history'. According to Wolfson, 'We cannot get the full meaning of what Benedictus says unless we know what has passed through the mind of Baruch.' Tracing Spinoza's metaphysics through its Jewish and other intellectual roots, he saw the philosopher as seeking influence in an exclusively Judaeo-Christian sphere. From Spinoza's texts, he argued, 'a religion of reason can be built up which in all essential respects would be like a rational religion of theologians'. Wolfson saw Spinoza as an unwilling outcast who, had he not been continually vilified,

> would undoubtedly have joined in the active life of the communities in which he lived . . . He would have become a substantial, respectable, and public-spirited burgher and a pillar of society. Perhaps, also, despite differences in theology, he would have joined the Lutheran church . . . in The Hague . . .
>
> I can picture him, once of a Sunday, at the invitation of the good old doctor [Dr Cordes, Colerus's predecessor], taking the services in the Church. He preaches a sermon which is an invective against 'the prejudices of the theologians of our time'. In it he inveighs against prevailing credulous beliefs in the spirituality of God . . . The sermon over, he pauses and says, 'Now let us pray.' And in his prayer he thanks God, 'the creator of the universe', for his bountiful goodness; he begs for the forgiveness of his 'sins', asks for divine enlightenment in the true understanding of 'Thy revealed Word', and petitions for divine grace in 'guiding us' in the paths of righteousness, to the end that 'we may inherit' life everlasting and enjoy eternal bless in the presence of 'thy glory'. As he is about to close his prayer, he catches a glimpse of a congregation and suddenly realises that he is in a Christian Church. Immediately he adds: 'In the name of Christ, the mouth of God, whose spirit is the idea of God, which alone leads us unto liberty, salvation, blessedness and regeneration.' Amen.

With canonization increasingly on the cards for Spinoza, it is small wonder that, when an entry had to be composed for the *Encyclopedia of Philosophy* of 1967, its writer felt he must direct his attention to specific philosophical claims, and rigidly divorce these from estimations of Spinoza the man. Yet, while there is fine detailed exegesis in this 1967 entry, we are ultimately little helped to see what it is we can usefully cull from Spinoza's thought.

> Spinoza . . . rationalist metaphysician, is of all philosophers the one whose life has least apparent connection with his work. . . . [His] manifest determination to think through his own thoughts, in relative isolation from others, accounts both for his independence from external influences apart from purely philosophical ones, and for his almost total lack of influence for long after his death . . . The self-enclosed character of Spinoza's thought constitutes the central difficulty in interpreting it. Not that Spinoza was uninfluenced by or was not reacting to either his immediate or his more distant predecessors . . . What Spinoza has left us is, because it is the most complete and hard-headed explosion of rationalist metaphysics, the best evidence of its impossibility.

Once understood, this passage tells me, it will be seen that Spinoza's metaphysical scheme is outdated, false, and unworthy of further consideration.

A new respect for Spinoza as an original thinker confronting issues of universal importance has infiltrated commentary on Spinoza during the past thirty years. The issues themselves are primarily addressed, as Spinoza would wish, yet their connection with his life is rarely entirely ignored, but is used to build bridges between the oddities of his culture and cast of mind, and our own late twentieth-century way of considering issues and people – the latter being a viewpoint which will almost certainly, in centuries to come, appear very odd indeed. Without the obituary element in exegesis we cannot refer *particular* thoughts of Spinoza's to general principles: if we ignore the man and his life we lack the data needed for submitting those ideas to the view *sub specie aeternitatis*. We are then brought up short at the chasm in understanding which opens up before us, and, as in the following engagement with latter passages of *Ethics* Part 5 of one of the shrewdest of recent Spinoza scholars, Jonathan Bennett, we find ourselves bereft of intellectual material with which to build bridges. Bennett had declared at the start of his acclaimed *Study*, 'I am not writing biography. I want to understand the pages of *Ethics* in a way that will let me learn philosophy from them.' The last stretch of *Ethics*, he found, defeated him.

> Most of the faults in *Ethics* occur while Spinoza is tackling real problems and are traceable to specific sources in the foundations of his thought. That makes his failures worth studying. But the final one-twentieth of his work [*Ethics* Part 5, Proposition 23 to the end] contains a failure of a different order – an unmitigated and unmotivated disaster. I would like to

excuse myself from discussing it, but my adverse judgement on it should be defended . . .

It is rubbish which causes others to write rubbish . . . Perhaps he was after all terrified of extinction, and convinced himself – through a scatter of perverse arguments and hunger for the conclusion – that he had earned immortality. Or perhaps [others'] suspicion of mysticism is right. . . .

Whatever mystical experiences Spinoza had, he ought to have written them off as *experientia vaga* – the mental side of a swirl in the cloud of particles constituting a human body. To accord them the dignity of important news about the whole reality should have been unthinkable for him. Perhaps it was. Perhaps Spinoza basically viewed later Part 5 not as telling the truth but rather as giving stern verbal expression to some ecstatic, uncontrolled, indescribable feelings . . . If that is right, then Spinoza in late Part 5 is using the materials of intellectual inquiry for cosmetic purposes, and this should be beneath him.

Either way, it looks as though some passive affect – fear or hope or excitement – clung stubbornly to the man and overcame his reason.

Such negativity arises when, in Voltaire's phrase, we stick to 'taking Spinoza's philosophy by the letter', that is, to allowing him the conceptual self-sufficiency he claimed for himself. Bennett's point is well made in that examination of Spinoza's life and character serve to confirm that certain logical flaws *are* integral to his thinking and *are* therefore ineradicable. But in locating the chains of ideas in secure evidence of Spinoza's actual vacillation of mind we make a more rational analysis of such passages than is possible if these are disregarded.

We may today get the most from Spinoza if we take the quite different approach of appealing not to 'the letter' of his work, but to his general treatment of issues which concern us. Then, I believe, we find answers which spring from the mainstream of his philosophical thought – his metaphysical theory of the interrelatedness within nature of all natural phenomena, physical and mental – from which he believed deductions covering all particular cases should be made. Many such deductions are shockingly relevant to current affairs and contemporary personal situations. I suggest that all the following focuses of contention are put in refreshing perspective – I do not say dissolved – if considered as activities or intentions operating in a determined and wholly natural universe: questions of civil disobedience, conscientious refusal, or mass political protest; the function of federalism; the role of monarchies; the retention of physical means of self-defence; the limitations and potentialities of personal power, and thereby the rationally-conceived status of celebrities; the possibility of social equity; the feasibility of convergence of agreement between members of disparate nationalities, cultures and diverse religious persuasions; the correlative rights of parents and children; the rights of animals; the anthropological foundations and legitimate social benefits of marriage; the mental and physical basis of sexual orientation, and the respective advantage of each kind to society; the implications of sexual licence and religious predilection on the part of individuals involved in the exercise of public duties; the allocation of public funds to the weaker or to the more intelligent members of society; the apt dispensation of charity to the dying; the inevitable logical trajectory of genetic engineering; the acquisition of organs for transplants and the manipulation of climatic conditions.

But Spinoza is also there for the petty personal issues which can blot out, although they are not, when viewed in relation to the whole, distinct from the greater social good which lies beyond them. His requirement was that we reason out our predicament either by investigating its causes or by appealing to some *common notion*. While it would be satisfying to be able to intuit the truth of our situation, the bulk of Spinoza's doctrine dictates that this option is not available to us. Instead, our decision-making procedures must consider each experience of pain, loneliness, guilt, fear, obsession, appetite, and financial or other anxiety as an event of kind so-and-so, taking into account our own internal drive. Moral dilemmas and practical choices are with equal profit rationally examined against this grid. We would, for example, reflect on career or other changes for ourselves and others on the basis of how a particular internal push is affected by its surroundings, and to what extent conditions in that immediate environment obey localised and atypical laws of nature. We would look at our emotional or sexual predicaments not only in terms of what the harm or good in doing x must be when any human, considered independently of a specific historical or cultural domain, does x, but in terms of what is the harm or good for a person of our disposition. It must not be forgotten that Spinoza, stunningly, vests the ultimate obligation of any individual wholly in that individual, *reasoning* self.

Reason: spiritual and physical homogeneity: universal interrelatedness and interdependence: advantage: survival. Spinoza's pronouncements on these themes presuppose neither a denial of self nor, if we remain with his doctrine of *common notions*, any preposterous presumption regarding our ability to limn the ultimate nature of the universe. Coleridge, who rejected much of Spinoza's doctrine, underscored, as I do, the value of this concept: 'How can common truths be made permanently interesting, but by being *bottomed* on our common nature?' Spinoza, denying anthropocentric understanding any epistemic merit if this consisted merely in a convergence of unreasoned human agreement, proposed instead an heuristic based on the belief that we learn most surely from what is common to all bodies, and that this interrelatedness extends beyond the commonality of merely human nature. This immense and entirely non-parochial philosophical bequest, generated by a physically fragile individual struggling to cope with alienation, grief, sickness and obsession in a small corner of seventeenth-century Europe, remains neglected by our – only partially differently – fragmented society.

APPENDIX

Spinoza's Illness

Consumption and phthisis are traditional terms for tuberculosis, but following Robert Koch's identification of the tuberculosis bacillus in 1882, the various forms of consumption and phthisis were classified by medical and public health authorities as a single disease, namely tuberculosis. Rosner and Markowitz argue that this conceptualisation obscures almost as much as it illuminates. There is probably a lack of understanding of the effect of non-bacterial consumption on those who suffered from 'the symptoms of coughing, wasting away and losing weight'. These were the symptoms described by Spinoza's earliest biographers, and considered the hallmarks of phthisis by the physician Abarbanel in 1665. Rosner and Markowitz explore the confusion between tuberculosis and other chronic respiratory illnesses as recognised as silicosis, and seen in mining, stone-cutting, and many other industries. They further examine how the narrow view of the bacterial origins of tuberculosis limited the medical profession's ability to diagnose and understand diseases caused by industrial dust. This is particularly the case when considering the illness of Spinoza, who ground glass while making lenses at home, probably in his only room, for twenty years. Failure to distinguish a lung disease distinct from consumption, or to acknowledge the specific ill effects of glass dust (containing silica), is shown in Abarbanel's judgement that 'Causes [of phthisis] may be carbon and metallic minerals.' Maxfield *et al.* described surveillance for silicosis in the United States, and found a definite association with silicosis associated with exposure in the glass industry, while Froines *et al.* also described a quantitative evaluation of worker exposure to silica in the United States. They included construction, chemical manufacture, stone, glass and clay manufacturing, as well as primary metal industries, and concluded that exposure to silica represented a continuing and significant problem in a number of US industries, including glass.

It is thus possible to speculate that Spinoza's illness was not only due to chronic low-grade pulmonary tuberculosis, but that he may have developed an additional silicosis from his exposure to powdered glass over many years. Since as far as we know there was no medical recognition of the harmful effects of inhaling glass particles, he himself is unlikely to have been aware that working with wet materials would decrease damage to the lungs. Spinoza's life-long exposure to (probably) cheap lamp oil and cheap tallow candles, as well as his habitual use of tobacco, would also have exacerbated his chronic pulmonary problems. Moreover, since his father was a first-generation Portuguese immigrant, who would have felt the cold in Holland, there may have been exceptional exposure to peat fires in the home from his birth. Spinoza's chronic lung disease probably explains his poor appetite, and his 'slight fever' would be compatible with chronic tuberculosis. Shortness of breath is associated with either disease.

SOURCE NOTES

All translations are mine, unless otherwise stated. Quotations from Spinoza are printed in *italics*; key phrases relating to the text are printed in **bold**.

ABBREVIATIONS

Spinoza's texts

CM *Metaphysical Thoughts*
E *Ethics*
KV *Short Treatise*
PPC *The Principles of Descartes's Philosophy*
TIE *Treatise on the Emendation of the Intellect*
TP *A Political Treatise*
TTP *A Theologico-Political Treatise*

A Axiom
Apx Appendix
Co. Corollary
D Demonstration (Proof)
Def. Definition
Ep. Letter in Spinoza's published correspondence. Translations are Shirley's, apart from Eps. 18, 19, 20, 22, 23, 24, 27, 48A and 48B, which are from the original Dutch texts. In these cases the translation is mine.
Exp. Explanation
L Lemma
P Proposition
Pref. Preface
S Scholium

Translation abbreviations

OPG: *Opera Posthuma* Gebhardt

C Curley
Es Elwes
S Shirley
W Wernham
Thus *Ethics* Part 1 Proposition 32 Corollary 2 appears as E1 P32 Co2: C 435

Spinoza's personal library

Within main brackets
1. Date of publication
2. Size of book
d duodecimo f foolscap m missing o octavo q quarto
3. Number according to *Catalogus van de Boekerij der Vereeniging Het Spinozahuis*, The Hague, 1914
4. In square brackets within main brackets, numbering according to *Inventaire des Livres Formant la Bibliothèque de Benedict Spinoza*, A.J. Servaas van Rooijen, The Hague, Paris, 1888
For example: Abravanel (Ebreo, Leone) appears as *Dialogos de Amor* (Venice 1568, q46 [22]).

The texts of René Descartes

CSM *The Philosophical*

Writings of Descartes, 2 vols, Translated by J. Cottingham, R. Stoothoff and D. Murdoch, Cambridge University Press, 1985
CSMK *The Philosophical Writings of Descartes, Vol III, The Correspondence, Translated by J. Cottingham, R. Stoothoff, D. Murdoch and A. Kenny, Cambridge University Press, 1991*

Other sources

CB *Confessieboek*, GAA
DTB Baptism, marriage and burial registers, ibid.
GAA Municipal Archives, ibid.
JB *Justitieboek*, ibid.
LBH *Livro Beth Haim* (Jewish burials), ibid.
NAA Notarial Archives, ibid.
PAA Archives of the Portuguese-Jewish Community, ibid.
PK Reformed Church Consistory Minutes, ibid.

ARA General Archives, The Hague
BW *Briefwisseling*
DNB Dictionary of National Biography

ESN Encyclopedia Sephard-
ica Neerlandica
EP Encyclopedia of Philoso-
phy
FQ Freudenthal *Quellens-
chriften*
HGA Municipal Archives,
Stadhuis, The Hague
HO Huygens *Oeuvres*

JE Jewish Encyclopaedia
JP Jelles's Preface to the
Posthumous Works
K Colerus: Dutch, 1705
KVNN *Kort Verhael van
Nieuw Nederlandts*
NNBW Nieuw-Neder-
landsch Biografisch Woor-
den-boek

OC Oldenburg Correspond-
ence
SR Servaas van Rooijen
TS Thijssen-Schoute 'Le
Cartésianisme aux Pays-
Bas'
VD/VT Vaz Dias & Van
der Tak
VPS *Vrye Politijke Stellingen
en consideratien van staat*

Book cover I have taken great care . . . TP14: W263
A man's true happiness . . . TTP III: W51

ACKNOWLEDGEMENTS, TECHNICALITIES AND A CONFESSION

xi   **'May still be . . .'** JP 218
xiii   **Mind** *the idea of the body*: E2 P15 D.
xiv   *Euclid, who only* . . . TTP V11: Es 113. *From the little I then* . . . Ep. 50, to Jelles,
June 1674: S 260. **Historie van Karel de 11**: 156 (38d). **Portraits of Spinoza**:
Ekkart's recent 'Spinoza in Portrait' throws doubt on Altkirch's judgements in
Spinoza im Porträt (1913). **Engraving most reliable likeness**: Ekkart 141. **Details
erased from letters**: C 162–3; Steenbakkers 69. **Place of birth**. The location is
uncertain, but the claim that Spinoza was brought up 'in the inner ghetto of
Flooyenburg' (Levin 27) has no foundation. Mundy ([1634–9] 70) suggests there was
no ghetto: *below*, 8.
xv   **Parents' ages**: *below 2 and 7.*

CHAPTER I

1   *I only know* . . . TIE [20]: C 13. *Men relate* . . . TTP VI: Es 92–3. **Aristotle's law of
non-contradiction**: *Metaphysics* 1.11 77a10–12. **The Spanish might** . . . (para.)
Parker xv and 179; Israel 3 111, 123; Gutmann 211–13; Zumthor 261–2. *Spanjaard*:
Van Deursen 202. **Southernmost towns** (para.) Israel 1 146–150, 123–44. Moryson
464; 'Troubles of Amsterdam' 20.
2   **Hispanic Jews and the Dutch economy**: *details in notes to 11.* **De Espinosas
trading**: VD/VT 126, 133, 145 quoting NAA records; Bloom 75, quoting De Castries:
also below, notes to 11. **Michael: Surname**: in Amsterdam records, Spiñoza, d'Spinoza,
De Spinoza, despinoza, Despinoza, Espinoza, Spinosa, De Espinosa, Despinosa,
d'Espinose, Spinoza. On gravestones: Espinoza, De Espinosa, d'Espinoza, D. Espinoza.
Age: 'about 38 years old' on 8 Oct. 1627; 'about 45 years old' on 10 Feb. 1633; 'about
46 years old' on 2 Nov. 1634: VD/VT 127–8, quoting NAA 634 f.24; 942; 641 f.71.
Lisbon merchant . . . **fled to Vidigueira**: Coelho 441, quoting ANTT *Inquisição*,
Conselho Geral, Papéis Avulsos N° 2609 (maço 7) and crediting Revah 2 135. Firm's
assets estimated in 1565 as 150,000 réis: Coelho 443, quoting ANTT *Inquisição de
Évora*, Processo N° 6041. **Michael was 'from Vidigueira'**: DTB 676. **Inquisition of
Évora 1596–8**: *below, notes to 4.* **Michael in Amsterdam**: First mention of him re.
the burial of his child, 3 Dec. 1623: LBH Pieterse 106. **Married Rachel, daughter of
Abraham Rodrigues Espinosa de Nantes**: VD/VT 135 and 138, citing NAA 1498.
See attendees at Rachel's funeral, LBH Pieterse 65. **Michael's father Isaac was 70 in
1614**: Coelho 441, quoting ANTT *Inquisição*, Conselho Geral, Papéis Avulsos N° 2609
(maço 7), 1614. **Warehouse** . . .**dried fruit** . . . **key**: VD/VT 145 and 166 citing NAA
941 15 July 1631, and NAA 975. Isaak PA 1052 5. **Synagogue** . . . **Abraham's**

house: VD/VT 121 citing the rate-book for 1631, 153–4. **Father's death and burial:** LBH Pieterse 137. **Sara** (7 Jan. 1625), **Rachel** (21 Feb. 1627), **Infants** (3 Dec. 1623 and 29 April 1624): LBH Pieterse 112, 65, 117, 106. **Plague dates:** Braudel 88. **Sabbath candle:** Roth 1 23 and 181; Hersch 71; Kamen 162.

3 **Abraham in Amsterdam by 1616:** VD/VT 117 (PA 1141 57). **'In the Low Countries . . .':** Wolf Lucien 88. **Spinoza's appearance:** Colerus 39: *below, notes to 32.* **Baruch:** PA 1052 5. **Bento:** VD/VT 158–63, citing NAA documents. **Jewish Latin scholars:** Silverman 1 11; VD/VT 156–7; Yovel 59; Zumthor 110. **Morteira a friend:** witness: VD/VT 120 and 126 (NAA 466, 1 Dec. 1625). **'Miguel's' Hebrew Grammar** (1523): ESN II 37. **Rachel's funeral:** LBH Pieterse 65. **'Mikael':** ESN II 39. **Ignorance of Law:** Dubiez 1; Roth 1 242 and Ch.vii *passim.* **'All of us who come . . .'** Roth 2 118. **'Michael' sole name:** VD/VT 113, 180–1 and 192; Vega 31.

4 **Aliases:** VD/VT 121; Gampel Chapters 4 and 5; Roth 1 390; Israel 3 364–5 and 434. **'It is a custom . . .'** Bloom 93, quoting Jacques Ricard, 1655. **Initial 'B':** 'B. de Spinoza' (Ep.15, 1663; 27, 1665 and 69, 1675); 'Bened. de Spinoza' (Ep.37, 1966); 'B. de S.' (Ep.40, 1667 and on the outside fold); 'Benedictus despinoza' (Ep.49, 1673), and 'B. Despinoza' (Ep.72, 1675). **Baruch scratched out:** PA 1052 5 (facsimile VD/VT 157). **Inquisition details:** Silva Rosa *passim*; Coelho 443–4, citing records of the Inquisitions of Évora and Coimbra, *Archivo Historico Portuguez*, Vol. IV, *Numeramento de Entre Tejo e Odiana*, and Revah 2. Poliakov 190–1, 234, 236, 242; Litvinoff 73; Kaplan 1 402–12 and 3 *passim*; Payne 106; Roth Chapter V and 180, 193; Kamen 187–9 and 303; Gampel, *passim*, especially 117–19. **Michael alias Gabriel Álvares (Dispinosa):** 1 Dec. 1625, NAA 646 and 942. **Michael was Pêro Roiz's second son:** ANTT Inquisiçao, Conselho General, Papéis Avulsos no. 2606. **Roiz an abbreviation:** PAA 114 47; VD/VT 123. **Álvares was his mother's maiden name:** Coelho 441 n.76, also citing Revah 2. **Alvares family of Vidigueira:** Coelho 442–4.

5 **Jews in Portugal:** Payne 207–8 and 229–30; Poliakov 201 and 233. **'All these people fled':** Coelho 441, quoting ANTT *Inquisição*, Conselho Geral, Papéis Avulsos Nº 2609 (maço 7) and citing Revah 2. **Family of Mor Alvares:** Coelho 444, quoting ANTT *Inquisição de Évora*, Processos No 7517 and 4676. *No traces . . .* TTP 111: W 63.

6 **Jews generally called 'Portuguese':** Howell 2 [1642] 128. Litvinoff 93; Roth 1 229. **Portuguese used:** VD/VT 195. **Spanish texts:** Quevedo (1660 q36 [12]) and 37 [13q]); Góngora (61 [37q]); Montalván (63 [39q]); Abravanel (Ebreo, Leone) (1568, q46 [22]); Diego de Savadra Faxado (1658) (40 [16q] 12q); Delgado (1627 106 [270]); Gracián Vol.3 (113 [340]); Calvin, *Institutes* (27 [3q]). **Spinoza's interest in Spain:** Deposition of Captain Miguel de Maltranilla, 9 Aug. 1659, Revah 1 33. Van Aerssen van Sommelsdijk's political propaganda *Voyage d'Espagne* (1666) d124 [6]). **'Bento y Gabriel Despinoza'** . . . **Spiñoza:** signature facsimiles Vaz Dias 2 23; Ep.6, April 1662: C 188. **Spanish cultural influence:** especially Benardete and Kaplan 2. **Hana Debora's parents:** (stated in *Spinoza: Troisième* 24 to be Maria Nunes and Baruch Senior). Maria Nunes married Henrique Garcês: DTB 665, 414. 'Baruk Senyori por outro nomo Henrique Garcês' buried on 13 March 1619: LBH, Pieterse 93. Also known as Manuel Mendes Cardoso: LBH Pieterse 26. **Maria Nunes mother of Josua and Jacob Senior** and **'the wife of Micael Espinoza':** VD/VT 193, citing *Livro e nota de ydades* by Isack ben Matatia Aboab, Ets Haim Library, Amsterdam. **Josua Senior 'son of Garcez':** LBH Pieterse 38–9. Hana Debora, if the eldest child, was at most 26 when Spinoza was born. **Michael's 3rd marriage to Esther 'from Lisbon':** 11 April 1641: DTB 676.

7 **Rachel's funeral dues:** LBH Pieterse 65. **Death of Henriques Garcês:** LBH Pieterse 93. **Wedding of David Senior** (b.1611) DTB 675/15. Nunes's name in the left margin follows the pattern of names of mothers made by the same registrar, and Verdooner (1 33) so classifies her. **Nunes and Garcês:** from Oporto or Ponte de Lima: Coelho 446–7, citing H.P. Salomon, *Os Primeiros Portugueses de Amsterdão*, 84, 11. **Manuel Bentalhado and Luis da Cunha:** ibid., citing ANTT *Inquisição de Coimbra*,

Processo N° 2894. Luis da Cunha, *Obra Devota* [32d] also listed FQ 164. **Da Cunha burials** in the Beth Haim: David Jessurum (1649) and Abraham (1655): ESN I 187. **Da Cunha wedding**: DTB 683/97. **Jesuit relatives**: Coelho 447, citing Révah 390, and records of the *Inquisição de Coimbra*, Processo N°ˢ 2894, 5385 and 2576. **Suárez** was at Salamanca University *c.* 1565–71: EP 830. **Spinoza's references to him**: e.g. *below, 167*. **Senior gravestone**: Vega 54. **Spanish bible** (1602 11 [11]). See Gracia Senior alias Isabel Henriques, widow of Duarte Coronel Henriques (PA 334, 826).

8 **Michael spoke Portuguese**: VD/VT 182, citing translation episodes 16 Aug. and 8 Oct. 1652, NAA 1029. **Esther's will** was in Portuguese: ibid. 194, NAA. **Michael's marriages**: Rachel *above, notes to 2*; Hana Debora and Esther: DTB 676/18. **Michael's gravestone** can be seen at the *Beth Haim* cemetery at Ouderkerk, Amsterdam: Photo: Vega 31. **Michael's synagogue offices**: VD/VT 130–1, quoting the *Libro dos Ymposta da Nação* and the *Livro dos Acordos*. **Power over rabbis**: Silverman 113. **Portuguese Messianism**: Payne 161: *below 40, 204, 285*. **Menasseh's** *Hope of Israel* (116 [370]). **Jews in Amsterdam**: In 1609 about 200 Iberian Jews; in 1630 about 1,000: Bloom 31; Israel 1423; by 1650, 400 families owned 300 houses: Baron 23, quoting Menasseh ben Israel 1655: most quote Menasseh's 1650s' report of '2000 souls, mostly from Portugal'. **'Marrano'**: Poliakov 218. **Chueta**: Roth 196 with n.11. **Sephardi**: identifying Sepharad with Spain is a matter of rabbinical interpretation based on Obadiah 1:20. *Rabbi arrested* 1603: Dubiez 1. **Ashkenazi**: In 1762 called 'Tudesques' by De Pinto: Baron 36 with n.44. **'The Jewes . . .'** Mundy [1634–9] 70.

9 *Hidalguia*: Benardete 40–2 and Yovel 38. **Marrano appearance**: Schwartz 328; Poliakov 151; Israel 2 142. **Spanish appearance**: Poliakov 116; Braudel 825–6; Litvinoff 83. **Ferdinand of Aragon** (1452–1526) descended from the Jewess Paloma of Toledo: Litvinoff 84. **Torquemada**: Roth 124; **Teresa**: Cox 157. **Luther and Erasmus**: Poliakov 220. **Willem the Silent**: an address translated in *Phenix* XIII (1707) 530, quoted by Kamen 253. **Jewish integration in Spain**: Yovel 88; Gampel Chs 4 and 5 and 117–19. **Dutch spoken at home** early 18c: Israel 2 199. **'Much as he may . . .'**: De Barrios quoted by Baron 20. See De Barrios's poems in *The Penguin Book of Spanish Verse*, intr. and ed. J.M. Cohen, 1956. **Warship and munitions**: Israel 3 342 and 346–7. **Catholic elements**: *below, 21 with notes*. **'In the hope'**: Bloom 23 with n.103. **Feast of Tabernacles**: Baron 32.

10 **Synagogue buildings**: Van Agt, *Synagogen in Amsterdam*. **Grotius's restrictions**: Arts. 9, 15: Meijer 117. **Beth Jacob**: Van Agt 11–13. Bloom 14 n.67 citing M.C. Paraira and J.S. Silva Rosa '*Gedenkschrift Talmud Tora en Ets Haim*', 1916. **Michael's signature**: VD/VT 140, 127; facsimile in Meinsma 1896 57. **Warnings on dress**: Israel 2 200. See also 'Anoniem Schrijven van Joodse Zijde': Meijer 141–3. **Wealthier merchants and court Jews**: Israel 2 140–2; **Carriage-mares and gilded ship**: Brereton [1634] 32 and 6–7. **Jews' loans**: Schama 593; Gans 47. **Palache**: Baron 50. **'Vloyenburg'**: VD/VT 139. **No residence restrictions**: Grotius, Art.6: Meijer 116. **'Sepulchers'**: Evelyn [1641] 11 42–3; Vega 25–60; Schama 594; Yovel 56. **Spanish manners**: Barlow 55; Howell 2 [1642] 70–1; 'Testimony of the Constable of Castille', 1604, Rye 261, n.90. **Also Portuguese**: Barlow 53, 151. **'He had a courteousness . . .'**: Lucas 63, 64. **Stock exchange (Bourse) and *Wisselbank* (1609)**: Baron 47; Wilson 25; Bloom 176. By 1620: Israel 3 421–2; also ibid. 372–84, 425, and 2 106–8 on specific areas of trading. **Antwerp**: VD/VT 122, citing Isak Prins, *De vestiging der Marranen in Noord-Nederland*, Amsterdam 1927. **Abraham's and Michael's accounts**: respectively 1628 and 1641–2/ 1651–2: VD/VT 127, 147 quoting Wisselbank ledgers (GAA). **Michael's partnership with uncle and cousin**: VD/VT 133 giving primary references: **piracy** [1617] ibid. 126; **storm damage, raisin-rot** [1632–3]: ibid. 133; **shipwreck** [1636] ibid. 145; **confiscation** [1651] ibid. 146.

11 **Michael's landlord was Willem Kick**: VD/VT 128, 175 quoting the rate-book for 1650–2 **Willem Kick, silk merchant**: Vroedschap II 731 (GAA Thes. Extra).

Michael's wealth: Rich neighbours: e.g. Dr Joseph Bueno and Manuel Rodrigo Monsanto: rate-book 1650–2, op.cit. Isaac de Pinto's mansion, diagonally opposite Rembrandt's, is pictured Gans 111. **Rabbis in business:** VD/VT 165. **Aboab:** Gebhardt 1923 275. **Cheap broadcloth:** Temple [1672] 142. **Luxury at home:** Mundy [1634–9] 71; Schama 320; Wilson 36; Zumthor 39. **'Given unto women':** Brereton [1634] 61. **'They allow brothel-houses . . .':** Barlow 63. **Jewish womanising in Iberia:** VD/VT 124; Gampel 109; Poliakov 135; *The Jewish Guide to Adultery*: JE X 120–121. **Apprentices:** Bloom 35, 110. **'Many Jews fleeing from Portugal . . .':** Feuer 3, quoting Arthur E. Kuhn, 'Hugo Grotius and the Emancipation of the Jews of Holland', Publications of the American Jewish Historical Society , XXXI (1938) 176. **'Abusing the daughters . . .':** Dutch Reformed Church report of 15 June 1623, Dubiez 7. **Intermarriage, sexual relations:** Grotius Arts. 27, 38: Meijer 120. **Actual relations:** Koen 35, 36, 38, citing Notarial records, *Confessieboek* RA 292 f.14 and JB RA 570 f.44v; Israel 2 200; Van Deursen 32. **Abraham's child:** VD/VT 119, 124, citing LBH and JB R.A.57294. **Abraham's age:** his younger brother Isaac was 'probably 53' in 1613: ANTT 2606; *above, notes to 4*. **Parnas until 1637:** VD/VT 122, 125, citing *Livro dos Ymposta da Nação* and PA 10525. **Passion des femmes:** Israel 2 202.

12 **Marrano women: 'Never go out'** (1731): Bloom 22 with n.101; **'restrained . . .':** Brereton [1634] 61. **Portuguese women:** Dom Francisco: Boxer 1 100; Pepys 25 May 1662. **'The men that are married . . .':** Barlow 63. Also Boxer 163, citing Brazilian historian Capistrano de Abreu, and Sonnet, M. 102. **Inés de la Cruz:** *The Penguin Book of Spanish Verse*, 311. **'The best book . . .':** Boxer 1 101. **'Who teaches . . .'** Eliezer's dates are not given, but Maimonides (1135–1204) quoted him: Abrahams 286. *Shulchan Aruch*: ibid. 287. **Miriam's mark:** 2 June 1650 (aged 21): DTB 680/243. **Ester and sister:** DTB 676 and 944. **Women's *mitzvoth*:** Abrahams 287; Roth 1 175. Poliakov 236.

13 **'Nothing in the . . .':** Unterman 133. See also ibid. 142, and JE XII 557–8. **'A man should . . .':** ibid. 557, quoting B.M.59a. **Dutch women's education:** Schama 408–13; see also Van Deursen 122–5; Sonnet 129. **'Logick Exercise':** Van Schurman (b. 1612) title page. **'Though women cannot . . .'** ibid. 26. **Descartes: on Van Schurman**, to Mersenne, 11 Nov. 1640: CSMK 156. **On Princess Elizabeth:** to Chanut, 1 Nov. 1645: CSMK 299. **'Infinitely wiser . . .'** More to Descartes, 11 Dec. 1648: Descartes, *Correspondance*. Ed. Adam, C. and Mithard, G., Vol. VII, Presses Universitaires de France, Paris, 1960. **Women in business/authority:** Schama 260, 404; Haley 3 111. **Marrano business women:** Benardete 74–5 cites only Doña Gracia Mendez, but see Isabel Henriques (*above, notes to 7*). **'Agree not with nature . . .':** Vivés translated by Thomas Paynell, in Clark, A. 37. Vivés son of persecuted *conversos*: Bergmann 129. **Dutch women's manners:** Schama 402, 438. Also Rye [1604] 261 n.90. **'The woman there . . .':** Felltham [1652] 24. **Dutch women's aggression, fines, cartoon:** Schama 88, 418, 421, 446–7.

14 *Inconstancy and deceptiveness:* E5 P11 S. *Common notions* the foundation for reasoning: E2 P40 S1; E2 P40 S2 [111]; E2 P44 D to C2. See also TTP V: W 99–101 and TTP VII: Es 104. *Philosophy is based* . . . TTP IV: W 123. **Imitating feelings:** E4 Apx XIII. *Inadequate ideas:* E2 P17 S; E2 P40 S2 [11] and [111]; E2 P41; E2 P42; E4 P66 S; E2 P41. *Political organisation:* TTP 111: W 65. *As for the fact:* TTP 111: W 63. See also TTP XVII: W 177. **Chinese pigtail:** TTP 111: W 63. *Womanish tears:* TTP Pref.: Es 4. *Womanish compassion, partiality, or superstition:* E2 P49 SIV C; E4 P37 S1. *Inconstancy, deceptiveness:* E5 P11 S. *Mental weakness:* TTP 11: Es 27; TP XI: W 443; *Inferiority:* ibid. 445; principles of Jewish religion *effeminate: Muliebris*: C 687.

15 *Did not the principles . . . (fundamenta suae religionis eorum animos effoeminarent):* TTP 111: W 63. *Common notions* agreed by all minds: E2 P38 Co. *Common human nature:*

TTP III: W 55; TP VII 27: W 359. 'The most part . . .': De la Barre 76, 78, 81. 'The delicacy of . . .': Malebranche Bk 2 Pt 2 'The Imagination of Women', 131–2. *All things . . . Reflection . . . It is . . .* TTP IV: W 67, 73–5. Related passages in E3 Pref. and TP 11 were published in the *Opera Posthuma*, 1677.

16 *All men have one and the same nature:* TP VII 27: W 359. 'Either because . . .': Lucas 72–3. *La Vie de Spinosa:* Lucas taken to be the author: see *Spinoza Troisième* 16, Wolf 2 19–24 and Wade 117. *Less fitted . . . uneducated peasants.* TTP 11: Es 27. Lawyer's visit . . . 'default . . .': 8 Sept. 1638: VD/VT 184: NAA. Michael's burial-site: Esther died 24 Oct. 1653; Michael 28 March 1654: gravestone inscriptions VD/VT 113. LBH ibid. 115. Rachel and Isaac: Rachel, Feb. 1627, Row 9, No.18; Isaac, April 1627, Row 9, No.20: LBH Pieterse 117, 139. Higher ground: Michael a sceptic: Levin 171–5.

17 Isaak died 24 Sept. 1649: VD/VT 113. Esther's will (23 Oct. 1652) VD/VT 179 and 182–3 (NAA). Advice from Odette Vlessing, Curator GAA. Notta dos Irmaos desta . . . ESN II 42. Ribca's mother: Rachel: Meinsma 78 (no evidence); Esther: Emmanuel 193; Hana Debora: daughter Hana, Emmanuel 193, 252, 326, citing DTB 699/6v. See also 690/12. Married Miriam's widower: tombstone inscription: Emmanuel 193. Translation into Portuguese, 16 Aug. 1652: VD/VT 194 (NAA 1029). Swift remarriage: Untermann 148. Nunes signature: DTB 665/ 414.

CHAPTER 2

18 *Anyone who saw . . .* Ep.23: OPG 4 152. These words reflect Aristotle's in the *Nichomachean Ethics* 1, 4 (C 8 n.3). *Ledikant:* Colerus 44, 101–2; Kortholt, Wolf 2 165; SR 111; VD/VT 163. Feather bags: Zumthor 43. Rembrandt's *lit* . . . Haak B186. 'Admitted to the bedroom . . .': *above, notes to 16.* Hana Debora died 5 Nov. 1638: VD/VT 113 (gravestone). Bento's birthday was 24 Nov. 'A wooden raft' before the Beth Jacob: VD/VT 140, citing the Register van Quijtscheldingen (NAA 183). Jewish burial ground: Vega 7, 13, 15; Pieterse xiii–xiv; Brereton [1634] 61; 50 ells from the nearest house: JE 111658. Sign at landing-stage: Vega 7 and 15: *see Plate 3.*

19 Complaints, picketing: Pieterse xiii–xiv. *Tarahah* and *rondeamentos:* Roth 1 190; Vega 22. Wife's space left blank: e.g. Vega 37, 59. Vivés: *De Institutione Foeminae Christianae,* 1523, translated into Spanish 1528 as *La mujer cristiana:* Bergmann 124, 129–31. Wood importing: Dubiez 5. 'Houtgracht' means 'wood canal'. Peat: Brereton [1634] 66; Mundy [1634–9] 64–5; Zumthor 278. Morteira's stipend: VD/ VT 152, quoting PA 1227. Oil, rape or linseed: Zumthor 46. Tobacco: Schama 172: Plague cure: Van Diemerbroek of Nijmegen: ibid. 197; recollection of a centenarian: *The Times* 18.6.1997. 'A great expeller . . .' Culpeper 184. Jews tobacco importers and spinners from 1630s to 1640s on: Israel 3 426. Industry dominated by marranos on the St Anthonie Breestraat: Schama 194. Pipes from Algeria 1651: VD/VT 146 (NAA 967/302). Plague: Van Deursen 239; Schama 146–7, 186. 'He did not enjoy . . .': Lucas 65; see also Colerus 73. Phthisis: JP 216; Hereditary: Letter from the physician Schuller to Leibniz, 6 Feb. 1677: FQ 202. Spinoza's pipe-smoking: Colerus 42, 92. Menasseh's printing-house: JE VIII 282.

20 'The commandment': Proverbs 6 v.23: Hersch 71. Glass lamps: Howell 1 [1633] 2 228; Evelyn [1641] 42. Beth Jacob: Van Agt 11–12. One synagogue an upper room: Brereton [1634] 68. Uniting of the 3 synagogues 1639: Van Agt 6–13. Sabbath: Brereton [1634] 60–1; Evelyn [1641] 1 142 and Howell 1 [1633] 2 228–9. 'One of their Rabbies . . .': ibid. 225, 228. 'For the Jews . . .': Howell 2 [1642] 128. Luria's influence: Van der Wall 173; Bernadete 81, 120. 'Sons of Aaron . . . Sons of Levi': Brereton [1634] 60–1; TTP XVII: W 163, 171.

21 **Marranos strange Jews:** Bernadete 65, 66, 165. **Women's gallery:** Evelyn [1641] 1 142. **Copied from the 1633 Lutherse Kerk:** Van Agt 7. See Veenhuysen's 'The Jewish synagogue on the Houtgracht': Schama 589; Roth 1 134. **Marrano music:** Bernardete *passim:* Yovel 20; Kaplan 2; Poliakov 117. 'The cantorial style places tremendous emphasis on improvisation and embellishment': notes to the BBC's 'Shalom Aleichem!' in *Sacred and Profane* 18 Feb.–31 March 1996. **'Organs are nott played . . .':** Mundy [1634–9] 68. **Dutch music:** Schama 61. **Aboab's harp:** Gans 67. **Love–song:** the *Lecha Dodi:* Benardete 82; words in Hersch 357–9. **Purim:** *Sacred and Profane* Notes 4: etching Gans 80. **Catholic elements:** Howell 1 [1633] 2 229; Yovel 20, 45, giving other examples found by Revah ('La Religion d'Uriel da Costa' 74–5). *Those things are good . . .* E4 P39. *Nothing forbids . . .* **enhancing health** . . . E4 P45 S. **Menasseh's ban:** Roth 2 54–6.

22 **'Their elders sometimes . . .':** Howell 1 [1633] 2 229. **Grotius's ban on weapons:** Art.11: Meijer 117. **'For entering the synagogue . . .'** (1639): PA 1997. **Jacob de Espinosa: synagogue charity:** VD/VT 132, 142 (PA 1142/241). **'Good payment'** of 220 guilders, 6 stuivers and 8 pennies: VD/VT 133, 143 (NAA 1498, 14 Jan. 1639. **'Between them a matter . . . the father of the said Jacob d'Espinosa':** ibid. 134, quoting J. Volkaertz, 26 Jan. 1639, and 134–6, 21 March 1639. *It is true . . .* TP VI 4: W 317 **'In his boyhood . . .'** Kortholt, Wolf 2 165.

23 **Track-covering:** Baron 58, 388–9 n.28; *also above, notes to 4.* **Safe-conduct passes:** Bernadete 87. **'It is Abraham . . .':** Baron 208, quoting a priest. **Caute:** *Plate 15 and below, notes to 233. The virtue of a free man:* E4 P69. **'The teachings of his father . . .':** Lucas 67. **'A ready and penetrating wit':** Colerus 3. **'Embarrassed his teacher':** Lucas 42. **'[His father] instructed him . . .':** Lucas 67–8.

24 **Ducat** = 3,60 guilders (florins) in 17c: Bloom 2, n.10 citing Antwerp Archives. **'Treasure'** stored in the *Wisselbank:* Riemersma 41–7. **'He knew the gravity . . .':** Lucas 50. *External acts . . . inward worship:* TTP XIX: W 205. See also TTP VII W 109. *Not to mock human failings:* E3 Pref.; also TP 1 4: W 263. *Descartes's principles . . .* Letter 81, May 1676: *inutilia . . . ne dicam absurda:* OPG 4 332.

25 **Rich but devout marranos:** e.g. Antonio Lopes Suasso; De Pinto: Vaz Dias, A.M. (i) 'Wie waren Rembrandt's Buren?' *Studia Rosenthaliana* JRG 7 (29) 17 Oct. 1930, 40, 43. (ii) 'Rembrandt en zijn Portugeesch-Joodsch Buurt-Genooten' ibid. JRG 8 (34) 20 Nov. 1931 122–3. **Rembrandt: complaints:** Schwartz 284; Vaz Dias i and ii; *above, notes to 25.* **Belshazzar** [1635], **Faust** [1652], **Piedra Gloriosa** [1655] based on the vision of Ezekiel: Schwartz 174–5; Štech 21. *The Learned Man (Old Rabbi), 1634* (National Gallery, Prague) reproduced in Michael (44) may be Joseph Solomon del Medigo, who visited Amsterdam in the 1620s and 1630s, but died in Prague. **Etching of Menasseh** (1636) was followed by a portrait (1637) by Rembrandt's pupil Govaert Flinck (The Hague, Mauritshuis). **Spinoza and Rembrandt** lived 100 yards apart. A link is suggested in notes to 58. **South Kerk:** the carillon [1638] praised by Vondel in an inscription above the stairs to the bell tower, is still played every Thursday. **Guilds' arms:** Brereton [1634] 67. **'Very sad nudity . . .'** [1646] quoted in Murris 190–1; also ibid. 195, 221.

26 **'Scripture . . . dispels . . .'** Calvin I vi 1. See also III xxiv 8; IV xiv 9. **'Lit up':** Colie 1 147. **'Christ, the Spirit . . .'** Balling 719. **Illuminated 'through the internal Spirit'** Calvin III ii 33. **'Till we have . . .'** ibid. I i 1. **Spanish on foot:** *above, 10, and below, 73.* **Family's clothes:** Spinoza's silver buckles: SR 115. **Canions:** Schwartz 159. Pepys 24 May 1660. **'The great ark':** Bayle, quoted Murris 76. **Dutch charity:** Haley 2 114–17. **Corrective training:** Schama Ch.1. **'. . . unnecessary vermin':** William Carr (English consul) *Reflections of the Government . . . more particularly of the United Provinces* (Amsterdam 1688) quoted Haley 2 116. **Lotteries** licensed and blessed by the church as charitable donation: Schama 306–7. **Religious tolerance:**

Mundy [1634–9] 68; Felltham [1652] 46. **Hidden Catholic churches**: e.g. Begÿnhof; Our Dear Lord in the Attic (Oudezijds Voorburgwal); Parrot (Rokin); Posthoorn (Brouwersgracht).

27 **'Refuge for Catholics'**: Letter to Mersenne, March 1642, CSMK 210. **'Wickedness of popery'**: quoted Van Deursen 286; also ibid. 293–4. **Marvell**: Marvell 97. **'A kind of king'**: quoted Murris 241. **'You may be . . .'**: Felltham 1652 44–5. **State faith etc.**: Grotius Art.2: Meijer 116. **'You must go . . .'**: pamphlet quoted Van Deursen 296. **'Anyone who did not . . .'**: ibid. See also Feuer 71. **'The Lord has not . . .'** Calvin IV xx 4 (see the *Institutes* in John Clarke's 1952 edition for Calvin's biblical support.

28 **Mennonites**: *below, notes to 53. If someone dresses* . . . KV 2 XII [3]. **'Better the instruction'**: Abraham 359. The words are Shylock's in Shakespeare's *The Merchant of Venice*, Act III Scene 1. **Inventory of Spinoza's clothes**: SR 113–15. **'Nose-cloths'**: Schama 319. **Catholic army**: Parker 13. See also Van Deursen 223–9. **'For the Catholic Faith . . .'**: Parker 200. **'Are we here. . . ?'**: ibid. 179.

29 **Groningen**: Marshall 87. See also Kaplan, Benjamin J.264. *'Goet ende bloet . . . klopjes*: Marshall 89. *Spieghel der Jeught, of Spaanse Tyrannie* 1615: Van Deursen 213: also ibid. 209; Geyl 2 227. **Catholic-Protestant relations in 17c**: Van Deursen Chs 14–16. **Vondel**: Geyl 1 211, 239. *If someone has been* . . . E3 P46. *Believed that their kingdom* . . . TTP XVII: W 175–7.

30 **Obscene charges**: Edwards and Moore in Wood, Diana (ed.) *Christianity and Judaism.* The Ecclesiastical History Society, Blackwell, 1992. *I marked the fierce* . . . TTP Pref.: Es8. **'In this large town . . .'** Letter to Balzac, 5 May 1631, CSMK 31. **Slave trader**: Murray 14. 20 out of 30 Jewish firms regularly engaged in the transportation and sale of slaves: Israel 3 440. **Fines for trading in gold and silver goods and exporting ducats**: Bloom 176 n.10, quoting a decree of 1661, and 177: *above, notes to 24.* **Lombards**: Reimersma 77 ff.; Howell 1 [1633] 2 224; Stouppe 34; Schama 590–1. **'I had imagined . . .'** (1640) Baron 54.

31 **'My business . . .'** Quoted Zemon Davies 510. A *stuiver* was worth $\frac{1}{20}$ of a florin or guilder: Schama 617. **The *Rasphuis***: Edward Brown 1668, quoted Meinsma 382 n.65. **Drowning cell**: Schama 19. **He 'had learnt . . .'** Lucas 65. **'A hundred Netherlanders'** Cats *Werken*, 301 ('Spiegel'), quoted Van Deursen 110. **Dutch punishments**: Schama 16–24, 583–5; Van Deursen 53–5; Wilson 58; Zumthor 252–6; Brekelmans 18. *Because he fears* . . . *He who gives* TTP IV: W 69.

32 *We can best* . . . E4 Apx IX. See also TP II. **The mindless mob**: Van Deursen 110, citing records of 1585 and 1621. *No society can exist* . . . TTP V: W 93. See also TTP XVI W 133–47; E4 P37 S2, E4 P54 and S, E4 P63. **'The most impudent . . .'** Brereton (1634) 55. **Spinoza's appearance**: Depositions of Father Tomás Solano and sea captain Miguel Perez de Maltranilla, who met Spinoza in Amsterdam 1658–9: Revah 1 32, 36; Colerus 39. *As far as sensual* . . . TIE [4]: C 8: *libidinem*: OPG 2 6. *Lust is also* . . . E3 Defs. of the Affects, XLVIII with Exp.: C 541. **Terence or Ovid**: C passim. **'Physical, sexual love . . .'** Feuer 218.

33 *Confusion de confusiones*: Joseph da Vega, 1688, in *Portions Descriptive of the Amsterdam Stock Exchange*, ed. H. Kellenbenz (Boston, 1957): Bloom 190–1; Schama 348–9. See also reports by Evelyn [1641] 46 and Felltham [1652] 48. The Bourse was behind and to the left of the artist (book cover painting). **'Tulipomania'**: Mundy [1634–9] 75: Schama 351ff; **Tulip vases**: a fine example at Het Loo. **Porcelain imports . . . Delft**: Schama 346, 318, 351. *Usually occupies the mind* . . . E4 Apx XXVIII. *Those who know* . . . E4 Apx XXIX. *Things like feasting* . . . TP X 5: W 435.

34 **Anatomies**: Zumthor 154; Murray ·18. Rembrandt's 'The Anatomy Lesson of Dr Tulp' (1632, Mauritshuis, The Hague) showed a criminal executed 31 Jan. 1632:

Schwartz 14. **Surgeons:** Wallace 3; Schwartz 14. The arm may also may have been painted at home: Schwartz 14. **Descartes:** living near Leiden in 1640: Baillet 198; Amsterdam, Summer 1631: Letter to Villebressieu: CSMK 32. *Treatise on Man*: Baillet 84–5, 91: CSM 179. **'Boasts that all . . .'** Philips van Limborch (Amsterdam University Library MS. M. 34.b. quoted Colie I 153. **'I, that is . . .** Mediation 1: CSM 2 54 (French version). **The pineal gland** (*Passions* I 31–44, CSM 1 340–4: *below 239*. **Withdrew claim . . .** belief depended on faith: Letter to Princess Elizabeth, Nov. 1645: CSMK 277, and Second Set of Replies to Objections, CSM 2 109. **Changed subtitle:** CSM 2 21. **Spinoza's earliest doubts:** KV *passim*, esp. Apx II; TIE [85]. **Sorbonne theologians'** objections were largely Father Mersenne's: Second Set of Objections to *Meditations*, CSM 2 88; ibid. 91. **'It does not seem . . .'** 2nd Objection, Third Set of Objections to *Meditations*, CSM 2 122, 126. Spinoza's earliest copy of *Meditations* may be in his 1650 Latin edition of Descartes's *Opera Philosophica* (48 [24q]).

35 **Descartes's mathematical standard of truth:** *Rules for the Direction of the Mind*, Rule 4: CSM 1 17–19 **Spinoza and mathematics:** his books: François Viète [1540–1603] (15); Johannes de Sacro Bosco (John Holywood) *Sphaera* (20 and 21); Van Schooten (Father and son, both Frans, both professors at Leiden 1615–45: 1646–60): *Mathematical Exercises*. (51 [27]q) and *Principles of Mathematics* 1651 (62 [38]q). Gregory, Jacques. *Optics*. London, 1663 (q60 [36]). Lansberghe, Phillipus van (1561–1671) *Commentaries on Astronomy and Maths*. (1630) (64 [40]q). Kinckhuysen, Gerard. *Algebra* (1661) (70 [46]q); ibid. *Geometry* (71, 72 [47, 48]q). Metius, Adrien (1571–1674): *Astronomy and Geometry* (3 vols in Dutch) (94 [15]o). De Graaf, Abraham (born Rijnsburg). *Mathematics* (1659) (112 [33]o). **'Something less than . . .':** Letter to Mersenne May 1630, CSMK 25. *Essence is to be sought . . .* TIE [101] C 41. *Sanctuary of ignorance*: E1 Apx: C 443. *Have caused the truth . . .* E1 Apx: C 441. See also TIE [22]; Ep.21: S 158. *I cannot wonder enough*: E5 Pref.: C 596.

36 **Spinoza's theory of mind deduced:** *Ethics* Pref. to Part 2. *A free man . . .* E4 P67. **Being free:** E4 P68 D: See also E4 PP 66–73. **Spinoza's Dutch:** for Akkerman its shakiness is charming: BW 12–13. *I really wish* . . . Ep.19, Jan. 1665: OPG 4 95G. **Talmud Torah** school: VD/VT 150–4, using records of the Ets Haim seminary; Roth 2 20–1. **Segregated instruction:** Grotius Art. 32: Meijer 119. **Michael's offices:** *above*, notes to 8. **Enrolment of his sons:** PA 10525. **Marie de Médicis's** visit: Schama 299, 301; Zumthor 187. See 'Water Revels for Marie de Médicis in Amsterdam' (1638, Bodleian Library, Oxford) reproduced in Schama 225. **Morteira at her Court:** Feuer 30; Israel 2 85. **Henrietta Maria 1642:** Menasseh's Oration: Baron 32–3 with n.39. **Michael *parnas* 1642/3:** VD/VT 131 (*Livro dos Acordos* A). **Menasseh published in 5 languages:** Roth 2 41.

37 **'Something of the five . . .'** VD/VT 153, from De Barrios *Arbol de las Vidas, c.* 1684. **Ladino:** Abraham 41; Benardete 129, 94 n.13, 117. **School hours etc:** *Spinoza: Troisième* 26, from Shabtai ben Joseph Bass *Sifté Yeshenim* (1680). **Practise Spanish at home:** Roth 2 21. **Abraham's house:** *above*, notes to 2. **Instruction-book,** the *Thesauro dos Dinim:* Roth 2 100–3. **'The most noble . . .'** ibid. 102. *I was imbued . . .* TTP IX, Es 139. **'The Amsterdam Jews . . .'** quoted from *A model of human life*, Feuer 14, first published in 1687 by the Dutch theologian Philips van Limborch in *The Remarkable Life of Uriel d'Acosta*, London, 1740. Parts of it cannot have been written by d'Acosta (e.g. his suicide). See accounts by Yovel 42–3; Feuer 13–14; JE 1 167–8. **Auto-da-fê watched by children:** Kamen 187–8. **Deuteronomy ritual:** Deuteronomy 18; Van Deursen 309 citing Meihuzen, *Menno Simons*, 137.

38 *. . . attack me, who utterly dread brawling:* Ep.6, April 1662: S 83. **Sinister figure:** suggested by Yovel 50; Roth 2 71. **'Exceedingly nasty':** Wilson 58. *No one, unless . . .* etc. E4 P20 S. **Pharisees . . .** TTP V: W 91; TTP VIII: W 193, 199). **D'Acosta's influence:** Wolf 2 475. *I saw that I was . . .* TIE [7]: C9.

CHAPTER 3

39 *Honour has . . .* TIE [4]: C 8. 'Spinoza showed . . .' Colerus 2–3. 'A brilliant . . . hard to solve . . .' Lucas 42. **Higher *medras*:** List for 1651: VD/VT 148 (PA 105/ 246.) See also ibid. 154. **Reference to *Talmud*:** Silverman 1 163–5 referring to TTP X and XI, where Spinoza comments on the inclusion or exclusion of the Apocrypha and other books. 'From an early age . . .' JP. See also Lucas 154. **Mathematics and science:** 'the Spanish Jews were trained [in] philosophy, astrology and medical science': Musaph-Andriesse 63. **Spanish and Hebrew:** *above, notes to 37.*

40 **Ets Haim society:** PA 105/25. 'Passed into adulthood . . .' Unterman 143. **Vivès . . . female silence:** Bergmann 128. **Women by nature gullible:** Zemon Davies 447. **How children learned:** E3 P32 S; Descartes: *Meditation* 1: CSM 2 12; *Principles* 1, 1: CSM 1 193. **Iberian Inquisition peaked in the 1650s:** Israel 3 48. **Messianic belief paramount:** Silverman 1 64, 78, 223. '**Ejected**': *below*, 205. **Mathematical knowledge:** *above, notes to 35.* **Jewish literature:** See especially the work of Feuer, Israel (2) Kaplan, Popkin, Revah, Roth 2, Silverman and Yovel.

41 **De la Peyrère.** I use the French form to distinguish him from the Amsterdam marrano Peyrera, over whose Yeshiva Menasseh presided. **Eskimos, etc.** Popkin 57 and 66. *Prae-Adamitae* (52 [28q]). Refuted by Grotius and burned: Popkin 65–6. cf. Paul's Epistle to the Romans 5: 12–15. **Morteira's *yeshivah*,** the *Keter Torah*, was held at the house of Isaac Penso from 1643 until Morteira's death in 1660, and continued there: Kaplan 1 426. **Morteira's background:** Salomon 131–2, citing Kaplan on Morteira's unpublished works. **Morteira's character:** De Barrios 5; Yovel 71–2; Israel 2 221. **Morteira's bans:** Lucas 50–3;

42 '. . . Philosopher is wicked': Yovel 73. *Paixoes* . . . 'laden with clear . . .' . . . *dolhuis*: Kaplan 611. **Puns:** VD/VT 155–6. *See 91 and notes.* Grant: VD/VT 151).

43 'His doubts embarrassed . . .' Lucas 42. **Isaak's death:** *above, notes to 17.* 'As he had a mathematical mind . . . a great enemy . . .' Bayle [1697] 290. **Denial of cabala heresy:** Menasseh in *Nishmat Hayyim*; Maimonides in *The Laws of Repentance*, Chapter 3: See Roth 2 98–9; Silverman 222. See Silverman 19 n.27, referring to sermons collected in 1645. Brann (p.110) cites Dunin Borkowski's discovery of Abrahan Alonzo Herrera's book *Door of Heaven*, written in Spanish and translated into Hebrew by Isaac Aboab (Latin version 1678) – a favourite sourcebook of Morteira's and Menasseh's. *I have read . . .* TTP IX: Es 140. *The Word of God . . .* TTP Ch. XII, Es 165 and 166.

44 *Elohim* and *Hatevah*: claimed by Solomon Rubin (1823–1910) who saw Spinoza as a Jewish thinker: Silverman 1 371–2, 395, Notes 190, 194. '**Searching** . . .' Testimony of Maltranilla, 1659: Revah 137. **i, ii, iii:** listed by Silverman 1 (29) as grounds stated in the *Shulchan Aruch*. **(a) (b) (c) (1639):** ibid. 30. **Article 33:** The 1939 Regulations (PA 1997): verbatim in De Castro.

45 '**Important Jews . . .**' Bloom 25–6 with n.113. '**Children of Jacob**': Intermarriage avoided; Baron 36 with n.44. **By no means a unified community:** Bloom 28. **1639 criteria for excommunication:** The *mahamad* should have been answerable to the magistrates on this: Grotius, Art.20: Meijer 118. **Duke's 3 charters:** Israel 2 108. **Freedom to print all but *Talmud*:** Grotius, n. to Art. 16: Meijer 124. '**Each may freely . . .**' Rabbi Uziel's letter quoted Schama 589. **Pogroms:** Litvinoff and Weinryb *passim*. *Sacred rites . . .* TTP IV 1: W 73. *And consequently . . .* TTP V: W 89.

46 *Religious inquisitions*: TTP XVIII: W 199. Kaplan 1 140, quoting Ribera. '**Little monsters**': Blok 484–5. **Jewish warning:** *Anoniem Schrijven van Joodse Zijde c.* 1617: Meijer 141–3. **Dutch hardship:** (para.) Israel 1 266–71 and 378–84; Geyl 1 126–7; Haley 2 75–6; Zumthor 249, 241, 256–7, 260: **Horrors of Dutch road transport:**

Murris 64, quoting Pavillon [c. 1680]). 'Worth a million . . .' Felltham [1652] 33 and 38.

47 Michael's account Aug. 1651–Jan. 1652: VD/VT 147 quoting *Wisselbank* ledgers (GAA). Cold, wet summer: Gutmann 215. Willem the Silent: Rowen I 31: TTP XVIII: W 203. Hostile regents reminded Willem II that 'the States were master in the land above His Highness': Geyl I 140. Rowen 3 3–5; Pontalis I 30–4; Schwartz, *passim*. Count Maurits: Geyl I 155. Frederik Hendrik: ibid. 150; Geyl 3 10–11. 'Great sovereign': Cats, *Werken*, Pref. to the 'Trou-ringh', quoted Van Deursen 8. See also Geyl 3 3, 11. Willem II: Pontalis I 36–8: Geyl 3 41–2; Israel 3 40, 98–9; Geyl I 11, 130. 'Servile officers . . .' Geyl 3 60, note 60. 'Church owls . . .' 'Troubles of Amsterdam' 4.

48 Money-lenders: Rowen I 26; Israel 2 23. Willem I borrowed from German Jews: Baron 19; the Stuarts were supported by marrano financiers: Feuer 33, citing Lucien Wolf; William III borrowed from Gabriel Lopez Suasso (1760s). After his move to England borrowed from London Jews: Israel 2 23. His haughty wife: Pontalis I 34–7; Geyl 3 54, 73, 74, 77. Charles's execution: Haley 2 78; Geyl 3 46, 56. Willem II's threats and plot: Rowen I 31–2; Pontalis I 46–8. 'Every merchant . . .' ibid. 43–51. In 'The Troubles of Amsterdam' [1650] 'every man upon his guard'. This pamphlet purports to be a dialogue between two ordinary Amsterdammers, but the quoting of letters, documents and Resolutions of State, and knowledge of costs, salaries and 'Incomes and Profits of the land' (p.4) show it to be a well-informed political attack not only on Willem II but on those in Haarlem, Leiden, The Hague, Rotterdam and Zeeland who supported him, and would have liked to see Amsterdam brought down (7, 20 and 28). See also Rowen I 34–6. Jews banned: Grotius, Arts. 40, 42: Meijer 120. Willem's death: Geyl 2 18. 'He hath cast . . .' 'Troubles of Amsterdam' 8–9. Miriam's wedding: *above, notes to 12.* 'Gave his consent' VD/VT 137.

49 'That it may be . . .' ibid. 144: 2 Dec. 1650: PA 19300. 'In almost all ages . . .' Calvin IV xx 24–5. Few nobles: Temple 2 [1672] 64. Councillors, burgomasters and aldermen: The Amsterdam town government consisted of 4 burgomasters (*burgemeesters*), 8 aldermen (*schepenen*) and 36 council men (*vroedschappen*). Council seats were held for life, while burgomasters and alderman were elected for terms of one year: Schwartz: Foreword. St Anthonie's dyke: Schama 38–9. Flooded Beth Haim: See Ruysdael's painting: Vega 14. Ruysdael moved from Haarlem to Amsterdam around 1655.

50 *Opera Philosophica* 1650 in 3 Parts (q48 [24]). Spinoza also owned Descartes's *Principles of Philosophy*, 1659 (34 [10q]); *Meditations on the First Philosophy* 1654 (44 [20q]); *Geometry* 1649 (47 [23q]); *Letters* 1661 (31 [7q]). 'Because he had . . .' Colerus 3. Spanish nuances: Meinsma 444; Steenbakkers 9; *above, 7.* 'Two hours . . .' Letter in Spanish, 31 Jan. 1648, quoted by Baron 57. In the early 1650s: *Esperança de Israel* (1650), *Nishmat Hayyim* (1651), *Piedra Gloriosa* (1655). Jewish physicians: Jewish surgeons were not allowed to perform operations on non-Jews in the Netherlands. No admission to the surgeons' guild until 1710: Bloom 67–8. First Jewish Leiden doctorate in medicine: Van Rooden 162. By 1656 10 Jews licensed to practise in Amsterdam: Revah 128. 'Go through . . .' Ep.8, Feb. 1663: S 90.

51 Miriam's death: 6 Sept. 1651 (gravestone): VD/VT 113, 179. Ribca married Samuel de Casseres: No record in Amsterdam, but her son Michael, son of Samuel, died 10 Jan. 1695, aged 40–2: Emmanuel 193, using records of the Portuguese-Jewish community of Curaçao. De Casseres died on 6 Sept. 1660: ibid. 193 citing PA *Livro dos Acordos* 245. 'Ribca de Casseres' was a witness at an Amsterdam wedding in 1687 (DTB 695/454) and an Anna de Casseres is found as a marriage witness in 1710 (DTB 707/220.) Bento Henriques: Disputes July 1639: NAA 1498 279–83. Cargo (pipes) July 1651: *above, notes to 19.* Ship reclaimed: NAA 967302. 'Our cargo ship': Amsterdam Historical Museum. Resentment of Dutch shipping domination: Hill

141; Rowen 116. 1st **Anglo-Dutch war** (1652–4). **Dutch sailors** 'The whip of Spain . . .' Felltham [1652] 38, also 40; Hill 45; Zumthor 241. **Michael's ship sold:** 3 Aug. 1652, NAA 1510. **Bills and translations:** VD/VT 194–5: 16 Aug. and 8 Oct. 1652, NAA 1029.

52 'An honest burial . . .' VD/VT 179, 188, NAA 1557. **Esther died** 24 Oct. 1653: (gravestone) VD/VT 113. **Ketubah:** VD/VT 182–3. **Womanish tears:** TTP Pref. 'Ever since he . . .' Colerus 96. **Ribca married:** above, notes to 51. 'Four Hollanders' incident: VD/VT 158–61, quoting documents 20 April, 4 and 7 May 1655, NAA 976B and 2198.

53 'Damages and interests . . .' VD/VT 160, 7 May, NAA 2198. **Jarig Jelles's home:** Van der Tak 2 11–13: NAA 1555, 1556 and 1557. **Probably met at the Exchange:** VD/VT 156. **Jelles Senior** (Tjebbes) Van der Tak 212: Register of Amsterdam Brokers' Guild 355/1066. **Mennonites:** Stouppe 49; Van Deursen Chapter 17 passim. 'The infection of sin': ibid. 309. 'His flourishing . . .' Geyl 2 223, quoting Riewertsz. in Knuttel, 'Ercus Walten en zijn proces', Bijdragen van Vaderlandsche Geschiedenis V, 1, 432.

54 **Jarig's gevoelens:** Confession: Ep.48A with BW Notes 488–9. See below, 261–2. **De Vries and family:** Vaz Dias 2 5, 6 and 7–8, citing Amsterdam documents and registers. **Vondel:** Van Deursen 68. **Schiedam:** Ep.19, Jan. 1665: S 132, 136. **Pieter Balling:** Poorter: 'Factoor Harlingen': GAA Poorters Register 1655–1700.

55 **Tromp's death:** 10 Aug. 1653: Geyl 2 34. **Deductie:** ibid. 105–8; Rowen 1 383–9. 'The people . . . ' Letter to the French ambassador in England, 1653: Rowen 2 47. See also Van Deursen 157ff. 'Not as a result . . .' Cicero 255–6: Pro Plancio 5–13. **De Witt's republic:** Rowen 1 133–8, 380–7. **Cats's poems:** Huizinga 65. By 1655 the illustrated edition had sold 50,000 copies: Zumthor 219. **Tromp:** 'mother washed . . .': Tromp quoted, Van Deursen 8. Warned that the ships were not fit: Geyl 2 33, quoting De Witt Brieven 195, 18 July 1653. **Vondel:** Price 36, 108; Schama 58; Murray 85, 95, 146 and 149. 'It is a work . . .' quoted Geyl 1 231.

56 **After much bloodshed . . .** TTP XVIII: W 201. **Cromwell's Ordinance** of 19 May 1649 declared England 'a Commonwealth or Free-State.' **Spinoza on Cromwell:** TTP XVI W 137. **De Witt:** Rowen 1 Chs 2–3 passim; Blok 221. **Tulp:** Schama 184. **Courting and marriage:** Rowen 1 100 'Good correspondence': Geyl 2 45, quoting Wendela's uncle, De Graeff van Zuidpolsbroek in a letter from L. Baeck to his cousin A. Hooft, 19 March 1655; Brieven van Hooft, IV 239. **Binnenhof:** Schama 226; Rowen 1 877; Schwartz 68. 'He had so little . . .' Lucas 51, 52.

57 **Spinoza: non-Jew friends before ban:** Meinsma 152; Feuer 5; Kasher 130–3; Klever 8 17–18; Silverman 167. **'Suppose [someone] . . .'** Reply to the Seventh Set of Objections to Meditations, printed with the Second Edition of 1642: CSM 2 324. 'Charmed with that . . .' Colerus 7. **Possession of Descartes's texts:** Kasher 117 and 130–2. **No Descartes in schools:** Synods continually objected: Zumthor 110. **Rembrandt:** Wallace 24; Swartz 119.

58 **Religious texts:** Stoye Ch.VIII esp. 227 and 233; Van Deursen 295, citing cases. **Free press:** ibid. 147. **Descartes's works** printed: CSM 1 109. **Bookshops meeting-places:** Meinsma 105, 103 referring to PK IX, 225, 226, 234, 235, 22 Nov.–27 Dec. 1657). **Spinoza on rabbis:** Notes 38 to TTP: W 253. See also Colerus 7–8. **Spinoza's languages:** Lucas 51–2. Spinoza owned Greek-Latin lexicons (3 and 83 [40]), 1652 and 1654); French–Latin–Spanish dictionary (26 2q); Latin–Belgian [Dutch] Dictionary (92 [130]). **Franciscus van den Enden:** Meinsma 2181 n.2; Meininger 8 n.2. **Bookshop:** Meinsma 183 citing Ledboer, Naamlist der Boekdrukkers, Dev. 1832, 32. 'In de Konst-winkel' in 1980 No.59: Meininger 16, citing S.C.A. Dudok van Heel, 1978. **Jesuit:** Archives of the Jesuit College at Drongen, Belgium: VD/VT 149, 156. **Married 1642** Clara Maria Vermeeren: Meinsma (p.202 n.6) cites Van Vloten Levensbode, XI 136. **Married in Amsterdam:** De Nazelle 99.

59 **Children:** Meinsma 182, citing baptismal records and other docs. **Professions: Physician:** NAA 3 204/37; Roukema 151; **Lawyer:** Jesuit records: VD/VT 176; De Nazelle (intr.) xiii. **'Catholic with Catholics':** De Nazelle [1680] 101. **'Seeds of atheism . . .'** Colerus 3. Refused confession at death: Apx, 'Judiciary documents relating to the trial of De Rohan': De Nazelle 263. **Anti-Catholic:** VPS 22. **Spinoza's understanding of atheism:** Ep.43: *below, 243–4.* **'Great penchant . . . little':** De Nazelle 99, 100. **Reason he left Jesuits:** ibid. 99. **Bankruptcy paid off:** Meininger 22: *Camer van Desolate Boedels te Amsterdam,* 16 July and 12 Sept. 1652 (GAA Act and Inventory), reproduced ibid. 155–63; see also De Nazelle 102–3. **'Somewhat lame and deformed':** *mank en mismaakt:* K3. The English and French versions of this are mistranslations. *Philedonius:* Meinsma 185–6; Meininger 34–43, reproducing title-page to the 1657 text. **Free love:** VPS 35–6. **Van den Enden spoke Spanish:** De Nazelle [1680] 98; Geyl 2 223. **Van Beyeren:** Valentiner 30–1; Meinsma 290. Meininger 17. Inventory of Van Beyeren's possessions, 10 Oct. 1649, ibid. 154. **'Latin and Greek':** Lucas 52. **'The new philosophy':** Meinsma 183–4. **Catholics:** teaching, 'publick charges': Zumthor 88–90; Temple 2 [1672] 104 and Apx. *'De Posthoorn:* no mention of Frans after the youngest child's baptism, 6 June 1651: Meinsma 182 and 203 n.12. **Clara Maria Catholic:** *below, 242 and notes.* **'Understood the Latin . . .'** Colerus 4. **De Witt unwilling to censure:** 'De Witt' 1 18, 69; Van Deursen 291; Rowen 1 436–9. **'United and bound . . .'** Geyl 2 107, quoting *Deductie* (1654).

60 **'The Latin . . .'** Kortholt, Wolf 2 165; Colerus 4. **'Although a clever . . .'** Geyl 1 231–2, quoting Cats, *Houwelick.* **'The richest . . .'** Colerus 3. **Clara Maria's portrait:** Meinsma 191 with n.50. **'Beautiful face':** Van der Goes in *Bruiloftsge-dichten:* Meininger 170. **'A great deal of wit':** Colerus 4. *Halachah:* 'rules': Alexander 195; 'following': Musaph-Andriesse 58. **'Lost son':** comment beside a copy of the ban, Amsterdam synagogue, 1990. **Michael's death:** *above, notes to 16.*

61 **No wealth tax (finta):** but *imposta* paid showing Spinoza was still trading: VD/VT 190, from the Journal of the *Gabay.* **Henriques, Pedro:** VD/VT 145 and 132: NA 953 and NA 1497, 8 and 30 June, 1638. Hana Debora died 5 Nov. 1638. **Kaddish:** Unterman 165; VD/VT 191: Journal of the *Gabay.* **'Took it upon . . .'** VD/VT 163, quoting Archives of the Orphan Chamber, Register of Guardianship C f.136, 5 Dec. 1655. **'Louis Crayer . . . Although the said Bento':** ibid.

62 *Ledikant: above, notes to 18.* **'His father's succession . . .'** Colerus 44. **Camel-hair . . . silver buckles and silver knife:** SR 111–16. **'The conduct . . . He could not . . .'** Lucas 44. **'[He] did not answer . . .'** ibid. 45.

63 *If it is your conviction . . .* Ep.21, 1665: S 151. **'Has God . . . Since nothing . . .'** Lucas 45. **First texts:** KV 1 II, 17, 18 and n.e: C70; CM 2, VII, C 327–8. **'Burning desire':** JP 216. **De Prado's arrival:** Revah 1 21; Ribera's (1653–5): Kaplan 1 138. **'The Rabbi that . . .'** Lucas 47. **'There was no precise . . .':** Silverman 1 63. **'The accused retorted . . .'** Lucas 49. **Another researcher:** Vlessing 206–10. See also Proceedings of 'The History and Culture of the Jews in the Low Countries', University College London, June 1997. **'Threatened the whole . . .'** Vlessing 208.

64 **'The son of . . .'** ibid. **1633 claim:** Seeligmann 19–20. **Text used after synagogue schism, 1618:** Salomon, H. P. 'La vraie excommunication de Spinoza', *Forum Litterarum,* APA-Holland University Press, Amsterdam and Marssen, 1984, 186–8. **'Commercial aristocracy':** Feuer 25–6: *above, notes to 11. Anoniem Schrijven* (*c.*1617): Meijer 99, 116–43. **'Harmful and heretical . . . our Holy Law . . .'** Kaplan 5 200–1; Kasher 118–19.

65 **De Prado's recantation:** Yovel 69, citing *Livro de Acordos da Naçam 5398–5440. Most men refuse . . .* TTP IV: W 83. *Could not . . . been the same . . .* TTP XII, Es 166. *Social organisation . . .* TTP III: W 57; TTP XVII: W 179–81. *Apology:* Colerus 31; Bayle [1697] 292–3, with note *D:* '. . . book of Van Til, minister and professor of Dordrecht, entitled *Her Voorhof der Heidenen voor alle Ongeloovigen geopent.* The Journal of Leipzig

331

for 1685 speaks for it.' FQ 25, 30, 54, 68, 224, 237 supplies all early references. 'Ejected . . . bad opinions . . . The Jews have': De Barrios 85: *below 205.* 'Whether he was . . . to repent . . .' Lucas 49–50. Menasseh - books: Offenberg 195. See also Meijer 34–6.

66 Synagogue 5 Dec. 1655: VD/VT 162 and 168, PA 29412. Ribera . . . 'Any land . . .': De Barrios: Kaplan 3 205–12, citing the *Livro de Acordos,* and 1, 223–4. Abstruse cosmological theories: especially *Nishmat Hayyim:* Roth 299; Dan 199–200; Fisch 228: *above, notes to 43.* Calvin: Jacob 40. Rabbi Nieto: Silverman 26. Ribera: 'Moses our teacher . . . is doing it . . .' Kaplan 1 143–4. Infringed *halachah:* ibid. 4–5. Aboab: Feuer 28–32.

67 Ribera's departure: Kaplan 1 145, crediting Révah. 'Nothing impious': Lucas 55. 'On leaving . . . kill him': Bayle [1697] 292. 'The old Portuguese . . . his clothes': Colerus 9–10. 1654 play 'The Fall and Destruction of Troy', from Virgil Book 1 Parts 2 and 10, staged at the wedding of a burgomaster's daughter: Meininger 25–6. Vondel's shop: No.39, later No.110: Murray 9. 'Kept still the coat': Colerus 10. 'One great mass . . . other sects': Deposition to the board of inquiry of the *mahamad:* Kaplan 1 141–2. De Prado led Spinoza astray: Gebhardt 1923, *passim.* Identical heresies: *below, 91.* De Prado's offences: listed in De Castro's 'Invective text against Prado . . .' *c.* 1663: Revah 1 21 ff.

68 'The world . . . impossible and irreconcilable': Kaplan 1 141–2 (quoting the pupil Monsanto) and 160. Consistent with Spinoza: Denial of Jewish destiny: TTP III, W53–5; ibid. 211 and n.111; of the superiority of the Jewish religion: TTP V: ibid. 89; ibid. 99; TTP XVIII: ibid. 193. The world eternal: the immortality of the soul: *below 91.* De Prado's recantation: *above, notes to 65.* Left for Antwerp etc.: Revah 140; Kaplan 1 157–9. A pension 'to engage . . .' Colerus 8–9, quoting F. Halma. VD/VT 170; Wolf 2 146. 'Not for ordinary . . .' Lucas 55. Morteira revenge: ibid. Reasons: see Kasher 119–20.

69 'Death or . . .' Kasher 129, quoting Grotius Art. 13: Meijer 117, 122. 'Repentance . . . excommunicate him': Lucas 50. *I hardly believe . . .* Ep.21, to Van Blijenbergh, Jan. 1665: S 151, 152. *When this imagination . . .* E3 P26 S. Pride = *superbia* or *philautia. Legitimate self-esteem . . .* KV 2, VIII: C111. *Self-esteem is really . . .* E4 P52 P and S.

70 'Prepare himself . . .' Lucas 52. *Cherem* = separation: Wolf 2 52. Van den Enden 'offered to . . .' Lucas 52. 'They do not force . . .' ibid. 51. 'Precentor blows a horn . . .' Lucas 53. See also Colerus 13–31 for allusions to Deuteronomy: 28; 1 Corinthians 5 and 16, and details of a 'third *herem*', given him by a 17c theologian of the University of Amsterdam, which has unmistakably Hispanic and cabalic elements but was not used to excommunicate Spinoza. Read from Ark: Kasher 98–9. 'The Lords of the Mahamad . . .' ibid., rejecting earlier translations e.g. VD/VT 170; Wolf 2 146. 'Evil': *má'as;* (Latin text *malas.*) 'Opinions and acts': *obras* (works).

71 'Abominable heresies': *horrendas herezías.* 'Holy men': in other translations 'saints'. Unsigned: Kasher 101. Six weeks: ibid. 102. *The same old song . . .* Ep.76, Dec. 1675: S 342.

CHAPTER 4

72 *I do not differentiate . . .* Ep.6, April 1662: S 84. *Man, as long . . .* KV 2 XVIII [9], C 129, with n.2 on *Godsdienst.* Latest Spanish publications: Savadra and Quevedo: *above, notes to 6.* Self-esteem: KV 2 VIII: C111. Clara Maria was born 1643: *above, notes to 59.* Bitter winter: Gutmann 217. 'Clara Maria Vermeren [*sic*]': 7 May 1657: DTB. 1056/95. Bankruptcy inventory: *below, notes to 74.* Frans 'remarried' between 1671 and 1673: De Nazelle 103, 107. 'Sweet and learned' etc.: Pieter van

Rixtel *Mengelrijmen*, 1169, 57: Meinsma 191. 'Having often occasion . . .' Colerus 4.

73 **Jewish girls married:** JE XII 556. **Daniel de Casseres** married Judith Moreno, aged 14 (DTB 691⁄214) on 14 April 1679. The marriage failed: Emmanuel 194. **Dutch girls married:** Schama 405. **Anna de Witt:** (1671) Rowen 1 503. **'Young daughters':** No older than 25: Van Deursen 84. **Jews Dutch subjects 1657:** Bloom xvii. **If a Jew was baptised:** Koen 34, with cases from records; Grotius Pref.: Meijer 110, 116 Arts. 36–7; **Encouraged** . . . Gans 87. **'Sr. Benedictus Spinosa':** Ep.8, 24 Feb. 1663: OPG 41. **'Civilly entertained':** Roth 2 251, citing Pocock's (1700) intr. to the English translation of Menasseh's *De Termino Vitae*. **A dignified pace:** Howell 2 [1642] 68–72; Barlow 55. **Hooghduytsen:** Schama 474; 587–91; **Frippery:** Howell op.cit. 24; Bloom 67 n.155. **Dutch food:** Schama 163, 158–9, citing *De Verstandige Kok* (17c.) and *Leering en Vermaak*, Amsterdam 1976.

74 **Beer and water:** Brereton [1634] 66; Boxer 295; Zumthor 72. **Spinoza: liked beer:** *below, 236*. **No appetite:** Colerus 36–8. See Appendix. **'Had been troubled . . .':** Colerus 91. **A physician acquaintance:** Letter from Schuller to Leibniz, 6 Feb. 1677: FQ 202. **'Put him up . . .'** Lucas 52. **Frans's former home:** *Akte uit de Camer van Desolate Boedels* (GAA): Meininger 158–61. **Boreel suggested teacher:** Silverman 19: in London throughout 1650s: Van der Wall 171. **In Greek:** New Testament (2): lexicons and grammars: 3, 9 (83 [40]), (107 [28]), (108 [290]). *I do not possess* . . . TTP X: Es 156.

75 **Jesuit natural philosophy:** If one 'had attended a Jesuit college, the lessons in Father Suárez's or Father Pereira's manual' would suffice as a general, pre-corpuscular theory, grounding: Redondi 62 (also 120, 129, 222–4) on the influence of Suárez and Pereira on scientists such as Galileo. **Descartes and Suárez:** EP 831; Leibniz also read Suárez with ease: Aiton p.13. Spinoza's Pereira text was not scientific, but a Commentary on Daniel (100 [21]o). **Spinoza's Classics:** Lucian (99 [20]o) Virgil (142 [24]d]; 152 [34]d; 153 [1671] [35]d), Tacitus (1607 [4], 157 [39]d) Livy (1609, 5), Aristotle (1548, f12) Aurelius (1539, 17) Hippocrates (1554, 86 [17]o) Epictetus (1596, 87 [8]o) Julius Caesar (101 [220] Seneca (Letters 103 [24]o and 126 [8]d; Tragedies (1541) 135 [17]d) Homer (Iliad 1572) [38]o) Pliny (1591, 134 [16]d) Ovid (3 vols. 138 [20d]; 139 [31]d) Curtius (141 [23]d) Petronius (1669, 93 [14]o) Plautus (143 [25]d) Cicero (144 [26]d) Justinian (146 [28]d) Virgil and Horace (m152 (34]d). **Books as gifts:** see e.g. Eps 6 to Oldenburg, April 1662 and 46 to Leibniz, Nov. 1671. *Zwartheid:* K30. **Moustache:** mentioned in 1659 (Revah 1 33) and just discernible in portraits.

76 **Niels Stensen (Steno):** Astronomy (f6). Anatomical Observations (Leiden 1662, d151 [33]). **Spinoza's Dutch:** *above 36.* **Frans's eloquence:** De Nazelle 100. *The authority of Plato* . . . Ep.56, Oct. 1674: S 279. Spinoza possessed no Plato (containing the philosophy of Socrates) but he had Aristotle's *Works* Vol.2 (1548, f12). **'Greatest light':** Colerus 7. **'Greatly useful':** JP 216. Descartes *a great man:* E5 Pref. **Kerckring, Theodor:** Banga 564. **Parents:** Vroedschap II 916; I 245–6 **Leiden entry:** Meinsma 189. **'Noble mathematician . . .':** *Spicilegium Anatomicum* (1670, q33 [9]) *Observatio XCIII* 177. **Joannes Casearius:** may be the Johannes Casier baptised in the New Church 4 Jan. 1643 (DTB 339⁄42). Heniger (p. 49 n. 87) accepts this. Meinsma (p. 241 n. 65) finds a Johannes Cassarius of Amsterdam registering to study philosophy 12 Sept. 1659 (p. 242 n. 66) and a Johannes Casear enrolling to study theology 21 May 1661 (ibid. 230). **Married as Casearius:** DTB 442⁄213. **Albert Burgh:** son of Coenraad Burgh, *Vroedschap* 1 453; Meinsma 430.

77 **Cause = reason** (*causa seu ratio*) equation made seven times in E1 P11 P2. **Medieval assumption:** See Allison 55 and Gullan-Whur 2 134–8. **'If a cause . . .'** *Principles* 3, 43, CSM 1 255. **Descartes, earliest principles:** *Rules for the Direction of the Mind* written 1628 or earlier, but not published until 1684 (in Dutch): CSM 1 17. *Discourse on the Method* available 1650. **For how can he** . . . KV II ii (C98). **From intellectual axioms** . . . TTP V: W 99. **Promise to discuss empirical method:** TIE [27] n.i.

78 'So clear and distinct . . .' Meyer, Pref. to PPC: C 225. *Axiom or [common] notion*: E2
P40 S1. **Cartesian common notions**: Postulate 3, 2nd Replies to *Meditations*: CSM 2
115; 'Comments on a Certain Broadsheet' CSM 1 305. *What is common . . .* E2 P37.
Common notions a doctrine of rational universality: In my view (Gullan-Whur
1996 47–8) Spinoza's doctrine resembles the Socratic 'one over many' in contradistinc-
tion to Platonic and Aristotelian views. For Spinoza, essences must exist *in rebus*, in
actual things: [TIE [19] [58], [76], [92–3] and [101]. Universals *do not exist nor have any
essence beyond that of singular things*: CM 2, VII. *Common notions* **first mentioned**:
Ep.4, Oct. 1661, S 68. *We must now establish . . .* E2 P44 D to C2. *Sub specie aeternitatis*
(or *durationis*): E2 P44 D to C2: E5 P23 S. I prefer 'aspect' to Curley's 'species'. *There
are no inadequate . . .* E2 P36 *Singular thoughts or . . .* ibid. *To the common properties . . .*
E5 P7 D; full quotation *below, 122*.

79 'Abraham Espinoza, *filho de Michael espinoza*': VD/VT 185: GAA *Desolate-
Boedelkamer*, 1657 (unnumbered); facsmile C (signature) Vaz Dias 223; *see also above*,
17. Serrarius: 'minister of the . . .' Van der Wall 165. **Worked with Menasseh**:
ibid. 168, 173–5. **Quakers**: Mennonites . . . tanner's garret: Popkin and
Signer 3; Braithwaite 407, 412. 'A very hard, obstinate . . .' Popkin and Signer 5,
quoting William Caton. *Inward . . . external* TTP XIX: W 205. See also TTP
V: W99.

80 **Spinoza no English**: Ep.26, May 1665: S 175. 'Lit': *above*, notes to 26. 'The
Enthusiasts . . .' Stouppe 60, 61, 62. 'The movement of . . .' Stouppe 61. 'I very
well remember . . .' Sewell 168. Also Fox 2 411; Braithwaite 408; Barclay 91.
'Singing, dancing . . .' ibid. 422. **English Ranters** first appeared in England in
1640–1: ibid. 414–23. **'Spoke themselves . . .'** ibid. 422–3. **'Passionate and giddy-
headed . . .'** Braithwaite 408, 409, 411–12, quoting William Sewel. **'Previously
written . . .'** Foreword to the Dutch version of the *Short Treatise* (C 59).

81 **Jelles suggested**: C 59 n.2. **Jelles . . . obedience**: *below 261–2*. **Spinoza, Quaker
terminology**: Kasher (p.136) suggests TTP XIV. **Fisher, translation** *A Loving
Salutation* etc: Popkin and Signer 5. Nothing indicates Menasseh knew about it (ibid.
4). **Margaret Fell: 'mother'**: ibid. 1; Fox 1 407. 'I have been . . . As touching . . .'
Popkin and Signer 6, 7. **Letters from Ames** 1657, 1658: ibid 1, 7. 'That by the Jews
. . . hath been a Jew': ibid.

82 **Eminent scholar**: Popkin, R. **Quaker women**: Boulding 12; Braithwaite 314.
'Beaming countenance . . .' Barclay 267. 'Greedily received': May 1658: Popkin
and Signer 8. 'The common people . . .' Letter to George Fox, husband of Margaret
Fell, Oct. 1658, ibid. 11. 'Turn your minds . . . Here you will come . . .' ibid. 32,
72. 'Keep your meetings . . .' [1657] Braithwaite 413. 'In their outpourings . . .
Stouppe 60, 62. **Serrarius . . . unlike primitive Christianity**: Feuer 50, citing Hull.
W.I., *The Rise of Quakerism in Amsterdam*, 27, 214–15, 234, 267. **'Stubborn Quakers'**:
KVNN 52. Stouppe said he would write only of Christian sects: Stouppe 33.
'Missionise': Silverman 26–7. Klever (3, 323) finds a clue in Borch's diary that the
translator was 'Wilhelmus' or William James, a Quaker.

83 **'Somebody who . . .'** Klever 8 24, quoting Borch. **'Interiorisation' of religion in
17c Holland**: Kolakowski 97, 99, 207. **'Spinosa quakers'**: Feuer 55, quoting *The
Diary of Robert Hooke (1672–1680)* ed. H.W. Robinson and W. Adam, London 1635,
368) *Christ's mind . . .* TTP IV: W 81. *The man who lives . . .* TTP V: ibid. 99. See also
TTP V: ibid. p.91; TTP VIII: ibid. 193. *The spirit of Christ*: Ep.43, 1671, S 241; TTP
V: W 105; also TTP XIV, V and VII; Ep.21: S 158. *Liberal Political Propositions*: VPS
28, 44. *As for Christian rites . . .* TTP V: W 99. **Matthew 22** vv 37–9: stressed by Jelles,
JP 226.

84 *The hate the Turks . . .* KV II iii, 'Of the Origin of the Passions in Opinion' (C 101).
Immersion at Collegiant centre, Rijnsburg: Barclay 90; Geyl 2 221; De Vries 18c

engraving. **Serrarius a mystic.** Van der Wall 165. *Very simple universal faith*: TP VIII
46: W 411. See also TTP XIV: ibid 119–21.

85   **Lodewijk Meyer:** Meinsma 146–50, with sources; TS 189, 253–5; Feuer 296.
Serrarius's rebuttal of Meyer: Van der Wall 166. **Treatise rebutted:** *Philosophia S.
Scripturae interpres* (1666): *below, 197–8. The kindness and esteem* . . . Ep.12, April 1663:
S 101. **Dutch Vocabulary** (*Nederlantsche woordenschat*) 1650; TS 254. **Theatre:** plays,
translations and imitations of French plays: *see below, 223* and TS 254 n.255. **Poem** . . .
wedding: Meinsma 149; Vaz Dias 25. **Meyer's influence:** Eps 12, 13 and 15, April,
July and Sept. 1663. **Geometricism v. mysticism:** Spinoza echoes the Greek
physician Galen in this: Steenbakkers 178, with references. **Long Leiden vacations:**
Lagrée in Meyer, 3. *Philodonius, Woman of Andros* and *Eunuchus*: Meinsma
185–8: Meininger 28–9. **Terence:** 'a dishonest comedy of Terence . . .' Not.
Naaldwijk, 14 July 1613, quoted by Van Deursen 152. **Pupil's withdrawals:** Colerus
(3–4) does not specifically blame the plays. Terence's English translator remarks that
they are still performed 'with omissions and adaptation': Sargeaunt x. **Iberian?**
ibid. vii.

86   **Spinoza's roles:** Klever 3 21 with n.13, citing Proetti, O. 'Adolescens lux perditus;
classici latini nell 'opera di Spinoza.' *Revista di Filosofia Neo-Scolastica* (77) 1985. **Van
den Enden thought marriage unnecessary:** VPS 35–6; KVNN 18–23. **Dutch
fathers:** Schama 541–4. **Spinoza and children:** Colerus 40. *Childish superstition*:
Ep.21, S 155; E2 P49 111.B.iv; E3 P2 S ii; E3 P32 S; E4 Apx XIII; Pref. to TTP (Es
4). *I added 'independent* . . .' TP XI, 3: W 443.

87   **'Ruinous pestilence':** Klever 2 623, quoting KVNN 28. See also VPS 23–30. **Dutch
historians who ignore:** e.g. Geyl 2 192, 116 quoting TTP X1X: W 217. **Leiden:**
Academisch Historich Museum. **Grotius:** NNBW 2 523. **Hobbes** (Oxford): Macpherson 15; **De Witt:** Rowen 1 13; **Kerckring** an *opsimath*: *Allgem. Deutsche Biographie*
Vol.15 626, citing Haller Bibl. Anat. 1570 or Bibl. Med. Pr.11 1268. **Spinoza's name
not found:** Révah 1 36, citing Leiden archivist. **Heereboord's unpublished
philosophy:** *below 106–7.* **Spinoza said to have studied at Leiden:** Deposition of
Tomás, 8 Aug. 1659: Revah 1 29–30. **Meyer 25:** Meinsma 149 with n.2. **Johannes
Hudde** entered Leiden to study medicine 1654. **Shared interest in Cartesian
mathematics:** Klever 3 24, quoting Borch; EP.36 to Hudde, *c.* June 1666. **Night-
study forbidden:** Van Deursen 134, citing Duker, *Gisbertus Voetius* 1,47. **Leiden an
industrial town** of 50,000 people: Schama 174, 569. Worst slums Leiden, Amsterdam
and Weesp: Zumthor 3, 10, 305.

88   **Van den Hove brothers:** Renier 124. *To pursue [honour]* . . . TIE [4], C 8. **Van den
Enden's chemistry:** De Nazelle 102; nitre project: Klever 8 28. **Sylvius** (Franciscus
de le Boe): King 93, 94. **'Perspective glasse' etc.:** Nicolson 139. Scheiner's *Astronomy
and Refraction*: (1617, q73 [49]). **'Imperfect instrument':** Hack 141–2, quoting
Jeremiah Joyce, *Scientific Dialogues*, London 1808. **Law of Refraction: Descartes:**
Optics Discourse 2: Refraction: CSM 1161; Letter to Mersenne, June 1632, CSMK 39.
Snell, Huygens: Clark G.L. 445–6. **Christiaan Huygens** (son of Constantijn
Huygens, art connoisseur, musician and Secretary to 3 Stadholders): *Theoremata* 1651;
pendulum clock 1657; Saturn's rings, 1657: Hartley 167–9.

89   *Opinion and advice*: Ep.36, *c.* June 1666: S 209–10. *Hooke's advice: Micrographia*,
1665, Pref. and Obs.VI (p.10). **Spectacles – lenses:** Descartes: Nicolson 159.
Zacharias Jansen (1609): Guthrie 189. **Lens-making details:** Twyman 8, 14–15,
29–34. **Jan Hendriksz. Glazemaker** TS 190 and n.116. *Catalogus bij een
tentoonstelling over de vertaler Jan Hendriksz. Glazemaker*, University of Amsterdam
Library, 1982, v–vi; also Thijssen-Schoute: 'Jan Hendrik Glazemaker, de zeventiende-

eeuwse Aartsvertaler' in *Uit de republiek der letteren* (The Hague 1967) 213 and 224. **Spinoza's textbooks on glass-cutting and optics:** Gregory, John, *Optica Promota* (1663, q60 [36]); Neri, Antonio, *Art of Glass Cutting* (1668, d121 [3]). **'Occupy himself . . .'** Klever 3 23–4, quoting Borch's Journal. **3-year course** for apprentices of the trade School for Optical Glass Work: Twyman 252. **Gentlemanly hobby:** Nicolson 22–6. **'I am convinced . . .'** Twyman 9, quoting Van Leeuwenhoek, Letter to Leibniz, Sept. 1715. **De Prado:** Revah 1 59.

90 **Depositions to the Madrid Inquisition, 8 and 9 Aug. 1659:** ibid. 1 31–40. Spinoza **'good philosopher'** ibid. 32. **De Prado 'small philosopher . . .':** Gebhardt 1923 285 n.1, quoting S66b. **'Dr Prado'** tall, Espinosa short, etc.: Revah 1 32. **'Who had abandoned . . .'** ibid. 33. The Lepers' Hospital was by the city wall on the Vloyenburg. **De Maltranilla's descriptions:** Révah 1 33. **'Content to maintain . . .'** ibid. 33.

91 **Spinoza's God was existential:** E1 P15. **Minds survive in part:** E5 P36 S. **Faith was not only unnecessary** . . . See below 184, 192. **'This world is . . .'** Kaplan 1 322–3, translating Peyrera's 1659 complaint, referred to by De Barrios and De Castro. **Hobbes on Spinoza:** *below, page* 200. **'The whole of philosophy . . .'** Pref. to the French edition of Descartes's *Principles of Philosophy*. CSM 1 186.

92 **'Pantheism':** Meinsma 144–5, quoting the pupil Rixtel. **Van den Enden, God or nature,** mind-body connection, determinism: Klever 6 628–9, citing KVNN 69; also 78 VPS 4, 40–1. **Spinoza,** *God, or Nature (Deus sive Natura):* E4 Pref. Also TTP III: W 53. Ep.6, April 1662; CM 2 vii, C 327–8. *Dios de la naturaleza:* Gebhardt 1923 286–7; Révah 1 42; Yovel 75–6. **'Extension arising . . .'** Bk 1, 'The Immortality of the Soul', Axioms XVII and XIX: More 28. **Descartes's response to this:** Letter to More, 5 Feb. 1649: CSMK 364 and 362. **More on Cartesian danger:** Colie 1 150. **On Spinoza:** while reading the unbound *Theologico-Political Treatise:* Letter to Lady Conway at Ragley, 1677, quoted Colie 1 74.

93 **Van den Enden 'a proto-Spinoza':** Klever 6 631; Klever 8 26. **'Communicated in manuscript . . .':** Borch's diary: Klever 6 618 with n.25; Klever 3 25–6. **'All the secret writings . . .'** Klever 6 618, quoting the pamphlet *Koeckoecx-zangh*, 1670. *It only remains* . . . KV 2 xxvi: C 150. *Intellectual love of God: kennis, of liefde Godts* VPS 44: Menasseh: *Nishmat Hayyim*. Spinoza's thesis, *below, Ch. 12*. **Adriaan Koerbagh:** qualified as a physician with *Disputatio medica inauguralis de Phthisi,* Leiden, 1659 (Vandenbossche 1 and n.217) and as a lawyer 1661 (ibid. with n.4). **Buxtorf's Hebrew dictionary:** (1618, f1); **Thesaurus** (1629, 091 [12]). *Some of the Hebrews . . .* E2 P7 S. Silverman (1 113) objects that this is Aristotelian, not Jewish doctrine.

94 *I do not differentiate . . .* Ep.6, April 1662: S 84. **Leibniz's remark:** Letter to Volder, 21 Jan. 1704: Loemker II 869. **De Prado questioned by Inquisition:** Kaplan 1 160. See also ibid. 329. **'Condemned the accused** . . . Lucas 55–6. **'Rid of the importunate . . .':** ibid. 56. **Morteira's death:** PAA: De Castro Vol. II. **Menasseh's death:** Katz in Kaplan 4 163.

95 **Jelles's house:** Van der Tak 3 21. It cost fl. 12300. **'He was able . . .'** Colerus 34–5. Monnikhoff [mid 18c] 22 (FQ 105) also believed he lived at Ouderkerk. **Ribca widowed:** ibid. 53 No.38. **First two treatises:** the *Short Treatise* and the *Treatise on the Emendation of the Intellect:* C 50: see Ep.6, c. April 1662: S 83. **Spinoza's took walks:** Ep.8 from De Vries, Feb 1663. *Man is a part . . .* CM 2 ix, C 333; CM 2 xii, C 342.

96 **'Someone'** with whom he went to Rijnsburg: Monnikhoff 22, FQ 105. *Collegianten:* Barclay 89–92. **Meeting-house** (1646) in the Rokin, near the Kalversteeg: Wagenaar 11, 204. **Coenraad van Beuningen:** second only to De Witt: described by De Witt in 1665 as the most able of all Dutch diplomats: Rowen 1 243, 612. **Converted when young:** Geyl 2 219. **Spinoza's move to Rijnsburg:** Borch was told that 'an

impudent atheist [Cartesian] Jew' was in Amsterdam in May, 1661: Klever 3 23. He was living in Rijnsburg when Oldenburg visited him, Summer 1661. 'In order to be less...' JP 216. Collegiant centre: Barclay 89–91. 'Religious conversations...' Geyl 2 219. Van Beuningen mad: below, 259. Daubed house with blood (late 1680s): Gans 87.

CHAPTER 5

97   *The way of understanding*: E3 Pref.: C 492. *I have therefore...* TP 1 4: W 263. **Canal, sea of Haarlem** Brereton [1634] 12 and 52–3; Temple 2 [1672] 78; Postmuseum, The Hague. 'The boat rowled...' Brereton 48; also Aglionby [1669] 362–3. **Lakes drained**: Zumthor 3 14–316. *Trekschuit*: similar to the horse-drawn barge in *Plate* 2. Description of *trekschuit* travel: Brereton 52–3. **'Vulgarly known'**: Moryson [1605–17] 470. **Every farmhouse**: Temple 2 [1672] 77–8.

98   **Clogs and shoes**: Zumthor 63. **Paint**: Paint Museum, The Hague. **Climate**: Murris 24–34: Mundy [1634–9] 72: Temple 2 69, 80–1, 89. **Dogs**: Zumthor 28. **French found...** Murris 32. **Descartes**: Letter to Balzac 5 May, 1631: CSMK 31–2. **High winds**: Ep.32, to Oldenburg, Nov. 1665. **Hispanic Jews town dwellers**: Bernadete 164. **Green plants**: E4 P45 S. *They tell of a...* KV II, iii: C 100.

99   *The common order of nature*: E2 P29 Co. *When we look...* E2 P35 S. **'Although he took...'** Lucas 57. *Whom I recently...* E2 P47 S. *For example a soldier...* E2 P18 S. **Rijnsburg**: Museum Guide *Oud-Rijnsburg* 1–2. **Collegiant meeting-hall at the Moleneind**: ibid. 2.

100   **Assembly 'of the free-minded'**: Aglionby [1669] 343. **'Infallible... in our hearts'**: Kolakowski 89, 93, quoting Camphuysen's tracts. **Katwijkerlaan cottage and inscription**: 4 lines from *Maysche Morgenstondt* (May Morning) by Dirck Camphuysen: Monnikhoff [mid 18c] 23 (FQ 106). Information on the stone from the Vereniging het Spinozahuis. **All sects received...** Barclay 89–91. **'Free table'**: ibid. 89–91. **Spinoza sold microscopes**: Klever 8 23–4, quoting Borch's Diary. **Hooman a Collegiant**: a legend originating in Monnikhoff 22: *above, notes to 96*. **'Apostles'**: Van Deursen 213. **'Filth'**: Levin 112 (no source).

101   **'Sect of the prophets'... known as 'Quakers'**: Barclay 90–1. **Van Beuningen: rarely in Holland**: Roldanus 64–6 and 119: *Vroedschap* 11, 1177. **Works completed while at Rijnsburg**: *Short Treatise* and *Treatise on the Emendation of the Intellect* probably drafted in Latin in Ouderkerk, brought to Rijnsburg to revise, then sent to the Amsterdam group (C 50): *below 136, with notes*, and Ep.8, S 87–8. Were the two works bound as a single treatise? If so, Rieuwertz (*below page 303*) split them up. **'He devoted himself...'** Kortholt, Wolf 2 166. *My late-night studies...* Ep.9, to De Vries, March 1663: S 91. **Heart and gemoed**: Kolakowski 98. *I shall consider...* E3 Pref. **Painting resembling De Witt**: by Samuel van Hoogstraten, 1670. See the jacket of *The Cambridge Companion to Spinoza* (Garrett). Ekkart (p.133) does not think it depicts Spinoza. **Regent black**: Rowen 1 582. **'Somebody who had...'** Klever 8 23–4, quoting Borch's Diary.

102   *A society of...* TIE [14]: C11. **'Unauthorised person'**: Bunyan 10. **Quaker 'risings'**: Pepys 7 Jan. 1660, 26 Oct. 1662 and 10 Aug. 1663. **'This morning I...'** ibid. 11 Jan. 1664.

103   **'This day I began...'** ibid. 22 Jan. 1660. Pepys was The Clerk of the Acts: Hartley 52. **Shoe 'laces'**: Bunyan 10. **'Wide canons'**: Pepys 24 May 1660. **De Witt**: Act of Seclusion 1654: Rowen 1 Ch.11; Campbell xliii, citing Aitzema; Renier (p.124) cites documents K7552 and K7660. **A plain man**: Temple [1672] 70–1. **Awkward Dutch**:

337

above, notes to 36. 'Affect polished . . .' Lucas 71. **Spinoza wrote in Latin:** C 48–50. Ep.17, to Balling originally in Spanish? C 352. **Originally in Dutch:** Eps 18, 19, 20, 21, 22, 23, 24, 27 (to/from Blijenburgh); Eps 34, 35, 36 (to/from Hudde); Eps 38, 39 (to Van der Meer); 39, 40, 41, 44, 50 (to/from Jelles); Eps 51, 52, 53, 54, 55, 56 (to/from Boxel). **Spinoza's Latin** had a 'terse elegance and compares favourably, both stylistically and grammatically, with much of the Latin written by his contemporaries': C 162 citing Leopold. **Von Tschirnhaus's Latin:** Steenbakkers 47–9.

104 *Some men* . . . Ep.13, to Oldenburg, July 1663: S 111. **De Witt a fellow mathematician:** The 2nd edition of Descartes's *Geometry* (Amsterdam 1659–61) included *Johannes de Witt de elementis curvarum linearum libri duo*: TS 209. **Cartesianism taught:** Geyl 2 106–9. **Philosophy 'ridiculous . . .'** Blok (p.278) does not say which brother. **'Unphilosophical . . . political thinker':** Rowen 1 Ch. 20 'The Unphilosophical Cartesian', esp. 400. **Adrian Heereboord:** Ordinary Professor of Theology: *Metaphysics in Philosophy and Theology.* Leiden, 7 Feb. 1658. **Important statements:** 2 substances etc. KV 1 II n.e: C 70. **God = Nature:** KV 1, II 1 and n.a: ibid. 65; 17, 18 and n.e: ibid. 70); Apx 1 and 11.

105 **Classical aphorism,** etc: See Steenbakkers 176 n.1. **Mixture:** especially Part 2 Chs I–VIII. *All-in-All:* KV 1 ii, *What God Is:* C 68 and 69. **Abravanel** (Ebreo, Leon, Arbarbanel). Born in Lisbon 1443. Fled 1483 to Toledo, then Naples, after his father was involved in a conspiracy: Abravanel ix. See also Benardete 67–8. Spinoza owned *Dialogos de Amor* (Venice 1568, q46 [22]). **'All that exists . . .'** Abravanel 46. **'Union in knowledge . . . desire':** ibid. 45, 48, 49. **'Human blessedness . . . activities . . .'** ibid. 36–7. **Philo 'manly reason':** Lloyd, Genevieve, *The Man of Reason: 'Male' and 'Female' in Western Philosophy*, London and Minneapolis, 1993, 23–3. *What a Union! What a Love!* KV ii–XXII: C 139. Mature definition of *the intellectual love of God*: E5 P32 Co.

106 **'Eternal object'** of love: Abravanel 3 and *passim:* **Spinoza's endorsement:** KV II v: C105; TIE [9–10]: C9. **'love and wanting possession':** Abravanel 3. **Lust:** KV I ii: C 74–5. **Erasmus:** KV I ii: C Meyer's apex of precision TS 189; Steenbakkers 17–18. **'Physics and ethics can . . .'** Steenbakkers 146. **'The mind, which has . . . geometrical method':** Pref. to *Parts 1 and 11* of PPC 1663: C 225–6. **First geometrical proofs:** KV Apx.1; Ep.2, to Oldenburg: S 62 with n.6. **Geulincx:** Steenbakkers 171 with n.6. *I wondered whether . . .* TIE [3] and [7] (C9).

107 **Heereboord:** 'the foundation, object . . .': 'Modes of Inquiry and Expression' in his *Logical Praxis*, 1657, quoted by Collins, James, *Spinoza and Nature*, Southern Illinois University Press, 1984, 78. **'Stove-heated room':** Nov. 1619: *Discourse on the Method* Pt 11, CSM 1116: **'Reviewing occupations':** ibid. Pt 111, CSM 1124. **Narrative,** etc.: Jonathan Rée (*Philosophical Tales*, Methuen 1987 1 and 25) finds a precedent in Dante's 14c *Comedy. The correct Method . . . Just as men . . .* TIE [31]: C17. **Sense perception,** etc. TIE [19, 20, 26]. *Modes of perceiving:* TIE [19]: see KV 2, 1 and 2: C 98. *Make accurate . . . define problems:* TIE [80]: C 35. *Half an orange . . .* TIE [56]: C 25.

108 *How* the senses deceive . . . TIE [78]: C 34–5. **Descartes's 'divine light':** Meditation 4: CSM 41. **Intuition:** highest kind of *perception* in TIE and KV. *The things I have . . .* TIE [22]. **Reasoning from good definitions,** etc. TIE [91, 93, 94].

109 **'Besides his preoccupation . . .'** JP 216. *We require no tools . . .* TIE [42]: C 21. **In earliest works:** Single, unified epistemology: KV I, 1 and II; TIE [92] with n.f. Equivalence of God and nature: KV I, II 1 and note a: C65; ibid. 17, 18 and n.e, 70; KV I iii, 1 and 2; TIE [75] with n.56; TIE [13] and [85]. *An idea is called . . .* CM I vi: C 312. **Rationalism** (my definition: see philosophy dictionaries). Descartes, Spinoza and Leibniz are commonly labelled 'rationalist' philosophers. *A philosopher is supposed . . .* Ep.4. *c.* Oct. 1662: S 67. **Missing the point:** Bayle 301 n.*N*. **'Rebellious marrano philosopher',** etc.: Shmueli in Shahan and Biro, 213 and 208–9.

110 **'Circles':** see Kolakowski 74; Francès *passim.*; Lagrée 2; Wolf 2 18. **Holy hypocrites:** KVNN 32. Heereboord's *Metelemata* (1680) is quoted verbatim in CM 11 XII (C

345). See also Curley's suggestions of Heereboord's influence in KV: C 80, 82 and 88; and to CM: C 301, 302, 304, 306, 320, 334, 337, 340, 341 and 345. **Leiden medicine:** Ep.8, from De Vries, 24 Feb. 1663. **Descartes's protest 1647:** TS 212 and 232.

111 **Adriaan Koerbagh:** Vandenbossche 1, giving the 1661 thesis reference. **Visits:** Balling: see Ep.8, 24 Feb. 1663 S 90. Meyer: invited 20 April 1663: see Ep.12 S 107. De Vries: Ep.15, 3 Aug. 1663 (*PS*). **Johannes Casear:** enrolled for theology 21 May 1661: *Album Studiosorum 1575–1875*, Nijhoff, The Hague, 1875. **Kerckring on alchemy:** *Commentarium in Currum Triumphalem* (1661, d 129 [11]). '**Most excellent microscope . . .**' Kerckring *Observatio XCIII: above, notes to 76*. **Looking for cases:** ibid. *Observatio XII*. **Anatomical observations:** *above, notes to 76*. **Years later Spinoza questioned:** Ep.40, to Jelles, March 1667. *The more I think . . .* Ep.72, to Schuller, Nov. 1675: S 331. '**Natural Magick**': Webster 64. On Newton, ibid. 9, 11 and 64–5.

112 '**Unicorn's horn . . .**' *Commentarium in Currum Triumphalem* Bk 15. '**They that doubt . . .**' Sir Thomas Browne *Religio Medici*, quoted by Webster 89. **Boyle's proof of atheism:** ibid. 92–4. '**King's-Evil . . .**'; **Charles II:** Guthrie 210, quoting John Browne *Adenochoiradelogia, or King's-Evil Swellings* (1654) and citing Raymond Crawfurd, *The King's Evil* (Fitzpatrick Lectures) 1911. '**Hair of the hare**': Van Deursen 238. **Pepys's charms:** Pepys, New Year's Day, 1665. The **reductive or eliminative materialist** claims that only truths about the brain make sentences about the mental true, that folk psychology is a primitive theory that should be replaced by neurophysiology, and that we should therefore abandon talk of beliefs, desires, emotions and so on, and talk instead about states of the body.

113 *The Method of proceeding . . .* TIE 25–7 with n.i: C 16. *Based on the pure power . . .* TTP V: W 99. **Sylvius:** King 96, 94 and 97. **Experiments:** Eps 39 and 41 (1667, 1669) optics and water pressure. Descartes on water pressure, Letter to Morin 1638, CSMK 122. **Bacon's death:** as told by Hobbes: Aubrey 192–3.

114 **Henry Oldenburg:** Background (para.): Hartley 183–5, 194. **Coccejus** (Johannes Koch): portrait 84 in *Icones Leidenses*. **Related by marriage:** John Dury of Kent, English millenarist, was Boyle's uncle and became Oldenburg's father-in-law in 1668: DNB XLII 96; Richard Popkin, 'Spinoza and the Jews' De Deugd, 181 n. 46. **Boyle 'very tall' at 6:** Aubrey 124. **Charles II:** Hartley 42–3. '**Spending time . . .**': Pepys 1 Feb. 1664.

115 '**With such reluctance . . .**' Ep.1, Aug. 1661: S 59. *Diligently to foster . . . I shall try . . .* Ep.2, c. Sept. 1661: S 61. **Hendry** on address (Ep.32): OPG 4 176: OC II 599. **Henry did not understand:** Ep.3, Sept. 1661: *below 127*. *The errors of others . . .* Ep.2, Sept. 1661: S 62. **Bacon's principles:** ibid. **Bacon's 'forms':** Bacon *Novum Organum* xxxv. '**Laying down the law to nature . . .**' ibid. 340.

116 **Bacon . . . Royal Society:** Hartley 9. **Hooke:** ibid. 124, 137–41. *Micrographia,* '**Treatise on . . .**': Ep.25, April 1665: S 174–5. Hooke's *Micrographia* was not found in Spinoza's library. The books he owned on optics, besides Descartes's treatise, were Scheiner's *Astronomy and Refraction: above, notes to 88*, and Gregory's *Optics above, notes to 35*. '**Our Royal Society . . .**' Ep.14, July 1663: S 118. **Boyle:** '**Book on Nitre, Fluidity . . .**' Ep.6, April 1662. *By Chemical or other . . .* ibid. S 78–9.

117 *Other experiments . . . I don't know . . .* ibid. 76. **Spinoza's experiment on fluidity:** ibid. 183, with n.39. On Spinoza's understanding of Boyle's work, and the validity of his own alternative experiments, see Hall. *The Learned Mr Boyle . . . For my part*: Ep.13, July 1663: S 111. '**We regard it . . .**' Ep.3, Sept. 1661: S 65–6. *If it seems advisable . . .* Ep.13, July 1663: S 116. **Spinoza added nothing original to optical theory:** Gabbey 150.

118 '**Sold pretty dear**': Colerus 33. **Huygens's ocular lens:** Gabbey op. cit. 151; Gray 386; Huygens 91 on lens preparation. **Van Leeuwenhoek:** Guthrie 458–9. Spinoza and Van Leeuwenhoek seem not to have corresponded, or met. **Leibniz:** '**Monsieurs**

Swammerdam, Malpigi... *New System, and New Explanation of the New System*: Parkinson 118. Spinoza's 'mill for grinding': SR 111 and 115. He 'observed also...': Colerus 42. Probably no workbench: Van Suchtelen I 475–6. 'Glasses in poor...' Van Rooijen 115. Tubing, usually brass, used in microscopes: Twyman 33. *Lunettes d'approche*: telescopic spectacles or binoculars. *Treatise on the Rainbow...* burned: JP 118; Kortholt, Wolf 2 169. The book entitled *Algebraic Calculation of the Rainbow* formerly ascribed to Spinoza is not now believed to be his: Gabbey 154, giving sources for the scientific debate on this.

119 *Nature herself is God*: TTP I: Es 25. *Nothing happens...* TTP VI: ibid. 84. *It is nonsense...* Ep.12, to Meyer, 20 April 1663: S 103. *If there were different...* KV 1 II n.e, C 70. *Bodies are distinguished...* E2 P13 L1; E2 P13 L7 S. *In the examination of...* TTP VII: Ep 104. *It [the worm] could...* Ep.32, Nov. 1665: S 193, 194.

120 Underlying force not explained: It is held by philosophers of science that even for Newton *explanation* of force is in scientific terms absent: Harré, Rom. *The Philosophies of Science*. Oxford University Press (2nd edition) 1985, 64. Spinoza's physics: Spinoza's thesis of modes of extension as units of force might seem to make his physics compatible with the claims of modern physics to a single unified force disseminated throughout nature, and with a mathematical physics that posits physical things as configurations of energy (Bennett 91–2). Other commentaries on Spinoza's physics: Gabbey 155–70; Lachterman 102–3; Savan *passim*; Woolhouse 115–16. Von Tschirnhaus asked for a 'General Physics': *below, 287 and notes*. Theory of motion: *below 171 and notes; 288 and notes*. Hands through a microscope... Ep.54, to Boxel, Sept. 1674.

121 Causes of passions: *We maintain that...* KV II, II: C99. See James, S. 1999. Descartes: *Passions* 1, 27, CSM 1338–9. *Tend to our destruction...* KV II III: C100. *He who uses his...* KV II VII n.c: C 110. 'Unpleasant listlessness': *Passions* 2, 92 and 100, and 116–42. 'I am not one...' Letter to Pollot, mid-Jan. 1641, CSMK 167. Descartes's 6–7-year-old daughter Francine died 7 Sept. 1640, and his father 17 Oct. *Womanish tears* and *womanish compassion*: *above, notes to 14*. Shared feelings inadequate understanding: E4 PP34, 35; TTP XVI: W 129 ff.

122 *An affect that arises...* E5 P7 D. *Good sense... thought of as such*: Ep.17, July 1664: S 125. 'He had the command...' Colerus 40. 'Concupiscent... that is a passion': *Passions* 2, 81, 91. *As far as the corruptible...* KV II v: C 105.

123 Good and evil: E4 Defs.; E1 Apx; *below, 161–3*. 'Attraction comes...' *Passions* 2, 90. *After the enjoyment* TIE [4]: C 8. This echoes the classical *post coitum omne animal triste est* quoted by Van Deursen (302), used as a platitude in 1603 (ibid. 86). *[Solomon] did wrong...* TTP II: Es39.

124 *The desire... As for marriage...* E4 Apx XIX, XX. Memory... unconscious ideas: E2 P18 S; E3 P2 Si and ii: C 497–8. Suicide: E4 P20 S. *Laughter and joking... I recognise a great...* E4 P45 S.

125 Vowed not to mock: E3 Pref.: C4 92; TP 1 4: W 263. *Risus*: E2 P35 D; E3 Pref.; E4 P35 S to C2; E4 P44 S; Ep.21. One translator... *irrisione* ? E4 P50 S: C 574 n.26. Another translator assumes ... 'derision', Ep.21: S 153. 'He was never...' Colerus 40. 'Was so pleased...' ibid. 42. *Cheerfulness, which I...* E4 P44 S. *While preparing to go...* Ep.4, Oct. 1661: S 67. 'I very much regret...' Ep.5, Oct. 1661: S 70. *Thirdly, things...* Ep.4, *c.* Oct. 1661: S 68.

126 *As for your contention...* ibid. S 68–9. One substance doctrine: Aristotelian... Cartesian... Ep.3, Sept. 1661, C169. Two men two substances: in a different sense this was so for Descartes: *Principles* Pt 1, 51: CSM 1210. Principal attributes: ibid. 53. See Woolhouse 15–17, also for the concept of substance generally in Descartes, Spinoza and Leibniz. *By substance...* E1 D3.

127 Leiden influence: see Ep.8, from De Vries, Feb.1663: S 89. Geometrical method: Ep.2, Sept. 1661, S 62 n.6. 'I warmly approve...' Ep.3, Sept. 1661, S 64. Visits to

Amsterdam: Klever 8 24 re. 3 April 1662; Ep.6 on nitre, written after *I was delayed at Amsterdam for some time* after moving in April: S 110.

CHAPTER 6

128 *In the mind . . .* E2 P48. *Nor can any . . .* CM 1 iii: C 309. **De Witt's success since 1654:** Stoye 146; **'G',** for **Guillaume:** Haley 2 vi, 124. **Charles asked for a commission:** Campbell I xxxix–xli. **De Witt: secrecy:** Rowen 1 248–52. **The Prince:** ibid. 367–86. William's words to Burnet: *Burnet's History of his Own Times*, 1 364, quoted in Campbell lxxxii. **The French on William:** Blok 245, quoting *Voyages de Mons. de Moncuys* ii, 127.

129 **De Witt's input in** *The True Interest:* Chapters 29 and 30: Rowen 1 391–2; Petry 163 n.18. In 'Witt, de', (*Indication,* 1669) Chapters 5 and 6 of Part III: Wildenberg 19–20. **'The weakness of Holland . . .'** 'De Witt' 2 11 255–6. **Handwriting of De Witt:** Rowen 1 393 gives examples of De Witt's alterations and additions. **Angry rebuttals:** Blok 265; Rowen 1 394. **1669** *Indication,* or *Aanwysing der heilsame politike gronden en maximen van de republike van Holand en West-Vrieslamd:* Wildenberg 121. **Spinoza owned** *A Political Discourse,* Pieter van den Hove, Leyden 1662: (q35 [11]) and *Consideratien van staat, ofte Politike Weeg-schaal,* Jan van den Hove (90 [11]). Petry (163, n.15) argues that both were edited by Pieter from Jan's papers. Jan, a political theoretician, died in 1660: Wildenberg 50. **Van den Enden's pamphlets:** *above, 93 and notes.* Also Marc Bedjai's unpublished 1990 Ph.D. thesis, 'Métaphysique, éthique et politique dans l'oeuvre du docteur Franciscus van den Enden (1602–1674): contribution à l'étude des sources des écrits de B. de Spinoza'. Dactylographié, Université de Paris, I-Pantheon Sorbonne, summarised in *Studia Spinozana* 6 (1990): Klever 6 622–3 n.31. See also Klever 2 620–3; Klever 7; Klever 9 Ch.2 and Klever 8 24–5. **He had not previously . . .** *Korte Verthoonighe van het Recht by den Ridderschap etc.* Meininger 20–1; Klever 6 618, citing Motley 11 xv 214. **Taxes:** VPS Pref. and 27. **'Great distaste . . .'** 'De Witt' 1 2 491; see Pontalis 2 172, 192–3. **Constitution . . . 117 articles.** KVNN Letter D (Klever 6 622). The text indicates that *Deductienen* A–G were written Dec. 1661–May 1662. The longest, A, was dated 20 Dec. 1661.

130 **Fourth kind of republic:** Klever 6 620: papers found in French and Latin: De Nazelle Apx. 241. **The sole foundation . . .** VPS 9 and *passim.* **'The whole people, together':** VPS 6, 16. **'Government by the people . . .'** VPS 12. **'Equal liberty'** (*even-gelijke vryheit*): VPS 5 and *passim.* **Van den Hove's exclusions:** Kerkhoven 6, citing *Politike Weeg-schaal* (*above, notes to 129*). **Resentment of regents:** VPS Pref.30–1. **Pasted note: 'It is especially . . .'** This unsigned comment matches Müller's in 1872: Mertens 724 n.39. **'I therefore understand . . .'** VPS 146–7.

131 *De Cive* **attacked in almost . . .** Wilson 176 n.135, with examples. *Leviathan* (1651) was translated into Dutch in 1667 and Latin (in Amsterdam) in 1668. **'A warre of all . . .'** *De Cive* Pref. [14]: Hobbes 134. **Two most certain maxims:** ibid. Epistle Dedicatory: 27. **Contracted only through fear:** ibid. 11 xvi: 58, and Ch. VI *passim.* **Forbade slavery:** KVNN 26. **Mores of the natives:** Klever 6 623–6, citing KVNN 18–23. **'Our time-honoured . . . important things':** VPS 21. **Rousseau's praise of early man:** Rousseau 1 *passim.* **Education:** *Émile,* Rousseau 2, Vols 8 and 9. **Educated . . . responsible adult:** Klever 9 35; VPS 17, 19. **'Common peoples' children' included:** VPS 35. **Leibniz's visit:** *Theodicy* Paragraph 376. Leibniz refers to Van den Enden as 'Affinibus'. He was called 'Master Affinius' in Amsterdam: De Nazelle (intr.) xiii. **Marianna** (b.1651): De Nazelle 118–9 and *passim.*

132 **Including females:** Klever 6 624 (See KVNN 55, 78–80 and VPS 36). **'M.V.Z.H':** Each petition ended *Was ondertekent* M.V.Z.H.: also Pref. to VPS and end of text. *Above all it is . . .* TIE [99]: *above, notes to 78. Wanen, gelooven* en *klare kennisse:*

341

VPS 238; compare KV 2 ii 'On What Opinion, Belief and Clear Knowledge Are': C 98–9. **TIE unfinished:** JP 250. **'Has much in connection . . .':** *above, notes to 131. Man is a part* . . . KV 2 XVIII: C 128; see esp. KV 2 Chs.XVII and XVIII: C 126–9, with n.2 on *Godsdienst.*

133 **'Equal liberty':** Kerkhoven 13: **'Pedagogical . . . temperamental':** Mertens 724, 738. **Disagreements** between Van den Enden and Spinoza: Mertens (p.724 and *passim*) opposes Klever's view that Van den Enden was a strong influence. *Society of the kind:* TIE [14]. **Powers of individual natures:** TTP XVI: W 125–9; Ep.50, to Jelles, June 1674. **Not equal:** E4 P54 S and P66 S; E5 P10 S: C 602; but see E4 Pref.: C 546; TTP XVI, opening paras.; *For by the laws* . . . ibid. W 129. **Van den Enden:** intense passions, etc. VPS 2. *The basis and aim:* ibid. 135. *De Cive (Elementa Philosophica)* Paris 1647 (d127 [9]). **1662 curb on Van den Enden:** Klever 3 319.

134 *The multitude* . . . TTP Pref: Es 11. *To deduce points* . . . TTP V: W 101. **Threat to Van den Hove:** Aug. 1662: Rowen 1 394. **'Sect-inclined' predicants** . . . KVNN 28; **Institutions:** VPS 28ff. **'Bitter . . . blackbook':** Klever 9 32–3. *Medea* . . . daughters Adriana Clementina (15) and Marianna (13): Meininger 30. **Plockhoy's 'First Co-operative Commonwealth':** Plockhoy (ed. Downie) 18, 20.

135 *Short work* . . . *I am naturally* . . . Ep.6, *c.* April 1662: S 83. *As you are* . . . KV 2 XXVI: C 150. *That petty man* . . . Ep.15, to Meyer, Aug. 1663: S 121. *I should like everyone* . . . ibid.: S 122. *The advantage of all:* **political aristocracy:** TP VIII 1–20. **Voting rights:** TP XI, 3: W 441–3.

136 **Reply on nitre:** Ep.6, *c.* April 1662. **'There are here atheists . . .'** Borch's Diary, 3 April 1662: Klever 724. *I have written* . . . Ep.6, *c.* April 1662: S 83. *Short Treatise* **abandoned:** It is said to have been rejected by Rieuwertsz as an unsatisfactory first draft of *Ethics.* The Dutch draft we now read, which may approximate to an early version, was not discovered until the 19c: Curley 46–50; Steenbakkers 125. First published 1899 in Meijer's *Werken: Catalogus* 2, 34. **'Previously written . . .':** KV Introductory Note: C 59. *Perhaps as a result* . . . Ep.13, to Oldenburg, July 1663: S 111. **'Had communicated . . .'** . . . **God or nature:** *notes to 92.* **Memory . . . rhetoric:** De Nazelle 97, 99, 100, 103.

137 **Meyer:** Ep.12A, Spinoza's point 2, July 1663. **'Prepossessed':** Lucas 57, 58. **Glazemaker's** *Alle de Werken:* TS192 with n.29. **'Naïve and primitive':** Akkerman, BW 18. **'Chatter and babble'** Pref. PPC: C 227. **Meyer's distraction:** ibid. C 228.

138 **'Excelled in the Cartesian . . .'** Klever 3 24. **First study group query:** Ep.8, Feb. 1663. **Ancient overnight bag:** SR 114. *Direct his life* . . . TIE [4] (C8). **Half-frozen canals:** Temple, Letter to Arlington, Dec. 1667: Haley 2 158, quoting State Papers. **Study group:** Letter 8 op.cit. **'Had no fear . . . little he had':** Lucas 64. **'It is scarcely credible . . .'** Colerus 36–7. **Ribca . . . estate:** VD/VT 171 (GAA, Supreme council in Holland, 7 May 1677); Colerus 100–1.

139 **Assisted passage:** no record of this. **'Simon de Vries of . . .'** Colerus 42–3; K 33. **'On the pretence'** – *voorgevende.* **Country landlord:** Voorburg is implied, since when Spinoza lived in The Hague, Simon was dead (d. 1667). **'To lay up no . . .'** Colerus 38. **'That Maxim of . . .'** Colerus 7.

140 **Casearius at Rijnsburg:** Eps. 8, 9, Feb., March 1663. **House gowns:** Zumthor 46, 58; Colerus 39. *Ledikant:* in Spinoza's room in The Hague: Colerus 101; SR 111, 113. **Casearius's signature:** DTB 17 June 1667. **Zeno's paradox:** an argument not found in any ancient source on Zeno is in PPC P6 S: C 270–1 with n.27. *Conserve of red roses:* Ep.28, June 1665. **'The conserve . . .'** Culpeper 139.

141 **'I have begun . . .'** Ep.8, Feb. 1663: S 90. **'As for our group . . .'** ibid. S 88. **'O fortunatum . . . sleeping near her . . .'** Sargeaunt 270–1. **'Fortunate, yes, most fortunate . . .'** Ep.8, op.cit. S 87. The Latin nowhere exactly matches Terence's. **Casuarius:** S 87 with n.44.

142 *My worthy friend* . . . *(Amice Colende)* Ep.9, *c.* March 1663: S 91; *vobis* – you (plural)

342

OPG 4 42. **No signed endings:** ibid. 95, 95. **'Show no respect...'** Feuer 55, 273 n.51, quoting a pamphlet of 1697 written by the physician J. Rodenpoort. **Homosexual claim:** Portnoy 122, 125. **'The abominable sin...'** Amsterdam... The Hague: Schama 601–2; also 475, 478, 601–6, with cartoons.

143 **'Unnatural':** ibid. 603, quoting Boon, L.J. 'Utrechtenaren: de sodomie-processen in Utrecht, 1730–32', *Spiegel Historiael* (Nov. 1982). **Calvinist theology:** Van Deursen 97. **'Moral':** ibid. 302; **Pregnancy, etc.:** ibid. 91–2. **De Witt:** Rowen I 102, quoting letters written in Feb. 1655. *There is no reason...* Ep.9, c. March 1663: S 91. *Which I had previously...* Ep.13, July 1663: S 110.

144 **Before Pts I and II:** C 222. *Having thus set out:* PPC III, Foreword: C 294–5. **'I shall even... so far from...'** Adam and Eve... *Principles* 3, 45: CSM I 256. *We only ascribe...* PPC III, Foreword: C 295. **'Our Author ended...'** Pref. PPC: C 228. **'Took care in...'** Colerus 3–4. **Jan to Utrecht:** Meinsma 184, citing the relevant *Studentenalbum*; Heniger 41. **Voetius: 'pernicious...'** Baillet 138; see Descartes's open letter to Voetius of May 1643: CSMK 220–4. *[In Amsterdam] some...* Ep.13, July 1663: S 110.

145 **'Obliged not to depart...':** 'opinion' – *sententia*. Pref. PPC: C 229. **Hudde:** Rowen I 417–18. See for example Letter 49 in Hudde's Brieven en Papieren (GAA). **Spinoza-Hudde correspondence:** Eps 34–6, 1666. **'More useful':** Blok 280. **De Witt's** *The Worth of Life Annuities compared to Redemption Bonds...* **More precise:** Rowen I 418. *I understand...* Ep.36, c. June 1666: S 206. *I understand that...* Ep.36, c. June 1666. **Witsen:** burgomaster 1653, 1658, 1662, 1667 and then Bailiff (head of police): NNBW 4 1471. Hudde's mother Maria was his first cousin: *Vroedschap* I Table 11.

146 *Since this is a...* Ep.12A, July 1663: S 108. **'The best and surest...':** Pref. PPC: C 224–5. *Most earnestly,* etc. Ep.15, to Meyer, Aug. 1663: S 121, 122. **'Atheists and...':** *above, 136.* **'I do not see...'** Letter to Mersenne, Oct. 1640, CSMK 155. **Transubstantiation:** Redondi Ch.9. **'The things done...'** Ep.67, Sept. 1675: S 305–6. **Pascal...** **'Would have liked...'** Pascal 640.

147 **'Rejects as false...'** Pref. PPC: C 229. **'The human Mind...'** ibid. **'Every thing in which...'** 2nd Set of Replies to *Meditations*, Defs.: CSM 2 114. **Minds 'created' substances:** *above, 126. A created thing...* CM Part II, X: C 334, cf. Aquinas, *Summa Theologica* Ia 45, I. *The builder is forced...* CM 2 VII: C 327–8. *Whenever people say...* ibid. 2 III: C 320. **Irreverent:** CM 2 III and 2 VII: ibid. 320, 327–8. *Perfectus: realitas sive perfectio:* E2 P1 S. *Since God's nature...* Ep.36 c. June 1666: S 208.

148 **Minds and bodies parts of God:** KV Pref. to Pt 2: C 94. **'Just as the human...'** Pref. PPC: C 229–30. *Hence, we also...* CM 2 XII: C 342. **'We must not fail...':** Pref. PPC C 230. **'Thrown us into total...'** Orcibal, Jean, quoting the theologian Nicole, in Dijksterhuis 97. **God not prior or certain:** Second Set of Objections to *Meditations*, by Mersenne, CSM 2 89. See Spinoza's caustic comment concluding PPC Pt 1.

149 **Huygens on Descartes:** TS 237, quoting notes made by Huygens on a desk calendar aged 15 or 16. **God's existence:** Huygens to Leibniz, July 1692: HO X 302. *Even though...* PPC Pt 1: C 237–8. **'Personalitas':** *below, 177. I believe that...* Ep.56, to Boxel, Oct. 1674: S 277. *By the guidance of God...* TTP III: W 53–5. **18c rumour:** McShea 38, citing Deborin, Alexander, 'Spinoza's World View' 102, In Kline George L. (Ed.) *Spinoza in Soviet Philosophy.* Routledge 1952. *The time of my moving...* Ep.12, 20 April 1663: S 107. *Keep silent rather...* Ep.13, July 1663: S 111.

150 **'Away with all fear...'** Ep.7, July 1662: S 86 G. *Odium theologicum:* Blok 278; Schama 172. **'I have not read...'** Arnauld, Letter 385, Nov. 1691: Lewis 177. *On condition that...* Ep.13, July 1663: S 110. **Cold, wet summer:** Gutmann 217. *Right from the...* Ep.13, to Oldenburg, July 1663: S 111. See Lucas 58–9. *Our friend...* Ep.15, 3 Aug. 1663 *(PS)*: S 122. *I composed it...* ibid. 121.

151 *The first and most...* Ep.2, Sept. 1661: S 62. **Defended Descartes:** Ep. 6 (C 175, 178,

343

182) and 13 (ibid. 210), both to Oldenburg. **Three letters to Meyer:** Ep. 12 (20 April 1663), 12A (26 July) and 15 (3 Aug.). **Title page PPC:** C 224. **Send Balling:** Steenbakkers 28, citing Akkerman 1980 171–2.

152 **Plague:** Biraben 129; Bell 51, 85, 178, 184, 246, 248. **Hebrew images:** ibid. 248, quoting 1 Samuel: 6. **'Tokens':** ibid. 127–8. **Visitation sites:** Biraben 420. **Comet . . . lindens to die:** Schama 147, citing *Afbeeldinge en Beschrijving van de drie aenmerckenswaerding wonderen in des Jaar 1664.* **'The plague has passed . . .'** Van Deursen 48, quoting Huygens, *Gedichten* 11, 107. *As for the omens . . .* Ep.17, July 1664.: S 125. *None of the effects . . .* ibid. 126. **'Child of Pieter Balling':** DTB KKH 2674. **Ballingh . . . living on . . . boat-cover:** DTB 1155/258.

CHAPTER 7

154 *The nature and efficacy . . .* TTP VII: Es 113. *The light of nature . . .* ibid. 114. *The idea that constitutes . . .* E2 P15. *Daniel Tydeman, painter:* Post-script to Letter 19: S 136. **Five years:** Monnikhoff [mid-18c] 24 (FQ 106): *below, notes to 24.* **The mail service:** PTT (Post Office) Museum, The Hague; Overvoorde *passim*; The Hague ibid. 370–80. *I wrote this . . .* Ep.32, Nov. 1665: S 196.

155 **'Lives in the country . . .'** Pref. PPC: C 227. *Still, my anxiety . . .* Ep.17, July 1664: S 125, 127. **Titles to Parts of *Ethics*:** Steenbakkers 30.

156 **'It is not wrong . . .'** Bayle 295. **'Very wicked author . . .'** Lewis, quoting 'Un Inédit de Du Vaucel': TS 120. **'Spinozism, which is . . .'** *Theodicy* 393. **'Certain friends . . .'** Stenonis, Nicolai, Letter quoted in Klever 3 27. **'The Reformer . . .'** Ep.67A, from Steno: S 313, 318; Sept. 1675 in S: 1671 in *Epistolae Stenonis*. Mentioned by Leibniz in his Letter to Gallois: *see below, 288.* **De Raey:** *below notes to 128.* **'Began to become famous':** De Raey, Letters 1687 and 1692: Klever 4 361. **'Spinoza's philosophy consists . . .'** *The Fourfold Root of the Principle of Sufficient Reason, c.* 1800, quoted in Curley 2, 154. **Some commentators:** Siebrand (216) thinks only Jelles, Balling and Meyer were Spinozists. I believe none of these accepted Spinoza's doctrine. *I have not thought . . .* Ep.21, Jan. 1665: S 158.

157 **Bouwmeester's poem:** *Ad Librum:* Steenbakkers 17. *I don't know whether . . .* Ep.28, June 1665: S 179. This letter was omitted from the *Opera Posthuma*: written on its back was 'Has no value': Steenbakkers 40. **Descartes to Mersenne:** Nov. 1640, CSMK 156: PTT Museum, The Hague: Overvoorde 80. *If you fear that . . .* Ep.28, June 1665: S 179. *I have previously . . .* ibid. Bouwmeester's *Improvement of Human Reason:* 1672, published by Rieuwertz: BW 47.

158 *We can make sure . . .* Ep.37, June 1666 (S 211), reiterating Bouwmeester's words. **'Thoughts are governed . . .'** ibid. *Clear and distinct perceptions:* ibid. See E1 P33 S. *Depend in the highest:* Ep.37: S 212. **No true accidents:** *above* CM2 XII: C 346; E2 P29. *Constant . . . distinguish:* Ep.37: S 212. **No more letters or translation:** Steenbakkers 17, but *see below, 302.* **With regard to the third . . .** Ep.28, June 1665: S 180. **Simon's contacts:** Ep.15, 3 Aug. 1663 (*PS*); **Plague May–June 1664:** Vaz Dias 2 7–8, citing burial records. **Herberg De Swaen:** now the Huize Swaenstein.

159 *Each thing, as far as it can:* E3 P6. Spinoza used this concept differently from the scholastics or Descartes: see PPC 2 P14. *I say that . . .* E3 Def. 2. **Van Limborch:** Meinsma 309 n.27. **Hudde-Locke debate:** Klever 5 328–55.

160 **'Above all . . .'** Ep.18, Dec. 1664: OPG 4 81. **Van Blijenbergh learned Latin:** Ep.20: OPG 4 125; S 150; NNBW 4 170. *I really wish . . .* Ep.19, Jan. 1665: OPG 4 95. **'Who is driven . . .'** Ep.18, Dec. 1664: ibid. 80. **'The Esteemed B.D.S':** ibid. 79: S 128. **Changed his name:** NNBW 4 170.

161 **'It follows then . . .'** Ep.18, Dec. 1664: OPG 4 83. *Very learned and . . .* Ep.19, Jan.

1665: OPG 4 86. *For myself, I cannot...* ibid. 88. *We know that...* ibid. 88–9. **Real demons:** Webster 89–94 on studies undertaken, or recommended by the Royal Society. **Spinoza on devils:** KV II XXV; Letter 76: S 341, 344. **Descartes's 'malicious demon':** *Meditations* 1: CSM 215. **Hedge garlic:** copy of William III's garden, Het Loo, Holland. **Cruelty hate/sadness:** E3 P41 S: see also E3 P64 D. **idea of a body...** see TTP XVI: W 127 ff. **'Not all possibles...'** 'Two notations for discussion with Spinoza': Loemker 1 262.

162 **'I have two general...'** Ep. 20, Jan. 1665: OPG 4 96–7. *D1. By good... D2. By evil...* E4 Defs. *Universal notion:* E2 40 S1: *common notions:* ibid. S2. *Because we compare...* E4 Pref.

163 **Carnal affection:** Ep.20, Jan. 1665: OPG 108. *When I read your first...* Ep.21, Jan. 1665: S 151. *If you had read ... a little thought...* ibid. S 152, 156. **At Schiedam:** Ep.19: OPG 4 86, 95.

164 *In a mathematical way:* Ep.21: S 158. *I considered you...* Ep.23, March 1665: OPG 4 146. *Each one must have...* TTP XVI: W 129. (*ne mente carere Videatur.*) *Clear and distinct only to...* E2 P40 S1. **In full consciousness:** *below 291–2.* See also Wernham's n.3 to TTP XVI: W 129. **'Since your letter...'** (Para.) Ep.22, March 1665: OPG 4 134–5. **Excuse me if...** ibid. 136.

165 **'Certainly those who stay'...** ibid. 141. **Discrete substances:** *above, 126.* **God is not composed...** CM 2 v: C 324. See also CM 2 ix: C 333. **One Substance thesis in** *Short Treatise:* KV 1, 2, and 2 Pref: in *Ethics:* Part I PP 1–13. **'I must be in Leiden... In my all-too great...'** Ep.22, March 1665: OPG 4 143–4. *I only repeated* Ep.23, March 1665: ibid. 145–6. *I shall now turn...* ibid.146. *Furthermore... Therefore...* ibid. 177–8. *And here I think...* ibid. 149.

166 *For now I say...* Ep.23, March 1665: OPG 4 152. **Six weeks:** Ep. 19, first sentence and PS. *My Ethics...* ibid. 151. **'The said Daniel Tydeman':** quoted FQ 118–19. **Lantman... De Landman:** HGA Alg. W.M.C. Regt. *Naamlist van Hervormde predikanten in Zuid-Holland,* Deel I, Classis Gravenshage 1/19–21; Deel III, Classis Leiden 21, 283, 6/570 to; Lexicon Biografische 3, 813. **Fiery Calvinist:** *below, notes to 260. Excessive authority...* Ep.30, Sept/Oct. 1665. **Regent black:** Rowen 1 582.

167 **'Under your guidance...'** Ep.8, Feb. 1663: S 88. **'Philosophers indeed...'** Calvin II.ii.2. **'But Augustine...** ibid. II.i.4. *Those whose philosophy...* TTP Pref.: Es 11. **Suárez:** 'Our philosophy must be Christian and the handmaiden of Divine Theology': *Metaphysicarum Disputationem* (1597), quoted Redondi 120. **'When I had the honour...'** Ep.24, March 1665: OPG 4 153. **Verbally, friendliest way:** Ep.27, June 1665: OPG 4 160.

168 **A great part of** *Ethics:* ibid. *I hope that when...* ibid. 161–2. **'Introduce a political religion':** Margin note in Van Blijenbergh's *De Waerheyt van de Christelijcke Godts-Dienst* etc (1674), quoted Klever, 'Spinoza interviewed by Van Blyenbergh', *Studia Spinozana* (4) 1988 318–19. **Blood-letting, diet.** Ep.28, June 1665: S 180.

169 *Vacillation of mind...* CM 1 iii: C 309. **'I believe that nothing...'** Ep.11, April 1663: S 99. **Letter on visit to Huygens:** *below, notes to this page.* **De Witt:** 200 'francs': Lucas 61. **Mathematics/ 'important matters':** Lucas first French edition: FQ 15. **Workload:** Rowen 1 506 and 660, quoting De Witt's letters. **D'Estrades's opinion of Van Beuningen:** Rowen 1 486–7. **Visions and prophecies:** *below, 259.* **Sent back to Paris** by resolution of 17 May, 1667: ibid. 655.

170 **'And there is nothing...'** Letter to De Witt, May 20, 1667: ibid. 656–7. **'Outbursts and threats':** ibid. 704, quoting Lionne. **French respect:** ibid. 244. **Dutch ambassador sent to France:** Ep.32, Nov. 1665. **Contempt for Van Beuningen's religious beliefs... eccentricity, spiritual instability:** *below, 259.* **Dispute:** Rowen 1 162. **Hofwijk:** Constantijn Huygens bought land for his 'Hofwijk' ('court-escape') in 1636. He also had a house in The Hague and an estate at Zeelhem (Züylichem):

Hofwijk Guide. **Hunting lodges:** for example, at Het Loo. **Huygens's appearance:** Plaquette by Jean-Jacques Clérion, reproduced in *Icones Leidenses* 100. **'A Crafts-man'** . . . Descartes to Mersenne, 5 April 1632, CSMK 36. **Ground lenses . . . rings of Saturn** Clark G.L. 445–6.

171 *He has told me* . . . Letter 26, May 1665: S 175. *I have seen* . . . Oldenburg to Moray, 7 Oct. 1665: OC II 549; Ep.30A, Sept/Oct. 1665: BW 224. *As to what you* . . . Ep.32, Nov. 1665: S 195. **Descartes's Rules:** above, notes to 77. On Spinoza's response to Descartes's theory of motion, and Huygens's *De motu corporum ex percussione* (1656, published 1703), Gabbey (167) considers Spinoza had 'an apparent disinclination or inability to disentangle and clarify a fundamental difficulty in Descartes's doctrine of motion' and that 'it is possible that Spinoza simply could not reconcile Huygens's empirically respectable collision theory with Descartes's, which he seems to have accepted (apart from Rule 6) to the end of his life' (Gabbey 188 n.55). **'Conjectures and fictions':** see *above, notes to 149. I don't yet know* . . . Ep.32, Nov. 1665: S 195–6. *Neri, Ars vitaria* (*above, notes to 89*) contains illustrations of handworking instruments only. **'When work of high class** . . .' Twyman 34. **Huygens's return:** Blok 281.

172 **'Jew':** HO VI, Letters of 14 Oct., 4 Nov. and 2 Dec. 1667. **'Israelite':** ibid. 9 Dec. 1667, 6 April and 11 May 1668. **Boyle's and Hooke's books in English:** Ep.26, to Oldenburg, May 1665. **Made brother responsible:** HO VI, Letters of 9 Dec. 1667 and 11 May 1668. **Resentment of Huygens's francophilia:** Geyl 2 228–9, and 195 on the 'Gallicisation of the Nobility' of the Dutch republic. **'It is true that** . . .' HO IV 11 May 1668. **Consulted by De Witt:** Huygens checked De Witt's *Elementa Curvarum Linearum* (*above, notes to 104*) at De Witt's request: Rowen 1413. On co-operation over applied physics, see *below, 175 and 245*. **Marine chronometer:** OC II, 1665; see n.4 to a letter of Sept. 1665, ibid. 500. **Huygens met Oldenburg** summer 1661: OC I xxxix. **Lost his address:** Letter 477, Moray to Oldenburg, enclosing a message, Dec. 1665: OC II 658. **'About the middle** . . .' Letter 409, 9 Sept. 1665: ibid. 505. This address was given to Huygens in a letter of 9 Sept. 1665: ibid. 505. Hall thinks this was Oldenburg's first letter to him since 1661: ibid. 449. **Secretary's description** . . . Moray to Oldenburg, Dec. 1665: ibid. 658. Letter from Helvelius, 22 May 1665: ibid. 396; Oldenburg to Huygens/Huygens to Oldenburg, Sept. 1665: ibid. 503 and 505. **Brusque messages:** e.g. via Moray, Letter 477, *above, this page*.

173 **Plague never reached Paris:** Biraben 420–1. **Decimated the Vloyenburg:** Kaplan 2 156. **Fled to Weyke:** letters from Iberian Jews only: ibid. 155. **'Sr Bento Gabriel de Espinosa . . . bills of exchange':** VD/VT 185, 189, quoting NA 2217. **Navigation Act** 1651, renewed in 1660 and 1663. **Plantations:** VD/VT 186, citing PRO Colonial Papers Vol.23, 99 & 98; Calendar of British State Papers, Colonial. 1669–74, nr 570, 234, and Friedenwald (p.71, No.5). **Ships for Amsterdam Jews:** VD/VT 186: Friedenwald, citing the above PRO documents; Israel 3 391. **Ribca emigrated between** 1679 and 1685: Emmanuel (194–5) reproduces the Hebrew inscription on her Curaçao gravestone. **Jews Dutch subjects 1657:** Bloom xvii. **Legal loophole,** etc. Baron 73 with n.84. **Amsterdam** *parnas: Register van namen van personen die een functie bekleed hebben bij de gemeente of éen van haar instellingen [1639–1939]*, 1755: PAA 334/157.

174 **2nd Anglo-Dutch naval war** 1665–7. **5 years of trading rivalry . . . looking for excuses:** 'De Witt' 2 9 238 and 244; Hill 142; Haley 2 37; Pepys 15 Feb. 1664. **Plague:** Bell 4. **'With all men** . . .' Pepys 23 Sept. 1664. **Amsterdam:** Haley 3 92; Blok 205. **'The most terrible** . . .' Wilson 213, quoting A. van der Donck. *I hear much about* . . . Ep.28, June 1665: S 180. **First plague for 20 years:** Bell 24. **Oldenburg's fear:** Oldenburg to Moray, 16 Sept. 1665: OC II 506. **Charles II:** Guthrie 208; Bell 16. **Quakers:** Bell 151, 182, citing C. Evans, *Friends in the Seventeenth Century*, 364, and

Beck and Ball, *The London Friends' Meetings*, 330. Will Caton, who had married a Dutch woman, died in the Amsterdam plague (1665): Fox 1 421.

175 **1665 bad for Dutch:** Blok 321; Haley 3 113; Geyl 2 89. **Recruiting sailors:** Rowen 1 576–7. **Workless poor:** Van Deursen 21. **Obdam** (Jacob van Wassenaer)... **Cannons heard:** Rowen 1 578–9, 589. **'Bold face'**... **Tromp's son:** ibid. 579–80. **'Witt's Diep'** episode; Campbell l-li; Rowen 1 581–2. **Huygens's hammock:** HO V 12 Aug. 1665. **Van den Enden's inventions:** 3 letters supplied by N. Japikse in *Chronicon Spinozanum* Vol.1. 1921, 113–17: Meininger, 44–58, with facsimiles 165–8. *Zeven Provinciën:* Richard Hough, *Man o'War: The Fighting Ship in History* 28–40, with illustrations; Rowen 1 586, 818. **An expert in naval warfare:** Campbell l; Rowen 1 583–6ff. **'As if with a finger':** ibid. 585, quoting De Witt's letter of Nov. 1665. **'The Dutch Fleet have...'** Oldenburg to Moray, 28 Sept. 1665.

176 *Serrarius:* See Ep.31, from Oldenburg, 12 Oct. 1665. Ep. 25 and Eps 28 to 33 exchanged April–Dec. 1665. **'Kircher's** *Subterranean...'* Ep.29, Sept. 1665: S 182. **'I believe... Some of our...'** Ep.31, 12 Oct. 1665: S 191. *There appears... The Dutch... The* Ep.32, Nov. 1665: S 196. **'The courage which...'** Ep.29, Sept. 1665: S 183 replying to 'your last letter, written to me on the 4th of Sept', now missing. *Philosophising ... human nature:* Ep.30, Autumn 1665. **Montaigne,** *The Art of Conversation,* referring to Hegesias in Diogenes Laertius, *Life of Aristippus:* Screech 1062. Montaigne's mother, Antonia López came from a *converso* family from Aragon: Benardete 50 n.12. See E3 Pref.: C 492; TP 1 4. **Translation of** *Ethics* **Pts 1 and 2:** by Balling: Akkerman 226.

177 *Inadequate and confused...* E2 P36. **'Personality':** *What theologians mean...* Ep.12 A, to Meyer, 26 July 1663: S 109. On this recently discovered letter (1974), see Offenberg. *The eternal part...* E5 P40 Co. **'For [Spinoza], the soul...'** De Careil 1140.

178 *The knowledge, Idea etc.:* KV Pref. to Pt 2: C 95. *In God [or Nature]...* E2 P3 and D. *The object of the idea...* E2 P13. **De Raey, 1654:** Dunin Borkowski 2 157, and TS 221–2. *The order and connection of ideas...* E2 P7. **Geulincx:** EP 3 323; Geyl 2 224: Meinsma 348 n.41. **'Occasionalism'** to the students of Sylvius and Bontekoe: TS 254 n.256. **'Occasional causes':** Malebranche Bk 6 Pt 2 Ch.3 448.

179 *The essence of the soul...* KV Apx 11 9. **Spinoza a materialist:** See e.g. *'Philopater' passim;* Clarke (1704) 27; Colliber (1734) Essay V 160 and Yolton, J. *Thinking Matter: Materialism in Eighteenth-Century Britain.* University of Minnesota Press, 1983, 4 16 45. **'For the universe...'** *Leviathan* 3, 34: Macpherson 428. **'It is still a matter...'** Ep.3, 27 Sept. 1661: S 64. *This one thing...* Ep.4, Oct. 1661: S 68. *Related to God's Nature...* E1 P32 C2. **Double 'aspect' theory:** Vesey 146 ff. *The thinking substance...* E2 P7 S. **Force in extension:** *above, 120. The power of the mind...* E2 P43 S: *The body cannot...* E3 P2. **Women deprived, etc.** TP XI 4: W 443–5.

180 *I shall send...* Ep.28, June 1665: S 180. **Original Part 3:** Steenbakkers 124; S 180 n.138. *We are driven...* E3 P59 S. See E4 PP 5, 6. **Withering comments:** *above, notes to 14; below, 272ff. There are certain ideas...* E2 P38 Co. *In the previous Chapter...* TTP V: W 89. *deduximus* = we deduced, rather than W's 'I derived'.

181 *Divine law* = happiness/blessedness/virtue: E2 P49 SIV A: Virtue/advantage: E4 P18 S: Power/virtue/advantage: E4 P20: Reason *or* cause: E1 P11 D; God *or* the power of Nature: E4 P4. **Tyrannical and vaporous uterus:** Berriot-Salvadore 349–51, 359, 362; Smith *passim.* **'Very far from...'** De la Barre 76, 78. **'A woman cannot learn...'** ibid. 113–14.

182 **'And there can be...'** ibid. 124 and 128. *I am fully entitled...'* TP XI 4: W 445. *The right and law of nature...* TTP XVI W 125 ff. **Amazons:** *Leviathan* XX, Macpherson 254. TP XI 4: W 443. **Had Spinoza by this time** (*c.* 1676) **read** *Leviathan?: above, notes to 131.* **Women's physiology: Aristotle and Galen:** Berriot-Salvadore

347

349–59; 'By nature': Crampe-Casnabet 325; Smith 100–7. Cold, damp field . . . Berriot-Salvadore 352 and 384. Womb caused most diseases: ibid. 360–1, citing 17c physicians Guibert and Mauriceau. Gullible, sensuous, etc.: ibid. 354; Smith 104. Ugly, etc. Berriot-Salvadore 354–5. Witchcraft: Homza 51. Dutch stopped executions: Van Deursen 252.

183 'The senses govern . . .' Diderot, *Critique de l'essai sur les femmes*, quoted in Crampe-Casnabet 324. *Anatomical Works* of Jean Riolan (1625 Paris, q30 [6]). 'The menstruous blood . . . Spermatick vessels . . .' Riolan Bk 2 Ch 27, 85 and 83. De Graaf: Berriot-Salvadore 366, 384. *No one has yet* . . . . . . E3 P2 S. *Axioma sive notio*: E2 P40 S1.

184 *No one is so vigilant* . . . TP VI 3: W 315. Killing animals *based more on* . . . E4 P37 S1. One Spinoza scholar . . . Matheron 384 n.69.

185 Partiality: E2 P49 SIV C; E4 P37 S1. *When you were* . . . Ep.76, to Burgh, Dec. 1675: S 341. *Nor are they thought* . . . E4 P44 S. *Men generally judge* . . . TP XI 4: W 445. *A king that is prey* . . . TP VI 5: Wernham (317) cites Van den Hove 1661 1 i 2 592. Part-justification: TP XI 4: W 445. Promise to treat the affects 'geometrically' E3 Pref.: *quotation on book cover.* Three primary affects . . . E3 P11 S. 'Primitive passions': *Passions* 11, 69: CSM 1 353. *With the accompanying idea* . . . E3 P13 S. *A vacillation of mind* . . . E3 P35 S. *So each one* . . . E3 P39 S. *If someone imagines* . . . *he is forced* E3 P35 and S.

186 *The latter reason* . . . E3 P35 S. *If someone begins to hate* . . . E3 P38 D. *Love of a harlot (meretricius* OPG 2 271): E4 Apx XIX: C n.40. 'Did soon perceive . . .': Colerus 4. Kerckring married Clara Maria: *below, 231 with note.*

187 'Another scholar . . .' Colerus 4. Inaccurate hearsay: *above, 76.* 'A necklace of pearls . . .' ibid 4–5. *He who imagines* . . . E3 P35 S. 'If he received' Colerus 42–3. Female genitalia . . . *Spicilegium Anatomicum*, 1670, *Observatione* XIX. Anecodotes: ibid. *passim.* 'Voetius has spoilt . . .' Letter to Mersenne, 11 Nov. 1640, CSMK 1 56.

188 'It was excellently . . .' Letter to Lady More: Van Schurman [1659] 43. Schama (411) claims Van Schurman married De Labadie, but this is unconfirmed by Stouppe (80) and Kolakowski, and denied by Klock (*An International Debate on Women in the Seventeenth Century*, Verloren, Hilversum, 1994) 147, 159. De Labadie: Kolakowski Ch.xi. Labadists were 'mortal enemies' of Cartesianism: ibid. 766. *Eukleria*: Baar 116, Kolakowski 741–66; Feuer 300–1. Kerckring's conversion: Colerus 5 (referring to Kortholt): Francès (244, no source) says Clara Maria imposed the condition. NNBW (2 663) says he became a Catholic in France. Visit to Paris: De Nazelle 125. No mention of baptism. 'Hauthum': Deed of Gift: VD/VT 177, quoting NAA 3204 f299 4 Sept. 1670. Cornelia Kerckrinck married Pieter Hunthum, merchant: Vroedschrap II 916; DTB 673/45. Wedding sudden: Meinsma 388–9; VD/VT 117. Poem: Van der Goes, *Bruilofsgedichten:* Meininger 170–1. 'Kind van Pieter Hunthum' 24 Nov. 1679: DTB 1134/8v; ibid. 26 Feb. 1681: DTB 1134/12.

189 *The more an affect* . . . E5 P3 Co. Also E5 P4 Co; E5 P10 S. Commit suicide . . . hidden causes . . . E4 P20 S. *No life is rational* . . . E4 Apx V. *For I do not presume* . . . Ep.76 to Burgh, Dec. 1675: S 342. *This doctrine* . . . E2 P49 IV Co. Hudde: proof for God's uniqueness: *above, 159.*

190 De Witt wrote despairingly: Letter to Vivien, 2 Oct. 1665: Rowen 1 421. Ban on *Indication of the Salutary, etc:* ibid. 435. Parish preachers: ibid. 421. 'Not the slightest . . .' ibid. 422. De Witt's vulnerability: ibid. 421ff. Devilish force: *below, 221.*

191 *The ministries of the* . . . TTP Pref.: Es 6–7. 'Spinozist': Heniger 41. *I am now writing* . . . Ep.30, Sept./Oct. 1665: S 185–6.

192 Oldenburg's encouragement: Ep.7, 1662; Eps.11 and 14, 1663; Eps.25 and 29, April and c.Sept. 1665. 'Odd philosopher . . .' To Moray, 7 Oct. 1665, OC II 549. 'Sgr

Spinosa . . .' to Boyle, 21 Nov. 1665, ibid. 615. **Concerning the agreement . . .:** referring to Ep.32, Spinoza to Oldenburg, Nov. 1665, quoted *above, 119.*

CHAPTER 8

193   *Faith has become . . .* TTP Pref.: Es7. **He had argued:** E2 P34 ff; E4 P35 and D. **Divination impossible:** TTP V: W 107. *Anyone who wishes . . .* TTP V: W 99–101. **Social and political principles** in E4: Ps 32–7, 70–3 Apx. *passim. Despotic statecraft:* TTP Pref.: Es 5.

194   *The necessity . . .* Ep.27, to Van Blijenbergh, 3 June 1665: OPG 4 161. Is metaphysics, for Spinoza, equivalent to physics? In the same letter Spinoza refers to *metaphysics* **and** *physics* (ibid., my emphasis) but the conjunction looks like *of* (that is, 'or', a disjunction) to me in Spinoza's handwriting (back cover of De Deugd). *Particularly relevant . . .* TP 11 1 ff.: W 267ff. *Belief in historical . . .* TTP Ch.IV: W 75. **1670 Synod petition:** Rowen 1 435. De Witt may never have read the book: ibid. 411. *Seeing that we have . . .* TTP Pref., Es 6.

195   *Theology is not . . .* TTP XV: Es 194. *I determined . . .* TTP Pref.: Es 8. *Whatever is . . .* E1 P15. **'Very well versed . . .'** Earbery Pref. and 114. **'Geen ketter'.** . . TTP XIV: W 111. **'The devil . . .'** *The Merchant of Venice,* 1 11 l.99. **'If what Spinosa . . .'** Colerus 61.

196   **'Teaches atheism cleverly . . .'** Letter from Van Limborch to Van Velthuysen (13 Sept. 1671) reproduced in Meinsma 518. **'Close examination . . . thoroughly . . .':** Ep.42, Van Velthuysen to Ostens, 24 Jan. 1671: S 225, 236. *Legitimate self-esteem . . . above, 72.* **'Generally so bred up . . .'** Pamphlet quoted by Schama, 266. *[My treatise] contains . . .* TTP XX: W 243. See also TTP Pref.: Es 11.

197   **Henry's advice:** Ep. 31, 12 Oct. 1665. **Mennonite press:** VPS was reprinted in 1665 by J. Venkel: Intr. to the British Library copy. Meyer's *Philosophiae Sacrae* (1666): TS 253–7, 255 n.258; Steenbakkers 105. **'Poses the question . . .** Lagrée 4. **Cartesians dissociated . . .** Steenbakkers 127 n.1. **Epilogue . . .** 'On God . . . the Church of . . .' Lagrée 249.

198   **Meyer as metaphysician:** TS 254 with n.256. *Hebrew Grammar: below, 285. Scripture very often . . .* TTP VII: Es 100. **Reorganised** Meyer's work: Lagree 9–10. **Made copies of his letters:** See debate in Steenbakkers 27. That the Latinity in the *Opera Posthuma* is not typically Spinoza's does not mean that he did not make the copies originally. **Echoes of Descartes in TTP:** *see below, 17, 218.* See Siebrand, especially 215 and 221. **Hobbes in TTP:** n.33: W 247. Spinoza refers to Hobbes in this context in Ep.50, to Jelles, June 1674: *below, 287.*

199   *That shrewd Dutchman V.H.:* TP VIII: W 397. **Geulincx's influence:** *Metaphysica Vera et ad Mentem Peripateticum,* copied from a student's notes, 1691. EP 323; TS 221–2 and 254 n.256. **Geulincx's *Ethics:*** EP 323–5. **'The late Prince . . .'** W 227, n.1. *By the guidance . . .* TTP 111: W 53. **Koerbagh's legal 'dictionary':** *'t Nieuw Woorden-Boek der Regten:* Vandenbossche 1. **'Very heretical . . . debauched lifestyle':** PK 225 and 227: 10 June and 1 July 1666.

200   **No connection with Spinoza:** Meinsma 352 n.83. **'Five little packets':** FQ 164. *Envy is nothing . . .* E3 P24 S. *Such, Philosophical Reader . . .* TTP Pref.: Es 11. **'Out throwne him . . .'** See Feuer n.16, 276–7 on the misprinting of Hobbes's remark in Aubrey 255. **The Van den Hoves drew on *Leviathan:*** Petry 153.

201   **A biographer's concern:** Feuer's *Spinoza and the Rise of Liberalism* adopts this approach. **Mistakes of apostles and Popes:** e.g., TTP V: W 99; ibid. 109. *The sole aim of philosophy . . .* TTP XIV: W 123. *He obviously means . . . merciful and so on.* TTP IV: W 79–81. See also TTP I: Es 18–19. *Scripture entirely confirms . . .* TTP IV: W 87.

202   **Hebrew history and Calvinism in foundation of Dutch Republic;** Van Deursen

206, Ch.14 *passim*; Schama 93–125. '**Our Moses**': Schama ibid. 110, 112. '**Ye Children of Israel**': ibid. 100. '**Millenarianism**': Webster 15–16, 48–49; Weinryb 211; Van der Wall *passim*. '**Although we cannot . . .**' Israel 286 n.27, quoting Wolf, Lucien.

203 '**Portuguese, with a . . .**' Dedication to *El Conciliador*, Pt 2: Roth 229. **De Labadie's millenarianism**: Van de Wall 167, 173. He came to Middelburg from Geneva in 1666: Kolakowski 741. **Van Beuningen**: *een sotte Duysent jaerist: Philopater* [1697] 121; Petry 167 n.75. **Zevi**: Israel 2 208–16; Weinryb 213; Bernadete 119–24. Yovel 191 cf. G. Scholem, *Sabbatai Sevi*, Princeton University Press, 1973, 518 ff. **Newton**: Webster 48; Elected Royal Society 1671. '**But I turn . . .**' Ep.33, Dec. 1665: S 199–200. *Did not the principles . . .* TTP III: W 63. *See above, 15.*

204 **Calvin on election**: Calvin III, xxi–xxiv. **Jews not 'chosen'**: *above, 29, 45, 65.* *Advantage/usefulness/interest* (*utilitas*): Curley translates *utilitas* as advantage or usefulness (e.g., C 700): Wernham as interest, advantage, utility or welfare (e.g., W 454). For a Jewish interpretation see 'Spinoza's Zionism', Yovel 190–3. **Zevi's apostasy**: Weinryb 214–15; Israel 2 212–13. '**Was not turned Turk . . .**' Van der Wall 167. *Only perceived God's . . .* TTP I: Es 24–5. See also TTP II: Es 27, 40. **Images adapted to singular imaginations**: TTP II: Es 38; TTP I–III passim. *Thus treating them . . .* TTP II: Es 39. *Moses did not . . .* TTP XIV: W 113.

205 '**Fear God . . .**' 1 Peter 2:17: Van Deursen 130. *Rites . . . adapted . . .* TTP IV 1: W 73. *Temporal welfare* TTP V: W 89. **TTP not taken to be addressed to Jews**: Strauss, L., quoted in Silverman 2 130. '**Benedito Espinosa . . .**' 'Eternidad de la Ley Mosaica', Respuesta 23, De Barrios 85. '**Since nothing . . .**' Lucas 45. *The law of Moses . . .* TTP I: Es 17.

206 *The story or parable . . .* TTP IV: W 83. *The first man . . .* TTP II: Es 35. **Apology reflected in TTP XIV**: Kasher 111–12; Mertens 732 with n.70. *Necessary articles . . .* TTP XIV: W 119–21. *So far I have* . . . TTP XVI: W 125. *The natural right . . .* TTP XVI: W 125. *A society can . . .* TTP XVI: W 133, 137. **Right to live through appetite**: TTP XVI: W 125–7; see quote *below, 260.*

207 *Contract* **rationally**: TTP XVI: W 133–5, 139–47, and TTP XVII: W 149. *Sovereign*: Wernham translates Spinoza's *summa potestas* (highest power) thus. See *below, 253. No society can exist . . .* TTP V: W 93. See also TTP XVI W 133–47 *passim*; E4 P53, E4 P54, E4 P54 S and E4 P63. *Purely theoretical . . .* TTP XVII: W 149. *When I said above . . .* TTP XIX: W 205. *Superstitious and ambitious men:* TTP XX: W 233–35. *My country's rulers*: TTP XX: W 243. *Danger to the peace* TTP XX: W 243. **Descartes on Hobbes**: Letter to a Reverend Jesuit Father 1643: CSMK 231. **Van Beckel**: Orangist oration: Petry 157. **Anti-monarchy in TTP**: TTP XVIII: W 199–203. *As for Holland . . .* TTP XVIII: W 203. Here Wernham translates *imperium* as sovereignty.

208 **Willem II's 1650 bid**: Wernham stresses (n.6, n.9) that Spinoza is arguing against the Orangist cause, but says oddly (n.8) that he means by 'the last count' Philip II of Spain. *Souverainiteyt*: Jongeneelen, Gerrit, H., 'An unknown pamphlet of Adriaan Koerbagh'. *Studia Spinozana* (3) 1987 405–14. *The corporate right . . .* TP II 17: W 277–9. *Take the city* . . . TTP XX: W 241.

209 '**In our country . . .**' Bontemantel's Journal: Meinsma 369. **D'Estrades to Louis**: Rowen 1 472, 781, March 1663 and June 1667. **Buat**: beheaded 11 Oct. 1666: Rowen 1622.

210 **2nd Anglo-Dutch war** (2 paras.): Rowen 1 Ch.28 *passim*; Campbell xxvi, xliv; 'De Witt' 2 9 244–5. **Ships burned and captured**: Pepys 15, 16 August 1666. **Forced to flee**: ibid. 16 Aug. 1666. '**England fears no potentate . . .**' Van den Hove: 'De Witt' 2 9 244. **Very cold winter 1666–7**: Haley 2 108. '**Day and night . . .**' Temple to Arlington, March 1666: ibid. p.82, quoting State Papers. **To abandon Spain** . . . ibid. Nov. 1667, quoting Courtenay. See also Rowen 1 482. '**A prying, pressing man**':

Letters from Louis to d'Estrades, Nov., Dec. 1664: Haley 2 p.52. **De Witt's errors:** ibid. 46–7.

211 **Carriage incident:** ibid. 46. **William 'Child of State':** Rowen 1 670–3, 646. **'Far greater power . . .'** Letter by unknown writer: Haley 2 108. **'Very just notions . . .'** Rowen 1 674, quoting J.H. Been. *Historische Fragmenten.* See also Campbell lxxxii, quoting Burnet's *History of his own times* 1 364. **William replied** . . . Haley 2 123–4. **Call for 'armour':** Rowen 1 670. **Pieter van den Hove . . . ruin:** 'De Witt' *passim:* Rowen 1 394: Petry 153 with n.21. **Demands for posts:** *Netherlands Proclamations, passim.* **William put off visit to Charles:** Rowen 2 160, 167.

212 **'In great straits . . . kingdom is undone':** Pepys 23 March, 10 June, 12 June 1667. **De Witt credited:** Rowen 1 597, 781. **'Mr Oldenburg, our Secretary':** 25 June 1667. *Living in solitude* . . . Ep.38, to Van der Meer, Oct. 1666: S 213. **Huygens: 1656;** see also correspondence with Hudde, May 1665. **Johannes van der Meer:** Van Suchtelen (Meinsma 344 n.8) suggests he was of a Leiden regent family, directed a financial-backing society, and corresponded with De Witt.

213 **Huygens: new moon:** HO VI, 7 May 1666. **Letters on optics:** 9 and 23 Sept; 14 Oct; 4 Nov; 2 and 9 Dec. 1667; 6 April, 11 May 1668. **Van Beuningen Amsterdam alderman 1668, until Aug.:** *Vroedschap* 2 1177. **Jelles's letters:** on optics and alchemy: Eps. 39, 40; water pressure Ep.41. *As busy as could be* . . . Ep.41, Sept. 1669: S 223. **'This same Simon . . .'** Colerus 43. **'Brother':** VD/VT 29. **Simon died 'a bachelor':** ibid. 8. **Part-shares, etc.:** valued at 7,191 fl.: GAA, Register of Collateral Succession, quoted in VD/VT 26.

214 **Moved to the Herenstraat** No.56 (now the Huygens Apothecary) in 1668: Voorburg GA and Town Guide. **Casier refused Smyrna post:** Meinsma 231: GAA (Nieuwe Kerk). **Married** 17 June 1668: DTB 442/213. **Appointed to Batavia:** Letters of the deputees of the Classis in Amsterdam to the Church Council of Batavia, 27 March and 19 Nov. 1668, and to the Church Council of Galle in Ceylon, 3 April 1668: Heniger 42. *Sparendam:* 12 April 1668: Meinsma 232 with source. **Installed by Sept. 1669:** Heniger 42. **'The Spinozist clergyman . . .'** ibid. 5. **His Latin:** Title-page of the Dutch *Hortus Malabaricus: In het Latyn bescriven door Johannes Casearius. Bedienaar des Goddelijken Woordes te Cochin:* ibid. 46 and passim. **'Feared that . . .':** ibid. 146, citing Vol.3 (1682) xv. **'Clear and distinct . . .'** ibid. 143, citing *Hortus* 1 iv. **'Consult somewhat . . .'** obligation to proselytise: Report of June 1675 and Letter of the Governor-General and Council of India to Van Reede and the Council of Malabar, 22 Oct. 1675: ibid. 44. **'Most learned and reverend . . .'** Tribute from Van Reede, Pref. to *Hortus* Vol.3 (1682) xv: ibid. 53. **Died sometime after May** 1677: ibid. p.46. See Boxer 2 on ship travel and conditions. **Name immortalised:** *Botany and History of the Hortus Malabaricus* (Ed. K.S. Manilai), A.A. Balkema, Rotterdam, 1980.

215 **Rokin: 'scandalous' assemblies:** PK XI, 192, 199, 206, 264, 283, 286, 288. (Meinsma 342, 352–3 nn.92–5.) PK XI 353 (5 Jan.) 361–2 (19 Jan.); 364 (26 Jan., 2 Feb.). See Meinsma 356–7. The *Protokollen* and *Confessieboeken* are at points faded and indecipherable. 1 **Corinthians 14:** PK XI 353. **Feb. 1688:** Vandenbossche 112; *Protokollen* XI 235. *Een Bloemhof* . . . Vandenbossche 2; Meinsma 332–8, 360–1; Vandenbossche 2; Siebrand 14. **'Theologians want . . .'** Meinsma 333 quoting *Bloemhof* on 'Miracles' and 'Metaphysics'. **'Ipstantie':** Vandenbossche 332; Meinsma 332. Compare Spinoza's One Substance: *above, 126.* **'Concubine':** Meinsma 339, with n.80: E4 Apx XX. **'In this consist . . .'** Meinsma 333, quoting *Bloemhof* on 'Paradise'.

216 **Spinoza's 'gospel':** Meinsma 333, also 328, 332. **'Someone'** . . . **'barbarous word':** Philips van Limborch's letter of Sept. 1671 to Van Velthuysen: Meinsma 519. **Socinian teachings:** Stouppe 54–5; *Een Ligt* 399, 328 and *passim.* **Contradictory:** Vandenbossche 12, 14–16. *Apart from the Socinians:* Ep.21, Jan.1665: S 157. *Bloemhof* **blamed for apostasy . . . Rokin:** Meinsma 295. **Adriaan's arrest demanded** 25 Feb.

1668: ibid. 360; Vandenbossche 1–2. **Adriaan's flight:** Meinsma 359, citing Bontemantel 436–7: Vandenbossche 3; **Second manuscript found:** Meinsma 362 with n.34. *Een Ligt:* found half-printed in Feb. 1668; not published until 1974. Koerbagh's books are not available in English. **'Consternation of soul':** PK XI 385: Meinsma 363. **Johannes Koerbagh:** (para.) Meinsma 360; PK XI 374, PK XI 383, 10 or 11 May: ibid. 362; PK XI 377–83.

217   **Receiving letters:** CB: Meinsma 361–2. **Witsen's demand:** Bontemantel: ibid. 363. **Adriaan's arrest:** Bontemantel 436–53: ibid. 363–5. Bontemantel's journal is the sole source of evidence for this account, except for a copy of the instructions for Koerbagh's arrest (GAA): Meinsma 381, Notes 48, 49. **Hudde:** present throughout trial: CB 116 ff; alderman 1668: burgomaster 1672: Meinsma 355 n.17. NNBW 11 175. **'Fox in the vineyard':** Blok IV 232. **Van Berckel . . . 'Spinosa':** CB116, reproduced in part FQ 119–20. See Meinsma 365–7. **Bontemantel's comments:** ibid. 367. **'Esdras':** CB 116: *Een Ligt* 86–7: Vandenbossche 8. Meyer: J.P. Belthouwer's response to Meyer's *PSSI*: Amsterdam 1673. Ezra revised the Books of the Prophets: TTP VIII: Es 129–32. **Buxtorf:** *notes to 93.* **'Schabinot':** *Hag Shavuoth:* Meinsma 381 n.52; *schechinat* or *schekinah:* Feuer 282 n.40.

218   *All-in-All: above, 105.* **'Ipstantie' matter and force:** *Een Ligt* 3, 6–7: Meinsma 332–3 with n.53. **Johannes Koerbagh:** denials: CB 117–19; Meinsma 367–8. **27 July 1668:** CB 119–20; Meinsma 368, citing Bontemantel 459; Vandenbossche 3; **JB:** Meinsma 382 n.62 claims a mention.

219   **'*Actum* 11 May':** 'D^to Van Beuningen': CB 117; transcript fragment FQ 120–1. **Van Beuningen in Paris** 29 June 1668: HO VI 227. **Burgomaster 1669:** *Vroedschap* 2 1177: Letters between Van Beuningen and De Witt, 2 and 3 Feb. 1669: Rowen 1 784. **Adriaan sent to *Rasphuis:*** A note at the end of Bontemantel: Dodt van Flensburg, *Archief* 11 367: Meinsma 370. **Removed 19 September:** Marginal note, ibid.; Van Moerkerken 73–4. **'The Lakes . . . repentant':** 6 Dec. 1668, PK XI 110; 10 Oct. 1669: ibid. 59. **Koerbagh's burial:** 15 Oct. 1669: DTB. **Witsen's burial** 16 March 1669: Meinsma 371. **'Ecclesiastical' . . . :** Bontemantel: Meinsma 368–9; CB 122 margin note: PK 3 Sept. 1669: Meinsma 372.

220   **Johannes's burial:** 11 Sept. 1672: ibid. p.374. **Three 'writers':** Vandenbossche 4. Aert Wolfgreyn (Aart Wolsgryn/Aard Wolsgryk) was the Amsterdam publisher of *Het Leven van Philopater* and *Vervolg van 't Leven van Philopater.* Colerus p.57; *below Ch. 9. Een Ligt* written 'To give a better explanation': Meinsma 365: CB 20 July 1668. **De Labadie:** Spinoza owned Wolzogen's *Refutation of Jean de Labadie* (1668, 133 [15]d). **In Amsterdam** 1669–70: Sambuc 10–11. **Before *Kerkeraad:*** PK XII *passim.* Said alternately to be the 'servant of Satan' (Kolakowski 759) and 'persecuted' (Sambuc 11). **60,000 followers:** Feuer 273, with sources. **Petitioning of Van Beuningen:** Stouppe 79–80.

221   *Faustbuch:* see bibliography. **Devils and demons:** Van Deursen 149–153. **'Hundreds . . . the devil':** Goeree *Historien* 665: Meinsma 371; Philips van Limborch, Letter to Jean le Clerc, 23 Jan. 1682; ibid. 526–7. **'One may very well . . .'** Musaeus, professor of Divinity at Jena, 1704: Colerus 79. **'Produced in Hell . . .'** FQ 194–5.

222   **Surveillance on printers** (including Christoffel Koenraad): PK XII 22–3. Meinsma's reference (p.376) to PK XI 126 seems to be mistaken. **Van Beuningen chairman:** PK XI 181. **Comedy:** PK XI 197. **Publication of TTP:** Meinsma 376, citing Land's research. **'Conrad himself . . .'** Colerus 56. **Van Limborch's opinion:** Stolle-sect. Hallman's Travel Notes: FQ 221. **'Never wanted his name attached . . .'** JP 219: see also E4 Apx XXV. **'I have reprehended . . .'** Letter from Schuller to Leibniz, 29 March 1678: Steenbakkers p.63. *Confession: below, 261.*

223   *Good friends . . .* Ep.44, to Jelles, Feb.1671: S 243. *Nil Volentibus Arduum:* Van Suchtelen 3 391, 393, 397, 398, 399; Meinsma 439–42. **'Calm . . .' . . . heresy trial:** Meinsma 329. *Men whose consciences:* TTP XX: W 239. *I have thus shown . . .* ibid. 243.

CHAPTER 9

224 *In a free man* ... E4 P69 C. See also above, 23. *Human power* ... E4 Apx XXIV. **5 Sept. 1669:** Ep.41, to Jelles. **The back room:** *below, 235.* **Driven:** *above, 191.* 'Which he preferred ...' Lucas 59. 'Not knowing which ...' *niet wetende van wat hout pijlen te maken* ... Roukema 151. **Left 1671:** ibid. 'A man of a very weak ...' Colerus 91. **1655 Ph.D. dissertation:** Abarbanel PA and X. **'The widow':** Colerus 36. When Colerus moved into No.12 Stille Veerkade with his family in Oct. 1693, on becoming the Lutheran pastor in The Hague (1693–1707: Meinsma 4), he would have been told of a 'widow'. **Lawyer:** Meinsma 385 n.103, citing M. Frederiks, *Nederlandsche Spectator*, 1871. **Willem van der Werve:** Colerus (36) says Van Velden; K 27 gives Van Velen.

225 'Distinguished by their ...' Colerus 35. See also 36 and 40–1; Lucas 63, 59, 63–4 and 73. 'Young girls of good ...' Stouppe 65. **While in Voorburg:** Colerus 35. 'Indolence': Saint-Évremond, Letter to Comte de Lionne: Des Maizeaux I lxxii. Aglionby [1669] 301. 'To imitate the French ...' Temple 2 [1672] 85. See also Van Deursen 161, quoting Charles Ogier's 1636 report. **Chess:** Zumthor 77. **Spinoza's chessmen:** SR 115. **Walk** ... *Huis ten Bosch:* Zumthor 75.

226 'I did visit ...' *Plays of William Wycherley* 37. **De Witt: dancing:** Campbell ix; see also Geyl 2 195. **'On foot ... of his house':** Temple 2 [1672] 70–1. **House: family:** Rowen 1 493–4. Pontalis 2 220–4. **Deaths:** Elizabeth June and Wendela July 1668: ibid. 497–8. 'I would rather ...' ibid. 504. **Anna married Herman van den Honert** 30 July 1675: NNBW 3 1467. **Triple Alliance Jan. 1668:** Rowen 1 169. **Van Beuningen's opposition:** Roldanus 119. **William, Council of State:** 2 June 1670: 'The wise arrangement ...' Calvin IV xx 8.

227 *Staatsgezind, Prinsgezind:* Rowen 1 381–2; Rowen 54 and 154. Rowen 1795. **Ban on** *Salutary Political Foundations:* 28 May 1669: ibid. 397. **Treaty of Dover:** Geyl 2 100–2. **'What was possible'** Rowen 1 727, quoting Mignet. **De Witt's stance:** Rowen 1 725–42; Haley 2 272–3, 280 with n.8. **William-Charles meeting:** Rowen 1 738 and 748–9. **Van Beuningen's return** Rowen 1 738. **'Pernicious book ...'** PK XII 110; see texts of the bans FQ 121 ff.

228 *This is not only* ... Ep.44, 17 Feb. 1671: S 243. **Principle of Cartesian physics:** TTP IV: W 67: PPC 11, 20. *I have already shown* ... TTP III: W 53; CM 11, 9: C332. **Calvin 1645:** John Calvin: *Contre la secte ... phantastique et furieuse des libertins qui se nomment spirituelz* (1545) in *Treatises against the Anabaptists and against the Libertines*, trans. and ed. Benjamin Wort Farley (Grand Rapids, Mich. 1982). *Libertins* **in The Hague:** Assoun 178. **Jacob, Intr. and Ch.1. Maxims 1623:** Assoun 175, citing d'Antoine, Adam. **Republican ideals top of list:** ibid. 176–8.

229 *Libertin érudit* and *libertin, politique* distinguished: ibid. **Hobbes** ... **Paris;** *below 290.* *The Key of the Sanctuary:* Catalogus 1 165. See also Lucas p.72. **Gabriel de Saint-Glen:** The '*Rotterdam*' (in fact Amsterdam) *Gazette:* Francès, M. 'Un gazettier français en Hollande: Gabriel de Saint Glen, traducteur de Spinoza', *Revue des sciences humaines*, 1955. See also Meinsma 429–30. **Lucas moved to Amsterdam 1671:** Meininger 83, citing Kleerkoper, M.M. **Adulatory author** ... *above, notes to 16.* **De Boulainvilliers:** Wade 117.

230 **Peyrère librarian:** Mongrédien 217. **Libertinism: broadened out from Calvin's sense:** Kaplan, Benjamin J., Introduction 2–5. **Sexual laxity:** ibid. 14 with n.24, citing 'John Calvin: *Contre la secte*.' op.cit. 159–362. 'As for the *libertins* ...' Stouppe 62–3: Stouppe said he wrote only of Christian sects: ibid. 33. 'Spinosa': ibid. 65.

231 *I do not here* ... Ep.43, February 1671: S 239. **Saint-Évremond:** Des Maizeaux 1 iv, xiv, xx, liv, lxi, lxv and lxxi; Vernière 16–18. **'Esteem'd and courted ...'** ibid. 11 141. **'Cast off the mask':** ibid. lvii. **Roman Catholic ... deathbed:** ibid. 1 civ. *Libertin* **consternation at *Ethics*:** Assoun 174.

232 **Cartesian-Coccejans were often more liberal than Coccejus** (d. 1669): TS 243–4. See

also Dibon 'Notes biographiques sur les Cartésiens Hollandais' 261 in Dijksterhuis. 'A great friend...' *Philopater* [1697] 149 and 150–2. The 'basic propositions' are in the Defs. of *Ethics* Part 1, with Propositions 14, 16, 17 and 18 (ibid. 151). See also Hubbeling (1982) 449–500 and Siebrand 220–1. 'Writ against the...' Colerus 85, 87. Wittichius would leave a posthumous refutation of Spinoza, *Anti-Spinoza, sive examen ethices Benedicti de Spinoza et commentarius de Deo et ejus attributis*, Amsterdam 1690. **Colerus's denial**: Colerus 85–7. **Aart Wolsgryn** the Amsterdam publisher of *Het Leven van Philopater* and *Vervolg van 't Leven van Philopater*. The writer was Johannes Duiker (Duijkerius): Hubbeling 493, citing Maréchal 1 5, 8, 17ff, 47 and 42ff. '**Zinospa**': Johan Melchior, of Frech, near Bonn, *Epistola ad Amicum, continens Censuram Libri, cui titulus Tractat. Theol. Polit.* Ultraj. 1671 (48) Pamphlet 9910 of the Royal Library: Meinsma 388 with Notes 3 and 4. Moreau claims that the first public attack came from Leibniz's teacher, Thomasius: Moreau in Garrett 409 (no ref.). **Ban 1674**: *below 261*. '**The book of Spinoza**': Letter to Van Velthuysen 13 Sept. 1671; *above 196*. **Van Limborch's condemnation**: *Theologia Christiana*, Amsterdam: Petry 169 n.105. **Lambert van Velthuysen**: Started studying medicine 1643: Meinsma 216 ff., with Notes.

233 **Regius**: Baillet 225. '**Political theologian**... I do not know... Ep.42 to Ostens, Jan. 1671: S 236, 225. '**Paradoxical theologian**': ibid. S 228. **Talked often**: Lamb. Velthuysii *Ultrajectensis Tractatus Moralis de naturali pudore et de dignitate hominis*, 1676 (Rotterdam 1680). '**Radical enlightenment**': Jacob Ch 1 and 48–52. **Rosicrucians**: ibid. 54ff. **Leibniz**: ibid. 55; De Careil 1 1–51 and 2 *passim*. **Locke, perhaps**: Jacob 118. **Lucas**: Wolf 2 26. *Caute* seal first used: Ep.46, to Leibniz, Nov. 1671: Wolf 1 441 annot.

234 **Michael French-speaking?**: VD/VT 130 (NAA 942). **Spinoza and Lucas's list**: *above, 58*. Spinoza's library included: French–Latin–Spanish dictionary (1599 q26 [2]); *Dialogues François* (0118 [39]); *La Logique ou l'Art de Penser*, Arnauld and Nicole (1662, d123 [5]); *Voyage d'Espagne* (1665 d124 [6]). **This man... whoever**... Ep.43, to Ostens, Feb. 1671: S 242. **Van Velthuysen's tracts**: Petry 155 with n.44; Geyl 2 115. '**He locates man's**...' Ep.42: S 227. '**Envisaged such a**...' ibid. 236.

235 *You are doubtless*... Ep.43: S 237. '**In the original**...': Shmueli 210. *It is in no... in what mire*... Ep.43: S 241, 238. *Lead unbridled lives... Does that man*... ibid. 238. *Love of God... the supreme happiness*... TTP IV: W 73: *below 281*. **Deism**: Ep.42, from Van Velthuysen: S 225. Orobio de Castro took it to mean denial of special providence, and the equation of God with the laws of nature: Silverman 163. See also Yovel 75; Colie 2 *passim*. *Evil cause*: Ep.43: S 237. *know that... Ii would be much*... Ep.69, Autumn 1675: 323. '**He spent**...' Colerus 36. **Back room**: ibid. **Spinoza's accounts**: ibid. '**Did not care**...' ibid. p.40.

236 **Beer**: Ep.70, from Schuller, Nov. 1675: S 328. *Repay in whatever*... Ep.72, to Schuller, Nov. 1675: S 331. '**Milk-soop... gruel**': Colerus 37. '**Like the serpent**...' ibid. p.38. **Moved to Hendrik van der Spyck's house** 1671: Colerus (38) says he was there over 5½ years: he died there 21 Feb. 1677. **Van der Spyck, Spijck, Spijk or Spyk** Konstschilder: HGA NA 686/205; Mr. Schilder: ibid. 671/21, 256; portretschilder, *Biografisch Woordenboek*, Krawn, Wurtbach, 641, 333–46. Military paymaster (*solliciteur-militair*): *below, 237* with HGA sources. **80 guilders**: Although Kortholt (Wolf 2 167) says 80 guilders 'quarterly', documents relating to the house at 72–4 Paviljoensgracht show he paid the Van der Spycks 80 guilders a year: Van Suchtelen 1 477. **Book-giving**: e.g., signed copy of TTP given to J. Klefmann: *Catalogus* (2) 18; Leibniz was offered a copy of TTP in Dec. 1671: S 246. **Barber**: Colerus 98. **Geulincx 'terribly poor'**: Balet 103. **Paviljoensgracht house**: bought by Hendrik's father 13 June 1669: Van Suchtelen 1 477. Now the Library and Reading-room of the Vereniging Het Spinozahuis. *See Plate 9*. **The *Heilige-Geesthofje*** still stands. **Moat ... Spui**: Map PTT (Post Office) Museum,

The Hague. **Hendrik's family:** wife Meinsma 400, citing ARA DTB. **Children:** Van Suchtelen 2 13, citing Campbell in *De Nederlandsche Spectator* 1880 (26) 206. See Colerus 40. **Carriages:** 17c engraving of the *Heilige-Geesthofje* in De Vries. **'Good republican':** Colerus 49. **'Affect polished . . .'** Lucas 71.

237   **'An eminent councillor . . .'** Colerus 39; K 30. The English version of Colerus wrongly narrows *raadsheer* to 'Councillor of State', as well as mistranslating Spinoza's reply. **'Quietly in his own chamber . . .' . . . 3 days:** Colerus 36, 41. **Longer:** *below, 258.* **'If he was very . . .'** Colerus 39–40. **Hendrik van der Spyck or Spijck:** a *solliciteur-militair* 1694, 1698 and 1707: HGA NA 919/609; 675/515; 1592/681; ARA Collectie Wolters. **The Hague's schuttersgilden:** Rosenberg 56, 398, 402; Rowen 1 878.

238   **Desk sent to Rieuwertsz after Spinoza's death:** Colerus 64–5. *I shall send . . . above, 180. I am now . . . above, 190. A man who is guided . . .* E4 P73 D. *The right way of living:* E4 P73 S and E4 Apx XXII.

239   **'On The Passions':** The anthology (not printed until 1765) was called *Instruction in the Poetics of Drama:* Steenbakkers 104, referring to a meeting of the arts society *Nil Volentibus Arduum* 16 Dec. 1670, at which this chapter was discussed. **The book:** Steenbakkers Ch.3, 'Lodewijk Meyer's catalogue of the passions (1670): between Descartes and Spinoza'. **Bouwmeester:** Steenbakkers 121–2. Descartes's *Passions of the Soul:* Hobbes *Leviathan:* ibid. 104 ff. **Spinozistic concepts:** examples of near-verbatim similarity, ibid. 114. **Pineal gland:** 'The part of the body . . .' *Passions* 31: CSM 1 340 ff. See also *Treatise on Man:* CSM 1 100, 106. **Steno's lecture 1665:** Steenbakkers 110–11, citing Cohen, Mozes Herman, *Spinoza en de Geneeskunde,* Amsterdam 1920. Spinoza owned Steno's *Anatomical Observations* (Leiden 1662, d151 [33]). **Sought Kerckring's advice:** Ep. to Jelles, 19 April 1673. **Descartes did not know the true nature . . .** Ep.2, Sept. 1661.

240   **'The passions are extraordinary . . .'** Meyer's definition; Steenbakkers 105. **'It is not the actuality . . .'** ibid. 108–9, quoting Meyer. On Spinoza and the passions, see James, S.(2). *logic . . . two sets of laws:* E 5 Pref: C 594; E3 P2 S [ii]. *In just the same . . .* E5 P1. **Aversion and enjoyment:** Steenbakkers 119–20. **Meyer's celibacy:** Meinsma 197. Meyer was 41 in 1670 and did not marry. **Van den Enden's school closed:** Meininger 68. **Perverter . . .** Colerus 3. **'Ill life . . . notorious Jew':** Roukema, quoted by Meininger 69.

241   **Poor businessman:** De Nazelle 100–1, 102–3. **Home mortgaged:** Meininger 24. **Fire and energy:** De Nazelle 99, 102. **'God preserve our land . . .'** KVNN 84. *Godt bewaer ons Landt voor Hongers-noodt, enz. Eynde.* **1665 pamphlet ended . . .** VPS 45, citing the historian Aitzema (1652). **Offered De Witt:** *above, 175* **Invited by the King of France . . .** Van der Goes, *Aen de Heere Franciscus van den Enden, Toen hij van zijne Majest: van Vrankrijk, tot Raedsheere en Lijftarts verkooren wiert. Gedichten,* Bilderdijk 11, 54, Amsterdam 1685: Meininger 63. In his *Spicilegium Anatomicum* (1670), Kerckring referred to 'Franciscus van den Enden, Christianissime suae majestatis medicum . . .' *Observatio* XXIV. **Talents:** by De Nazelle 97–8, 105, 115. **French officer . . .** De Nazelle Apx. 244. Frans is said to have 'raised objections' at first: ibid. **Plot:** *see below, 267.* **One or more daughters:** Meininger (72) implies 3. De Nazelle (103) says he left 2 in Amsterdam, and that he took only 'his youngest daughter' (Marianna) to France: ibid 95, 107. But Mme Dargent 'his daughter' (ibid. 245) was in the school when Van den Enden was arrested (154 n.1). **Journey to Paris:** De Nazelle 105–7. **The IOU:** The debtor was the artist Joan Spilberg. Bond cashed 13 Sept. 1670: VD/VT 176–7: NAA 3204 f.92. **Kerckring's wealth:** Meininger 61. **'Solid financially':** VD/VT 176. **'Little creatures':** Banga 566–7, quoting Morhof, who visited Kerckring in 1669. **'Anatomical cabinet . . .'** Meininger 64, quoting Van der Goes, *Bruiloftsgedichten* (in full ibid. 170–1); Banga 565.

242 **Skills:** NNBW 2 663–4. **'Unreliability', 'plagiarism':** Banga 565 and 670, quoting Swammerdam. *Also Haller, above, notes to 85.* **Hunthum (Hauthum):** *above, 188, and below, notes to this page.* **Marriage:** DTB 334: text, Meinsma 390. Signature facsimiles: Meinsma 1896 332. **Cupid, etc.** Van der Goes, *Bruilofsgedichten:* Meininger 171. See also ibid. 64–5. **'Pass through the clouds . . .'** ibid. **Marianna 'put' in a convent** 31 Aug. 1674: De Nazelle 135. **2 daughters left:** ibid. 103. **1680 document:** 19 July NAA 2259/197. **Travel, son, deaths:** Meininger 66, quoting *Allgem. Deutsche Biographie.* **'Of suspect morals':** above, Haller, notes to 87. Meininger 66. **'Sister, or a servant':** Meinsma 503 n.55, citing *Allgem. Deutsche Biographie.* s.v. (Dutch version 1 v.). **Catharina Bode,** widow of Pieter Hunthum: 11 Sept. 1703: DTB 1134/56. **Pieter Hunthum,** husband of Catharina Linthijner, buried 25 June 1706: DTB 200. **'Elders of the Lutheran . . .'** Colerus 3–5. **Van der Spyck** an elder of the Lutheran community: HGA NA 1067/549.

243 **'More letters had been found . . .'** 1710: Dr Hallmann's *Journal of Travels,* quoted in FQ 231 ff. See also annotation to Ep.48A, Spinoza to Jelles, 19 April 1673: Wolf 1 443. *Atheists are usually . . .* Ep.43, Feb. 1671: S 237. *Recently paid me . . .* Ep.44: S 243. **Wittich:** just arrived at Leiden. Wolf (1 439) says only six points marked the space, and suggests Kranen, Cartesian professor of philosophy at Leiden. *Homo Politicus:* (S 243) According to Barbier's 1824 *Dictionary of Anonymous Works,* this book was published anonymously in 1664, and written by Christophorus Rapp, Chancellor to the Elector of Brandenburg: BW 485–6. But Meinsma refers to a rare list of Spinoza's papers (a copy of which was sent by Schuller to Leibniz) where the work is claimed to be a 2nd edition, published in 1648, its author 'Franciscus Datisius': Meinsma 393. *The restless and . . .* Ep.44: S 244. *It is not out of necessity . . .* ibid. The fable is from Diogenes Laertius's *Lives of the Philosophers:* S 244 n.234. **One commentator:** Jonathan Israel: Proceedings of the Amsterdam *Herdenking* 1997, Vereniging Het Spinozahuis. **Jelles, endowments:** *below, notes to 302.*

244 **Oath of allegiance:** 22 Jan. 1671: Friedenwald 71, citing Document No.5. **'Prepare a bill . . .'** 22 June 1671: VD/VT 187, quoting Public Record Office, London, Calendar of British State Papers, Colonial, 1669–74, no.570234. **Land grant to 'Abraham Spinosa' and Moses Yessurun Cardosa:** Andrade 134, citing County of Surrey (Jamaica) Liber 4 f.149, 20 Sept. 1672. **'In consideration that . . .'** ibid. 136. **Amsterdam** *parnas: above, notes to 173.* **Abraham/Gabriel** signatures: *above, 79.* **Earthquake:** Andrade 7, 221: Doc. 334/157.

245 **35,000 men:** Moorman 147–50, chiefly citing Rousset's *Vie de Louvois.* **'Huygens and Hudde':** April 1671: Rowen 1 417; HO VII, 57–78; 95–8; 103–4. **De Witt: onset of French aggression:** Rowen 1 737–742; 760–62; 768–70; 763, 766 and 778–80; Haley 1 277–8. **Dutch army:** Rowen 1 809–10. **William . . . 20,000 men:** Wicquefort IV 283. **Doing a deal . . .** Barlow was told this as a fact: *below, 248.* **William . . . Captain General:** Rowen 1 805–9.

246 **'Was a man who . . .':** Pontalis 2 361. **'All military matters':** Extracts from the Register of the Resolutions of the Heeren Staten van Holland en West Friesland, in their gathering of Monday 27 June, 1672: Tracts, 1786, BL 934 d3, 116–18. **Complaints about army payment system:** Wicquefort IV 587–88. **Changes in the role of** *solliciteur–militair,* 1673 and 1676: Zwitzer, H.L. *De Militie van den Staat,* van Soeren & Co. Amsterdam 1991, 92–4. *Sovereignty was always . . .* TTP XVIII: W 203. Temple 2 [1672] 57. **Kings must sometimes . . .** Calvin IV xx 11. **Passions:** E2 P34 ff; E4 P35 and D; TTP XVI: W 129 ff. **Views plain in TTP:** esp. Ch.XVIII: W 203. **3rd Anglo-Dutch naval war:** Rowen 1 816, 820. **Cornelis . . . monitored:** ibid. 505, 819. **France declared war:** ibid. 812. **Course of the war:** ibid. 822–7. **Sole Bay:** May (English dating); June (Dutch dating). **Pamphlets:** ibid. 853. **Embezzlement:** ibid. 840–1; 854–5. **Retraction:** Moorman 280. **Territory**

offer: Rowen 1 838. **Hot dry summer:** Gutmann 217. **Summer invasion from** 12 June: Rowen 1 831–5; Pontalis 2 309–12; 'The terror . . .' **6,000 calvary** . . . *Negociations* 12 with n.2.

247 **De Witt attacked:** Rowen 1 841–3. **Utrecht taken:** ibid. 849; Pontalis 2 317; Geyl 2 121–7. **Van Velthuysen:** Meinsma 420; Geyl 2. **Land flooded** 15–20 June 1672: Rowen 1 837; Moorman 167, 190–8. '**Gracht, trench or channel**': 'De Witt' 2 14 291; see Rowen 1 392. **Zuyder Zee:** Mignet 29. **Edict overturned** 3 July: Rowen 1846. **William Stadtholder of Holland and Zeeland,** 9 July 1672: ibid. 844–5. **Cornelis's arrest:** Rowen 1 864, 872, 889. **Visit to Prince:** 31 July 1672: ibid. 857. **Resignation and claim:** ibid. 853–5; Moorman 283. **20 Aug. 1672:** Rowen 1 873–82; Campbell lxxviii; Moorman 283–90. **Officers of the Blue Flag:** Wicquefort IV 487–8; Pontalis 2 487, 492.

248 '**Land Prince**', etc. Rowen 1 882. '**By the canaille** . . .' Moorman 290, quoting Van der Goes. Pontalis 2 487, 492. Rowen 1 880. **Cannibalism:** ibid. 882 (many primary sources); Pontalis 2 494; Campbell lxxix. See relics in The Hague's Historical Museum. '**Great joy** . . .' Pontalis 2 495, quoting an eye-witness account. '**Had taken some of** . . .' Barlow [1673] 234. **Willem 'turned pale':** Wicquefort IV 536; Pontalis 2 504, quoting De Benthem. **Amalia:** Rowen 1 886; Pontalis 2 505. **Huygens on De Witt:** Letter to Lodewijk Huygens, 4 Sept 1672, HO VII 218. *The mob is terrifying* . . . E4 P54 S. This comment inverts Tacitus's *In vulgo nihil modicum, terrere, ni paveant:* OPG 3 319; see TP VII: 27. '**He shed tears** . . .' Lucas 65.

249 '**Had been prompted** . . .' A note by Leibniz: De Careil 1 lxiv. '**But his host** . . .' ibid.

CHAPTER 10

250 *One man has another* . . . TP II 10: W 273–5. See also E4 P70 D. **3rd Anglo-Dutch naval war** (1672–4): Haley 2 287; Haley 3 102–5, citing Barbour, *Capitalism in Amsterdam in the Seventeenth Century,* Baltimore 1950 101–2, and *English Historical Documents* viii, 1660–1714, ed. A. Browning (1953) 854. **Sole Bay:** *above, 246.* '**Cabal**': initials of ministers Clifford, Arlington, Buckingham, Ashley (Shaftesbury) and Lauderdale: dissolved 1673. '**Thus ended one** . . .' Temple 1 vol. 1 381. '**The people are** . . .' Felltham (1652) 26, 29–30. '**Dutch courage**': see Brewer for about 20 other such insults. '**For pickled herring, pickled** *heeren* **changed** . . .' Marvell 96.

251 **William's cussedness:** Il possédait . . . l'opiniâtreté de ses ancêtres . . .' etc.: *Negociations* 75. **If the land were taken:** Macaulay 206 (no source.) 'If they had not . . .' De Gremonville: Pontalis 2 333. **De Witt's murder** Rowen 1 888. 'This affair': Pontalis 2 498. **Share prices:** Pontalis 2 319 and 497–8. **No easy victory:** Rowen 1 747–8 and Haley 2 288. *La Religion des Hollandois:* Letters written in May 1673, sent to a publisher 19 May: Meinsma 421, 433 n.15. **Utrecht** . . . **Catholics:** Kaplan, Benjamin J. 277. **Sacrament processed:** 22 May 1673: Geyl 2 138–9.

252 '**A very bad Jew** . . .' Stouppe 65. **No Dutch refutation:** ibid. 107–9. **Van Mansveldt's refutation:** Meinsma 432. *Juif renégat:* Stouppe 107. '**Writ several letters** . . .' Colerus 46. *Not worth reading* . . . Ep.50, to Jelles, June 1674: S 260. **Spinoza's copy:** (1674 q65 [41]). '**[Stouppe] was so much** . . . Colerus 46–7.

253 **Siege of Maastricht:** Gutmann 218; Letter from Louis, 1 July, 1673: *Negociations* 192. '**Nothing is to be** . . .' Pontalis 2 352, quoting Louis, in camp at Arnhem, 25 June, 1672: *Negociations* 85. **Religion the monarch's affair:** TTP XIX: W 205. *Everyone knows* . . . TTP XIX: W 217. Louis carped especially over Vatican claims to land and revenues: Williams, 266. **Hobbes and Catholicism:** *Leviathan* IV 44: Macpherson 632; ibid. IV Ch.XLVII, and last 3 chapters *passim:* '**Darknesse**': ibid.

704. *Modern sovereigns* . . . TTP XIX: W 225. 'The determination to flood . . .'
Mémoire de Louis XIV, Rousset, *Vie de Louvois* 1 Apx.

254 *Obedience is less* . . . TTP XVII: W 151–3. *Hope of some greater good:* TTP V: W 95.
'Who would not . . . ?' Bramhall, John. *A Defence of True Liberty from Ante-cedent and
Extrinsicall Necessity*, London 1655, quoted Hampton 190. **Monarchy unsuitable** . . .
TTP XVIII: W 199 (IV) and 203. *Inward piety* . . . TTP XIX: W 205. *The attempt to
make* . . . TTP XX: W 229. *Liber pestilentissimus:* Letter to Leibniz, 12 April 1671: FQ
193. **Louis-Joseph de Bourbon-Condé:** Family a cadet branch of the royal family.
Noblesse. 'Mon cousin le prince de Condé': Louis XIV, 1 July 1673; Negociations 192.
Soldier, etc: Mongrédien 200, 213, 222, 225, 229. **Wound:** Moorman 193. **Re
Stouppe:** Mongrédien 200; Moorman 325, quoting Russet *Vie de Louvois* 435–44.
Calvinist burghers: Mongrédien 224. **Religion affair of State:** Macaulay 1 160.
'Ravished . . . thousand honours': Mongrédien 197.

255 **Condé's conversion:** ibid. 229, 235. *Men holding high* Ep.13, to Oldenburg, July 1663:
S 111. **Journey to Utrecht:** Pontalis 2 329; Moorman 202; Meinsma 424, 425 citing
Booth, *Notes Quotidiennes* and *Journael*. Meinsma believes, solely on the basis of
coincidental dating, that Spinoza was accompanied to Utrecht by Everard Booth. Booth
would in 1674 return to his home town of Utrecht as a provincial councillor: *De
Verdediging van Nederland in 1672 en 1673*, Jhr. J.W. van Sypestein en J.P. Bordes.
Langhuysen, The Hague, 1850; *Vroedschap* 11 813. **Condé left:** 'An order from . . .':
Lucas 63. Wicquefort (IV 570) says he left 5 July. Vernière, citing G. Cohen's research
in the Musée Condé Chantilly, claims 15 July, and believes Spinoza reached Utrecht by
28 July: Vernière 24. Gutmann 218; Meinsma 426, citing Booth *Notes quotidiennes* 114
and *Journael* 204. 'M. de Luxembourg . . .' Lucas 63.

256 **'He submitted to it** . . .' Lucas 63. 'The Tractatus . . .' Ep.70, from Schuller,
[Autumn] 1675: S 325. **Thought better** . . . Ep.69, quoted *above* 235. On Nieuwstad
see Meinsma 427. **A six-line note:** Ep.49, 14 Dec. 1673. **Night mail:** Ep.49, marked
'Hagse nacht post' and signed 'Benedictus despinoza'. The provinces of Utrecht,
Gelderland and Overijssel were cut off for two years: Moorman 180. *It seemed to me* . . .
Ep.50, to Jelles, 2 June 1674: S 260. *Theologen . . . everywhere* . . . Ep.68, to Oldenburg,
Sept. 1675: S 321; also used in Ep.21, 28 Jan. 1665: BW 185. BW's editor suggests
hoogleraren (professors), or *boekverkopers* (booksellers). *Sçavanten:* TS 243–4.

257 *Cartesianen* . . . *the stupid* . . . Ep.68, Sept. 1675: S 321. **Condé returned to France
from Maastricht:** Wicquefort IV 570. 'After some weeks . . .' Lucas 63. 'Monsieur
Stouppe . . .' Colerus 48. See FQ 32–3 for an assertion that Spinoza did meet Condé.
'All [the Prince's] power . . .' Louis Morelli, quoted Mongrédien 225. **French
atrocities:** Wiquefort LXXIII, *Touchant ce qui s'est passé dans les villages de Bodegrave
et Swammerdam et les cruautés inouïes, que les français y ont exercées.* **Maurits** . . .
herrings: Van Deursen 19, citing Brandt and Centen *Historie*, 1 289. 'Always aimed
at . . .' Colerus 49. **Treasury gold** sent by De Witt: Rowen 1 835.

258 'After his return . . . was afraid . . .': Colerus 48. 'Spinosa put [Hendrik] . . .'
Colerus 48–9. 'Spent the greatest . . .' Colerus 41. **Once he did not** . . .' Lucas 60;
also JP 218, referring to the testimony of the people 'with whom he lodged'. **'Friends
persuaded him** . . .' Lucas 63. **Burgh and Van Beuningen cousins:** Francès 93.
William contrived downfall: Pontalis 2 430 ff. **De Witt's cousin** Ascanius van
Sypesteyn: ibid. 506–7.

259 'Some lavish . . .' 'De Witt' 3 1 334. **Van den Hove:** Rowen 1 395–6. **William
autocratic:** Wicquefort IV 620, 624; Geyl 2 147–52; a 'despot': Moorman 293. 'The
Majesty of Orange . . .' Pontalis 2 511. 'As dead as I . . .' Temple 1 Vol. 2 395.
Letter of 14 April 1676. Van Beuningen at peace talks with Willem July 1672:
Wiquefort IV 454. 'A great creature . . .' Rowen 1 846. **Persuaded** . . . Rowen 1
859–60. **Eternal Edict:** ibid. 679. **William wanted Van Beuningen:** Moorman
235ff, 257, 261–2, 271, 295. **Rapport and quarrel:** ibid. 348 with n.1. **Van Beuningen:**

1672 pamphlets: *Beklagh over de Bedroefden Toestant in de Nederlantse Provintien* (Amsterdam 1672): Knuttel, *Pamfletten* 10237. *Eenige Prophetien en Revelatien Godst's Aengaende de Christen werelt in deze eeuw* (1672): ibid. 9932. **Dream about Louis,** 'par le Sieur van Beuningen', 19 Nov. 1689: Knuttel 13336. **'Ridiculous ... thousand-yearist':** Philopater 121. Van den Enden also talks of 'domme duizent-jarige rijks-gezinden'': KVNN 52. **Paid for publication of the German mystic Boehme:** Kolakowski 715 n.169. **Psychosis:** *Vroedschap* II 514; Petry 167 n.75; Roldanus 160. **Last papers:** Knuttel 13339, 49, 72, 70, 71.

260 *I doubt very much:* Ep.73, to Oldenburg, 1 Dec. 1675: OPG 4 308. *Reges* = King. Shirley (S 333) misses Spinoza's pun on King's Evil. **Most 'violent' preachers:** Simon Simonides and Thaddeus de Landman: *Mignet* 23, quoting Cerisier *Histoire Générale* VII 359–60; Wicquefort IV 613–14. *See above, 166.* **Sovereignty ... stadholder rule:** *The people of* Holland ... TP IX 14: W 427. *Comitatus* means a throng or retinue, later a court, place or seat of an emperor. I have altered Wernham's translation slightly to accommodate this. *By the right and ...* TTP XVI: W 125 – a principle restated in TP II, 2–3, 4, 7. **Appetite the essence of man:** TP II 5: W 269. See also E3 Def. Affects 1 Exp.: C 531; E3 P9 S. *The power of the mind ...* E5 P20 SV. *It is clear ...* E5 P42 S.

261 **Ban 19 July 1674:** FQ 139 reproducing *Groot Placeat-Boek* III 523f. *Opera Posthuma* banned 25 June 1678: FQ 179–81 (*Groot-Placaet-boek* III 525ff). *When the state ...* TP X 10: W 439. **Machiavelli:** *Discourses* iii, 24. Noted by Wernham (439 n.2) and others. *If men are puffed ...* TP VII 27: W 359. **Confession of the Universal Christian Faith**: printed by Rieuwertz, Amsterdam, in 1684 as *Belijdenisse des algemeenen en christelijken geloofs, vervattet in een brief aan NN, door Jarig Jelles*, extracts from which form Ep.48A in S and BW. **'Stop the mouth ...'** Ep.48A: BW 303. **'Conditions ...'** Jacobius Acontius, *Stratagematum Satanae Libri Octo* (1565) BW 489–90. Jelles writes of his adherence to the 'judgement of Jacobus Acontius': (*na het ordeel van Jacobus Acontius*) Ep.48A: BW 304. **Spinoza's influence:** Jelles quotes Hooft's poem from his *Gedichten* of 1636, so endorsing Hooft's Calvinist belief in predestination: JP 264. See Spinoza's early distinction between Providence and Calvin's Predestination in KV I V and VI: C 84–5. The BW's notes. to Ep.48A indicate weak parallels in Jelles's and Spinoza's texts, as does Kolakowski 217–25.

262 **'Going into details ...'** refused critical examination: Ep.48A, BW 303–4. **Three accounts:** in BW only, but see Wolf's notes: Wolf I 442–3. **'Friend outside the town'** ... *I have read ...'* Ep.48B: BW 306. **Bayle:** Bayle 302; see also FQ 32 n.1. **'On page 5 ...'** Ep.48B, 19 April 1673: S 255. **'He who has the Spirit ...'** ibid.

263 **'To accept a regular ...'** Ep.47, 16 Feb. 1673. **The Prince-Elector:** See Meinsma 407 and Wolf I 441, quoting the learned courtier Urbain Chevreau, who claims to have shown the Prince the PPC: *Chevraeana*, Amsterdam [1700] II, 99. See also Clair, *Cahiers Spinoza* II, 209–10. *If I am to find time ... I do not know that ...* Ep.48, March 1673. **Heidelberg university burned down ...** Meinsma 409 n.76, crediting Wilhelm Bolin, *Spinoza, ein Kultur-und Lebensbild*, Berlin, 1894. *Men whose consciences ...* TTP XX: W 239. **Satisfaction of mind:** E5 P32 P and C.

CHAPTER 11

264 *Most esteemed Sir ...* Ep.56, to Boxel, Oct. 1674: S 279. **5-Part Treatise ready:** *below, 256.* **Freedom of mind, or blessedness.** E5 Pref. **Syrups ... oak** (*Symphyto Dodonaei*) ... 'Tendency to violent ...' Abarbanel XXIV and XXVII.

265 *Your letter ...* Ep.52, Sept. 1674: S 262. *I beg you to ...* ibid. *Here I shall ...* ibid. 263. *I am surprised ...* Ep.54, Sept. 1674: 267. *One the one hand ...* ibid. 267–8.

266 'I say that . . . As to their . . .' Ep.55, Sept. 1674: 274, 272. *That your conjecture . . .* Ep.56, Sept. 1674: S 278. This letter's final words head Chapter 11, above. **Treaty of Nijmegen**, 1678, returned Maastricht and all other gains: Williams 458. *Patricians will never . . .* 'Violence . . .' Des Maizeaux 11 141. *A man who is guided . . .* E4 P73.

267 **Successful school in Paris:** Meininger 71 and 95–8. **New 'wife':** De Nazelle (p.107) admired the 53-year-old Catherina Medaens, but was not sure there had been a marriage contract. **Husbands for 2 daughters:** Meininger 72, citing Dozy, R. *Frankrijks ellende onder Lodewijk XIV*, Paris 1865. **Louis de Rohan:** *Noblesse* Vol. XVII 508 and 467–8. **Quillebeuf plot:** De Nazelle 112 with n.1. **Franco-Dutch republic:** See 19c sources cited by Feuer 20 n.40, and the *Plan de gouvernement* or 'fourth kind of republic' admitted by Van den Enden during his trial to have been given to de Latréaumont in Amsterdam: Klever 6 620. **Arrests:** Du Cause de Nazelle was the betrayer: De Nazelle 150. See also French and Dutch newspapers of Sept.-Nov.1674 quoted by Meininger 87, citing Krämer, 73–4 and 113. **'The trial of De Rohan':** Reports from the *Amsterdamsche Courant* No.38, 20 Sept. 1674 until No.49, 6 Dec. 1674: Meininger 172–6. Lucas moved to Amsterdam from Rouen in 1671: Meininger 83, citing Kleerkoper. **Journalist Lucas** is not said to have written for the *Amsterdamsche Courant:* Wolf 2 25. **'Born in Antwerp . . .'** *Amsterdamsche Courant* No 46, 13 Nov.1674, Meininger 174; Meinsma 461. **Hanged:** De Nazelle, Apx 263. Rhetoric: '*Spraekmeester*': *Amsterdamsche Courant* op.cit. Meininger 174; De Nazelle 100.

268 **'A spirit from . . . the reputation':** ibid. 97. **'Sorry that the mild . . .'** Meininger 122, quoting Bodemann, E. (ed.) *Briefwechsel der Herzogin Sophie von Hannover mit ihrem Bruder* Leipzig, 1885. **Brother's letter:** 17 Nov. 1674: ibid. *Completely distracted . . .* Ep.58, Oct.1674: Wolf 1 294 *OP*. **Unwell that Oct.:** Ep.58, Oct.1674. **Downstairs:** *below, 287.*

269 **'Though there is nothing . . .'** Lucas 73. **Count von Tschirnhaus:** Meinsma 431–2 and 435. **Plague deaths 1669:** Coccejus: NNBW 1 616; Guelincx: Meinsma 431 with n.63. **Reply to von Tschirnhaus:** Ep.58 op.cit. **On motion:** Ep.59, from von Tschirnhaus, 5 Jan. 1675.

270 *Since my views . . .* Ep.60, Jan. 1675: S 291. **Prevarication in TIE:** TIE [27] with n.i: C 16. *It belongs more . . .* KV 1 ix: C 91. *Every particular . . .* KV Apx 2 [14]: C 155, and Ep.6, April 1662: C 182. See Lachterman 81–3, and *above, 120.* **2 Defs.:** Ep.63, 25 July 1675, and Spinoza's reply Ep.64, 29 July 1675. **Plan to publish *Ethics* in 1675:** *While I was engaged . . .* Ep.68, Sept.1675: S 321. **Von Tschirnhaus's army service . . . reputation:** Meinsma 432, 436. **'Will you please . . .'** Ep.65 (from London) 12 Aug. 1975: S 301.

271 **'Reply to the Preceding':** Ep.66, 18 Aug. 1675: S 302. (The calendar difference lengthens the gap between these letters by 10 days.) *We neither . . .* E2 A5. *If the object . . .* E2 P13 D. *Thus, most excellent Sir . . .* Ep.64, July 1675: S 300. **Wet summer:** Gutmann 219. **From Tschirnhaus's first letter:** Wolf 1 454 annot.

272 *No connection with the others . . .* Ep.66, Aug. 1675: S 302. **'Mr Boyle and Oldenburg . . .'** Ep.64, 25 July, 1675: S 297. **'Very profound insight into . . .'** Ep.61, June 1675: S 293. **'Since . . . it is your':** Ep.62, July 1675: S 294.

273 **Burgh at Leiden:** enrolled 20 Feb. 1668: Meinsma 430. **'Should anything worthy . . .'** Ep.67, 3 Sept. 1675: S 303. **Burgh's earlier views:** Ep.76, Spinoza to Burgh: S 340. **Conversion:** described in *Oeuvres de Messire Antoine Arnauld*, Paris-Lausanne, 1778–81 (1) 861 sq. This was a re-edition of *L'Apologie pour les Catholiques contre les faussetés et calomnies d'un livre intitulé La Politique du Clergé de France*, 1674. See Meinsma 430 and 447, n.57. **Steno's *footsteps*:** Ep.76, Spinoza to Burgh, Dec. 1675: S 340. **Barefoot:** *Oeuvres de Messire . . . op.cit.* **'The more I have . . .'** Ep.67, 3 Sept. 1675: S 303. **'Deadly arrogance':** ibid. S 305. **'Do you then dare . . .'** ibid.

274 'I have written...' ibid. 312. **Joined a mendicant** ... *Oeuvres de Messire*, op.cit. 11
476. *What I could* ... Ep.76, to Burgh, Dec. 1675: S 340. 'To the Reformer...
While public peace ... I see shrouded... And although...' Ep.67A, from
Florence, Sept.1675: S 313–4. On dating see *above 156*. 'I shall not speak...' ibid. S
318. 'Scrutinise... For it is a religion...' ibid. 318.

275 'I am indeed fully... As first-fruits': ibid. S 310, 320. *Point out* ... Ep.68, Sept/
Oct. 1675: S 322. *Put in writing* ... Ep.69: S 323. 'Your writings': Ep.70, 14 Nov.
1675: S 327. **Leibniz: background and research:** Aiton 9–25, 48.

276 'He would wager ... insinuated himself...' *Theodicy* Para. 376: (Ed. Farrer,
1952.) **Helped Arnauld with Hebrew, etc.:** De Nazelle 101. **Arnauld's opinion of
Leibniz:** Arnauld to the Landgraf Ernst von Hessen-Rheinfels, 13 March 1686: quoted
Barber 13. **Essay on optics:** *Notitia Opticae Promotae, The Complete Works of Leibniz*,
11, 1768: Wolf 1 253, 440; BW 486. 'Among your other...' Ep.45, Oct. 1671: S 245.
Spinoza's reply... Hudde: Ep.46, Nov.1671. 'In metaphysical studies...'
Ep.70, [Autumn] 1675: S 327. *I believe I know* ... Ep.72, 18 Nov. 1675: S 330–1.
Letters missing: details, Steenbakkers 40–2. *See above, notes to 157*. **Leibniz's
condemnation of TTP:** e.g. in a letter to Thomas of Jan. 1672 he referred to its
'monstrous' opinions: FQ 194. *Greet that friend* ... Ep.72: S 331.

277 'Strange metaphysic...' *see below, 288*. 'Which have proved ... I refer in
particular...' Ep.71, 15 Nov. 1675: S 329. **Notes to the French TTP** (*La Clef du
Sanctuaire*): Lucas 60–1 nn.7, 8. *I entertain an opinion... However, as to* ... Ep.73,
Dec. 1675: S 332. *This, I believe* ... Ep.73: S 333. *As to the additional* ... ibid. 333.

278 **Henry's protests:** Ep.74, 16 Dec. 1675. *At last I see ... Christ did not appear...*
Ep.75, Dec. 1675: (Dutch dating 1 Jan. 1676: BW 408): S 337, 338. *The passion,
death* ... Ep.78, Feb. 1676: S 348. 'Been assured that...' Bayle 320. *This
inevitability* ... Ep.75: S 337. *I will concede* ... Ep.76, 1675 (Dutch dating Jan. 1676): S
340. *The title of mysteries ... prince of evil...These absurdities* ... ibid. 341. **Tiernan:**
ibid. with n.378.

279 *O mindless youth* ... ibid. **Shirley's** *deprived of understanding* does not, in my view,
capture the Latin of OPG 4 319. *You can give* ... ibid. 342. *You have become* ... ibid.
344. *Single cause* ... (see also E5 P42 S). 'There is an easy...' Ep.67: S 305. *When
you were in your senses* ... Ep.76: S 341. *Do you take it* ... ibid. 344. *The organisation
...* ibid. 343. *Examine the histories* ... ibid. 344. *Cartesian principles* ... Ep.81, to Von
Tschirnhaus, 5 May 1676: OPG 4 332. **Extracts:** Eps.60, 66, 81, 83 (Jan.1675–July
1676).

CHAPTER 12

280 *Love towards God* ... E5 P16. *To have shown* ... TP VII 2: W 335. **The wise man:**
E5 Pref.: C 594. *Salvation* ... E5 P36 s. **Unconscious ideas:** *see above, 121.
Intellectual love of God* ... E5 P32 C and P33. *Which cannot be* ... E5 P19 SV,
referring to E5 Ps 15–16: C 606. **Remedies for the affects:** E5 Pref. **The first of
these** ... E5 P3 and Co; E5 P10 S..

281 *A last kind of knowledge* ... KV 2 ii [3]: C 99. **Perception we have** ... TIE [19 (4)], [22].
Love toward the eternal ... ibid. [10]. 'God's existence is...' *Almost all the
knowledge* ... PPC 1 P5 and S. *The man whose main* ... TTP IV: W 71. **Dominion of
reason over affects.** E5 Pref.: C 595.

282 *How much more powerful* ... E5 P36 S: C 613. **Particular essences** ... E5 P25 P; E2
P40 S2; TIE [101]. *The more we understand* ... E5 P24. *The essences of singular* ... TIE
[101]. *We call that clear* ... KV 2 11: C 99. *There seems to be* ... *The things I* ... TIE
[102], [22]. 'As I gather...' Yovel 165. **Mathematical examples:** TIE [22] and E2

P40 S2 [1V]. 'Salvation': Yovel 167–9. *Who understands himself . . . Love towards God . . .* E5 P15 P and P16.

283   **Active intellect:** Abravanel 36–7, 45. **Maimonides:** EP 5 131, 132. Spinoza owned his *Guide to the Perplexed* (*Moreh Nebuchim*) (1515, f19), which does not contain this view. **Sephardic-cabalic-Neoplatonic** . . . For extensive information, see Kaplan 2. Maimonides was born in Córdoba, Spain: EP 5 129. Abravanel in Lisbon: *above, 105.* Ebreo's (Abravanel's): Kristeller 10. **Rational view:** EP op.cit. **Union with God's mind:** Jesuit *Spiritual Exercises:* Cox 150. **Salamanca university:** e.g., St Peter of Alcantara, Juan de Avila, St John of the Cross: ibid. 154, 164. 'A 'great precursor . . .' Peers 322. **References to Suárez:** ibid. **Santa Teresa:** Hosea 2: 19–20: Silverman 2 129–1; Psalms: Cox 42–44, 78; Bernadete 77, 83. 'A glorious folly . . .' Peers 126, quoting *Vida* Ch.XVI and *Obras* i 117.

284   'Active Intellect . . . Knowing and loving . . .' Abravanel 45 and 47. 'Broke through the . . .' Feuer 222. 'Eagle . . . excellent men': Van Schurman 26. **Aboab's (Pereira's)** *yeshiva:* VD/VT 153, 155, citing De Barrios *Arbol de Vida* [*c.*1684]. 'Time indeed . . .' Abravanel 64. 'Born of reason . . . not restricted . . .' ibid. 57–8. 'Jesus . . . imagination': TTP II: Es 41. *Communed with God* . . . TTP I: Es 19; see also TTP IV: W 79 (with n.2), 81, 83. **New synagogue** designed by Elias Bouman: Dubiez 9–10, citing *Livro dos Acordos* 1671. It cost 186,06ofl. See 'The Portuguese Synagogue in Amsterdam' by Emanuel de Witte (Rijksmuseum, Amsterdam). **Dimension of churches** . . . TP XIII 46: W 411. **Reinstatement of Stadholder rule:** Israel 2 Ch.VI 'The Court Jews 1650–1713', 123–44, esp.127.

285   *I myself know* . . . Ep.76, Dec. 1675: S 343. Judah (Christian-born Don Lope de Vera y Alarcon) was burned by the Inquisition in Valladolid in 1644. Menasseh wrote about him in *Hope of Israel* [1650] ibid. and Wolf 1 474. 'Had always had it . . .' JP (Latin text only) 253. 'Up to this point . . .' ibid. 255. *There are many . . . Hebrew Grammar* 36. *They wrote a grammar* . . . ibid. 36. **Reference to a 2nd part:** ibid. 2. **Maimonides:** *above, notes to 268.* **Del Medigo,** Joseph. *Sepher Tabuith Hechal* (1659, q53 [29]); *Abscondita Sapientiae* (q54 [30]); *Sefer Elim* (numerology, 1627, q55 [31]). *Hagadah Pesach* (1505, f24). **Hana married Samuel Idanha:** Emmanuel 252 and 326, DTB 669/12. *Saudade:* Payne 244, 161; Yovel 24.

286   *Perhaps, if I live* . . . Ep.83, to von Tschirnhaus: July 1676: S 355. *The intellectual Love* . . . E5 P33. *Death is less* . . . E5 P38 S. *For the eternal* . . . E5 P40 Co.. *God's love of men* . . . E5 P36 C; Abravanel 33, 250. 'An entity of geometrical . . .' Feuer 215–6. **The Love towards God, etc.:** E5 P20. 'Self . . . streak of masochism . . . a form of self-hatred . . .' Feuer 216, 218. *The power of the intellect* . . . Title to E5. 'Hatred of the body . . . love is rarefied . . .' Feuer 219. 'There was a component . . .' ibid. 221.

287   'Had become almost constant . . .' Lucas 73. **Fever . . . tubercolosis:** See Appendix. 'Came down': *Hy lag ook niet te bedde, maar was de laatste morgen nog beneden, ook sliep hy in geen Ledekant, maar in een bedstede op de voorkamer:* K 77. Colerus 95 distorts this. *I thank you* . . . Ep.84 [undated] 1676: S 357. **Jelles** . . . **Hobbesian politics:** Ep.50, June 1674. **The scholar who thinks** . . . Akkerman, *Studies* 273 n.70. 'How, from Extension . . .' Ep.82, June 1676: S 353. *I think I have* . . . Ep.83, July 1676: S 355. **'General Physics'** and motion, and Spinoza's reply in Ep.60, Jan, 1675: *above,* 269.

288   **Leibniz:** A paper he called *Pacidius Philaletes seu prima de motu philosophia:* Letter to Kahm, Nov. 1676: Aiton 67. 'Did not see . . .' De Careil 1 lxiv. **Defended Descartes:** *above, 171.* 'Composition of the continuum . . .' theory of monads: For Leibniz there were infinitely many substances, which after 1695 he called 'monads': *Monadology* (1714): Parkinson 179ff. **Microscopy connection:** Aiton 69. 'Strange Metaphysic . . .' Letter to Gallois, 1677: Loemker 1 259; FQ 206. 'Everything happens . . .' Letter of 30 April 1687: Parkinson 65 and 68. 'Spoke with

[Spinoza] . . .' Letter to Gallois, op.cit. **Leibniz's proofs:** *That a most perfect being exists:* in 2 parts: Nov. 1676 and 2 Dec. 1676: Loemker 1 259–62. See also *On Freedom c.* 1689, paras 9 and 12.

289   **This wrangle** . . . See, for example, Walker, Ralph, 'Sufficient Reason', *Proceedings of the Aristotelian Society* (XCVII) 1997. **'Such a God** . . .' Leibniz: Loemker 1 262. **'The philosopher is not a citizen** . . .' Wittgenstein, L. *Zettel.* Ed. G.E.M. Anscombe and G.H. von Wright. Blackwell, 1981, 455. **'A short time before** . . .' JP 248–9.

290   *The causes and natural* . . . TP I 7: W 265. *I have shown that* . . . TP I 5: W 265. *Multitudo:* Wernham gives 'a people'. *Repentance is not* . . . E4 P54. *To have shown* . . . TP VII 2: W 335. *Men are necessarily* . . . TP I 5: W 263; E4 P4 Co. **'The Reason of State** . . .' Béthune, *Le Conseiller d'Estat*, Paris [1633] 326, quoted by Skinner 429. **Duc de Rohan:** died 1638; married to Marguerite de Béthune: *Noblesse* 351, 353. **'Our own interest** . . .' Rohan 1639: *De l'interest des princes et estats de la Chrestienté* 132–3, translated in Skinner 428. **'Forasmuch as the laws** . . .' *De Cive* 111 25: Hobbes 172.

291   **'Means to obtain** . . .' *Leviathan* 1 10: Macpherson 150. **If 'interest requires** . . .' ibid. 1 11 166. See Skinner 426–7. **Second-best democracy:** see McShea 132. See also Feuer 40. *In certain persons only* . . . *whose private interests* . . . TP VII 4: W 337 and VIII 15: W 381. *Those who confine* . . . TP VII 27: W 359.

292   *Pride is characteristic* . . . TP VIII: W 409. *The sudden overthrow* . . . TP IX 14: W 427. *Constitution established* . . . *Supported by reason* . . . TP X 9: W 437. Wernham refers to Aristotle, *Politics* 1295 ª40. *It is really* . . . TP VIII 44: W 409. *By a stronger* . . . TP X 10: W 437. *First, in a well-organized* . . . TP X 10: W 439.

293   **'Inveterate irreverence** . . .' Green 67. *Devotion to some* . . . *true knowledge and* . . . TP III 10: W 293. *Nobody can give up* . . . TP III 8: W 289–91. *Right* . . . *law of the commonwealth* TP II 3: W 287. *It is quite inconceivable* . . . TP III 3: W 285. *Men hold rights* . . . TP II 15: W 277. *Peace cannot be* . . . TP III 7: W 289. **Heroics of Van den Enden:** esp. TP 111 8, last lines. *All patricians* . . . TP VIII 46: W 411. *Although everyone* . . . TP XIII 46: W 411.

294   **Christ not mentioned** . . . or in *Ethics. Love finds its supreme expression* . . . TP III 10: W 293. **'Your religion's all right** . . .' Colerus 41; K32. The English version is inaccurate.

295   *Did not the principles* . . . *above, notes to 15.* **Women controlling:** De la Barre 124 and 128: *above, 181.* **Women** *gemeenten biedenaars:* KVNN 52–9. *Absolutely* . . . TP XI 3: W 443. **Spinoza's exclusions:** See also TP VIII 14: W 381. **Jan van den Hove** (1662): Kerkhoven 6 and 10, citing *Consideratien van staat ofte Polityke Weeg-schaal.* Wernham believes Van den Hove (111, 4, 564–5) excludes the same classes as Spinoza: TP VIII, 14: W 381 n.2. **Stricture on women standard:** Kerkhoven 4–5, citing D. Haks, *Huwelijk en gezin in Holland in de 17de en 18de eeuw. Processtukken en moralisten over aspecten van het laat 17de – en 18de eeuwse gezinsleven*, Assen, 1982, 157. Saint-Évremond: Des Maizeaux 1 xcii–xciii. *If nature had made* . . . TP XI 4: W 443.

296   **Women would abuse rights:** Matheron 377, 381. *If we also consider* . . . TP XI: W 445. **Spinoza realised the cruelty** . . . Matheron 381. **Exaggerates** . . . 'as is often said': ibid. 379 and 380. *We understand nothing about* . . . Spinoza's note f to TIE [19 (3)]. **'Something':** *'Il y a quelque chose*, qui les désavantage dans le jeu des rapports de pouvoir que sont condamnés à entretenir tous les membres du genre humain sous le régime de la passion': Matheron 378.

297   **Theory of the elements and humours:** Gullan-Whur 1 21, 38 and Ch. 5, esp. 99–101. Spinoza describes a standard feature of the melancholic: in E4 P35 S: C 564. **'Every man and woman** . . .' **'He began to find himself** . . .' **'I would not deny** . . .' **'Think on fulfilling** . . .' Abravanel 356–7 and 467–8.

298   *The definition of those* . . . E3 'Defs. of the Affects' VI. Exp. Kristeller (9) believes Spinoza may have had Ebreo (Abravanel) in mind, but as Curley points out, 'the

conception of love here objected to goes back as far as Plato's *Symposium*'. '**Take heed that . . .**' Jewish hymn: the *Lecha Dodi: above, 21. Paixoes: above, 42.* '**Powerful eagle . . .**' Peers 159, quoting Teresa's *Vida: Obras* Vol.1. The eagle . . . Gullan-Whur 1 147 ff.

299 *Who has bewitched . . .* Ep.76, Dec. 1675: S 342. *Uneducated countrymen . . .* TTP II: Es 27. *Nor is this contrary . . .* TTP II Es 27. **Ribca's claim:** C 100–1; VD/VT 171 and FQ 165–7, quoting ARA NAA.

300 '**The inventory of a true . . .**' Colerus 101. See Van Roojien, 111–16. The books in the Rijnsburg museum-library replicate those listed in the inventory. '**Strong temper . . . outbursts**': Shmueli 209, 210, 211. '**Enslavement**': Feuer 218. See also Popkin, 'Another Spinoza'. '**Sallow**' . . . 'avait un teint olivâtre et quelque chose d'Espagnol dans son visage': Leibniz (1700): FQ 220. Schuller expected the death (Letter to Leibniz, 6 Feb. 1677: FQ 202), but knew Spinoza did not anticipate dying since he made no will: Letter of 26 Feb. 1677: FQ 202. '**His landlord . . .**' Colerus p.91. '**If he happened . . .**' ibid. 40. '**Trivial . . . embarrassing:** Steenbakkers 69.

301 **Meyer an editor:** *Philopater* [1697] 55; see Steenbakkers 18–19 (Monnikhoff and Bayle) and 25–8, 35. **Not an editor:** ibid. 25, citing Meijer (1897) 606, and Gebhardt. '**That friend of Schiedam**': Colerus 97. There was also a sale of Spinoza's effects in Oct. 1677: Colerus 101; FQ 172–3. **Leibniz:** 'famous Jew': 1700: Otium Hannoveranum, op.cit. **Considered coming:** Steenbakkers 61, citing *Akademie-Ausgabe* 3rd series, 2 No.40118. **A copy of *Ethics* stolen:** Steenbakkers (56–8) gives this story thorough examination. **Leibniz's copy** 1678: Friedmann 190. **Half-barrel:** *above, 236 and notes.* **Initials L.M.:** Steenbakkers 59–60. '**That very evening . . .**' Colerus 92–3. A *dukaton* was a half-ducat. **Schuller present:** The name 'Georgius Hermanus' is crossed out on the first inventory of 21 Feb. 1677; Schuller's names were Georg Hermann: Steenbakkers 59. See also FQ 156 n.4. **Conflicting accounts:** Letters to Leibniz and Von Tschirnhaus, 26 Feb. 1677, and from von Tschirnhaus to Leibniz, 17 April 1677, cited or quoted in Steenbakkers, 56–60 (also FQ 203–7). **Raked through . . .** Letters from Schuller to Leibniz, 29 March and 19 Sept. 1677, quoted ibid. 61–2. **Inherited rare books:** 'ad meas manus devoluta est': Schuller to Leibniz 29 March 1677: ibid. 56, with n.162.

302 **Editors of Latin version:** Steenbakkers 16. **Schuller's Latin . . . Bouwmeester:** ibid. 17. **Dutch version:** ibid. 16. **Balling's contribution:** Akkerman 1980. **Dead within six years:** *see dates beside names in index.* '**Profane, blasphemous . . .**' Ban of 25 June: FQ 179–81, quoting *Groot Placaet-Boek* 111 525 f. *Ethics:* Alternative Parts titles listed: Steenbakkers 30. **Meyer weakened JP:** Sections 30, 52: Akkerman *Studies* 267 n.30, 269 n.52. '**Pulpit**' style: ibid. 266. **Altered Jarig's judgements:** ibid. 248–9, 272 n.70. **New Testament quotations** listed ibid. 254–6. '**Had not death . . .**' JP 216. See also Colerus 74, and *above, 118. Treatise on the Rainbow:* JP 218: 'several years earlier . . . hidden': Meyer, JP 219. 'The testimony . . .' letters . . . JP 218. '**Had withdrawn himself . . .**' JP 216. '**All that could be collected . . .**' ibid. 218. *Oranjeappel* orphanage. Steenbakkers 39–41, listing 13 letters found there. Jelles gave 300 fl. to this orphanage when it was set up in 1675: Wolf 1 410. A mortgage bond was given to a Frisian Mennonite orphanage in 1681: Van der Tak 3 20 (NAA 2009).

303 '**Essential . . . universal**': Ep.48A, BW 303, 304. *Symbool* = set of articles of belief. '**On Sunday . . .**' K 75. '**Stoical or unfeeling**': K 77. **To talk to Schuller . . .** K 77; Steenbakkers 59–60. *Curse or laugh . . .* E3 Pref. See also TP I 4: W 263. **Grand funeral:** billed to Rieuwertz: Colerus 97. '**Many illustrious . . .**' ibid. 98. **De Witt** buried there: Wicquefort IV 532. **Spinoza buried** 25 Feb. 1677: K 80. In rented grave No.162: FQ 156 Doc. 66. His remains were moved 12 years later to some unknown place in the graveyard: Van Suchtelen I 477.

POST MORTEM:

304   The vilifications: *above, 150, 195, 222*. A presumptuous Neo-Cartesian: *above, 155–6*; Pollock 353–4. 'Disciples and imitators . . . stealing gradually . . .' Leibniz (1704): *New Essays on Human Understanding*, trans. and ed. Peter Remnant and Jonathan Bennett, Cambridge University Press, 1981, 262.

305   Locke as refugee: Bourne, H.R.F, *The Life of John Locke*, Harper, New York, 1876, Vol.II, 17–24; *The Correspondence of John Locke*, ed. E.S. De Beer, Oxford University Press, 1976–1989. 8 Vols. I, xxiv–xxxi. 'God, spirits . . . modifications' etc: *An Essay Concerning Human Understanding* (1690), collated and annot. by Alexander Campbell Fraser, 2 Vols, Dover Publications, 1959, Book II Ch. XVIII: Fraser Vol.I, 229 n.2. An imagined material God: ibid. Book IV Ch.X: Fraser Vol. II 316 n.2. Accusation of Spinozistic atheism: ibid. quoting William Carroll, 1706. 'The author of the finest . . .: Leibniz, *New Essays*, op.cit. 55. 'Pitiful or unintelligible: Leibniz: *Doctrine of a Universal Spirit*, 1702: Loemker II, 902. 'Well held up to ridicule . . .': ibid. 908. 'It is not true . . .: Bayle 300. 'An ill look' . . . 'bore a character' . . .: Colerus 90, quoting the *Menagiana* printed in Amsterdam in 1695. It was written by 'Mr Menagius' of Paris's French University: K 93. Mockery of grace, 1704: FQ 221. 'Those who were acquainted with him' . . . 'All who have refuted . . .: Bayle 295.

306   'It is not as easy . . .: ibid. 295–7. 'It must not be forgotten . . .: ibid. 300. Bayle probably refers to Spinoza's descriptions of the devil and hell as *absurdities*: Letter 76, to Burgh: S 341, 344. He may have had no access to the arguments on the necessary non-existence of the devil, and the lack of necessity for positing a devil, of KV II XXV, since the *Short Treatise* was not included in the *Opera Posthuma*. 'Wild imaginations . . .: George Berkeley: Dialogue 2 in *The Principles of Human Knowledge, With Other Writings*, ed. and intr. G.J. Warnock, Fontana Paperbacks, London, 1962, 199. 'Anything at all . . .: ibid. 'Hideous hypothesis': David Hume: *A Treatise of Human Nature*, Analytical Index L.A. Selby-Bigge, 2nd Edition with text revised and notes by P.A. Nidditch, Clarendon Press, Oxford, 1978, Bk. 1 Pt.IV §V, 241. 'Two different systems': ibid. 242. 'Bayle's dictionary': ibid. 243. 'Then a little Jew . . .: Les Systèmes', *Satires c.*1722, in *Oeuvres Complètes de Voltaire*, Paris, 1877, X, 170–71.

307   'Spinoza, in his famous book . . .': ibid. 171 n.1. 'Bayle, taking Spinoza's philosophy to the letter. . .': ibid. 171 Note 1. Count de Boulainvilliers: Pollock 363. 'Thing-in-itself': Immanuel Kant, *Critique of Pure Reason*. Trans. Norman Kemp Smith, second impression with corrections, Macmillan Education Ltd, London, 1987, A30, B45. 'Rationalist extravagance': *Prolegomena and Metaphysical Foundations of Natural Science*, trans. Ernest Belfort Bax, George Bell, London, 1883, Appendix 133. 'If I am to call myself . . .': Lessing in conversation with Jacobi, 5 July 1780: trans. in Pollock's Chapter XII, 'Spinoza and Modern Thought', 366.

308   'He does not prove the existence. . .':. Letter 172, to F. Jacobi, 9 June 1785, in *Letters from Goethe*, trans. M. von Herzfeld and C. Melvil Sym, Edinburgh University Press, 1957 pp. 157–8. 'Profound thinker . . . mild and benevolent countenance . . . Ether . . . Substance with Spinoza . . . Neither are extension and thought . . . death blow to morality . . . The allegations of those . . . Those who defame . . .': *Lectures on the History of Philosophy* (1837), Vol III, trans. E.S. Haldane and Frances H. Simson, Routledge and Kegan Paul, London and Humanities Press, New York,, 1968, 254, 289, 269, 279, 281–2.

309   Spinoza and the Romantic movement: see, for example, Craig, Edward, *The Mind of God and The Works of Man*, Oxford University Press, 1987, 144–58; Beck, Lewis White, *Early German Philosophy: Kant and his Predecessors*, Belknap Press of Harvard University Press, Cambridge, Mass., 1969, 359, 386. 'It is too true . . .': Samuel Taylor Coleridge, 'Biographia Literaria: *Coleridge*, Poems and

Prose selected by Kathleen Raine, The Penguin Poetry Library, 1967, 176. **Ethics one of the 3 great works . . .'**: ibid. Ch.ix, Note 17 (1847). **'The common fountainhead'** etc: 'Anima Poetae', ibid. 142. See also Wordsworth's 'Lines written a few miles above Tintern Abbey', 13 July 1798: *William Wordworth*, The Oxford Authors, ed. Stephen Gill, Oxford University Press, 1988, 134. **Spinoza a panpsychist**: see, for example, Naess, Arne, 'Spinoza and the Deep Ecology Movement', Eburon, Delft, 1993, 10. **'That our modern natural . . .:** *The Works of Friedrich Nietzsche* Vol.X, 'The Joyful Wisdom', trans. Thomas Common, T.N. Foulis, Edinburgh and London, 1910, 290, 337. **George Eliot's translation of Ethics**: begun 8 Nov. 1854: Rosemary Ashton, *George Eliot: A Life*, Hamish Hamilton, London, 1996, 130. **'Never to beat and bruise . . .'**: *The George Eliot Letters*, ed. Gordon S. Haight, Oxford University Press, 1956, Vol. IV (1862–68), letter to Clifford Allbutt, 30 Dec. 1868, p.499.

310 **'By the way, when Spinoza comes out . . .'**: ibid., Vol.II, 233, letter to Charles Bray, 26 March, 1856, p.233. **G.H. Lewes's biography of Spinoza**: printed in *The Westminster Review*, 1843, and reprinted as a pamphlet. **Eliot's translation** was eventually published as *Ethics, by Benedict de Spinoza*, trans. George Eliot, ed. Thomas Deegan, Institut für Anglistik und Amerikanistik, Universität Salzburg, Austria, 1981, 311. **'Ever since I first read Pollock's book . . .'**: letter to Lady Ottoline Morell (11 Dec. 1911) quoted in Monk, Ray, *Ludwig Wittgenstein: The Duty of Genius*, Jonathan Cape, London, 1991; Vintage Books 1991, 68. **'The noblest and most lovable. . .'**: *A History of Western Philosophy*, George Allen and Unwin, London, 1946, Chapter IX, 'Spinoza' 592. **'Logical monism was incompatible . . . In forming a critical estimate . . .'**: ibid. 600–601.

311 **'The value of such work . . .'** *Mysticism and Logic: including A Free Man's Worship*, Unwin Paperbacks, 1976, 107. **'Spinoza is concerned to show . . .'**: *A History of Western Philosophy*, 601. **'I do not know . . .:.** ibid. 597. **Concurring with Pollock**: ibid. 597; Pollock 43, final paragraph. **Societas Spinozana**: Van Suchtelen 1, 477. **'Secret of peace'**: 'Ultimate Religion' in *The Philosophy of Santayana*: Selections, ed. and intr. Irwin Erdman, Charles Scribner's Sons, London and New York, 1936, 572. **'The conception of eternal truth'**: ibid. 578. **'Animality qualified by reason' man's essence'**: ibid. 579. **'Here we touch the crown . . .'**: ibid. 578. **'From [man's] animality . . .'**: ibid. 579.

312 **'Chose to follow . . .'**: H.A. Wolfson, *The Philosophy of Spinoza*, Cambridge, Mass, 1934, II, 330. **'We cannot get the full meaning . . .'**: ibid. I; Preface, vii. **'A religion of reason . . .'**: ibid. II 355. **'Would undoubtedly have joined . . .'**: ibid. II 351–2. **Mouth of God**: *os dei*: TTP IV, trans. by Wernham as 'instrument of God': W 78. **The idea of God . . . which alone leads us . . .:** E4 P 68 S; E5 P36 S. **'Spinoza . . . rationalist metaphysician . . .'**: MacIntyre, Alastair, EP Vol.1, pp.530–1, 541. **'I am not writing biography . . .'**: Bennett 15. **'Most of the faults in *Ethics* . . .:** ibid. 357, 374, 375.

315 **'How can common truths . . .'**: 'To William Wordsworth', *Coleridge*, op.cit., 131.

316 **A small corner of north-west Europe**: Spinoza would be pleased to know that The Hague will house a permanent, independent and international criminal court for trying crimes against humanity.

APPENDIX:

317 **Rosner, D. & Markowitz, G.** 'Consumption, silicosis, and the social construction of industrial disease.' *Yale Journal of Biology and Medicine.* 65 (5): 481–98, 1991 Sept.-Oct. **Abarbanel, Josephus.** *Disputatio medica inauguralis de Phthisi.* 1665. Leiden

Dissertations 1652–60 BL 1185.g.4 (12). **Maxfield R.**, et al. 'Surveillance for silicosis, 1993 – Illinois, Michigan, New Jersey, North Carolina, Ohio, Texas and Wisconsin.' *MMWR CDC Surveillance Summaries.* 46 (1): A13–28, 1997 Jan.31. **Froines, J.R.** Wegman D.H. Dellenbaugh, CA. 'An approach to the characterisation of silica exposure in U.S. Industry.' *American Journal of Industrial Medicine* 10 (4): 345–61, 1986.

WORKS USED IN WRITING THIS BIOGRAPHY
Additional accreditations are made in the source notes

Annot. = *annotated*
BL   = *British Library*
Ed.   = *edited*
Int.   = *introduced*
Trans. = *translated*

THE WORKS OF SPINOZA (1632–77)

Treatise on the Emendation of the Intellect. Written *c.* 1656–62; first published posthumously in the *Complete Works*, 1677. Translation used: *The Collected Works of Spinoza*, Volume 1, ed. and trans. Edwin Curley. Princeton University Press, 1985
Short Treatise. Written *c.* 1656–62; first published 1899. Translation used: Curley, op.cit.
The Principles of Descartes's Philosophy. First published Amsterdam, 1663. Translation used: Curley, op.cit.
Metaphysical Thoughts. The Appendix to *The Principles of Descartes's Philosophy*, and first published with it in 1663. Translation used: Curley, op.cit.
A Theologico-Political Treatise. First published, 1670. Translations used: (1) *Spinoza: The Political Works.* The Tractatus theologico-politicus in part and the Tractatus politicus in full. Ed. and trans. with int. and notes by A.G. Wernham, Oxford University Press, 1958 (2) *A Theologico-Political Treatise and A Political Treatise*, trans. from the Latin with an introduction by R.H.M. Elwes, Dover, New York, 1951
A Political Treatise. Written *c.* 1676–7; first published posthumously in the *Complete Works*, 1677. Translation used: Wernham, op.cit.
Ethics. Begun *c.* 1661; first published posthumously in the *Complete Works*, 1677. Translation used: Curley, op.cit.
Compendium Grammaticus Linguae Hebraecae. First published posthumously in the Latin edition of the *Complete Works*, 1677. Translation used: *Hebrew Grammar*, Ed., trans. and int. Maurice J. Bloom, Vision Press, London 1963
Spinoza's Correspondence (1661–76). Seventy-five letters were published in the posthumous *Opera Posthuma*, 1677. Others have since been discovered, and the total presently stands at eighty-eight. Translation and Latin text used:
  The Letters, trans. Samuel Shirley, with Introduction and Notes by Steven Barbone, Lee Rice and Jacob Adler, Hackett Publishing Company Inc., Indianapolis/Cambridge, 1995
  Spinoza Opera, ed. Carl Gebhardt, Carl Winters, Heidelberg, 1925

PRIMARY SOURCES:

ABARBANEL, Josephus, *Disputatio medica inauguralis de Phthisi* [1655] Leiden dissertation, 1652–60 BL

ABRAVANEL, Judah [Ebreo, Leone], *The Philosophy of Love* [*Dialogi d'amore*], trans. F. Friedeberg-Seeley and Jean H. Barnes, Soncino Press, London 1937

AGLIONBY, William (FRS), *Present State of the United Provinces of the Low Countries*, printed for John Starkey in Fleet Street, London 1669

AKKERMAN, F. (JP: Jelles's Preface to the *Posthumous Works*), (1) *Studies in the Posthumous Works of Spinoza: on style, earliest translation and reception, earliest and modern edition of some texts*, thesis: University of Groningen, Groningen, 1980.

ALGEBRAIC CALCULATION OF THE RAINBOW 1687. Int. G. ten Doesschate. De Graat, Nieuwkoop, 1963.

ANDRADE, Jacob A.P.M., *A Record of the Jews in Jamaica*, ed. Basil Parks, The Jamaica Times, Kingston, 1941

AUBREY, John, *Brief Lives chiefly of Contemporaries set down . . . Between the Years 1669 and 1696*, (Selections) ed., int. and annot. Anthony Powell, Cresset Press, Oxford, 1949

BACON, Francis, *The Philosophical Works*, text, trans. notes and prefaces of Ellis and Spedding, ed. and intr. John M. Robertson, Routledge, London, 1905

BALLING, Pieter, *Het Licht op den Kandelaar*, in English translation as *The Light upon the Candlestick* in William Sewell, *A History of the Rise, Increase and Progress of the People called the Quakers*, London, 1722

BARLOW, Edward, *Barlow's Journal of Life at Sea in King's Ships*, Vol. 1 (1659–77), Hurst and Blackett, London, 1934

BARRE, F., Boulain de la, *The Woman as Good as the Man: Or The Equality of Both Sexes*, trans. from French into English by A.L., licensed 20 August 1676, printed in London, 1677

BARRIOS, Daniel Levi de, *Triompho del Govierno Popular de la Antiqedad Holandesa*, Amsterdam, 1683

BAYLE, Pierre, *Historical and Critical Dictionary* [1697], (Selections) trans., intr. and annot. Richard H. Popkin, The Bobbs-Merrill Company Inc., Indianapolis 1965

BRERETON, William (Bart), *Travels in Holland: The United Provinces*, ed. Edward Hawkins, Printed for the Chetham Society, 1844

CALVIN, John, *A Compend of the Institutes of the Christian Religion* (English trans of John Allen, 1813), ed. Hugh T. Kerr, Lutterworth Press, London, 1964

CAMPBELL, John, *Historical Memoirs of Cornelius and Johan de Witt*: see WITT de

CASTRO, D.H. de, *De Synagogue der Portugeesch-Israelitische Gemeente te Amsterdam*, Belinfante, The Hague, 1875

CATALOGUS van de Boekerij der Vereeniging Het Spinozahuis. (1) compiled by J. te Winkel, The Hague, 1914

CATALOGUS van de Bibliotheek der Vereniging het Spinozahuis te Rijnsburg. (2) compiled by J. M. Aler, E.J. Brill, Leiden, 1965

CICERO, Marcus Tullius, *Res Publica: Roman Politics and Society according to Cicero*, selected and trans. W.K. Lacey and B.W.J.G. Wilson, Oxford University Press, 1970

CLARKE, Samuel, *A Demonstration of the Being and Attributes of God: More Particularly in Answer to Mr Hobbes, Spinoza and their Followers*, The Boyle Lecture 1705: the substance of Eight Sermons preached in St Paul's in 1704, 10th edition, Janus Knapton, London, 1766

COELHO, António Borges, *Inquisição de Évora. Dos Primórdios, A 1668* – Vol.1, Caminho Lisboa, 1987

COLERUS, Johannes, *Korte, dog waaragtige Levens-beschrijving van Benedictus de Spinosa* [1705], Martinus Nijhoff, The Hague, 1910. Reproduced in FREUDENTHAL

COLERUS, John, *The Life of Benedict de Spinosa* [1706], Martinus Nijhoff, The Hague, 1906 Reproduced in POLLOCK

COLLIBER, Samuel, *Free Thoughts Concerning Souls*, int. John Yolton, reprint of the 1734 edition, Thoemmes Antiquarian Books, Bristol 1990

CONFESSIEBOEK Gemeentearchief Amsterdam (GAA): Film No.1841

CULPEPER, Nicholas, *Complete Herbal and English Physician*, reproduced from an original edition published in 1826, J. Gleave and Son; Manchester. Privately printed by Harvey Sales, 1981

DESCARTES, René, (1) *The Philosophical Writings of Descartes*, Trans. John Cottingham, Robert Stoothoff and Dugald Murdoch, 2 vols, Cambridge University Press, 1985

DESCARTES, René, (2) *The Philosophical Writings of Descartes*, Vol. 111, *The Correspondence*, trans. John Cottingham, Robert Stoothoff, Dugald Murdoch and Anthony Kenny, Cambridge University Press, 1991

EARBURY, Matthias, *Deism Examin'd and Confuted. In an Answer to a Book intitled, Tractatus Theologico Politicus*, London, 1697

ENDEN, Franciscus van den, (1) *Kort Verhael van Nieuw Nederlants*, Amsterdam, 1662

ENDEN, Franciscus van den, (2) *Vrye Politijke Stellingen en Consideratien van Staat*, Amsterdam, 1665. See KLEVER (7)

ENDEN, Franciscus van den, (3) *Vrye Politijke Stellingen*, int. Wim Klever, Wereldbibliothek, Amsterdam, 1992.

EVELYN, John, *The Diary of John Evelyn* [1641], 6 vols, Clarendon Press, Oxford, 1955

FAUSTBUCH, *The Sources of the Faust Tradition from Simon Magus to Lessing*, Philip Mason Palmer, and Robert Pattison More [1939], Cass, London, and Octagon, New York, 1966

FELL, Margaret: see POPKIN and SIGNER

FELLTHAM, Owen, *A Brief Character of the Low Countries*, printed for Henry Seile, London, 1652

FOX, George, *The Journals of George Fox*, 2 vols. ed. N. Penney, Cambridge University Press, 1911

FREUDENTHAL, J., *Die Lebensgeschichte Spinoza's: In Quellenschriften, Urkunden und Nichtamtlichen Nachrichten*, Van Veit, Leipzig, 1899

FRIEDENWALD, Herbert, *Material for the History of the Jews in the British West Indies*: Publications of the American Jewish Historical Society (5), 1897

GLÜCKEL OF HAMELN, *The Life of Glückel of Hameln, 1646–1724, Written by Herself*, trans. and ed. Beth-Zion Abrahams, Thomas Yoseloff, New York, 1963

GROTIUS, [Groot, Hugo de] *Remonstrantie Nopende de Ordre Dije in de Landen van Hollandt ende Westvrieslandt Dijent Gestelt op de Joden*, Coster, Amsterdam, 1949

HEEREBOORD, Adriaan, *Metaphysics in Philosophy and Theology*, Leiden, 7 Feb. 1658

HOBBES, Thomas (1) *De Cive* [1642]. The English version, entitled in the first edition *Philosophical Rudiments Concerning Government and Society*, ed. Howard Warrender, Clarendon Press, Oxford, 1983

HOBBES, Thomas, (2) *Leviathan* [1651] ed. with introd. C.B. Macpherson, Penguin Classics, Harmondsworth, 1986

HOOKE, Robert, *Micrographia: or some physiological descriptions of minute bodies made by magnifying glasses, with observation and inquiries thereon*, facsimile of first edition [1665], Dover, New York, 1961

HORTUS INDICUS MALABARICUS [1678–86], 3 vols, Leiden University Botanical Library

HOWELL, James, (1) *The Familiar Letters of James Howell*, 2 vols [c. 1662–33], ed. W.H. Bennett, for David Stott, London, 1890

HOWELL, James (2) *Instructions for Forraine Travel* (dedicated to the young Prince Charles, later Charles II, printed by TB for Humprey Mosley, London, 1642

HUYGENS, Christiaan, (1) *Oeuvres Complètes de Christiaan Huygens, publiées par la Société Hollandais des sciences*, vols V and VI, Martinus Nijhoff, The Hague, 1888–1950

HUYGENS, Christiaan, (2) *Treatise on Light*, rendered into English by Sylvanus P. Thompson. Dover, New York, 1912, 1962

JELLES, Jarig: Preface to the *Posthumous Works*: see AKKERMAN

JUSTITIEBOEK, Gemeentearchief Amsterdam (GAA): Films 1735 and 1736

KERCKRING, Theodor, (1) *Commentarium in Currum Triumphalem*, Leiden, 1661

KERCKRING, Theodor, (2) *Spicilegium Anatomicum* (Anatomical Investigations), Amsterdam, 1670

KNUTTEL, P.C., *Catalogus van de Pamfletten verzameling berustende in de Koninklijke Bibliotheek*, The Hague, 1978

KOERBAGH, Adriaan, *Een Ligt Schijnende in Duystere Plaatsen/Om te verligten de voornaamste saaken der Gods-geleertheyd en Gods-dienst/Ontsteeken door Vreederijk Waarmond/ondersoeker der Waarheyd. Anders Mr. Adr. Koerbagh/Regts-gel. en Genees-Mr, t' Amsterdam/Gedrukt voor den Schrijver.* Int. Jaar/1668, ed. Hubert Vandenbossche, Brussels, 1974

KORTHOLT, Sebastian, Preface to Christian Kortholt's *On Three Great Impostors* [1700]. Extracts in WOLF (2) op.cit.; in Latin, FREUDENTHAL (pp. 26–8); reference is to WOLF (2)

LEIBNIZ, G.W. (1), *Philosophical Writings*, ed. G.H.R. Parkinson, J.M. Dent & Sons, London, 1973

LEIBNIZ, G.W. (2), *Theodicy*, trans. E.M. Huggard from C.J. Gerhardt's edition of the *Collected Philosophical Works*, 1875–90, J.M. Dent & Sons, London, 1952

LEIBNIZ, G.W. (3), *Philosophical Papers and Letters*, Vol. 1 ed. and trans. Leroy E. Loemker, Reidel Publishing Company, Dordrecht, 1969

LEIBNIZ, G.W. (4), Critical remarks (1706–10) found with a book by Wachter, in *A refutation recently discovered of the philosophy of Spinoza*, trans. O.F. Owen, Constable, London, 1855

LUCAS, J.M., credited with being the author of *The Life of the late Mr de Spinosa*, in WOLF (2)

MAIZEAUX, M. Pierre des, *The Works of Monsieur de St Evremond*, 3 vols, 2nd edition, corrected and enlarged, London, 1728

MALEBRANCHE, Nicolas, *The Search After Truth*, trans. Thomas M. Lennon and Paul J. Olscamp. Ohio State University Press, 1980

MARVELL, Andrew, 'The Character of Holland', *The Poems and Letters of Andrew Marvell*, Vol. 1, ed. H.M. Margoliouth, Clarendon Press, Oxford 1927

MEIJER, J. see GROTIUS.

MEYER, L., *La Philosophie interprète de l'Ecriture Sainte (Philosophiae S. Scripturae Interpres: Exercitatio paradoxa in qua veram philosophiam etc.)* [1666]. Traduction etc. par Jacqueline Lagrée et Pierre-François Moreau, Paris, Intertextes Éditeur, 1988

MIGNET, F.A.M. *Negociations Relatives à la succession d'Espagne sous Louis XIV. Collection inedits publies par ordre du Roi etc.* Series 1, 2 vols, Histoire Politique, Imprimerie Royale, Paris, 1840–2

MONNIKHOFF, Johannes, mid-18th-century biography of Spinoza, Royal Library, The Hague. Extracts reprinted in FREUDENTHAL pp.105–8

MORE, Henry, *A Collection of Several Philosophical Writings*, Vol. 2. Garland Publishers, New York, 1978

MORYSON, Fynes, *An Itinerary . . . containing his ten yeers travell.* Vol. IV [1617] Glasgow, 1907–8

MUNDY, Peter, *The Travels of Peter Mundy in Europe and Asia (1608–1667)*, Vol.4, Travels in Europe 1639–47, ed. Richard Carnac Temple (Bart), Hakluyt Society, London, 1925

NAZELLE, du CAUSE de, *Mémoires du temps de Louis XIV* [1680], with an Appendix, 'Judiciary documents relating to the trial of de Rohan', Int. and ed. E. Daudet, Librarie Plon, Paris, 1899

NEGOCIATIONS: see MIGNET

NETHERLANDS PROCLAMATIONS (1655–72), vol. 2, London BL

OLDENBURG, Henry, *The Correspondence of Henry Oldenburg*, ed. A. R. and M. B. Hall, 11 vols, University of Wisconsin Press, Madison, 1965–77

PASCAL, Blaise, *Ouvres Complètes*, Présentation et Notes de Louis Lafuma, Éditions du Seuil, Paris, 1963

PEPYS, Samuel, *The Diary of Samuel Pepys Esquire, FRS*, Simpkin, Marshall, Hamilton, Kent & Co., New York 1825

PIETERSE, W.Chr. *Livro de Beth Haim*, copy of the original text with int. notes and index, Studia Rosenthaliana, Van Gorcum, Assen, 1970

PHILOPATER, het leven van: see MARECHAL (2)

PLOCKHOY, Pieter Cornelius, pioneer of the First Co-operative Commonwealth, *A way propounded to make the poor in these and other nations happy, enz*. [1659], His Life and Work, commentary, John Downie, London, undated – between 1918 and 1939

PORTUGUESE-JEWISH COMMUNITY (PA) Gemeentearchief Amsterdam (GAA 334)

PROTOKOLLEN van der Kerkeraad. (PK) Gemeentearchief Amsterdam (GAA 376)

ROHAN, Henri, Duc de (1), *De l'interest des princes et estats de la Chrestienté*, Paris 1639

ROHAN, Henri, Duc de (2), *Discours politiques* (1646), not published: see SKINNER

ROUKEMA, Roeloff, *Naamboeck der Beroemste Genees-en Heelmeesters van alle eenwen*, 1706, Amsterdam University Library

ROUSSEAU, Jean Jacques (1), *A Discourse on Equality*, trans. int. and annot. Maurice Cranston, Penguin, Harmondsworth, 1984

ROUSSEAU, Jean Jacques (2), *Émile*, Vols 8 and 9, *The Works of Rousseau*, Paris, 1822

RYE, William Brenchley (Ed., intr. annot. and etchings), *England as seen by foreigners in the days of Elizabeth and James 1*, Benjamin Blom, New York, 1967

SCHURMAN, Anna van, *The Learned Maid, or Whether a Maid may also be a Scholar*, A Logick exercise written in Latin, with some epistles to the famous Gassendus and others, trans. into English, John Redmayne, London, 1659

SERVAAS VAN ROOIJEN, A.J., *Inventaire des Livres formant la Bibliothèque de Bénédict Spinoza*, W. C. Tengeler, Paul Monserrat, The Hague, Paris, 1888

SEWEL, William, *The History of the Rise, Increase and Progress of the Christian People Called Quakers. Written originally in Low Dutch and Translated by himself*, 1722 BL

SILVA ROSA, J.S. da, *Catalogue of the Portuguese and Spanish Gedruchten Judaica*, Bibliotheek Ets Haim, 1933

STOUPPE, Jean-Baptiste, *La Religion des Hollandois*, Pierre Marteau, Cologne, 1673

TEMPLE, William (1), *The Works of Sir William Temple*, 2 vols, J. Round et al. London, 1740

TEMPLE, William (Bart) (2), *Observations Upon the United Provinces of the Netherlands* [1672], ed. G.N. Clark, Clarendon Press, Oxford, 1972

TERENCE, *Plays*, Vol.1, with an English translation by John Sargeaunt, Loeb Classical Library, William Heinemann, London, 1912

TROUBLES OF AMSTERDAM THE: Or the Disturbed Amsterdammer: With his true Warning, Counsel, and Answer upon Bicker's Troubles, Anonymous, Amsterdam, BL E.615. (20) 1650

VAZ DIAS, A.M. and VAN DER TAK, W.G. (VD/VT) (1), *Spinoza; Merchant and Autodidact*, (reprint from *Studia Rosenthaliana*, Vol. XVI No.2, 1982

VAZ DIAS, A.M. and VAN DER TAK, W.G. (2), *De Firma Bento y Gabriel de Spinoza*, E.J. Brill, Leiden, 1934

VAZ DIAS, A.M. and VAN DER TAK, W.G. (3), *Spinoza and Simon Joosten de Vries: Jarich Jelles's Life and Business*, Eburon, Delft, 1989

VERDOONER, Dave and HARMEN, Saul, *Trouwen in Mokum: Jewish Marriage in Amsterdam (1598–1811)*, 2 vols, Koningklijke Bibliotheek, Den Haag

WAGENAAR, Jan, *Vaderlandsche Historie*, 21 vols, 1749–59

WICQUEFORT, M. Abraham de, *Histoire des Provinces Unies des Pays Bas*, Amsterdam (no publisher given) 4 vols Frédéric Muller, Amsterdam, 1864

WYCHERLEY, William, *The Plays of William Wycherley* (ed. Peter Holland), Cambridge University Press, 1981

'WITT de', John (truly by Pieter de la Court [van den Hove]), *The True Interest and Political Maxims of the Republic of Holland*. In English, trans. from the original Dutch, with the

Historical Memoirs of Cornelius and Johan de Witt, by John Campbell, printed for J. Nourse in The Strand, London, 1746. Actually *Indication of the Salutary Political Foundations and Maxims of the Republic of Holland and West Friesland* [1669]

WOLF, A. (1), *The Correspondence of Spinoza*, trans., intr. and annot. Russell and Russell, New York, 1966

WOLF, A. (2) (ed., trans., intr. and annot.), *The Oldest Biography of Spinoza*, Kennikat Press, Port Washington and London, 1970

WOLF, Lucien (WOLF, L.), *Menasseh ben Israel's Mission to Oliver Cromwell*, Macmillan and Co., London, 1901

SECONDARY SOURCES

ABRAHAMS, Gerald, *The Jewish Mind*, Constable, London, 1961

AGT, F van, *Synagogen in Amsterdam*, Staatsuitgeverij's Gravenhage, 1974

AITON, E.J., *Leibniz: A Biography*, Adam Holger, Bristol and Boston, 1985

AKKERMAN, F. (2), 'J.H. Glazemaker, an Early Translator of Spinoza', in DEUGD, de

ALEXANDER, Philip S. (ed. and trans.), *Textual Sources for the Study of Judaism*, Manchester University Press, 1984

ALLISON, Henry E., *Benedict de Spinoza: An Introduction*, revised edition, Yale University Press, 1987. (First published by Twayne Publishers, G.K. Hall and Co., Boston, 1975)

ASSOUN, Paul-Laurent, 'Spinoza, les libertins français et la politique (1665–1745)', *Cahiers Spinoza III*, Editions Réplique, Paris, 1980

BAAR, Mirjam de, *et al* (eds.), *Anna Maria van Schurman (1607–1678)*, Walburg Pers, Zutphen 1992

BAILLET, Adrien, *Vie de Monsieur Descartes* [1691] Collection 'Grandeurs', La Table Ronde, L'Imprimerie Knapp, Paris, 1946

BALET, Leo, *Rembrandt and Spinoza*, Philosophical Library, New York, 1962

BANGA, J., *Geschiedenis van de vroegere Geneeskunde in Nederland*, Schiedam, 1868

BARBER, W.H., *Leibniz in France, from Arnauld to Voltaire, A Study in French Reactions to Leibnizianism, 1670–1760* Clarendon Press, Oxford, 1955

BARCLAY, Robert, *The Inner Lives of the Religious Societies of the Commonwealth*, Hodder and Stoughton, London, 1876

BARON, Salo Wittmayer, *A Social and Religious History of the Jews*, Vol. XV ('Dutch Jerusalem'), Jewish Publication Society of America, Columbia University Press, Philadelphia, 1973

BELL, Walter George, *The Great Plague in London in 1665*, Bodley Head, London, 1924; revised 1951

BENARDETE, Mair José, *Hispanic Culture and Character of the Sephardic Jews*, 2nd, corrected and augmented edition, Sepher-Hermon Press Inc., New York, 1982

BENNETT, Jonathan, *A Study of Spinoza's Ethics*, Cambridge University Press, 1984

BERGMANN, Emilie, 'The Exclusion of the Feminine in the Cultural Discourse of the Golden Age: Juan Luis Vives and Fray Luis de Léon', in SAINT-SAËNS

BERRIOT-SALVADORE, Evelyne, 'The Discourse of Medicine and Science', in ZEMON DAVIS

BIRABEN, Jean-Noël, *Les Hommes et la Peste dans les pays européeans et méditerranéens*, Vol. 1, Mouton, Paris, 1975

BLOK, Petrus Johannes, *History of the People of the Netherlands*, Vols III and IV, trans. Ruth Putnam, New York, 1900. G.P. Putnam's Sons

BLOOM, Herbert I., *Economic Activities of the Jews of Amsterdam in the 17th and 18th Centuries*, Kennikat Press, New York, 1937

BOAS, Marie, *Robert Boyle and Seventeenth Century Chemistry*, Cambridge University Press, 1958

BOULDING, Elise, *The Underside of History: A View of Women through Time*, Vol. 11, revised edition, Sage Publications, Newbury Park, California, 1992

BOXER, C.R. (1), *Mary and Misogyny: Women in Iberian Expansion Overseas 1415–1815: Some facts, fancies and personalities*, Duckworth, London, 1975

BOXER, C.R. (2), *Dutch Merchants and Mariners in Asia 1602–1795*, Variorum Reprints, London, 1988

BRAITHWAITE, William C., *The Beginnings of Quakerism*, 2nd edition, revised by Henry C. Cadbury, Cambridge University Press, 1955

BRANN, Henry Walter, 'Spinoza and the Kabbalah', in HESSING

BRAUDEL, Fernand, *The Mediterranean and the Mediterranean World in the Age of Philip II*, Vol. 2, William Collins, London, 1973

BREKELMANS, Michael, *De Gevangenpoort*, De Walburg Pers, Zutphen, 1985

BREWER'S DICTIONARY OF FAME AND FABLE, revised by Ivor H. Evans. Cassell, London, 1978

BRIEFWISSELING: Spinoza, trans. and annot. F. Akkerman, H.G. Hubbeling and A.G. Westerbrink, Wereldbibliotheek, Amsterdam, 1977

BUNYAN, John, *The Pilgrim's Progress*, with a biographical note by Gwilym O. Griffith, Lutterworth Press, London, 1947

CAROSSO-KOK, M. and LEVY VAN HALM, J. (eds.), *Schutters in Holland: Kracht en Zenuwen van de Stad*, Wanders, Frans Hals Museum, Zwolle, 1988

CARROLL, Berenice A. (ed.), *Liberating Women's History*, Theoretical and Critical Essays, University of Illinois Press, 1976

CLARK, Alice, *The Working Life of Women in the Seventeenth Century*, George Routledge, London, 1919

CLARK, G.L. (ed.)., *The Encyclopaedia of Microscopy*, Chapman and Hall, London, 1961

COLIE, R. (1), *Light and Enlightenment*: A Study of the Cambridge Platonists and the Dutch Arminians, Cambridge University Press, 1957

COLIE, R.L. (2), 'Spinoza and the Early English Deists', *Journal of the History of Ideas* (1959)

COX, Michael, *Mysticism: The Direct Experience of God*, Aquarian Press, Wellingborough, 1983

CRAMPE-CASNABET, Michèle, 'A Sampling of Eighteenth-century Philosophy', in ZEMON DAVIS

CURLEY, E.M. (2), *Spinoza's Metaphysics: An Essay in Interpretation*, Harvard University Press, 1969

DAN, Joseph, 'Menasseh ben Israel: attitude toward the Zohar and Lurianic Kabbalah', in KAPLAN (4)

DEUGD, C. de, (ed.), *Spinoza's Political and Theological Thought*, North-Holland Publishing Company, Amsterdam, Oxford, New York, 1984

DEURSEN, A.T. van, *Plain Lives in a Golden Age. Popular Culture, Religion and Society in Seventeenth-century Holland*, Cambridge University Press, 1991

DICTIONARY OF NATIONAL BIOGRAPHY, Smith, Elder and Co. London, 1895

DIJKSTERHUIS, E.J. *et al.*, *Descartes et le Cartésianisme Hollandais*, Presses Universitaires de France, 1950

DUBIEZ, F.J., *The Sephardi Community of Amsterdam*, trans. C.F.L. Los, published and sold by the Jewish Synagogue, Amsterdam (undated)

DUNIN BORKOWSKI, Stanislaus von, *Spinoza*, Vol. 2, Aschendorff, Münster, 1933

EKKART, Rudi, 'Spinoza in Portrait: The Unknown Face', in *De Steen Vliegt (A Stone in Flight)*, Art et Amicitiae, Amsterdams Fonds voor de Kunst, Vereniging Het Spinozahuis, Rijnsburg, 1997

EMMANUEL, Isaac S., *Precious Stones of the Curaçao Jews, 1656–1957*, Bloch Publishing Company, New York, 1957

374

ENCYCLOPEDIA OF PHILOSOPHY, 8 vols, ed. Paul Edwards, Macmillan and Free Press, London and New York, 1967

ENCYCLOPAEDIA SEPHARDICA NEERLANDICA, 2 vols, ed. J. Meijer, Uitgave van de Portugees Israëlietische Gemeente te Amsterdam, 1949

FEUER, Lewis Samuel, *Spinoza and the Rise of Liberalism*, Beacon Press, Boston, 1958

FISCH, Harold, 'The Messianic Politics of Menasseh ben Israel', in KAPLAN (4)

FOUCHER DE CAREIL, A.L. (1), *Refutation inédite de Spinoza par Leibniz*, Paris, 1854

FOUCHER DE CAREIL, A.L. (2), *Leibniz et la philosophie Juive et la cabale*, Paris, 1861

FRIEDMANN, Georges, *Leibniz et Spinoza*, Gallimard, Paris, 1946

FRANCÈS, Madeleine, *Spinoza dans les pays néerlandais de la seconde moitié du XVIIe siècle*, Félix Alcan, Paris, 1937

GABBEY, Alan, 'Spinoza's Natural Science and Methodology', in GARRETT

GAMPEL, Benjamin R, *The Last Jews on Iberian Soil* (Navarrese Jewry) 1479–98, University of California Press (Berkeley), 1989

GANS, M.H. *Memorboek: platenatlas van het leven der joden in Nederland van de middeleeuwen tot 1940*, Bosch and Kenning, Baarn, 1971

GARRETT, Don (ed.), *The Cambridge Companion to Spinoza*, Cambridge University Press, 1996

GEBHARDT, Carl, 'Juan de Prado', *Chronicon Spinozanum* III (1923)

GEYL, Pieter (1), *The Netherlands in the Seventeenth Century*, Vol. 1 (1609–48), Cassell History, London, 1981. First published by Williams and Norgate, 1936, as *The Netherlands Divided*

GEYL, Pieter (2), *The Netherlands in the Seventeenth Century*, Vol. 2 (1648–1715), Ernest Benn, London, 1964

GEYL, Pieter (3), *Orange and Stuart* (1641–72), Weidenfeld and Nicolson, London, 1969. First published by N.V.A. Oosthoek's Vitg.-Mij, Utrecht, 1939

GRAY, Peter (ed.), *The Encyclopaedia of Microscopy and Microtechnique*, Van Nostrand Reinhold, New York, 1973

GREEN, T.H., *Lectures on the Principles of Political Obligation*, Longman, Green, London, 1917

GRENE, Marjorie and NAILS, Debra (eds), *Spinoza and the Sciences*, Reidel, Dordrecht, 1986

GULLAN-WHUR, Margaret (1), *The Four Elements*, Century Hutchinson, London, 1987

GULLAN-WHUR, Margaret (2), 'A perspective on the Mind-Body Problem, with particular reference to the philosophy of Spinoza', Ph.D. thesis (unpublished), University of London, 1996

GUTHRIE, Douglas, *A History of Medicine*, Thomas Nelson and Sons, London, 1947

GUTMANN, Myron P., *War and Rural Life in the Early Modern Low Countries*, Princeton University Press, 1980

HAAK, Bob. *Rembrandt: His Life, Work and Times*, trans. from the Dutch by Elizabeth Willems-Treeman, Thames and Hudson, London, 1969

HACK, Maria, *Lectures at Home: Manufacture of Glass, etc.*, Darton and Harvey, London, 1834

HALEY, K.H.D. (1), *The Dutch in the Seventeenth Century*, Thames and Hudson, London, 1972

HALEY, K.H.D. (2), *An English Diplomat in the Low Countries: Sir William Temple and Johan de Witt, 1665–72*, Clarendon Press, Oxford, 1986

HALEY, K.H.D. (3), *The British and The Dutch*, George Philip, London, 1988

HALL, A.R. and M.B., 'Philosophy and Natural Philosophy: Boyle and Spinoza', in *Mélanges Alexandre Koyré*, Hermann, Paris, 1964

HAMPTON, Jean, *Hobbes and the Social Contract Tradition*, Cambridge University Press (Paperback Library), 1988

HARTLEY, Sir Harold (ed.), *The Royal Society: Its Origins and Foundations*, The Royal Society, London, 1960

HENIGER, J., *Hendrik van Reede tot Drakenstein (1636–1691) and Hortus Malabaricus*, A.A. Balkema, Rotterdam and Boston, 1986

HERSCH, J.H., *Daily Prayer Book*, Soncino Press, London, 1976

HESSING, Siegfried (ed.), *Speculum Spinozanum 1677–1977*, Routledge and Kegan Paul, London, 1978

HILL, Christopher, *The Century of Revolution (1603–1714)*, first published 1961, Thomas Nelson and Sons, London; Abacus, London, 1978

HOMZA, Lu Ann, 'To annihilate Sorcery and Amend the Church: A new Interpretation of Pedro Ciruelo's 'Rebrobación dea las supersticiones y hechicerías [sorcery]', in SAINT-SAËNS

HUBBELING, Hubertus G., 'Philopater. A Dutch Materialistic Interpretation of Spinoza in the Seventeenth Century', *Spinoza nel 350° Anniversario della Nascita*, Atti del Congresso (Urbino 4–8 ottobre 1982: Proceedings of the First Italian International Congress on Spinoza), ed. Emilia Giancotti, Bibliopolis, Naples, 1985

HUIZINGA, J.H., *Dutch Civilisation in the Seventeenth Century*, William Collins, London, 1968

ICONES LEIDENSES: *De portretverzameling van de Rijksuniversiteit te Leiden*, Rijksuniversiteit Universitaire Pers, Leiden, 1973

ISRAEL, J.I. (1), *The Dutch Republic and The Hispanic World 1601–61*, Clarendon Press, Oxford, 1982

ISRAEL, J.I. (2), *European Jewry in the Age of Mercantilism*, Clarendon Press, Oxford, 1985

ISRAEL, J.I. (3), *Empires and Entrepots: The Dutch, The Spanish Monarchy and the Jews 1585–1713*, The Hambledon Press, London, 1990

JACOB, Margaret C., *The Radical Enlightenment: Pantheists, Freemasons and Republicans*, Allen and Unwin, London, 1981

JAMES, Susan, 'The Passions in Metaphysics and the Theory of Action', in *The Cambridge History of Seventeenth Century Philosophy*, Cambridge University Press, New York, 1998

JEWISH ENCYCLOPEDIA (12 vols), Funk and Wagnalls Company, New York and London, MDCCCCI

KAMEN, Henry, *Inquisition and Society in Spain in the sixteenth and seventeenth centuries*, Weidenfeld and Nicolson, London, 1985

KAPLAN, Benjamin J., *Calvinists and Libertines: Confession and Community in Utrecht, 1578–1620*, Clarendon Press, Oxford, 1995

KAPLAN, Joseph (1), *From Christianity to Judaism. The Life and Work of Orobio de Castro*, Littman Library, Oxford University Press, 1989

KAPLAN, Joseph (2), 'On the Relation of Spinoza's Contemporaries in the Portugese Jewish Community of Amsterdam to Spanish Culture and the Marrano Experience', in DEUGD

KAPLAN, Yosef (3), (ed.) *Jews and Conversos; Studies in Society and the Inquisition*. The Magnes Press, Hebrew University of Jerusalem, 1985

KAPLAN, Yosef (4), (ed., et al) *Menasseh ben Israel and His World*, E.J. Brill, London, 1989

KAPLAN, Yosef (5), 'Karaites' in Early Eighteenth-Century Amsterdam', in KATZ and ISRAEL

KAPLAN, Yosef (6), 'Deviance and Excommunication in the Eighteenth Century. A Chapter in the Social History of the Sefardic Community of Amsterdam', in MICHMAN

KASHER, Asa and BIDERMAN, Shlomo, 'Why was Baruch de Spinoza Excommunicated?', in KATZ and ISRAEL

KATZ, David S., 'Menasseh ben Israel's Christian Connection: Henry Jessey and the Jews', in KAPLAN (4)

KATZ, David S. and ISRAEL, Jonathan I. (eds.), *Sceptics, Millenarians and Jews*, E.J. Brill, Leiden, New York, 1990

KERKHOVEN, Jaap, *Spinoza's clausules aangaande uitsluiting van politieke rechten in hun maatschchappelijke context*, Eburon, Delft, 1991

KING, Lester S., *The Road to Medical Enlightenment, 1650–1695*, History of Science Library, Macdonald, London, 1970

KLEVER, Wim (1), 'Spinoza interviewed by Willem van Blyenbergh', *Studia Spinozana* 4 Walther & Walther Verlag Alling, Germany, 1988

KLEVER, Wim (2), 'Spinoza and Rieuwertsz', *Studia Spinozana* 4, Walther & Walther Verlag, Alling, Germany, 1988

KLEVER, Wim (3), 'Spinoza and Van den Enden in Borch's Diary in 1661 and 1662', *Studia Spinozana* 5, Walther & Walther Verlag, Alling, Germany, 1989

KLEVER, Wim (4), 'Spinoza's Fame in 1667', *Studia Spinozana* 5, Walther & Walther Verlag, Alling, Germany, 1989

KLEVER, Wim (5), 'Hudde's Question on God's Uniqueness: A Reconstruction on the Basis of Van Limborch's Correspondence with John Locke', *Studia Spinozana* 5, Walther & Walther Verlag, Alling, Germany, 1989

KLEVER, Wim (6), 'A New Source of Spinozism: Franciscus van den Enden', *Journal of the History of Philosophy* 29, Washington University, St. Louis, 1991

KLEVER, Wim (7): see VAN DEN ENDEN (3)

KLEVER, Wim (8), 'Spinoza's Life and Works', in GARRETT

KLEVER, Wim (9), *Mannen rond Spinoza (1650–1700)*, Uitgeverij Verloren, Hilversum, 1997

KOEN, E.M., 'The Earliest Sources Relating to the Portuguese Jews in the Municipal Archives of Amsterdam up to 1620', *Studia Rosenthaliana* (4) 1970, Van Gorcum, Assen

KOLAKOWSKI, L., *Chrétiens sans Eglise, la conscience religieuse et le lien confessionel au XVIIe siècle*, Gallimard, Paris, 1969

KRISTELLER, Paul Oskar, 'Stoic and Neoplatonic Sources of Spinoza's *Ethics*', *History of European Ideas* (5) Pergamon/Elsevier, Oxford, 1984

LACHTERMAN, David R., 'The Physics of Spinoza's *Ethics*', in SHAHAN and BIRO

LAGRÉE: see MEYER

LEVIN, Dan, *Spinoza, the Young Thinker Who Destroyed the Past*, Weybright and Talley, New York, 1970

LEWIS, Geneviève, 'Observations sur la Philosophie de Descartes', in DIJKSTERHUIS

LEXICON BIOGRAFISCHE, Index van de Benelux, compiled by Wilhelmina Van der Meer, K. G. Saur, München, 1997

LITVINOFF, Barnett, *The Burning Bush: Anti-Semitism and World History*, Collins, London, 1989

MACAULAY, Lord, *The History of England*, Vol.1. *From the Accession of James the Second*, Macmillan and Co., London, 1913

McCONICA, James, *Erasmus*, Past Masters Series, Oxford University Press, 1991

MACPHERSON: see HOBBES (2)

McSHEA, Robert G., *The Political Philosophy of Spinoza*, Columbia University Press, New York and London, 1968

MAHONEY, Edward J. (ed.), *Philosophy and Humanism*, E.J. Brill, Leiden, 1976

MARÉCHAL, G. (1), *Een gedrochtelijk lasterschrift: de spinozistiche romans over het leven van 'de spotterigen Philopater'*, M. A. thesis, Instituut voor Neerlandistiek, Universiteit van Amsterdam, 1981

MARÉCHAL, G. (2) *Johannes Duijkerius: Het leven van Philopater: Vervolg van 't leven van Philopater*, Rodopi, Amsterdam, 1991

MARSHALL, Sherrin, *The Dutch Gentry 1500–1650*, Greenwood Press, New York, 1987

MATHERON, Alexandre, 'Femmes et serviteurs dans la Démocratie spinoziste', in HESSING

MEININGER, Jan V. and SUCHTELEN, Guido van, *Liever met Wercken, als met Woorden* (De levensreis van doctor Franciscus van den Enden, leermeester van Spinoza, complotteur tegen Lodewijk de Veertiende), Heureka, Weesp, 1980

MEINSMA, K.O., *Spinoza et son Cercle*, Vrin, Paris, 1983. First published in Dutch as

Spinoza en zijn kring, The Hague, 1896; trans. into German: *Spinoza und sein Kreis*, Berlin, 1909

MERTENS, F., 'Franciscus van den Enden: Tijd voor een herziening van diens rol in het ontstaan van het Spinozisme?', *Tijdschrift voor Filosofie* (56), Hoger Instituut voor Wijsbegeerte (Katholieke Leuven) Leuven, 1994

MICHMAN, Jozeph (ed.), *Dutch Jewish History*, Vol. III, The Institute for Research on Dutch Jewry, Hebrew University of Jerusalem. Van Gorcum, Assen, The Netherlands, 1993

MOERKERKEN, P.H. van, *Adriaan Koerbagh (1633–1669): Een Strijder voor het Vrije Denken*, De Vrije Bladen, (2) 1948, G.A. van Orschot, Amsterdam

MONGRÉDIEN, Georges, *Le Grand Condé: L'Homme et son Oevre*, Librarie Hachette, Paris, 1959

MONTAIGNE, Michel de, 'On the Art of Conversation', in *The Complete Essays*, trans. M.A. Screech, Penguin Classics, Harmondsworth, 1993

MOORMAN, Mary (Mary Caroline Trevelyan), *William the Third and the Defence of Holland, 1672–4.* Longmans, London, 1930

MURRAY, John J., *Amsterdam in the Age of Rembrandt*, University of Oklahoma Press, 1967

MURRIS, R., *La Hollande et Les Hollandais* (au XVIIᵉ et au XVIIIᵉ siècles), Librarie Ancienne Honoré Champion, Paris, 1925

MUSAPH-ANDRIESSE, R.C., *From Torah to Kabbalah. A Basic Introduction to the Writings of Judaism*, Oxford University Press, 1982

NEHER, André, *Jewish Thought in the Sixteenth Century*, Litmann Library, Oxford University Press, 1986

NICOLSON, Marjorie Hope, *Pepys' Diary and the New Science*, The University Press of Virginia, 1965

NIEUW-NEDERLANDSCH BIOGRAFISCH WOORDENBOEK, 10 vols, Leiden, 1911–37

NOBLESSE, Dictionnaire de la., Vol. XVII, Schelsinger, Paris, 1872

OFFENBERG, A.K., 'Letter from Spinoza to Lodewijk Meyer, 26 July 1663', in HESSING

OVERVOORDE, J.C., *Geschiedenis van het Postwezen in Nederland voor 1795*, Sijthoff, Leiden, 1902

PARKER, Geoffrey, *The Army of Flanders and the Spanish Road, 1567–1659* (The Logistics of Spanish Victory and Defeat in the Low Countries' War), Cambridge University Press, 1972

PARKINSON, G.H.R.: see LEIBNIZ (1)

PAYNE, Stanley G., *A History of Spain and Portugal*, Vol. 1, University of Wisconsin Press, 1973

PEERS, E. Allison, *Studies of the Spanish Mystics*, Vol. 1, Sheldon Press, London, 1927

PETRY, M.J., 'Hobbes and the Early Dutch Spinozists', in DE DEUGD

POLIAKOV, Léon, *The History of Anti-Semitism*, Vol. 1: From the Time of Christ to the Court Jews, trans. from the French by Richard Howard, Elek Books, London, 1966

POLLOCK, Frederick, *Spinoza: His Life and Philosophy*, C. Kegan Paul and Co., London, 1889

PONTALIS, G.A. Lefèvre, *Johan de Witt: Grand Pensionary of Holland, or Twenty Years of a Parliamentary Republic*, Vol. 3 trans. S.E and E. Stephenson, Longmans, Green, and Co. London, 1885.

POPKIN, R.H. (1), 'The Pre-Adamite Theory in the Renaissance', in MAHONEY

POPKIN, R.H. (2), 'Another Spinoza', *Journal of the History of Philosophy*, [34], University of California, Los Angeles, January 1996

POPKIN, R.H. and SIGNER, Michael A. (eds), *Spinoza's Earliest Publication? The Hebrew Translation of Margaret Fell's Loving Salutation to the Seed of Abraham among the Jews, wherever they are scattered up and down the Face of the Earth*, Van Gorcum, Assen 1987

PORTNOY, Ethel, *Bange Mensen: Een Haagse vertelling*, Meulenhoff, Amsterdam, 1996

378

PRICE, J.L., *Culture and Society in the Dutch Republic during the 17th Century*, Batsford, London, 1974

REDONDI, Pietro, *Galileo: Heretic*, trans. Raymond Rosenthal, Allen Lane, The Penguin Press, Harmondsworth, 1988

RENIER, G.J., *The Dutch Nation: an Historical Study*, Allen and Unwin, London, 1944

REVAH, Israel S. (1), *Spinoza et le Dr Juan de Prado*, Mouton, The Hague and Paris, 1959

REVAH, Israel S. (2), *Annuaire, École Pratique des Hautes Études*, Mouton, The Hague and Paris, 1964–5

REVAH, Israel S. (3), 'Les origines juives de quelques jésuites hispano-portugais du XVᵉ siécle', in *Études ibériques et latino-americaines: IV Congrès des Hispanistes Français*, Mouton, The Hague and Paris, 1968

RIEMERSMA, Jelle C., *Religious factors in Early Dutch Capitalism 1550–60*, Mouton, The Hague/Paris, 1967

ROLDANUS, Cornelia Wilhelmine, *Coenraad van Beuningen: Staatsman en Libertijn*, doctoral thesis, Amsterdam, 1931. The Hague, 1931

ROODEN, P.T. van, *Theology, Biblical Scholarship and Rabbinical Studies in the Seventeenth Century: Constantijn l'Empereur (1591–1648) Professor of Hebrew and Theology at Leiden*, E.J. Brill, Leiden, 1989

ROSENBERG, P.T.E.E. in CAROSSO-KOK

ROTH, Cecil (1), *A History of the Marranos*, 1932; 4th edition, with a New Introduction by Herman P. Salomon, Hermon Press, New York, 1974

ROTH, Cecil (2), *A Life of Menasseh ben Israel: Rabbi, Printer and Diplomat*, The Jewish Society of America, Philadelphia, 1935

ROWEN, Herbert H. (1), *John de Witt, Grand Pensionary of Holland, 1625–1672*, Princeton University Press, 1978

ROWEN, Herbert H. (2), *Johan de Witt: Statesman of the True Freedom*, Cambridge University Press, 1986

ROWEN, Herbert H. (3), *The Princes of Orange: The Stadholders in the Dutch Republic*, Cambridge University Press, 1988

SAINT-SAËNS, Alain (ed. and int.), *Permanence and Evolution of Behaviour in Golden-Age Spain: Essays in Gender, Body and Religion*, The Edward Mellen Press Lewiston/Queenstown/Lampeter, 1991

SALOMON, H.P., 'Haham Saul Levi Morteira en de Portugees Nieuw-Christenen', *Studia Rosenthaliana* (10), Van Gorcum, Assen, 1976

SAMBUC, Felix, *Jean de Labadie, sa vie et ses écrits*, Jean-Hein-Edouard Heitz, Strasbourg, 1869

SARGEAUNT: see TERENCE

SAVAN, David, 'Spinoza: Scientist and Theorist of Scientific Method', in GRENE and NAILS

SCHAMA, Simon, *The Embarrassment of Riches*, William Collins, London, 1987

SCHWARTZ, Gary, *Rembrandt: His Life, his Paintings*, Viking, London, 1985. First published in Dutch under the title *Rembrandt, zijn leven, zijn schilderijen*, 1984.

SEELIGMANN, S., 'Spinoza Amstelodamenis', *Amstelodamum* 2 (Feb. 1933)

SHAHAN, Robert W. and BIRO, J.I. (eds), *Spinoza: New Perspectives*, University of Oklahoma Press, 1978

SHMUELI, Efraim, 'The Geometrical Method, Personal Caution, and the Ideal of Tolerance', in SHAHAN and BIRO

SIEBRAND, H., 'On the Early Reception of Spinoza's *Tractatus Theologico-Politicus* in the context of Cartesianism', in DE DEUGD

SILVERMAN, R.M. (1), 'The Jewish reception of Spinoza: reactions to Spinoza's challenge to traditional Jewish thought', Ph.D. thesis, The John Rylands University Library of Manchester, 1988

SILVERMAN, R.M. (2), *Baruch Spinoza: Outcast Jew, Universal Sage*, Symposium Press, Science Reviews, Northwood, 1995

SKINNER, Quentin, *Reason and Rhetoric in the Philosophy of Hobbes*, Cambridge University Press, 1996

SMITH, Hilda, 'Gynaecology and Ideology in Seventeenth-Century England', in CARROLL

SONNET, M., 'A Daughter to Educate', in ZEMON DAVIS

SPINOZA: troisième centenaire de la mort du philosophe (A catalogue of primary references), ed. A.K. Offenberg *et al.*, Institut Néerlandais, Paris, 1977

ŠTECH, V.V., *Rembrandt: Etchings and Drawings*, Hamlyn, London, 1963

STEENBAKKERS, Piet, *Spinoza's Ethica from Manuscript to Print* (Studies on text, form and related topics), Van Gorcum, Assen 1994

STOYE, J.W. *Europe Unfolding 1648–1688*, Fontana History of Europe, London, 1988

SUCHTELEN, G. van (1), 'The Spinoza Houses at Rijnsburg and The Hague', in HESSING

SUCHTELEN, G. van (2), *Spinoza's sterfhuis aan de Paviljoensgracht*, J. N. Voorhoeve, The Hague, 1977

SUCHTELEN, G. van (3), *'Nil Volentibus Arduum: Les Amis de Spinoza en travail'*, Studia Spinozana Walther & Walther, Verlag, Alling, 1987

TAK, W.G. van der (2 and 3): see VAZ DIAS (2 and 3)

THIJSSEN-SCHOUTE, C. Louise. 'Le Cartésianisme aux Pays-Bas', in DIJKSTERHUIS

TWYMAN, F. (FRS), *Optical Glassworking* (an abridged edition of the author's *Prism and Lens Making* compiled for optical lens-makers), Hilger and Watts, London, 1955

UNTERMAN, Alan, *The Jews: Their Religious Beliefs and Practices*, Routledge and Kegan Paul, London, 1981

VALENTINER, W.R., *Rembrandt and Spinoza*, Phaidon, London, 1957

VANDENBOSSCHE, Hubert, *Adriaan Koerbagh en Spinoza*, E.J. Brill, Leiden, 1978

VEGA, L. Alvares, *Het Beth Haim van Ouderkerk aan de Amstel*, Van Gorcum, Assen, 1979

VERNIÈRE, P., *Spinoza et la Pensée Française avant la Revolution*, Presses Universitaires de France, Paris, 1954

VESEY, G.N.A., 'Agent and Spectator: The Double Aspect Theory', in *The Human Agent*, Macmillan, London, 1968

VLESSING, O., 'The Jewish Community in Transition: From Acceptance to Emancipation', *Studia Rosenthaliana* (30), Van Gorcum, Assen, 1996 (1)

VRIES, Theun de, *Spinoza: biografie*, De Prom, Amsterdam, 1991

VROEDSCHAP van Amsterdam, De (1578–1795) 2 vols., Johan E. Elias. Vincent Loosjes, Haarlem, 1903–5

WADE, I., *The clandestine organisation and diffusion of philosophic ideas in France*, Princeton University Press, 1967

WALL, Ernestine G.E. van der, 'Petrus Serrarius and Menasseh ben Israel: Christian Millenarianism and Jewish Messianism in Seventeenth-Century Amsterdam', in KAPLAN (4)

WALLACE, Robert, and the Editors of Time-Life Books, *The World of Rembrandt 1606–1669*, Time-Life Library of Art, Amsterdam, 1971

WEBSTER, Charles, *From Paracelsus to Newton: Magic and the Making of Modern Science*, Cambridge University Press, 1982

WEINRYB, Bernard Dow, *The Jews of Poland*, A Social and Economic History of the Jewish Community in Poland from 100–1800, The Jewish Publication Society of America, Philadelphia, 1972

WILDENBERG, Ivo W., *Johan & Pieter de la Court* (1622–60 and 1618–85): Bibliografie en receptiegeschiedenis, APA Holland Universiteits Pers, Amsterdam and Maarsen, 1986

WILLIAMS, E.N., *The Penguin Dictionary of English and European History* (1485–1789), Penguin Books, Harmondsworth, 1980

WILSON, Charles, *The Dutch Republic*, Weidenfeld and Nicolson, London, 1968

WOOLHOUSE, R.S., *Descartes, Spinoza, Leibniz: The concept of substance in seventeenth-century metaphysics*, Routledge, London, 1993

YOVEL, Yirmiyahu, *Spinoza and Other Heretics: The Marrano of Reason*, Princeton University Press, 1989

ZEMON DAVIS, Natalie and FARGE, Arlette (eds), *A History of Women in the West*, Vol. III. *Renaissance and Enlightenment Paradoxes*, The Belknap Press of Harvard University Press, 1993
ZUMTHOR, Paul, *Daily Life in Rembrandt's Holland*, English translation, Weidenfeld and Nicolson, London, 1962

INDEX

Entries do not include names listed in the bibliography and source notes